WALTHER RATHENAU

WALTHER RATHENAU

*Industrialist, Banker, Intellectual,
and Politician*

———

Notes and Diaries 1907–1922

———

Edited by
Hartmut Pogge von Strandmann

The Notes and Diaries were translated by
Caroline Pinder-Cracraft
in conjunction with
Hilary and Hartmut Pogge von Strandmann

CLARENDON PRESS · OXFORD
1985

Oxford University Press, Walton Street, Oxford OX2 6DP

Oxford New York Toronto
Delhi Bombay Calcutta Madras Karachi
Kuala Lumpur Singapore Hong Kong Tokyo
Nairobi Dar es Salaam Cape Town
Melbourne Auckland

and associated companies in
Beirut Berlin Ibadan Nicosia

Oxford is a trade mark of Oxford University Press

Published in the United States by
Oxford University Press, New York

Introduction, appendices, comments, insertions, and this translation
© Hartmut Pogge von Strandmann 1985

Revised and extended edition.

Originally published in German under the title of
Walther Rathenau: Tagebuch 1907–1922
Düsseldorf: Droste Verlag 1967
© 1967 Droste Verlag und Druckerei GmbH, Düsseldorf

Rathenau text © 1967 Gotthold Müller Verlag, München

British Library Cataloguing in Publication Data
Rathenau, Walther
Walther Rathenau: industrialist, banker,
intellectual and politician: notes and diaries
1907–1922.
1. Rathenau, Walther   2. Politicians—Germany
—Biography   3. Businessman—Germany—
Biography
I. Title   II. Pogge von Strandmann, H.
943.08'4'0924   DD231.R3
ISBN-0-19-822506-7

Library of Congress Cataloging in Publication Data
Rathenau, Walther, 1867–1922.
Walther Rathenau, industrialist, banker,
intellectual, and politician.
Translation of: Tagebuch 1907–1922. Translated by
Caroline Pinder-Cracraft in conjunction with Hilery
and Hartmut Pogge von Strandmann.

Bibliography: p.
Includes index.
1. Rathenau, Walther, 1867–1922.   2. Statesmen—
Germany—Biography.   3. Germany—Politics and government
—1871–1933.   I. Pogge von Strandmann, H. (Hartmut)
II. Title.   III. Title: Notes and diaries, 1907–1922.
DD231.R3A2713 1985   943.085'092'4   85-7188
ISBN 0-19-822506-7

Typeset by Joshua Associates Limited, Oxford
Printed in Great Britain
at the University Press, Oxford
by David Stanford
Printer to the University

To the 'splitters and lumpers' in St. Antony's College
and Balliol College 1962–1970

CONTENTS

List of Abbreviations   ix

Editorial Note   xi

Introduction: Walther Rathenau, a Biographical Sketch   1

The East African Journey   27
  Notebook 1907   30
  Extracts from the 'Report on the Development of the
    German East African Colony'   49

The South African Journey   60
  Notebook 1908   62
  Extracts from the 'Report on the State of the
    South West African Colony'   78

Diary for 1911   93

Diary for 1912   142

Diary for 1913   175

Diary for 1914   181

Notes on 1915   195
  Journey to Kovno. Thursday evening,
    18 November to Monday morning, 22 November 1915   195
  Interview with General von Falkenhayn,
    Chief of the General Staff   205
  Conversation with Gerard, United States Ambassador   207

Notes on 1916   209
  Talks with Colonel House, Ambassador Gerard,
    and Foreign Secretary Jagow   209

Notes on 1917   212
  First Talk with General Ludendorff   215
  Discussion with Chancellor Bethmann Hollweg,
    Secretary of the Interior Helfferich, and
    Councillor Wahnschaffe   218
  Second Talk with General Ludendorff   222

Notes on 1918 233
  Rathenau's Letter Drafted for Prince Max von Baden
    to send to President Wilson 235

Notes on 1920 237
  The Kapp Putsch 239
  The Spa Conference 243
  A Visit to the Italian Ambassador 249

Notes on 1921 250
  Commentary on a Proposal regarding Allied
    Reparations Demands 251
  The Negotiations with Loucheur at Wiesbaden 252
  Plan for a Visit to Paris 266
  Conflict over Troop Transports to Upper Silesia 267

Rathenau's Talks in London and Paris 273
  Rathenau's First Journey to London 273
  Rathenau's Second Journey to London 283
  Rathenau's Visit to Paris 286
  Negotiations with the Reparations Commission in Paris 288

Notes on 1922 290
  Conversation with the French Ambassador Laurent 292

Rathenau's Membership of Supervisory Boards
  of Joint-stock Companies 1907–1922 296

Bibliography 299

Biographical Index 311

General Index 333

LIST OF ABBREVIATIONS

AEG	Allgemeine Elektrizitätsgesellschaft
AR	Aufsichtsrat
BA Koblenz	Bundesarchiv Koblenz
BBC	Brown, Boveri & Compagnie
BEW	Berliner Elektrizitätswerke
BHG	Berliner Handelsgesellschaft
DUEG	Deutsch-Überseeische-Elektrizitätsgesellschaft
ELG	Elektrizitäts-Lieferungs-Gesellschaft
HAPAG	Hamburg-Amerika-Packetfahrt-Aktiengesellschaft
KRA	Kriegsrohstoffabteilung
MAN	Maschinenfabrik Augsburg–Nürnberg
MEW	Märkisches Elektrizitätswerk
PA Bonn	Politisches Archiv Bonn
PRO	Public Record Office
RK	Reichskanzlei
RKolA	Reichskolonialamt
SPD	Sozialdemokratische Partei Deutschlands
UEG	Union Elektrizitäts-Gesellschaft
ZStA	Zentrales Staatsarchiv

EDITORIAL NOTE

Rathenau's diaries and notes were referred to for the first time in Count Kessler's biography. It seems likely that he saw the original handwritten version, because he referred to Rathenau's handwriting as 'uneven and excited' during the time of his father's serious illness in 1912.[1] However, Kessler's quotations are not always identical with the version used here: either Kessler or the editor of the 'private print' changed the text slightly without indicating why he did so. Although he mentions the diaries for the period between 1911 and 1914 he does not reveal whether they were complete or not, but knowing Rathenau's propensity to keep notes about events, conversations, and meetings with celebrities it is likely that the material used for this edition does not include all that left by him for the years between 1907 and 1922.

The source for this edition is a 'private print', produced by the Government's printing shop in 1930. As the correspondence of the printers has not survived the last war it is difficult to give any precise reason as to why the diaries were printed in this form and which criteria were used to prepare the material for the edition. Two members of the former Rathenau Foundation assume that it was Rathenau's sister, Edith Andreae, who selected and authorized the print.[2] Only a few copies were produced and even fewer survived the war. One copy, marked number seven, was acquired by the Hamburg State Library in 1947, and has been used for this edition. The Library catalogued it in the ordinary way although a 'private print' is not a proper publication. I came across it when I used the catalogue to prepare a seminar paper for Professor Fritz Fischer.

A complete edition of Rathenau's notes and diaries would only have been possible if his papers were still available. The eventual fate of these papers remains a mystery, but it is more than likely that they were destroyed at the end of the last war. Originally Rathenau's library and papers were kept by the Rathenau Foundation in his former house in Berlin-Grunewald. When the NSDAP came to power the foundation was dissolved and the private papers taken by Rathenau's sister to Bavaria. Between 1933 and 1939 the Imperial Archives in Potsdam tried to obtain them, and when Edith Andreae and her husband Fritz left Germany in 1939 the papers were confiscated by the Gestapo. Two years after the end of the Second

---

[1] Kessler, *Rathenau*, p. 159.
[2] Private communication by Professor Edwin Redslob and Professor Arnold Brecht.

World War Fritz Andreae wrote that the 'Gestapo came to the
Rathenau House in the Grunewald and confiscated all documents,
scripts etc., supposedly in order to transfer them to the Imperial
Archives in Potsdam'.[3] The evidence from Potsdam shows, however,·
that the Imperial Archives asked the Gestapo to confiscate the
papers before the Andreaes emigrated from Germany in 1939.
So it seems likely that the Gestapo acted twice, the first time soon
after the seizure of power, and the second time in 1939. The first
raid probably cleared Rathenau's former house in Berlin of everything that the Andreaes had not already managed to take to Bavaria.
The second time the Andreaes lost the rest, except for a few letters.
The Imperial Archives noted that in the second raid the Gestapo found

the complete collection of Rathenau's papers in twelve boxes in a small location
in Upper Bavaria. There they were secured by the State Police in Munich at the
request of the Imperial Archives. Repeated and urgent reminders were sent to
the State Police and the Gestapo in Berlin, to demand from the State Police in
Munich a transfer of the confiscated Rathenau papers to the Imperial Archives
but to no avail.[4]

In May 1940 a note was filed which reveals that the 'Rathenau
papers are with the SS-Hauptamt where Dr Löffler works on them.
Further information about their fate is promised by Dr Turowski
soon.'[5] With the help of the Canadian historian, Michael Kater,
I was able to trace Dr Löffler in Heidelberg. Dr Löffler maintains
that he asked Dr Turowski in May or June 1940 to help him to study
the Rathenau papers in the Imperial Archives.[6] As far as he remembers, Turowski answered him 'that this was impossible because some-
body high up had reserved the papers for himself; this person would
release the papers to be worked over at an appropriate moment'.
Dr Löffler also claims that he had no connection with the SS-
Hauptamt and that he lost contact with Dr Turowski after 1941.[7]
Michael Kater is able to substantiate Löffler's remarks to the extent
that he does not believe that Löffler had worked with the Rathenau
papers, as this would have shown in the documents, and that Löffler
probably had not worked with the SS-Hauptamt.[8] So the only other
person who might be able to give some further clues as to what
happened to the Rathenau papers during the remaining years of

[3] *Die Welt*, 14 March 1947, Fritz Andreae to Professor Rauers.
[4] ZStA Potsdam, Reichsarchiv 438, 16 August 1939. Private communication by the
ZStA Potsdam.
[5] Ibid., 3 May 1940.
[6] Private communication by Professor Hermann Löffler, 21 September 1974.
[7] Ibid., 27 December 1974.
[8] Private communication by Professor Michael Kater, 20 August 1974.

the war is Dr Turowski, and nobody seems to know what has happened to him.

In the Central State Archives of the GDR in Potsdam it was suggested to me that a part of the documentary material of the SS-Hauptamt had been transferred to Breslau to escape the air raids in Berlin. A flying visit to Warsaw in 1973 resulted in a letter from the Director of the Major Committee for Studies of Hitler's Crimes in Poland (Główna Komisja Badania Zbrodni Hitlerowkich w Polsce), Professor Pilichowski, saying that no trace could be found of any Rathenau papers among the collection of German documents.[9] A brief visit to the State Archive in Wroclaw/Breslau did not yield any positive information either. In fact, when one archivist was asked about the existence of any Rathenau papers she referred to a dictionary of place-names (in which the original German names of towns and villages had been translated into the present Polish ones). Obviously the name of Walther Rathenau did not mean much to her.

The Federal Archive in Koblenz suggests in its note to the small collection of the Nachlass Rathenau in its possession that the papers might have landed in the Gestapo archives in Berlin-Wilmersdorf where they would have been destroyed at the end of the war. It seems more than likely that apart from a few letters in private hands and the small collection in Koblenz the great bulk of the Rathenau papers no longer exists.

Thus the diaries preserved through the 'private print' are of special value. The diaries fall into three categories; the African notebooks of Rathenau's journeys to East, South, and South West Africa in 1907 and 1908, the diaries for the years 1911 to 1914, and the accounts of conversations between 1915 and 1922. There are also a draft of a letter to President Wilson and a drafted reply to Allied reparation demands in 1921. In addition Rathenau's two memoranda about his visits to Africa have been included in an abbreviated form because Rathenau's journeys and his influence on colonial policy have been neglected. They also show to what use he put his notes. Most of the diaries were not intended for publication—they are not written in the polished style which usually indicates the author's wish for future publication. Rathenau wanted to keep them as an *aide-mémoire* in case he should wish to write his memoirs. An exception might be the East African notebook, which Golo Mann, in his review of the German edition, has called one of the most beautiful pieces Rathenau ever wrote.[10] Some of it

[9] Private communication by Professor Pilichowski, 15 October 1973 and 2 January 1974.
[10] *Die Zeit*, 28 February 1968.

was written in hexameters, so it may have been designed for a wider readership, or merely for his own amusement. The accounts of his talks with a number of politicians were largely written for possible publication, a case in point being his second discussion with Erich Ludendorff, from which, however, he only published some extracts.

The English translation is based on the German edition of 1967. The editorial explanations of certain events and the comments have been revised and extended in the English edition, taking into account new publications and new sources.[11] In a number of instances it has also been possible to throw new light upon brief references Rathenau made in his diary. Additional archive material has been found in the Staatsbibliothek in Hamburg, the Public Record Office, the Ministère des Affaires Étrangères in Paris, the archives of the firms Felten & Guilleaume Carlswerk AG in Cologne, the Gutehoffnungshütte AG in Oberhausen, the Krupp AG in Essen, the Mannesmann AG in Düsseldorf, and the Thyssen AG in Duisburg. The archives of Siemens and the AEG provided new and important material, as did the Bundesarchiv in Koblenz and the Militärchiv in Freiburg. I am very grateful to the archivists and librarians for their support.

In addition to those whom I have already thanked for their generous help with the German edition I want to mention the names of Dr Michael Geyer, Dr Ottoarndt Glossner, Dr Hans-Dieter Hellige, Bodo Herzog, Dr Guenther Holzer, Dr Charles Medalen, Dr Helga Nussbaum, Ernest Rathenau, and Professor Ernst Schulin. Professor Volker Berghahn, Dr Leslie Mitchell, Alexander Murray,

---

[11] These editorial comments are brief, and have by no means exhausted the subject. It is hoped that the text will become easier to understand by the provision of background material. Criticism of the text has been kept to a minimum. Two sections which have been included in the 'private print' have been omitted in this edition. The first one is a supposed report by Rathenau about a journey to Geneva in September 1921: as Rathenau could not have been in Geneva at that time the report must have been written by someone else. After some research the original was found in the Federal Archives in Koblenz: it was a report by the banker Dr Erich Alexander. The second section is a short communiqué about the Wiesbaden Agreement which also was not written by Rathenau.

Not all events mentioned in the diaries can be explained, but, where possible, references to secondary literature have been made which mention the same events. Articles and book-titles have also been included to show where the subject-matter has been discussed further or where Rathenau's diaries have been quoted.

The Biographical Index is not complete because it proved impossible to gather all the necessary information. I hope I have kept the number of errors to a minimum. Names have been corrected if there was no doubt about their identity and initials have been decoded where possible. Footnotes explain the cases where doubt continues to exist and give the names of people who have been referred to only by their title. Small alterations in the German text have been made to increase readability. The dates have been checked against available evidence and corrected, and have been put in an uniform way throughout the text. Where English has been used in the original text it has been left uncorrected and put into italics.

and Professor John Röhl have helped in a very efficient way preparing certain sections of the final English manuscript, for which
I am very grateful. I am also greatly indebted to my wife, who spent
a great deal of time and effort in going over the editorial sections and
checking the translation. At times she may have wondered whether
the name of Rathenau would become an inseparable part of our life,
as the preparatory work for the English edition seemed to be never-
ending. I also would like to mention here Professor James Joll,
the late Professor John Gallagher, and Dan Davin, without whose
initial encouragement I would not have tried to plan an English
edition.

INTRODUCTION: WALTHER
RATHENAU, A BIOGRAPHICAL SKETCH

The economy shapes our destiny. In a few years time the world will recognize that politics do not determine the ultimate.

(Walther Rathenau's speech in Munich, 28 September 1921.)

During the years before the First World War Berlin had become one of the most dynamic industrial, financial, and cultural centres in Europe. It was also the political capital of the German Empire which in turn was one of the few leading powers in the world. As in any other major capital there were in Berlin illustrious, powerful, and sometimes outstanding men in the fields of industry, finance, and politics, who contributed much to the glamour of the metropolis. But only a few of Berlin's citizens were as influential in all of these spheres as was Walther Rathenau. His rise within Berlin society was accompanied by newspaper articles which heralded him as the coming man, and by 1914 he had become one of the city's celebrities. His social life, as revealed to some extent in his diaries, has even been compared with that of the Emperor holding court.

But who was Walther Rathenau? [1] Anyone who would like to find out can nowadays turn to an encyclopaedia, a well-stocked library, or even a large bookshop where one of the many modern studies on Rathenau in either German or English may be available. This was not the case eighty, seventy, or even sixty years ago. After the First World War Rathenau's books were widely circulated, but it would not have been easy to find out much about the author himself. A look into *Wer ist's* (the German *Who's Who*), published in the years before the First World War, would have revealed nothing: Rathenau was not in it. Only in 1922 when he was Foreign Minister

---

[1] Studies about Rathenau since 1975 include: Schulin, 'Die Rathenaus—Zwei Generationen jüdischen Anteils' (1976); D. G. Williamson, 'Walther Rathenau: Realist, Pedagogue and Prophet' (1976); Kallner, *Herzl und Rathenau* (1976); Schulin (ed.), *Walther Rathenau. Hauptwerke und Gespräche* (1977); D. G. Williamson, 'Walther Rathenau and the KRA', (1978); Schulin, *Walther Rathenau, Repräsentant, Kritiker und Opfer seiner Zeit* (1979); Loewenberg, 'Walther Rathenau and Henry Kissinger' (1980); Joll, 'Walther Rathenau— Intellectual or Industrialist?' (1981); Pogge von Strandmann, 'Rathenau zwischen Wirtschaft und Politik' (1981); Hellige (ed.), Rathenau–Harden (forthcoming); Pogge von Strandmann, *Grandmaster of Capitalism*, (forthcoming).

Recent books and articles in which Rathenau figures prominently are: Baudis and Nussbaum, *Wirtschaft und Staat* (1978); Pogge von Strandmann, *Unternehmenspolitik und Unternehmensführung* (1978); Wulf, *Hugo Stinnes* (1979); Buddensieg and Rogge, *Industriekultur* (1979); Pogge von Strandmann, 'Rapallo—Strategy in Preventive Diplomacy' (1981).

did the editor put in a reference to him; and it was so brief that it was obviously made without Rathenau's approval.

Yet many people wanted to know more about him, as he was a public figure and had been so for some time—during his lifetime alone his books and pamphlets reached a sales figure of about one quarter of a million copies. Many newspapers carried information about his industrial and political activities, and so regular newspaper readers would have been aware that he was the nominal head of the Allgemeine Elektrizitätsgesellschaft (German General Electric Company: hereafter AEG), one of Germany's largest industrial empires and the biggest electrotechnical group, and that he was a supervisory-board member of about forty companies. They could begin to follow to some degree his political career when he became the head of the Kriegsrohstoffabteilung (War Raw Materials Department: hereafter KRA) at the beginning of the First World War, an appointment which proved to be of considerable importance for Germany's economic war effort. And again, after the war they could read that he was appointed, in spring 1920, to the Second Socialization Commission, which was to examine the left-wing demand for nationalizing sectors of German industry; that he joined the German delegation for the Spa Conference about reparation payments in July 1920; that he became a member of the Provisional Reich Economic Council; and finally that he was appointed to advise the Government on the preparations for the London Reparations Conference of March 1921. Shortly afterwards, in May 1921, he joined the Cabinet of Chancellor Joseph Wirth as Minister of Reconstruction. He made headlines when he concluded the Wiesbaden Agreement with France in October 1921, but left the Government in the same month and continued to work for it as special envoy on reparation questions, first in London, then in Paris and finally at the Cannes Conference of January 1922.

By the time he became Foreign Minister at the end of January 1922 most people interested in politics had some notion of Rathenau as a politician without knowing much about his life. He was not a popular figure and was often attacked for the discrepancy between his rather luxurious life-style and the austere messages in his writings. Some, however, thought highly of his intellect and expected much from the involvement of a top industrialist in politics. Yet Rathenau himself steered away from publicity; he did not address crowds and turned down many invitations to give speeches. Although he was regarded as a good speaker he did not appear very often in the Reichstag, let alone speak there. He was much more what has been termed a *Honoratiorenpolitiker* (a local dignitary involved in politics because of his position) than a people's tribune. Even before entering politics he preferred to view the political and industrial world from above rather than below. Consequently he tended to know ministers better than ordinary deputies; he remained a somewhat distant figure in business circles, and did not seek contact with AEG workers or employees.

Rathenau's contempt for any suggestion that he should consciously seek publicity, and his negative attitude towards the trimmings of modern politics, do not, however, explain why it was difficult to find out more about him. His industrial, literary, and political activities would each have warranted an entry into any *Who's Who*, and no doubt he was repeatedly sent the appropriate forms by various editors, but he evidently refused to comply with their requests: he was too proud and too vain. It seems he had such a high opinion of himself that he hoped to achieve publicity without appearing actively to seek it. Earlier on in his life he had published his articles under pseudonyms in the magazine *Die Zukunft*, but there were far more concrete reasons for this than a wish to avoid personal publicity. He feared the consequences for his industrial and political career if he were associated too closely with a journal which sharply criticized the political establishment of Wilhelmine Germany. He later dropped the anonymity and republished some of these articles in two collections of essays, when, under altered circumstances, it had become more important to him to see his name in print.[2] Then he might even have been able to bask in this gradually increasing publicity, had it not been for the sometimes very critical reception of these books. He found this difficult to cope with and was therefore pleased when his name became well known later on in life. Despite this rather late boost to his pride he remained intolerant of the schemes which lesser mortals, as he would have regarded them, employed to become known, so until after his death relatively little was known about his life.

What information could a *Wer ist's* reader have gained had Rathenau allowed the publication of an entry about himself? The earliest date for an entry would have been the year 1893, when he became managing director of the Elektrochemische Werke (Electro-Chemical Works) in Bitterfeld, in the Prussian province of Saxony. But in any case, no *Wer ist's* edition between 1893 and 1922 would have provided substantial information about Rathenau: it would at best have given some initial clues for further investigation to anyone interested in him. A fuller biographical sketch might read as follows.

[2] *Impressionen* (1902) and *Reflexionen* (1908).

Walther Rathenau was born in Berlin on Sunday, 29 September 1867, the day of the German patron St. Michael and the day before the most important Jewish holiday, the New Year's Day. He was never interested in astrology, but later came to believe that this constellation of events was not without significance.

His father, Emil, who had also been born in Berlin, ran a prosperous machine factory in the north of the city, which he had bought, together with a partner, two years before Walther's birth.[3] Emil Rathenau trained as an engineer, first in Hanover and later in Zurich. His first job was at Borsig in Berlin, but soon he went to England, spending two years there with three different firms. Rapid business expansion of his machine factory forced Emil to go public with his enterprise soon after the Franco-German war, but when his house bank collapsed in the crash of 1873 he decided to sell the business. After satisfying all his creditors he was left in 1875 with a fortune of about 900,000 marks, but without any occupation. During the next few years he became a restless and enquiring *rentier*, looking out constantly for a new field of activity. Ordinary industrial investment was not of great interest to him: he was sufficiently ambitious to wish to be able to affect the lives of ordinary people. The opportunity came when he saw Edison's electric bulb at the Paris Exhibition of 1881. He bought Edison's patents and two years later founded the Deutsche Edison-Gesellschaft (German Edison Company) in collaboration with his greatest potential competitor, Siemens. Faced with enormous financial and technical difficulties, to which were added a number of patent lawsuits, he was forced to cut his ties with the American Edison companies and to put his relationship with Siemens on to a new footing.[4] The result was the setting-up of the AEG on a broader financial basis. From then onwards the AEG expanded and gradually became a success. Once its last contractual links with Siemens were dissolved in 1894, Emil Rathenau was ready to overtake all his rivals in Germany in making the firm the predominant electro-technical enterprise in the country.

When the AEG was founded Walther was twenty years old. He had witnessed, at close range, the stress experienced by his father while he grasped a new idea and established a new enterprise against strong competition. He also knew that his father was fighting against the stigma of supposed failure, because he had been wrongly blamed for the collapse of his original machine-building factory. Terms

---

[3] Riedler, *Emil Rathenau und das Werden der Grosswirtschaft*; Pinner, *Emil Rathenau; 50 Jahre AEG* (written in 1933, published Berlin 1956).

[4] Kocka, 'Siemens und der aufhaltsame Aufstieg der AEG'.

like 'money', 'capital', 'loss', 'profit', 'production costs', 'organization', and 'management' were important in Walther's life during
his early years. He seems to have found it hard to cope with his
father's restlessness, and to have been, as a result, closer to his
mother. In any case, as she took care of her children's education,
a relatively intimate relationship developed between mother and son.

Walther's mother, Mathilde, née Nachmann, tried to provide
her children with as wide-ranging an education as possible. Music,
painting, poetry, and the standard works of European literature were
very much part of the Rathenau daily life. She was born in Frankfurt
where her father, a banker, had committed suicide when he faced
bankruptcy in the aftermath of the Franco-German war. Her style
of life has often been contrasted with that of her husband's, who
was not used to luxury and believed in a rather Spartan existence.
Certainly the contrast between life in Frankfurt and in an industrial
district in the north of Berlin, on the premises of her husband's
factory, must have been striking, but they were not short of money,
nor was Emil a philistine. Both parents were of relatively wealthy,
educated Jewish middle-class stock, but while Emil devoted most of
his time to his business, his wife took care of the arts and kept in
touch with those members of the family who were of a more artistic
disposition than her husband.[5]

Walther Rathenau remained unmarried. He had one brother,
Erich, four years younger than him, who died in January 1903, and
one sister who was born in 1883. She married the banker Fritz
Andreae in 1902 and had four daughters by him.

Walther Rathenau attended the prestigious Wilhelms-Gymnasium
in Berlin. Some of his earlier education had taken place in Frankfurt, but this had been only short-term. His mother's interest in his
education led her to engage governesses. Walther was fond of one
French governess and indicated that he would like to look after
her when he was grown up. His school career was unremarkable,
and he did not strike his teachers as being a particular gifted man;
the lack of regard was mutual. At the age of seventeen he passed
his *Abitur* (the equivalent of A-levels). His best subject was German
literature and language, in which he passed with a B grade. He went
straight to university to read sciences, first at Strasbourg and later
at Berlin. Altogether he spent five years at university and eventually
passed his doctoral examination in physics, writing a thesis on light
absorption by metals.[6] He complied with his father's wish that he
specialize in electro-chemistry, and therefore attended a one-year

---

[5] The well-known painter Max Liebermann was Walther's cousin once removed.
[6] *Die Absorption des Lichts in Metallen.*

course at the Technical University of Munich. At the end of 1890 he began his military service with the heavy cavalry guards in Berlin. The individualist Rathenau seems to have enjoyed his time in the army and would have liked to become an officer. But he was unable to obtain a commission, partly because he was a Jew and partly because he came from an untitled, non-landowning background. If he had been willing to join a non-cavalry regiment somewhere in the provinces he might have been able to fulfil this ambition, but apparently he was not.

Rathenau's parents were both Jews, but only maintained tenuous ties with Judaism, and their son Walther followed them in this respect. However, his attitude was more ambivalent. Occasionally he emphasized how much he stood above any religious conviction, but at other times he admitted the extent to which he had been formed by religious ideas. While he never formally accepted Christianity, he often underlined his belief in the Gospels and the divinity of Jesus, and even went as far to dissociate himself, in a magistrate's court in Berlin, in 1895, from his former 'Mosaic belief'. But he refused to be baptized because this would have gained him social advantages which had nothing to do with his convictions. Conversion would also have meant making a concession to the official policy of discrimination in Prussia. He was extremely sensitive about being a second-class citizen, yet he advocated assimilation and hoped for equality. He called himself a 'German of the Jewish tribe' but was not in favour of Jewish solidarity.[7] Above all, he regarded himself as a German; everything else was of lesser importance. He was an anti-Zionist and urged the German Jews: 'Let others found a state in Palestine: nothing draws us towards Asia.'[8] However, he continued to be fascinated by Judaism. In 1903 he made the effort to learn Hebrew, and later complained that he did not know enough about Judaism. He always remained conscious of his Jewish background, not because he was especially attached to it but rather because he was reminded of it when equality with other Germans was denied. When, after the war, it was possible for him to obtain high office he wrote: 'What binds me to the Jews is at the most a sense of common derivation,—not even family feeling'.[9] Despite the rise of anti-Semitism he expected the process of assimilation to be complete within a relatively short time.

His industrial career may seem to have been easily achieved,

[7] Rathenau, *An Deutschlands Jugend* (Berlin, 1918), pp. 9 f.

[8] Rathenau, *Briefe*, vol. ii, p. 76, Rathenau to Apfel, 16 November 1918.

[9] Schulin (ed.), *Walther Rathenau. Hauptwerke und Gespräche*, p. 788, Lore Karren-brock's notes of a conversation with Rathenau, 11 May 1919.

but this was not so. The early stages were fraught with doubts as to whether he had chosen the right path, and with strong longing for financial independence. After finishing his military service he joined, at his father's suggestion, the Aluminium Industrie, an AEG-subsidiary, at Neuhausen in Switzerland, set up to produce aluminium industrially by way of electrolysis. He passed his industrial apprenticeship when he was able to convince the AEG to set up the Elektrochemische Werke with a capital of two million marks in 1893.[10] The enterprise was to produce electro-chemical goods on a large scale. Because of the availability of cheap energy through lignite coal in the Prussian province of Saxony the new factory was established in Bitterfeld. Later another plant was built in Rheinfelden on the Upper Rhine to make use of hydroelectric power there. Walther Rathenau was made managing director of the company and the two plants. The extension of this enterprise was financed by a new rights issue of the Elektrochemische Werke in 1896, worth two million marks, which the AEG took over completely.[11] Of the total, one and a half million marks were to be used in Bitterfeld and half a million in Rheinfelden. As a result expansion took place at home and abroad, but competition with the strongest rival, Chemische Fabrik Griesheim Elektron (Griesheim Elektron Chemical Works), which was superior in one particular aspect of industrial electro-chemistry, led Rathenau to advise the AEG to avoid a cutthroat struggle and seek an arrangement with the competitor. This was done to the satisfaction of both sides in 1898.[12]

Through the management of the Elektrochemische Werke, Walther had sufficiently qualified himself to join the board of directors of AEG in May 1899, but he continued to be managing director of the Elektrochemische Werke at the same time. His new task consisted of constructing power-stations in Germany and abroad. Three years later, at the height of the recession and the structural crisis in the electro-technical industry, he resigned from the board. The reason was the rejection by the board of his scheme for a take-over of the rival firm of Schuckert, on the grounds that the project did not aim at a level of centralization which the AEG and Emil Rathenau insisted upon for their operations. In the event, Siemens took over the ailing Schuckert concern on the lines Walther had suggested. However, the negotiations with Schuckert had one important result: Walther discovered his *métier* in industry. He found that he was less interested in managing a plant on a day-to-day basis or running a

[10] *Fünfzig Jahre AEG*, p. 99.
[11] AEG-Archiv, AR-minutes, 16 April 1896.
[12] *50 Jahre AEG*, pp. 138 f.

section of a group than in organizing the financial side and planning the strategy for the group or even the entire branch of that industry. When he left the AEG he was offered a highly important post on the board of AEG's main bank, the Berliner Handelsgesellschaft (hereafter BHG), which led him to become a member of a number of supervisory boards in industry and banking. From this vantagepoint he began to work for concentration in the electro-technical and electrical supply industries. He was able to renew earlier efforts for a merger with the Union Elektrizitäts-Gesellschaft (Union Company: hereafter UEG), another rival of the AEG. This time he succeeded, and was subsequently invited to join the AEG's supervisory board.

When the steam turbine began to replace other sources of power he bought himself into the very successful Brown, Boveri & Compagnie (hereafter BBC). But the AEG's domination was to last only for a short while. In any case he continued to work for closer integration in the entire electro-technical and electrical supply industries. He staged another coup in 1910, when the AEG purchased the majority of the shares of Felten & Guilleaume–Lahmeyerwerke AG in Cologne and Frankfurt.

By 1911 the electro-technical industry was increasingly dominated by a 'duopoly', the AEG and Siemens, and it was Walther Rathenau who negotiated for more formal co-operation with Siemens; but the emergence of a trust which raised the spectre of a monopoly was prevented by public pressure. In recognition of his coup with Felten and Guilleaume and his general dynamism he was elected vice-chairman of the AEG's supervisory board in 1910, and chairman when his father fell ill, in December 1912. However, he did not prove skilful enough in pursuit of his aim to follow in his father's footsteps and take over the post of managing director after the latter's death in 1915; instead he became 'president' of the AEG, a more powerful chairman of the supervisory board.

In the face of the rising power of the steel industrialists during the First World War and the rapid expansion of Hugo Stinnes's industrial empire, Rathenau tried to arrange mergers with Krupp, the Gutehoffnungshütte—a steel-making enterprise—and the South German machine-building firm Maschinenfabrik Augsburg–Nürnberg (hereafter MAN). But his attempts failed; instead it was Hugo Stinnes who was able to bring about a joint venture with Siemens and thus form the biggest industrial conglomerate of the time.

For over twenty years, from 1899 to 1921, Rathenau was involved in several industrial enterprises and his influence often proved to be decisive, as in the case of the Mannesmann-Group or as in the merger between the Delbrück and Schickler banks. However, his main interests remained with the AEG, the BHG, the Elektrobank in Zurich, the Berliner Elektrizitätswerke (Berlin Electricity Works: hereafter BEW), and Felten & Guilleaume in Cologne.[13]

His political career was relatively successful during the early years of the Weimar Republic. He was a cabinet minister twice, in 1921 and 1922, he was involved in the preparation of, and attended, several international conferences, and he went on special missions to London and Paris. He was also an active member of the Second Socialization Commission, failed to win a seat in the National Assembly, and tried to mediate during the Kapp Putsch of 1920.

Before the war Rathenau went on two semi-official visits to East Africa (1907) and South Africa (1908). In 1910 he negotiated on behalf of the Mannesmann brothers in Paris about their claims in Morocco. A year later it looked for a short while as if he would be nominated as a candidate for the Reichstag elections of 1912. It did not happen; but he was then able to comfort himself by pointing to his good contacts with the political decision-makers of Wilhelmine Germany. During the war he organized the KRA, tried to increase war production, and in November 1918 brought about, together with Stinnes, the agreement between leading industrialists and trade unions about future co-operation between them in the fields of economic and social policies.

Rathenau was a member of the board of the Scientific Electro-Chemical Society, he supported the Berlin Secession, which was a group of artists, as well as the Schiller Foundation which tried to help young authors. He also founded the Emil-Rathenau-Foundation after his father's death in 1915. His membership of other societies is not known, but it is probable that he kept his commitments down. He voted for the National Liberal Party before 1914 and became a member of the German Democratic Party after the war.

His major publications include *Zur Kritik der Zeit* (*Criticism of the Age*), published in 1912, *Zur Mechanik des Geistes oder Vom Reich der Seele* (*The Mechanism of the Mind*) published in 1913, and *Von Kommenden Dingen* (an English version was published under the title *In Days to Come* by George Allen and Unwin in 1921), published in 1917. Previously two volumes of essays appeared: *Impressionen* (1902) and *Reflexionen* (1908). Apart from a considerable number of articles in various newspapers and the magazine *Die Zukunft*, several pamphlets and booklets were brought out, among which the best known ones include *Die Neue Wirtschaft*

---

[13] For further details of Rathenau's industrial career see Pogge von Strandmann, *Grandmaster of Capitalism*, and Rathenau's diaries *passim*.

(*The New Economy*), published in 1918, *Der Neue Staat* (*The New State*), published in 1919, and *Die Neue Gesellschaft* (*The New Society*), published in the same year. The first edition of his *Gesammelte Schriften* (*Collected Works*) was printed in five volumes in 1918. Between 1917 and 1920, according to Count Kessler, Rathenau's biographer, 'Walther Rathenau became the most widely read and most passionately discussed of German writers'.

Rathenau liked playing the piano, often playing duets with his mother later in his life. He also wrote poetry and painted. He had talent as an artist, but was not sufficiently gifted to become a professional painter. He liked riding, and is supposed to have tried to impress the Kaiser with his abilities when they once met in the Tiergarten. He also liked bathing. He travelled widely and had a strong interest in architecture. He knew Europe reasonably well, and spent short periods in America and Russia as well as his two journeys to Africa.

Most of his life was spent in Berlin. Only as a student did he live for a short while away from the city, in Strasbourg and Munich. He worked for a short while in Neuhausen in Switzerland, and when he moved to Bitterfeld he only rented a five-roomed flat, which he gave up upon his appointment to the board of the AEG in 1899. In Berlin he first chose a flat in the Victoriastrasse, in the smart Tiergarten district, while his parents continued to reside at the AEG's headquarters in the Schiffbauerdamm. In 1909 he bought the former Royal Country House in Freienwalde on the Oder River, and a year later built himself a house in the wooded district of Berlin-Grunewald. His parents then moved to the Victoriastrasse and Walther kept a *pied-à-terre* in his parents' new house.

He was a member of the Aero Club and the Automobile Club, and during the war he joined two political clubs: the Deutsche Gesellschaft 1914 and the Mitwoch Gesellschaft, both founded in 1915. He was also a regular guest in some of the Berlin salons which revived the traditions of those which existed in the late eighteenth and early nineteenth centuries. These salons were a meeting-point for diplomats, officers, artists, and writers: financiers and industrialists like Rathenau could not often be encountered there because it was taken for granted that they were not very interested in cultural matters, and assumed that they would not fit easily into the socially exclusive world of these salons which focused very much on the life of the Imperial Court.

Wer ist's of 1922/3 carries a brief mention of Rathenau, reporting that he died on 24 June 1922. By this time he was widely known, and after his assassination every newspaper carried details of the murder plot, the funeral, the political consequences, the hunt for the murderers, their capture, and their trial. Rathenau was killed in his open car on Saturday morning, at about 10.45 a.m., shortly after he had left his house in the Grunewald to drive to the Foreign Office in the Wilhelmstrasse in the city centre. His assassins, who had been waiting for him in another open car, overtook his car, forced it to slow down, and then shot him at close range with an automatic weapon. A hand grenade was thrown into the car for good measure. After the explosion the assassins drove off at high speed and a nurse who happened to be near the scene jumped into Rathenau's car; the unhurt chauffeur took them both back to Rathenau's house. He died on the way, or shortly afterwards. His murderers, Kern, Fischer, and Techow, were young, right-wing, anti-Semitic officers who saw in Rathenau a dangerous man who, through political success, could make the Weimar Republic more acceptable to a great number of people who initially nourished resentful or even hostile feelings towards it.

It may not have been easy for the interested contemporary to find out a great deal about Rathenau's personal life, but by the outbreak of the First World War, or at the latest by 1920, the special role he played as a link between industry and politics had become apparent. Yet it would have been difficult to discover, behind the closed doors of finance and industry, to what extent Rathenau was actually involved in those spheres. Most of the authors who write about Rathenau—and there are a great number of them—have emphasized the role of the intellectual, the visionary, the social-political philosopher, and the politician, but rarely has his role as industrialist, or industrial organizer, as he preferred to think of himself, been the subject of extensive research. Yet his industrial experience and his reflections about it form the basis of his role in politics as well as in the world of letters and ideas.

Industrialists in late Bismarckian and early Wilhelmine Germany did not belong to the group which was placed at the top of the social ladder. Army officers, diplomats, university professors, and even bankers usually commanded more respect than manufacturers. However, the situation gradually changed when industrial enterprises began to expand more rapidly: size impressed, and the wealth accompanying it did not fail to make an impact on socially dominant circles. Of course it was increasingly recognized by the public at large that Germany's status as a world power rested more on its industry and its industrial growth than on agriculture and commerce. This development was not universally welcomed, but observers could not help being impressed by the growing economic power the industrialists represented. Apart from labour disputes, strikes, and social problems, the educated public knew little about the organization of industry and the emergence of large groups. Rather than trying to understand business operations it was easier to be interested in the man behind the large companies—and it did not matter much whether the growing industrial empires were in the hands of managers or run by family entrepreneurs. Thus the lives of tycoons like Krupp, Stinnes, and Thyssen began to fascinate the public.

Rathenau's industrial career particularly impressed those who had a considerable appreciation of the scope of Germany's industrialization and the growth of new industries in the field of electro-technology. Yet before the war the interest in the captains of industry was only at an early stage, and perhaps nowhere near American standards. A few years after the war the situation seemed to have changed completely. The Foreign Minister, Gustav Stresemann, called the industrial tycoons the kings of his time.[14] Obviously their social prestige had grown and their political power was recognized, but in the eyes of a large section of the public they still had not reached the top of the ladder. The rising prestige of industrialists during the war and shortly afterwards was matched by a strong anti-capitalist and anti-industrial feeling in large sectors of the population. Industrial power was regarded as a dark force which with its drive for maximum profitability was the cause of human misery and frustration. Industry had strengthened materialism, and had forced agriculture to step down from its socially dominating position, reducing its economic importance and weakening the rural population. But since the debate in the 1890s of *Industriestaat* versus *Agrarstaat* there was hardly anyone who advocated a return to pre-industrial life,[15] and although the industrialists were satisfied with the outcome of the controversy, some of them had no wish to reduce the importance of agriculture and its power as a political ally.

However, industrialists were not able to take over political positions previously held by men who were much more closely attached to the agrarian world, and naturally there were several captains of industry who wanted to see their growing economic power somehow translated into strong political influence. They were no longer satisfied with interest groups or parties in the Reichstag, preferring direct contact with members of the Government and leading officials. Above all many industrialists felt that their growing economic power ought to have a political equivalent. Of course they were able to

[14] Bernhard (ed.), *G. Stresemann, Vermächtnis*, vol. ii, p. 300.
[15] Barkin, *The Controversy over German Industrialization.* See also Hellige (ed.), Rathenau–Harden.

influence a number of political decisions, but they desired a much greater role in shaping the course of German politics. Walther Rathenau was in the forefront of those entrepreneurs who wanted to be more involved in high politics and who were very much aware of the general industrial demand to have a greater say in political matters.

Especially in his writings, Rathenau revealed a desire for moderate reforms which might nevertheless enhance industrial influence. He was convinced that society as a whole would benefit from the influence of those whose business operations were largely dictated by an economic rationale. He believed that the degree and regularity of their influence would have to be increased because other economic and social groups exercised political influence disproportionately to their position in the national economy. Max Weber had observed that industrialists were underrepresented in the parliamentary bodies of Wilhelmine Germany; Rathenau shared this opinion, but he went a step further and wanted the captains of industry to wield much more political influence because he identified industrial interest with 'national interests'.[16] For him the State was still too autonomous and state bureaucracy too narrow-minded to understand the ongoing process of industrialization and to allow the leaders of that process adequate political power. Of course there existed contacts between industrial interest groups and ministries, especially when a new piece of legislation was prepared, regardless of whether the initiative originated in the public or the private sector. However, there was no guarantee that regular consultation would take place, nor were the leading industrialists sure that their opinion would be sought. Rathenau wanted a type of 'co-operation' with the State which went beyond existing levels. The bureaucracy's belief in its own competence, the interdepartmental rivalry, and the competition among industrialists in the economic and political spheres did not make any change easier, but the prevailing capitalist economy was felt to make the State more dependent on the market leaders of the most important economic sector than it had hitherto been.

Rathenau's proposals, made to the Imperial Secretaries of the Interior and the Treasury, for the introduction of a Reich monopoly in the electrical supply industry were opposed by the Prussian Ministry of Public Works at the instigation of three dominant Ruhr industrialists.[17] Obviously, state bureaucracy was as divided as industry. The Imperial bureaucracy was often in a position of rivalry

[16] Weber, 'Der Nationalstaat und die Volkswirtschaftspolitik', p. 18.
[17] Baudis and Nussbaum, *Wirtschaft und Staat*, vol. i, pp. 112 ff.

with the administration of the German states, and the latter often found itself under pressure from provincial and local institutions. Industry, on the other hand, was not only divided between the large groups on the one side and small and medium-sized enterprises on the other. It was also divided between different types of industry like the electro-technical and steel industries as well as between the personal ambitions of industrial tycoons.[18]

Industrial development became even more complex from the 1890s onwards. Industry began to contribute more to the gross domestic product than agriculture, forestry, and fisheries. More workers were employed in industry than in agriculture, and more people lived in cities than in small towns and villages. In particular, the growth of large cities with more than 100,000 inhabitants— the minimum required for a town to be called *Grosstadt*—was matched in industry by the growth of large companies which employed more than 5,000 people. In 1887 there were about ten of those; twenty years later this figure had grown five times, eleven of the companies in question employing more than 20,000 people. By 1913 there were at least five companies with more than 50,000 employees each.[19]

In general, the complexity of industrial development does not easily allow concepts like 'state monopolistic capitalism' or 'organized capitalism' to be used.[20] They presuppose a far greater amount of uniformity in the political and economic behaviour of industrial enterprises as well as a more easily identifiable pattern of interaction between industry and State than actually existed. In fact the changes Rathenau wished for were closer to what these theories were trying to establish than the existing reality.

As might be expected, Rathenau welcomed the development towards an industrial society. He did not think it feasible to feed the growing population in Germany other than by the full industrialization of the country. He was aware of the fact that life might be more pleasant for some people in an agrarian society, but industry and technology provided the only means of keeping Germany in the forefront of the leading nations. To him agriculture was a type of industry, although an antiquated one: he considered it to be too dependent on industry to offer a successful alternative. It seemed pointless to him for Germany to try to become self-sufficient in food if her working capacity could be used more efficiently in

[18] Pogge von Strandmann, 'Widersprüche im Modernisierungsprozess Deutschlands'.

[19] Kocka and Siegrist, 'Die hundert grössten deutschen Industrieunternehmen'.

[20] See the latest East German contribution by Baudis and Nussbaum, *Wirtschaft und Staat*; also Nocken, 'Corporatism and Pluralism in Modern German History'; Hentschel, *Wirtschaft und Wirtschaftspolitik im wilhelminischen Deutschland.*

industry. The danger to food imports in wartime could be over-come by an alliance system which was based on an internationally agreed division of labour, and which might also help to overcome nationalism and chauvinism. 'And this would be a more worthwhile goal', he wrote to Maximilian Harden, the editor of *Die Zukunft*, 'than the usual diplomacy and possible warfare about Crete and the Straits.'[21]

In the debate about the relative merits of the industrial and agrarian state it was often held that the power behind industry consisted of the big banks which largely controlled industry. Rathenau did not deny that this had earlier been the case, but was convinced that during the 1890s such control was being reversed, and that the representatives of large industrial companies had gained a predominant influence over the banks.[22] He took this to be another proof of his belief that the process of industrialization was speeding up in Germany. He expressed this conviction in a letter to Harden: population growth, he argued, led to industrialization and capitalism which were the only secure foundations for a powerful modern state.[23] And as Germany had become a strong nation it was high time that industrialists were more directly involved in the decision-making process in politics. For Rathenau the German Empire was a fully fledged capitalist country which had, in contrast to Britain, a strong agricultural sector. He did not believe that capitalism in Germany was essentially different from British, French, or American capitalism. When he compared Germany with other countries in these terms at all it was to express his belief that industrial capitalism in Germany was more advanced than in other industrial countries except perhaps America. Britain's relative industrial decline was described by Rathenau in 1906: he blamed the trade unions, the quality of engineering training, and the lack of management skills.[24] He also castigated the resistance to innovation and the way in which industry was financed.

The British industrialist, he wrote, would repeatedly ask himself, when new investment was required, 'will it pay?', and in the mean-while his existing plant became outdated. The existing campaigns of 'Buy British' did not make economic sense to him, and were worse than the abolition of free trade because they were too subjective. He saw Britain's future in the tertiary sector and in administering a third of the world.

---

[21] Hellige (ed.), Rathenau–Harden, Rathenau to Harden, 15 October 1897.
[22] Pogge von Strandmann, *Unternehmenspolitik und Unternehmensführung*, pp. 27 ff.
[23] See fn. 21 above.
[24] Rathenau, 'Englands Industrie', *Gesammelte Schriften*, vol. iv.

However, his belief in German industry was not matched by a corresponding admiration for the political consciousness of his fellow industrialists. He criticized the industrial bourgeoisie for its political indolence; that is to say for not joining forces to pave the way for greater industrial influence in politics. He was less interested in democratic developments, but wanted to achieve, through a wider application of liberal constitutionalism, greater influence on politics at the expense of the agrarians. He hoped that the division within the middle classes and liberal parties could be overcome by a general recognition of the importance of industrial aspects in politics. His political enemies were the Social Democratic Party (hereafter SPD) and the agrarians, but he thought that the official hostility towards the labour movement should be replaced with a flexible attitude. He aimed at the integration of the socialist voters into the State, not because he wanted to practise social harmony but because he was keen on national efficiency which could not be achieved with policies directed against a third of the electorate, namely the SPD voters. If integrative policies meant a move towards more democracy he would have been in favour of it, unless industrial predominance could somehow be assured by other means. To him, industry remained the key factor in the economy, in politics, and in society.

However Rathenau did not want simply to replace the previous agrarian predominance with an industrial one. He saw industrial domination as a transitory phase to achieve a greater 'spiritualized' period in human history. Industrial growth was not to be an end in itself, but the material basis for something like a 'spiritual elevation'. Therefore it was possible for him to be dualistic: to condemn the materialism of his age and at the same time regard it as necessary for a higher, non-materialistic achievement. The men who were to lead society to a new spiritual life would belong to an élite which would be mainly middle class. They would probably have made their career in industry. The justification for their leadership would lie in their selection through competition and in the historical triumph of the middle classes rising through the industrial revolution. Rathenau displayed a strong belief in Social Darwinism and this included a racialist component based on the thoughts of Gobineau. Thus he was convinced that the northern European middle classes would eventually dominate the world.

The more important industry became in his life, the more he was willing to leave behind his earlier belief in Nietzsche's philosophy. As he moved away from Nietzsche he also shed his admiration for the Prussian Junkers. In the last years before the war he advocated a new selection system for the army, the civil service, and the Government in general. The aristocracy might have played a significant and worthwhile role in the past, but Rathenau did not think that their predominance was justified any longer. To him, the rise of the manager in industry and banking typified a much sounder system which should be extended to other spheres of society. It followed from this that he joined those who called for modest political reforms such as the redrawing of constituency boundaries, the abolition of the three-class franchise in Prussia, and a different taxation system. The aim was not to weaken Wilhelmine Germany but to strengthen it. Like Friedrich Naumann, he held that reforms would enable the Government to conduct a more vigorous and imperialist foreign policy. On the domestic side, 'harmful' social divisions could be reduced if social reforms could have as a component the attempt to achieve the 'realm of the soul'. A 'harmonious' society would be the result. This would eliminate the polarization between 'capitalism and proletariat' and instead introduce a 'solidarity of production'. 'Creativity' and 'ethical standards' would figure more prominently.[25]

In a way, he was trying to soften the impact of continuous industrialization by striving for ethical achievements which would reconcile him to the crass materialism of industrial growth. Therefore he wanted to abolish luxury, to restrict unnecessary demands, to tax away excessive private affluence, and to introduce an uncompromising inheritance tax. 'Distribution of property', he wrote, 'is not a private affair, any more than is the right to consume.'[26] He continued that 'richness should be replaced by prosperity which in turn is based on creativity and responsibility for one's work or one's own society'. The striving for profits should be replaced by industrial power and influence, and the workers should be allowed to participate in management. Finally, he hoped to eradicate poverty and establish the principle of equal opportunitites. This, in short, was his programme for the post-war economy which he put forward in his book *In Days to Come* and which he elaborated more in his pamphlets about the state, society, and the economy.

To sum up, he considered that it was not sufficient to advocate industrial growth without creating the conditions under which a large number of people could benefit from a stimulation of consumption. He did not want to start with the demand side of the economy, but put production first so that a stimulated demand could follow. However, it would only be worth while going ahead with his proposals if at the end industrial materialism could be replaced by a high

[25] Rathenau, *Von Kommenden Dingen* (ed. by Schulin), pp. 327–34.
[26] Ibid., pp. 343–81.

degree of 'spiritualization'. The world would benefit from industrialization and living conditions would improve. Nevertheless, with his
own industrial experience he was fully aware of the industrial
dynamism which would penetrate all aspects of life and thus promote growth without any clear ulterior purpose. To control this
dynamism he rejected competition as wasteful, preferred well-
integrated large industrial units because of economies of scale,
and believed that the employed captains of industry would be better
suited to responsible economic expansion than the owners of
personal enterprises. He assumed that the former especially would
be more interested in the welfare of society as a whole and therefore
should be involved in politics.

But there was another reason why he thought that certain industrialists should be more concerned than others. As the electricity
generating industry had to plan consumption and create appropriate
facilities on a wide scale in collaboration with local and provincial
authorities, Rathenau was ready to think more in terms of co-
operation with the State than many other members of the business
community. In his position he had to concern himself more with the
economic situation, the potential areas for development, the living
standard of the consumer, and the question of public control. The
technical needs of interconnecting power plants demanded the crossing of political boundaries, and made a regulating central authority
at least desirable. As a result, Rathenau's interest in politics in Berlin
was strengthened, and it brought him into close contact with
Prussian and Imperial governmental institutions. Personal inclinations apart, he was also drawn into the political sphere by circumstances. In this respect other industrialists, be it in the chemical, the
machine-building, or the heavy industrial sector, started from different assumptions when they turned towards politics.

However, there is no evidence to suggest that Rathenau pursued a
markedly different line towards his own AEG workforce from that
of other industrialists towards theirs. Unlike other employers he did
not favour the so-called yellow, non-socialist trade unions, but he
supported the pension funds for white-collar workers, discount
facilities for the workforce, education schemes for gifted workers,
and tied accommodation facilities for loyal service. Rathenau was
also concerned with the improvement of working conditions, but
mostly because he thereby hoped to increase productivity. Like his
father he believed that the existing economic situation at the time
should govern the AEG's relationship with its workforce.[27] Both
father and son were anxious to avoid any disruptions at work,

[27] Pinner, *Emil Rathenau*, pp. 404 f.

therefore both were willing to negotiate with the trade unions. Walther was convinced that a capitalist rationale devoid of any signs of hostility should be the guiding principle for the firm's labour policies.

When political judgement was required, he again revealed greater acumen than many of his colleagues. During the revolutionary days of November 1918 it was he who persuaded his fellow industrialists to concede the eight-hour working day to the trade union leaders. After 1918 he welcomed the formation of factory councils and their participation in the meetings of supervisory boards, but he did not concern himself with wages or the question of adequate remuneration for labour. He continued to believe in the market as a regulator for settling wage demands, and regarded strikes as wasteful. Before the war he had little sympathy for Social Democrats and trade unionists, and this did not change much after the war, but he was willing to recognize them as a political factor and to co-operate with them as he had done before the war. Only in an abstract, macro-economic sense did he talk about labour in a more positive way; the details of labour relations within the AEG-group were left to other board members to deal with. Indeed, had he ever wanted to carry out social experiments within the AEG, or companies where he had a relatively strong position, he would have met with insurmountable opposition and would have ruined his own career in industry. He has often been accused of not practising what he preached, but although there may be some justice in the criticism, it does not take his position within the AEG sufficiently into account. He was dependent on a majority for introducing any reforms, and could hardly expect to command any support for what would have been regarded as mere eccentricities. So all he did in this respect was to help some workers to further their education, and even this was never done on a systematic basis. Generally he left reforms for the future and satisfied himself by pointing out that he had provided some guide-lines and thoughts as to how society ought to proceed.

One of his aims was to abolish the 'proletariat', or rather to abolish the conditions which helped to create it. Obviously he did not think of changing the ownership of the means of production: to him a distribution of wealth and equal opportunities would be sufficient to eradicate the conditions which caused the existence of the 'proletariat'. Because of this line, and his unwillingness to back a return to the pre-1914 economic order, he was often accused by industrial colleagues of being a 'socialist'. They did not try to distinguish between Rathenau's views and socialist theories; they often believed that he intended to nationalize large-scale industry.

But they were mistaken. Rathenau aimed at a corporatist economy, and intended to institutionalize industry in branch organizations similar to the war corporations he had helped to set up in 1914–5. Industrial enterprises ought to remain in private hands and 'the function of the state should not be', as he wrote at the end of November 1918, 'to possess and to suppress free initiative, but to regulate and to balance . . .'.[28] A month later he again stressed his conviction: 'through a free [market] economy and free ability we shall attain new wealth'.[29] This was not socialism, but several industrialists were terrified that a powerful insider, one of their own kind, had failed to join the campaign for a return of the economy to pre-war conditions, and was speaking instead in favour of a close and institutionalized co-operation with the state. The steel industrialists of the Ruhr even started a press campaign against him in the spring of 1918. They overlooked the fact that Rathenau wanted to introduce into the post-war situation those elements of capitalism which he cherished. He shared their platform when he rejected the introduction of a planned economy, but they in turn opposed his idea of a 'regulated capitalism'. Their willingness to collaborate with the State did not extend beyond the pre-war pattern, while Rathenau regarded the former peace economy as 'anarchy'. He wanted to save the large-scale industrial enterprises from the threat of socialism because to him they were the most valuable result of capitalism—he compared them with sophisticated works of art which needed to be preserved. They should become what he called 'objective enterprises' under a 'depersonalized ownership.[30]

In Rathenau's view the organizational structure of large-scale industry bore a strong affinity to the organization of the State. If large-scale industry and the State grew more alike then it would be easier to overcome the pre-war dualism of State and economy. This process would be helped by all industrial matters becoming political matters, and the greater part of politics being reduced to its economic denominator. He wanted to replace the pre-war State with a decentralized and functional one which would become the centre of all economic life. Although the task of reconstructing the economy and society after the war would let industry and government become nearly interchangeable, he recommended for industry 'self-administration, not a state-run economy, free initiative, not bureaucracy, power to create order, not

---

[28] Rathenau, *Nachgelassene Schriften*, vol. i, p. 89.
[29] Ibid., p, 92.
[30] Rathenau, *Von Kommenden Dingen* (ed. by Schulin), p. 375.

INTRODUCTION: WALTHER RATHENAU

arbitrariness'.[31] In any case the central role of industrialists in politics would be assured.

The industrial opposition to Rathenau's ideas was divided into two groups. One consisted mainly of small and medium-sized enterprises, and objected to his emphasis on large companies; and the other found its support chiefly in heavy industry. This group suspected that he was out to curtail its expansion and its growing influence. Of course their opposition was not always consistent, and Rathenau himself was willing to bury the hatchet on occasions in order to co-operate with the captains of heavy industry. Thus the Stinnes–Legien Agreement of 16 November 1918 between the Trade Unions and large-scale industry found Rathenau and his industrial and political antipode, Hugo Stinnes, on the same side.[32] They extended their accord to the setting-up of the Zentralarbeitsgemeinschaft (Central Working Community of the German Commercial and Industrial Employers and Employees). However, there was another dimension to the rivalry between the coal and steel industrialists and the President of the AEG. The former wanted to preserve their predominant position which they had substantially extended during the First World War. They also intended to influence politics from their position of strength. Rathenau, on the other hand, had constantly tried to challenge and resist the rise of the steel industrialists in whom he saw a threat to the independence of the large groups in the manufacturing industry. The need for cheap raw materials and semi-finished products made the electro-technical and the machine-building industries vulnerable to heavy-industrial vertical integration, which aimed at bringing under its control the entire process from steel-making to the final product. Rathenau's plan to introduce a functionally organized economy also aimed at preserving the manufacturing industry's independence against a heavy-industrial 'price dictatorship' combined with expansionist moves among steel industrialists.[33] The rising power of the steel industrialists gave Rathenau's wish for industrialists to enter politics a new dimension. It was a matter of some urgency that industrialists from the manufacturing sector should join politics; the chances for it were generally better after 1918 than before 1914.

Whether one takes Rathenau's writings, his political career, or his daily affairs into account, his industrial experience dominated every

[31] See for a number of similar sources, Rathenau, *Nachgelassene Schriften*, vol. i, pp. 90 ff.; *Reden*, pp. 144 ff., 'Die Neue Wirtschaft', *Gesammelte Schriften* (ed. 1929) vol. v, pp. 202 ff.
[32] See now Wulf, *Hugo Stinnes*, pp. 87–107.
[33] Pogge von Strandmann, 'Widersprüche im Modernisierungsprozess Deutschlands', pp. 236 f.

aspect of his manifold activities. He was *un homme industriel.* He understood the significance of science and technology, was well aware of some of the economic complexities, and realized the social problems. He remained an optimist with regard to industrial progress but was not blind to inherent dangers, and was therefore keen to lead a campaign against materialism. However, his occasional far-sightedness did not enable him to provide original solutions. He was a synthesizer rather than an innovator. He told his publisher Samuel Fischer 'that the law of my existence dictates that I do not develop ideas, but listen to them'.[34] His originality lay in recognizing the importance of certain ideas and projects and in supporting them. Thus he was not the only man to suggest that the wartime supply of raw materials should be centrally organized, nor was he the only industrialist to advocate the normalization of relations with Soviet Russia. In the first case credit has to be given to his employee Wichard von Moellendorff, and in the second it was Rathenau's industrial colleague at the AEG, Felix Deutsch, who favoured an economic *rapprochement* with Russia after 1917.[35] But whoever may have been the source of his initiatives, he saw himself as the translator of these suggestions into actions, and more specifically into political actions. In the first case it was he who approached the Prussian Minister of War, Erich von Falkenhayn, in August 1914, in order to propose an organization for raw materials and in the second it was he who eventually signed the agreement with Soviet Russia at Rapallo in 1922.

Another view of the development of Rathenau's ideas can be gained from his experience of a mixed economy in the electrical supply industry. Rathenau had first-hand evidence of how the city of Strasbourg had wrested control from the AEG over the regional power-station and supply company in 1910.[36] As a result, the city and the AEG were able to co-operate to their mutual satisfaction, especially in their efforts to extend the power-supply company's influence over the whole region of the Upper Rhine. Rathenau used this co-operation as a model when he elaborated his plans for a state monopoly, but without much success: the plans were shot down by Ruhr industrialists, who as the greatest generators and suppliers of electricity mobilized the Prussian ministers against them.

Despite this pre-war failure Rathenau did not give up any of his

[34] Rathenau, *Briefe*, vol. ii, p. 202. Rathenau to Fischer, 27 November 1919.
[35] D. G. Williamson, 'Walther Rathenau and the KRA'; Pogge von Strandmann, 'Rapallo —Strategy in Preventive Diplomacy'.
[36] Ott, 'Privatwirtschaftliche und Kommunal(Staats)Wirtschaftliche Aspekte beim Aufbau der Elektrizitätswirtschaft'.

plans. Instead he developed them into a general system and made them the pivot of his wartime books, after he had gained further experience in setting up the KRA. When he established this interventionist institution he was quite aware of certain implications which would affect his position. He fully realized that he was helping to undermine the pre-war liberal economy. Thus he confessed in a letter that he was contributing 'to the overthrow of the gods to whom, before August 1914, the world prayed, a world to which I belong and through which I became what I am: an individualist'.[37] He also recognized that this might be the beginning of Europe's decline.

In March 1915 Rathenau left the department he had helped to set up eight months earlier. From that point State control of the privately organized economy had begun to expand. The general attitude among business men was acceptance of the inevitable. This resignation was made easier by an improving profit situation which calmed down most opposition although it did not alter the basic desire to return to the *status quo ante bellum* when the war was over. In any case the structure Rathenau designed was a mixture of state *dirigisme* and business self-administration. It would have been difficult to manage a war economy on mixed lines without the existence of large industrial groups, cartels, and syndicates. Alternatives were ruled out because any greater state interference would have been strongly resented by industry, and a private market economy could not have responded quickly enough to the urgent and one-sided demands of the war situation. Rathenau was impressed by the achievements of his own design and firmly believed that it had to be transferred into the post-war world in some form appropriate to meet the exigencies of demobilization, the change to a peace economy and the revival of the world market. He was not enthusiastic about the desirability of a mixed economy, but thought that any other economy would face even greater difficulties in the post-war world. Precisely because of his pragmatism, which was based on some substantial experience, he was attacked by his fellow industrialists, who regarded him as a traitor to their cause and therefore more dangerous than an exponent of socialist ideas.

However, Rathenau found some response among the educated middle classes and among workers, especially in the Ruhr district, where they did not follow the line the party leadership of the Majority Socialists and the Independent Socialists had taken towards him. Rathenau may have been aware of these reactions, but it was not to

[37] Meridies-Stehr (ed.), *Hermann Stehr–Walther Rathenau*, pp. 26 f. Rathenau to Stehr, 14 August 1914.

the workers that he wished to address himself. If he had a group in mind at all it was the young,[38] but as there was no generally organized youth movement there was no forum for any action on the lines hinted at by Rathenau. He expected to be called upon by the post-war political leadership, on behalf of the nation, to put certain ideas into practice to save Germany from disaster. He was very disappointed when this did not happen, but made no effort to influence directly the rank and file of the refounded parties in the autumn of 1918. This enabled the emerging leadership of the middle parties to neglect his ideas because they were considered to be too vague and too difficult to be absorbed easily into party programmes. His wish to be drawn into the centre of politics presupposed a publicity campaign at the grass roots. But this would have meant that he would have had to give up his position in industry and banking in order to increase his credibility with the public, and he was not prepared to mount such a campaign. True to his style he wanted to enter politics from the top, but he had to wait until May 1921 for the fulfilment of this ambition, when Chancellor Joseph Wirth appointed him Minister for Reconstruction.

By the autumn of 1918 it had become clear that he would not be asked to enter politics at a very high level, so he tried to improve his position by continuing to write. On the industrial side he attempted to limit the expansion of the steel industrialists, and especially of Hugo Stinnes, by exploring possible alignments of the AEG with Krupp, the Gutehoffnungshütte, and the MAN. Neither strategy worked. During 1919, once the revolutionary events were over, he was politically isolated. His anti-socialist views made it impossible for the Social Democrats to use him, and the middle parties disliked his so-called socialism. On the industrial side it was Hugo Stinnes who landed the major post-war coup when he merged his already vast empire with the AEG's rival Siemens. Rathenau's industrial grand design had failed, and from then onwards the AEG was on the defensive and could only hope that it would not be squeezed too much by its rivals.

Although he left the task of protecting the AEG to a large extent to Felix Deutsch, Rathenau kept his prestigious industrial positions to facilitate his entry into politics at a higher level. His industrial card remained his only trump once he gave up publishing his ideas after 1919. His interests moved to the management of the industrial and economic side in politics. In this field he was able to impress and convince, and thus become more acceptable to, the middle parties, especially as he appeared to have shed some of his more

[38] Rathenau, *An Deutschlands Jugend.*

radical proposals. His doctrine that successful politics depended upon an efficient industry paved the way for his ministerial appointments in two Coalition Governments based on middle-party support. As he regarded a sound industry as the most important factor for a revival of Germany as a Great Power he was also acceptable as a politician to several leading industrialists, although they never forgave him for some of his writings.

As he was trying to establish industrial primacy in German politics, the Weimar Republic was in this respect more acceptable to him than Wilhelmine Germany had been. Part of him would have preferred a modernized and reformed monarchical Germany to have survived: nevertheless, he was satisfied with the situation because his wish for the involvement of more industrialists in politics had been realized, and because his own entry into high politics was the fulfilment of a life-long ambition.

In his novel *Contro-passato prossimo*, Guido Morselli pursues what he calls an 'alternative reality'; he lets Rathenau become Chancellor of a victorious Germany and later Foreign Minister of a united Europe.[39] In these positions Rathenau works less for his industrial interests and more for his general concepts. It is hard to say how realistic such a vision is. Obviously Rathenau could have had a greater chance to elaborate some of his ideas in detail if he had lived beyond 1922, but whether he would have found that his sense of realism would have been stronger than his idealism remains an open question.

In the event, Rathenau only became Foreign Minister of a defeated Germany for a period of five months. This time-span was too short for him to effect any reforms in the Foreign Office, but it is clear that under him economic questions figured more prominently than under his predecessors.[40] Did his past in the business world mean that he was an industrialist in politics, or a politician who had at last found his *métier*? This question has occupied the minds of several authors, among them Albrecht Mendelssohn-Bartholdy, who wrote that 'Rathenau, when it came to politics, was an industrialist first and last'.[41] Robert Michels, on the other hand, has tended to emphasize large-scale industry as the power base for Rathenau's influence in politics.[42] James Joll has weighed up the industrialist against the intellectual and has concluded 'that he was a successful industrialist who thought he was an intellectual'.[43] If Rathenau

[39] Morselli, *Contro-passato prossimo*, Milan 1975.
[40] See also Doss, *Das deutsche Auswärtige Amt*, pp. 303 ff.
[41] Mendelssohn-Bartholdy, *The War and German Society*, p. 224.
[42] Michels, *First Lectures in Political Sociology*, p. 95.
[43] Joll, 'Walther Rathenau—Intellectual or Industrialist?', p. 61.

was mainly an industrialist, he was also of necessity a politician at the same time, because of the particular position of the electro-technical and generating industry. This was the starting-point for his scheme to bring the two spheres, industry and politics, closer together. He also aimed for a rationality in politics brought about by economic considerations centred on the idea of an institutionalized co-operation between State and industry. He was well aware that the large enterprises would benefit most from his plans, and justified this by pointing out that what was good for the market leaders would benefit society as a whole. A regulated super-capitalism based on large-scale industry was to his mind the panacea for all social, economic, and political troubles of the post-war world. And he believed that he himself was well equipped through his position in industry and politics to guide Germany to a revival as a Great Power, although he overestimated the positive effects of industry on politics, and the actual possibilities open to captains of industry if they entered politics.

This expectation has to be seen against the background of the change in Imperial Germany from an agricultural to an industrial society, and the fast growth of industrial empires in the electro-technical, chemical, and steel industries. As one of the most success-ful industrialists, Rathenau defended capitalism in a flexible way at a time when it was threatened by the social and political upheavals in post-war Europe. His main concern was to safeguard the prosperity and continuing expansion of large-scale enterprises. He was a political industrialist who, drawing upon his own experience in the business world, was able in his writings to reflect upon the political and social implications of the ongoing process of industrialization. Combining as he did the position of a highly skilled practitioner of the capitalist economy with the role of an ideologue of industrial capitalism he may justly be called a grand master of capitalism.

THE EAST AFRICAN JOURNEY

Until recently, Rathenau's journeys to Africa with the Colonial Secretary, Bernhard Dernburg, have been neglected. There are three reasons for this: his motives for going were not known; it was not possible to establish any connection between the journeys and the rest of his life; and historians have generally paid little attention to colonial policy during the last eight years before the First World War. The fact that the industrialist and banker Rathenau accompanied the former banker Dernburg had, therefore, hardly been noticed.[1] This has now changed. Some recent studies on East Africa have underlined the effects of their visit on the formation of Germany's colonial policy.[2] Together with the newly appointed Governor of East Africa, Albrecht Freiherr von Rechenberg, they developed a programme by which for some time the emphasis in colonial policy was altered. A more efficient infrastructure was to be developed, and African agriculture was to be greatly improved. Peace, economy, and reform were to be the guide-lines which would characterize a new phase in colonial policy, the 'Dernburg era'.[3] However, owing to political opposition in Berlin as well as among the white settlers in the colony the chances of success were somewhat reduced. Dernburg, Rechenberg, and Rathenau held similar views on imperialism. Dernburg and Rechenberg shared Rathenau's opinion that the Government should initially provide the capital to build up an infrastructure which would then attract private investment. The biggest project of this kind which was envisaged was the construction of the so-called Central Railway from Dar es Salaam to Lake Tanganyika. All three were advocates of this scheme, but while Rathenau and Dernburg assumed that a railway line would generally develop the area through which the railway would be built, Rechenberg insisted that an efficient local transport system was necessary to strengthen the local African peasant economy.

As neither Rechenberg, Dernburg, nor Rathenau had shown any great enthusiasm for the colonies before 1906/7 it seems justified to assume that their concern reflected the increasing interest in colonial policy in Germany after 1904. The importance of the colonies had grown because of the war in South West Africa (1904-7) and the Maji-Maji revolt (1905-6), and by the so-called colonial scandals—the public's concern about the maladministration of the German colonies. The Chancellor, Bernhard, Prince von Bülow, was able to dissolve the Reichstag in December 1906 by exploiting a colonial issue, using a difference of opinion with the Centre Party regarding a supplementary budget

---

[1] Federn-Kohlhaas, *Rathenau*, pp. 55 ff.; Kessler, *Rathenau*, pp. 138 f.; Böttcher, *Walther Rathenau. Persönlichkeit und Werk*, pp. 84 ff.; Fürstenberg, *Carl Fürstenberg*, p. 471; Berglar, *Walther Rathenau*, pp. 9, 47, 132; Stoecker (ed.), *Drang nach Afrika*, pp. 144, 149; Gann and Duignan, *The Rulers of German Africa*, p. 53.

[2] Schnee, *Als letzter Gouverneur*, pp. 92-5; Austen, *Northwest Tanzania*, pp. 77-80; Iliffe, *Tanganyika*, pp. 79 ff.; Tetzlaff, *Koloniale Entwicklung*, pp. 222-32; Bald, *Deutsch-Ostafrika*, pp. 196 ff.; Smith, *The German Colonial Empire*, pp. 197-202. On Dernburg, see Schiefel, *Dernburg*, pp. 66-73; Medalen, 'Capitalism and Colonialism', pp. 220-38.

[3] Neither the previous inspection tour to East Africa by the Colonial Director, Paul Kayser, in 1892, nor the later ones to West and South West Africa by the Colonial Secretary, Wilhelm Solf, in 1912 and 1913, are of the same significance. Kayser, *Reise nach Ostafrika*; Vietsch, *Wilhelm Solf*; Newbury, 'Partition, Development, Trusteeship'.

and a reduction in the number of troops in the South West as the occasion for doing so. It looked as though the time was ripe for mounting a successful election campaign, on national and international issues, against the Social Democrats and the Catholic Centre Party. As in the elections of 1884, imperialist aims were to rally the educated and propertied classes behind a programme of backing the policies of the Wilhelmine State. In the long run, colonial policy was to serve to integrate the nation, if necessary against the Social Democrats. Thus it was no accident that *Sammlungspolitik* (rallying the right-wing forces into a national bloc), and questions regarding colonial policy, dominated the election campaign of 1906–7. The tactical goal of the so-called 'Hottentot Election' of January 1907 was to strengthen Bülow's reputation, which had suffered on account of his Morocco policy and consequential developments abroad. Bülow hoped to repeat, by his election policy, the success that Bismarck had had in his colonial elections of 1884 and in the Cartel elections of 1887. Like Bismarck's, Bülow's bloc included Conservatives and National Liberals— although this time the left-wing liberal Progressives joined in as well—and, as in the period between 1887 and 1889, the National Liberals pressed for a more active execution of colonial policy.

After the victory of the 'Bülow bloc' at the polls, a Colonial Office was set up in May 1907 and Bernhard Dernburg became its first Colonial Secretary. The appointment of the banker Dernburg as Colonial Director in September 1906 had already made clear Bülow's resolution to give colonial policy a decisive turn and to carry out the colonial programme he had framed in December 1904. With characteristic energy, Dernburg advocated a colonial policy administered from an economic point of view. He thus initiated an era in which, for a few years, the commercial and fiscal points of view seemed to dominate. He cleaned up a few colonial scandals, annulled monopoly arrangements, and brought the budget for 1907 through the Reichstag; he followed this up by planning to go to the African colonies to take stock of the situation personally. He intended to go first to South West Africa and then to East Africa. At the end of May 1907 the plan was changed and it was decided to go only to East Africa.[4]

It is not quite clear when Dernburg persuaded his friend Rathenau to accompany him on his fact-finding tour to East Africa. The first reference to a trip to Africa is to be found in a letter from Maximilian Harden to Rathenau. Harden obviously assumed that Rathenau would not be in Berlin over the following twelve months because he might be 'with the blacks'.[5] It is likely that Dernburg had sounded Rathenau out provisionally soon after he had been appointed Colonial Director, and probably again later, during the election campaign, about a possible joint trip to Africa, without, however, being able to promise anything definite. First the Bülow bloc would have to win the elections, then Dernburg would have to be promoted to the position of Colonial Secretary, and finally Dernburg's programme would have to be accepted by the Reichstag.

It suited Rathenau, who was to leave the banking concern, BHG, on 1 July 1907, that nothing definite could be arranged until May. When the invitation finally came it offered him the opportunity—without obligation, and without severing his ties with business affairs—to become more involved in politics. He had already published his political manifesto in an article, 'Die Neue Ära', which appeared in the *Hannoverscher Courier* shortly after the Reichstag

---

[4] BA Koblenz, RKolA, Personalakten Dernburg, D, 2/5, ii, Dernburg to Woermann, 16 May 1907 and Dernburg to Rechenberg, 31 May 1907.

[5] Hellige (ed.), Rathenau–Harden, Harden to Rathenau, 20 October 1906.

elections.[6] In this article he rejected existing political categories and stressed moral, intellectual, and economic forces as the decisive instruments of international politics. He advocated a moderate liberal course. For future domestic politics he recommended a 'middle-class evolution' which could bring industry to the centre of political power. The article and the journey to East Africa were the first cautious steps towards participation in politics. Soon he found himself in the same circle as people like Ballin, Kirdorf, Gwinner, Gutmann, and Schwabach, who stood in the antechambers of politics and who were thus often able to influence the execution of policy to a not insignificant degree.

When Dernburg finally submitted his plans for the trip, Bülow agreed with them. The Chancellor must have been especially pleased to see Rathenau go as well, because he seems originally to have played with the idea of appointing Rathenau as Colonial Secretary before he approached Dernburg.[7] It is not exactly known what caused Bülow to give up this plan, or even why he had had it in mind in the first place. At any rate, he left himself the opportunity of appointing Rathenau to public office later, after the latter had commended himself by personal service to the Reich.

The final negotiations between Dernburg and Rathenau regarding the tour were soon concluded. On 12 June 1907 Dernburg informed the Chancellor officially that Rathenau was prepared to accompany him 'out of interest in the affair and at his own expense'.[8] Dernburg proposed to include Rathenau, who held no official position, in 'all conversations concerning economic matters'.

The final preparations for the journey were completed in less than a month. On 6 July Rathenau went to see Bülow to discuss the tour. Seven days later those taking part in the expedition left Berlin to embark on a German East Africa Line steamer at Naples on 15 July, except for Rathenau who had left on 10 July for Marseilles, where he boarded the boat earlier. Just before he left Marseilles, Rathenau sent Harden a farewell note in which he confessed to

---

[6] The first hints that Rathenau might leave the BHG are in a letter (ibid.) from Harden to Rathenau, 10 June 1906. After some hesitation Rathenau finally announced his resignation from the bank on 19 June 1906; it was to take effect on 1 July 1907. Rathenau had not quite decided what to do next, and Harden recommended him for public office in an article: 'If I were Chancellor, I would consider this man very carefully. He could become useful in London, New York and also in a large colony.' *Die Zukunft*, 28 July 1906. The article 'Die Neue Ära' is reprinted in Rathenau, *Nachgelassene Schriften*, vol. i. Rathenau had discussed his manifesto with Dernburg and Harden two days after the dissolution of the Reichstag, but because of Harden's sharp criticism it was not published as an article until after the elections.

[7] Bülow, *Denkwürdigkeiten*, vol. ii, p. 266. In a letter to Harden on (probably) 27 July 1906 Rathenau had written: 'No, dear friend, no Bülow can take a crust of bread from me, if it is a case of sending me dishonourably to the Colonial Office, to the negro women and other tasks which I cannot carry out.' BA Koblenz, Nachlass Harden, 85 a. See also Medalen, 'Capitalism and Colonialism', p. 111.

[8] ZStA Potsdam, RK 1663, Dernburg to Loebell, 12 June 1907. Bülow agreed that Rathenau's business experience would be very useful for colonial policy. Bülow to Dernburg, 12 July 1907, Schiefel, *Dernburg*, p. 67. Rathenau had informed Harden on 1 June that he was going to accompany Dernburg to East Africa. He went on to say that he had laid down no conditions and hoped that Harden would not consider him 'foolish'. In concluding he said that 'above all the definite break between old and new . . . [was] important' to him. BA Koblenz, Nachlass Harden 85 a. The agreement was put in a letter to Rathenau on 8 June and accepted by him on 10 June. BA Koblenz, RKo1A, Personalakten Dernburg, D, 2/5, ii.

feeling a bit anxious.[9] The party included, besides Rathenau and Dernburg: Lieutenant-Colonel Quade of the Department for Colonial Troops, Construction Councillor Baltzer, Count Henckel von Donnersmark as aide-de-camp, the landscape painter Wildhagen, whose passage was paid for by Dernburg and Rathenau privately, two low-ranking colonial officials Krüger and Hille, and one personal servant Friedrich Mau. Forty journalists originally applied to accompany Dernburg on his journey, yet finally only seven went along: O. Bongard (*Leipziger Neueste Nachrichten*), C. Alberti-Sittenfeld (*Berliner Morgenpost*), Hornung (*Kölnische Zeitung* and *Strassburger Post*), V. Storz (*Generalanzeiger Düsseldorf und Elberfeld*), Toeppen (*Berliner Lokalanzeiger*), A. Zimmerman (*Wolff Telegraph Bureau*), and E. Zimmermann (*Schwäbischer Merkur* and *Allgemeine Zeitung Chemnitz*). As well as these, Beck of the *Neue Photographische Gesellschaft*, Kliemke, director of the Deutsche Bank and the East African Railway Company, Schubert, a manufacturer from Zittau, and Wilkins, a member of the Colonial Council and a timber merchant, all took part in the expedition.

Notebook 1907

15 July, Monday. Naples. Museum. Photographers. Breakfast with Consul-General von Hartmann. Asemeier's house and garden. Car trip to Camaldoli. Summer in Italy: chestnuts, plane trees, monastery garden, circular seat, a priest on *Usurpazione*,[10] phyloxera. Back along the Corso. Tennis club, dinner by the bay, dusk. Embarkation 9.30 p.m.; departure along the gulf.

16 July, Tuesday. Dawn, Stromboli. Two villages trustfully in the bosom of the volcano; the crater. Circle of the Lipari Islands.
    Noon: Straits of Messina. Etna in the mist. The circle of Messina's harbour. Reggio [di Calabria].
    Calabria: naked mountains, brown and reddish-yellows, craters and peaks.
    The land retreats.

17 July, Wednesday. Early heat, moderate at noon. Blue tones, warm wind. Crete invisible.
    Party table and birthday jokes on the upper deck.
    Evening: Naval officers' reception.

18 July, Thursday. Sunrise: copper and greyish-blue, behind, a wall of mist rises up; red, Egyptian orb. Then shining high; daytime colours.
    Evening: colonial troopers.

[9] BA Koblenz, Nachlass Harden 85 a (undated), Hellige dates the letter 13 July.
[10] i.e. the seizure and dissolution of the Papal States (1870).

19 July, Friday. Noon, green sea. 3 o'clock, Port Said.

Hoary old consul;[11] his dealings with Omar and Ali. Harbour trip. Casino. Bastard nature of the city.

Evening atmosphere. The ship: three airy decks in the grey calm of the harbour. Reflecting coloured lights; dark hulls pass by. From the side a cross-section of the city: music and lights.

Network of moonlight on the water. Ships with searchlights far off in the bosom of the canal: drawing near, moving away.

Silent departure, gliding slowly, carried by the evening breeze into the dark of the land (a lake to one side).[12]

20 July, Saturday. Morning in the canal. Two deserts, salt lakes, green threads of artificial vegetation. Threefold blue of sky, sea and canal: shining streaks of gold, rose and violet.

The land of wandering through the wilderness.

At noon the canal opens into the bay. Shining light-green, blue-shadowed surface, bordered in a wide arc by cliffs through which light can be seen. Like a narrow ribbon Suez weaves itself into the distance. Black ships in the harbour: they stay behind; we steer into the Red Sea. Late evening, distant vision of the coast: Sinai.

21 July, Sunday. Night on deck under the stars. Moderate heat, rougher sea. The busy maritime life of the Red Sea. Islands, craggy and bright at sunrise. Towards noon, a long cliff, flat and dominated by a lighthouse. Surprise at the moderate increase in temperature.

22 July, Monday. Night on deck; sultry heat.

Evening: broad swell; the apparent heaviness and indolence of the water.

Behind an iron-grey screen of dust the sun shines pale and wintry.

Misty-grey sky, brooding heat. On the water the gigantic, densely black shadow and reflection of the column of smoke.

23 July, Tuesday. Night on the bridge. Beautiful star phenomena. Greyish-white night sky, illuminated only at the zenith. The stars seem to be broad, moon-like patches.

Maximum daytime temperature, 38 °C.

24 July, Wednesday. Night on the bridge. Quiet and somewhat cooler. Hot throughout the day: early on, volcanic islands; a harbour formed from a crater, surrounded by tri-coloured, rubbly mountains.

[11] H. Bronn.
[12] Lake Mensale, to the west of Port Said.

Noon: Perim,[13] the key to Bab-el-Mandeb, fortified by the English.
Evening: 9 o'clock, Aden.

Black, grey and misty-coloured vanishing mountains enclose the
bay. Milky, muddy sea.

The rowing-boat, handled by six slender Somalis, shoots through
the water.

Silence on the shore. Silhouettes of Negroes and Arabs perched
up high. Away by car. Silent tracks, brown, barren, bereft of vegetation. In the wavering moonlight figures pass by.

Narrow high-turreted gorge, closed over by arched bridge. Entrance
to the crater which encloses the ancient city in a mighty arc; in
the rock Abel's grave. Deserted squares, dead streets. In front of
the houses, stretched out on litters, the sleeping inhabitants:
gleaming white cloth on black limbs; the image of a city ravaged
by plague.

Goats and their kids rest on low walls.

We draw near the deepest fold of the crater. White chapels shine
in the enormous furrows of the cliff. Climb by bridges and footpaths
to the enormous basins of the reservoirs. They serve to collect rain-
water; allegedly built 700 BC.

Back past the camel market. The animals lie like dark patches on
the brown earch. The business city.

Exit through the rock passage. Camel waggons meet head on.
They are hauled back on their reins right to the last ones at the
exit. The gurgling of the throttled animals, the skittishness of the
horses.

Past '*The Last Retreat*', along the sea, to the guest-house.

25 July, Thursday. Early, 4 o'clock, from Aden. A prosaic view of
the Romantic. The mountains are colourlessly grey; ahead the
quarantine island.

26 July, Friday. Noon. Somali coast, then Cape Guardafui. As forecast: from complete stillness to rough sea; behind the second cape
begins the monsoon. Storm in clear air. Abrupt drop in temperature
from 36 °C to 26 °C.

27 July, Saturday. Monsoon in a bright sky, weaker and stronger.
Sultriness and coolness alternate.

30 July, Tuesday. 5 o'clock in the morning. Equator. In the afternoon

[13] A fortified island in the Straits of Bab-el-Mandeb, British since 1857. It belonged to
the Aden Protectorate.

baptism [i.e. the crossing of the Equator ceremony] of the crew
(relief of *Seeadler* and *Bussard*).[14]

1 August, Thursday. Before sunrise. The ship lies in motionless
water, encircled by islands and coasts. Dark green fleece of richest
vegetation, dissolving at sunrise into sharper forms of palms, the
rounder ones of deciduous trees, bungalows surrounded by verandas.

Ashore at Kilindini.[15] First steps in foreign plant life. Night
shadows, feather-duster-like grasses, leathery-leaved bushes, reddish-
yellow paths, fiery red acacia-like blossoms.

Trolley-cars, rickshaws pulled by Negroes. Road to Mombasa:
round, blackish-green mango trees, from a distance like chestnuts,
in groups, in perspective. Bread-fruit trees. Trees with yellow
blossoms. Bluish-red rivers of bougainvillaea. Then plantation-
like maize. A farmhouse in a tropical garden: foliage of every colour.

First houses, old Portuguese fort, Indian quarter. Two merchants
bartering without success. Cool, empty vestibule; tradesmen squatting
on couches adding up accounts and entering up their books. Oriental–
Latin houses; outside staircases. Indian doors, worked in Zanzibar.
White walls, blue shutters.

Stillness of the town. Silent walk of the Negroes.

Negro-types—red, brown, black. Half-castes. Goanese. Children.

Negro quarter. White mud huts, shaggy rush roofs, broad paths.
Village-like. Big trees. Fair-ground bustle.

Costumes: blue, white cloth with gigantic patterns of stars and
checks.

Funeral: the bier carried into a Mosque-hut, 'La-lai-wa-la-lai'.[16]

The image of two Negresses doing their hair. Basin of oil, ridgy
coiffure of little plaits. Stench of fish (shark), spices, Negro goods
laid out on display. Lunch at the club. Conversation about dressing
the *boys* in uniforms.

Ladies as masters.

Reflections on colonial psychosis. The white man as master, in
contrast to his oppressed home situation. Saluting. The police
present arms. Reward and punishment.

Negro melancholy. Their eyes. Silence, *tristitia*, and gaiety.

English officials: Bell, Anderson, Baker; compare with Zanzibar.
African fruits: mangoes, papai [papaw].

[14] On board the steamer *Feldmarschall* were the relief crews for the small, old, un-
armoured cruisers *Bussard* and *Seeadler*.

[15] Originally a Portuguese settlement, to the south of Mombasa.

[16] Presumably Rathenau did not take down the words properly. Possibly a song which
can mean 'lay to rest' in Swahili; but a connection with the word Allah is also possible.

2 August, Friday. Early, Tanga. First visit to German territory in Africa. Broad streets, garden plots; a cement paradise. Negro school: geography and arithmetic. The roll-call. German language. School band. Carpenter's shop. Everything under the aegis of the guided tour of Governor von Rechenberg. Also: von Winterfeld, Nötzel.

Evening: the long coast of Zanzibar. Flat and green. Later, bungalows, palaces, ruins. At last the town, shining in the evening sun: Venice and Constantinople. Sultan's palace in the centre. Lofty, turreted, fantastically built-about with climbing verandas. Chains of light in the dusk. At the cape white terraces with dark trees.

3 August, Saturday. Entered Dar es Salaam. Surprise as the harbour unfolds. Reception formalities. Breakfast with the Governor. Afternoon excursion. Mango trees in bloom, park-like landscape; a departure from the artists' traditional hieroglyphs of palms and bluish-yellow hues.

Very low tide, mud-bank. Graveyards. Burning corpses of heathen Indians. Negro village. Women predominate. The fair-like quality. Quintessence and caricature of the city, which turns out to be the paradise of the inferior race.

Covered market. Comparison of the black crowd clothed in white and white men clothed in black. Favours the former.

Danger for mediocre whites, who see in superiority and submissiveness not responsibility but rather satisfaction for their inclination to tyranny. The former serf can become citizen, but not a master.[17]

Askari barracks. Live with wives and children. Classical layout: court surrounded by halls; in the middle, the hall of the women. Dark rooms. Display by the Askari. Egyptian picture of great beauty. The movement of their eyes. Something monumental about the race.

Stables of the zebra–horse hybrids belonging to the colonial troops.

Repair shops, shipyards and customs houses. Dinner at the Governor's.

---

[17] Although Rathenau has given this statement a rather general meaning, he applies his experience chiefly to German conditions. See his 'Report on the Development of the German East African Colony' which follows. In a letter to Stefan Zweig of 22 July 1909 he returned to his view concerning the inability of Germans to govern: 'Colonizing means governing from conviction. Our people govern from inclination, that is, like upstart servants. It is not true, as they say, that to govern one must be able to obey. This maxim is true of commanding, not of governing. Our people can command, not govern.' Rathenau, *Briefe*, vol. i, p. 67.

4 August, Sunday.[18] Morning, Protestant church. Lunch at the Governor's. Evening, dinner with the colonial troops.

5 August, Monday. Morning, Askari drill till 10.30. Question of suitability for these physiques. Hospital, mortuary. Lunch-time, Governor. 4 o'clock, visit to Seid Chalid, the deposed rightful Sultan of Zanzibar. White antechamber, ceiling beams of round timber. Roughly carpentered, dark-stained doors and window shutters. Free-standing, narrow staircase. Reception room on the first floor similar. Yellow table-cloth, colourful carpet, divan with big flowers, two easy chairs, other chairs. Against the wall a telescope, portraits of his father and grandfather, sabre. The Sultan in a blue and red turban, black robe, white shirt, sandals. Beautiful, dignified, 40 years old. Sometimes a quick, scarcely audible laugh; otherwise very serious. Coffee. In the doorway two servants: brown jackets, brown faces of a different shade of brown. Two small sons come in. They leave their sandals outside the door. The smallest, the [son] of an 'Abschi' (Abyssinian woman), somewhat Negroid.

Then to the former Wali.[19] Old Testament scene. Carpet laid under the overhanging roof. Room on the ground floor: carpets, otherwise white. Sofas against the walls. Tables with pastries. The image of the Arabs of old. One man, rose-coloured, outside. The crowd, standing in the sun and squatting in front of the door. In the inside corner three old men. Black, green, red, white. Yellowish turbans. Heads of prophets. Next to me, Jesaias—little, sharp, dark. Coffee; sherbet = raspberry-water.

A drive. Young coconut plantations. Distant views. Valley of the Spring. Surrounded by oil-palms, which do not grow anywhere else here. The path alive with people fetching water. Whitish, limy water, scooped out with coconut ladles. Loading up the vessels: Rebecca.

Cloud phenomena. Rosy-yellow.

Visit to the Catholic mission.[20] In the evening, reception for the colony at the Governor's.

[18] That same say he wrote to Harden: 'this primeval country is enigmatic and fantastic. Heat and stones have kept us company: today everything lies in a Sunday calm.' BA Koblenz, Nachlass Harden 85a, 5 August, 1907.

[19] The former Wali was Soliman bin Nasr el Lemke. The visit served to enhance the Arabs' standing, and, indirectly, to express thanks for their non-participation in the Maji-Maji Rising (1905–6). Since 1891, Arabs had been drawn into the German administration to an increasing degree, by the system of akidas, who were Muslim administrative officers.

[20] Missionaries of the Benedictine Missions Society took over the Catholic mission in Dar es Salaam in 1888.

6 August, Tuesday. Walk through the Negro quarter. Oil press, turned by six camels. Primitive manufacture. Blindfolded. Covered market. Drive through the shambas[21] with District Officer Böder.

Afternoon: shooting by the Askari. Evening, 12 to dinner on *Seeadler*. Great fatigue.

7 August, Wednesday. Stomach upset. Nevertheless drive with Böder 7–10.30 a.m. Communal farm, Aulep. Coconut plantations; native cattle crossed with European breeds. Catholic mission farm. Two sisters. *Simbasi* = among the lions.[22] Aquarium, polyp. Excused lunch with the Governor. In bad shape afternoon and evening.

8 August, Thursday. Better in the morning. Departure 7 o'clock for Zanzibar. On the way plan for Safari altered.[23] Arrived 11 o'clock.

Brief survey of the town. Behind the gleaming, Venetian façade the bowels [of the town], tangled yet rich and full of life. Nile-green streets in the sun. Dark business streets. Deserted suburban alleys, with graves and huts. Indians as merchants: lying, crouching, squatting in loose, white garments, their feet in their hands. Craftsman holding his work with his foot.

Squatting women. Bluish-green silk trousers, orange gown, rose-coloured jacket, shawl and cap. Colour combinations. Inexpressibly beautiful children. Adults: men fat and well-developed, women lean like gypsies. Trade in spices, cotton, tinware, fruit, canes. Wholesale merchants in cool ante-rooms with money-boxes. Market.

India, Arabia and Africa rub shoulders; in appearance, in customs, in race; half-naked, herculean Negroes, Arab scribes and dandies, noble Indians and beggars.

Noon. *Lunch* on the roof of the African Hotel. Airy, fantastic, delicate stairways, awnings.

Afternoon drive to the clove plantations. Past the lagoon, Guadalquivir![24] English playing-fields. Then *Paul et Virginie* countryside.[25]

---

[21] African orchards and kitchen gardens.

[22] Today Sibasi is Msimbazi, a village in the Suburban District of Dar es Salaam.

[23] Originally it was planned to visit next the southern and then the northern coastal stations, and thereafter Zanzibar, Kilimanjaro, and the Usambara countryside. But the trip to the south was abandoned in favour of travelling on the recently opened first stretch of the German Central Railway to Lake Tanganyika. Now they were to travel by British Uganda Railway to Lake Victoria and from there make for Tabora on foot. Officially it remained open whether the overland route from Tabora to Dar es Salaam or the British Uganda Railway should be taken on the way back. But already from Lake Victoria Rathenau wrote to his parents that the expedition would return by the Uganda Railway to Mombasa and Tanga. Rathenau, *Briefe*, vol. ii, Appendix, pp. 63 f., Rathenau to his mother, 16 August 1907.

[24] River in southern Spain; Arab term for a big river valley.

[25] Bernadin de Saint-Pierre (1737–1814) wrote this novel in 1783.

A park of mangoes. Colourful shrubs. Palms like fans. Huts among the foliage. Clove trees: half laurel, half birch.

Abandoned observation-point. View over palm-fields and in the misty distance, the sea.

Evening, dinner at the consul's.[26] Night on board.

9 August, Friday. 10 o'clock, audience with the Sultan.[27] Palace and exhibition. Stairs, gallery, mirrors, chandeliers, red furniture; everything badly fastened into and on to the walls. Eight mantelpiece clocks.

Arab interpreter. Coffee. Visits: to the general, English consul.[28] Returned by both. Lunch with the consul.[29]

Shopping in the afternoon. Then by steam train to the Indian club, where the locomotive breaks down. Hospitality with dozens of sweetmeats, tea, coffee. Finally yellow bouquets. Aga Khan founder of the sect.[30]

Evening in the German Club. Talk about the plague which broods over everything. Dozens of unsuspecting plague victims spread the infection through the city. The club itself is in the plague area. Sinister roofs and alleys from the balcony.

The representative of the firm of Hansing on Negro fashions. The story of Achmed Buntia: 'Assanti, A.B.'—'Many thanks A.B.', as the motto on a piece of cloth. The vanity and economy of a charming custom. Every month a couple of cloths are treasured up, to be used in old age as a romantic souvenir.

In the evening, a rout at the Sultan's. Conviviality on the veranda. The English as hosts. The motionless punka. Night on board. Departure 2 o'clock.

10 August, Saturday. 8 o'clock, arrival Dar es Salaam. Packing.
Lunch-time, 2 o'clock, departure for Mombasa.

11 August, Sunday. Mombasa. *Boma*: old Portuguese fort. Mules and luggage loaded on. Departure, Uganda Railway.[31]

[26] Ostman von der Leye.

[27] Ali Seid.

[28] The English general was Brigadier-General A. E. Raikes, the English consul Sir Basil Cave.

[29] See fn. 26.

[30] Aga Khan founded the sect of the Hodjas, a branch of the Ismailis. They belonged to the Shi'ites.

[31] The 572-mile long Uganda Railway was built between 1896 and 1902. The total cost, including the interest on loans, came to £7,909,294, 12s. 6d. The railway was built primarily for strategic purposes.

1 o'clock. Rich country. Palms, mangoes, bread-fruit trees. Later on thorns, bush and thicket. Mountains draw nearer. Red earth.[32]

Night. Steppe-fire, circling and advancing. Bush so thick that it seems impenetrable. Voi.[33] Outlines of Kilimanjaro. Uphill. Cool.

12 August, Monday. 5 o'clock, steppe country begins. 6 o'clock, sunrise. Weakly suspended in red haze. Cold. Landscape expands into Campagna. Isolated blue mountains spring up. Volcanic. Aerial perspectives.

Animal world makes its appearance. Lone hyenas. Gazelles in pairs. Herds of gnu and hartebeest.

Purple-red grass. River bed. Stands of trees. Mountains pile up.

Animals in herds. Blue birds, herons, ostriches and buffalo: antelope by the hundred. Zebras.

Flat steppe. Cornfields of a similar colour. In between, scorched earth.

Sun at its zenith. Warm, mountain air. Natives approach. Barter with the Askari for copper wire and bangles. Proud Masai.

1 o'clock, mid-day, Nairobi. Americanizing railway town. H. A. F. Currie.

13 August, Tuesday. 1 o'clock, left Nairobi. Native plantations. Yellow flowers predominate. Sharp reddish-yellow. Land of the Kikuyu.[34] Forests close together. Creepers canopy gorges. Uphill.

Broad beds of dried-up lakes. Fiery-red earth. The Central African Rift Valley (from the Dead Sea) comes closer. Distant mountains come into view. The abyss appears. Immense plain deep down. Ringed around by snow-topped mountains. In the centre, a citadel of a volcano. Descent, in huge serpentines. Temperature increases.

Across the plain. Steppe and vaulting sky. In the evening sun the reflection of a lake appears. Herds of zebra grazing.

Lion-steppe (at Gilgil) as night falls. Scarred earth with short grass transforms the yellow into gloomy grey. Uphill again. Night. The blacks cook. Overnight at Nakuru.

14 August, Wednesday. 4.30 in the morning, train leaves Nakuru. Forests so woven over with lianas that the shapes of the trees are hardly recognizable any more: a solid sea of green. Cedars stand out. Scarred, bast-like, twisted trunks; thin, grey tree-tops.

Upwards to the height of the pass 2,400 m. First: forest meadows

---

[32] Laterite soil.
[33] Town on the Uganda Railway.
[34] The Kikuyu (a Bantu people) are Kenya's largest tribe.

surrounded by hills. One would think it Germany but for greyer trees, rough leaves, different plants. Then mountain meadows, swampy, reddish; sorrel.

Descent through forest and steppe into a valley surrounded by mountains. 3 o'clock in the afternoon, Port Florence (Kisumu), Victoria Nyanza.[35]

Spent the night on board *Clement Hill*.[36]

15 August, Thursday. Negro market. Kawirondo and Nandi tribes.[37] Completely naked. Beautiful women, for the first time. Departure in the afternoon. Among islands, like Capri. At night, the noise of hippopotamus, crocodiles surface, invisible.

16 August, Friday.[38] High sea. Boundless. Afternoon, 4 o'clock, Entebbe. Climb the hill between gardens in blossom. Avenues of solanum trees (nightshade) of all shades of violet. Botanical garden. Tea, coffee, cacao, mastafere, hibiscus, frangipani. A mass of roses which flower three times.

Rebuilding of Government House on the highest hill. View of an expanse of meadows with round trees: hill after hill rings the background, fading away into an ever more delicate grey. Between them, in countless bays, the mother-of-pearl colour of the water that reflects the evening clouds and the subdued light of the sinking sun, which melts thereafter into the silver horizon. Coolness and calm.

Gaze for a long while from the veranda over the darkening meadowland, that loses all its tropical harshness in the falling dusk and reveals what is common to all silent lands on earth.

All around, the domain of the tsetse fly.

17 August, Saturday. Smooth trip across the lake. Evening: mist and lights of Bukoba. Rode at anchor.

---

[35] Lake Victoria.

[36] Clement Hill was the first Superintendent of African Protectorates in the Foreign Office. The steamer was named after him.

[37] Tribes belonging to the Nilo-Hamitics.

[38] In a letter of the same day to his mother, Rathenau mentioned that his brief notes amounted to several dozen pages. He complained that too much time was lost through official engagements, but emphasized that the journey 'is progressing in the best way and on good terms', and described the trip on the Uganda Railway. Regarding his impressions of Lake Victoria he wrote: 'When I, here on the deck of this big steamer, glance across the wide, blue surface, I can hardly grasp this is an inland sea in deepest Africa, immediately under the Equator, and that beneath this surface are innumerable hippopotamuses and crocodiles.' Rathenau, *Briefe*, vol. ii, Appendix, p. 63.

18 August, Sunday. Reception in Bukoba. The first sultan:[39] red cloak held by two servants, yellow gown, green waistcoat, cap. Second sultan: black gown with gold. Third sultan: Kahigi by name, white uniform, white helmet. Arrived later. Strong, dark black, something of a beard, decisive appearance. Welcomed by the women. The men greet one by squatting down and stretching out their hands four times.

A purely Negro town for the first time. The quarter of the round huts. (Captain von Stümer.)

To the mission in the afternoon.[40]

19 August, Monday. Ride to Kahigi. Over three mountain ridges. Women working in the fields. Clothes made of rushes. Head-cloths held on with a band. Men in loincloths. Old Testament parallels.

On the heights, the ruler's houses. Guest-house to the left. Gate and forecourt. Understand Egyptian courts: the rows of identically dressed people are the only décor.

The house: four rooms. Furnishings: linoleum carpet and rugs on the floor. Table to one side with three alarm clocks, two oil-lamps, two brushes, a soap-dish, an umbrella. Table in the centre: pink silk cloth. On the walls two posters, two mirrors, a humorous calendar picture.

In the back room, a bed with mosquito netting, a dismantled bed. In front of it, five wives. One yellowish-red silk, two green silk, two reddish-brown silk.

Nearby, new building.

Back on to the *barasa* (terrace). Negro dance. Group of players with long pipes and tassels. Groups of flautists; like horns. Group of drummers with leopard skins. Above all the jester, horn trinkets, bagpipe. Group of dancing women; singing led by the eldest.

Ox slaughtered, bananas cooked, camp.

Departure through an avenue of the entourage. View over the sea (lake) with bays, islands, foothills.

20 August, Tuesday. Drive to Mwanza. Arrived 4 o'clock in the afternoon. Unusual stratifications of granite on islands and hills. Blocks: one on top of the other, tumbled down, piled up, sticking out in sharp points, spread broadly around. Islands inhabited by crocodiles. Big Negro quarter. Square and round, mud and straw huts. *Boma* by the roadstead; headquarters on a granite hill.

[39] The first two sultans were probably Mutahngarwa of Kiziba and Nyarabamba of Ihangiro.
[40] The Marienberg station was founded by the White Fathers in 1892. The Order was established by Cardinal Lavigerie in 1868. The German mother-house was at Trier.

Councillor Stieglich from the Ministry of Commerce in Saxony, and Böhm, an agriculturist, joined the party travelling from Mombasa to Mwanza. On arriving in Mwanza Quade was sent back to the South West African border area because of Morenga's return.[41] From Mwanza, Dernburg, Rechenberg, Rathenau, Henckel-Donnersmark, Staff Surgeon Engeland, Lieutenant Schön, Wildhagen, and Krüger set off on their march to Tabora. Among the journalists Bongard, Hornung, Storz, Toeppen, and Zimmermann took part. But on the way Toeppen and Zimmermann left the party for health reasons and went back to Mwanza.

The expedition covered the distance between Mwanza and Tabora in twelve days, although eighteen had been allowed for. They went on foot or rode on mules, and followed the telegraph lines to keep in touch with events in South West Africa. After stopping in Tabora for three days the expedition returned back to Mwanza but chose a route lying further to the east. This took them only fifteen days and was also accomplished sooner than had been planned.

21 August, Wednesday. Afternoon, 5 o'clock, set out on Safari. Eight Europeans, five European journalists, two European servants, 300 bearers, *boys*. Askari, eight donkeys and mules, one portable chair.

Evening, camp. Bearers arrive, with a roll of 'drums' on their packs. Askari bed down the animals. Bearers set down their burdens. *Boys* pitch tents. Groups cooking, opening crates. *Boys* busy about the tents.

Fire flames up; dusk and moon. Smoke rises, scent of green wood. Last Post sounded. Fires glow. Boys warm their hands, fry up leftovers of meat. Night. Lightly covered; heads, bodies, feet, they lie around the fire crowded together in rows. From time to time, a movement, a deep breath drawn. The cool of the night.

22 August, Thursday. Reveille at 5 o'clock. Off at 6 o'clock. Between granite bluffs.
Safari.
Breaking camp. Bugle-call before sunrise. Red glow of dawn. Fires still burning. Baggage party on the move. Bearers step up. Tent struck; packs shouldered. Edges strengthened with sticks wrapped around with mats.

Now they stand in rows. Sing-song and chatter. Askari fall in. March begins.

Sunrise. Red rays behind mountains. Up hill.

Harvested maize fields with deep, crooked furrows. Then steppe.

[41] For Morenga's release in June 1907 and the joint Anglo-German hunt for him later, see Drechsler, 'Jacob Morenga'. On 25 August 1907 Dernburg informed Bülow of his counter measures because, owing to Morenga's reappearance, the Chancellor and the Kaiser were very apprehensive about the prospect of renewed fighting in the colony. Only one day (23 September) before Quade arrived in South West Africa Morenga had been killed by a joint Anglo-German action. BA Koblenz, RKo1A Personalakten Dernburg, 2/5, iii, Dernburg to Bülow, 25 August 1907 and Lindequist to Dernburg, 24 September 1907.

Dry, yellow, ungleaned stalks towering as tall as a man. Like corn-fields, but with signs of infertility. In between, patches of black, scorched earth.

Then *pori*[42] on hill ridges. A dried up wood of acacias and thorn bushes. Grey, the branchy tree-trunks; yellow, the dried up grass. Patches of thicket; occasionally light-green shoots, thrusting their way out of the roots.

Over hills and scorched valleys. Piled up blocks of granite appear. Then, a wide view. The *pori* hills, greyish-green, soft yet rugged. Scattered in the valleys, light-green patches of water indicate bananas, maize, and palms.

At the water-oases, villages. The fenced farmsteads enclosed by poisonous euphorbia hedges. The mud houses are round with thatched roofs; a circular passage surrounds the oven-like bedroom. Women and children squat on the dry earth. Provisions stored in clay and wickerwork.

Midday-rest.

The heat has risen from 12° to 28 °C. The first arrivals reach camp at twelve o'clock. Askari with flags. Then comes the first column of bearers, carrying victuals in crates, singing and beating on the crates with sticks. Then those carrying the tents with long green loads. Lastly the food for the baggage gang. Askari bring up the rear.

Meanwhile the women of the place fetch water in gourds and pour it into big black earthenware pots. From time to time they dance a *ngoma*.[43] A child demonstrates a *ngoma* like a ventriloquist. Dialogue between a mother and a crying child. A hut is built for the mules and donkeys. The tents are up, the camp is ready. Old Testament conditions. The men trail off to work with hoes, to plough and to weed. Women take turns with the field-work. Unseamed clothes of one piece: skirt and bodice. Skins, too, as clothing. Bangles on their arms and knuckle-bones as ornaments. Often a metal band (and cloth) around the crown of their heads.——Threshing.

Women's call of welcome: Li-li-li. Dances on the paths. Rare, shared enjoyment. David. Tunes in a minor key.

Youth, old age and death for thousands of years. Without tradition and history. Contrast with the Jordan tribes whose names, traditions, songs and laws still rule the world today.

1 September, Sunday. Entry into Tabora. 37,000 people. Accommodation at the *Boma*. Panoramic view. The hills, in a wide circle, are in gradations like stage scenery. Stories of lions and people. Of

---

[42] Term for sparsely-wooded country.
[43] Swahili word for drum.

Simba-Watu (lion-man). Of the python who devours the wildcat and is chained up in the morning. Of five lions in the camp. Of the lioness who breaks into the hut through the roof. Of the lion who roars and drives the prey to the lioness. Of the laughing of the hyenas. Of their cowardice: the *Schenzis*[44] drive them off with firebrands. Of the lion who prowls through the streets in daylight and carries off children.

4 September, Wednesday. Set out from Tabora by the easterly road back to Mwanza. 3.30 in the afternoon.

5 September, Thursday. Camped with the sultan,[45] who had been a *boy*; produces his testimonial: 'Leaves service to ascend his father's throne.' The farmstead surrounded like a casemate. Shady wild figs outside.

10 September, Tuesday. Safari. On the way: strange Bibi Mtau, old woman, horrible. Story of the burnt down palisades.

Healing centre for eye ailments. The abatis next to the tree, on a ladder. The tree as a source of healing.

Beautiful valley. Deeply embedded, dried up river. Umbrella acacias. Grass as tall as a man. Bird song. Monkey-bread trees.

Story of the lion who carries an ass, tossing it up and down. A leap over the stockade with an ox in his muzzle.

Wild sow. Guinea-fowl, cranes, dwarf antelope. Traces of leopards, kiboko, cats, baboons.

14 September, Saturday. On *pori* paths. Narrow track, hard like a channel. Endless patches of yellow stalks billow up on both sides. Trees, in a park. At close range nothing but thorns. Prickly bushes, acacias; the spherical archings of the thorny branches of a bush, which bears ruby-red, brush-like blossoms. Track narrows; grasses as tall as a man. Then, creviced, black, the deepest bottom [of the valley] opens up. Scorched patches, groups of taller trees, granite plateaux. Then a sudden view. On the horizon, sky-blue, sharp peaked chains of hills, thrust back by light, greyish-blue swellings. In front of them, rounded yellow surfaces; patches of green bushes mark villages. Herds of cattle to the fore; to the left, a sharp point of brownish-grey, patchy *pori*-land cutting into the plain. At its fullest arch, the sky's sphere threaded through with light cloud-flakes. Our native sky, which blends the contrasts.

[44] Swahili word for garbage, but also for people who are in no way respected.
[45] Probably a sub-chief of the Wanjamwesi.

15 September, Sunday. Postscript to 'Patriarchal Air and Atmosphere'. People with string-like little plaits, reminiscent of Pharoahs' tombs. Strings of blue glass beads on dark upper arms. The fine creases of much-used linen. Change of loincloth. Sandals tied between big and second toe. Songs with weak rhythm, tight modulation (reflection on the long notes and, therefore, meaningful expression of our folk-songs. The long duration of the same mood in contrast to the rapid change of the southerner.) Palms as a symbol and as décor.

Postscript. Story of Kasimoto. 'I am called Selim.[46] I love to work and will satisfy you. Therefore, call me Kasimoto.' (Ardent work.)

16 September, Monday. Thunder in the distance. Then, first rain. Scent of the countryside. Sprouting green.

18 September, Wednesday. Eight hour march from Missungi to Mwanza. Captain Merker. Concerning the Masai.[47] An old Semitic people.

Tradition of Moses, the father a stutterer. Inauguration of the week. Story of *Kerio* (paradise). Mother cult. 'Mother and father.' (Missionary pupils.) Nicholas Bay. Salesman: 'Books like this are only published once.'

On the origins of the risings.[48] The huts of their forefathers. Pilgrimages of 400 to the *Fumo* for the sake of the *Dana.* To men: invulnerable; the guns will spew water. To women: grains against deformity and pestilence. Then prophecy is changed. The brave will rise up, the cowards be consumed by an inner fire.

Story of the Negro boy, who brings the captured hyena into the tent. Of the monkey on the tree who watches over the herd (long-tailed monkey). Of the missionary, the leopard and the terrier. Of the lion in the sleeping-car. Of the Masai, who demands to fight on an equal footing, with bows.

---

[46] Swahili word for laziness.

[47] The Masai are not an old Semitic, but rather a Nilo-Hamitic pastoral tribe.

[48] Governor Rechenberg's predecessor, Count Götzen, had tried to establish religious motives for the Maji-Maji Rising. Maji-Maji is a Swahili word for water, which was supposed to make men invulnerable against their enemies. Yet, already, Rechenberg and Dernburg did not share Götzen's opinion. In a communication to Chancellor Bülow, in which Dernburg criticized a travel report by Councillor von Miquel, Dernburg mentioned that the 'attempt, made in the south of the protectorate under Count Götzen, to use forced labour for public works in the year 1904–5' had 'led to that frightful rising in which 75,000 were sacrificed'. ZStA Potsdam, Reichskanzlei 924, Dernburg to Bülow, 14 February, 1908. J. Illife agrees with the economic origins of the uprising but adds that the movement later acquired an ideological content which was introduced by prophetic religious leaders. Illife, 'The Organization of the Maji-Maji Rebellion'.

19 September, Thursday. In the evening, after sunset, Shirati.[49] 500 Wagaya warriors. In the shifting moonlight, innumerable black figures. Head-dresses a yard high. Tower-like skins fantastically built up with ostrich feathers. Black crowns like the bearskins of the English guards. On some of them the feathers surround the head like a wheel. Thick boas[50] around neck and shoulder; gleaming bangles around their arms and wrists: necklaces of snow white mussel-shells on their breasts. Figures by Donatello. So too are the painted buffalo-hide shields, worth many cattle. A forest of twelve-foot lances with yard-long heads.

Surrounded by these nocturnal figures in waving feathers, tinkling necklaces. Then, throughout the ranks the shields are set up between two rows of men.

At last, the war-dance. To the sound of the wooden tuba. Alone, in groups, advancing, creeping, leaping, dancing, spears swinging, covering the retreat, forward. Moving around the shields; war cries; rushing forward in a mass.

Tumult of war dies away. Silence. Reflect on their culture and on the sleeping sickness (Glossina) which is destroying this people and their Homeric world. [Their] 'lack of needs' which is to be 'fought'.

Journey, Lake Victoria, Port Florence. 48 hours Uganda Railway: Mombasa, Tanga.

24 September, Tuesday. Tanga Railway: Muhesa, Zschaetzsch. Manihot[51] plantation. Kihuui,[52] Prince Albrecht Plantation. Sisal.

25 September, Wednesday. Climb to Amani. Sisal fields, then bushy forest. Vegetation seemingly like ours, different in every detail. Dark green, impenetrably thick bushes; creepers hanging down from trees; interchange of dense shadow and sun. Then, bridged over by foliage; hanging flowers, yellow and white; red and fiery-red blossoms against dark leaves alongside the path.

Climb. Tree trunks taller and smoother; boulders almost covered over; distant view over wooded valleys; descending mist, blue distance.

Tallest primeval forest. Tree trunks anchored on gothic bases, fluted; others smooth and straight as candles, sky-high; bearing a ceiling of light crowns. Wreathed half-way up with polypody,[53] lower

[49] Town on the eastern shore of Lake Victoria.

[50] Feather scarves.

[51] Some species of the plant produce raw rubber (caoutchouc), others edible roots (manioc).

[52] Railway station in the Usambaras.

[53] Kinds of ferns growing on moist rocks, walls, trees, etc.

half clothed in leafy creepers. Ground covered with large-leaved plants; deeply down-hanging clusters of flowers crowned with leaves. Scent of the forest. Tropical aroma. Silence. Twilight. Wreathed around with emerald green depths. Crystal-clear living water. Endless silence and lifelessness in endless life. Candelabra-like polypody.

Coming out into the open, a sideways glimpse of the white tree-trunks.

26 September, Thursday. Amani.[54] Garden and study centre.

Bomole, a mountain with a view. The loosely-organized tree-dungeon below. Sharp, piled up, carved out rocks shine blue out of the mountain clefts. Play of sunlight nearby. Distant view on two sides; blue plain dissolving into the sea. Flying clouds, dipping down into the evening.

27 September, Friday. From Amani to Niussi. Path high up on the mountain ridge. View over the plains. Greyish-brown of the *pori*. Railway Niussi–Mombo. Beautifuly rounded valleys. Repulsive activities of the adventurers.[55]

28 September, Saturday. Over mountain and valley to Wilhelmsthal.[56] Changed character of the landscape. West Usambara, the northern area, 1,800 m.

29 September, Sunday. Ten and a half hours march. Cedars of the *Schumewald*.[57] Hermann's Plateau. Seems suspended in the air. To one side, the stage-scenery to steep rocky cliffs, opening like craters. The eye, accustomed to thickets, suddenly opens when confronted by sudden distance. From the depths peaks rising up from below, flowing away into the distance higher up. Slightly scented air, covering the depths, accentuating the pure line of the mountains. Light blue to violet. Mirror surface of a lake on the furthest horizon. Camped the night in front of the forest ranger's house. Four o'clock, Negroes shuddering with cold.

[54] Biological and agricultural research station, founded in 1902, which had acquired particular importance for its agricultural developments.

[55] Small European settlers and game-hunters are probably meant. But it is also possible that Rathenau referred to Carl Peters's behaviour which led to the latter's dismissal from a specially created post as 'Commissar' in 1896.

[56] Present-day Lushoto.

[57] Large forest reservation in the Usambaras.

30 September, Monday. Descent. Detour to Kwai.[58] German cattle ranch.

1 October, Tuesday. Kwai, Wilhelmstal, Mombo. Train to Tanga. Arrived in the evening.

2 October, Wednesday. Tanga. Late evening departure for Sadani.

3 October, Thursday. Early, Sadani. Cotton-fields. Evening departure.
   Carried into the sea. Dusk. Gliding over the water. Coolness from above. Rippling waves. Feeling of weightlessness. The way the Negroes walk in the water.
   The warm reflection of the sea's surface. Darkening. Arion.[59] Drawing near to the ship. White forms in the water. Sea ghosts.

4 October, Friday. Early, Dar es Salaam.

The diary breaks off with their arrival in Dar es Salaam, although the return journey on the steamer *Prinzregent* did not begin until 13 October. The last days were taken up with talks in Dar es Salaam and an expedition on the branch railway to Morogoro to discuss the further construction of the Central Railway.[60] Before drawing up his report, Rathenau had specifically stated to the journalist Adolf Zimmermann that he saw no economic need for new private capital investment in the colony. It was a matter of expanding opportunities for trade in East Africa. Zimmermann had then reproached the 'Super-Secretary of State', as he described Rathenau in his writings, for sharing the ideas of Eugen Richter (left-wing liberal) and for having no understanding of Young Germany's expansion requirements. Colonial Secretary Dernburg shared Rathenau's opinion when he expressed his view of East Africa to Zimmermann: 'It is an unyielding country if one abandons it to its natural destiny; a bad country for European experiments. A good country for merchants; a bad country for settler-farmers. The small settlers here will always be particularly badly off. For they cannot raise crops for export, nor even for the food market here because the blacks do not buy any.'[61]
   Rathenau and Dernburg reached Berlin on 30 October 1907. They both

---

[58] Domain tenant [Domänenpächter] Illich in Kwai had explained to Dernburg during his visit that he was in favour of the settlement of German farmers in East Africa. To Dernburg's question whether German farmers get on in East Africa, Illich had replied that the first generation would 'perish', but the next generations would acclimatize. ZStA Potsdam, RK, 924, Dernburg to Bülow, 14 February, 1908.
[59] Legend has it that the Greek poet was rescued by a dolphin when, on a journey from Sicily to Corinth, he threw himself into the sea to elude the murderous threats of the sailors.
[60] On 9 October 1907 Dernburg cabled to Bülow that the first 'important' point of the Central Railway had been reached: to open the 'highly populated and promising centre of the colony'. BA Koblenz, RKo1A Personalakten Dernburg, 2/5, vii.
[61] Zimmermann, *Mit Dernburg nach Ostafrika*, pp. 86 and 125. See also Tetzlaff, *Koloniale Entwicklung*, pp. 222-32.

immediately began work on their reports on the journey which formed the basis for the reform programme. Rathenau sent his report to Dernburg on 15 November. In his covering letter he wrote:

'. . . the thoughts in the accompanying pages are not new to you. At dawn on the march, in front of our tents in the evening, on the train from Uganda, crossing lake Victoria and the Indian Ocean, during our long hours of discussion these sentences emerged, were examined, approved, sometimes rejected, and dug up again. It can and should no longer be determined today which one of us first suggested or exclaimed anything. Our opinions should remain set down in unison as witness to our joint labour, concern and confidence. . . .'[62]

Some days later Dernburg transmitted Rathenau's report and his letter to the Chancellor together with his own memorandum. Dernburg emphasized that all that he had anticipated from Rathenau's accompanying of him 'had been amply fulfilled'.[63] In conclusion he stressed Rathenau's sacrifices and exertions and asked the Chancellor 'to procure an imperial decoration'. Rathenau had paid for the whole trip nearly 6,000 marks, out of which his servant was paid, and 1,000 marks of which formed his contribution to enable Wildhagen to go with them.[64] While the report to the Kaiser was being prepared, Wahnschaffe, the councillor in the Chancellery, tried to prevent Rathenau being decorated. He referred to the fact that the BHG, of which Rathenau had been a member, sustained commercial relations with the Polish Central Co-operative Bank which was obstructing Germany's policy in East Germany.[65] But Bülow did not allow his purpose to be deflected by this cross-fire.

Rathenau's report and the petition for a decoration were laid before the Kaiser. On 28 November, Bülow presented Rathenau to him. The records are not clear whether the Order of the Crown, Second Class, was conferred on Rathenau on this occasion or at the investiture ceremony on 18 January 1908. Finally, Dernburg and Rathenau were both invited to a ministerial dinner at Bülow's in December.[66]

Rathenau harked back to his experiences in Africa in a letter to an acquaintance when he wrote: '. . . when looking back on the beautiful and free life in Africa, it seems to me that work involving great responsibility in virgin territory is one of the most beautiful [tasks] that modern life enables an active man to undertake.'[67]

---

[62] ZStA Potsdam, RK924, Rathenau to Dernburg, 15 November 1907; see also Rathenau, *Briefe*, vol. i. pp. 51 f.

[63] ZStA Potsdam, RK 924, Dernburg to Bülow, 22 November 1907. Two days later Bülow thanked Dernburg for his letter and on 25 November he also asked him to let him see Rathenau's accompanying letter. BA Koblenz, RKo1A Personalakten, 2/5, iv, Bülow to Dernburg.

[64] For a letter presenting Rathenau with the costs, see ibid. Dernburg to Rathenau, 28 November 1907.

[65] ZStA Potsdam, RK 924, Wahnschaffe to Bülow, 23 November 1907.

[66] Ibid., Report to the Kaiser, 23 November 1907. Bülow's marginal comment on the copy.

[67] Rathenau, *Briefe*, vol. i, pp. 58 f. Rathenau to Lieutenant Winterer, 12 January 1908.

Extracts from the 'Report on the Development of the German East African Colony'[68]

Many of the misgivings most frequently stressed regarding the economic presuppositions of German East Africa must be conceded. The whole country lies in a tropical zone and climate. Its most valuable product, its human population, is large but sparse; its population density is some twelve to fifteen times less than that of our own country. Population growth makes but slow progress, impeded as it is by endemic and epidemic disease.

The country is not rich in water. Only two large rivers carry a substantial volume of water into the Indian Ocean. A considerable part of the country consists of steppe; great waterless plains in the interior with meagre, *pori*-type vegetation. Stands of forest are insignificant in number and moderate in extent, and this contributes to irregular irrigation.

Mineral deposits have been discovered sporadically, but offer little prospect of exploitation. Mining enterprises are very small. The only natural highways are the lakes, and the biggest of these is linked to the coast by the English Uganda Railway. The German railways only open up part of the coastal area; for example, the Usambara plantation district. Roads hardly exist and must be of secondary importance as long as coastal fever and tsetse fly render the country impassable for draught and pack animals. Native tracks and old caravan routes are the arteries of communication and allow only human strength as a means of transport. Funds invested for plantations were on a considerable scale, for settlements on a modest one. But this expenditure has hitherto had no returns. Only isolated enterprises which have gone ahead and cultivated special plantations can look forward to good profits in the coming years.

Commercial statistics represent a not unfavourable total trade of 35 million marks. Nevertheless this is considerably reduced if the value of non-recurring investments and administrative costs corresponding to import and export figures is set aside. The figure should, as an index of the value of the net commercial exchange, run to about 24 million marks, a respectable figure in itself, especially if its steady growth is taken into account, but not in relation to the size of the country and the number of its inhabitants.

So the country must be considered as essentially undeveloped,

[68] ZStA Potsdam, RK 924. The memorandum was first published in Rathenau's *Reflexionen*. Harden then published extracts of it in *Die Zukunft*, vol. 63 (1908), pp. 290–308, leaving out the passages in which Rathenau attacked the German planters and settlers. The memorandum was republished in Rathenau, *Gesammelte Werke*, vol. iv, and again in *Nachgelassene Schriften*, vol. ii.

and the difficulties which stand in the way of development must continually be borne in mind.

If the question is raised today as to the point of a colony, a variety of answers will be given. Some would demand a territory to absorb surplus home labour: a place of refuge for emigrants. This point of view, which corresponds to the ancient colonial concept, cannot be generalized for our time. The population of our homeland is a treasure which can and may only be diminished by serious economic crises. Even if present industrial progress is only to some extent maintained, the opposite task of securing new sources of human strength for Germany looms far larger.

Another definition of the end-purpose of colonization would be the creation of new outlets for export goods. This answer would certainly be true if it were possible to maintain a constant monopoly of markets. The example of Great Britain shows that this is only possible to a limited extent. Our outlet remains the world market. If we can compete successfully here we shall not lack for other markets even in the struggle against hypothetical and material protective tariff systems. If we cannot do so, then we cannot hope to foist over-priced products on our own colonies.

Worth more attention would be the opinion that every country should produce its own raw materials either at home or overseas. But even this view is not final. For, on the one hand, the international market in raw materials stands open to every country, and, on the other hand, the German consumer will pay dearer for his basic products in order to benefit a colony than he would otherwise pay for them elsewhere.

Without mentioning any further attempts to define the purpose of colonies, an obvious parallel can be drawn to illustrate the view advocated here. An industrialist may link various aspirations to the success of his life's work: ambition, the striving for power and wealth, the hope of outstripping his competitors, the intention of creating an influential social position for his children. None of these tendencies will influence him in his individual operations. He will frequently forgo obvious profits in favour of his higher objective, and see this objective as the building-up of his enterprise until it is large, full of vitality, and flourishing. If this aim is realized, he knows that the viability of his enterprise will allow him to realize all his individual desires. When necessary, he can impose on it the burden of an enhanced standard of living, more representative and more scientific undertakings, the maintenance and employment of qualified people.

Analogous to this picture, let us suppose an ideal colonial situation, where the country, with the development of all its resources, is flourishing. It will satisfy all the individual desires of the mother country according to time and need, whether it is a question of imports and exports, of immigration and settlements, of administrative expenses and pensions, of political and mercantile influence. The circumstances of this flourishing, however, would have to be so defined that a population, corresponding in size to the area, could, by fully exploiting all their economic resources and while satisfying all reasonable needs, translate their existing natural resources and products into market commodities; that these commodities could reach the world market without any loss of value due to transport costs and be able to compete; and that further development should adequately advance the achievements of technology along peaceful lines.

In this supposition, setting aside transcendental considerations, lies the true economic justification for imposing on foreign peoples metropolitan government, ways of thought, and work. In addition, old civilized nations are responsible to their descendants for not allowing the natural resources of the earth to lie anywhere idle or inaccessible.

There are two approaches to economic development: the first sees the labour force of the country as an essentially passive resource; the other sees the resources as destined for independent operation. The first way, which assigns constructive work to the European, and mechanical work to the native, is that of an economy based on plantations and settlements; the second, which entrusts management and negotiation to the European, independent work and agriculture to the native, is that of commercial development. The real emphasis must lie between the two methods, which do not altogether exclude each other, but which, apart from their economic consequences, obviously correspond to different historical conceptions. It can now be stated that in the present discussion it is attempted to place the emphasis closer to the commercial than to the agrarian type of economy.

At the very centre of the discussion the question arises whether the Negro is capable of increasing his material needs, and whether he possesses enough ability and perseverance to satisfy his needs by independent work.

Not only is the Negro not without needs but he is also decidedly covetous, provided that he is brought in contact with new and comprehensible things to possess, and acquires the idea that they are within his means.

With the exception of a few uprooted nomadic tribes, which

progressive pacification has deprived of the prerequisites of their livelihood, the coloured people provide their own subsistence by means of traditional small-scale cultivation, which they are ready to expand by planting new products if the possibilities of rapid yield can be demonstrated to them. Wherever the effects of the traffic of the English Uganda Railway can be felt in German territory, production increases as well as a knowledge of, and demand for, goods. Where old and primitive traffic conditions prevail, production remains limited and, since the women do much of the work, the men are left with time to idle. But it is precisely here that those who recruit able-bodied people, who would otherwise live by their own tillage, succeed in getting them to work in the plantations, because the desire for gain has been sufficiently aroused. It is well known that the perseverance of the European is not inherent in the Negro. But whoever gets to know the native as a farmer can hardly maintain the assertion that he is not capable of cultivation on his own.

If on the one hand the native does not always live up to the view of those who attempt to characterize him as economically of age, yet at the same time there are several ideas current about the nature of plantations and settlements that remain to be verified. A general preliminary remark might also be made here.

Germany lacks a gentry, that is, a middle class that is gentlemanly by character and breeding, such as is spread over England. The German middle class is used to subordination, and educated in recent years to co-ordination and federation; the practice of authority is attained only in isolated cases, and not, on the whole, among those classes who seek a new home as colonists. Cultivation in Negro territory, however, depends on a very wide-spread ability to lead; and if the position of the coloured man, in most of the colonies under review, cannot be described as without rights, yet the employer is and remains responsible only to himself for much that he does. For a white immigrant a peculiar transformation of his position takes place when he first steps ashore—he finds himself a kind of superior to innumerable people. This, together with the physical effect of the tropics on the nervous system, the discomforts of many an enforced abstinence and the consequences of its transgression, the difficulties in the way of maintaining family life, and, finally, the adjustment to completely new, often apparently paradoxical, conditions—all these factors work together to generate an uncertain, nervous, heated atmosphere, lead to brutality and excess, confuse the business mind, and are finally vented in passionate accusations and imputations. When the number of those affected by these hardships is multiplied, particularly when managers, highly paid and temporarily employed in the country, are passing through, manifold unpleasant pictures of a distorted colonial life are to be observed. It might also be noted that the contagious influence of such conditions, to which government officials also occasionally succumb, has probably been the cause of many an impropriety with which the system of civil administration has normally been charged.

The German immigrant, consequently, works in difficult circumstances from the outset. So a balance could only be achieved by means of nature being abundantly productive. Neither the history of the working of plantations up to now, nor observation of those of today, allow such compensation to be, generally speaking, recognized.

In summing up one's impression of the character of plantation economy, it can be said that the results hitherto and the outlook for the immediate future are poor, in so far as it is not a question of large-scale capital investments which are, for their part, in some measure the product of speculation or of fluctuations of the market. This impression does not accord with the expectations of those who hoped that a plantation would combine personal work and initiative with relatively modest investment. Investment opportunities for lage-scale German capital can, however, be found: investment in the colonies themselves would possibly be more profitable if mercantile, mining, and industrial developments were later to emerge.

It is frequently asserted in favour of a plantation economy, and against a native economy, that the former produces a considerably greater turnover, reckoned per head of workers. This assertion would only become meaningful if in relation to this turnover, and above all in relation to capital expended, correspondingly higher returns were demonstrated. Otherwise it would be most desirable, according to this economic doctrine, to train all Negroes as goldsmiths or to use them to operate costly machines, when the turnover per head can, of course, be stepped up at will without regard for the final result.

Settlers and planters are partly in the dark about their uncertain situation and partly aware of it. Because they wrongly identify the source of their woes, they often try to make the conditions of work, and occasionally even government measures, reponsible. There are unanimous complaints about high wages, without it being possible to establish a scale of what is cheap and what is dear in relation to the statement 12 Rs = 16 marks per month. Even in such cases complaints are passionately expressed, cases in which, as with coffee, a raising or lowering of the rate of pay is almost irrelevant to the final result. The grievances about an adequate labour supply are more justifiable. This question, and various kinds of prohibited self-help among employers, will be touched on more closely in dealing with the native question.

If, in accordance with the preceeding observations, the native and his productivity have drawn nearer to the central point of the colonial interest, if he himself is considered the country's most valuable asset, then a purposeful system of government will have to emanate from various points simultaneously, in order to release the forces which are embodied in a sound policy for the welfare of the natives.

To begin with, the treatment of the native will have to be so directed that he can lead a peaceful, active, and gainful life while unreservedly acknowledging supreme German authority.

Afterwards, the country's conditions and methods of production will have to be examined and improved, so far as this is possible, by government measures. A further problem, whose solution would doubtless be efficacious, is the opening-up of the country to external and internal commerce.[69]

Finally, in order to secure the mechanism of government, and as a prerequisite for the solution of all remaining problems, it must be arranged that the power of the civil service, which at every turn faces the most difficult, and in Germany unknown, problems, should remain, by means of proper organization and selection, suited to meet these problems.

But with these considerations it must continually be borne in mind that economic aims are attained by economic methods. Together with every advancement of and solicitude for the native population, this principle must remain the guide, untarnished by sentimental and emotional politics.

A country of nearly ten million inhabitants is to be held in check by a few hundred white men and a couple of battalions of coloured troops. Next to the innate indolence of the black man, only his boundless respect for the energy of the European, for the power of the latter's country and the magical power of his remedies, produces this paradoxical effect. The respect is increased through the fear which the Conquistadores of the country have awakened by sharp, often brutal, behaviour. It might be remarked, parenthetically, that there is a certain justification for many a course of action which is difficult to imagine at home. Consequently, if fear and respect are the foundation of our position of power, the possibility of equal treatment of white man and black man is excluded; it can also certainly be claimed that [such] respect, even in the ethical sense, is strengthened through the exemplary leadership of the European.

[69] Rathenau meant railways and sea communications.

That this inequality should extend to the administration of justice is based on the fact that punishments involving honour or liberty have no effect on the Negro, and that the arrest or sentencing of white men by coloured is inadmissible to this way of thinking. It must be recognized that we exercise racial justice in the colonies and could not at this time survive without it. But the black man is all the more entitled to demand that he should be secure within his justice, that inroads from the field of European law should not take place, and that they [the Europeans], within their field of law, should equally be subject to an inexorable justice. These demands are today unfulfilled.

It has already been mentioned that as soon as the European steps on African soil he finds himself a sort of superior to his black brother, and in fact a superior without responsibility. He will be decidedly strengthened in this view by the maxims and advice of well-meaning compatriots, many of whom, on the very first day of their stay, acquire a *kiboko* (a hippopotamus whip), which is carried as a walking stick and is used as a means of communication.

As a legal penalty, corporal punishment is still indispensable. The English also still make use of it, and indeed—it would appear from court records—on a far larger scale than statistics indicate. By order of the Secretary of State certain safeguards, which are designed to work in a restrictive way, have been added to sentencing and to the execution of legal corporal punishment. Furthermore, corporal punishment exists in a quantitatively limited, but otherwise fairly unrestricted, form under the name of the 'disciplinary right' of plantation owners and caravan leaders. Every employer, it is true, has the right to exercise a moderate amount of discipline. It must be admitted that a liberal and completely unacceptable use is made of this authority to punish, which of its very nature excludes the right of appeal. Indeed, maltreatment of black men by white men occasionally goes beyond this level of authority. Judicial action against such transgressions rarely takes place or is ineffectual; in fact, no judicial sentence has been passed for more than a year.

Redress is needed here in several directions. The right of plantation owners and caravan leaders to punish must be limited, or at least subjected to safeguards similar to those affecting the execution of judicial sentences. The rights of employers to flog could be modified by prohibiting the use of any instruments, however made. Finally, the extent to which prosecution of Europeans for the maltreatment of Negroes can be made more effective will have to be considered.

But what is most gratifying is the fact that the white man who finds himself in a land that has not yet been opened up, that is inhabited by undeveloped peoples, regards himself as the bearer and transmitter of part of the cultural heritage of the West. This consciousness would be the more beneficial if everywhere the serious responsibility that attaches to this mission was felt completely. But that this is by no means always the case emerged from several experiences in Usambara and Morogoro. Yet it is worth noting the special interpretation on which the interested party bases his cultural task: he is called to train the Negro to work, and indeed this is clearly understood to be plantation work. The interpretation goes further—[this is] an argument which was put forward on an official occasion: just as the German child has to go to school, so too the black man has to undertake regular work in European enterprises.

These views, which former Governments probably did not share, yet tolerated, have occasionally and sometimes continuously produced results reminiscent of kidnapping and serfdom. As the government archives at Tabora show, at the beginning of this century natives were forcibly led off by recruiting sergeants and [their] huts burnt down. The scale on which these incidents occurred need not be determined; they stand on a par with the compulsory purchase of cattle that led, years ago, to the closing of Ruanda and Urundi to European visitors.

To sum up, may I once again put forth schematically the main suggestions touched on in the course of this discussion. The following points are at issue:

1. With regard to overall economic policy: shifting the emphasis in the direction of native agriculture.

2. With regard to the native question: different regulation of the power of Europeans to punish, and protection of the coloured man against maltreatment; modification and supervision of the work contract, as well as the recruiting system; creation of an office corresponding to the *Native Commissioner*.

3. With regard to the agriculture of the country: an extensive afforestation programme; a search for new, and protection of existing, sources of water; a topographical survey, if possible with the aid of missionary establishments; the establishment of a Regional Agricultural Office connected to the Regional Institute at Amani.

4. With regard to the communications system: establishment of a railway-building programme, beginning with the central railway between Morogoro and Tabora, and completion of the Usambara railway; creation of a network of country roads in accordance with the flow of traffic to the railways.

5. With regard to the administration: reorganization of municipal finance; establishment of the colonial service as a career; an increase in the number of senior officers in administrative posts.

In view of the expenditure of time and money required to realize this programme, it is justifiable to ask the following question: what benefits can the colony derive from a new economic policy, and would they be adequate?

At the beginning the colonial task had been defined as leading the territory, by means of its own strength, to a position where all its human and physical resources are developed. This definition requires an ideal situation which can only be approximated to. But even this approximation can only be reached after travelling a long road. For this is the prerequisite [of such an approximation]: the development of the native economy, which today finds itself in an indeed promising, yet primitive, condition, into a powerful economic factor. That such a development is possible is proved by any serious examination of the country. If any new colonial policy succeeds in pointing out and smoothing the path [of such developments], it will have fulfilled its greatest current task.

As the first stage of an advance, and one which lies in the immediate future, one could designate the stage at which the colony reaches a level which is *self-supporting*, where its budget can be balanced on the basis of its own [economic] strength. If the attempt to lift the burden from the government-owned enterprises is successful, then the arrival of this stage is only a matter of accounting. Should the Reich then decide to shoulder the costs of the acquisition and defence of the colony—compensation to the German East Africa Company and the war budget—then a financial balance would occur and expenses would be covered by its own revenue. In this way the colony will benefit, for once it has matured into a self-sufficient economic organism it can lay claim to an independent financial policy. For it can cover larger, non-recurring investments by its own loans, without Imperial guarantee; the Reich is relieved of anxiety for one of its most considerable passive undertakings; and, to some of the critics of colonialism, the expense and possession of protectorate territory is justified.

This external justification does not, however, exempt from examination the serious question of whether the value of East Africa to the Reich corresponds to the expenditure of money and blood which it cost. The difficulty of predicting the kind and sequence of advantages which the mother country will derive from the colonies was mentioned at the outset. If, none the less, one

wanted to hazard a conjecture about the thick veil that deprives us
of a view of future world developments in technology, economics,
and commerce, one would be tempted to assume that liberation
from foreign raw materials will give the next epoch of colonial
economy its significance. A period of syndication and monopoliza-
tion of the most important basic products began about twenty
years ago and will last as long as the number of deposits of such
products as coal, petroleum, iron-ore, zinc, and cotton only just
corresponds to the volume of world demand. During a period like
this, particularly if it coincides with an era of protective tariffs
throughout the world, the danger exists that some countries will
remain confined to the working of their own raw materials, while,
conversely, each of its deposits of raw material helps to stabilize
the corresponding industry.

Leaving aside these considerations, which include too much that is
conjecture, it must nevertheless be borne in mind that there is no
more powerful monopoly than to own land. If a businessman, acting
on the assumption that for every German born so many square yards
of the area of Berlin are needed, acquires a piece of land in the
business section of the city, it is a matter of indifference to him
whether this will later be used for a department store, a bank, or a
ministry: he owns his share of a monopoly and, of all the possibilities
it contains, he is certain that it will appreciate in value as long as the
development of the Reich lasts and the law protects his monopoly.
That the monopoly of real estate for private purposes is far exceeded
by the monopoly of real estate by the state goes without saying.
For in the latter case change of ownership takes place considerably
less often. The division of Africa was the work of a few decades and
its main features may remain valid for hundreds of years. That
Germany was, in fact, able to share in this division will be appreciated
in years to come. For the overpopulated areas of Asia will, after
a period of strong external consumption, go back to satisfying their
economic needs themselves, to processing their mineral resources
for their own requirements; they will compete in the world market
and lay claim to economic independence, while the enormous areas
of Africa and her productive potential, which will be in need of
management, will remain at the disposal of the civilized nations for
the foreseeable future.

It is constantly regretted that our possessions are considerably
inferior to Egypt and the Cape. Commercial considerations are not
promoted by sharing this view. It must be taken into account that
Egypt, owing to its history and physical characteristics, is not really
African, and that the Cape Colony has needed several hundred

years of Dutch and English management to attain its present prosperity.

Neither Germany's political nor its industrial position could have been achieved if the question, whether or why other countries were geographically better situated than we, had been a constant preoccupation. We owe our existence to ideal and ethical values and to a law, according to which a certain sterility of conditions is necessary to attain and permanently maintain a strong situation.

So we may look confidently at the last question: whether the German is equal to the colonial task. That certain deficiencies of education and background cling to us, especially in the middle classes of the population, must be admitted. It must also be recognized that we are lacking in other colonizing qualities: the homogeneity of race and way of life; the naïve and unshakeable sense of superiority; the stubborn hold on the language; the living strength of tradition—qualities which immediately transform every land touched by the Englishman into a part of Great Britain. But on the whole, the work of colonization demands qualities which the German possesses in rich measure: courage and devotion; idealism and perseverance. The evolution of Germany in the nineteenth century depended on the fact that the ideological and philosophical disposition of the German people, which had spent itself for centuries in transcendental speculation, suddenly was recognized as having enormous real value, because it was set adequate problems in science, technology, and organization. Thus we may hope that education for colonization will once more open to the German soul a field that corresponds to its earthly mission. But German policy will need the results of this education when the second and perhaps last division of the culturally deprived countries takes place: the period of colonization of the territories governed today by decadent races and states.

THE SOUTH AFRICAN JOURNEY

The colonial budget for 1908 and the first great railway programme had hardly been approved by the Reichstag when Dernburg set off on his South African journey. The objective was, as Dernburg wrote 'to study the British native policy, the experiences in exploiting water resources and the possibility of reducing the colonial budget by extending the railway lines in the South West'.[1]

Rathenau accompanied him again. Just a day before he left Rathenau complained to a friend that he would probably fare in Africa as he had the previous year.[2] He feared he would collect 'a great number of notes' and would let them get cold 'like omelettes that are not eaten straight away'. The contrast between his impressions in Africa and his life in Germany was presumably too great for his briefly jotted notes to prompt him to any literary creation over and above the compilation of his three memoranda. Although he had firm and well-founded opinions about several African problems he does not seem to have maintained a great interest in them in later years.

His notes on the second journey are much briefer—perhaps South Africa, as a land of European settlement, fascinated him less, perhaps it was due to strain and dissension. In a letter to his father he described the trip in South Africa as a bit more monotonous, and he was somewhat weary of the fact that every meal became a social occasion. It is, however, more likely that he used most of his spare time to draft his memorandum 'Remarks about England's Present Situation' after his talks in London. In the diary only his conversation with Jameson is recorded at any length, but the remaining notes must have been sufficient to write his memorandum, among the readers of which were Bülow and the Kaiser.[3] He summarized his impressions about Britain in the conclusion of this:

'Thus we see England today burdened with two main anxieties: one economic

[1] BA Koblenz, RKolA, Personalakten Dernburg, 2/5, iv, Dernburg to the Duke of Mecklenburg (President of the Colonial Society), 4 May 1908. The Reichstag had agreed to build 1,467 kilometres of new railways in Africa.

A similar journey, but of an unofficial nature, had taken place earlier. The Central Association of German Industrialists had sent a commission to visit both British and German South West Africa. Kaelble, *Industrielle Interessenpolitik*, p. 6. Recent literature on Rathenau's journey to South and South West Africa includes: Schnee, *Als letzter Gouverneur*, pp. 95 f.; Schiefel, *Dernburg*, pp. 73–80; Medalen, 'Capitalism and Colonialism', pp. 291 f., 318–22, 326–9; Smith, *The German Colonial Empire*, pp. 205 f.

[2] Rathenau, *Briefe*, vol. i, p. 60, Rathenau to Dr Goldmann, 9 May 1908. A day later Harden wished him well in a letter: 'New experiences, new work for Germany: how enviable. Look after yourself, dear Walther, and return home as flourishing, youthful and clear-sighted as after your first "campaign". Then you must provide us with an equally masterly report.' Hellige (ed.), Rathenau-Harden, 10 May 1908.

[3] Rathenau, *Briefe. Neue Folge*, pp. 112 f., Rathenau to his father, 19 June 1908. The memorandum on England was published for the first time in his book *Zur Kritik der Zeit* (Berlin 1912). Bülow quoted the memorandum extensively in his memoirs. Bülow, *Denkwürdigkeiten*, vol. ii, pp. 427 f. See also Cecil, *Ballin*, p. 169. Apparently it was Ballin who, in February 1909, reminded Bülow of Rathenau's memorandum, sent to the Chancellor in June 1908.

and one colonial, for which there are two remedies. One remedy—protective tariffs—is without doubt basically practicable; the other remedy—naval expansion—is appropriate and is suitable, but perhaps not so easily carried out as it seems at first glance. The English navy is in fact exceptionally popular, the nation's greatest pride; . . . but the country is not as generous as before and it has never been willing to make sacrifices. Even if a national balance with the repayment of debt standing at £18 million seems splendid, the surplus is still only a result of war taxes which are still being paid and paid reluctantly. England could, with its great national prosperity, support a considerably increased budget. But it does not want to pay heavier taxes any more than it wants to bear the burden of universal national service. The pampered country has been doing bad business for years and lives, by our standards, beyond its means: new taxes are there [considered] the most disagreeable expense . . . . Doubtless England can strengthen its fleet, will strengthen it, and must strengthen it—but its present exorbitant[ly expensive] position of superiority can not be maintained in the long run.

'It is especially worth noticing that both these anxieties, industrial and colonial, cause the nation to look across to Germany. Here is the competitor, the rival. It soon comes up in all conversations with informed Englishmen, sometimes as a compliment, sometimes as a reproach, sometimes ironically: you will outstrip us, you have outstripped us. And to this add a third reason, which we here at home do not always bear in mind: Germany, as it is judged by the foreigner. From the outside one peers into the cauldron of nations that is the Continent, and becomes aware of a people, surrounded by stagnating nations, a people of restless activity and enormous powers of physical expansion. Eight hundred thousand new Germans every year!. . .

'Thus all English discontent is substantiated and localized—and there is plenty of discontent since the last war—in the notion of Germany. And what appears among the educated as a motivated conviction is expressed among the people, among the youth, in the provinces, as prejudice, as hatred and wild fantasy to an extent that far exceeds the measure of our journalistic apperception.

'It would be feeble and superficial to believe that small kindnesses, visits by deputations, or press campaigns, could quiet a discontent that wells up from such deep springs. Only our policy taken as a whole can possibly create in England at least this impression: that on Germany's part there exists no ill-feeling, no fear, no need for expansion, no offensive posture. The masses will not be convinced by this, but it will probably preserve in their governments a sense of responsibility . . . .'

The days in London also served to prepare the first conference to establish the frontiers of the north-west in East Africa.[4] Dernburg's plan for colonial co-operation with England was confirmed during their friendly reception in London.[5] Dernburg and Rathenau were again accompanied by Count Henckel von Donnersmark and Schlüpmann, a technical adviser at the Colonial Office. Among the accompanying journalists only Oskar Bongard's name can be established.[6]

[4] Louis, *Ruanda-Urundi*, pp. 44–58.

[5] ZStA Potsdam, RKo1A 1462, Dernburg to Bülow, 15 May 1908.

[6] Because of the attacks against Dernburg in the press a year earlier, ridiculing his antics, Oskar Bongard was the only journalist allowed to accompany the expedition. See Bongard, *Staatssekretär Dernburg*. Apart from Count Henckel von Donnersmarck, the engineer

Dernburg and Rathenau also wanted to learn from the British and South African organization about diamond and gold mining, since it was generally expected that diamonds would be discovered in the German colony. In addition to the discussion about colonial policy, Rathenau wished to consider further the affairs of the Victoria Falls Power Company which was dominated by the AEG.[7]

Notebook 1908

12 May, Tuesday. London.

Arrived at 8 o'clock. Dinner with von Stumm, Lord Crewe, Winston Churchill, Cassell, Prince Stolberg, Schwabach.

13 May, Wednesday. Marquess of Winchester to lunch. Banking Association banquet in the evening. Between Fitzgerald (London-Union Bank) and the Deputy Governor of the Bank of England.[8]

Bank not administered by bankers. *Common sense* rather than specialized knowledge. Sir Felix Schuster, Haldane. Late evening at Dr Jameson's. Conspiratorial interior. Old colonel, assistant, journalist Stead. Jameson takes negative position.

Ideal advantages from English colonies. Extreme conciliation to preserve them. Protective tariffs[9] the only economic measure. (Winchester, quoting Rhodes.)

Jameson's theory of racial equality.[10]

Fleet for protection—perhaps for fighting the colonies.

Naval rivalry.[11] Difficulty of the ratio 2:1 against Germany.

Schlüpmann, and the official Krüger, Rathenau had asked his own servant Hermann Merkel to come with him. The servant of the previous journey, Friedrich Mau, was also with them.

[7] Weinberger, *An den Quellen der Apartheid*, pp. 134–71. The author examines at length the AEG's domination of the Victoria Falls Power Company. See also Christie, 'The Electrification of South Africa'.

[8] Reginald E. Johnston. The Marquess of Winchester was a member of the board of the British South Africa Company and chairman of the Victoria Falls Power Company, which was a subsidiary of the AEG. Rathenau wrote to Harden on the same day, but did not mention anything about his activities in London. Hellige (ed.), Rathenau–Harden, 13 May 1908.

[9] Jameson revealed himself as in agreement with other Dominion statesmen who supported Chamberlain's plan for the introduction of preferential tariffs.

[10] Rathenau reported, in his memorandum on England, that Jameson was decidedly in favour of the coloured people's right to self-government and advocated 'non-racial politics'. As Prime Minister of Cape Colony Jameson had spoken up for retaining the Coloured's right to a parliamentary vote, which had been introduced in 1852, but curtailed in 1893. When the Union was founded a selective right to vote was admitted, which remained in force until 1936. In 1951 the right to vote of the coloured population of Cape Province was abolished.

[11] The naval rivalry between Germany and England underwent its first critical phase during this year. Wilhelm II and Edward VII met at Bad Homburg on 11 August 1908 to discuss the naval question. Rathenau believed that England could not, in the long run, maintain the ratio of naval strength of two to one against Germany. In his opinion the naval rivalry contributed to the anti-German feeling of the Imperialists, who saw in the fleet and England's unchallenged maritime supremacy a guarantee of the unity of the Empire.

Disinclination to tax. Military Associations give evidence of short-ages. Repayment of £18 million debt. African danger: whites and blacks. Indian danger. Why do the Germans not find their way back home.[12] Citizens and subjects. Classes. The forms in which the administration is encountered. Authority.

Loss of confidence by the natives in South West Africa?

When driving through the tracts of South Africa (bush, veldt, rhenoster) envisage future corn production. Reasons for the past: water.

War as the cause of Cape Town's prosperity.

Questions: perhaps centuries to develop. Whether for whites or coloureds?

1. Dutch–English
2. Whites–Blacks.
The critical point of the proportions of the population.[13]

Unification on the basis of a compromise regarding franchise (civil rights)? What is the goal? Probably: greater independence. [Jameson] alleges: savings. Which cannot be made if the more reasonable form of a federal state is chosen.[14] Otherwise: dis-appointment, because of lack of interest by parliament in conflicting needs.

Unification with the exclusion of Natal.[15] (Malcolme junior). Consequences for South West Africa.

Durban: manifestly richer hinterland. One million blacks, 90,000 whites, 90,000 Indians. Zulus. The quality of its sugar, tea, coal, etc.

Black man's or *White man's colony*? Undecided as regards Natal. Definition: stability in terms of generations.

14 May, Thursday. Wallace Collection. A most banal selection of the most valuable things. Tate Gallery. The originals of all popular reproductions. Lunch with Chartered Company.[16] Duke of Abercorn,

---

[12] This remark had led, in the seventies and eighties of the previous century, to the German desire to steer the stream of emigrants to German colonies or territories under German political influence. The wish for 'national emigration' came into being at this time. See Walker, *German Emigration.*

[13] The proportion of the black to white at this time was roughly 4:1, and of Boer to English, 6:4.

[14] The Union of South Africa was founded on the basis of a decentralized unitary state.

[15] The right to vote of its coloured population divided Cape Colony from Natal. The latter opposed the plans for union because it did not want to grant its coloured population the right to vote. In addition the predominance of the Boers in the Union was feared.

[16] Through the African Concessions Syndicate, the Chartered Company had granted the concession to build a hydroelectric power-station and a coal-fired power-station in the Rand to the Victoria Falls Power Company (founded in 1906). The Victoria Falls Power Company also bought the right to acquire the General Electric Power Company and the Rand

able, business-like dinner. Evening, Cassel. The stairway like an opera house; the halls and dining-room like an American hotel. Tadema tells dinner-party stories. Semon, Morowitz. *Skat* [German card game] till 2.30 a.m.

15 May, Friday. City in the morning; Seligmann tea company. Afternoon visited by Colonel Unsworth of the Salvation Army. Evening at Wernher's with people from the Chartered Company.[17]

16 May, Saturday. Afternoon, departed Southampton at 5 o'clock. Fog.

18 May, Monday. Sun and a clear sky.

19 May, Tuesday.[18] Cloudy. Level with Lisbon. Dunning, Beak, Dartnell, Lamont, Neame.

2 June, Tuesday. Cape Town. Early. Mount Nelson Hotel. Lunch at the City Club. Evening, Governor's House. Sir Walter Hely Hutchinson. Merriman. Farrar. Town without seasons. Southern American. Table Mountain half-veiled.

3 June, Wednesday. Moved to the Governor's House. Morning, *Panther* and *Sperber*; information about Walvis Bay.[19] Lunch with Merriman, Mount Nelson. Visited Mullins, General Manager, Africa Bank, Evening, dinner-party at the Governor's (Sauer, Graaf, etc.).

Central Electric Works. By early 1907 the AEG held most of the preference shares and debentures in the Victoria Falls Power Company. Weinberger, *An den Quellen der Apartheid*, p. 142.

[17] After the take-over of the UEG by the AEG in 1904 the London banking house of Wernher, Beit and Co., which had been a business partner of the UEG, established closer relations with the AEG. This was important for the AEG, as this bank formed the link with the Chartered Company. The bank also owned a substantial share in the biggest group of gold mines, Rand Mines Ltd., which had not fully electrified their mines. The Rand Mines negotiated with several groups for a supply of electricity to the mines: as the AEG aimed at a monopoly the Rathenaus were worried at the prospect of costly new competition. Emil Rathenau wrote a letter to this effect to Sir Julius Wernher on 9 April 1908, asking him to use his influence for favouring the Victoria Falls Power Company. Christie, 'The Electrification of South Africa', p. 74.

[18] On that day Rathenau wrote to his mother, informing her that he had found his stay in London very interesting and added that he had low expectations of his forthcoming journey. Rathenau, *Briefe*, vol. i, p. 61.

[19] This remark is revealing because both before and after the journey it was officially stated that the acquisition of Walvis Bay would not be discussed.

4 June, Thursday. Visits to Merriman and Sauer regarding Walvis Bay. Lunch at the Governor's. Evening, walk. Ideas regarding water-colonization. Manuring and drainage. Evening, with Consul-General von Humboldt.[20]

5 June, Friday. By car to Somerset West. Dynamite factory. Evening, Governor.

6 June, Saturday. Graaff's car to Deltafarm (Pickstone) and Schoen Gesicht (Merriman). Evening, club and Deutsches Haus.

7 June, Whit Sunday. To Cape Point and Groote Schuur[21] with Lady Hely Hutchinson. Afternoon, tea with the Governor. Evening, departure.

8 June, Monday. Train journey. Veldt. Yellowish-red aloe. Evening, Mossel Bay. Tea with Consul Matarée. Then on to George, where spent the night in the carriage.

9 June, Tuesday. Departed George in three Cape waggons, four horses, over Montagu Pass. Rain up to the heights. Then Truter's Farm. Thence in cars (Dr Russel, Mayor Olivier) into the wider alluvial valley of Oudshoorn. Ostrich-farms, Raubenheimer's among others, 100 kilometres. On ostrich breeding. Sitting-hours during incubation: males 9–4, females 4–9; 20 eggs; 42 days. In the evening, to the train where we spent the night; Olivier entertained.

10 June, Wednesday. Early, car trip. Fields of cactus. 11 o'clock

[20] On the same day Rathenau wrote two letters, one to his mother and one to Harden. In his letter to his mother he described Cape Town, which reminded him of America. He wrote: 'All business life is depressed here; at the moment people are beginning to have hopes again, [but] it is doubtful if the improvement will last. Although the people are very friendly to us we have the feeling that Germany has only a few friends nowadays, the fewest in England. It will take a long time before the relationship is good again.' Rathenau, *Briefe. Neue Folge*, p. 111. To Harden he wrote that he did not understand the situation in South Africa, despite the fact that they had tried to sift an enormous amount of material: 'The day is strenuous and instead of peace in the evening we have to have buffet dinners with strange and indifferent people and thin suet.' (Rathenau translated 'small talk' as *schmaler Talg*.) Hellige (ed.), Rathenau–Harden, 4 June 1908.

Dernburg sent back accounts of his conversations with various South African politicians about South West African questions. He mentioned Rathenau's presence only once, when reporting his talk with Merriman and Sauer. It is also likely that Rathenau took part in the discussions with Lord Selbourne on 19 June. PA Bonn, Südafrika, Generalia, vol. 65. I am very grateful to Dr Hellige for providing me with copies of these documents.

[21] After a period of decay Groote Schuur was rebuilt, at Rhodes's request, by the architect Sir Herbert Baker. It became then the residence of the Prime Minister.

departure, special train. Little comfort. As cold as the previous night. Rock-climbing party from Toover Water (Magic Water).

11 June, Thursday. Very early arrival Port Elizabeth, Mayor Mackay, Consul Rolfes, etc. Accommodation at the club. Drive round. Feather and Wool Exchange. Information about qualities of feather from Mosenthal. Noon, Mayor's lunch at the club. Afternoon, trip around the roadstead. Evening at Rolfes's, Liebermann, then supper at the Liedertafel;[22] ball at the *Town Hall*.

12 June, Friday. With the *Magistrate* (Staatskommissar)[23]—trial. Black police. Prison. Then to Mosenthal. Lunch with Rolfes, Grand Hotel. Afternoon, Main Street. 4 o'clock embarked *Armandale Castle*. Departure, 7 o'clock.

13 June, Saturday. Early, East London. Open roadstead. By basket to the lighter. Sightseeing tour: park, market. Insignificant town. *Town Hall*; German Association—veteran atmosphere. Speech by Malcolmess. Breakfast with Jungheinrich (in Malcolmess's firm). Departure, 3.30 p.m.

14 June, Sunday. Afternoon, 2.30, Durban. Reception: Ponsonby, the Governor's secretary, Captain Coleman, ADC. Sightseeing tour by car. Resembles Zanzibar. Evening, club; then dinner-party, Marine Hotel. C. P. Robinson, English Jew.

15 June, Monday. Minister Hitchins: railway workshops, harbour, loading equipment. *Lunch* at the club. Car trip with mayor.[24] Walk. 5.30 departure for Pietermaritzburg. Arrival 9.30. *Government House*, Governor Sir Mathew Nathan.

16 June, Tuesday. 12 o'clock, opening of Parliament by the Governor. Afternoon, expedition with eight mules to Kaffir reservations. Three kraals. Evening, dinner for 42 people.

17 June, Wednesday. Agricultural institute at Sidara. Evening, dinner for 30 people.

18 June, Thursday. Morning, visits. Noon, Prime Minister Moor to

[22] The name of the first men's choral society founded by Karl Zelter in 1809.
[23] Charles Bell.
[24] Charlie Henwood.

Lunch. Afternoon, arrival of Lord Selbourne. Evening, ball at the *Town Hall.*

19 June, Friday. Morning, Selbourne. Afternoon, polo. Evening, small dinner-party. Departure 9.30 p.m.[25]

20 June, Saturday. Drive through the Transvaal. Majuba Hill.[26] Fertile land, some irrigation. 6 o'clock, arrival Johannesburg. Entrance to the town similar to Oberhausen. Germiston. Park Station. Carlton Hotel. Consul's dinner-party: Reyersbach, Spengel, Francke, Consul Frank; later, Sir Lionel Phillips.[27]

21 June, Sunday. 9 o'clock by car to May Consolidated. Small, old plant. Simmers Deep. New American installation: 300 8-ton stamps a day. Cost: £325,000. 1 stamp £1,000. Then patience. Lost our way. Sad situation. Victoria Falls Power Station, Major Bagot.[28] Back at 6 o'clock. 8 o'clock, dinner with Reyersbach.

22 June, Monday. Morning, descend into the Robinson Mine. Work has begun at Main Reef (hitherto Main Reef Leader and South Reef). Lunch with Sir Lionel Phillips. View over 'Sachsenwald'. Afternoon,

[25] On this day Rathenau wrote to his father about the progress of the journey. He described Durban as the most beautiful African harbour town on the Indian Ocean, and again complained about the great number of social occasions he had to endure. Rathenau, *Briefe. Neue Folge*, pp. 112 f.

[26] Zulu expression for 'Mountain of the Doves'. On this mountain between Natal and Transvaal the British suffered a defeat during the first Boer War, on 27 February 1881. The peace negotiations, which had begun before the battle took place, led to the Pretoria Convention which established British suzerainty over the Transvaal.

[27] Sir Lionel Phillips and Louis Reyersbach were directors of Hermann Eckstein & Co., the largest mining group in the Transvaal. This group was Wernher, Beit and Co.'s biggest partner in the Rand Mines Ltd. The Victoria Falls Power Company had founded the subsidiary the Rand Mines Power Supply Company, which was to supply the Rand Mines. The contract between the latter two companies has been called 'probably the largest ever given in the history of electrical enterprise'. (Christie, 'The Electrification of South Africa', p. 77.) Most of the machinery came from the AEG. The Marquess of Winchester wrote in his memoirs that on one trip to Berlin he placed orders with the AEG 'for what in those days was the equivalent of the cost of a battleship'. (Ibid.)

[28] This was presumably the turbo-dynamic power-station which had just been completed by the Victoria Falls Power Company at Brakpan near Johannesburg. A larger station at Simmerpan was under construction. By this time it had become clear that the Victoria Falls could not produce sufficient hydro-electric power for supplying the Rand. Since the Transvaal Government favoured the use of Transvaal coal, Reyersbach agreed to a station to be built at Rosherville Dam. So the original name of the company was changed in 1909 into the Victoria Falls and Transvaal Power Company. By the end of this year the company had won supply-contracts for all the gold-mines except two, the Farrar-Mines in the East and the Robinson Mines in the West. See Weinberger, *An den Quellen der Apartheid*, pp. 153–63; Christie, 'The Electrification of South Africa' pp. 79 f. The account given in Fürstenberg, *Carl Fürstenberg*, p. 492, is obviously incorrect.

Corner House. Premier,[29] diamond sorting. Evening, Mayor's banquet (Carlton). 250 people.

23 June, Tuesday. Early, 7.15, to Premier. Arrived waterworks 11.30, mine 2.30. 7,000–8,000 workers. Excavators suggested. Production costs: 6s. per carat. 10 million tons processed per annum. Evening, own dinner-party at the hotel. Then Liedertafel.[30]

24 June, Wednesday. Early, 7.45, to Pretoria. 9.30 arrival. At the station, Botha, Smuts, Hull (Agriculture). Morning, the town, zoological garden. Lunch, Consul.[31] Afternoon, Theiler Institute.[32] Inflamed eye. Poultices until the evening. Then Lord Methuen, Roberts Heights. Present were Botha, Smuts, de Villiers, Delarey (who had captured Methuen), Sir George Farrar, among others. Friendly conversation with Smuts. Picture of Napoleon with an inscription by Methuen's father, *'This is Bony to whom I have been introduced in 1808'.*[33]

25 June, Thursday.[34] Morning, visited Botha, who first talked about the war, then assembled the Cabinet. Hull, de Villiers, Solomon. Rissik. Story of the *fat train* at Christmas. Krüger only wanted old generals. Acquisition of cattle before the conclusion of peace (Vereeiniging).[35] Noon, lunch with the mayor, Dr Savage, 150 people. Afternoon, Entomological Institute. Excellent system for

[29] Premier is the world's biggest diamond mine. (There was also a diamond mine of the same name near Kimberley.) The competition between De Beers and the Premier Company had reached a peak in 1908. Rathenau took advantage of his visit to the mine to make a business proposal to Fürstenberg—namely, to raise a loan on Premier diamonds, as Rothschild had done for De Beers. Fürstenberg, *Carl Fürstenberg*, p. 475.

[30] On the same day Governor Schuckman cabled to Britain about the diamond finds in South West Africa.

[31] Erich Reimer.

[32] Biological Institute, chiefly concerned with bacteriology. The Institute became well known on account of its anti-locust campaigns. It was founded by Sir Arnold Theiler.

[33] English in the original. It must have been Methuen's grandfather (1779–1849). Methuen's father was born in 1818.

[34] On the same day Rathenau wrote to Carl Fürstenberg that the itinerary envisaged a sea-voyage from Cape Town to Lüderitz Bay. (Evidently this plan was changed, and the over-land route via Upington to South West Africa was adopted.) The letter also contains information concerning the good position of the gold-mining industry, the critical situation of the diamond industry because of the competition between De Beers and Premier, the impending foundation of the Union of South Africa, and the economic recession in Natal and the Cape after the end of the Boer War. He also told Fürstenberg that the labour question in the mines was solved. The last Chinese workers had been replaced by Africans, which lowered the gold-production costs from 30 shillings per ton to 18 shillings. According to Rathenau, rationalization could bring down wage costs further. In conclusion he expressed his satisfaction with the composition of the group in which he was travelling. Fürstenberg, *Carl Fürstenberg*, pp. 473 ff.

[35] The Peace of Vereeiniging, which ended the Boer War, was signed on 31 May 1902.

eradicating locusts. Then Parliament. Hull's speech. Tea with the opposition (Farrar).[36] Evening, our dinner-party at the club. Botha, Smuts etc. Departure 12.30.

26 June, Friday. Noon, Bloemfontein. Evening, 6 o'clock, Kimberley; Hirschhorn, Oats, etc.

27 June, Saturday. Sanatorium. Morning. War Memorial; Rhodes Memorial; club; Kimberley Mine. Wernher's and Beit's accommodation-cottages. Diamond ghetto. Mine's hellish abyss, 1,800 feet deep, pierced through primeval rock. Shaft next to it. (In the office: pictures of old Kimberley; Anthony Trollope—'Devil's harp'.) Similar installations at De Beer's mine. Side-shaft a mile long. Breakfast at Alexandersfontein. Afternoon, stud farm at Mauritsfontein. Battlefield at Magersfontein.[37] Return journey via Wesselton mine. Observation: bowels of the earth, green, 30,000 human beings, compounds of corrugated-iron cliffs to produce ½-ton of stuff which is useless. *Facies Hippocratia*. Stones in stock worth £7 million. Dilemma: close down?

28 June, Sunday. Morning, battlefield at Carter's Ridge.[38] Lunch with Hirschhorn. Afternoon, expedition to the River Vaal. Landscape. Diamonds recovered from the river. Dinner at the Sanatorium.

29 June, Monday. Morning. De Beer's installations. 1. Pulsators. 2. Washing plant. 3. Central Office. 4. Wesselton, blasting. Afternoon, telegram exchange concerning the inland trip. Departure, 11.30 p.m.

30 June, Tuesday. Morning, 9.30, Mafeking.[39] Bechuanaland Protectorate. Drive through Negro reservation. Clean villages. Hides bought. Visited Commissioner.[40] Departure, 1 o'clock. Surroundings more tropical. *Pori*. Mountains. Thick dust at night.

[36] The opposition to Botha came from the nationalist side of his party (Het Volk), the Progressives, and the Labour Party. These three groups had raised objections to the resolution in favour of union. The leaders of the Progressive Party were John Percy Farrar, Sir James Fitzpatrick, and Lindsay.

[37] On 11 December 1899 the Boers warded off a British attempt to raise the siege from south of Kimberley. It was here that Lord Methuen was taken prisoner. See the diary entry for 24 June 1908.

[38] Engagements took place here, south-east of Kimberley, between 25 and 28 November 1899, which then led to the battle of Magersfontein.

[39] Railway junction for the Cape–Bulawayo and the Durban–Johannesburg–Mafeking lines. Boer units besieged the place for 217 days (October 1899–May 1900). Mafeking was defended by General Sir Robert Baden-Powell.   [40] Francis W. Panzera.

1 July, Wednesday. Early, still *pori*-landscape. 1.30 p.m. arrived Bulawayo. Small, spaciously laid-out country town. Museum, club, tobacco factory. Most important thing—conversation with *Native Commissioner*, Taylor. Evening, dinner-party at the Grand Hotel.

2 July, Thursday. Motor excursion to Matopo Hills.[41] Granite peaks, extraordinary weathering. Rhodes's grave imposing in its solitary cliff. Lunch, Matopo Hotel. Evening, mayor's (Basch) dinner at the Grand Hotel.

3 July, Friday. Morning, trial—a case of indecent assault. Volunteer training house as hospital. King's House on the old site at Lobengula's.[42] Midday, 12.30, departure for Victoria Falls— landscape hardly changed; dust, especially at night.

4 July, Saturday. Early, 7.15, Victoria Falls. To the railway bridge; grandiose view. Then to the rain forest opposite the great fall: a mile long, 400 feet high. Theory of the plateaux. Drive up the Zambezi towards Livingstone. Indian landscape. Trolley for five miles. Livingstone newly laid out; gardens. The house of the Administrator, Codrington, who was ill. Chapel and endowment of the Founder [Livingstone]. Midday, 11.30, departed Livingstone, 12.30 left Victoria Falls.

5 July, Sunday. Train. Lindequist and Rechenberg instructions discussed.[43] Kaffir wood-carvings in Shashi. Eyes painful.

6 July, Monday. Train. Evening, Kimberley. Supper with Hirschhorn. Departure, 1 o'clock.

7 July, Tuesday. Arrived Britstown 11 o'clock. Car to Smart's farm. New installation of a dam of 100 million cubic metres. To irrigate 4,000 hectares. Cost supposed to be £80,000. Afternoon, Houwater —small-scale irrigation of 800 hectares; capacity 5 million cubic metres. 500 hectares of lucerne, 200 of wheat and of fruit.

[41] When he died in 1902 Rhodes was buried in the Matopo Hills at 'The World's View'. Jameson was buried in the same place.

[42] King of the Matabele, who granted large concessions to the British South Africa Company in 1889. Between 1893 and 1894 he rebelled in vain against the Company's rule.

[43] The Colonial Under-Secretary, Lindequist, visited German East Africa at this time. In a telegram to Rechenberg, Dernburg said that the local 'native policy' was so appropriate that it would be worth while studying it for a few weeks. Rechenberg agreed, but argued for a postponement of such a study. BA Koblenz, RKo1A, Personalakten Dernburg, 2/5, iv, Dernburg to Rechenberg, 2 July 1908; ibid., Rechenberg to Dernburg, 4 July 1908.

8 July, Wednesday. Morning, 8 o'clock, arrived Prieska. Convoy separates. Henckel, Bongard, servants to Cape Town. Car 1 (Hirschhorn's Fiat, 40 hp): Dernburg, myself, Hirschhorn. Car 2 (Oats): Schlüpmann. Midday, Cape Asbestos Mine, across the River Oranje. Car 2 breaks down. Schlüpmann transferred to the Fiat to get to Draghoender. On the way sandhills, horses harnessed, pushed. Arrived at Draghoender in evening. Krüger junior (Moses), a storekeeper and farmer. Stayed the night.

9 July, Thursday. Early, to Springpitt (Krüger senior) with the Fiat and Bleloch's car, which had turned up. Both had flat tyres. Then set out for Upington (100 miles). Midday Fiat broke an axle. Bleloch's car took us on. Re-packed. 2 o'clock, set off again. 4 o'clock, car stuck. Sand dune. Sandruchens Farm. Help fetched. Tyres. Horse-drawn car catches up with us. Spent the night. Farmer's family called Bockys. Bad accommodation.

10 July, Friday. After heavy thunder-shower (first rain in July for 25 years, after 14 months drought) set off in Bleloch's car. Beforehand, basic discussion of South West [Africa]. Afternoon, 3 o'clock, Lieutenant von Hanenfeldt with a car. 4 o'clock, Upington. Saw Fletcher. Evening, Mayor Bergman's dinner-party. Magistrate May. Beforehand, visited all the ladies. Evening, speech.

11 July, Saturday. Car to Areachap.[44] Arrived 1 o'clock. Mine. Evening, four in the tent.

12 July, Sunday. 8 o'clock, on horseback. 80 kilometres, mostly trotting. Arrived Swart Modder 6 o'clock. Saw Harris. Heimann. Stayed the night.

13 July, Monday. Morning, left Swart Modder on horseback at 2 o'clock. 70 kilometres. Evening, 9 o'clock, camp.

14 July, Tuesday. Early, 4 o'clock, rode off. Arrived frontier (Nachab) 8 o'clock. Set off again 10 o'clock. Arrived Ukamas 1.30. From Prieska–Upington: 240 kilometres; Upington–Ukamas: 250 kilometres.

Apparent blood poisoning. Afternoon, fever began. Slept a little at night.

15 July, Wednesday. Departure 9 o'clock. Noon at Heirachabis

---

[44] Copper-mine near Upington.

Mission Farm—Father Lipper. Evening 7–8 o'clock rest, Nachab, then continued journey. Arrived Warmbad 6 o'clock in the morning.

16 July, Thursday. Governor von Schuckmann, Commander von Estorff. Morning sightseeing. Afternoon ride.

17 July, Friday. Warmbad. Bondelzwarts,[45] Johannes Christian. School. Afternoon, ride.

18 July, Saturday. Set off on horseback early, 6.30 a.m. Noon, Gabis. Then Bondel reservation, Drijhoek. Evening, 6 o'clock, Kanus. 80 kilometres.

19 July, Sunday. Noon, 1 o'clock, left Kanus on horseback. Evening, nine o'clock, rest camp. Then night ride. Then camped for night.

20 July, Monday. Early, 4 o'clock, departure. Beautiful morning ride. 10 o'clock, Tsawisis, half-caste farm without a house. Water. Rest until 2 o'clock. Set off on horseback. Evening, five *holoog*, military post, then 8–10 o'clock night ride to the camp site (25 kilometres).

21 July, Tuesday. 4 o'clock, set off, morning ride as far as Chamaites; breakfasted there. Set off on horseback 9 o'clock; rode to Seeheim; arrived 1 o'clock. Warmbad–Seeheim: about 250 kilometres. Inauguration Seeheim-Keetmanshoop railway.[46] Arrived 4 o'clock. Evening, hotel, new bandage.

22 July, Wednesday. Morning, District Office; lunch, mess; afternoon, Little Naawte, compound, drive, school. Evening with District Officer Schmidt.

23 July, Thursday. Departure by car, 8 o'clock, Great Naawte. Returned, 6 o'clock.

24 July, Friday. Departure, 6 o'clock, to Brakwasser; thence to Bethanie; small settlements; District Commander; waterfall. Afternoon, ride to Buchholzbrunn; on by train to Lüderitz Bay.

---

[45] Belonging to the Nama tribe. They fought the Germans between 1904 and 1907.

[46] The Lüderitz Bay–Kubub line was opened in 1907. The financing of the railway to Kubub and Keetmanshoop had led to difficulties in the Reichstag, which was also at this time demanding a reduction of the number of troops in the colony; Bülow used these issues as an opportunity to dissolve the Reichstag on 13 December 1906.

25 July, Saturday. Early, 4 o'clock, Lüderitz Bay, Kapps Hotel. Morning, railway, harbour. Lunch, mess. Afternoon, diamond fields.[47] Evening, mess.

26 July, Sunday. 8 o'clock, boat trip round the harbour; Dias Point. Lunch with District Officer Brill. Afternoon, diamond mine. Evening, mess.

27 July, Monday. Departure by train, 6.30 a.m. Arrived Keetmanshoop. Departed 7 o'clock.

28 July, Tuesday. Car. Departure 8 o'clock. Arrived Berseba 1 o'clock. Hottentot territory. Lieutenant Linsing. Stayed with the grocer Kries.

29 July, Wednesday. Dep. Berseba (car) 6.30 a.m. Via Tses to Gröndorn, thence by cart to the blue-ground site of Gibeon pit. Absurd undertaking. On by car to Gibeon, arrived 4 o'clock. Total 145 kilometres. Accommodation District Officer von der Groeben. Evening, hotel.

30 July, Thursday. Departure, 5 o'clock, in carts and on horseback. Arrived Satansplatz 10 o'clock, to Tsubqarris (Voigts farm) at 2 o'clock. On the way von Koenen's Farm. Stayed the night with von Kleist.

31 July, Friday. Rest day on account of the Governor and Dernburg. Morning, pleasure-ride.

1 August, Saturday. Early, 6 o'clock, set off on horseback to Maltahöhe. Morning, von Heinitz's Farm. Then Karichab, arrived 4 o'clock. Sandstorm. Lodged officers' house.

2 August, Sunday. Departure, 7 o'clock, in cars which had come from Gibeon. Morning, Hermann's Farm. Breakdown. Evening, Tsumis (choice of half-caste woman).

[47] These were fields discovered by chance by an official of the Deutsche Kolonial-Eisenbahnbau- und Betriebsgesellschaft (German Colonial Railway). The importance of the find was such that both the parent company, Lenz and Co., and the BHG became interested in exploiting the fields. Rathenau and Dernburg also decided to offer the sole exploitation of government lands to the Frankfurt-based Metal-Gesellschaft which accepted their proposal. The two men then set to work to found a mining monopoly similar to that of De Beers. Medalen, 'Capitalism and Colonialism', pp. 320–42. For the leading role of the BHG and the Diamantenregie, see ibid., pp. 343–6; Fürstenberg, *Carl Fürstenberg*, p. 467.

3 August, Monday. Arrived Rehoboth noon. Brief encounter with Henckel's party. First Lieutenant Hültscher, District Commander. Without a bandage for the first time, but with a plaster.

4 August, Tuesday. Early, departure by car. Morning, Harris. Went for a trot [on horseback] until 4.15 p.m. because second car broke down.
   Windhoek posting-station. Lodged with the Governor. Evening, small dinner-party.

5 August, Wednesday. Morning, shopping. Evening, civil servants' and officers' mess.

6 August, Thursday. Morning, discussed farmers, then native question and police (Major von Heydebreck), municipal constitution (Major Külz). Afternoon, the military. Evening, Governor's dinner-party.

7 August, Friday. Morning, the economy, mining. Afternoon, ride to sandstone works and Little Windhoek. Evening, beer party at the Governor's.

8 August, Saturday. Morning, medicine, economy, etc. Lunch with von Vietsch. Afternoon, Veterinary Institute. Beer evening *Krug zum grossen Kranz*. Telegrams composed.

9 August, Sunday. Lunch, officers' mess. Evening, supper with the Governor. Count Hoensbroech, one-year volunteer.

10 August, Monday. Early, 6 o'clock, departure by state railway.[48] 10 o'clock Osoana. Rode to the small settlements, then to Okahandja. Breakfast. On to Okasisi, von Dewitz's Farm. Evening, 10 o'clock, Karibib Hotel.

11 August, Tuesday. 7 o'clock departure by Otavi Railway. 12 o'clock arrive Omaruru. Meal with District Officer von Frankenberg. Afternoon, ride. Evening, von Frankenberg and beer party.

12 August, Wednesday. Early, 5 o'clock, departure by Otavi Railway. Lunch-time, Otjiwarongo. Afternoon Otavi; evening, Tsumeb. Accommodation with director Hassinger.

---

[48] The state railway between Swakopmund and Windhoek was constructed as a field railway in 1896. Because of certain stipulations concerning monopoly agreements with the South West Africa Company it was even, to begin with, operated with horses. When the Otavi Railway was built the old line became superfluous as far as Karibib.

13 August, Thursday. Early to Otjikokoseo. Machine-gun practice Afternoon, mine and foundry. Evening, hotel.

14 August, Friday. 8 o'clock to Otavi; then train to Grootfontein. Arrived afternoon. Accommodation, Rothe Hotel.

15 August, Saturday. Early, drive (carts) to Halberstadt's farm. Evening with Director Tönnesen (South West Africa Company).[49]

16 August, Sunday. Early, train to Otjiwarongo. Arrived 2 o'clock. 4 o'clock, on with Henckel and Saldern by car to Okanjande. Von Veltheim, von Reibnitz. Arrived 5 o'clock.

17 August, Monday. 6 o'clock by car to Waterberg. Arrived 1 o'clock. Hildebrandt, District Officer. Return trip 3 o'clock. 6 o'clock, eight kilometres from Okanjande, car collapsed. On foot. Arrived 9 o'clock.

18 August, Tuesday. 5 o'clock, left Okanjande. 6.25 left Otjiwarongo. Train. Arrived Karibib 5.30 p.m. Beer party.

19 August, Wednesday. Departure, 6.30 p.m., by train to Swakopmund.

20 August, Thursday. Steamer to Walvis Bay.

21 August, Friday. Banking conditions. Beer party.

22 August, Saturday. Departure, 12 o'clock, *Bürgermeister*.[50]

As after their first journey Dernburg and Rathenau wrote up their reports. By the beginning of October, Rathenau had already sent a privately printed copy of his report to Bülow. The Chancellor passed it on to the Kaiser and thanked Rathenau very formally.[51]

This time Rathenau had to wait for a decoration, despite the fact that his relations with Bülow were very good. During the *Daily Telegraph* Affair, after the important meeting between Bülow and the Kaiser on 17 November, Rathenau

[49] The South West Africa Company (founded in 1890) made an arrangement with the Diskonto Bank in 1902 and founded the Otavi-Minen- und Eisenbahngesellschaft (Otavi Mining and Railway Company), which then built the railway, over 500 kilometres long, to develop the Otavi Mines. The negotiations between the Diskontogesellschaft (Diskonto Bank) and the Rhodes Group, which was behind the South West Africa Company, had far-reaching consequences affecting great parts of Africa south of the equator. See Pogge von Strandmann, *Imperialismus am grünen Tisch.*

[50] The ship belonged to the Woermann Line.

[51] ZSta Potsdam, RK 927, Bülow to the Kaiser, 4 October 1908.

sent the Chancellor a flower arrangement with the card: 'To the saviour of the fatherland'. Consequently Rathenau was invited to dinner at the Bülows, where he was involved in further attempts at mediation between Bülow and Harden in the Eulenburg affair.

At the end of December, Dernburg approached the Chancellor and told him that Rathenau was in a very 'sulky and disappointed mood' over the question of an order; he attributed the delay to Dernburg, and that was probably why he planned to publish his memorandum on South West Africa.[52] Dernburg saw this as a further obstacle to investing him with an order, and as complicating his own policy, which had become more benevolent in its attitude to settlers. Rathenau's report, on the other hand, was sharper and more critical than Dernburg's, the exact opposite to their reports on East Africa the year before. Bülow declared he was prepared to dissuade Rathenau from his plan and would request a decoration in a short while. After Wilhelm von Loebell, the Permanent Under-Secretary in the Chancellery, had stated his reasons—mainly Rathenau's personal links with Harden—for not conferring on him the order of the Red Eagle, Second Class, Bülow made it quite clear to him that he wanted to decorate Rathenau 'because he is a very capable, useful person, and to show that we do not always treat unbaptized Jews as pariahs. If we do not give Rathenau some plaster or other (order or counsellor) he will be very demoralized.'[53] Bülow also pointed out that Rathenau's abilities made it desirable 'that he should not deny his services to us at a later occasion'. He saw no real obstacle in the Rathenau-Harden connection with the Moltke trial that Loebell had referred to, and even defended Rathenau's record in the Moltke and Eulenburg affairs.[54] Obviously Bülow realized that Rathenau did not support Harden unreservedly. In fact, Loebell did not object to a decoration in principle, and even went so far as suggesting that Rathenau could receive the title *Geheimer Legationsrat* as well, but did not consider the present time suitable. Councillor Wahnschaffe supported Loebell by pointing out that Rathenau's memorandum about South West Africa 'contains a very sharp criticism of our conduct of war in South West Africa [and] talk of atrocities in our native policy. If that were printed in *Die Zukunft* a decoration of Dr R. by the Kaiser would become even more unlikely.'

Bülow accepted Loebell's advice and decided to postpone conferring a decoration. He then asked Rathenau to come and see him and explained that it would be inopportune, at the moment, to publish his memorandum. Thereupon Rathenau gave up the idea of publication and thus kept the chance of being decorated later. With that the political side of the dispute was settled. However, relations between Rathenau and Dernburg remained strained. From the correspondence between them, which went through the Chancellor's office, it became quite clear that Rathenau had regarded Dernburg as an obstacle to his getting a 'decoration for his evening dress', as he described the order, or a

[52] Ibid., Dernburg to Bülow, 24 December 1908.

[53] Ibid., Loebell to Bülow, 27 December 1908; Bülow to Loebell, 27 December 1908; Loebell to Bülow again, the same day.

[54] Bülow had approached Harden in 1907 and 1908, through Rathenau, to persuade him to be more moderate in the case against Moltke and the Eulenburg affair. For instance, on 20 October 1908 Bülow asked Rathenau to tell Harden to drop the date for a court-hearing in the Moltke-Harden trial. For this see the documents in the Bülow Papers, BA Koblenz, Nachlass Bülow 32; Rogge, *Holstein und Harden*; Joll, 'Rathenau and Harden', pp. 124 ff. For the various developments in the affair, see Hellige (ed.), Rathenau-Harden.

title.[55] Although relations between the two had worsened on the last journey, Rathenau's suspicion was groundless because Dernburg had approached Bülow for a decoration as early as September.[56] On 31 December Dernburg tried to assure Rathenau that he was not motivated by personal reasons in preventing a publication of his memorandum.[57] It was understandable that Dernburg should not want to see Rathenau appearing in print first, especially as Rathenau's report could have embarrassed Dernburg's efforts to come to terms with the settler farmers. But Rathenau's vanity appears all the more astonishing when later he tried to create the impression that he placed no value on such superficialities.

Bülow followed up the question of a decoration after the *Daily Telegraph* Affair and after his resignation as Chancellor.[58] Thanks to his efforts, Rathenau was invested with the order of the Red Eagle, Second Class, in January 1910.[59]

Reconciliation between Rathenau and Dernburg soon followed, though the old intimacy between the two was never completely restored. According to Lili Deutsch's account, Rathenau considered the journey with Dernburg a 'catastrophe', because Dernburg kept on disregarding him.[60] Rathenau's vanity must have suffered badly when Dernburg, in his capacity as Colonial Secretary, stood in the centre at official receptions, while Rathenau had to stay among his retinue.

At the end of his journeys, Rathenau did not gain the prestige he presumably hoped for—decorations or titles—which would have helped him along his road to power. Furthermore, Bülow's own difficulties were so greatly increased after the *Daily Telegraph* Affair that he gave up his plan to liberalize top administrative posts.

On the personal side, the trip to South and South West Africa had been more exhausting than the previous one. Rathenau never looked back on it as he had with a certain nostalgia on his travels in East Africa. He told Harden afterwards that 'his head was still full of bushes, sand and African small cattle. All this has to be weeded first before I regain my horsepower.'[61] He was glad that Africa had released him: owing to blood-poisoning 'there was a period of time when I thought this evil land would keep me'. In contrast to his East African visit, Rathenau had this time been involved in many business affairs which affected the AEG or the BHG. The major ones concerned the Victoria Falls Power Company, the Otavi Mines, which were to supply the AEG with copper, and the discovery of diamonds, in which Rathenau took interest as banker and as board member of the Frankfurt-based Metall-Gesellschaft, whose official name was Berg- und Metallbank (Mining and Metal Bank).

---

[55] ZStA Potsdam, RK 927, Wahnschaffe to Loebell, 28 December 1908; ibid., Wahnschaffe to Bülow, 4 January 1909, and the enclosure there of Rathenau to Dernburg, 12 December 1908.

[56] Fürstenberg, *Carl Fürstenberg*, p. 471.

[57] ZStA Potsdam, RK 927 and BA Koblenz, Personalakten Dernburg, D, Nr. 2/5, 23.

[58] BA Koblenz, Nachlass Bülow 115, Bülow to Rathenau, 28 September 1909. Bülow, *Denkwürdigkeiten*, vol. iii, pp. 40-5.

[59] Ibid., pp. 91 f. BA Koblenz, Nachlass Bülow 115, Rathenau to Bülow, 15 January 1910.

[60] Pfeiffer-Belli (ed.), *Kessler. Tagebücher*, p. 553. See also Bülow, *Denkwürdigkeiten*, vol. iii, pp. 40 f. Dernburg first visited Rathenau again in 1912. See diary entry for 26 October 1912.

[61] Hellige (ed.), Rathenau–Harden, Rathenau to Harden, between 15 and 20 September 1908.

Extracts from the 'Report on the State of the South West African Colony'[62]

Any review of our territory in South West Africa should begin by assessing the countries of South West Africa as a whole. For the physical and economic homogeneity of the sub-continent unites the six colonial states in an integral complex within which political frontiers are fortuitous and, therefore, frequently altered. But, on the other hand, within this homogeneity the country exhibits contrasts of every possible shade within a limited range: from colonization dating back two hundred and fifty years to colonization dating back twenty years; from a totally black population to an almost wholly European one; from an age-old nomadic economy to a large-scale industrial mining economy; from a bushman's kraal to a great seaport; from the rule of chieftains to the parliamentary organization of the state—gradations and transitional stages can be found which are historically, physically, and culturally based and disclose uses, implications, and prospects for our German territory.

Yet, no matter how significant such explanations may be for the tasks of today, they leave unanswered the question central to all African policy. Is a lasting, successful colonization of this continent by Western peoples possible? The Egyptians, Phoenicians, Romans, Goths, Arabs, Portuguese, Dutch, French, and English have owned great parts of the country and yet left behind only vanishing traces of higher civilization. Nowhere has true colonization, as in North and South America, or in Australia, been achieved. The broadest tracts of land belong to the forces of nature; vast areas belong to the animal kingdom. The natives have made no steps in the direction of civilization. Wherever it has been forcibly set in motion they were driven towards racial intermingling, slavery, or annihilation. The Europeans, on the other hand, whom this country has taken in, seem with each generation to become more estranged from their homeland: they create new communities, new genetic characteristics, and, not infrequently, new racial mixtures. Africa, to this day, despite all the colours on the map, is not a colonial continent. And even the economic results, modest hitherto for the colonial powers, are, given the enormous scale of investment, operations, and sacrifice, minimal or negative.

The Protectorate[63] is not one of the middling, let alone one of the best territories of South Africa. Of its 835,000 square kilometres of area, about 500,000 are reckoned economically viable. The Namib

---

[62] Published in Rathenau, *Nachgelassene Schriften*, vol. ii.
[63] Of South West Africa.

coastal strip is desert and the Amboland remains for climatic reasons unsuitable for European settlement. Annual rainfall only exceeds the South African average in a small region in the north-east. To the south-west it gradually decreases to very insignificant and irregular yearly averages, so that in parts of the south one can hardly talk abut normal rainfall. Two perennial surface-rivers empty into the sea; the southern frontier river Oranje, neither of whose banks we possess, and the northern river Kunene, which flows through Amboland. Artificial accumulation of water, and dams, pose considerably greater difficulties than in, say, Cape Colony and in the Transvaal, because rain-water reservoirs have to be distributed over enormous catchment areas and hydraulic works remain dependent on irregular river supplies.

Of the country's mineral deposits—which, though not rare, are mostly insignificant as far as present experience can tell—one, the Otavigesellschaft copper-mine, is being exploited on a modest scale and with large-scale capital expenditure. At present this enterprise has no financial results to show, though it should be possible to produce them by reorganizing the company. The diamond-fields discovered at Lüderitz Bay, mentioned above, are worth consideration; so possibly are the marble-quarries near Karibib and the copper-fields in the Khan area. Although prospectors roam through the whole country, and the natives have got used to paying attention to any unusual-seeming mineral, discoveries which stand up to serious examination are rare, and the country's geologists do not expect any surprising revelations for the present. Nevertheless, hope of future mining developments remains, even though intensive exploitation can only be considered for minerals of high specific value, since the country's consumption will always remain insignificant while freight rates to the coast will generally be heavy.

In order to assess the native's position it is advisable to bear in mind the internal evolution of the Protectorate since the hoisting of the German flag. The northern part of the country, called Damaraland, was owned by the Hereros, a hard-working pastoral tribe whose flocks, though admittedly over-valued in relation to their size, were the constant envy of their neighbours. The Hereros were considered courageous but peaceful people, vigorous and intelligent. Because of their tall, slim build they were reckoned one of the most beautiful tribes of Africa. In contrast to them were their hereditary enemies the Hottentots who lived in the south, in Namaland. A curious mongrel race, yellowish in colouring, half negroid, half mongoloid in type, small in build, skilful, crafty, unfaithful, and work-shy, they led a life of hunting and cattle-thieving. Until the conclusion of the

Protectorate Treaties both peoples lived in complete independence under the rule of their chiefs. The Protectorate Treaties themselves do not imply that the Reich seized possession but rather, as the name says, that there was a relationship based on protection and friendship. The nucleus of the agreement was the fact that whites were allowed to remain in the country. To what extent the treaties were understood by the natives according to their own way of thinking, and what conception they could have had of simultaneous sales of land, given the scale of their ideas and the fact that they were not aware of the concept of private ownership of land, must remain undetermined. Certainly the most intelligent of them foresaw the decline of their freedom and indeed of their tribes. This is demonstrated by the deeply thought-out letter, full of forebodings, which Hendrik Witboi, paramount chief of Namaland, sent on 30 May 1890 to Kamaherero, paramount chief of Hereroland.

An attempt has been made to establish the personal policy of the chiefs, or even religious motives, as the reason for the Herero and Hottentot rebellions—events which were, indeed, to the native way of thinking, not rebellions but legitimate *orlogs*, that is to say, feuds. It is difficult to agree with this point of view. If, in a vast country inhabited by peoples to whom abstract ideas or even national feeling are unintelligible, all men, from first to last, reach for their weapons and risk property and life, one can suppose that a commonly experienced severe economic pressure was the cause. This pressure existed, since both through the careless management of Chief Samuel Maharero and through the economic immaturity of his fellow-countrymen, the tribe of the Hereros, in particular, had fallen into a serious predicament.

Farmers[64] and traders, often one and the same person, had come into the country. The farmers demanded the ownership of land; and because the settlement societies, which had meanwhile acquired a large part of the country in the form of concessions, refrained from selling in the way the prospective purchasers intended, they sought to get the biggest possible share of the land left in the tribes' possession by bargaining with the chiefs. The traders ran a credit business that was facilitated by the natives' uncontrollable inclination to buy, and took their cattle in payment. A well-meaning but badly drafted credit ordinance from the colonial administration jeopardized all outstanding debts, encouraged the traders to ruthless execution, and displaced, in the utmost confusion, the natives who had had to give up one watering-place after another and who were, in any case, anxious to preserve their own livestock. It is useless to

[64] European settlers in South Africa were referred to as farmers.

heap moral reproaches on the traders for their actions, which were completely admissible according to European ideas of granting credit, although this was a case where one of the contracting parties was economically under age; and it is equally one-sided to regard the massacres with which the Hereros began the war as a crime which the whole tribe must still expiate to-day.

The war was begun in a manner very much in contrast to that of the English, who had shown in the Sudan how a native war can be organized by engineers and architects firstly, so as to wage the decisive battle with colonial troops later. Thus, at the peak of the decisive period [of the native war against the Germans], of 15,000 combat troops scarcely more than 3,000 faced the enemy, while the remainder were needed for communication and supply services. Even the expeditionary campaign, which was conducted by the commanders and men with enormous sacrifice and admirable courage and endurance, suffered from European ideas which envisaged a war between nations rather than the massacre of natives. Thus the winning of positions was thought important, although it was incomprehensible to the natives why the surrender of this hill or that should represent a defeat for them. On the other hand, driving away native cattle was considered despicable [by the Germans], but this, together with the heavy damage it would have caused, really would have affected morale. Then, at a certain time, the war was waged so as to contrive a sort of African Sedan, and by means of a vast encircling movement the final catastrophe was brought about. It is to be deeply regretted for the present condition of the country that, backed up by the fantastic notion of an alleged pan-African Bantu threat, the total extermination of the colony's most single valuable possession, its native population, was contemplated. With the assertion that it had been forbidden, in the highest places, to give pardon, all peace negotiations were refused and orders issued not to take any prisoners.

Although the African Sedan failed at the Waterberg, the Hereros were driven into the Sandfeld and the greatest atrocity that has ever been brought about by German military policy took place: a whole nation, with its women and children, languished for weeks in mortal agony. That intransigence as a principle turned out to be impracticable is shown by the course of the war with the Bondels, who, militarily undefeated, concluded the peace of Heirachabis through the intervention of the Catholic Mission.

At the end of the war the military advance was accompanied by equally unhappy measures against natives who had voluntarily surrendered. The system of deportation and concentration camps extracted heavy sacrifice. Thus, of the 1,800 Hottentots interned on Shark [Haifisch] Island, 1,200 perished within 6 months. These measures resulted in the opinion, which was widespread in English territory and was openly expressed by the highest authorities in Cape Colony during the negotiations for the surrender of Simon Cooper, that our natives had lost confidence in our government.

The state of being a prisoner of war—for that is what the detained men, women, and children were called after the war was ended—has been abolished. However, even today the position of the native cannot be considered more than that of a helot, here and there bordering on that of a slave. This position is not the result of the terms of the decree which today controls the position of the native but is, without doubt, the result of interpretation and application. That the native can at any time and in any place be stopped and questioned by any white man is a humiliating measure, but one which has no far-reaching consequences—so long as the white man is sober. That the native is only allowed to own land and cattle with the Governor's consent means that in general he is allowed to own neither land nor cattle, a measure which might be narrowly construed to protect the interests of the individual farmer from competition, but which seems particularly hard on the Herero, who is used to working exclusively at breeding cattle and to living on cow's milk. Rather more serious are the provisions concerning work contracts, which, though indeed unobjectionable according to European ideas, do not make the legally untutored native sufficiently aware of his rights; while the most varied means remain by which the employer, who has the advantage of greater power, insight, and public credit, can continue using forced labour. Thus the employer, as well as failing to give a period of notice, can make accusations of guilt which are easily concocted, given the custom of payment in kind. He can also make the frequently-heard allegation that the worker, whose submissiveness has to be observed in order to appreciate the irony of the accusation, had in fact threatened him with violence. Indeed, plenty of cases occur in which disagreeable working conditions are successfully terminated by the worker. There are even cases in which the worker has run away from his master without justification. Finally, there are cases in which the runaway, though without formal justification, is nevertheless not forcibly returned to his master by sensible police authorities because his master is known to be brutal or insolvent. But this does not mean that labour conditions as they exist today must not be described as partial and preferential in interpretation and operation.

The surviving remnants of the two great native nations are encamped in kraals, as the collections of beehive huts are called. Estimates of their number vary between 20,000 and 40,000: women, naturally, greatly predominating. Private kraals are scattered on the farmers' estates; state kraals are to be found outside the so-called towns, and the number of inmates is considerably in excess of the white population. From these labour reservoirs, which remind one to some extent of the slave-camps of the classical world, the whites supply themselves with servants according to need and in return for the customary local wages. The storekeeper takes servants, workers, washerwomen; the soldier, batmen; the authorities, road workers. Frequently, and despite preventative measures by the authorities, these encampments receive visits at night by whites which lead to unpleasant scenes. Departure from the state kraals is allowed in theory but is, however, dependent on evidence of means of subsistence elsewhere, which can rarely be produced.

The oppressed condition of the native is reflected in his outward behaviour. It is unpleasant and humiliating for strangers to observe how these people, timidly and with the expression of poor sinners, press themselves to one side at the approach of a European, and submissively doff their caps in front of every white man. Nowhere are the innocent cheerfulness and trust, which are characteristic of natives in English colonies, to be seen. It has the outward appearance of slavery, as seen in the beer-dreams of the petty philistine. To consider the native question, or any other problem, merely in a moralizing way, is not the task of this discussion, which should not deliberately depart from an economic and political point of view. Should, then, the final question be formulated thus: is the condition of our natives in keeping with the interests of the Reich, the Protectorate, and the white settlers? Quite apart from the fact that it is not in keeping with the interests of the Reich if the only white colony among its possessions is seen abroad, particularly in neighbouring states, as a creation built on the extermination and oppression of natives, the question must be answered in the negative on purely economic grounds.

Any agricultural colony needs a native labour supply. We have no right, nor is it in our interests, to hope or to work to induce part of our home population to expatriate itself for the purpose of forming a white proletariat in a Protectorate to do that work which normally falls to the lot of the natives in other colonies and for which they, for climatic and ethnic reasons, are better qualified. It must therefore be ensured that a healthy stock of native elements is preserved in the country, living in accordance with their natural capabilities, and able to increase in numbers.

It is instructive to examine by what means the English handled the native question in South Africa and how, it may be claimed, they solved it. They start from the assumption that the Negro, accustomed from time immemorial to an unstable way of life and irregular pressure to work, prompted only by immediate needs, and endowed by nature with less concentration and perseverance than the European, cannot be trained in a trice to persistent, continuous work, which always remains the same, on the Western pattern. They therefore put him in a position where he can pursue his customary way of life for part of the year, while at the same time he is forced by automatically exerted pressure into periodic work for a farmer or an industrial plant. This happens, on the one hand, by means of large, inalienable native reservations on which the native can, under the protection of his headmen or chiefs, pursue his usual employment or unemployment for as long as he likes; on the other hand, however, he has to produce a tax, which is not too insignificant and which obliges him to work for at least part of the year. The tax is collected by the headmen and handed over to the Native Commissioner who is, at the same time, in close touch with the natives, and the advocate of their interests with the government departments. At the same time, in newly colonized territories where settlement by white elements is relatively sparse and the power of the thickly settled natives is still unbroken, the system of settling annuities on the chiefs according to influence and territory, which can make them loyal servants of the British Government and at the same time cause them to watch over their subjects and neighbouring potentates carefully, has been proved as a means of keeping the peace and of sharing interests.

So there are only two different sorts of places for the native to live: either on a reservation or with his employer. By means of a painstaking pass and registration system, control is exercised to prevent him roving about the country unemployed. Those who say our system inclines very closely to the British one are right, in so far as the pass system also plays an important part in our system. But with this difference: that with us the mitigating correlations—the reservations and the protection of the advocate—are disregarded.

Had the English system been introduced at the beginning, or had a native policy of whatever kind been at all consistently pursued on the basis of ethnic considerations, it is probable that the extinction of our tribes might have been avoided. Beginnings were made: thus under Leutwein's governorship negotiations about founding reservations took place; they were interrupted by the beginning of the war.

If one were to introduce English native policy into German South

West Africa straightaway, in all its entirety, several difficulties would result. It is practicable on the largest scale in Amboland, which is about to be opened up because of recently ratified treaties with the chieftains. Here the establishment of considerable reservations and the creation of commissioners and pensions for chieftains are urgently advised; indeed, it would be desirable to avoid completely all contact with traders and contractors for the time being. Under these conditions it will be possible to avoid a third great war and preserve intact the Ovambo tribes whom we urgently need for the economy of the Protectorate. For even if their land is hardly suitable for settlement, its 60,000 inhabitants will represent a valuable asset for us—in so far as they begin to get used to a sort of labour migration. They are certainly going to provide the labour force for the future mining industry, just as they already form the main tribe providing workers for the Otavi mines; and, with increasing colonization, they will fill in the gaps in the labour market in Herero and Hottentot country.

The introduction of a reasonable native policy is complicated by the situation of the Hereros and Hottentots. Neither of the tribes—with the exception of the Berseban Hottentots who wisely kept out of the uprisings—retains any livestock worth mentioning on which they could support themselves in any reservations that might be set up. It is true that, if it were possible, they could save during a period of employment and use this to acquire cattle. However, the breeding of cattle, as mentioned above, as in practice prohibited; moreover, their disastrous inclination to buy everything that is put up for sale continues as before and so, given the prevalent system of credit, they time and again slip back into dependence on the storekeeper. A further complication arises with the Hottentots, who are hunters and thieves by origin and are as little inclined to cattle-breeding as to any regular work.

Nevertheless, the necessary institutions must be established now: that is, commissioners as well as reservations. And among the commissioners' tasks will be that of studying the economic obstacles and of working towards their elimination, perhaps even along the lines of suitable provision of credit.

The Hottentots' situation demands particular care. Perhaps this is the place to take a more general look at the condition of the south and in this connection to discuss the problems and methods of defending the country.

Despite the decimation of the natives, and despite strict supervision in locations and kraals, the south cannot yet be thought of as pacified. Simon Cooper and Klein Jakobus, the one with more, the other with fewer adherents, roam on the other side of the English border and keep our administration and natives in a state of unrest. The Bondels, disarmed and subject to strict controls, submit unwillingly to this situation and remain an essentially unreliable element. But above all, throughout the south, cattle-thieving by roving bands against the farmers settled there never ceases.

This cattle-stealing represents almost the only item of interest for the security service in the south. Theft of cattle is reported to the nearest military station which immediately dispatches an officer and several troopers, and often a native guide and tracker as well, in a patrol which follows the fleeing thieves for days. In many cases pursuit is in vain because the report came too late. In other cases it is useless because the report was a false alarm; the missing cattle have turned up again. From time to time the thieves are caught and, because they 'offered resistance', shot down; and the cattle are returned to the owner in a state of exhaustion. The episode has cost him nothing; it occasions the military authorities considerable expense, which annually amounts to many times the value of the total number of cattle so protected. For, quite apart from the expense of maintaining horses and the wear and tear on them, the density and strength of military posts is forced up to a scale quite out of proportion to the funds invested in the country or even to the number of white settlers there.

The military defence of a country against external enemies— possibly also against internal enemies, if these should make their appearance as a belligerent mass—on the one hand, and the protection of the country against crime and disturbance of the peace, on the other, are two completely different problems which cannot be solved using the same means. Defence is the duty of the troops, security the duty of the police or *gendarmerie*. The troops will have to maintain and exercise their military fitness in integral units; the *gendarmerie*, distributed across the country in detachments and squads, will have to acquire a knowledge of the country and learn sympathy with the natives, skill in tracking, and mobility. To use troops for *gendarmerie* service means misuse, and cannot have satisfactory results. Apart from the heavy demands of military training, the troops cannot, in their short period of duty, satisfy the demands for experience, for knowledge of the people, for knowledge of their languages, and of the country, which the professional *gendarmerie* must provide. Equally, the military sense of the commanding officer must suffer in a service which makes him the tool of the civil authorities in trivial property matters and at the same time never grants him any official authority over those people entrusted to his protection.

The English long ago effected the separation of the regular troops, the *Imperials*, from the *gendarmerie*, the *Mounted Police*, although the regular troops' long period of service guarantees them increased knowledge of the country and independence of action. It is astonishing how police squads, weak in numbers and strength, can control large areas of the English colonies. Certainly the English make use of a large range of indispensable native auxiliary troops, because they have learned by experience that only a native with fellow tribesmen and tribeswomen can maintain the close contact that is necessary for reliable information, and that only he has the incredible tracking ability which far excels all other means of investigation in this rainless country. Among our troops, on the other hand, the use of native forces is limited as far as possible because it is thought that intelligent troops can, with good will, learn in a couple of years the skills the natives have acquired over the centuries.

Furthermore, our Protectorate also has the beginnings of a *gendarmerie*, under the name of a police force. But this is made up of officials who are in fact recruited from among older people, some of whom can be recruited to military service. Quite apart from the fact that strict military organization and discipline cannot be expected from this force, it remains unusable in the country's security service because the policeman's civil functions absorb all his energy. It seems hard to believe, but the truth is that by far the greatest part of the work done consists of serving official and judicial writs. This anomaly is understandable if one realizes that in the colony an average of two civil actions are brought against each white man and that legal proceedings, taking no account of exceptional colonial circumstances, unravel themselves with all the complicated forms and court procedures of the homeland. One might also bear in mind that delivering a message in this vast, thinly settled country frequently means days, indeed weeks of riding, and that because of the mobility of the addressees many of the expeditions peter out unsuccessfully.

It might be noted in passing that the country is in urgent need of law reform, and reform of trial procedure, in particular, branching out and having petty cases summarily dealt with by changing the code of law. It must be emphasized that a civil police force cannot carry out the duties of a military *gendarmerie*.

If it may be hoped that painfully acquired experience in the handling of natives will lead to peaceful development of our relations with the Ovambos, then there is no place for a regular military campaign in German South West Africa in the foreseeable future. For the number of surviving Hereros or Hottentots cannot field any opposition which would justify a real state of war. Therefore, leaving aside the fantastic notion of a land war with England, the importance to the Protectorate of regular troops is considerably diminished and even the present figure, reduced to almost 2,500 men, does not represent the minimum which the necessary reserve could reach. The internal security of the country, on the other hand, will demand the attention of the authorities for a long time to come, and necessitate supplementing the Protectorate force with a militarily organized *gendarmerie*.

The white population includes a noteworthy percentage of hardworking, indeed self-sacrificing, people. There are many farmers, tradesmen, and missionaries who perform their jobs with devotion and idealism despite privations, isolation from other people, and dangerous circumstances. This does not preclude speaking openly about the weaknesses of the colonial population, because understanding is the first step to improvement.

Next, the general passion for lawsuits must be mentioned. It must be termed highly abnormal that in a country of 8,000 white inhabitants almost 8,000 lawsuits occur annually such that, since each case presumes two parties, two suits fall to the share of each inhabitant, whether man, woman, or child.

Another of the white colony's faults is spreading intemperance. It has already been mentioned how compensation for the lack of an ideal standard of living and for the monotony of the way of life is sought in material pleasures. To this must be added the manifold lack of any family life and domesticity among the predominantly male population. This can explain, though not justify, the fact that in some places there is a tavern for every ten, in others for every six, inhabitants, and that the consumption of spirits, reckoned per head of population, reaches the enormous annual total of 600 marks. It is true that this is owing to the high price of drink in that country, which is the result of transport costs, taxes, and retail sale. Yet even reckoned quantitatively the figures remain alarming. Thus beer consumption amounts to 3,500,000 litres a year. It is significant that the tax on spirits is at the moment the state's only net receipt for German South West Africa worth mentioning.

Our neighbours have, to a high degree, been aware of the seriousness of alcoholism in colonial countries. The English live considerably more soberly than we do; the abstemiousness of the Boers is well known. The moral dangers of drink are evident if one considers that the white man demands the most unreserved recognition of his authority from the blacks to whom in his drunkenness he becomes dangerous and at the same time despicable. Intercourse with native

women, to which we owe a dangerous racial problem and unsatisfactory sanitary conditions among natives and whites, particularly
among the troops, mostly occurs in the context of alcoholic excesses.

In the broader context of alcoholism crime statistics must be
mentioned, which amount, including those for trespassing, to 3,600
prosecutions. So that of every two colonists one, on average, is
charged each year. Here it should be remarked that not only is there
a difference for whites and blacks in the execution of sentences, but
also, in contrast to English usage, in the competent courts and in
the jurisdiction over criminal cases. It is therefore inevitable that the
idea is growing among natives that they alone are subject to a more
severe justice than the white man, who as a rule gets off scot-free.

Along with these ethical characteristics an intellectual peculiarity
of the colonists must not be concealed, one which is to some extent
explained by the composition of the population and its lack of
traditional customs and experience. Only a minority worry about
the circumstances in which their businesses were set up and the
conditions in which they operate.

It is evident that the conditions described, at a time of limited
development, cannot usher in a comfortable or calming atmosphere.
And, because German South West Africa is a land of small people,
of limited means and narrow vision, dissatisfaction does not lead to
introspection and increased activity but rather to stringent and not
always intelligent criticism, first of the government, then of the
constitution.

Yet, for a more distant future, one may not ignore the fact that a
colonial population cannot indefinitely receive its laws, instructions,
and officials from the homeland. The independence of a self-
sufficient life, disengaged from the homeland, demands an increased
measure of self-government. As soon as German South West Africa
stands on its own feet economically, is one generation richer in
political experience, begins to produce a population of native-born
colonists, the time will have come to let this country achieve similar
constitutional standards as its political neighbours. The country
must become an export country in order to maintain a profitable
economy.

Whoever pictures to himself the origin, history, and present
position of the South West African Protectorate surveys a series
of disappointments and failures heavier than any to which the new
Reich has been subjected. Unfortunately they are not undeserved,
for the German colonial policy of the first years can no longer
be spared the blame for inadequate knowledge of the country
and for inconsistent and uneconomic actions.

Originally founded by a not particularly important trader who hoped for a business in guano, copper, and useful plants, and saw his hopes disappointed, the Protectorate was built up as the enterprise of a trading company vested with sovereign power. The company came to grief and then, in 1889, the Reich undertook the protection of all private estates which did not belong to a colony, whilst they, in order to maintain their previous value, needed to be supplemented with new territory which was the property of tribes independent of any protectorate treaties. If this step was to have any political or economic meaning, the transition from Protectorate to colony would have to take place. It took place, but without being acknowledged and appreciated as such. It happened, not under the direction of a deliberate and effective policy, but far more through headstrong action by private interests, through gradual sequestration of native lands, later through combating the so-called rebellions, finally through war. The transformation of an impossible creation, the militarily guaranteed Protectorate, into the normal form of a crown colony was the cause of heavy sacrifice. Therefore, it might be noted in parenthesis, the now meaningless label—Protectorate—should disappear from the name of the colony, for the name German South West Africa or German South Africa would be more suitable.

That the demarcation of the country was undertaken in a manner which did not constitute a magnificent testimony to our geographic information at the time, was mentioned earlier.

If one thinks of the sacrifice that South West Africa has exacted from us, then what is inestimable must be spoken of first. Two thousand German soldiers fell in this country. Those are the heaviest losses the German Reich has sustained since it was established. Because of a temporary change in the policy of the war, which aimed at the extirpation of the natives, one of the noblest of African tribes, the Herero people, was almost wiped out. The black population as a whole was reduced to a fraction, and their livestock destroyed, with the exception of the hitherto inaccessible Ovambos. The bare cost of the war swallowed up 400 million marks; almost 100 million marks poured into the country in subsidies and investments, so that almost 80,000 marks of *Reich* funds devolve on the head of each white man living there, quite apart from the approximately 3,000 marks of interest rates for the annual deficit.

If one were to set this unprecedented expenditure against the present statement of assets the picture would not prove any more favourable. A country of vast dimensions, it is true, able to be productive, but depopulated and hardly settled by whites. One type of production [agriculture] in its first beginnings, not yet ready to export, has not yet quite found its right market. The farmers need considerable capital until the economy is finally set on its feet. Indebtedness and latent crisis in the commercial class; stagnant business. At present almost 3,000 men are necessary for the defence and security of the country, that is, 1 man for every 3 inhabitants. The Reich's subsidies, including the cost of the Protectorate troops, amount to 25 million marks.

This description finds the country in its darkest period, after the end of a serious war, at the end of an unfortunate political era, and at the beginning of the painful business of building up the economy. The existing economy can be expected to consolidate itself and reach a standard of production fit for export, such that commerce can withstand pressures on it and mature into a healthy export business, the mining industry forge ahead from its many beginnings to a profitable output, and for the size and expense of the country's defence be further reduced, and with them the burdens which are incumbent upon the Reich. With increased production, tariffs and taxes will accrue to the country's revenue which will reduce the deficit and gradually lead to the control of its own finances by the country's administration. If one reflects that the German is one of the thriftiest managers in the world, and is accustomed to creating out of comparatively unfavourable preconditions organizations and industrial works which compete with the best situated and the most favoured enterprises, so one should have confidence in the beginnings of a development which can be seen everywhere, and encourage its continuance.

On the other hand, it must not be forgotten that according to our present level of knowledge this development is not unlimited. South West Africa is, unless undreamed-of treasures are concealed in her flanks, a poor country. Should the value of agricultural products ever in years to come reach 100 millions or even higher, these amounts are still not as important as the current figures of one or other of our industrial concerns at home with far smaller investment. Also the number of people who can find a livelihood in the country, whether it is now more or less than 100,000, is not greater than the number our industrialists of large-scale enterprises are used to dealing with.

Furthermore, it is evident that the country's development is not a matter of a few years. It is useless here, to use a Bismarckian phrase, to hold a lamp under the ripening fruit. For the next few years large investments are not necessary; the opening up of Ovamboland must follow peaceful paths. Railway construction on a considerable

scale is not at present suited to this country, which needs ameliora-
tion more than reorganization. The government programme should
consist in strengthening the country by means of internal organization and reform. And, indeed, this is where the problems of native
legislation, defence, judicial reform, and the credit system take
first place.

The question whether the possession of South West Africa means
good or bad business for us—whether this country should be
retained or given up—must never be considered again. Through
the German blood spilt on its fields it has become a part of our
homeland and German land must remain sacrosanct.

South West Africa is our only white colony. The German name
has been pledged to the country; it is for us to prove that German
civilization is equal to colonization. The country is ready to receive
our civilization; it is healthy, very suitable for Germans to live in,
and productive. The peculiar magic that emanates from it and calls
back many who are homeward-bound does not just issue from its
clear sky and blue mountains, but above all from the pure horizon
that extends the vision and elevates the spirit to greater resolution
and freer action. And here lies the significance of what South West
Africa owes to us. In Germany there is a lot of discipline, a lot of
order, a lot of knowledge, and a lot of work. But the times demand
more and more determination, human understanding, initiative, and
responsibility from the individual. England owes a good part of its
superiority to colonization; so too may our colonial beginnings,
perhaps, lead to a new education for Germans.

DIARY FOR 1911

No diary entries have survived for the years 1909 and 1910, and the number of letters dating from these two years is not large. After his two journeys to Africa, Rathenau developed his activities in the industrial sphere and met with success in several matters relating to the expansion of the AEG concern. The most important coup he was able to bring off was the acquisition of the majority holding of Felten & Guilleaume-Lahmeyerwerke.[1] Apart from this he busied himself as a 'marriage-maker', bringing about a merger between the banking houses of Delbrück and Schickler.[2] It was this period too which saw the purchase of Schloss Freienwalde (1909) for a price of 262,000 marks, and the laying of the foundation-stone of his house in the Grunewald in Berlin (1910).[3] His estimated annual income rose from 205,000 marks in the summer of 1908, to 295,000–300,000 marks in 1910, while his assets approached the two million mark.[4]

In the field of politics he regretted very much that Bülow was dismissed, especially as he had been in agreement with the Chancellor's attempt to reform the taxation system. When Bülow left Berlin he went for the summer to Norderney and Rathenau became one of his first visitors there. It was then Rathenau who suggested to him that he should write his memoirs in the style of Macaulay's essays. On that occasion both men also discussed the question of Rathenau's decoration again. Thus Bülow wrote to his Under-Secretary Loebell: 'I would be really obliged to you if you were to leave the splendid Walther Rathenau in no doubt that we have done all we could to obtain for him the order, which he deserves so much. This seems necessary to me in view of possible counteractions by Dernburg.'

Six days later Bülow repeated his plea on Rathenau's behalf and this time added a letter to Valentini, which Loebell was to deliver in a closed envelope. 'Perhaps you will find the opportunity to inform Rathenau personally of my positive feeling for him,' he wrote. Loebell obliged and received on the 12 August Rathenau's very enthusiastic reply. In his letter Rathenau payed homage to the 'great man' Bülow and asked Loebell 'to continue to show his goodwill of the last few years as he intended to continue the warmest devotion to him and willingness to serve'.[5]

When Bethmann took over the Chancellorship, Rathenau did not miss the opportunity of sending him a congratulatory letter.[6] He has often been accused

[1] After the transaction the Lahmeyer branch in Frankfurt was sold and the Cologne-based cable works took on the old name of Felten & Guilleaume Carlswerk AG. The AEG remained the major shareholder until 1920. See also fn. 22 below.

[2] Hellige (ed.), Rathenau–Harden, Rathenau to Harden, 24 December 1910.

[3] The contract was signed on 21 September 1909. Rathenau was allowed to keep the title 'Royal' for the Schloss which had been built in 1795 with the aid of the architect David Gilly. Schmitz, *Schloss Freienwalde*; Fürstenburg, *Carl Fürstenberg*, pp. 477 ff.; Hellige, (ed.) Rathenau–Harden, Harden to Rathenau, 15 September 1909.

[4] Staatsarchiv Potsdam, Rep. 30, Berlin C. Tit. 94.

[5] Bülow, *Denkwürdigkeiten*, vol. iii, pp. 39 and 43 f.; Hiller von Gaertringen, *Fürst Bülows Denkwürdigkeiten*, p. 36; BA Koblenz, Nachlass Loebell 10, Bülow to Loebell, 1 August 1909 and 6 August 1909; ibid., Rathenau to Loebell, 12 August 1909.

[6] Hellige (ed.), Rathenau–Harden. Hellige quotes Rathenau's telegram of 14 July 1909.

of buying Schloss Freienwalde simply to become Bethmann Hollweg's neighbour, but the negotiations for the purchase of the estate were well under way when Bethmann Hollweg took over his new office.

At the beginning of 1910, on the occasion of the investiture ceremony on 18 January, Rathenau received the long-awaited order of the Red Eagle, Second Class. (He already held the order of the Red Eagle, Fourth Class, and the Order of the Crown, Second Class. In addition he was awarded the Star to the Order of the House of Orange, and later the War Merit Medal, and the Iron Cross, Second Class. The latter two were given during the war in recognition of his service to war industry.) Rathenau thanked Bülow for his goodwill and intervention in the matter of the decoration, and repeated his regrets about the latter's resignation in the summer of 1909:

'Regarding the loss that we all suffered when you left, my feelings must be set aside. But I feel even more cast down by the anxieties which I have for the distant future. Not that I see a single outside threat; we carry our threat within us, because our expansion is taking place faster than evidence of our power abroad allows. He who makes such big claims must pass examination no matter who his examiners are to be. These melancholy thoughts allow me to keep hoping one thing, that your Highness will assume the task of counsellor and faithful Eckehart of the nation whose steward you were for so long.'[7]

Apart from his business activities and his efforts to equip himself with the outward signs of his rising social status, Rathenau made a further attempt to qualify for high political office. In May 1910 he went to Paris to mediate on behalf of the brothers Mannesmann—who by this stage had no longer anything to do with the well-known steel group of the same name—with the Union des Mines Marocaines, controlled by Schneider–Creusot, regarding reciprocal claims to mining concessions in Morocco.

On the occasion of Edward VII's funeral in London the Kaiser had talked to the French Foreign Minister, Stéphan Pichon, on 19 May about the mining claims and the setting-up of an independent court of arbitration.[8] In a letter to Rathenau, Harden conjectured that the Kaiser would have mentioned Rathenau as mediator to Pichon.[9] Rathenau was equally concerned about the Kaiser's possible indiscretion in London, which could jeopardize his task in Paris, and he told Harden that 'the whole thing depended on the attitudes of the entrepreneurs [the Mannesmanns], and I fear here the consequences of past mistakes. I shall go to Paris with little hope. The only pleasure in the thing is your friendly reception of my intended expedition, which I really only undertake *par titre d'information.*'[10] On his trip to Paris, Rathenau passed through Frankfurt to consult Wilhelm Merton whose concern, the Metall-Gesellschaft, was a partner of the Union des Mines. Rathenau was a member of the supervisory board of the Metall-Gesellschaft and thus had a good reason for going to see Merton.

Whatever the legal standing of the concessions that the Mannesmanns had obtained from the Sultan may have been, in Germany the interests of the

[7] BA Koblenz, Nachlass Bülow, Rathenau to Bülow, 15 January 1910. Bülow, *Denkwürdigkeiten*, vol. iii, pp. 91 f.

[8] *Grosse Politik*, vol. 29, p. 56, Bethmann to Wilhelm II, 18 May 1910.

[9] Hellige (ed.), Rathenau–Harden, Harden to Rathenau, 23 May 1910. Tardieu, *Le Mystère d'Agadir*, pp. 48 ff.

[10] Hellige (ed.), Rathenau–Harden, Rathenau to Harden, 23 May 1910.

Mannesmanns had become a major political issue and Rathenau's trip to Paris was warmly welcomed by the German Foreign Office.[11] It was hoped that a successful solution would eventually stave off the mounting attacks of the 'national opposition' against the policies of the Government. If, however, Rathenau's mission failed and the brothers could be blamed for the failure, it was hoped that the criticism could be silenced. When in Paris Rathenau wrote to Harden: 'The complications are unbelievable, the prospects still poor . . . But the most complicated thing of all is the behaviour of the crazy brothers who madden each other, never let telephone and telegraph out of their hands, and throw themselves heart and soul into back-stairs politics, half Sherlock Holmes, half Monte Cristo.'[12]

At the beginning of June, after arduous negotiations, Rathenau reached an agreement with the representative of the Union des Mines, M. Darcey: Morocco was to be divided into two spheres of interest. The territory north of the 35th parallel was to go to the Mannesmanns, that south of the line to the Union. Rathenau seemed to have achieved everything the Mannesmanns wanted except the financing of their Moroccan enterprise and possible French credits. Yet the agreement was rejected by the Mannesmanns. Their demand for the reopening of negotiations was met by a French refusal and Rathenau's resignation as mediator and departure back to Berlin.[13] At the end of June the Mannesmann brothers summed up Rathenau's activities: 'Dr Rathenau was most zealous in his efforts to restore our confidence in the support of the German Government and to convince us that by accepting the agreement with the Union Marocaines we could count on energetic representation on the part of the German and French Governments, although there was nothing about this in the draft agreement.'[14]

A month later the Mannesmanns tried to recommence their campaign. They intended to publish an account of the Paris negotiations. For that they needed Rathenau's approval, which they were unable to obtain because in their drafts they constantly misrepresented the reason for their rejection of the proposed agreement. While the failure of the Paris negotiations damaged the interests of the Mannesmanns, their refusal to agree in turn made it very difficult for Rathenau to exploit his mission and to foster his political career. The débâcle in Paris may have damaged his chances of candidature in the forthcoming Reichstag elections of 1912: the Mannesmann brothers had a number of political friends among the right-wing National Liberals who may have prevented his candidature.

On the industrial side, Rathenau used his mission to Paris to sound out the willingness of Schneider–Creusot to co-operate in supplying the AEG with steel, pig-iron or iron ore. Together with Richard Lindenberg, who had suggested Rathenau to the Mannesmanns, the AEG had founded the Elektro-Stahl Gesellschaft (Electro-Steel Company) which produced steel after the Héroult system. This was supposed to enable the AEG to become independent from the supplies of the German steel magnates. Moreover, he wanted to find out whether Schneider-Creusot had any interest in joint constructions of hydro-electric power-stations.

[11] For a detailed account of Rathenau's mission to Paris, see Pogge von Strandmann, 'Rathenau, die Gebrüder Mannesmann und die Vorgeschichte der Zweiten Marokkokrise'.

[12] Hellige (ed.), Rathenau–Harden, Rathenau to Harden, 31 May 1910.

[13] H. Pogge von Strandmann, 'Rathenau, die Gebrüder Mannesmann und die Vorgeschichte der Zweiten Marokkokrise', p. 262.

[14] Ibid., pp. 264 ff.

3 January, Tuesday. Berlin. Vereinigung Rheinischer Elektrizitäts-werke[15] [United Rhenish Electricity Works] established. Morning, BHG. Let Bassermann preside. Lunch at club.[16] Discussed his pro-gramme with Bassermann. Advised him to gain control of the Hansa-bund,[17] to brush aside the right-wing liberal elements, to come to an understanding with the Social Democrats for the elections.[18] He was pleased to hear that he held the key position in politics.

4 January, Wednesday. From 12 to 1.30 p.m. at the Treasury at Wemuth's request. Discussed Reich monopolies, particularly electricity,[19] petroleum, matches, potash, and coal. Estimated electricity receipts at 25 millions. He wants to talk to Bethmann. Afternoon at Fürstenberg's. Complaints about Ahrens's unsuit-able letter regarding taking over Dr Mosler's places on the super-visory boards.[20] Afternoon, aesthetic tea with Blüthgen, Lyceum

[15] An association of the electrical power-stations in the Upper Rhine. Ernst Basser-mann was on the supervisory board of one of these, and it is likely that this was why Rathenau let him chair this meeting. Bassermann had nothing to do with the BHG.

[16] The Kaiserliche Automobilclub, founded in 1899.

[17] An alliance of commerce and industry, founded in 1909, with decidedly anti-agrarian leanings. It resulted from the failure of Bülow's financial reforms and the demise of the Bülow bloc, and tried to reduce the influence of the Agrarian League and favoured a Liberal bloc in the coming Reichstag elections. Stegmann, *Die Erben Bismarcks*, pp. 176–95; Mielke, *Der Hansa-Bund*; Eley, *Reshaping the German Right*, pp. 297–301. In 1912 twenty-one National Liberals and thirty-eight left-wing Liberals were elected with the Hansa Bund's support.

[18] Both Bebel and Bassermann refused to collaborate in the elections of 1912. Whatever Bassermann's private views may have been, he held the middle position in a party which was deeply divided. All he was willing to support were a number of election alliances between National Liberals and Progressives. Reiss (ed.), *Von Bassermann zu Stresemann*; Heckart, *From Bassermann to Bebel*; White, *The Splintered Party*; Sheehan, *German Liberalism*.

[19] Rathenau began to develop his idea of an electricity-supply monopoly when he realized that free competition between power-station networks would lead to an un-economic use of resources. While thinking about the subject, two factors caused him to crystallize his plans: the monopoly gained by the Victoria Falls Power Company, in supply-ing the Rand with electricity, and the successful bid by the city council of Strasbourg for the majority holding in the Strasbourg Power-Station Company. In the first case the monopoly was legalized by the Power Act of 1910. In Strasbourg, under the guidance of the local administrator, Walter Leoni, a mixed enterprise was set up, whose majority capital was in the hands of the city while the AEG managed the company and supplied it with all the machinery. See Christie, 'The Electrification of South Africa'; Ott, 'Privatwirtschaftliche und Kommunal(Staats)wirtschaftliche Aspekte beim Aufbau der Elektrizitäts-wirtschaft'. Some of Rathenau's letters and memoranda about the electricity monopoly are published in Rathenau, *Nachgelassene Schriften*, vol. i. H. Nussbaum edited Rathenau's proposal of 13 November 1913 for the first time in 'Versuche zur reichsgesetzlichen Regelung der deutschen Elektrizitätswirtschaft'. See also Nussbaum, *Unternehmer gegen Monopole*, pp. 72–99 and Baudis and Nussbaum, *Wirtschaft und Staat*, vol. i, pp. 112 f. The monopoly is mentioned in the diary on 7 January, 6, 7, and 18 February, 27 April and 13 July 1911, and again on 12 and 13 March 1914. For a discussion of state monopolies with regard to electricity and the other items see Blaich, *Kartell- und Monopolpolitik*.

[20] Eduard Mosler left the BHG and joined the Diskontogesellschaft. See also Hellige (ed.), Rathenau–Harden, Harden to Rathenau, 22 October 1910.

Club.[21] Caricature. *Conférencière*, the actress who used to play the lady's maid at the Court Theatre. Evening with Heinemann.

5 January, Thursday. Morning, basic agreement with Klöckner regarding Aumetz-Friede–Felten & Guilleaume.[22] Under consideration: supply contract based on cost price and a share of profits, share exchange of 10 millions. Evening Harden here (Esplanade)[23] to dinner, stayed till 1.30 a.m.

6 January, Friday. Afternoon, Deutsch-Überseeische Elektrizitäts-Gesellschaft [German Overseas Electricity Company] —meeting concerning shares and loans.[24]

7 January, Saturday. Exhaustive report concerning the electricity monopoly sent off to Wemuth. Justificatory visit from Ernst Körting, jun.[25] Agreement to separate the construction from the manufacturing. Noon, Hauptmanns to lunch at the Auto Club. Read him the article against Kohler which was going to the printer.[26] Afternoon, visited Lili Deutsch. Harden turned up as well.[27] Tenor of my article disapproved of.[28] Evening

[21] The original club was founded in London in 1903. The aim was to foster international friendship amongst educated women, and female education.

[22] In 1910 the AEG acquired the majority holding in Felten & Guilleaume Carlswerk AG, and it became Rathenau's most important task to secure a long-term supply of steel and iron for Felten. Several firms were approached, among them Klöckner. Despite the basic agreement mentioned here, the deal was not accepted because of differences over profit margins.

[23] Together with the Adlon and the Eden, the Esplanade belonged to the top hotels in Berlin.

[24] A company founded in 1898 by the AEG. Like the Deutsche Bank the AEG held a share of only 16 per cent, but carried out the majority of the construction orders for the company. The London bank Wernher, Beit and Co. held 10 per cent of the share capital. The DUEG was Germany's most successful overseas enterprise: its joint-stock capital grew from 10 million marks in 1898 to 150 million marks in 1914. The company mainly operated in South America. Seidenzahl, *Hundert Jahre Deutsche Bank*, pp. 125–31; Strobel, 'Die Gründung des Züricher Elektrotrusts', pp. 328 f. Rathenau refers to a meeting of the supervisory board of which he was a member.

[25] The electro-technical branch of the Gasmotorenfabrik Körting (Körting Gas-Engine Works: founded in 1871) was separated from the company and taken over by the AEG in 1902. Moreover, the Körting company went public in 1902. Together with the BHG the AEG was the majority shareholder. However the growing importance of steam turbines made the liaison between the AEG and Körting less important.

[26] See the editorial insertion below. The article against Kohler was the first part of a series of three articles entitled 'Staat und Judentum' which Rathenau republished together in 1918 in a new edition of *Zur Kritik der Zeit*. See also Kallner, *Herzl und Rathenau*, pp. 337–48. The first article was originally called 'Erwiderung auf einen Artikel des Herrn Geheimrat. . .'. Only later did he use the title 'Staat und Judentum' for the whole series. All three articles were published for the first time in *Der Tag* on 2, 4, and 16 February.

[27] Rathenau later complained about Harden's calling on Lili Deutsch. Kessler, *Rathenau*, p. 159.

[28] Harden objected to Rathenau's disapproval of Jews converting to Christianity. Harden

Wilhemite[29]-dinner (25th Anniversary) at Lantsch, Potsdamer Brücke.[30] Glatzel relates the incidents of his departure from Henckel, whom he portrays in a derogatory fashion.—The Prince's letter: 'I would understand your action if someone wanted to protect himself, should business go through an unfavourable period.' 'You are shortening my life.' Talked to Glatzel until 4.15 a.m. He must make an effort to come to terms with existence, since absolute positions do not exist. Advised him to go to the Schaaffhausener Bankverein [Schaaffhausener Bank] as a director.[31]

8 January, Sunday. Morning at new building (as every day).[32]

9 January, Monday. At Deutsch's suggestion published article, 'Judentaufen' [Baptism of Jews] in *Montags-Zeitung*.[33] Approved by Goldberger, Fritz Rathenau, Ludwig Stein, Martin Beradt, M. Weiner. Discussion at the Stock Exchange. Evening with Schwabach.

Rathenau had already, in his first article, spoken out against the baptism of Jews if it was only to secure material or social advantage. Apart from that, he was of the opinion that accepting the demand for the baptism of Jews represented submission to Prussian Jewish policy. (See diary entries for 7, 9, and 17 January 1911.) In the second article, 'Sendschreiben an Herrn von N.', Rathenau argued against the view that the German Jew was 'different in character' to and worth less than his 'autochthonic fellow-countryman'. Rathenau, then, no longer completely

published an anonymous letter in *Die Zukunft* of 11 March in which the author rejected Rathenau's assertion that conversions were merely made for opportunist reasons. He agreed with Rathenau in condemning the official encouragement of conversion, but maintained that Rathenau overlooked the difficulties in establishing full equality: 'For the resistance against complete equality has deeper roots than Rathenau believes and this [resistance] is not only upheld by those whose ancestors fought the battles of the Alte Fritz [Frederick the Great].'

[29] Old boys club of the Royal Wilhelm Gymnasium, which was regarded as an institution of spick-and span people (Lackstiefelputzer) because of the high proportion of wealthy families which sent their sons to it. At the turn of the century about one-third of the pupils were Jewish, the rest Protestant.

[30] Well-known wine bar.

[31] The bank was established in 1848. It was the first Prussian joint-stock, investment, and credit bank. Its main field of activity was the Ruhr district. Its co-operation with the Dresdner Bank was dissolved in 1908, but it needed the support of the other banks. In 1914 it was taken over by the Diskontogesellschaft.

[32] Rathenau had built himself a villa in the Grunewald at 65 Königsallee, which he moved into on 17 January. In designing the house himself he borrowed elements of the styles of Gilly and Schinkel. He drew the plans for the ornaments and did the decorations inside together with the Swiss painter Karl Walser. His architect was Johannes Kraaz. Kessler, *Rathenau*, p. 148; Rathenau, *Briefe*, vol. i, p. 78, Rathenau to Rötger, 31 March 1911, and vol. ii, pp. 104 f., Rathenau to L. Jahn, 12 June 1912.

[33] *Die Welt am Montag* was founded by Karl Ploetz and Felix Holländer. Franz Oppenheimer had been editor-in-chief since 1897. The paper was later taken over by the Scherl Newspaper Group.

identified himself with his notorious article 'Höre Israel', in which he had reproached the Jews for being different. Rathenau's argument against the verdict of inferiority was that there was too great a tendency to generalize and to take the uncultivated Jew as representative of all the others. He countered the charge of liking innovation, often levelled against Jews by conservatives, by asserting that one can only reproach the Jew with liking innovation when this has been misapplied. As he saw it, the verdict which the ruling class in Prussia brought against Jews was based on fear of competition. He believed that the aristocracy had indeed created and sustained the Prussian state, but 'today they [sustain] it no more, because both Prussia and the Reich [have] become industrial states'. (See diary entries for 20, 21, and 30 January, 2 and 4 February 1911.) In the third article, 'Erwiderung auf das Schreiben eines befreundeten Gutsbesitzers', he contested the verdict of 'inter-nationality'. Rathenau referred to the fact that in Germany neither political nor religious centres existed for Jews as they did for Danes, Poles, Alsatians, and Catholics as well. In conclusion he remarked that he would 'fight against pseudo-Germanic exclusiveness' and against 'the injustice that [occurs] in Germany', for he 'saw shadows rising up, wherever [he] turned.' (See diary entries for 6, 12 and 16 February 1911.)

Rathenau's articles raised a lot of dust and provoked much discussion. Out of this a book emerged in 1912, entitled *Judentaufen*, to which Sombart, Erzberger, Naumann, Wedekind, H. Mann, Ewers, Kohler, and Dehmel, to name but a few, had contributed articles.

10 January, Tuesday. Visit from Bodenhausen and Count Schwerin. Discussed regulation of patents and experiments. Lunch with Berthold Körting and Deutsch at the club; dinner there with Bodenhausen and Schwerin; with them later to the beer party, Sezession.[34]

11 January, Wednesday. Gift from Schickler, Pourtalès, Delbrück and Joerger: French *Empire* clock, as a thank-you for the merger.[35] Letter from Klöckner about Aumetz-Friede. Evening, talk on copper by Moellendorf of the AEG;[36] conversation with Mamroth, then party at Edith Andreae's. Talked to Reinhardt, suggested some spectacular scenes for his Volksbühne [People's Theatre].[37] Vollmoeller,

[34] Artists' association in Berlin founded by Max Liebermann in 1899. Many foreigners exhibited at the Berlin Sezession, including Blanche, Latouche, Monet, Pissaro, Vuillard, and Rodin.

In December 1910 Bodenhausen and Rathenau had met for the first time. At that time Bodenhausen was full of admiration for Rathenau. Bodenhausen-Degener (ed.) *Briefe der Freundschaft*, p. 192. [35] See p. 93.

[36] Moellendorff, who in August 1914 suggested to Rathenau the organization of the wartime raw materials, was at this time the head of the research laboratory of the metal section within the AEG. Apparently it was Harden who had called Rathenau's attention to the qualities of this engineer. He later became an expert in supplying the AEG with raw materials and also tested Taylorist methods. Hellige (ed.), Rathenau-Harden, Harden to Rathenau, 23 November 1911.

[37] The Freie Volksbühne was founded in 1890. It was intended as a working-class theatre with low-priced tickets, but this was a rather loose definition, and it gradually moved closer to the more traditional Freie Bühne, merging with it in 1913.

Saenger, the latter proposed bringing out a weekly paper with Naumann. My objection: I do not see any fresh blood [to work for it].[38]

12 January, Thursday. Lunch-time, dress rehearsal of *Ratten*.[39] Strong Act II. Risky on account of complicated plot—three small children—and double story, the more cheerful side of which is rather weak. Excellent performance by the actress Lehmann. Then (4 o'clock) ate at the Adlon. Made Kyser's acquaintance. Rather superficial remarks. Evening, exercised option on Tschöpelner-Braunkohlenwerke [Tschöpeln Lignite Works].[40] Schiffbauerdamm, piano duets.[41]

13 January, Friday. Première of *Ratten*. Partial success, especially after Act II. Adlon afterwards. Diffuse atmosphere. Conversation with Kyser, Ivo and Gerhart Hauptmann.

14 January, Saturday. Felten & Guilleaume committee, supervisory board, then committee again. Stormy session because of Tronto.[42] Theodor von Guilleaume vehement, von Kleist's demand is provoking, Hagen insulting to Emil Rathenau. Revoke; against that, withdrawal cannot be rectified. Evening at club with Vollmoeller.

15 January, Sunday. Morning at Harden's. Marx, Jänecke.[43] Evening, at the club with Hugenberg. Discussed Felten & Guilleaume merger

[38] No such newspaper came into being.

[39] Successful play by Gerhart Hauptmann; written in 1909–10.

[40] The joint-stock company, founded in 1905, was amalgamated with the Vereinigte Lausitzer Glaswerke (United Lausitz Glass Works) in 1911, a company in which the AEG held an important stake.

[41] Rathenau often played the piano with his mother. See Joll, *Three Intellectuals in Politics*, p. 62.

[42] Tronto was the name of a power-station, on the river Tronto in Northern Italy, which was built by Felten & Guilleaume in conjunction with an Italian firm. The power-station was expensive to build and was burdened with a heavy deficit from the outset. Because of its loss-making position it was excluded from the takeover by the AEG. The row over what portion of the losses should be borne by Felten & Guilleaume and what portion by the major shareholders alone brought to the fore at least Kleist's opposition to the take-over by the AEG in 1910. Eventually the two brothers Guilleaume were persuaded to bail out Tronto, which left the Felten group with a reduced loss of 1.2 million marks. In order to pay their debts they sold their AEG shares to Felten & Guilleaume. FG Archiv, AR-Minutes, 14 January 1911 and 16 February 1911. See also the agreement between Rathenau and the Guilleaumes. Through his marriage, Kleist had also become a major shareholder with Escher Wyss before that company was taken over by Felten & Guilleaume in 1906. Consequently Kleist obtained a number of Felten & Guilleaume shares.

[43] It is possible that Jänecke's joining the supervisory board of Körting was discussed. The aim was to prevent Ernst Körting's brother Berthold from becoming a member. Jänecke was Ernst Körting's son-in-law.

with Krupp: (*a*) community of interests, combining of profits, (*b*) merger with Rheinhausen by setting up a leasehold company for both works.[44]

16 January, Monday. Evening at Stern's. Saenger, who repeated his offer, and Frau von Hartmann at dinner. Afterwards, late at the hotel with gay women.

17 January, Tuesday. 'Von Diezelsky' letter about the Jewish article.[45] Evening at Leonie Schwabach's. Dutch Ambassador[46] has proposition regarding the Princess's grave. Talked to Szögeny about Mannesmann (Khevenhüller, Alberts).[47] Smart society: Carolath, Taxis, Countess Lehndorff and daughter, Radowitz, Senden. Then soirée at Fürstenberg's, Bellini 'mind reader', insipid performance. First night in the Grunewald.

In 1911, after Schloss Freienwalde had come into Rathenau's possession, Queen Wilhelmina expressed her desire to transfer the remains of Princess Pauline of Orange-Nassau (1800–6), buried there, to Delft. The Princess was the daughter of King William I of the Netherlands (1772–1843, Reigning Prince 1813, King 1815–40), and of the Prussian Princess Wilhelmine (1774–1837), the daughter of Friedrich Wilhelm II. According to a statement made by Count Eulenberg Rathenau was obliged to look after the Princess's tomb. He questioned this obligation, but tended the grave most meticulously. Only after some hesitation was Rathenau prepared to carry out the Queen's wish, because he prized the tomb as a decoration in his park. After the Kaiser had also given his consent, the remains were transferred to Delft in a bronze casket on 6 April. The monument on the tomb was by Schadow and now stands in the church in Delft. By way of thanks Rathenau received another decoration, the Star to the Order of the House of Orange.[48]

[44] Since the autumn of 1910 Rathenau had also negotiated with Krupp in order to merge the two firms. On 9 December 1910 Felten & Guilleaume rejected the provisional scheme Rathenau had arranged. In his talks with Hugenberg of Krupp Rathenau tried to improve the terms under which both companies would co-operate, but obviously without much success. The reason why Krupp was unwilling to meet the wishes of the Felten company became clear a few days later when Krupp took over the Westfälische Draht-industrie (Westphalian Wire Industry) for 25 million marks. FG Archiv, Discussion on 9 December 1910; Krupp Archiv, WA IV 1264. Rathenau revived his plans of a merger with Krupp in 1919.

[45] Rathenau answered the letter on 28 January 1911. He addressed his letter 'Send-schreiben an Herrn von N . . .' and published it in *Der Tag*. See the editorial insertion on pp. 98 f.

[46] Baron Willem Gevers.

[47] It is likely that Rathenau was referring to his mission on behalf of the Mannesmann brothers to Paris in the previous year and not to the Mannesmann subsidiaries in Austria which belonged to the Mannesmann Company in Düsseldorf.

[48] Private information from the archives of the Royal Household, 's-Gravenhage, Netherlands. See also diary entries for 17 and 21 January, 12 and 15 February, 2, 3, 6, 7, 18, and 20 March, and 6 April 1911.

18 January, Wednesday. Edith Andreae's birthday; present—water-colour by Walser. Hagen's, vom Rath's letters answered reassuringly. Lunch, von Arnswaldt, Edith and Fritz Andreae, children.

19 January, Thursday. Anniversary of Erich Rathenau's death. Morning, Schöneweide.[49] Afternoon, particulars of new staff. Göring (Spain), Fänder (Lausitz) and others.

20 January, Friday. Essay in answer to Diezelsky. 'Staat und Juden-schaft'.[50] Visit from Hagen—compromise proposal.[51]

21 January, Saturday. Morning, walk in the Grunewald for the first time. Diezelsky finished—lunched at the palace with Eulenberg and discussed Dutch Ambassador. Letter. (Afternoon, Zapf, Zander.) Evening, set off for Bingerbrück and Düsseldorf to [join] the National Bismarck Memorial jury.

The plan to build the National Bismarck Memorial at Bingerbrück kept artists, art experts, donors, and millionaires busy for the whole year. The competition for the monument had been announced a year before, to enable as many artists as possible to take part. Entries were submitted up to the end of the year. During the month-long tug of war over the entries the jury twice decided on the Hahn–Bestelmeyer design of a Siegfried in a classically designed round temple, who—leaning on his sword—was supposed to interpret Bismarck's thought. Yet neither the majority of the supporters, nor the main committee would accept the jury's verdict. Altering the composition of the jury—Klinger, Stuck, and Muthesius were added—brought no change. Finally the prize was won by a design by Kreis, who had assisted Wallot in the building of the Reichstag. His plan of a monumental construction was supported by Bethmann Hollweg, the National Liberals, and industrialists from the Rhineland. However, the discussion over the National Memorial did not end there, but dragged on until the Second World War without the memorial ever being built.[52]

22 January, Sunday. Early, Bingen, Rochus chapel. Lunch-time, Elisenhöhe, Bingerbrück. The small, ruined-summer-house model for the memorial. Jury: Kalckreuth, Lichtwark, Tuaillon, Gaul, Clemen, Dessoir, Fischer, Dill, Hoffmann, Kirdorf, Schmidt, Schumacher, Flossmann, myself. In the evening, to Düsseldorf.

[49] The AEG's cable and wire factory to the east of Berlin.
[50] The article 'Staat und Judentum', part three, is meant.
[51] See diary entry for 14 January 1911 and fn. 42 above.
[52] See *Entwürfe zum Bismarck-Nationaldenkmal auf der Elisenhöhe bei Bingerbrück*, pub. by the Denkmalsausschuss; Dessoir and Muthesius, *Das Bismarck-Denkmal*; Lichtwark and Rathenau, *Der rheinische Bismarck*. See diary entries for 22 to 26 January, 11 February, 24 June, 20 and 21 November, and 4 December 1911; also for 26 January and 1 and 14 February 1912.

23 January, Monday. At the art gallery, 374 designs. Lichtwark chairman at my suggestion. About 100 selected. Evening, at von Wätjens. Wife, née Vautier, daughter: Frau Clemen. Then, Malkasten.[53] Reminiscent of *Meistersinger*. Performance: Stradella scene etc.[54]

24 January, Tuesday. Further selections. Short-listed about 45. Evening, *Götterdämmerung*, then Wätjens.

25 January, Wednesday. Final short list about 11. Evening, city's dinner at the Park Hotel.

26 January, Thursday. Morning, final decision. Made two speeches in favour of *Siegfried Dolmen*. Which was thereupon almost unanimously accepted. Afternoon, smaller prizes and wording. Telegram to Hahn—Apollo Theatre.[55] Eulenberg invited. Departure.

27 January, Friday. Zander, Fritz Andreae about the *Vossische Zeitung*.[56] Advised him to interest the Hansabund through the Darmstädter Bank. Dernburg sends his exposé on Eastern Asia.[57] Two books from Kyser. Visit from Endell who praises the house and declares his intentions. Afternoon, Engelhardt (Seville), then had to take the chair at the Kaiser dinner at the Aero Club.[58] Metaphysical discussion with Nernst. Had taken Jung (Halle) along and proposed to him lease of the electrical power-station in Halle.[59] Reply sent off to Diezelsky.

28 January, Saturday. Afternoon, discussed engaging Bodenhausen

---

[53] A Düsseldorf artists' association founded in 1848, which in 1860 obtained a building for theatrical performances and festivities and which still exists today.

[54] Probably a reference to Friedrich von Flotow's opera *Alessandro Stradella.*

[55] Built by the Düsseldorf architect Hermann vom Endt. It was opened in 1899 and was considered the most modern and one of the biggest multi-purpose theatres in Germany. Presumably Hahn worked there at the time.

[56] At about this time the proprietors of the liberal paper *Vossische Zeitung*, Voss's heirs, began to negotiate its sale. After an interval with the newspaper publisher Huck and the Speyer-Ellissen Bank, it was finally taken over by the Ullstein Publishers at the end of 1913. De Mendelssohn, *Zeitungsstadt Berlin*, pp. 170 and 174.

[57] After resigning as Colonial Secretary in 1910, Dernburg undertook a fact-finding tour of China and Japan. Subsequently he became a member of the supervisory board of the Deutsch–Ostasiatische Bank (German Far Eastern Asiatic Bank). His report about the journey has so far not been found but he published some ideas in 'Östliche Wirtschaftsfragen'.

[58] A club founded by the newspaper owner August Scherl.

[59] Probably the power-station which supplied the electricity for the tramway system in Halle and which had been built by the AEG.

with Fürstenberg.[60] Sought him [Bodenhausen] out at the Kaiserhof. Discussion continued in the Grunewald. Evening at Lili
Deutsch's.

29 January, Sunday. Morning, Bodenhausen telephoned in agreement. Lunch at Fürstenberg's who thanked me with delight.

30 January, Monday. Diezelsky agrees to publication. General meet-
ing of Deutsch-Überseeische Elektrizitäts-Gesellschaft. Telephoned
Marx (of *Tag*),[61] who accepts the article. Evening at Varnbüler's.
Talked to Lichnowsky about colonies. Hofmannsthal and wife,
Keyserling, Tatistschew.

1 February, Wednesday. 11 a.m. Klöckner, AEG.[62] Main features
of the agreement, supply contract and acquisition of shares in the
Lothringischer Hüttenverein [Lorrain Steel Mill]. Klöckner to lunch
at Schiffbauerdamm. Afternoon visit from Spieker. Conversation
about gospel propaganda. Evening at club. Keyserling, and Vollmoeller who dedicates *Wieland* [der Schmied]. In the end alone with
him. Suggestions for a social libretto.

2 February, Thursday. First half of the Diezelsky correspondence
in the *Tag*. Evening at Friedlaender's: Prince Heinrich, Henckel,
Prince von Fürstenberg, etc. Talked to Henckel about Glatzel whose
retirement he regrets, to Moltke and Krätke about the Jewish article
and Jewish question.

3 February, Friday. Lunch-time, Hans Heinz Ewers at the club. Talk
about the will's realm of existence. Girlish physiognomy, rather
affected, rough manner. Evening, 8 p.m., at Bethmann's, took Miss
von Pfuel in. Music: Chelius and wife, Grünfeld played. Bethmann

---

[60] The BHG had run into difficulties because the Hohenlohe group (Fürstenkonzern)
changed over from the BHG to the Deutsche Bank, and the Niederdeutsche Bank (Lower
German Bank) in Dortmund collapsed. It was suggested then that Fürstenberg should take
in a partner who might become his eventual successor. Rathenau suggested Bodenhausen,
but Krupp offered Bodenhausen the improved position as a permanent director; previously he had only been a deputy director. See the diary entries for 10, 28, and 29 January
and 17, 18, and 21 February 1911.

[61] An illustrated daily newspaper founded by August Scherl in 1900. Edition A bore
a red mast-head and is therefore called *Der Rote Tag*. Its readers were from predominantly
educated, conservative circles.

[62] Once the plan to obtain steel supplies for Felten & Guilleaume from Klöckner had
come to nothing, Rathenau tried to secure iron and steel from Klöckner for the AEG.
Since the summer of 1910 he had negotiated with various firms to buy steel outside the
existing syndicates, on a long-term basis.

on the Jewish article. Satisfied with foreign policy (Russian).[63] With Chelius about Hauptmann, Rantzau, von Bülow (Holstein).

4 February, Saturday. Jewish article, Part II, in the *Tag*. Evening, Harden here until 12 p.m.[64]

5 February, Sunday. Walk by Grunewald lake. Lunch at Frau Dohme's. Max Liebermann, then Orlik to see the house. Evening, Mamroth, conversation about the article, I complained about the indolence of the Jews. Commonplace performances after dinner. Read Kyser's *Medusa*.

6 February, Monday. Capito & Klein, supervisory board.[65] Letter about Jewish question from Zelter. Lunch-time, rehearsal Act II of Vollmoeller's *Wieland*. Evening, soirée at Bethmann's. Talked to Günther, Wahnschaffe, Hoffmann, Varnbüler, Mutius, Bassermann, Bethmann. Bassermann asked me whether I would consent to stand as National Liberal candidate. Under-Secretary Kühn asked me about my discussion with Wermuth concerning the electricity monopoly. Thoroughly in favour. He wants Leoni to come.

The invitation to become a National Liberal candidate for the Reichstag, which remained largely unknown at the time, afforded Rathenau another opportunity to devote himself to politics, even if this time as a deputy and not on the Government side. His position in the Reichstag would in any case have been affected by his relations with several members of the Government as well as by his relations with industry and the banking world. Rathenau was indeed prepared to be a candidate for the National Liberal Party, but he wanted to be nominated by the Progressives at the same time. Kessler recalls how: 'After some weeks of disappointing negotiations he withdrew his name. His decision seems to have been determined by reports from his constituency: the name Rathenau was like a red rag to a bull, because he was a Jew and because of his well-known opinions.'[66] Kessler's argument does not seem very convincing,

[63] After the Potsdam interview of November 1910 the rumours about a Russo-German agreement persisted. It now seemed possible to increase Britain's distrust of Russia's policy in Persia, and to manœuvre Russia and England apart. At this time it still seemed feasible to break up the *entente* before Germany took further steps which would have the opposite effect. Hauser, *Deutschland und der Englische–russische Gegensatz*, pp. 127–36; Taylor, *The Struggle for Mastery in Europe*, pp. 463 f.

[64] Hellige (ed.), Rathenau–Harden, Harden to Rathenau, 6 February 1911. During Harden's visit Rathenau showed him his new house and they talked about August Scherl, and the fact that the latter's manager wanted to obtain for him the Star to the Order of the Red Eagle Second Class. They also discussed Bethmann Hollweg's foreign policy.

[65] An enterprise of the sheet metal industry with which the AEG co-operated to produce an alloy for transformers. Rathenau was a member of the supervisory board. The company was later taken over by Krupp.

[66] Kessler, *Rathenau*, p. 152. Mielke, *Der Hansa-Bund*, p. 308.

because Rathenau's writings could only have been known to a limited circle, and not much had appeared by then. His position as an industrialist and as a partisan of a liberal bloc (possibly even attracting Social Democratic votes) could have influenced the local National Liberal election committee. But then the National Liberal, Dr Bollert, was elected there on the platform of both liberal parties. The stumbling-block to Rathenau's being nominated seems to have been his 'manifesto' which he published in 1907 under the title 'Die Neue Ära' and to which he held four years later. Although the 'manifesto' was acceptable to the party leadership, this appears not to have been the case at the local level, where it was opposed by the committee and the local press.[67] Furthermore, it seems that Rathenau did not want to join the National Liberal Party and insisted on remaining somehow independent. Even that was perfectly acceptable to the right-wing party leadership, but must have given the impression to the local party committee of being very affected.

7 February, Tuesday. General meeting Lausitz Glass.[68] Increase of capital. Little opposition. Leoni notified.—Letters from Ballin, Zweig, Erzberger, Hauptmann. Afternoon, visit from Zimmermann, who has become Scherl's manager and would like to procure him the Star to the Order of the Red Eagle, Second Class.[69] Gave him an introduction to Hollmann. Evening, Theodor Wolff and later Liebermann.

8 February, Wednesday. Visited von Kardoff. Afternoon, at Kemmann's, Cauer. Read *Wieland*, Sternheim's *Don Juan*.

9 February, Thursday. Morning, Wiens, Elektrochemische Werke annual balance.[70] Lunch at the club: Hoffmansthals, Count and Comtesse Kalckreuth, Gabler, Vollmöller I and II,[71] Kardorffs. Later at home with the Hoffmannsthals (then Fricke, Frantzen). Evening, at home. Kern's book.[72]

10 February, Friday. With Gabriel Seidl. Morning, AEG concerning Victoriastrasse.[73] Lunch at club; afternoon, visitors in the Grunewald.

[67] D. G. Williamson, 'Walther Rathenau: A Study', pp. 144 f. Williamson points out that the *Oder-Zeitung* in Frankfurt on Oder did not publish any article hostile towards Rathenau. See also the diary entries for 3 and 10 April, 8 and 16 May, 8, 22, and 26 June 1911.

[68] Vereinigte Lausitzer Glaswerke at Weisshammer, founded in 1905. Its capital was increased from 3 million marks to 3.5 million marks. The company belonged to the AEG empire.

[69] See fn. 64 above. Rathenau turned to Admiral Hollman to satisfy Scherl's ambitions.

[70] The Elektrochemische Werke was founded in 1893 and Rathenau became its first manager. The company, which belonged to the AEG, had factories in Bitterfeld and Rheinfelden; it was very successful once teething problems had been overcome. *50 Jahre AEG*, pp. 391 ff. See above, p. 7.

[71] The reference is to Karl Vollmöller's brother Hans.

[72] Berthold Kern's book, *Weltanschauungen und Welterkenntnis* had just appeared.

[73] 3 Victoriastrasse was the place where Seidl built the house for Emil Rathenau.

Appreciative judgement. Evening, left for Düsseldorf. In the carriage, Reinhardt junior to whom I suggested play-reading evenings for the Kammerspiele [Theatre Workshop].[74]

11 February, Saturday. Düsseldorf. Discussion with Hagen, Rath, Theodor von Guilleaume about the Tronto difference. Suggestion for settlement. Opening of the Bismarck Competition exhibition. Rheinbaben's speech prejudiced against Hahn: the common man's understanding. Stroll. Verbal explanation to Rheinbaben. Lunch at Kirdorf's table, Park Hotel. Prince von Wied. Afternoon, big committee; evening smaller committee meeting. Gave general explanation: masses cannot pass judgement on the memorial. Rejected mandate to inform the Kaiser. Evening, with Hahn and Bestelmayer, who accompanied me to the train.

12 February, Sunday. Back in Berlin. Second 'Staat und Judentum' article completed. Visit to Tuaillon's, who had, however, left town. Then to Harden. Met Dr Jolles. Afternoon, Edith Andreae here. Evening at Friedlaender's. The ladies *en tête*. Conversation with the Dutch Ambassador about the Princess. He has received a report of the 1806 burial. The monument is by Schadow (1813) and the grave in a 'vault'. With Jagow, Kampf, von Kardorff, Solf.

13 February, Monday. Spinning mill meetings,[75] AEG, agreement with Felten & Guilleaume regarding Tronto. Zander.

14 February, Tuesday. Spinning mills again. Lunch with Henri Guilbeaux at the club (recommended by Zweig). Soft, professional aesthete, compromise Frenchman—but bearable. Afternoon, visitors. Missed Count Kalckreuth. Evening, finished Sternheim's *Don Juan*. Deeply moved.

15 February, Wednesday. At the Dutch Ambassador's, Baron Gevers: he translates an account of the Princess's burial. Visit from Glatzel who disclosed the reasons for his break with the Prince. Afternoon, Scheffler to see the house. Pinched and vexed. Evening, club: Kleefeld. Left for Cologne.[76]

16 February, Thursday. Cologne, to junk-shops. Then at Max von

[74] The Kammerspiele of the Deutsche Theater began at Maximilian Harden's suggestion in 1906. Gottgetreu, *Harden*, p. 221.

[75] Rathenau was a member of the supervisory board of certain cotton-spinning mills, presumably in order to promote the electric motor for driving spinning machines.

[76] For a meeting of the supervisory board of Felten & Guilleaume, 16 February 1911.

Guilleaume's. Preliminary discussion, absolutely refused to alter the Berlin agreement to their advantage.[77] Lunch there, imposing house, now completed in French hotel style. Meeting at the Schaaffhausener Bankverein. Then at the hotel with Emil Guilleaume who gave an account of the beginnings of the business. Experiences in England.[78] Journey home 4.19 p.m. On the train: Lindner. In the *Tag*: 'Judentum', part II.

17 February, Friday. AEG meeting about Schlesische Kleinbahnen [Silesian Light Railways].[79] Drewes to be dismissed. Afternoon, Bodenhausen about his employment contract. Evening at Deutsch's. Music. Cool atmosphere.

18 February, Saturday. 10 a.m. Bodenhausen with Fürstenberg. Ahrens brought in later. Letters concerning 'Judentum'. Evening, Cassirer. Grotesque stories about Jagow.[80] Lunch at the club with Bodenhausen. Afternoon, Leoni in the Grunewald. Wermuth had sent for him at my suggestion. He is not much taken with electricity monopoly. Tried to explain to him. Questionable success. Evening, at Cassirer's, because of his Jagow story (letter to Tilla Durieux).

19 February, Sunday. Wrote to Cassirer again: advised returning the letter *sans phrase*. Visitor, von Vietsch from South West Africa. Lunch at Kardorff's with Bruhns. Afternoon, Kardorff here, then Mrs von Wätjen and Mrs Haller came. Evening at Richter's, took in Mrs von Hindenburg. Ended up at Fürstenberg's. Gloomy day. End of correspondence with . . .[81]

[77] The Guilleaume brothers tried to improve the conditions under which they had agreed to bail out Tronto, but Rathenau remained firm. See fn. 42.

[78] Felten & Guilleaume was an old enterprise which had started in 1829. It had copied a number of manufacturing processes from England. One of the Guilleaume family had worked in England at that time for industrial-espionage purposes. His notebook with the relevant sketches has been preserved in the company's archives.

[79] An enterprise re-established in 1908. In 1909 the AEG held 75 per cent of its shares. It was a tramway linking various city centres. Drewes was an engineer who had worked with the company.

[80] At this time Police Commissioner Jagow's censorship of the theatre was assuming fantastic proportions. He intervened at a rehearsal of von Sternheim's *Die Hose* and invited himself to Tilla Durieux's home for further talks. As the press made a scandal out of the incident, Jagow challenged Tilla Durieux's husband, Paul Cassirer, to fight a duel with him. The story was the incentive for Sternheim to write the play *Bürger Schippel.*

[81] The reference is probably to a temporary break in his correspondence with Lili Deutsch, but it is possible that Rathenau refers to Raoul Richter's wife, Lina, née Oppenheim, whose mother was Louise née von Saucken-Tarputschen. According to Ida Dehmel Rathenau had loved two women: Lili Deutsch, and Lina Oppenheim before she married Raoul Richter. Private communication of Dr Ernest Rathenau to his sister Mrs Ellen Ettlinger (19 July 1967) and myself (6 April 1968).

20 February, Monday. Morning, visit from vom Raths who, at my suggestion in Dusseldorf, is interested in Bitterfeld.[82] At Reicke's request brought him and Erzberger together at the club at lunchtime. Discussed Tempelhof Field. Afternoon, Elektro-Stahl supervisory board.[83] Evening, at Riedler's, talk to Stumpf about his direct current motor[84] and to Wassermann about my symbiotic theory [Symbiontentheorem].[85] We agreed to enter into a correspondence.

21 February, Tuesday. Letter from Hauptmann about the Jewish campaign. Hofmannsthal wrote about Dr Karl Michaelis. Bodenhausen about his discussions with Bohlen.[86] Evening with Nostiz at his parents' house (Hindenburg). With Kessler, then at the club. Jagow affair. Friendly settlement.

22 February, Wednesday. Lunch at the club with Kessler. Afternoon, Klingenberg and brother here, then Weiss. Evening at the club with vom Rath about Bitterfeld.

23 February, Thursday. Drew up the financial account of the Planiawerke [Plania Works] with Hennig.[87] Oswald about the steel supply to Felten & Guilleaume.[88] Lunched with Centuriones, Schiffbauerdamn. Afternoon, Hamspohn about Jewish agitation. Final BHG meeting. Evening, at Ahrens's.

24 February, Friday. Lunch at Langwerth's with Lancken. Lancken reports on Pichon's perilous situation. 3.20. left for Zurich and Italy.

25 February, Saturday. Early, 9.45 a.m., Zurich. Baur. Visit

[82] The Elektrochemische Werke in Bitterfeld at this time had invented a process of making synthetic rubies.

[83] Together with the R. Lindenberg AG and the Aluminium Industrie Neuhausen, the AEG founded the limited Elecktro-Stahl Gesellschaft in Remscheid in 1905. The new company introduced the Héroult system to make steel in an electric arc furnace.

[84] Direct current motors were essential for the electrical equipment of submarines, which gradually became a growing business. AEG Business Reports 1910/11.

[85] Rathenau published his ideas in an essay 'Physiologisches Theorem' in an appendix to *Zur Kritik der Zeit*. He believed that the organism of animals and human beings was not to be perceived as a 'cell state', but as a state of independently living beings. Rathenau, *Briefe*, vol. i, p. 87, Rathenau to Heimann, 15 December 1911.

[86] Gustav Krupp von Bohlen und Halbach. See fn. 60.

[87] The Planiawerke were established in Vienna in 1895 with a joint-stock capital of 2 million marks. The company produced carbon and carbon brushes required by the electrical industry.

[88] Oswald was head of the blast-furnace plant Rombacher Hütte in Lorraine, and also managed the iron and steel trading firm of Carl Spaeter in Koblenz. He was a member of the supervisory board of the BHG.

Kreditanstalt [Credit Institution], then inspect the Escher Wyss factory.[89] Difficult decision. Afternoon, Kreditanstalt; evening, dined with Dr Frey. Left for Genoa at eleven o'clock at night.

26 February, Sunday. Bad carriage, nasty journey. Early, 6.45 a.m., Milan. On to Genoa. Arrived Miramar 11.40 a.m. Picked up by Königsheim, lunched with him. Went on immediately in an open car, in beautiful weather, to Portofino. 3 p.m. at Hauptmann's in the Villa San Martino. D'Albert had lived there with his last wife. A walk on the peninsula, tea at the harbour, finally 'carousal' at the Villa. Hauptmann about his ship novel and the *Novelle*.[90] He describes the plot of the seduced cleric. D'Albert plays a Chopin fantasia on a wretched *pianino*. About 9 p.m. return home with the d'Alberts who live in Pegli. Hauptmann seriously wishes I would abandon industry for literary work. Scruples not accepted.[91]

27 February, Monday. Preparatory meetings: morning, Officine; afternoon, Officine and Unione.[92] In between, lunch at Labò's.

[89] This Swiss machine-building company had been acquired by Felten & Guilleaume in 1906. Since the autumn of 1909 the board had discussed whether it ought to sell the plant, which did not prosper sufficiently. However, Felten & Guilleaume wanted to keep a stake in the growing market for steam turbines and Escher Wyss sold the successful Zoelly-turbine. From 1907 onwards over-capacity led to a sharp competition with the other turbine producers; consequently prices fell. A price cartel, supported by the fourteen firms which were involved in making steam turbines, was rejected by the AEG which produced turbines as well and which used its overall strength—in particular its ability to offer the equipment necessary for large industrial installations, as well as the turbines themselves—to squeeze the smaller companies out of business. Apart from this sales practice the AEG, Siemens, and BBC reached certain agreements which left Felten & Guilleaume's Escher Wyss outside. Despite the sharp competition on the turbine sector Rathenau decided against a sale of Escher Wyss, presumably because the Swiss company had good business connections with France. Strobel, 'Zur Einführung der Dampfturbine auf dem deutschen Markt 1900 bis 1914'.

[90] *Atlantis* appeared in 1912 and *Der Ketzer von Soana* in 1918.

[91] Rathenau must have been pleased by Hauptmann's wish, for he often toyed with the idea of retiring from business life. When he came from Bitterfeld in 1899 he resolved 'to withdraw from industry to do literary work'. A few months after his stay with Hauptmann he wrote to Stefan Zweig that he considered his activities as an author as 'life', and those as an industrialist as 'play'. Rathenau, *Briefe*, vol. i, p. 84, Rathenau to Zweig, 28 November 1911. Yet he realized that he could only write if he continued to work in industry. Thus he wrote to Lili Deutsch: 'Whether it would be right to sever my links with industry, I dare not decide. My last three works: the [two] African ones and the one about traffic, which all have their merit, would never have been done if I had not been living the life of this world.' Kessler, *Rathenau*, p. 160.

[92] Officine Elettriche Genovesi, (Genoa Electrical Works), Genoa. The company was founded in 1895 with a capital of 3 million lira. Its main task was to provide electricity for the tramways in Genoa. The financing of the enterprises in Genoa was arranged by the Elektrobank in Zurich which was founded to some extent for this very purpose.

The three tramway companies in Genoa were merged in 1901. The Unione Italiana

Evening, Sampierdarena Centrale.[93] Ball at the hotel (Croce Rossa), provincial splendour. We stand by the lift looking on. Unusual dreams, wanderings. A husband's complaints—the small-town actress.

28 February, Tuesday. First breakfast with Plieniger. Packed. 11 a.m. Officine. Afternoon, Unione. Evening, left for Milan with Emil Rathenau and Zander. Arrived late, Palace Hotel; bad reception, Deutsch, Jordan, Pollak.

1 March, Wednesday. Morning, Brera,[94] deeply impressed by Bellini and Luini. Study of Venetian portraitists. Varnishes; frame's effect when picture is close. Question whether life-size. Lunch-time, Cova, then Sviluppo meeting.[95] Dinner at Joel's, then Scala première, *Cavaliere della Rosa.*[96] Moderately unsuccessful; futuristic pamphlets after Act II.[97] Went home and packed.

2 March, Thursday. Very early departure over the Gotthardt. With Emil Rathenau and Pforr. Sombart's Jewish book.[98]

3 March, Friday. Early in Berlin. A lot of work. Lunch, guests in the Grunewald for the first time: Fürstenbergs, Bodenhausens, Langwerths, Kessler. Afternoon, Eilender. Dinner with Kessler at the club: Hardts, Richters, Bodenhausens, Mutzenbecher junior; later Harrachs, Mrs von Thüngen. Letter from Eulenburg regarding the Kaiser's consent to transferring the Princess's remains.

4 March, Saturday. Hennig about Redlich's mismanagement.[99] Lueg. Grievances about Guilleaumes appeased. Dr Frey, Wiens. Afternoon, Hardts and Harrachs to tea here. Countess's resemblance to her sister

Tramways Elettrici took over the other two companies. All three belonged to the AEG and the Elektrobank. *50 Jahre AEG*, pp. 133–7. In 1906 the city of Genoa decided to take over the company, and the AEG's general influence declined in Italy. Through the Elektrobank Walther Rathenau remained a member of the supervisory boards of the Italian companies. Ibid., p. 187.

[93] Autonomous commune in Genoa for whom the AEG had to arrange a special supply of electricity, for which the installation was free of charge, as had often previously been the case in Genoa.

[94] Palace in Milan.

[95] Società per lo Sviluppo delle Imprese Elettriche in Italia (Development Company for Electrical Printing Machines in Italy), Milan.

[96] Richard Strauss's opera *Der Rosenkavalier.*

[97] See Joll on Marinetti in *Three Intellectuals in Politics.*

[98] *Die Juden und das Wirtschaftsleben* (München, 1911).

[99] This is a reference to the Planiawerke in Silesia.

(Lichnowsky).[100] Evening, visited by James Simon. Agreement regarding the Jewish demonstration. Proclamation drafted later.

5 March, Sunday. To Freienwalde in the rain. Sunshine there. Work in the grounds until afternoon. Back in the evening.

6 March, Monday. *7 March*, Tuesday. Final Abo meetings.[101] Visited Eulenburg at the Ministry of the Royal Household about his letter (Princess). Beautiful room. Evening with Schuster.

8 March, Wednesday. Midday, left for Laufenburg with Schuster, Klingenberg.[102]

9 March, Thursday. Laufenburg, meetings and inspections until afternoon. Evening, to Strasbourg.[103]

10 March, Friday. Meeting [with the directors] of the power-station. Antiquary Brion. Lunch at Valentin's; Löwe had invited Sattler. Afternoon, hurried walk through old courtyards and alleys with Sattler. Another meeting, then Wangen. Drive to Basle. Salomon's sentimental lamentations.[104]

[100] Harrach's and Lichnowski's wives were both called Countess von Acro-Zinneberg before their marriages.

[101] Electrical power-station in Abo, Finland. The headquarters for the company were in Berlin.

[102] The power-station at Laufenburg had been founded in 1908. At that time it belonged to the Gesellschaft für Elektrische Unternehmungen (GESFÜREL) which itself had been a sub-sidiary of the UEG. See fn. 117 below. The UEG had been taken over by the AEG in 1904, but the GESFÜREL remained independent. But obviously the equipment for the hydroelectric power-station in Laufenburg in Switzerland had to be bought from the AEG. Moreover, the AEG held the purse-strings of Laufenburg through the Schweizer Kreditanstalt, the Schweizer-ische Bankverein (Swiss Bank Association), the Zurich Elektrobank, and Felten & Guilleaume.

[103] The AEG obtained the concession to build a power-station in Strasbourg and set up a company in 1895. The enterprise prospered so that the city decided to buy the company for 22 million marks when the concession had run out in 1910. But this proved to be too expensive, and it was arranged with the Elektrobank that the city would take over 40 per cent of the joint-stock capital. The city then managed to buy another 11 per cent on the open market without anyone noticing, and thus held the majority. Initially Rathenau was shocked by the coup, but later came to accept it, as the city supported his plans for monopolizing the supply of electricity from the Swiss border up to the Saar region. Rathenau made a special reference to the AEG-controlled Saar-Elektrizitäts-Gesellschaft (Saar Electricity Company) at the supervisory board meeting in Strasbourg on 10 March. Contrary to Rathenau's plans, the state of Baden built a power-station by the Murg and thus pushed a wedge between the Saar and the AEG's interests in Southern Baden. Ott, 'Privatwirtschaftliche und Kommunal(Staats)wirtschaftliche Aspekte beim Aufbau der Elektrizitätswirtschaft'. See also fn 19 above.

[104] Professor Salomon was chairman of the board of the Lahmeyer Werke in Frankfurt. He had joined Felten & Guilleaume when the latter took over Lahmeyer, and was ousted when the AEG stepped in. It had been due to him that Felten & Guilleaume got involved with Tronto and with Escher Wyss.

11 March, Saturday. Early, from Basle to Baden, to Brown, Boveri meeting.[105] Bond issue. Contract with Sulzer.[106] Lunch at Boveri's. Travelled back to Basle with Simonius and Sarasin. [Talked] about old Basle houses. Between the stations to the Petersplatz: Hessian house. Departure from the Baden station.

12 March, Sunday. Early to Berlin. Morning, at the auto club constituing the committee for the Nietzsche memorial.[107] Kessler, Kohler, Raoul Richter. Noon, 21 guests for lunch, Heykings, Harden, Emil Rathenau, Matilde Rathenau etc.[108] Telegram from Hauptmann.

Afternoon, first visit to Haller's. Evening, at Paul von Mendelssohn's, marionettes. Napoleonic court's four categories for invitations: *les ennuyeux, les nécessaires, les élégants, les oubliés.*

13 March, Monday. Afternoon, Fricke about settlement, then Henckel at the AEG.

14 March, Tuesday. Plania annual balance. In the evening rehearsal of Kyser's *Medusa*.

15 March, Wednesday. Schultz-Knaudt.[109] Lunch at Rosenberg's.

---

[105] In 1904 the AEG merged with BBC through an exchange of shares. The AEG controlled 6.5 million Swiss francs out of a total of 12.5 million. Both companies exchanged their patents for constructing steam turbines. Thus the AEG saved the costs for developing a large turbine which had been produced with some success by BBC. BBC gained through its liaison with the AEG the backing of the banks. In 1905 BBC's capital was raised to 16 million francs and the AEG increased its share to 8.7 million francs. After 1906 the AEG sold its majority and gradually its entire holding except for a small amount which was kept in the portfolio of the Elektrobank. Thus Rathenau continued to be a member of the supervisory board. The differences between the two companies reached a peak in 1911 when BBC informed the Baden Ministry of the Interior of Rathenau's monopoly plans in that area. Strobel, 'Zur Einführung der Dampfturbine auf dem deutschen Markt 1900 bis 1914', p. 466.

[106] The Swiss machine-building company Sulzer abandoned in 1911 the construction of large steam turbines, and either BBC or more likely the AEG, offered Sulzer some compensation for withdrawing from the market. Ibid., p. 469.

[107] At their previous meetings Kessler must have sounded out Rathenau about how the project should be realized. Kessler had secured the co-operation of Maillol and van de Velde. The memorial was to consist of a temple, a large stadium, and a gigantic Apolline statue, made by Maillol using Nijinsky as a model. Kessler thought that about a million marks would be necessary and he was able to win Henri Lichtenberger, André Gide, Anatole France, d'Annunzio, Gilbert Murray and H. G. Wells, among others, for the committee, but by the end of 1913 the project came to grief, partly because Nietzsche's sister now opposed it, despite her earlier support: 'The aping of Greekdom through this rich, idle mob from the whole of Europe is horror to me.' Burger (ed.), *Hofmannsthal-Kessler*, pp. 323 ff. Kessler to Hofmannsthal, 16 April 1911.

[108] At Rathenau's lunch-party were also Lili Deutsch, Fürstenberg, Walser, and Max Liebermann. Hellige (ed.), Rathenau–Harden, Harden to Rathenau, 12 March 1911.

[109] A rolling mill, established in 1889, with a joint-stock capital of 5 million marks. On Rathenau's initiative it was taken over by Mannesmann in 1914. Pogge von Strandmann, *Unternehmenspolitik und Unternehmensführung* pp. 106–14.

Afternoon, 4 p.m., *Faust II*, Deutsches Theater until 12 p.m.[110] Great scenic achievement. Bethmann with family.

16 March, Thursday. 1 p.m. at Hollmann's. The Kaiser present. Talked to me about Mannesmann,[111] Freienwalde, the Princess, England, death of Edward VII, jewels, cotton, architectural styles (against Schinkel), reluctance to fight. At table, stories. Afternoon, Schlesische Elektrizitätswerke [Silesian Electricity Works].[112] Then Zander. Evening at Hermann Dernburg's. Talked to Bernhard Dernburg about Hansabund with reference to Kleefeld's visit. He is preparing a pamphlet against von Sydow on the admission of foreign stocks.[113]

17 March, Friday. Lunch at Riezler's at the Esplanade Hotel with Councillor Göppert. Lively controversy concerning foreign shares. Afternoon, Hallers to tea. Evening, with vom Rath at his hotel [and] with Brüning. Sale of power-station provisionally put off.[114] —Bought Chinese porcelain.

18 March, Saturday. Morning, Trippensee, then Baron Gever's visit, then Firle. Afternoon, walk in the Grunewald; evening, painful leave-taking.

19 March, Sunday. Lunch here: Varnbülers, Sarres, Bülow, Matuschka, Frau vom Rath. Afterwards to Gaul. Evening, Dr Bruhn here, whom I sounded out about engagement as Bodenhausen's successor.[115]

[110] Harden had recommended the performance to Rathenau. Baroness Spitzemberg noted that 'society' was full of admiration for 'the performance of Faust, Part II'. Vierhaus (ed.), *Spitzemberg Tagebuch*, p. 527.

[111] Rathenau's mission to Paris in 1910; Princess Pauline of Orange-Nassau was buried in Freienwalde.

[112] The AEG had a substantial stake in this enterprise. Its full name was Schlesische Elektrizitäts- und Gas AG (Silesian Electricity and Gas Company) with a nominal capital of 14.7 million marks in 1913. The company supplied nearly the entire industrial region of Upper Silesia with power.

[113] In 1911 Dernburg published his pamphlet for the Hansabund, *Kapital und Staatsaufsicht*. The Prussian Minister for Trade wanted to restrict the launching of foreign issues on the German Stock Exchanges. Rathenau and Dernburg objected to this type of isolationist state intervention. Feis has praised Dernburg's pamphlet: 'This short volume is the most effective argument against the exercise of government control written in Germany before the war'. Feis, *Europe, the World's Banker*, p. 171; Schiefel, *Dernburg*, p. 147.

[114] The Main-Kraftwerke (Main Power-Station) was founded in 1910 with a joint-stock capital of 2 million marks, of which Felten & Guilleaume took over nearly 1 million marks. In 1912 Felten & Guilleaume sold its share, because it did not fit into Rathenau's scheme for concentrating the AEG's interest in specific areas.

[115] Bruhn did not want to take up a position in the BHG. He stayed with Krupp and followed in Bodenhausen's footsteps.

20 March, Monday. Baron Gevers transmits Queen's gratitude.[116] Gesellschaft für Elektrische Unternehmungen [Electrical Enterprises Company] annual balance.[117] Afternoon, Bodenhausen's visit. Then meeting with Salomonsohn and Waller at the AEG about Peter.[118] Accepted my programme. Dinner, 8 p.m., with Kessler at the club. Then Varnbüler's, Countess Matuschka's birthday. At 2 a.m. Mrs von Varnbüler begins to dance in front of Kessler, Schad-Rossa and myself. Dubious situation. Ended 3.30 a.m. At the same time public meeting of the Society for the Preservation of Jewry [Verein zur Erhaltung des Judentums].[119] Lecture on article in the *Tag* by Rabbi Fink. Geitner represents me.

21 March, Tuesday. Lunch at Richter's. Mrs Richter ill. Frau Kolbe. Kessler, Bodenhausen, Hardts. *Der Starr.*[120] Evening, at the club with Storz.—Work in the garden.

22 March, Wednesday. Kleefeld telephones with the Hansabund about Dernburg's pamphlet. At the AEG, then Wolff-Zitelmann, and Friedlaender; to lunch at his place with Goldschmidt-Rothschild senior and Kiderlen. Afternoon, with Weinberg concerning, MEW,[121] Konschewski, finally Salomon until 8.30 p.m.

23 March, Thursday. 12 a.m. take-off, Johannestal, with police club —flight over Köpenick, then Grünau. Commanding officer: Captain Dinglinger.[122] Afternoon, with Landau about Franz Mine.[123] Hahn's letter about Bismarck memorial.

[116] Queen Wilhelmina.

[117] The GESFÜREL is the oldest and most important holding company in the electrical industry. It was founded in 1894 with a capital of 15 million marks. The GESFÜREL belonged to Isidor Loewe and the UEG. When in 1904 the AEG took over the UEG the GESFUREL remained independent, but through the Elektrobank the AEG had some say in its affairs. Rathenau was a member of its supervisory board.

[118] The central German rubber-goods factory, Louis Peter AG, Frankfurt, was established in 1905. See Dresdner, *Industrielle.* The AEG tried to obtain a stake in the company because of its production of tyres, which the AEG wanted to use for its production of cars and aeroplanes.

[119] The association's full name was Verein zur Erhaltung des überlieferten Judentums. It was a small traditionalist, orthodox, and Zionist body. I am very grateful to Dr Peter Pulzer for providing me with this information.   [120] So far not identifiable.

[121] In 1909 the AEG founded the MEW with a capital of 2 million marks. The plan was to supply the growing industries along the canal from Berlin to Stettin, but this had to be altered because of opposition from Siemens. So the company expanded eastwards and towards Mecklenburg.

[122] A year later the AEG started with the production of aeroplanes, mostly for military purposes. *50 Jahre AEG*, pp. 181 and 426 f.

[123] The pit belonged to the Rybniker Steinkohlenwerke (Rybnik Colliery), which had strong links with the Ostbank für Handel und Gewerbe (Eastern Bank for Trade and Commerce). The main bank for Rybnik was the BHG which also had strong links with the

24 March, Friday. Afternoon, Haller here. Evening, at Lepsius's.

25 March, Saturday. Mad letter from Trebitsch who proposes a magazine.

26 March, Sunday. Caught a cold. Long walk—Kaiser Wilhelm Turm, Pechsee, Teufelssee. Part of the way with Baltzer who was on horseback. Noon, 23 people to lunch, Kolbes, Hallers, Kysers, Behrens, Lepsius, Weiss, Edith Andreae, etc. Afterwards, walk with Hallers. After dinner to Jordan's. Staudt.

27 March, Monday. Morning, Zander. Afternoon, Seville and Barcelona.[124]

28 March, Tuesday. Early walk. *Mechanik des Geistes*.[125] Lunch with Fricke, Körting annual balance. Evening, at the club with Kessler. Controversies.

29 March, Wednesday. Early, 'Bons' Consul Marx here about Schweig.[126] *Modus procendi* suggested, lunch at the AEG with Lord Mayor Marx and Waller; final agreement about Peter, Frankfurt.[127] Afternoon, discussion at the AEG about foundation of Saar region [power-station].[128] Then goodbye to Hallers. Evening, Schiffbauerdamm with Ilse, Heykings etc. Talked to Ilse about Jews and the middle class in the army and the administration.

30 March, Thursday. Morning, Solingen;[129] afternoon, Elektrizitäts

Ostbank. Friedländer-Fuld governed the expanding empire of Rybnik. Achterberg, *Berliner Hochfinanz*, pp. 49 f.; Fürstenberg, *Carl Fürstenberg*, pp. 261 f. See also fn. 188 below. The AEG was also interested in the Silesian coal-mine in order to secure coal supplies for its more eastern power-stations.

[124] The Compañia Sevillana de Electricidad (Seville Electrical Company), Seville, and the Compañia Barcelonesa de Electricidad (Barcelona Electrical Company), Barcelona, belonged to the AEG, which had passed on the majority of its shares in these two companies to the Elektrobank. Rathenau was a member of the supervisory boards of the two Spanish companies thorugh his board-membership of the Elektrobank. Between 1891 and 1896 the AEG became the predominant enterprise in the electrification of Spain, a position the AEG was able to maintain until 1914.

[125] A reference to his work on this book, which he published in 1913.

[126] Schweigsche Glas- und Porzellanwerke (Schweig Glass and Porcelain Works). Rathenau and Marx were members of the supervisory board.

[127] See diary entry for 20 March and fn. 118 above. On the same day an article, written by the AEG, appeared in the *Frankfurther Zeitung* in which the group's expansion was defended. Nussbaum, *Unternehmer gegen Monopole*, p. 98.

[128] The Saar-Elektrizitäts Gesellschaft was founded by the town of Saarbrücken and the AEG in 1912. With the help of this foundation Rathenau hoped to build up a regional supply monopoly stretching from the Saar to the Swiss border. See also fn. 103.

[129] Rathenau was a member of the supervisory board of the Solinger Kleinbahn AG.

Lieferungs-Gesellschaft [Electricity Supply Company] and Rheingau.[130] Letter from Roetger, who is settling here. Carl Hauptmann
sends two volumes of *Napoleon*.[131] Schröder sends elegy.[132] Very
warm weather.

31 March, Friday. Walk. Brüning writes on progress in the N-pro-
cess.[133] Afternoon, Märkisches Elektrizitäts-Werk. Evening at Fried-
länder's. Lord Chatham sings.[134] Talk to Toni Ruprecht, who tells
me the strange story of her dream about her dead brother.

1 April, Saturday. Early, visit from architect Lessing. Excited general
meeting of the BHG, Gottschalk and Werthauer sharp attacks. Afternoon, with Waller and Mosler, Peter contract—AEG revised. Evening,
Klingenberg.

2 April, Sunday. Morning, Roetgers pays a visit about building a
house. Lunch, 16 guests. Haber, Wittings, Ahrens, Sterns, etc.
Schlüpmann stayed longer. Afternoon, drove to Dahlem. Evening,
Friedlaender 10 p.m.

3 April, Monday. Foundation of Saar Elektrizitätswerk [Saar Power-
Station]. Löwe general meeting.[135] Lunch, 17 guests again. Holl-
manns, von Hindenburg, Frau Delbrück, Brahm, Kessler, Kleefeld,
Friedlaenders etc. Kleefeld stayed to talk about Reichstag again.
Afternoon, Schlesische Kleinbahnen.[136] Evening, Stern and Kyser
lecture, then in a large party at Steinert's.

4 April, Tuesday. Drive to Zeipau about 'Franz' mine planned and
cancelled. Evening, at Stern's with Heilbuth, Hitz, Brahm.

5 April, Wednesday. Lunch with Bodenhausen, Aldon [Hotel].

[130] The ELG was founded by the AEG in 1897 with a joint-stock capital of 5 million
marks as a holding company. It was to finance the construction of power-stations. The company was totally owned by the AEG. The Rheingau-Elektrizitätswerke (Rheingau Electricity
Works) were founded in 1906. They were built by the AEG and later taken over by the
Main-Kraftwerke. Rathenau was a member of the supervisory board of Rheingau.
[131] Carl Hauptmann's work on Napoleon I had just been published.
[132] Either Schröder's contribution to *Deutsche Chansons* (pub. 1911) or his *Elysium.
Gesammelte Gedichte* which appeared a year later, is meant.
[133] This may be a reference to the nitrogen-fixation process which was developed by
Haber and Bosch.
[134] So far no evidence has been found for the existence of a singing Lord Chatham.
[135] Rathenau was a member of the supervisory board of the company, which was known
at the time for its involvement in the armaments and munitions factories in Germany. The
Loewe Group had controlled the UEG until it had merged with the AEG, and it still had
a considerable influence on the GESFÜREL.   [136] See fn. 79 above.

Afternoon, Körting, annual balance meeting. Conversation with Fürstenberg regarding successor. He wants to engage Walter Merton.[137]

6 April, Thursday. With Chamberlain van den Bosch, Gevers, Friedlaender to Freienwalde. Handing-over of the Princess's remains. Lunch. Star to the Order of the House of Orange. Telephone message for Friedlaender: Prince Bishop Kopp had declined for dinner. Amusing situation. Evening, dinner at Friedlaender's. Kopp present, had been rounded up by Hutten. Talked to Havenstein/Solf—about his wishes for German East Africa—, von Bülow.[138]

7 April, Friday. In Bitterfeld to inspect the Bitterfeld–Dessau railway.[139] Afternoon, with Fürstenberg about Merton, etc. Evening, visit from Eloesser about Brahm succession. Advised him to build a new house, and that with Dernburg.

8 April, Saturday. The AEG about Peter again, new differences.— Lunch-time, bought old clocks at Prächtel. Afternoon, 6 p.m., club, Kessler, Schwabach, memorial.[140] Evening, at Lotte Cassirer's. Large, boisterous party, Durieux.

9 April, Sunday. Warm and fine again after extreme cold. In the Grunewald for a long while.

10 April, Monday. Morning, Nischwitz, Seiring (on behalf of Miss Kaulitz), who tells about his position in the Lingner advertizing business (Odol).[141] Evening, at Brahm's with Theodor Wolff, who reports Hansabund enquiry regarding my possible candidature.

11 April, Tuesday. Mannesmann, suggestion concerning steelworks.[142]

[137] Walter Merton accepted Fürstenberg's invitation to join the BHG as the latter's potential successor, but after a few years he changed his mind and subsequently joined the bank's supervisory board.

[138] The next day Solf sent Rathenau the minutes of the Budget Committee 'in which you will find the record of my sins and my defence . . .'. BA Koblenz, Nachlass Solf, 124.

[139] On 18 January 1911 the first Prussian overhead electric railway line was opened between Dessau and Bitterfeld. The electrification of the railways would have made greater progress if it had not been for the resistance of the military circles.

[140] Nietzsche Memorial; see fn. 107 above.

[141] The Lingner Werke produced a mouthwash called Odol.

[142] Meeting of the Mannesmann supervisory board of which Rathenau was a member. The suggestion that a blast-furnace plant be established was followed up, but it was three years before the final decision was made and eighteen years before Mannesmann was able to produce its own steel. See Pogge von Strandmann, *Unternehmenspolitik und Unternehmensführung*, pp. 77–82.

Lunch at the club with Klöckner. Talked to James Simon, who is commissioned to sound me out by the Association of German Jews [Verband Deutscher Juden].[143] Partly turned it down. Finished 'Politik, Humor und Abrüstung' [Politics, Humour and Disarmament] article for the Easter number of the *Neue Freie Presse*.[144]

The article contained two basic ideas which were intended to limit the sovereignty of the State: that a country's armaments should be in relation to its 'inner power complex' and that 'bellicose tensions' should be relieved by fixed quotas of armaments. Apart from that, he proposed that a fixed correlation should be established between a country's military budget and its total expenditure.

'Damage is bound to result from a national or commercial policy which is always defensive. An efficient business man knows that each day brings difficulties and misunderstandings, whereas unexpected strokes of luck rarely occur. It is not enough to order chaos, overcome inconveniences: new nets must constantly be cast out, so that of a hundred opportunities, one is realized ....
National business and private business can be compared in this respect ....

'The Bismarck era has left us in an all too saturated position. Germany was like a business man to whom someone had paid a lot of money for his business. The fear of losing some of it now prevents him from taking on something new. After living a fairly miserable, rather adventurous but hopeful life up to 1870, he woke up as a well-to-do, satisfied bourgeois; hemmed in, it is true, by inconvenient boundaries, with no room to spare, which had henceforth to be defended; the neighbouring states being in a similar position, defending their boundaries. The time for expansion was past; our geographical situation a rather restricted one. Then a stupid mistake was made; to find a parallel it would be necessary to delve far back into history: we allowed the popular voice of a neighbour to utter oaths of vengeance in every idle moment, and we got used, through a mistaken courtesy, to accepting this remarkable situation of unilateral threats as a justifiable peculiarity, until it assumed the character of a generally sanctioned prescriptive right, which today, as one of the strongest realities of world politics, cripples part of our capacity for action.

'German policy has remained defensive since Bismarck's departure. We have not concluded a single effective business deal of our own, and, what is more serious, have not once found a larger, more satisfying aim for our politics. We should have added a more convincing formula to our innumerable protestations of our love and peace [than we have done]—because we do not know what we want for ourselves.'

Rathenau then considered the question of disarmament. He thought that since Germany had reached its expansionist stage too late, it could at least take the initiative in the matter of disarmament, and thus do the world a useful service. He ended his article by saying: 'If, moreover, support can be given to the idea

---

[143] The Verband Deutscher Juden was founded in 1904 as a Jewish lobby to influence policy-making and legislation. Presumably the association wanted to know whether Rathenau was willing to write another article, or to give a talk, or to join the association by taking over an office.

[144] Reprinted in *Zur Kritik der Zeit*.

that there can be no fact or reality in the world, no matter how confusing which cannot with goodwill and humour be turned to the good, then the wish of this peace-seeking Easter meditation will have been fulfilled.'

12 April, Wednesday. Plania general meeting. Afternoon, Konschewski. Evening, 9.30 p.m., visit from Lancken who was on his way to Potsdam.[145]

14 April, Good Friday, to *18 April*, Tuesday, at Freienwalde. Friday, Kessler and Gustav Richter to stay.

19 April, Wednesday. Nitrum meeting at Höchst.[146] Lunched at von Brünings in Frankfurt. Then viewed house of his mother's family, corner of Mainzer Landstrasse and Westendstrasse, that had belonged to my grandfather.[147] Afternoon, at junk-shops and Lahmeyer's[148] then by train with Gnauth and von der Herberg. Got out at Andernach;[149] with Konschewski to Tönisstein; quarters for the night.

20 April, Thursday. Morning, at Burgbrohl.[150] Difficult work. Afternoon, to Cologne; from there travelled by Rheinuferbahn [Rhine Embankment Railway] to Bonn and back. To Berlin [at] 9.40 p.m.

21 April, Friday. Strange dream in the sleeping-car: social gathering Unter den Linden (literary club?). Someone comes (Theodor Wolff?) and reports that the première is a real success. Contents intimated to

[145] Lancken, councillor at the Paris Embassy, came to report on French policy, for the situation in Morocco had become critical: military intervention in Fez was imminent; Cambon had expressed the idea of territorial compensation for Germany to Caillaux; and Delcassé was able to influence policy again through his position as Minister of the Navy.

[146] Joint laboratory set up in order to further nitrogen fixation. Out of this laboratory grew, during the war, the Elektro-Nitrum AG Rhina near the large AEG-run, power-station at Laufenburg.

[147] Rathenau's grandfather Isaak Nachmann (1816–70) was married to Ida Stiebel (1820–74).

[148] The Elektrizitäts AG vorm. W. Lahmeyer & Co. was founded in two stages between 1890 and 1893. The manufacturing side of Lahmeyer was merged with Felten & Guilleaume in 1905. Five years later Felten & Guilleaume sold the Lahmeyer dynamo factory in Frankfurt to the AEG. At the same time the Elektrobank acquired a share in the Lahmeyer Company by offering Elektrobank shares for Lahmeyer shares. Thus Rathenau became a member of the Lahmeyer supervisory board. See fn. 104 above.

[149] After the meeting of the Lahmeyer supervisory board Rathenau travelled with the leaders of Felten & Guilleaume from Frankfurt to Andernach. He met them again on the next day in Cologne. They discussed the efforts Felten & Guilleaume had made so far to obtain its own supply of steel. After this discussion Rathenau asked for details in order to calculate the viability of purchasing a blast-furnace plant. FG Archiv, A/I/9–0307, Rathenau to Zapf, 21 April 1911.

[150] Brohltal Stein und Ton-Industriegesellschaft (Brohltal Stone and Clay Industrial Company), established in 1899.

Emil Rathenau: very factual, without inner coherence. I have to go to the Grunewald. Drive abandoned since road (Charlottenburger Chaussee?) torn up on both sides, the car could not go any further. Walk along the embankment in front of the covered market, opposite Schiffbauerdamm.[151] Someone is sitting on a beam over the river sawing off his right foot.[152] The saw looks like a thin, gleaming red streak. 22 Schiffbauerdamm, the lights in the windows go out, it is very late, I am very frightened. Burning anxiety and concern for Emil Rathenau. At this moment a blueish-red meteor (shooting star), which goes down over the Reichstag. I turn into the Neue Wilhelmstrasse, Fritz Friedlaender next to me. I complain that Emil Rathenau does not look well. He says, 'Yes, his cheeks have sunk in a lot.' Wake up in a great fright; the train stops. Arrive in Berlin at 7.02. Worked in the Grunewald with Geitner, then alone. Beautiful spring weather. Evening, at Harden's till late.

22 April, Saturday. Thiederhall.[153] Afternoon, at Frau von Mendelssohn's. Evening, read *Crinett* by Hindenburg.[154] Important material for getting at the ideas of the Prussian nobility.

23 April, Sunday. Early to Freienwalde with Dora Hitz. Afternoon in the wood. Then Endell and wife to tea.

24 April, Monday. At Freienwalde. Physiological theorem to Wassermann.[155]

25 April, Tuesday. Early to Berlin. Afternoon Zander. Books forwarded by Kyser and Ewers.

26 April, Wednesday. Morning, visit from Mosler. Letter sent off to Wassermann. Afternoon, Tschöpeln general meeting, take over chairmanship.

27 April, Thursday. Supplementary suggestion concerning electricity monopoly and retort to Leoni's elaboration to Wermuth.[156] Read in the last few days: Eulenberg, *Sonderbare Geschichten*; Schäfer,

---

[151] The AEG's headquarters and his parents' former residence.
[152] Reference to the amputation of his father's foot a year later.
[153] Rathenau was a member of the supervisory board of the AG Thiederhall, in Thiede, which produced potash. The enterprise was established in 1893 with a capital of 4 million marks.
[154] Kessler, *Rathenau*, pp. 51 f.
[155] See fn. 85 above.
[156] See fn. 19 above.

Anekdoten (Béarnaise!); Kyser, *Titus*;[157] *Faust* (popular edition);
Ewer's *Gedichte*;[158] Larsen, *Japan im Kampf.*
Afternoon, Sezession. Slevogt, Daumier.

28 April, Friday. Ampère Gesellschaft [Ampère Company].[159] At
the club with Zander, Salomon, Haas. Elektrische Kraftwerke Baku
[Baku Electrical Power-Station].[160] Evening, Lili Deutsch.

29 April, Saturday. General meeting Solinger Kleinbahn [Solingen
Light Railway] and Schlesische Kleinbahnen.[161] Discussed Frankfurt–
Wiesbaden contract with Salomon and Zander. Evening, at Edith
Andreae's.

30 April, Sunday. *1 May*, Monday. At Freienwalde. Fruit blossom.

2 May, Tuesday. Returned. Evening, at von Mendelssohn's. Klinglers,
Robert and Franz von Mendelssohn play Beethoven opus 59, no. 3
and Schumann Quintet.

3 May, Wednesday. Morning, in the Grunewald. Lunch at the club
with Zapf.

4 May, Thursday. Morning in the Grunewald. Sketched.

5 May, Friday. Grunewald. Niles general meeting.[162] Mrs von Mendelssohn, Dora Hitz, Landauer to tea.

6 May, Saturday. Afternoon, to Freienwalde.

8 May, Monday. Back early. AEG with Klöckner and Grossberg. Afternoon, Erlangen about the lock-out.[163] National Liberal Party (Fuhrmann, dated 5 May) enquiries whether I want to be a candidate.

---

[157] *Titus und die Jüdin*, a tragedy in three acts.
[158] *Magonni Nameh. Gesammelte Gedichte*, Munich 1910.
[159] The Society was to promote the standardization of measures in the electrical
industry.
[160] The AEG had built the power-station at Baku a few years before.
[161] See fnn. 79, 129, 136 above.
[162] Deutsche-Niles-Werkzeugmaschinenfabrik (German Niles Machine Tool Factory),
founded in 1892. Rathenau was a member of its supervisory board.
[163] The lock-out was preceded by a strike of 400 textile workers who were members of
the socialist trade union. The employers retaliated by planning a lock-out, which was to
start on 20 May, of the 70 textile workers of the firm Weber & Ott in Erlangen. I am very
grateful to Dr Richter of the Stadtarchiv Erlangen for providing me with this information.

9 May, Tuesday. Haas, von Bodenhausen to lunch. With him at Fürstenberg's in the evening.

10 May, Wednesday. At the club with Kleefeld about candidature.

11 May, Thursday. Whole day, compensation negotiations AEG–Felten & Guilleaume Dynamowerk.[164] Balance completed. Evening, at Felix Deutsch's with Sombart, Behrens, Gnauth, etc.

12 May, Friday. (Konschewski, Trippensee. Afternoon, Stein und Ton.[165] Letter from Fuhrmann.) Letter from Theodor Richter about Meister Ekkehard.[166]

13 May, Saturday. Early, 9 a.m., to Freienwalde with Mrs von Mendelssohn and Mrs von Grunelius.

14 May, Sunday. Lunch-time visit from Hauptmanns. Afternoon, Deutschs and Sombart until evening.

15 May, Monday. Freienwalde.

16 May, Tuesday. Early to Berlin. At Joël's, Adlon [Hotel].[167] Supreme Court hearing of Friedmann-Quilitz's commission case.[168] Kuntze, Firle. Evening, visit from Fuhrmann who offers Frankfurt-on-Oder at the behest of the National Liberal Party.

18 May, Thursday. ELG general meeting. Afternoon, BHG. Walter Merton elected. Evening, at Lili Deutsch's.

19 May, Friday. Lindenberg, Eilender.

20 May, Saturday. Weisswasser, on account of the Arnimscher Opalglaswerke [Arnim Opal Glassworks].[169]

[164] For the forthcoming annual general meeting and the meeting of the supervisory board on 24 May the details of the take-over of the Lahmeyer factory in Frankfurt by the AEG had to be agreed upon, so that a unanimous report could be presented. See also fnn. 22 and 148 above.   [165] See fn. 150 above.
[166] On 5 May 1911 Rathenau had briefly thanked Richter for a quotation from Meister Eckhart. Rathenau, *Briefe*, vol. i, p. 80.
[167] Professor Karl Joel had written to Rathenau about 'Staat und Judentum' and Rathenau had replied on 5 May 1911. It was made clear that if Joel were in Berlin they would meet to discuss the problem. Rathenau, *Briefe*, vol. i, pp. 78 ff. In this edition Rathenau's reply is wrongly attributed to Joel's comments about *Zur Kritik der Zeit*.
[168] Dispute over the percentage paid for arranging mergers.
[169] The enterprise was taken over by the Vereinigte Lausitzer Glaswerke. Rathenau was a member of its supervisory board.

21 May, Sunday. Freienwalde, Kleefeld.

22 May, Monday. Back at lunch-time. Afternoon, Salomon.

23 May, Tuesday. Firle, Kretschmar, Zander, Schoder, Wiens. Lunch at the club with von Hindenburg. Afternoon, Zander, ELG. Evening, at Mrs Schwabach's with Mrs von Boddien. Varnbülers.

24 May, Wednesday. Felten & Guilleaume. Morning, committee; afternoon, board of directors. Evening, the Grönvolds visited.

25 May, Thursday. Ascension Day. Left by car 7 a.m. Lunch at Zwickau. Afternoon, visited Nostiz at Auerbach. Evening, Hof.

26 May, Friday. Left early, 7.30 a.m. Lunch Regensburg, Grüner Kranz [Hotel]. Evening, 6 p.m., Munich, Continental [Hotel]. Spent evening with Hahn.

27 May, Saturday. Off 8 a.m. via Rossenheim; 12.30 a.m. at Innsbruck. Afternoon, at Bozen 5.30 to 6 p.m. In Trient at 8.15 p.m. Flat tyre in front of the garage. Spent the night Hotel Trento.

28 May, Sunday. Early, flat tyre, [Italian] frontier, tyre bought with much difficulty in Verona, lunch in Modena. Early cathedral, side façade with portal and balcony. Evening, Bologna. Extremely lively.

29 May, Monday. Via Castiglione and Prato to Florence. Lunch at Arezzo. San Francesco being restored. Evening, Perugia. Impressed again by the square between the church and the town hall. Little preserved from early times that is more beautiful.

30 May, Tuesday. Via Todi, San Gemini, Otricoli, Narni, Città Castellana to Rome. The oak woods of the Apennines. Campagna in blossom. Heavy downpour. The rainfall of the last two days has brought pleasant coolness after the heat in Bologna. Freshness of the vegetation. Arrived 12.30 p.m. Afternoon, Villa Malta.[170] Left cards. Then exhibition in the rain. Evening, 8 p.m. Villa Malta with Mühlberg and von Bülow, nephew. Prince Bülow tells of Bismarck's last meeting at the Ministry of State.[171] Great justifying

---

[170] Bülow's residence. Rathenau's first visit to Bülow's house in Rome had taken place in April 1910.
[171] The meeting took place on 27 March 1890. For the minutes see Bismarck, *Die Gesammelten Werke*, vol. xv, pp. 519 ff.

speech: Bötticher's reply. Condolence. Then someone asks: the King of Saxony had arrived incognito; whether ministers should leave cards at the palace. Answer: drive there in second class cabs, sign names as Müller and Schulze. On the practicability of a Reich's embassy to the Vatican.[172] Bülow very much in favour. On the aggressive patriotism of Germans. The Prince found the Liberals very 'considerate', because they did not ally themselves to the Social Democrats for the elections. In 1907 the Centre [Party] procured the Social Democrats 10 seats.[173]

31 May, Wednesday. Morning, Castel Sant'Angelo, then Ranieri, Galeria San Giorgio; afternoon, 4.30 p.m. excursion. Via Appia.

1 June, Thursday. Morning, Museo delle Terme. Lunch, 1 p.m., at the Prince's. Alone, the Princess had a cold. Stayed until 5.30 p.m.

Bülow recalls how in the winter of 1909 he had expressed to Loebell his intention of bringing an unbaptized Jew into a high state office, so as to give the problem another aspect.[174] He had in fact only known one important minister: Miquel. Difficult choice to make—if possible, not a parliamentarian, and, if possible, a noble. Briand was a radical journalist (Justice), married to a restaurant-keeper's daughter. As if Stadthagen [SPD] married Miss Ewest and became a minister. High estimation of the French ministers. When Bethmann was to become Minister of the Interior Heydebrand said: unsuitable. He was a muddled philosopher, one needed a 'truncheon' for the Ministry of the Interior. He regrets not having demanded 2 thousand millions during the financial reform, in order to link it at the same time to a great work of social reform.[175] At the time of the annexation of Bosnia Grey went fishing in Scotland. He appears

[172] In 1920 the Nunciature in Berlin was established at the suggestion of the Nuncio Pacelli. The first German Embassy to the Vatican was established in the same year.

[173] The Social Democrats and the Centre Party had not worked together during the 1907 Reichstag elections. 'Politics had made them bed-fellows, but they chose not to sleep together.' In the final ballot the South German Centre Party helped the SPD to win eight seats. Crothers, *The German Elections of 1907*, pp. 168–71. In his memoirs Bülow spoke of at least a dozen. *Denkwürdigkeiten*, vol. ii, p. 278.

[174] It is possible that Bülow had expressed such an intention since he argued along similar lines for Rathenau's decoration in December 1908, but in any case it is likely that Bülow would have met very strong opposition if he had nominated an unbaptized Jew for a high office.

[175] In November 1908 a Government Bill for financial reform was proposed which was to bring in about 500 million marks from various direct taxes, of which 100 million were to be raised by estate duty. The Conservatives put up a successful fight against these demands, and the triumph of agrarian interest led to the dissociation of the Liberals from the Conservatives and the end of the Bülow Bloc. See Witt, *Die Finanzpolitik des Deutschen Reiches*.

to consider his attitude towards Austria against Russia as his greatest foreign success.[176]

Dietrich von Hülsen said to him: now HM wants to make the biggest blockhead commander of the Foot Guards Regiment. (Alexander? Forgotten.) Why? Because once a year he has to sit next to the commander at table for two hours and he does not want to sit next to an unsympathetic person. The Kaiser, who was pleased with Tschirschky and Schoen, has obliged him to retain both these totally incapable people for so long. Afternoon, at Jagow's. Then San Pietro in Montorio and Pincio.

2 June, Friday. Morning, correspondence. Then at Centurione's. Then Villa Borghese exhibition. Afternoon, 4.30 p.m., the Prince collects me [to go] to the Villa Palazzo Mattei.[177] The Pasha's 101 reasons why he did not buy the villa (above all—fever and remoteness). Painful incident with Prince Wied whom he holds on to while he [Wied] wants to join the ladies. Finally, in a huff, 'I do not want to detain you'.

On Christianity and the Roman religion. Abolition of state religion not undesirable. Enthusiasm for Paul and Jews as propagandists. Sudden thought: what would Marcus Aurelius have said if someone had prophesied to him that a Jewish craftman's son would stand on his column.

About Victor Emmanuel on his death bed, who asked for time for reflection on whether he would regret having taken Rome.[178] He asks: Hell? Priest: No, not for the scion of so great a house; but probably purgatory. 'Then he would have to let it come to that, for Rome was much too important a possession.'

About the present ministers. Great interest as to what Posadowsky is doing or has in mind. Monts very incompetent; he (Bülow) was to blame for the mistake. I: dearth of aims in domestic and foreign policy. Admitted. Yet his policy had had an aim: place in the sun, fleet, world power.[179] Nothing any more.

[176] The Revolution of the Young Turks induced Austria to transform the existing occupation of Bosnia and Herzegovina into annexation. This move prompted Russia to seek compensation. The Austrian ultimatum to Serbia and the indirect German ultimatum to Russia in March 1909 forced Serbia and Russia to recognize the annexation.

[177] A palace built by Moderna in 1616. The title 'Pasha', which follows, possibly refers to Bülow's pomposity.

[178] Victor Emmanuel II had had the Papal States occupied on 20 December 1870.

[179] Bülow had already conceived these aims in foreign policy during his first year as Chancellor. Bethmann Hollweg, in a defensive position, had had a memorandum drawn up in January 1910 'which showed that since he had entered office there had been no departure from the guiding principles which had been in force up to then and which had been laid down by his predecessor, particularly not in the direction of greater compliance abroad'. The Second Morocco Crisis was to confirm that. ZStA Potsdam, AA, Handel 4615, 31 January 1910.

On Alsace. I: I would have preferred a monarchy, in order to win the Alsatians.[180] Frenchness attracts them as being the more 'refined'. Germanism must therefore become the more distinguished.[181] Whole-hearted agreement.

On the three phases of the Kaiser's judgement: first, admiration; then, disappointment; then, pity.[182] In the second phase Miquel had said to him: politically colour-blind. Holstein: *He lives in a fool's paradise.*[183] Explanation: his parents' and grandmother's dislike of Bismarck had strengthened his desire to work without a minister. I: ministers' impossible position in Germany, have to serve two masters (monarch and parliament), whereas elsewhere they are only dependent on one.

Brought me to the hotel at 7 p.m. Evening, dined alone with Jagow until 12 p.m.

3 June, Saturday. Morning, Trastevere and St. Peter's. Afternoon, 4.30 p.m., collected Jagow, with him to the exhibition, then to Albano (Alhambra [Hotel]), back at 11 p.m.

About Donna Laura [Minghetti]. She said of Blaserna, *'che cazzo'.*[184] In Venice, fearing a collision with the steamer, *'squarcia coglione'.*[185] Barrère told how she met Coquelin and he kept on praising *'la Vertu'*. Finally she becomes furious and says, *'moi, je n'ai jamais été vertueuse, et j'en suis fière'*, which (rightly) made a certain heroic impression on everyone.

She had told the Kaiser she loved him in mess dress. She now tells how he always came in short tunic, with heavy hips, and she said, *'si j'étais plus jeune, vous me feriez dégringoler'.*

Of Bülow she says, *'Berhard fait un secret de tout. Il vous prend le bras, vous mène à la fenêtre et vous dit: n'en parler pas, mais voilà un petit chien qui fait pipi.'*

On Holstein. Monts had sent a report from Rome: France wanted to make concessions regarding Morocco (at Delcassé's orders). Holstein had put the report away: 'Monts wants to be ambassador

---

[180] In 1871 the provinces of Alsace and Lorraine were subordinated to the sovereignty of all German princes and cities. The constitutional law of 26 May 1911 bestowed on the two provinces an equal and free franchise for the Landtag, a nominated upper house, and three seats in the Bundesrat. This was a late but decisive step towards a policy of integration.

[181] Bismarck had a similar aim in 1885. Frauendienst (ed.), *Bismarck. Die Gesammelten Werke*, vi c, p. 321, Bismarck to the Crown Prince, 25 June 1885.

[182] There does not seem to be any evidence for the three phases in Bülow's relations with Wilhelm II.

[183] For Holstein's remark see Bülow, *Denkwürdigkeiten*, vol. i, p. 57.

[184] Translated: 'What a cock.'

[185] Translated: 'It hurts one's testicles.'

in Paris'.[186] Bülow had been completely in Holstein's hands. Holstein believed he could, if need be, persuade the Kaiser to go to war with France.[187] Admitted the only aim of policy was the Baghdad Railway. Germany's lack of diplomatic prestige. Nevertheless, Mühlberg's bearing in the last conflict energetic (just the reverse says Bülow, 'conciliating').[188] He said: Let us imagine we are like doctors at the sick-bed of a dying man. Something must happen or he will die. King of Italy was excessively democratic and anti-clerical.[189]

At dinner, discussion on the Jewish question.

4 June, Sunday. Whitsun. Dedication of the memorial.[190] During this, excursion to Tivoli, Olevano, Palestrina. Evening, at Bülow's with Kehr, Count Tattenbach, Frantzius. The Princess had a cold, not at table. From the tower the fireworks in the Pincio [Gardens].

5 June, Monday. Morning, churches, correspondence. Negri comes to see me several times. Said goodbye to the Centuriones. Evening, at Bülow's again. With Kehr, Nast and wife, Mietzl (Austrian military attaché), music, farewell.

6 June, Tuesday. Left 8.30 a.m., excursion to Capraola. Then Viterbo, Montefiascone; in Orvieto at 1.30 p.m. The whole town digs old ceramics out of the *pozzi*.[191]

7 June, Wednesday. Early from Orvieto via Montepulciano and Picara to Siena. There, quite by chance, met Rudolf Borchardt at lunch in the Aquila Nera [Hotel.][192] Alone to the cathedral and town hall, then at 4 p.m. accompanied Borchardt to his country estate. Thence at 6 p.m. via Siena to Florence. Arrived in the evening.

8 June, Thursday. In the streets and at junk-dealers. Extremely hot. Evening, lovely excursion along the Mugone, up to the pass,

[186] *Grosse Politik*, vol. 22, p. 362, Monts to Holstein, 2 May 1905; Rich and Fisher (eds.), *The Holstein Papers*, vol. iv, pp. 339 f., Holstein to Radolin, 8 May 1905. The aim of humiliating France and testing the *entente* with Britain could not, in Holstein's opinion, be reconciled with a policy of offering compensations to each other. Namier suspected this document, which was discovered by Willequet, to be an invention. See Willequet, *Le Congo Belge et la Weltpolitik*, pp. 430 ff. and Namier, *Vanished Supremacies*, p. 132.

[187] Rich, *Holstein*, vol. ii, pp. 698 f.

[188] The Bosnian crisis.

[189] Victor Emmanuel III.

[190] Unveiling of the national memorial to Victor Emmanuel II, to commemorate the fiftieth anniversary of the foundation of a united Italy.

[191] Etruscan tombs. Orvieto is the Etruscan Volsinii, destroyed by the Romans in 280 BC.   [192] Black Eagle.

back via Fiesole along a steep path. A lot of correspondence. Reports from Geitner about the constituency.

9 June, Friday. Exhibition (portraits) Palazzo Vecchio. Considerably impressed by Ghislandi. Lunch at Count Harrach's Villa Ridolfi, Marignolle. Afternoon, with Count and Countess Harrach to Villa Bombicei (despite High Renaissance, most delicate architectural feeling), thence Villa Caruso, Baroque. On the way back in a Ridolfi tenuta [land holding], a silkworm farm. Dinner at Harrach's. —Hasty return journey necessary on account of Geitner's news.

10 June, Saturday. Morning, in San Marco. Deeply impressed, as before, by the monastery rooms with Angelico's pictures. Noon, Harrachs to lunch at Donnay's. With Hans Harrach to Andrea del Castagno's *Last Supper*. Left 3 p.m. over the Futa Pass to Bologna. Arrived, 6 p.m.

11 June, Sunday. Left 7.30 a.m., flat tyre. Stopped in Parma, cathedral, baptistry, junk-dealer. Lunch at Piacenza. Afternoon in Pavia and the Certosa.[193] 5 p.m. Milan, Hotel 'Milano'.

12 June, Monday. Morning, Zander and Königsheim. Afternoon, 2 p.m. meeting at the polytechnic with Colombo, Negri, Scotti, Conti, Mangili, Rossi, Zander, Königsheim regarding agreement among the water power companies. 6 p.m. hasty departure.

22 June, Thursday. Afternoon, 5 p.m., meeting of the National Liberal Party leadership. Breithaupt, Fuhrmann, Dr Leidig (Zentral-Verband der [*sic*] Industriellen [Central Union of Industrialists]). From Frankfurt—Dr Wintzer (*Oder-Zeitung*). District Court President Mathis. Want very much to put me up as a candidate, with the exception of the *Oder-Zeitung*. Declaration: I abide by my decision to withdraw because the discussion has produced no new incentive.

23 June, Friday. Evening, left for Wiesbaden.

24 June, Saturday. Bismarck Memorial. Jury discussion, committee, decision-making committee, bigger general meeting. Had my way that the successful artists should be able to submit new plans and that these would be judged by the jury. Evening, with Tuaillon, Lichtwark, Kalckreuth, then return journey. At Frankfurt, Salomon on the train.

[193] La Certosa di Pavia; a monastery.

25 June, Sunday. Arrived, drove immediately to Freienwalde. Lunch, Jordan, visited Roland-Lücke together.[194]

26 June, Monday. Telephone: letter from Trowitzsch to Breithaupt, position unchanged. Frankfurt-on-Oder, therefore, definitely out of the question. Letter from Ballin: Kaiser very pleased about my candidature; regards it as a great sacrifice, etc. Afternoon, visit from Lili Deutsch.

27 June, Tuesday. Back to Berlin. Deutsch-Überseeische Elektrizitäts-Gesellschaft, Valparaiso,[195] Zander, Hulse, Goldschmidt, who wants me to join his supervisory board. With him to the Diskontogesell-schaft, with Mosler and Lord Mayor Marx. Evening, left for Cologne.

28 June, Wednesday. Felten & Guilleaume supervisory board and general meeting. Departed 4.24 p.m. with Emil Rathenau and Hagen. Arrived Berlin midnight.

29 June, Thursday. Tired and run down. A lot of work. Afternoon, Rybnik.[196] Evening, walk.

30 June, Friday. Inspected Löwe factory. Afternoon, Dr Rothe.

1 July, Saturday. Lunch-time, Freienwalde with Mathilde Rathenau.

2 July, Sunday. Emil Rathenau's visit.

3 July, Monday. Back to Berlin. 'Eitel' [Vain] delivered. Observations and accustoming of the dog. Afternoon, Fänder. Evening, at Max Liebermann's.

4 July, Tuesday. Walk with Eitel. Firle. Lindenberg.

5 July, Wednesday. Evening, to Dr Guthmann, Cladow.

6 July, Thursday. Morning, AEG factories with Jordan.

8 July, Saturday. To Freienwalde.

[194] Roland-Lücke was a leading member of the Hansabund and the Bund der Indus-triellen (League of Industrialists); he was also a candidate of the National Liberal Party for the forthcoming elections. It is likely that Rathenau wanted to consult him in connection with his own candidature. See Mielke, *Der Hansa-Bund*; Ullmann, *Der Bund der Industriellen*.

[195] The DUEG's subsidiary, The Chilean Electrical Tramway and Light Company, managed the electrical enterprises in Valparaiso.

[196] See fn. 123 above.

9 July, Sunday. Visit from Kleefeld. Advised him to set up some positive aims for the Hansabund: (1) electoral reform for Prussia, (2) redistribution of constituencies for the Reich.[197] Both under the motto: Constitutionalism.

With Kleefeld to Friedlaender in Lanke. Thence in haste to Berlin and the station. In the train—Riesser, to whom I suggested the same. He stayed in my compartment until 12.30 a.m. Apart from that I recommend Eich to him for the Hansabund, to replace Roetger.[198]

10 July, Monday. Essen. Goldschmidt meeting until evening.[199] Evening, dined at Bodenhausen's; then to Düsseldorf.

11 July, Tuesday. With Riesser again, who is also staying at the Park Hotel. He wants to follow up my proposals, both regarding electoral reform and constituencies, and regarding the Eich matter.[200] Riesser offered me a directorship of the Hansabund; refused. Capito & Klein meeting until 1 p.m. 1.35 p.m. left for Berlin. Extremely hot. Arrived 9.14 p.m.

12 July, Wednesday. Revised correspondence. Major Glynn.

13 July, Thursday. Redlich, Hennig. Afternoon, Leoni about electricity monopoly—then Lili Deutsch. Evening, Leoni again.

14 July, Friday. Afternoon, left for Baden in extreme heat. Leoni accompanied me as far as Halle. Electricity draft has been drawn up in principle at the Treasury.

15 July, Saturday. Morning, Brown, Boveri, Baden.[201] Atmosphere

[197] The breach, which occurred in June, between the heavy industrial leadership of the Zentralverband deutscher Industrieller (Central Association of German Industrialists) and the Hansa Bund because of the Bund's anti-agrarian election policy, drove the Bund a little further to the left. Moreover, the reform of the Prussian franchise and the redrawing of constituency boundaries became the Bund's election slogans. Thus Rathenau's suggestion was incorporated in the Bund's election platform in order to focus the political interest of the middle classes. Bertram, *Die Wahlen*, pp. 102-7; H. Kaelble, *Industrielle Interessenpolitik*, pp. 130 ff. and 184 f.; Stegmann, *Die Erben Bismarcks*, pp. 239-43; Mielke, *Der Hansa-Bund*, pp. 141-59.

[198] Mielke, *Der Hansa-Bund*, p. 94.

[199] The Theodor Goldschmidt AG at Essen was established in 1847 and was transformed into a joint-stock company in 1911. The AEG was interested in its electrolytic and aluminium processing. Rathenau was a member of its supervisory board.

[200] Pogge von Strandmann, *Unternehmenspolitik und Unternehmensführung*, pp. 64 f.

[201] Rathenau refers to the difficult position the BBC found itself in, when it paid a dividend of only 7 per cent. Boveri, *Ansprachen und Betrachtungen*, pp. 22 ff.

more depressed than before. 7%. Afternoon, departed. With Rödiger and Favreau.

16 July, Sunday. Arrived 7.36 a.m. at the Anhalt Station. Then on to Freienwalde. Visited by Bodenhausen.

17 July, Monday. Visited by Gaul [who stayed] until the evening.

18 July, Tuesday. Afternoon, to Berlin. Riesser telephones: (1) I ought so to influence Bassermann through Bülow that he moves to the Left. (2) I ought to organise articles defending him in the newspapers. Declined.[202] Evening, at Hamspohn's, von Huhn, Heinemann.

19 July, Wednesday. Firle, Hennig. Evening, met Strauss who then came to tea at 10 p.m. with Stucken and wife, Heimann and wife, Marschalk and five ladies.

21 July, Friday. To Freienwalde for a longer stay.

22 July, Saturday. Morning in Berlin for the foundation of the Ozon Gesellschaft [Ozon Company].[203]

23 July, Sunday. Deutsch, Moslers, Gutmann, Zimmermann to lunch. Unbearable heat. Afternoon, thunderstorm.

25 July, Tuesday. Afternoon, 5 p.m., to tea at Bethmann's at Hohenfinow until 7 p.m. He enquired after the Hansabund. Advised him regarding Alsace (1) if possible—dynasty, (2) careers for young Alsatians.[204]

Regarding the Morocco negotiations—about which he spoke with little confidence—conditional concessions must be demanded, 'in case France establishes herself administratively or militarily, or

[202] Using Bülow in the suggested way must have struck Rathenau as absurd. It was believed that the party would split if Bassermann threw his weight behind one of the factions, and Rathenau was also well aware of Bassermann's balancing act in the National Liberal Party. Rathenau no doubt turned down Riesser's second request for a number of reasons, but one was that his contacts with the press were not all that good, and his relationship with Harden was cooling off. Moreover, Rathenau did not want to be identified too closely with the Hansabund.

[203] The company was set up to purify the drinking water in Paris and St. Petersburg. The partners in the enterprise were Siemens, the AEG, Felten & Guilleaume, and a French company. The starting capital was 500,000 roubles.

[204] See fn. 180 above.

keeps troops there longer than x years—compensation in the form of territorial acquisitions'.[205]

Bethmann exhaustively on Alsatian constitution. He deplores the franchise, but has reached three results: (1) Upper house according to his desire. There are already a hundred candidates for this. (2) The administration can continue if the budget is not forthcoming. (3) Strengthening of the Kaiser's power by martial law. Bülow has written to him and expressed his hesitations on the franchise. He answered him thus: a later Reichstag would probably not have conceded him as much.[206]

28 August, Monday. Evening, 8 p.m., to dinner at Hohenfinow.

After dinner I showed pictures of Freienwalde—where the children had been with Pastor Freitag—and Grunewald.

Talk about Jagow's decree regarding woman's hats, which Bethmann whole-heartedly approves of.[207]

Then on the balcony in the dark. Discussed uneasiness of the Stock Exchange and among the public. I said: England's attitude, above all, has caused annoyance; Lloyd George, Asquith, Cartwright.[208] Bethmann agrees; does not think Cartwright's *dementi*

---

[205] The gunboat *Panther* was sent to Agadir on 1 July to protect alleged German interests from French encroachments. The mission caused the Second Morocco Crisis. After Lloyd George's Mansion House speech (21 July), Bethmann's lack of optimism was understandable. On 12 August 1911 Rathenau wrote to Harden about his conversation with the Chancellor: 'In that awkward situation I had—very confidential this—made the suggestion: no compensation in [the form of] unknown tropical mandates. Only statement from France: if we still retain troops in Morocco in 1915 *or* possess administrative authorities *or* any other controls, Germany will be indemnified. I get the reply: These premises are difficult to define. I answered: No, just look at Egypt and draw up a list of the characteristics of English Government. France *can* only control the country by means of administrative measures. That cannot continue from Paris indefinitely. I like conditions the other party grows into, against his will and contrary to his expectations.' Harden wrote back: 'I miss one thing in your smart and clever proposal: kind and amount of compensation [France] would have to pay in 1915. If I understand you correctly you don't really want one, only a trick. I share your opinion. What has been planned now, is, as the entire bargain, scandalously stupid, so that you can explain it only through the personalities involved.' In *Die Zukunft* Harden had advocated war against France or an alliance with either Britain or France. Hellige (ed.), Rathenau–Harden, Rathenau to Harden, 12 August 1911, and Harden to Rathenau, 15 August 1911. Similar ideas had been mentioned in the *Frankfurter Zeitung* (18 July); Wernecke, *Der Wille zur Weltgeltung*, pp. 31–88.

[206] Bethmann obviously did not approve of the general suffrage in the Reichstag elections. Therefore he had limited the democratic franchise in Alsace by means of legal stipulations. To a certain extent the upper house provided a Conservative counterbalance to the Landtag. The retention of the old budget was a guarantee against possible obstructionist policy. A military dictatorship was immediately possible in the event of war. See also Bethmann's defence of the Kaiser's rights before the Reichstag on 3 December 1913 during the Zabern Crisis. Zmarzlik, *Bethmann Hollweg*, pp. 95–101. See fn. 180.

[207] The decree was directed against the wearing of over-large hats.

[208] Rathenau referred to Lloyd George's Mansion House speech of 21 July 1911, Prime

holds water (consequently is not clear about the authorship). Agadir was necessary just because of England: the Morocco Question welds England and France together and must therefore be 'liquidated'. Condemns war-mongering, because we are at a most unfavourable moment as regards alliances. Admits to difficulties in the negotiations, hopes no danger will ensue. Remembers my opinion and suggestion in July: this solution would not have been popular. That can be seen from industry's demands regarding rights in Morocco. I commented in detail: privileges for commerce could not be formulated and would later be enforced if the Protectorate were set up, therefore one should not impede the negotiations for the sake of a soap bubble.[209] In the present situation one would have to limit oneself to the hinterland of the Cameroons. He believes that a strong party group stands behind Mannesmann; Kirdorf, Stinnes, etc. I tried to refute this.[210]

Then general topics, depressed atmosphere. As I left Bethmann accompanied me to my car. On the steps, 'I wish these times were over. Now this Cartwright incident.' I said, it had always been his strength not to lose his nerve. Only the negotiations should be brought quickly to an end. The formulation of rights in Morocco should not be taken to heart. He: 'I tell you this confidentially. It is somewhat *for show* (verbatim).[211] We cannot yield too much'. I: 'But we can never quite please public opinion, for which the hinterland question is most important.' He: 'We don't know how valuable the strip is. But we must insist on (1) a stretch of coast,

Minister Asquith's speech of 27 July 1911, and the unauthenticated interview given by Sir Fairfax Cartwright, the British Ambassador in Vienna, which appeared in the *Wiener Neue Presse*, on 25 August 1911. *Grosse Politik*, vol. 29, pp. 237–44. The article in the *Wiener Neue Presse* was sharply critical of German policy regarding Morocco. *British Documents*, vii, Appendix V, The Cartwright Interview, pp. 837–45. See also von Schwabach, *Aus meinen Akten*, pp. 220–4; Wernecke, *Der Wille zur Weltgaltung*, pp. 92–7; Fischer, *Krieg der Illusionen*, pp. 125 ff. and 132 ff.

[209] Rathenau's suggestion was not followed up. Instead a guarantee of commercial and industrial rights was drawn up which later was used as a defence against the criticism of the Moroccan Agreement made by some steel industrialists.

[210] Rathenau's attempt to correct Bethmann's opinion was based on his personal knowledge of the attitude of some German industrialists, particularly in connection with the case of the Mannesmann brothers. The Mannesmanns had not only lost industrial support but also that of the Pan-Germans. See Pogge von Strandmann, 'Rathenau, die Gebrüder Mannesmann und die Vorgeschichte der Zweiten Marokkokrise', pp. 267–70.

On 22 July Thyssen and Kirdorf asked Kiderlen to secure German interests in Morocco, and while both stood behind the Mannesmanns, Krupp did not. Fischer, *Krieg der Illusionen*, pp. 127 ff.

[211] After the Potsdam interview, at which it was hoped to manœuvre England and Russia apart, the object of the Morocco Crisis in foreign policy was to break up the *entente*. Kiderlen had obtained Bethmann's consent to his Moroccan initiative by making him believe that he could use a success in the coming Reichstag elections.

(2) access to the Belgian Congo.'[212] Once home I wrote him a letter: the leading traffic expert at the Colonial Office (Schlüpmann) had told me on Sunday that the port of Duala would suffice for all communications with the hinterland trade.[213] Freienwalde, and Berlin by day. Work on *Kritik der Neuzeit*. At Freienwalde until Friday *15 September*. Finished *Kritik der Zeit* up to concluding chapter.[214]

Saturday, *16 September*, to Saturday, *30 September*, in Westerland. Final editing. Negotiations with Fischer. Then in Berlin. With Hauptmann a lot, whose novel in proof had accompanied me in my retreat. Meanwhile Grete Hauptmann at the clinic slowly recovering from the operation.

20 October, Friday. With Hauptmann again, at the Adlon. I suggested the title *Atlantis* to him, which he accepted.[215] At Harden's, who was celebrating his 50th birthday. *In floribus*. Rather embarrassed about certain valuable presents. Did not want to name the donor of a gold timepiece (Ballin?). Evening, appointment with Varnbüler at the club. On Eulenburg etc. He believes that Bülow co-operated in his downfall through Holstein. He was present at Liebenberg with Lecomte, Leszinsky, etc.[216] Supposedly the most harmless conversation. As Japan and Russia were being discussed someone took Lecomte aside. Varnbüler later went to see Eulenburg, at the Kaiser's and the Chancellor's order, to ascertain what position he would take in the case!!![217]

[212] The so-called 'antennae' of the Congo (the New Cameroons) were to be the first stage in further acquisitions intended to link the Cameroons and East Africa ('Kiderlen Bridge'). It was the beginning of an expanding Central Africa policy which depended to some extent on the Cameroon–Congo Railway project. The breakdown of the Franco-German negotiations regarding this scheme was one of the reasons for sending the *Panther* to Agadir. Kiderlen hoped he would be able to coerce the French into an agreement about this project. Görlitz (ed.), *Der Kaiser*, p. 87.

[213] As an expert on colonial transport systems, Schlüpmann had accompanied Rathenau and Dernburg on their South African journey in 1908. He, moreover, kept in mind the plan, which originally came from Georg von Siemens, for an East–West trans-African railway.

[214] *Zur Kritik der Zeit* is meant.

[215] See fn. 90 above.

[216] Rogge makes the same accusation against Bülow. Rogge, *Holstein und Harden*, pp. 12–17. Holstein was certainly not the instigator of Eulenburg's fall. Ibid., p. 11.

[217] Ibid., pp. 164 and 212. It was also probably the occasion of that visit of Varnbüler's which is mentioned in Bülow's *Denkwürdigkeiten*, vol. ii, pp. 312 f. Apparently Varnbüler took part in the plot to topple Bülow in October and November 1906. Lecomte's relations with Eulenburg were of great interest to Holstein and Harden because he might have conveyed information about Germany's policy during the First Moroccan Crisis to Paris. See especially Hellige's footnotes in Hellige (ed.), Rathenau–Harden, Harden to Rathenau, 6 June 1907 and 8 May 1908.

21 October, Saturday. Lunch at the club with Hauptmann, Ivo as well as Benvenuto.

22 October, Sunday. Went riding again for the first time. Afternoon at Hauptmann's, Adlon [Hotel]. Grete Hauptmann considerably better.

23 October, Monday. Out riding early.

30 October, Monday. Evening, Sternheim here, whom I had met two days previously at Reinhardt's. That evening (after *Penthesilea*)[218] we had been at the club (with Hardt).

31 October, Tuesday. Zander in Berlin, Wiens, Rothe.

1 November, Wednesday. Märkisches Elektrizitätswerk, 5.2 Million expansion agreed with the AEG. Lunch at Heimann's and Fischer's. Agreed about *Kritik der Zeit*. Afternoon, Niles. That night (11.38) to Ratibor (reminiscing).

8 November, Wednesday, or Thursday, *9 November*. A few minutes with Bethmann at the Reichstag after his Morocco speech.[219] With Sternheim and Wassermann several times.

12 November, Sunday. Those [Sternheim and Wassermann] with wives and Holländers to dinner.

13 November, Monday. Mrs [von] Wassermann here, then Kleefeld.

16 November, From Thursday evening, until Thursday *23 November*, early, in Augsburg.[220] (Lechwerke; earth tremor on the way there), via Zurich to Bodio, Basle, Cologne, Strasbourg.

20 November, Monday, and Tuesday, *21 November*, Second Bismarck

[218] Play by Heinrich von Kleist (written 1808), performed at the Deutsche Theater.

[219] Bethmann gave his first speech in the Reichstag on 9 November and the second on 10 November 1911, so Rathenau must have seen him on 9 November. A day later he wrote to Bethmann supporting the Chancellor's stance, although he made it clear that he was 'not enthusiastic about the concluded bargain' with France. Rathenau to Bethmann Hollweg, 10 November 1911 in Hellige (ed.), Rathenau–Harden, Harden to Rathenau, 27 September 1911.

[220] Lech Elektrizitätswerke [Lech Electrical Works] Augsburg. The company was founded by the Lahmeyer group in 1903 with a joint-stock capital of 4.5 million marks. Through the take-over of Felten & Guilleaume and the Lahmeyer factory in Frankfurt Rathenau became a member of the supervisory board of Lech Elektrizitätswerke.

Memorial Competition. Hahn first again. Kalkreuth and Kirdorf are absent, Kirdorf has resigned the chairmanship. Therefore Stuck and Klinger. Evening, next to Klinger for a long while in the tavern until 1.30 a.m. Saxon—jovial—lecherous sort. He has all the documents about Stauffer-Bern. Commonplace swindles. A prisoner in Rome from October to December he never asked after the Escher woman. Ravaged by syphilis (*impotentia semialis, alternum scrotum* atrophied).—Tells also of students who came early to play a Beethoven sonata to him, whilst he still had dolly birds (plural) with him.

22 November, Wednesday. Jury in Strasbourg concerning the point of entry of the new boulevard; with Seidel and Grässel.

23 November, Thursday. Back to Berlin. Negotiations regarding Schweig-Unternehmungen [Schweig Enterprises]. General meeting, lignite coal: Fricke. Came upon Ewers' book *Alraune*.

27 November, Monday. At the club with Rechenberg. On his chances as Secretary of State.[221]

28 November, Tuesday. At the club with Collier and wife. They were addressed by Bodenhausen. On Germany.[222] A lot of work. Spinning mills, proof-reading, Lindenberg. Felten & Guilleaume general meeting regarding Collart purchase.[223]

[221] Lindequist, the Colonial Secretary, who did not agree with the bargain with France and who felt himself passed over by Kiderlen, was eventually allowed to resign on 9 November 1911, three months after he first tried to. ZStA Potsdam, RK 1663. Thereafter the Governor of German East Africa, Rechenberg, had some chance of succeeding him. However, as a member of the Centre Party and an opponent of the white settlement in East Africa he had no chance in the face of National Liberal and Free Conservative opposition to his colonial policies. On his return from Africa it was too late to stand for the forthcoming Reichstag elections, so he had to wait a year to win a place in the Reichstag through a by-election. Schnee, *Als letzter Gouverneur*, pp. 106–14; Iliffe, *Tanganyika.*

[222] Collier published *Germany and the Germans from an American Point of View* in 1913. A German translation appeared a year later. Burger (ed.), *Hofmansthal–Bodenhausen, Briefe*, p. 130.

[223] Since May 1911 Felten & Guilleaume had tried to bring its various negotiations for the securing of its own source of steel supply to a successful conclusion. The last candidates among the steel companies were Krupp, the Rombacher Hütte, and the newly founded ARBED (Aciéries Réunies de Burhach-Eich-Dudelange). Émile Mayrisch, its new managing director, proposed a partial merger with Felten & Guilleaume which ran counter to the AEG's strategy. In the middle of October Zapf went to Luxemburg to inspect a steel plant which had come on to the market. FG Archiv A/I/9–0307, Zapf to Rathenau, 16 October 1911. Before Zapf's visit Rathenau had favoured the construction of a blast-furnace plant together with other steel-consuming manufacturing companies. FG Archiv. 122, Board Meeting 19 October 1911. On 10 November Zapf informed Rathenau about the details of the inspected steel plant Jules Collart in Steinfort. Meanwhile no agreement could be found with Krupp, ARBED, or Oswald from the Rombacher Hütte. FG Archiv 122, Board

1 December, Friday. Lunch with Bruhn who said goodbye,[224] and Zander. Emil Rathenau back from Constantinople. Evening, at the club with Erzberger regarding Rechenberg. Interesting disclosures about Catholic dogmas. Erzberger confesses every four weeks. Debate about the danger of Papism. Erzberger in favour of collaborating with the Liberals.[225]

2 December, Saturday. Felten & Guilleaume, deliberations and decisions regarding Collart.[226] Afternoon, at Mosler's about Bergmann,[227] then Elektrische Werke Bitterfeld [Bitterfeld Electricity Works]. Finally at Rechenberg's about Erzberger.

3 December, Sunday. Lunch at Mrs von Bodenhausen's (Baroness Wendelstadt, Countess Degenfeld, Hofmannsthals, Colliers, Kessler, Schröder, Heymel). Evening, to Cologne.

4 December, Monday. In Cologne. Morning, art committee. Afternoon, big Bismarck Memorial Committee. Gave two big speeches.[228] Decision against us, for Kreis.

Meetings 14 and 17 November 1911. On 28 November Zapf wrote to Rathenau informing him that the board was ready for preliminary talks with him about a deal with Collart. FG Archiv, A/I/9-0307, Zapf to Rathenau, 28 November 1911. Rathenau may have been of the opinion that it was necessary to convene a general meeting for the purpose of approving the planned purchase of the plant in Luxemburg.

[224] Until 1914 Bruhn tried to increase Krupp's influence in China.

[225] If Erzberger meant his suggestion seriously then this was to counter the threat of the Grand Bloc (Liberals and SPD) spreading from Baden to the rest of Germany. In Hesse and in the Rhineland an understanding was however reached between the Centre Party and the National Liberals. Bertram, *Die Wahlen*, pp. 44 and 79–82. See also White, *The Splintered Party*.

[226] The meeting took place at the AEG's headquarters and consisted of the members and committee of the supervisory board. As Krupp did not want to give up any of its wire production it was decided to form a special committee which would begin to negotiate with Jules Collart in Luxemburg. FG Archiv, 122. Rathenau was a member of this committee.

[227] Bergmann Elektrizitäts Unternehmungen (Bergmann Electrical Enterprises) emerged as a result of two electro-technical firms being merged in 1900, with a capital of 1 million marks. When the company was reorganized in 1910, Kleist of Felten & Guilleaume tried to avoid a take-over of the latter by the AEG through a merger with the fourth biggest group in the industry—Bergmann. Ever since 1910 the AEG and Siemens had tried to gain control of the Bergmann Group. In 1911 the Bergmann Group ran into cash-flow problems, and the AEG as well as Siemens made a bid for the Group. In order to avoid the emergence of the AEG as the leading electric-technical company, especially after the take-over of Felten & Guilleaume in 1910, the Deutsche Bank enabled Siemens to take control of the Bergmann Group, although the AEG was involved as well. The intervention of the Deutsche Bank had been prompted by Siemens. See also the diary entries for 2, 13, and 14 March 1912.

[228] See Rathenau's section 'Das Denkmal der Unreife' ['The Memorial of Immaturity'] in Lichtwark and Rathenau, *Der rheinische Bismarck*. See fn. 52 above.

5 December, Tuesday. Unforeseen journey to Luxembourg and Steinfort, to Collart.[229] Negotiations regarding the purchase of the blast-furnaces and mines. Evening, back to Berlin.

7 December, Thursday. Evening, at Mrs Dohme's.

8 December, Friday. Morning, at Seidl's, Victoriastrasse. Then Körting till evening. Continuous severe stress, added to that proof-reading.[230] Another journey to Cologne to conclude the contract with Collart regarding Steinfort. Lunch at Collier's with Reinsch, Solf, American Ambassador, etc.[231] Finished proof-reading.

17 December, Sunday. Colliers, Reinschs, Hitz, Justi, Endells, Rechenberg to lunch in the Grunewald. Evening, at 10.10 p.m. to Frankfurt regarding Laufenburg and Unione.[232]

18 December, Monday. Frankfurt. Meetings from 9 a.m. to 8 p.m. without a break. Evening, to Cologne.

19 December, Tuesday. Cologne. Felten & Guilleaume supervisory board agrees to purchase of Collart.[233] To Essen at midday. Rain, dreary afternoon, read: Michaelis, *1812*.[234] Evening at Bodenhausen's.

20 December, Wednesday. Morning Goldschmidt supervisory board.[235] Midday, left for Berlin with Deutsch and Mosler.

22 December, Friday. Evening, Harden here; brings *Köpfe*[236] and

---

[229] The special committee started serious negotiations after the Krupp deal had come to naught. See fn. 223 above.   [230] *Zur Kritik der Zeit.*

[231] John Leishman.   [232] See fnn. 92 and 102 above.

[233] At this meeting the purchase, at a price of 6,838,000 marks, was concluded. Felten & Guilleaume paid with its own shares. The meeting also decided to put Escher Wyss on to a sound footing. For this purpose a committee was set up consisting of Gnauth, Zander, Deutsch, and Rathenau. The committee met on 12 January 1912 with Director Zoelly present, and recommended that the capital be reduced from 10 million francs to 6.5 million francs. The difference of 3.5 million francs was used to cover the losses. On 1 and 2 February Deutsch, Zander, and Gnauth met in Zurich, and after a thorough inspection of the company concluded that restoration to profitability would be difficult but not hopeless. Deutsch in particular suggested a reform of the invoice and receipt system. It would also be necessary to invest another 600,000 francs. Business prospects in France looked good for Escher Wyss, and therefore Felten & Guilleaume went ahead with the programme suggested by the committee. FG Archiv, V, vol. 13, Gnauth's report 7 February 1912.

[234] Sophus Michaelis, *1812. Der ewige Schlaf* (Berlin, 1912). Michaelis was a Danish poet and this book was translated by Marie Herzfeld into German.

[235] See fn. 199 above.

[236] Harden's four volumes about various personalities. They appeared between 1911 and 1924; the first twenty copies were bound in leather.

a paper-knife for Christmas. Tells the story of how, during the interval in negotiations, Kiderlen went to Chamonix with his French girl-friend. At their departure she left a letter lying about, intimate in content, critical, what is more, of Cambon. The letter came into the hands of the barber. This was discovered by Suse, also in Chamonix, who telegraphed Harden, who wrote a letter to Kiderlen. Kiderlen replied that he wanted to call on Harden immediately but had to go on a journey. Suse succeeded, following Harden's instructions, in securing the letter without handing over any money. But three days later, Kiderlen, as he was expressing his thanks, also remarked that the indiscretion had in fact been intentional(!).[237]

23 December, Saturday. Evening, Deutsches Theater. *Offiziere* by Unruh.[238] Much impressed, wrote to him.—Christmas present from Carl von Bülow, Kleefeld.

24 December, Sunday. Lunch and dinner, Schiffbauerdamm.

25 December, Monday. To Freienwalde. Evening, to Munich and Neubeuren.[239]

26 December, Tuesday. Arrived midday. Present: Bodenhausen, Countess Degenfeld and mother, Price Collier who had come with me, Heymels. Later, Thursday evening, Hofmannsthals and Behn. Left Friday morning. In Munich at Bernheimer's, Sternheim at Höllriegelskreuth.[240] Evening, with Hahn. Departed.

30 December, Saturday. Evening, at von Hindenburg's. Miss von Olfers tells about 1840. Tieck, lame, with dark-blue eyes, reads 'Blaubart' out loud. Bettina lives in In den Zelten.[241] Young girls paint in her house. Her dress consists of a square of material through

[237] At the end of August Kiderlen went on a trip from Geneva to Chamonix with the Russian Baroness de Jonina. *Grosse Politik*, vol. 29, p. 337; Hallgarten, *Imperialismus*, vol. ii, pp. 255 and 262. It has not yet been established whether German policy was prejudicially influenced by Kiderlen's escapades.

[238] Rathenau congratulated Unruh with the words: 'Prussia has not been so glorified for a long while. The time will come when it will thank you.' Rathenau, *Briefe*, p. 86, Rathenau to Unruh, 15 December 1911. The date must be wrong. The editor of the *Briefe* should have put 23 December as the date for the letter. The first performance took place on the 15th, but Rathenau did not see that performance. Unruh remembers that Rathenau also invited him to dinner in the Automobilclub for a Friday, which must have been the 29th of December. Schulin (ed.), *Walther Rathenau. Hauptwerke und Gespräche*, p. 672.

[239] Freiherr von Wendelstadt's residence. He was Bodenhausen's brother-in-law.

[240] Sternheim's residence.

[241] In den Zelten was a district in the centre of Berlin.

which she pokes her head. Frankfurt dialect. Her daughters are not like her. Goethe's letters have been turned over to the Oriollas who keep them under lock and key. Bettina is painting a battle of the Amazons. Varnhagen, vain, disagreeable. The family doctor tells how Varnhagen had often beaten Rahel 'black and blue'. Olfers's mother had a great regard for Rahel. Friedrich Wilhelm IV and Wilhelm I gave small parties.[242] Diplomats were not invited. Typical of the atmosphere at court: Count Platen said, as Ambassador von Müller (the Hague) was mentioned; he belongs to the Bülow's set too. He has played the piano at Nordeney.[243]

31 December, Sunday. Morning, Franz Oppenheimer came to call. About a factory and living-centre near Berlin.[244] I disclosed to him that we had pursued the idea ten years before and dropped it because of opposition from the Social Democrats. Lunch-time, on the same subject with Emil Rathenau. We want to put the idea forward again. Evening, 6 p.m., Ludwig Stein to tea. He tries to win me over to *Nord and Süd* which he has taken over.[245] His alleged conversation with Bülow and wife, 'whether Walther could become a minister in Prussia'.[246] I told him I would never have entered Government service.

[242] The contents of this passage are very similar to a letter written to Lili Deutsch, which Kessler published in his biography. Here it is the sister of the authoress Marie von Olfers who tells the story and certain participants are different. Kessler—without giving a date—refers to the letter as an 'early' one in the correspondence between Rathenau and Lili Deutsch. So it looks as if there were two different occasions on which German romanticism was mentioned. Kessler, *Rathenau*, p. 52 f.

[243] Bülow's summer residence.

[244] Buddensieg and Rogge, *Industriekultur*, pp. 129 and 132 ff.

[245] Stein planned a special edition of his paper *Nord und Süd* which was to improve the climate between Britain and Germany. The issue was published in August 1912.

[246] The position was more likely to be that of a Secretary of State than a Prussian minister. See the diary entry for 1 June 1911.

DIARY FOR 1912

1 January, Monday. Afternoon, 5 o'clock, tea at Mrs Collier's. Strange conversation with Baroness Schröder. Evening, at the theatre (*Fünf Frankfurter*)[1] with Sternheims; then at the club for a long while.

Very busy. Schlesische Kleinbahnen, Nieske, Wiens, Michaelis, Carl Stein (Deutz), Firle etc.

3 January, Wednesday. Evening, at Wölfflin's. Talked to Sering. Also: Goldschmidt, Justi, Lepsius, etc. Justi tells how Mrs Weissbach spent an hour talking intensely to Wölfflin about her husband. Finally he answered: I'll have to go to Wertheim's soon, Rosa says crockery has become expensive.[2]

4 January, Thursday. AEG. Fricke-Heinlein.

11 January, Thursday. *Zur Kritik der Zeit* published.[3]

In this book Rathenau criticized the effects of industrialization, the 'mechanical age', as he called it: the loss of ideals, and the cultural stagnation compared with the previous rich variety of life. He put these changes down to 'mechanization', or in other words to the development of capitalism. Apart from Marx, whom Rathenau had read much earlier, in the 1890s, it was Werner Sombart and Max Weber who influenced him in his view of the causes of capitalism, although Rathenau did in fact provide a different explanation. Unlike those two writers, Rathenau describes the process of industrialization, and its effect on all aspects of life. To him the reason for all this was the rapid increase in population during the last century. This growth made industrialization inevitable, and consequently the 'lower' strata of society moved upwards and gradually pushed aside the Nordic upper groups. Social change and industrialization were made possible through science and technology, which to Rathenau were intellectual disciplines and as such all-important to him personally.

Rathenau's observations on social change were based on a racialist point of view emanating from Gobineau and Chamberlain. Thus the imaginative Nordic race was threatened by the rise of previously inferior races, who were largely responsible for the modern 'soulless' world. Although Rathenau was pessimistic about the immediate future he was in the long term a social optimist. He

---

[1] Comedy by Carl Rössler about the rise of the Rothschild family.
[2] A. Wertheim GmbH, a famous Berlin department store.
[3] Kessler, *Rathenau*, pp. 100 and 114 ff. G. Jenne, 'Sein Philosophieren', in Harttung *et al.* (eds.), *Rathenau. Schriften*. See now Schulin (ed.), *Walther Rathenau. Hauptwerke und Gespräche* for a new edition of Rathenau's book, an evaluation of the reviews, and an interpretation of the work. See also J. Joll, *Three Intellectuals*, pp. 83-9; Berglar, *Walther Rathenau*, pp. 112-29.

considered that the otherwise deplorable effects of industrialization could be overcome, provided it was able to remove economically-based hardship. This would be desirable in order to achieve a higher spiritual level. So his concept of 'mechanization' was a means to an end—a way to the 'evolution of the soul'. Industrial capitalism offered in Rathenau's mind the chance of a better society which would replace the materialism of his age.

The book was widely read, and its edition, outside the Collected Works, reached the figure of 20,000 by 1922. Many reviews appeared. They dealt either with general aspects, the development of capitalism, or his racialist views. Rathenau's attempts to link social change to a racialist outlook attracted strong criticism, not so much because some of the reviewers did not share his views, but more because Rathenau's exposition was not sufficiently systematic. Among Pan-German critics his pessimism about the future of the Nordic race was rejected, and his method of using Chamberlain's ideas was resented.

Rathenau's book belonged to a genre of works which helped people to cope somehow with the rapid changes they witnessed every day. It was not surprising that Oswald Spengler later said that he learnt much about the character of the 'present crisis' through reading *Zur Kritik der Zeit*.

12 January Friday. Election day.[4] Evening, at Harden's till 1.30 a.m.

14 January, Sunday. Afternoon at Mrs von Hindenburg's, who asks for advice. Evening at Stern's (Grönvolds back).

15 January, Monday. Tschöpeln. Lunch at the Auto Club with Dehmels and Heymel. Evening Justi and Wille here.

16 January, Tuesday. In Köslin with Zander, Jeidels, Konschewski.[5]

17 January, Wednesday. Afternoon, 4.30 p.m. at Mrs vom Rath's, music. Evening, 10 p.m. at Baroness von Schröder's. Two von Bronsarts.

18 January, Thursday. Wiens. Lunch at the club; Collier reads out his article on the press. Evening, Müller with the financial statement (*circa* 4 million).[6] Max Liebermann.

[4] Main election for the Reichstag. The subsequent second ballot took place on 20, 22, and 25 January. On 12 January Rathenau also met Gnauth from Felten & Guilleaume to discuss the purchase of Collart and the situation of Escher Wyss. When he was with Harden they discussed the elections and the third Moltke–Harden trial, and probably mentioned Lili Deutsch. A day later Rathenau wrote to Harden: 'Odd times, in which the people hold once more their fate in their hands! History works with dramatic means.' Hellige (ed.), Rathenau–Harden, Rathenau to Harden, 13 January 1912.

[5] Paper factory in Köslin which the BHG had been trying to put on to a sound footing for some time. Fürstenberg, *Carl Fürstenberg*, p. 135. See also Fürstenberg, 'Erinnerung an Walther Rathenau', in Kessler, *Rathenau*, p. 436.

[6] This sum was probably the difference between the undeclared net profits and the amount paid out in dividends by the BHG. On the same day Harden wrote to Rathenau,

19 January, Friday. Schöneweide.[7] A lot of letters about the book: Bethmann, Burchardt, Gaul, Ballin, Hofmannsthal, etc.

20 January, Saturday. Lunch at the Justi's with Wille about arrangement of the Casa Bartholdi and Schinkel rooms.[8] Afternoon with Oppenheimer at the AEG about the town project.[9]

21 January, Sunday. Lunch with Ilse (Lieutenant-Colonel) Schiffbauerdamm; afternoon, visit from Henckel, still half paralysed. Then to Fischer's for the first time.[10] Peter Nansen, Emil Ludwig, Christophe. Evening, Holzmann here.

22 January, Monday. Zander, aircraft. Evening, news from Geitner about the second ballot.[11]

24 January, Wednesday. Evening, at Paul Herz's. Talked to Lewald who thinks that a swing to the Left is necessary.

25 January, Thursday. Krebs, Nischwitz. Evening at Hollmann's. Hutten-Czapsky said of Korn, who was present, 'the only man who can say whether Krupp is still alive'.[12] He takes Schorlemer to be the next Chancellor and thinks that the question was acute in the autumn.[13]

---

thanking him for his book. Then he commented on the election results of the first ballot in which the National Liberals had only won four seats and the Progressives none. 'For the people with modest means a difficult time lies ahead. It hurts more, really deeply, that our country will [now] be described in the world as a cage guarded by *Junker* and clerics.' Hellige (ed.), Rathenau–Harden, Harden to Rathenau, 18 January 1911.

[7] This day was the anniversary of the death of Erich Rathenau, Walther's younger brother. The grave was in Schöneweide. Just before his departure for Schöneweide Rathenau dropped a note to Harden telling him that the Government reckoned on a majority of the so-called opposition parties of 210 seats, with the SPD capturing 120. Ibid., Rathenau to Harden, 19 January 1912.

[8] At the National Gallery, Berlin.

[9] See diary entry for 31 December 1911.

[10] He enjoyed going to the house of his publisher. He met there among other authors Gabriele Reuter, Annette Kolb, Oskar Loerke, Jakob Wassermann, Richard Dehmel, Otto Flake, Hermann Bahr, Emil Ludwig, Franz Blei and possibly George Bernard Shaw. The company at Fischer's also separated him more from Harden.

[11] The first ballot had produced 206 mandates, the second ballot of 20 January 78, and that of 22 January 80.

[12] After the death of Friedrich Alfred Krupp in 1902 a rumour circulated that he had not died but fled from Essen. He had been accused of being a homosexual. Korn was his private secretary.

[13] A remark of the Chancellor's in September 1911 might indicate that he had feared that the Kaiser would drop him. Görlitz, *Der Kaiser*, p. 91. See fn. 7 above for a prediction by the Government.

At 12 p.m. Geitner telephones the latest results of the final ballot: 198 anti-bloc votes.[14]

26 January, Friday. Letter to Lichtwark agreeing to publication.[15] Afternoon, Fürstenberg regarding annual balance BHG 9½% [dividends].[16]

27 January, Saturday. Wiens, Rothe, Lambert's appointment; 5 p.m., anniversary dinner in honour of the Kaiser at the Aero Club, presided. Speech. Home at 9 p.m.

28 January, Sunday. 23 gentlemen to lunch. Wölfflin, Brahm, Grönvold, Reicke, Heimann, Kardorff, Ewers, Lörke, Collier, Harrach, Gaul, Behrens, Walser, Kyser, etc.

30 January, Tuesday. Kunze, Zapf.[17] Evening at Leonie Schwabach's. Afterwards at the Esplanade [Hotel] with Mumm.

31 January, Wednesday. Fricke; lunch at Paul von Schwabach's. Amusing scene: Oppenheimer talked to Friedlaender about bills of exchange which his son was taking to school. I explained to both of them how the next generation would not have to learn *Collynamen*[18] by heart and would be able to devote themselves to their inclinations.

1 February, Thursday. Evening, Lichtwark to dinner. Publication of *Der rheinische Bismarck* decided on.

2 February, Friday. Julius Hofmann to dinner.

4 February, Sunday. Afternoon with Pauli, Esplanade [Hotel]. Evening, big *fête* at Friedlaender's. Letter from Bülow.[19]

---

[14] At the final ballot on 25 January the last 33 deputies were elected. The National Liberals, Progressives, and Social Democrats won 198 of 397 seats over all. Thus the Centre-Conservative bloc was defeated.

[15] See p. 102.

[16] See fn. 6 above. On the same day Rathenau informed Zapf of his preference among the applications for the directorship of Collart. FG Archiv, A/I/9–0307, Rathenau to Zapf, 26 January 1912.

[17] After the meeting with Zapf Rathenau informed Felten & Guilleaume that he wanted certain changes in the statutes of Collart to enable the subsidiary to raise capital on the German market. Ibid., Rathenau to Felten & Guilleaume, 30 January 1912.

[18] So far it has not been possible to establish the meaning of this expression.

[19] The letter has not been found.

5 February, Monday. At the club with Zander. Evening at Brahm's, birthday. Next to Else Lehmann. Fischers, Schlenther, etc. Talked to Wolff: proposed to him, should the National Liberals fail, an alliance with the Centre for constituency reform.[20]

8 February, Thursday. Evening, Sternheim at the club.

9 February, Friday. Engelhardt, Zander, Frey, Salomon, Laufenburg, Elektrobank, etc.

10 February, Saturday. Lunch at the club, Harrach, Sternheim, Heymel. Evening, Russian ballet.[21] Karsavina, Nijinsky. Deeply impressed. At the Kaiserhof [Hotel] till late with Brahm and Fischers.

11 February, Sunday. Lunch at Holzmann's. Justi, Quast. Then to Endells'. Marcus Behmer. Evening at Mrs von Boddien's. Varnbülers, Mutzenbechers, Sierstorpff. Finally, at Harrach's. Bethmann and wife. Depressed. Concerned about the middle-class parties.[22] Haldane's visit apparently not a success.[23]

12 February, Monday. Spinning mills. Club: Harrach, Collier, Heymel, Bodenhausen. Evening: Eysler. Party of screaming people.

13 February, Tuesday. Spinning mills. Lunch at Hollmann's. Kaiser had long conversation with Simon and myself, without other witnesses. The Kaiser's train of thought was as follows: 'The English tell and stomach the truth. Haldane discovered it and was very depressed. The English realize that they will have to reckon with

---

[20] The redrawing of the constituency boundaries was a Liberal aim, as the existing system favoured the countryside and hence the Conservatives.

[21] Diaghilev's ballet.

[22] The question was whether the Liberal parties and the Centre Party would support Government policy.

[23] Haldane, the British Secretary for War, visited Berlin from 8 to 11 February 1912 to discuss the possibility both of Germany cutting down its ship-building and of a political settlement between Germany and England. In a letter to the Kaiser Ballin wrote that Haldane was pleased with his reception in Berlin, 'although at the same time he felt that more might have been done in view of the great concessions expected from England'. (Letter of 9/10 February 1912.) The Kaiser commented: 'Donnerwetter das ist stark!' [Damn it all, that's strong!]. Because German concessions were small Haldane seemed unable to consent to a political agreement such as Bethmann had in mind. As a result Haldane was only prepared to discuss at home a promise by both powers to observe neutrality if either power were attacked in a war of aggression. Cecil, *Ballin*, p. 190; Fischer, *Krieg der Illusionen*, pp. 182–92; Steinberg, 'Diplomatie als Wille und Vorstellung'; Kennedy, *The Rise of Anglo-German Antagonism*, pp. 450 ff.

our fleet. They seek an agreement. Haldane received the answer: political questions will have to be clarified first. Churchill's speech[24] was very unpleasant for Haldane. Churchill, a daredevil, spoke on his own account. This was different from Lloyd George who at that time had been asked by the Cabinet.[25] The situation of the summer puts the whole thing in another light: France, not England, is the disturber of peace. Intrigues by both Cambons. England will not let herself be continually misused. Interesting digression on Alfred von Rothschild.[26] "My most honoured friend." Looks like the deceased Sagan.[27] Came to him to say: the house of Rothschild trusts in the Kaiser's love of peace and is at his disposal in France and England. He did not understand this until the autumn. But now Rothschild has gone to Grey on behalf of the City and has told them that he would not get any money for the war (?!). Grey, an unscrupulous diplomat, had made the mistake of acting against the tradition *to take the opposition in confidence*, of not informing anyone of his plans. Neither with regard to the plan to increase the number of those raised to the peerage,[28] nor with regard to the war. His high decoration (Garter) merely signified a retreat.[29] The Kaiser only wanted to go to Cowes again, then he would settle everything. The King trusted him. His plan was: United States of Europe against America.[30] The English are not unsympathetic to this. Five states (incl. France) could do something. The French are afraid now. Kiderlen has made the same mistake as Grey, against the Kaiser's advice: *Not to take England in confidence* [sic].'[31]

[24] In a speech made in Glasgow on 9 February 1912 Churchill described the German fleet as a luxury.

[25] See diary entry for 28 August 1911. Lloyd George's Mansion House speech of 21 July 1911.

[26] Rothschild had probably, together with the Radical Liberals, opposed any intensification of the Morocco Crisis.

[27] Louis, Duc de Talleyrand-Périgord.

[28] In order to put through the House of Lords the Parliament Act, which was to guarantee Parliament greater independence from the veto of the House of Lords, Asquith's Liberal Government contemplated having a large number of peers created. After the Parliament Act was passed by the House of Lords in August 1911, the Government gave up the idea of reforming the House of Lords. Ensor, *England*, pp. 420–31.

[29] It was neither Grey's thwarted desire to reduce the hereditary element in the House of Lords, nor his supposed war plans, that brought him the Order of the Garter, but rather his efforts for a peaceful settlement of the Morocco Crisis. See also the diary entry for 16 February 1912.

[30] In contrast to earlier remarks of this kind by the Kaiser, England is here drawn into a plan for a European Federation. Rathenau shared this opinion and published it later, on 25 December 1913, in an article 'Deutsche Gefahren und Neue Ziele', which was reprinted in Rathenau, *Gesammelte Schriften*, vol. i. See also Fischer, *Krieg der Illusionen*, pp. 201 ff. In Britain similar ideas were published by Sir Max Waechter.

[31] So far written evidence of the Kaiser's advice has not been found. Generally speaking the Kaiser was not pleased with the way Kiderlen handled the affair right from the beginning,

Then on Italy for a long while.[32] The Italians' desperate situation. A railway could not be built because of sand. Oasis only a few acres large. An airman reconnoitred an Arab camp of 40,000 men in the south. Italian officers good, soldiers mediocre. Reason for the war: Banca Romana [Banca di Roma] and a colonel's report to the speculators' advantage. In desperation the colonel, 'like Judas', sought and found death in war. Italian losses: 7,000. Mistake of the Curia to talk about a 'crusade'; this was the cause of the [Muslim] Holy War. Curia had an interest in the Banca Romana. He was rather pleased with the Italian situation, but this 'in strictest confidence'.

Clear, pointed presentation throughout.

Evening, at von Schröder's. Harrach, Comtesse Keyserling, von Mackensen.

14 February, Wednesday. Thiederhall, Elektro-Stahl. *Der rheinische Bismarck* published. Freienwalde photographs to the Kaiser, Nischwitz, Zander, etc. Evening, Mamroth.

Very heavy work-load for days, engaged almost every minute of the day.

16 February, Friday. Ballin says: Bethmann will go after the English negotiations have been settled.[33] Successor: Marschall (?). Grey got the decoration because he carried out the English Morocco guarantee

---

neither was he kept well informed by Kiderlen. See the Kaiser's numerous marginal comments on German Foreign Office reports, PA Bonn, Frankreich 102, 8, vol. i. Mortimer, 'Commercial Interests and German Diplomacy in the Agadir Crisis', p. 450. For Kiderlen's offers of resignation see Jäckh (ed.), *Kiderlen-Waechter*, vol. ii, pp. 128–34; Fischer, *Krieg der Illusionen*, pp. 123–7.

[32] The war between Italy and Turkey was provoked by the Italian occupation of Tripoli in September 1911. While the German Foreign Office backed Italy as Germany's ally, the Kaiser favoured the Turks. In the Peace Treaty of Lausanne in October 1912 Libya became an Italian colony. Turkish resistance, backed by the Senussi, virtually restricted the Italian conquest to the coastal areas. Before the war the Banco di Roma had, at the suggestion of the Italian Government, been making investments in Tripolitania. These were not sufficiently successful and the bank then forced the Government to give it active support. The anti-clerical Government thus supported clerical enterprises, as Jagow put it. *Grosse Politik*, vol. 30/1, pp. 26–9, Jagow to Bethmann, 1 March 1911; ibid., p. 31, Jagow to Bethmann, 13 June 1911; ibid., pp. 288–97, Marschall to Bethmann, 7 February 1912.

[33] For further Anglo-German negotiations after Haldane's departure from Berlin see Cecil, *Ballin*, pp. 190–6. The failure of the Haldane mission and Bethmann's delaying tactics regarding the Navy Bill made his relations with the Kaiser increasingly difficult. A telegram directly from the Kaiser to Ambassador Metternich enabled Bethmann to tender his offer of resignation on 5 March 1912. Jäckh (ed.), *Kiderlen-Waechter*, vol. ii, pp. 159–61; Görlitz, *Der Kaiser*, pp. 116 f. The real reason was that the Kaiser demanded that Bethmann publish the Navy and Army Bills. The Chancellor scored a success when the Kaiser, faced with the threat of Bethmann's resignation, temporarily abandoned his demand. Fischer, *Krieg der Illusionen*, pp. 188 f.; Gutsche, *Aufstieg und Fall*, pp. 94 f.

peacefully. Now the guarantee relationship had been dealt with and England was free as regards France.

17 February, Saturday. Fischer is preparing a new impression of *Kritik der Zeit.* A lot of comments on the *Rheinische Bismarck* in the papers.

18 February, Sunday. Lunch at Hindenburg's. Afternoon at Countess Schlippenbach's. Evening at the club with Lichtwark. After dinner Lewald, von Miller, Albert come and sit with us. Lewald against Wermuth's policy.[34] Thinks he ought to go. Delbrück said to him about Posadowsky's first speech, he didn't believe that Posadowsky had had himself elected to be a 'Deputy'.[35]

Weather warm and springlike. [My] mood changing. What a dish I'll make for the young dons in 1950! I can't make anything of my own age, it does not seem to produce any causes which attract me.

19 February, Monday. Evening at Fritz and Edith Andreae's.

20 February, Tuesday. Schweiz negotiations. Firle. Evening, Stehr to dinner.

21 February, Wednesday. BHG commissioned to make financial statement for Elektrotreuhand [Electrical Mortgage Bank.][36] Evening, Kröpelins to dinner.

22 February, Thursday. BHG meeting for annual statement. Before that, Felten & Guilleaume and Treuhandbank [Mortgate Bank for the Electrical Industry].[37] Evening, at Mrs Begas with Kandt, Schmitz, etc.

[34] Wermuth had eventually agreed to Army and Navy Bills despite the fact that he favoured the army. He had handed in his resignation but was convinced by Bethmann that he should stay, when the latter offered him the introduction of the death duty. Wermuth's original opposition had also been motivated by considerations of fiscal policy, for his principle—'No expenditure without adequate revenue'—seemed to be in danger. Fischer *Krieg der Illusionen*, pp. 195–201.

[35] In 1912 Posadowsky had been elected to the Reichstag for the first time, but he did not join any party.

[36] The Elektrotreuhand AG was founded jointly by Siemens and the AEG in 1908. Its joint-stock capital amounted to 30 million marks of which 25 per cent were paid in. The company was to advance credits to the central and local administration for the construction of electrical installations. The surety offered in return was to enable the company to issue bonds.

[37] The Treuhandbank für die elektrische Industrie was founded by the Felten Group in 1909 with a joint-stock capital of 25 million marks. It was to gain orders for Felten & Guilleaume when the recession of 1908 began to make itself felt, but the company took up its operations too late to prevent Felten & Guilleaume-Lahmeyerwerke from sliding into the red. Although the AEG did not need another financial institution when it took over Felten & Guilleaume, the Treuhandbank had won enough customers to make it worthwhile for the AEG to take over 40 per cent of its capital in 1911. The Elektrobank controlled another 12 per cent. Rathenau had also helped to reorganize the bank so its survival was assured.

23 February, Friday. Evening, to Milan, southern express. Arrived 10.20 a.m.

24 February, Saturday. Evening, 8.20 p.m. at Cova's with Frey and Zander.

25 February, Sunday. Morning, Sviluppo meeting. Afternoon, visited Joëls. News comes of the suicide of a friend of theirs. Evening, Scala: *Isabeau* by Mascagni, mediocre.[38] Phenomenal tenor, new discovery—de Muro.

26 February, Monday. Early, 9 a.m., to Genoa, Miramar [Hotel]. Afternoon, Officine and Central [power-] stations.

27 February, Tuesday. Officine; afternoon, Unione; 5 o'clock to Sestri by car, then to Portofino.
    9 p.m., visited Hauptmanns, Castello Paraggi; his enthusiasm for projected management of the Lessingtheater-Ensemble.[39]
    Stayed the night at vom Mumm's, San Giorgio. Together with von Huhn and the Twombley couple.

28 February, Wednesday. Lunch with Hauptmann's at Mumm's. Afternoon, back to Genoa with Huhn. Late that night at Bellinzona. Caught a bad cold.

29 February, Thursday. Early walk through Bellinzona, then to Bodio. Lunch-time, on to Strasbourg. Arrived 10 p.m. To Leoni's.

1 March, Friday. Afternoon, toured the new medical buildings, then Laufenburg meeting. Left 7 p.m.

2 March, Saturday. Early, 7.36 a.m., in Berlin. DUEG general meeting. Conversation with Gwinner about Bergmann.[40] Report to Emil Rathenau. Afternoon, visited by Emil Ludwig.

3 March, Sunday. Morning, to Gross-Besten to collect the dog (supposedly trained).[41] Evening, at Gaul's.

[38] The opera was performed for the first time in 1911.
[39] The Lessingtheater was established on the Friedrich-Carl-Ufer in Berlin in 1888. It was, like the Volksbühne, a 'contemporary theatre'.
[40] See diary entry for 2 December 1911, and fn. 227, above.
[41] The reference is probably to the dog Eitel which Rathenau had already taken to a trainer once before. See diary entry for 3 July 1911.

4 March, Monday. Lunch, at Countess Schlippenbach's, with Hey-kings, Schotts, Countess Bethusy. Then to Burchardt's where Zweig had invited Verhaeren, Reinhardt, Holländer, Stucken.

Afternoon, Grunwald called about the Lessingtheater-Ensemble. Evening, Philharmonie, Mass in B Minor.

5 March, Tuesday. Norddeutsche Seekabel Werke [North German Sea Cable Works].[42] Afternoon, conference on organization of Schweighütte [Schweig Glass and Porcelain Works] and Aktien-Hütte. [United Lausitz Glassworks].[43] Evening at von Arnswaldt's. Discussion with Sudermann. Lunch-time, visit from von Rechenberg.

6 March, Wednesday. Evening, at Bethmann's. Present: Countess Harrach, Schoen and wife, Countess Wolkenstein, Mrs von Beth-mann, née Countess Harrach, Rantzau, Stumm, Mrs von Speck.

Long conversation with Bethmann about Rechenberg. Bethmann tells how the Kaiser had played the *Rheinische Bismarck* off against him (Bethmann). Little optimism about England.[44] Dernburg makes tentative approaches.[45]

8 March, Friday. Evening, after Paul von Mendelssohn, left for Cologne.

9 March, Saturday. Cologne, visits throughout the day from candidates for Collart directorate.[46]

10 March, Sunday. By car to Antweiler, clay works.[47] Lunch at Altenahr. Then Ringen clay-pit; travel home from Coblenz.

[42] From 1899 Germany began to install its own sea cables to America. Felten & Guilleaume took the lead and founded the Deutsch-Atlantische Telegraphengesellschaft [German Atlantic Telegraph Company]. To produce the new cables Felten & Guilleaume and the Deutsch-Atlantische Telegraphengesellschaft set up the Norddeutsche Seekabelwerke in Nordenham in 1899.

[43] Both works were at Weisswasser and belonged to the AEG. The Vereinigte Lausitzer Glaswerke had been founded in 1905 and the Schweigsche Glas-und Porzellanwerke in 1910.

[44] After the failure of the Haldane mission the Chancellor saw little possibility of continuing the discussions at a promising level although he asked Metternich and Ballin to maintain good relations with the English Government. Cecil, *Ballin*, p. 192; Görlitz (ed.), *Der Kaiser*, pp. 117 f.

[45] Rathenau had become estranged from Dernburg during and after the second journey to Africa in 1908. See pp. 76 f.

[46] On 2 March Rathenau had written to Zapf, suggesting that the interviews should be held on the 9th, two in the morning and two in the afternoon. FG Archiv, A/I/9–0307, Rathenau to Zapf, 2 March 1912.

[47] Ibid.; Rathenau informed Zapf that he had to inspect the claypits on 10 March 1912.

11 March, Monday. Abo, Rheingau, Königsberg.[48]

12 March, Tuesday. Lausitz general meeting;[49] lunch at the club: Monnier and Count Pourtalès. Afternoon, Bitterfeld Electrochemische Werke. Evening, at the club with Blei and von Unruh.

13 March, Wednesday. Discussion with Berliner about Bergmann.

14 March, Thursday. The same thing with Gwinner.

15 March, Friday. In Cologne on account of the Land- und Seekabel-Werke [Land and Sea Cable Works].[50] Plan for new rights issue. Afternoon and evening, Düsseldorf; opera: *Martha.*[51] Ridiculous impression.

16 March, Saturday. Berlin.

17 March, Sunday. Morning, Schiller Foundation meeting.[52] Lunch at Privy Councillor Müller's. Then Kalckreuth to tea in the Grunewald.

18 March, Monday. Evening, Schäfer, Heymel, Behn to dinner.

19 March, Tuesday. Telegraph companies. Lunch at Hiller's (invited by Reinsch), Hirst, editor of the *Economist*. Evening, at Varnbüler's. Talked to Stumm. I advised him to let a clear answer be made through the press to yesterday's speech by Churchill.[53] Disarmament is possible as soon as the *entente* with France is made harmless through assurances of neutrality.[54] He complains about the plans for the fleet.

[48] All three power-station companies had been founded by the ELG, a subsidiary of the AEG.

[49] The company did not generate its own electricity, but merely distributed it. It had been founded by the ELG.

[50] The Land- und Seekabel-Werke had been founded in 1898. By 1905 Felten & Guilleaume had gained complete control of the company.

[51] An opera by Flotow, of which Rathenau had a low opinion. Rathenau, *Briefe*, vol. i, p. 94. Rathenau to Kroepelin, 25 February 1912.

[52] A foundation set up in 1859 to promote German writers.

[53] In his speech to the House of Commons on 18 March 1912 Churchill declared that England would immediately follow the example of a German moratorium in naval expansion. If Germany did not build her next three ships, then England would be spared the building of five ships. With them, so he argued, Germany could have won a greater maritime victory than it could normally have hoped for.

[54] Rathenau shared the opinion of Ballin, Bethmann, Kiderlen, and the Kaiser. They aimed for an English promise of neutrality in the event of a European war. But unlike the others Rathenau did not envisage a German attack on France.

22 March, Friday. At the club with Prof. Wolf (Breslau)[55] and Storz. Declined Wolf's strange proposal for mutual criticism. Evening at Mosler's.

23 March, Saturday. At Dehmel's suggestion letter and communication to Strübe (H. Burte).[56]

24 March, Sunday. Lunch, Fürstenburg.

25 March, Monday. Schulz-Knaudt, Oberschlesische Kleinbahnen [Upper Silesian Light Railways].[57]

26 March, Tuesday. Freienwalde, waterworks.

28 March, Thursday. To the Minister of War about aircraft.[58] Afternoon, Permutit;[59] evening at Friedlaender's. Article for *Neue Freie Presse*.[60]

In his article 'England und Wir' Rathenau accepted wars as inevitable phases in a nation's life: 'Wars of fate are examinations which a nation has to go through in order to pass on to the next [higher] form.' He raised the question whether Germany could maintain its position as a naval, colonial, and world power without a war with England: 'Germany has no political ambitions. It is satisfied with a bare sixth of European influence . . . But it cannot avoid securing its consumption and sales as well as protecting its trade and its colonies. These are however functions of a sea power; thus Germany is forced to claim the status of a sea power.' He evaded answering the question by observing that Germany's fate depended on what the other powers decided. Because the initiative had to come from England, he went on, the decision to reach an agreement on neutrality between the two countries could only be made in England. Only then would Germany be in a position to follow the English lead with a suggestion for bilateral arms limitation. If England did not propose a treaty of neutrality to Germany, and if the *entente* continued to exist, then, concluded Rathenau,

[55] It is possible that Rathenau had borrowed certain ideas about a *Mitteleuropa* from Wolf, who was the founder of the Mitteleuropäischer Wirtschaftsverein (Central European Economic Association).

[56] On 21 March Dehmel had written to Rathenau and had asked him for financial support for Strübe. Rathenau complied and informed Dehmel of his willingness to help, on the 22nd. Staatsbibliothek Hamburg, Nachlass Dehmel.

[57] Rathenau represented the AEG's predominant influence on the board.

[58] The Minister of War was J. von Heeringen. For Rathenau's considerable interest in the development of the aircraft industry, see D. G. Williamson, 'Walther Rathenau: A Study', p. 124. See diary entry for 23 March 1911 and fn. 122.

[59] The Permutit AG on whose supervisory board Rathenau sat was founded in Berlin in 1902. One of its main tasks was to develop machinery for purifying and softening water, cleaning swimming-pools, and treating sewage.

[60] 'England und wir, eine Philippika' [England and ourselves: A Philippic], *Neue Freie Presse*, Vienna, 6 April 1912; Rathenau, *Gesammelte Schriften*, vol. i.

'we have to regard Britain as an enemy'. To remove England's supicion that
Germany would attack France in the event of an Anglo-German treaty of
neutrality, Rathenau referred to the 'credit which the German Reich had
politically gained in its mission as a peace-power'. Apart from that, Rathenau
believed that the risks and industrial upheavals caused by a war were so high
that both represented an effective deterrent.

He then analysed, on a broad level, the basis of current Anglo-German
tensions:

'England, the cleverest and most truly political nation on earth, understands the
situation fully. England does not really hate us, but she feels that our ascent
represents a fourfold danger. Firstly, she is under the impression she has been
technically and industrially outstripped. Secondly, she feels obliged to intervene
against every dominating continental power which emerges. Thirdly, her colonial
structure would be shaken from within if supremacy at sea lost its value as a
historic dogma. Fourthly, the armaments race is becoming too expensive and,
given a constantly changing technology, success uncertain. The war which
England would have to wage would thus be a preventive war . . . If the war
were to end in decisive defeat for Germany, England would have only a few
years of peace.'

Further wars would follow 'until this rivalry was eliminated by the course of
world developments. We need not consider any other outcome of the war. But
whatever the result the United States would reap the main benefits, and the
American economy would develop on such a different level that possibly all other
economies would be subordinated to it.'

Rathenau argued that a situation like that would be new for England. 'For
England has, for two hundred years, been used to having all problems brought
before her curial throne and to deciding them at leisure. . . . a policy of phantasy,
passion, adventure and desperation was alien to the Doge-like wisdom of this
country.'

Rathenau asked himself what could be done in a situation like this: 'England
feels threatened because we are arming; England is arming because she feels
threatened; we are not arming because England is arming but we will not stop
arming ourselves as long as England is arming: a vicious circle.' As he saw it,
the only way out of this dilemma would be if England were prepared to offer
an agreement of neutrality which could coexist with the *entente cordiale*. He
believed the first step had to come from England because the 'political symmetry'
in Europe favoured Britain, and Germany was not allied with any of Britain's
enemies. If England would offer an agreement of neutrality then Germany and
Britain should manage to find a way to disarm. Obviously Rathenau did not
want to see that Germany appeared aggressive and expansionist. To him
Germany was in too vulnerable a position 'to move along the path of adventure
and violent expansion'. To preserve peace 'England would have to offer us
both hands'.

29 March, Friday. Frey, Rybnik, Russisch-Eisen [Russian Iron
Industry].[61] Plieninger-Diskonto [-gesellschaft]. Evening, at Prince
Donnersmarck's. After guests' departure long talk about the industrial

---

[61] The company was founded in 1900.

town to be founded. The same day Glatzel's case was settled in the Court of Appeal.

30 March, Saturday. BHG general meeting. Evening, at Fürstenberg's, then at Robert von Mendelssohn's.

31 March, Sunday. Morning, visited Karl Joël at Schlachtensee: mother and sister. Afternoon, at Mrs Harden's.[62]

1 April, Monday. MEW, Solingen.

2 April, Tuesday. Löwe general meeting. Diezelsky. Zander. Nischwitz. Run down and exhausted for several days now.

7 April, Sunday, to *13 April*, Saturday. Week of severe disappointment, which perhaps explains the preceding condition. Sunday at Freienwalde. 'England und Wir' in the *Neue Freie Presse*. Wednesday, I discovered that Lili Deutsch,[63] passionately embittered, has handed over to Harden that letter of mine from 1908 which expressed unfriendliness. Thursday morning, talked the matter out with Harden. He sends me the letter that afternoon. It is dated 22 March and talks about the terrible article against Dernburg which condemned and endangered my policy.[64] The acrimony of the letter can be explained by the excitement of the moment. All the more shocking that she handed it over in a cool, calculated way. I wrote a long, very conciliatory and cordial letter to Harden and travelled to Frankfurt.[65]

[62] It is not quite clear whether Rathenau refers to Harden's companion or to his wife. Harden divorced his first wife the actress Josefine Katharina Joost in 1898. He then lived with Selma Aaron, the daughter of a Berlin banker, marrying her in 1919 or 1920.

[63] In the privately printed edition the letter C stands for Lili Deutsch.

[64] In *Die Zukunft* of 21 March 1908, vol. lxii, pp. 410-14, Harden had ridiculed Dernburg because the latter had distanced himself in public from Harden and his position in the Eulenburg affair. Harden then went on to criticize Dernburg's colonial policy and his judgement that East Africa ought to remain a colony for the Africans. Rathenau was furious about Harden's criticism because he identified with Dernburg's colonial policy. After all, he had worked it out with Dernburg and Rechenberg and he now saw that his chances of a political career were being threatened. On 22 March 1908 Rathenau wrote a very embittered letter to Lili Deutsch, in which he complained about Harden. Rathenau's letter to Harden on 18 April 1908 healed the rift between the two men, but Harden did not know of Rathenau's letter to Lili Deutsch. (Hellige (ed.), Rathenau-Harden). See also H. Schnee, *Als letzter Gouverneur*, pp. 92 f.

[65] The letter referred to was dated 11 April 1912. In it Rathenau apologized for the tone of his letter of four years ago, but he made it clear that it was Harden's article which had caused all the trouble. Rathenau also blamed Lili Deutsch for passing on his letter to Harden four years after the incident. Finally he asked Harden to forget it all. For the resulting estrangement between Harden and Rathenau, see Joll, 'Rathenau and Harden'; Berglar, 'Harden und Rathenau'; D. G. Williamson, 'Walther Rathenau:, A Study', pp. 110-14; Hellige (ed.), Rathenau-Harden.

On the 13th, when I returned home, I found the answer, equally conciliatory, but mentioning most unpleasant details as between Lili
Deutsch and Harden before the letter was handed over. I was incapable of replying again. Saturday, Schlesische Elektrizitätswerke.

14 April, Sunday. Lunch at Cassirer's with Kardorff. Afternoon at
von Schröder's.

15 April, Monday. Morning, Körting; afternoon, Niles; evening, von
Unruh and departure for Cologne.

16 April, Tuesday. Cologne, Felten & Guilleaume.[66]

17 April, Wednesday. Back early; noon to Henckel's for lunch:
Princess,[67] personal physician, von Bismarck. Princess highly-
strung Russian, arrogant to begin with, then amiable. The Prince has
a mild attack. She shouts: Stand up and walk around the table.
Eclipse of the sun observed through pane of glass smeared with
soot. Monograms designed at table. Her age: self-conscious, rather
parvenu reference to the *Gotha* [handbook of the German and
European aristocracies]. Her position consists in 'guaranteeing' the
Prince's health. Nothing can happen to her: never ill, never confined
to bed—but as far as she is concerned it would not matter anyway.
Carolath's secretary dealt with, with regard to invitation. Talked to
the Prince about his land-plots. Also about Oberschlesische Elektritäts-
werke [Upper Silesian Electricity Works]. He grumbles about
Ratibor. He advises buying Begas's Prometheus: 'good speculation'.
The block of marble alone costs 45,000 marks, which is the price of
the sculpture. One 'would thus get the labour for nothing'.

18 April, Thursday. Evening, to Essen.

19 April, Friday. Goldschmidt, Essen. Returned with Mosler.
Evening, Berlin.

20 April, Saturday. Recommended Rechenberg to Mosler.

21 April, Sunday. Freienwalde. Waterworks nearly completed.
Rounded hilltop built.

[66] A meeting of the committee of the supervisory board was followed by a meeting
of the full supervisory board. In both meetings the results of the previous year, the acquisition of Collart, the sale of the share in the Treuhandbank, and the reorganization of a subsidiary in Nürnberg were discussed. FG Archiv.
[67] Katharine née von Slepzow; her previous marriage to Muraviev ended in divorce.

22 April, Monday. Evening at Varnbüler's. Cambon relates how Kiderlen has *'toute sorte de bêtes'*, among them *des hibous.*[68] He has *'lui envoyé des lapins'*, as feed, which was perhaps meant to call to mind *'poser des lapins'*.[69]

Varnbüler tells how Kiderlen and Cambon had exchanged photographs after the Morocco negotiations. Kiderlen wrote: *Au terrible adversaire et charmant ami.* Cambon: *Au charmant adversaire et terrible ami.*[70]

23 April, Tuesday. Rothe, von Simson, etc.

Somewhat less work. Arranged Victoriastrasse apartment.[71] Permutit—negotiations—frequent visits from Unruh.

28 April, Sunday. At Freienwalde, where the waterworks are being finished. Trees begin to blossom. Plans for Rixdorf-Gesundbrunnen underground railway, real estate business there, Gross-Schönebeck railway (Liebenberg).[72] Visit from Oppenheimer. Begin riding in the Grunewald and Tiergarten.

2 May, Thursday. At the club with Oppenheimer, van Eeden, Upton Sinclair, Gutkind.

3 May, Friday. Letter from Lili Deutsch. She wants to come to see me about things 'which are as serious for me as for her, perhaps more serious [for me]'.[73]

4 May, Saturday. Dream: In a twilight garden with a woman. Someone

---

[68] Probably means that Kiderlen had mad ideas, yet occasionally quite wise ones.

[69] Perhaps a reference to the fact that he had bluffed Kiderlen.

[70] Jäckh cites the dedication in a slightly different form. Cambon: 'A mon terrible ami!' Kiderlen: 'A mon aimable ennemi!' Jäckh (ed.), *Kiderlen-Waechter*, vol. ii, pp. 140 f.

[71] Rathenau took over the upper floor of his parents' house which was built by von Seidl in the Prussian classical style of the early nineteenth century.

[72] In 1894 the AEG had, in partnership with Philipp Holzmann, founded a company for the construction of underground railways. As it was generally held that Berlin's soil was unsuitable for underground tunnels, the AEG had first to prove that this was feasible. Only after a protracted struggle did the AEG manage to obtain the concession for building an underground line for most of the section from Gesundbrunnen to Neukölln. The contract was signed with the City in 1912 and building permission was granted in 1913. The delay was mainly due to land speculation. The projected line was 10.6 kilometres long, of which 1.6 kilometres were built as an overhead railway (see diary entry for 24 February 1914) and 9.3 kilometres as an underground one.

[73] On 5 May Rathenau wrote to Harden that he had received a letter from Lili Deutsch two days previously. She had asked whether she might come and see him, for it concerned 'things which are probably as serious for you as they are for me. Or rather, even more serious.' Rathenau added that he had written putting her off, 'but, as it was difficult for me, in an almost affectionate way'. Hellige (ed.), Rathenau–Harden, Rathenau to Harden, 5 May 1912.

calls to me 'my play is being put on'.[74] I turn round and step on to a dark stage. Everything silent and disordered. Auditorium empty and seats displaced. A director comes, I ask him: was the incident so bad? Contradicting his earlier shrieking, which I remember, he replies in an objective, natural and unsurprised manner. 'Yes, particularly since the public thronged to the box-office to get their money back.' Without any astonishment or regret I say: 'It was just at the wrong time', [and] turn to face the view which is opening up in the middle and step out alone into a sunlit garden (not the previous one) light-hearted and gay. At this instant Hermann wakes me.[75]

Evening, at von Schwabach's, long conversation with Cambon: he laments the bad state of relations. Kiderlen's only concern is for his own foreign success. '*Il faudrait causer*', to moderate the clauses.[76] He fears the moment when the Congo is handed over. It could certainly be held up for two years. I should talk to Bethmann.

5 May, Sunday. To Freienwalde with von Unruh. There: Fischer, Heymel, Justi, Annette Kolb.

Return journey with von Unruh. He suddenly suffers a nervous attack, especially headache. Drove him home; got doctor, nurse, medicaments; stayed till midnight.

Then reply to Lili Deutsch: 'Unable to see you. Please do not insist.'

6 May, Monday. Lunch-time, trip to Laufenburg with Schuster and Zander planned.[77]

7 May, Tuesday. Meeting at Solbad from 9 a.m. to 5.30 p.m. Then got together with Strübe: first power plants, then to Basle, finally to both Veltliner markets.[78]

8 May, Wednesday. Morning, Wangen 1.57 p.m. Return journey with Salomon.

[74] Presumably a reference to *Blanche Trocard*, a play by Rathenau which has never been performed. The play was privately printed at Strasbourg in 1887, and re-edited by E. Redslob in 1947.

[75] Hermann was Rathenau's valet.

[76] The first part of the French Congo was handed over to Germany on 1 October 1912. It was renamed New Cameroons.

[77] In his letter to Harden on the previous night he also mentioned that he had to go to Switzerland to inspect the progress made at Laufenburg, and to attend supervisory board meetings. Hellige (ed.), Rathenau-Harden, 5 May 1912.

[78] Strübe described Rathenau's visit to Laufenburg in Burte, *Mit Rathenau am Oberrhein*. He also mentioned that Rathenau had sent him his two books *Reflexionen* and *Zur Kritik der Zeit* on 30 March 1912. See diary entry for 23 March 1912.

9 May, Thursday. Early, Berlin, moved house with mother.[79] Evening, my father returns from Vienna, suddenly, after nerve-racking telegrams. Anxiety about his condition.

10 May, Friday. Afternoon, visited Stein. Evening, serious diagnosis from Israel. God grant recovery.

11 May, Saturday. 12 o'clock, Israel–Asch consultation. Danger confirmed. There at lunch-time and in the evening.

12 May, Sunday and *13 May*, Monday. Acute anxiety.

14 May, Tuesday. Improvement. Gangrene apparently decreasing. Still danger, particularly as regards saving his foot. Evening, at Solf's request, a long conversation at his flat about German South West [Africa].[80]

15 May, Wednesday, to *19 May*, Sunday. Variable condition, rather better on Sunday; therefore, in the afternoon, with Fritz von Unruh to Freienwalde where the waterworks are finished.

20 May, Monday. Change for the worse. Decision to operate.[81]

21 May, Tuesday. Morning, 9.30 a.m., operation. Extreme danger continues.

22 May, Wednesday, to *26 May*, Sunday. For the first days constant danger of coma. At the clinic three times a day. Meetings cancelled, work sent to Victoriastrasse. Friday, danger of coma lessened. Atmosphere most gloomy.

[79] See fn. 71 above.

[80] On 18 May 1912 Solf thanked Rathenau for his memorandum on South West Africa. For extracts from the memorandum see pp. 78–92. Solf went on to say: 'I read the piece with great enjoyment and lively interest and will study it again in detail on my journey [to South West Africa]. I value it all the more in that, unlike the conventional treatment of colonial questions, it illuminates the nature of present problems as seen from above and deals with the essential points. I found several thoughts, that had already frequently occupied me in my colonial past, came up again in your piece in sharp relief, and I fear that I may almost acquire the reputation of a plagiarist if perhaps you later on notice congruencies with remarks made during my future political activities. Meanwhile we are hardly likely to quarrel over priority, since for you, as for me, the attempt to reach a beneficial goal had a common motivation.' BA Koblenz, Nachlass Solf, 124.

[81] Rathenau had to take this decision and after the operation he wrote to Harden, who always had a great admiration for Emil Rathenau, that his father had not yet realized that his foot had been amputated. Hellige (ed.) Rathenau–Harden, Rathenau to Harden, 21 May 1912. Apparently Emil Rathenau was so incensed when he heard about the amputation that he threw a stick at his daughter. Kessler, *Rathenau*, pp. 158 f.

28 May, Tuesday. New dressing. Progress of healing apparently surprising.

31 May, Friday. Israel informs my father of the loss of his foot.

1 June, Saturday. Deep depression.

2 June, Sunday, to *9 June*, Sunday. Health slowly improves; continues very weak. Friday, after a bad night, psychological reaction.
    Several evenings with Hauptmanns. At the club and Hotel Adlon.

6 June, Thursday. Schickler celebrates 200th anniversary of foundation. Long conversation with the Kaiser. On Emil Rathenau's health. Gave him a detailed account of how I brought Delbrück and Schickler together, which had been concealed from him.[82] Then on France, Cambon. About Marschall. He had published the press notices on the Franco-English alliance, the origins of which the English presume to be Paris.[83] On my *Neue Freie Presse* article and on the *Rheinischer Bismarck*. Finally, for a long while, on the opera-house.[84] I advised removing the churchyard wall of the Moltke memorial.[85]

8 June, Saturday. Evening, von Hofmann, Hauptmanns, von Unruh to dinner, Grunewald.

9 June, Sunday. Lunch at Sarres's at Neu-Babelsberg. Bode, Sydow, Türken, etc.

10 June, Monday. At the club with Joël, Felix Deutsch, Zander.

11 June, Tuesday. Weisswasser until the evening. 6.27 p.m., travelled back from Spremberg.

12 June, Wednesday. Lunch at Hutten-Czapsky's, Joël, Wahnschaffe, Rosen, Huhn. Dernburg, Below, etc. Early, consultation with His. Attempts made to walk.

[82] For the merger see diary entry for 11 January 1911. Delbrück was the Kaiser's private banking house.
[83] Probably this is a reference to the naval consultations between France and England in the early summer of 1912 which led to the exchange of letters between Grey and Cambon in November 1912.
[84] Rathenau and Harden had criticized the plans for a new opera house as being too pompous. Both resented the Kaiser's interference. Hellige (ed.), Rathenau–Harden, Harden to Rathenau, 25 March 1912.
[85] Rathenau's advice was not taken up because the new opera-house was not built.

14 June, Friday. In Lauchstädt with von Unruh. Spent the night in Halle.

15 June, Saturday. To Berlin and Freienwalde.

16 June, Sunday. Hauptmanns and Sternheims at Freienwalde.

17 June, Monday. To Hamburg and Brunsbüttelkoog.

18 June, Tuesday. Regatta dinner. Short conversation with the Kaiser before dinner.[86]

19 June, Wednesday. Afternoon, Berlin.

20 June, Thursday, *21 June*, Friday. A great deal of work. Article for *Nord und Süd*.[87] Berliner Elektrizitätswerke (coal fields), Zander, Zapf, etc.[88]

In this article Rathenau repeated his idea that an understanding between Germany and England could only be reached by means of mutual arms limitation. He claimed that the greater the 'parallelism and symmetry' between the two countries, the more successful limitation of armaments would be. Yet, as he saw it, England was upsetting the symmetry between the two countries by her alliance with France and her aim of preserving the balance of power in Europe. In his article he envisaged two possible ways of altering this situation: either by means of a reciprocal treaty of neutrality or by means of a war launched by England, 'resulting from English needs'. He believed, however, in the English nation's love of peace, which allowed him to hope that war would be avoided and that the momentary trial of strength would, as in a sports competition, 'be concluded with a handshake'. Rathenau's final judgement was that 'both nations are behaving, if the danger of the entertainment is taken into account, like perfect spectators'.

22 June, Saturday. Freienwalde until *24 June*, Monday morning. Von Unruh stays on there.

25 June, Tuesday. Evening, to Paris.

26 June, Wednesday. Afternoon, 4 p.m., Hotel Meurice.

---

[86] The Elbe Regatta was the occasion of the Kaiser's visit.

[87] 'Den Finger auf die Wunde', reprinted in Rathenau, *Nachgelassene Schriften*, vol. i.

[88] The BEW and the AEG developed plans to supply the capital with electricity generated by lignite coal from Spremberg (see diary entry for 11 June 1912) and Bitterfeld. It was hoped that in this way Berlin might become independent from the Westphalian Coal Syndicate.

27 June, Thursday. Morning. Internationale Bergwerksgesellschaft [International Mining Company] talks at the Grand Hotel.[89] Lunch at Monnier's, 33 rue de Monceau. Became acquainted with Bénac. Afternoon, meeting at the Banque de l'Union.[90] Then at Schickler's.

28 June, Friday. Early visit from Waterbury who reported from London. Lunch-time, departure. Evening, Cologne.

29 June, Saturday. Düsseldorf, at Heye's. Afternoon, Brohltal.

30 June, Sunday. Early, Berlin, then Freienwalde.

5 July, Friday. Visit from Dehmel, club. Evening, Pauli to dinner.

6 July, Saturday. To Freienwalde with Pauli.

7 July, Sunday. Morning, visited at Freienwalde by Arnhold and Kranold, then Sternheim. Left at 12 noon for Baden.

8 July, Monday. Brown, Boveri meeting. On the journey from Basle to Baden Simonius told about his experience on the *Titanic*.[91] Afternoon, to Schloss Bürgeln with Strübe.[92] Evening, back to Basle.

9 July, Tuesday. Early, to Frankfurt. Afternoon, Homburg, to reserve accommodation at Dr Pariser's sanatorium.

10 July, Wednesday. Early, Berlin.

11 July, Thursday. Afternoon, visit from Bourdon (*Figaro*).[93] Evening, at Fürstenberg's after dinner.

20 July, Saturday. Afternoon, to Freienwalde. Unruh has been there for about three weeks.[94]

23 July, Tuesday. Spent the night in Berlin.

[89] The company was founded in 1906. Rathenau was a member of its supervisory board. He probably tried to find out whether the company could supply Collart with coke.

[90] The Banque de l'Union Parisienne was Schneider–Creusot's main bank. It had interests in the armaments business as well as in Russian industry and in Serbian capital investments. Hallgarten, *Imperialismus*, vol. ii, pp. 309, 466, and 477.

[91] Simonius was one of the survivors of the *Titanic* disaster of 15 April 1912.

[92] In his account Strübe-Burte has dated the visit to Schloss Bürgeln as 7 May.

[93] See Bourdon, *L'Énigme allemande*, pp. 164–77.

[94] Unruh completed there his drama *Loius Ferdinand, Prinz von Preussen*.

24 July, Wednesday. 8.17 a.m. Emil Rathenau left for Homburg. Evening, at Freienwalde again.

25 July, Thursday. Dined at Hohen-Finow. Chancellor satisfied with Russia.[95] He trusts the Tsar; they want peace, but have no sympathy for Germany. Sazonov said: France is dying away. Bethmann only hopes for a *modus vivendi*.

Asked what I meant by what I had called political goals.[96] He saw no such goals for Germany. Long discussion on this after dinner. I put forward: (1) Economy. Customs unions with Austria, Switzerland, Italy, Belgium, Netherlands, etc., at the same time closer association.[97] (2)Foreign Policy. Key to it: Franco-German conflict by which all nations profit. The key: England. Disarmament impossible today.[98] Next, increase the tension of the situation— although dangerous—, moreover, undermine England's position in the Mediterranean. Then alliance.[99] Goal: *Mittelafrika*, Asia

[95] Bethmann Hollweg was referring to the Kaiser's meeting with the Tsar at Baltischport 4-6 July. On the Russian side the Prime Minister Kokovtsov took part as well as Sazonov; on the German side there was Bethmann Hollweg. After the conference Bethmann visited Petersburg and Moscow. *Grosse Politik*, vol. 31, pp. 439-44, Bethmann's note of 6 July 1912. See also his letter to Eisendecher, ibid., p. 449, and Fischer, *Krieg der Illusionen*, p. 222.

[96] It was already evident from his conversation with Bülow on 2 June 1911 (diary entry) that Rathenau wanted a programme in foreign as well as in domestic policy. At the beginning of the year he wrote in a letter: 'What we need is—aims in foreign policy, ideas in domestic policy.' Rathenau, *Briefe*, vol. i, p. 90, Rathenau to Friedegg, 27 January 1912; Fischer, *Krieg der Illusionen*, p. 203.

[97] The aim of a series of customs unions with Germany's neighbours was not so much an intensification of Caprivi's trade policy, but rather the beginning of a new concept of *Mitteleuropa*. Rathenau aimed at a counterbalance to American, Russian, and British economic power. The *Mitteleuropa* concept may have developed out of the 'greater Germany' tradition, yet for Rathenau it was based essentially on considerations of world politics. To him Germany's demand for hegemony on the continent was legitimized by Germany's industrial power. The conflict in the Balkans crystallized his wishes into political goals. Meyer, *Mitteleuropa*, pp. 82-115; Fischer, 'Weltpolitik', pp. 324-9; Böhme, *Deutschlands Weg zur Grossmacht*, pp. 597 ff.; Kaelble, *Industrielle Interessenpolitik*, p. 156; Zechlin, 'Deutschland zwischen Kabinettskrieg und Wirtschaftskrieg', pp. 398-401; Gutsche, 'Zur Mitteleuropapolitik der deutschen Reichsleitung', p. 92 and Mader, 'Europapläne und Kriegsziele Walther Rathenaus', pp. 198 ff., both in Gutsche (ed.), *Studien zur Geschichte des Deutschen Imperialismus*.

[98] Rathenau thus abandoned the opinion put forward in his article 'Politik, Humor und Abrüstung'. (See diary entry for 11 April 1911 and the subsequent editorial insertion.) His remark also showed that he did not really believe in disarmament, but wanted to burden Britain with the political initiative in this respect.

[99] Unlike Rathenau, the Chancellor did not really believe that it was possible to coerce Britain into an alliance with Germany. In a letter to Marschall, Bethmann had referred to the incompatibility of an expansionist Germany policy with a *rapprochement* with England. He was of the opinion that 'the task of bringing off a political agreement with England, while at the same time passing the Navy Bill which originated in a fighting mood regarding England, is like squaring the circle.' ZStA Potsdam, RK 1710, Bethmann to Marschall, 10 April 1912.

Minor.[100] (3) Domestic. Reform of parliament. Prussian franchise. Reich constituencies.[101] Proportion.[102] These are all ways to a full parliamentary system.

Bethmann in overall agreement; arguing against 3 (*a*) inferiority of the Reichstag, lack of political personalities. Reply: No one wants to enter a mere debating machine. (*b*) [He] : we have the most perfect self-government (municipal, country, provincial). Reply: Only as far as the kitchen, not as far as the drawing-room.

I went on to explain. He could not very well dispute that change would come. Answer: No(!). Hence: either it would come as a result of unfortunate circumstances, or 'heroically' amid sunshine, through a new Hardenberg. Wahnschaffe(!), who was listening, admitted this was by far the more preferable.

Bethmann urged me three times, the last time as he accompanied me to the car, to elaborate my ideas regarding electoral reform for him. Each time I declined: he has better people for that among his staff.

4 August, Sunday. Dr Schröder paid a visit. Telegram from Dr Pariser, Homburg: 'Threat of gangrene.' My reply answered at 4.30 a.m. Set off for Homburg at 6 a.m.

5 August, Monday evening, till *9 August*, Friday evening. Homburg. Condition unchanged.

10 August, Saturday. Berlin. Evening, Freienwalde.

18 August, Sunday. Sternheim's visit.

19 August, Monday. Early, to Berlin. Afternoon 3.35 p.m., to Zurich.

20 August, Tuesday. Zurich. Elektrobank annual balance. To Frankfurt at night.

21 August, Wednesday. Early to Homburg. 11 a.m. Mathilde Rathenau leaves. Depressed mood.

[100] Negotiations concerning German expansion in Africa and the protection of German influence in Asia Minor continued from the time of the Second Morocco Crisis up to the outbreak of the First World War.

[101] Rathenau repeats his liberal demands.

[102] It is not clear whether he refers to proportional representation for the Reichstag and thus advocates a change of the franchise.

22 August, Thursday. Afternoon, consultation with Garré. More promising. Left in the evening.

23 August, Friday. Early, Berlin, Geitner, visited Edith Andreae, Konschewski; afternoon, Körting; evening, 9 p.m., Freienwalde.

25 August, Sunday. Visit from Deutsch.[103]

26 August, Monday. Schöneweide.

29 August, Thursday. Evening, to Breslau.

30 August, Friday. 10 a.m., visited the Oberpräsident[104] [leading provincial official] about the Schlesische Kleinbahn. Departed 3.24 p.m.

31 August, Saturday. Morning, to Freienwalde.

4 September, Wednesday. Fetched my father from Homburg. Taken seriously ill on the journey.

5 September, Thursday. His and Israel diagnose pneumonia. Serious danger.

6 September, Friday. Moved over to Victoriastrasse. Gradual improvement. Out of danger after a week.

19 September, Thursday. To Westerland. First nice weather for months.

Fortnight in Westerland; at the beginning took meals with Ilse Dernburg and Mrs Bernhard, later alone. Work with Geitner finished. Controversy with *Zeit im Bild*.[105] Sent *1813* to Harden.[106]

---

[103] Rathenau had invited Harden to come as well, but Harden was suffering from tonsillitis. It is very likely that Rathenau wanted to discuss the question of his father's succession in the AEG with Deutsch and Harden so as to uncover any plot that might exist between the two against him. Hellige (ed.), Rathenau-Harden, Rathenau to Harden, 25 August 1912.

[104] Von Günther.

[105] Correspondence between Rathenau and the paper *Zeit im Bild*. The editor, Alfons Goldschmid, polemicized against the success of Rathenau's book (no. 36, 29 August 1912). Rathenau replied four times (9, 17, 25 September, and 13 October 1912). In the end he agreed to a competition: one thousand marks were to be offered to the person who would be able to discover a single new idea in Rathenau's book. Rathenau wrote to Harden: 'If you reproach me for my follies with regard to the press, I must admit that you are completely right. I am gradually coming to your estimate of this agreeable profession and have

[See p. 166 for n. 105 cont. and n. 106].

4 October, Friday. Evening, four of us at Bülow's, with Dr Meinecke.[107]
After he left, alone with the Prince till 12 p.m.

Princess[108] describes her first presentation to Kaiserin Augusta. In
a wheelchair, mummy-like, staring eyes (1887); the Perponcher
woman made conversation. The door opens, and bent and small,
Wilhelm I wobbles into the room on a cane. 'I wanted to see the
eyes that young Bülow has fallen in love with.' I asked: 'small?'
She maintains that that was the impression. The Prince confirms:
'Lehndorff commissioned him to procure a top hat in Paris for
Wilhelm I. The hatter said: that is a small child's measurement.
Check-back: it was true.'

Old story about Körber: In the corridor the Czech asks the
German: 'What did he promise you?' I cannot tell you that. But
he gave me his word that he will not keep the promise he made
to you.

At his first meeting with the Ministry of State Bismarck developed
his ideas on the German question 'to the umpteenth detail'. There
was nothing about it in the minutes on the following day. He called
the Secretary of State to account. 'I thought your Excellency
would rather it were omitted', and looked at him with a benevolent
smile.[109]

just today received another definite proof of the accuracy of your opinion, which I suppose
I shall follow up with another stupidity simply and solely for reasons of temperament.'
Harden had advised Rathenau not to react. Hellige (ed.), Rathenau–Harden, Harden to
Rathenau, 24 September 1912 and Rathenau to Harden, 24 September 1912; Schulin (ed.),
Walther Rathenau. Hauptwerke und Gespräche, pp. 511 f. and p. 526; Rathenau, *Briefe,*
vol. i, p. 109, Rathenau to M. K., 1 October 1912 and to Hermann Kroepelin, 2 October
1912.

[106] The poems *1813* which dealt with the German war of liberation were published
in *Die Zukunft,* vol. lxxxi, 1912, pp. 128–36, under Rathenau's anagramatic pseudonym
Herwart Raventhal. On 21 September Rathenau had asked Harden whether he would like
to print them. Harden wanted them and tried to dissuade Rathenau from using a pseudonym (24 September). On 25 September Rathenau sent the poems and hoped that Harden
would think well of them. Three days later Harden replied that he liked them, and
Rathenau was very grateful for his appreciation (29 September). The verses were Prusso-
phile and patriotic; nevertheless Rathenau preferred them to be published under a pseudonym because 'precisely at this moment I give great offence to officials and competitors
and suppliers. I am afraid that if I am caught writing poems, no one will ask me for any
estimates but will ask for rhymed business reports instead.' (25 September.) Obviously
Rathenau did not want to be ridiculed at a time when he hoped to become his father's
successor in the AEG. For the letters between Harden and Rathenau, see Hellige (ed.),
Rathenau–Harden.

[107] At Bülow's house in Hamburg-Flottbeck.
[108] Maria di Camporeale.
[109] Bismarck's first meeting with the Ministry of State took place on 24 September
1862. The official keeper of the minutes was Hegel, in the State Ministry. (Information
from the ZStA, Merseburg.) Keeping the minutes was not the responsibility of a Secretary
of State; later it fell to an Under-Secretary of state.

We talked about Bethmann.[110] By way of illustration he tells about his uncle, General Loën. At the front he had only risen to first lieutenant, then was promoted to brigadier while serving at court and was supposed to command the brigade. The aide-de-camp whispers every command to him. On the way home the General says: I can see things are going quite well and it is not difficult at all.

Very deprecating about Marschall.[111] He had revoked the Re-insurance Treaty. He was responsible for the Krüger Telegram.[112] In his last year as Chancellor the Kaiser said to him: 'this man from Baden prevailed on me over the telegram.' Marschall openly admitted that he had moderated it. There was a proposal in mind which amounted to a kind of duel in Africa between the Kaiser and the Queen.

Regarding Agadir: it was definitely known abroad that we had given way in July 1911. Tittoni had said to him: what a change in France's conduct compared with 1905![113] One could not grasp that this situation was only seven years behind us.

In 1887 Bismarck had explained that a war with France was use-less.[114] Toul and Verdun could not be taken. One could restore Poland and divide it up again 12 years later. But what use would that be?

Bülow had twice been faced with war. 1905 (Delcassé) and 1909 (Bosnia). Both times relatively promising. In 1905 France was weak. Russia involved in Japan. England possibly passive.

In 1909 Austria would have been forced to cope with Russia. Germany would have had France to deal with; England was uncertain.

In 1911 the situation was much worse. Complications would have begun with England; France would have stayed passive, would have

[110] Although Bülow advocated Bethmann's appointment, he had never had much of an opinion of him as a statesman. The antipathy was mutual. Vierhaus, (ed.), *Spitzemberg Tagebuch*, p. 544.

[111] Marschall had contributed to the revocation of the Reinsurance Treaty in so far as he belonged to the group around Holstein and Eulenberg who opposed Bismarck. Rich, *Holstein*, vol. i, p. 320; Röhl, 'Staatsstreichplan oder Staatsstreichbereitschaft?' pp. 614 f. Rathenau had not thought much of Marschall. In a letter to Harden on 25 September he commented on Marschall's death: 'I did not know Marschall. I only know one thing: he died rather expediently.' Harden had judged him to be 'insincere down to his testicles'. Hellige (ed.), Rathenau–Harden, Harden to Rathenau, 24 September, and Rathenau to Harden, 25 September 1912.

[112] The telegram in which the Kaiser congratulated Krüger, the President of the Transvaal, on the successful defeat of the Jameson Raid, was Marschall's idea; he wanted to divert the Kaiser from worse plans. The Kaiser had, however, sharpened the wording of the telegram. P..A. Bonn, Marschall Tagebuch, 3 January 1896; Rich, *Holstein*, vol. ii, p. 469; Vierhaus (ed.), *Spitzemberg Tagebuch*, p. 340; Röhl, *Germany without Bismarck*, p. 165 f.

[113] France had stepped down in the First Morocco Crisis. Bülow considered Delcassé's dismissal in 1905 as his success.

[114] Bismarck's rejection of the idea of preventive war against France and Russia between 1885 and 1888 had at the time, however, met with much opposition.

forced us to attack. That would not have provided the *casus foederis* with Austria—which even Aehrenthal declared to the delegations—; against that Russia was under an obligation to co-operate.

I said that in the last decades all foolhardy enterprises had been successful. He agrees: during the disorders in Crete King George had come to him and said: What would you do if I took a yacht, sailed to Crete and allowed myself to be proclaimed? Bülow had not taken the matter seriously, but had been convinced that it would have worked.[115]

5 October, Saturday. Dehmel to lunch at the Atlantic [a Hamburg hotel]. Afternoon, Kalckreuth fetched us in his car to his property near Harburg. There later, Lichtwark and sister. The Countess's drawings.   .

Evening, 8 p.m., at Ballin's. 38 people, Bülow and wife. Took in Mrs von Selchow. Discussion about the Balkan War.[116] Painful situation: Ballin in disagreement with some of the guests.

6 October, Sunday. 8.52 a.m., departure. Lunch-time, Berlin. After-noon, talk to Emil Rathenau about his arrangements. I advised postponing everything until 1 January, which he accepted.[117]

As a result of the dietetic arrangements agreed upon [his] con-dition (sleep, interest) improved. Intensive work.

9 October, Wednesday. Evening, Joël to dinner.

[115] In February 1896 a revolt in Crete, encouraged by Greece, had broken out against Turkish rule. Crete was occupied by a raiding party led by Prince George of Greece. At the Peace of 4 December 1897 the island became autonomous, with Prince George as Governor. In 1908 Crete was annexed by Greece and came into Greek hands definitively in 1913.

[116] The First Balkan War between the Balkan states of Bulgaria, Greece, Montenegro, and Serbia on the one hand, and Turkey on the other, increased the risk of a European conflagration.

[117] After the worst of Emil Rathenau's illness was over it was clear that the head of the AEG had to decide whether he would resign or share his responsibilities. Walther tried to influence his father so that a solution favourable to himself could be worked out. However, Felix Deutsch regarded himself as the natural heir to the general directorship of the AEG: he could look back on thirty years of close and successful co-operation with Emil Rathenau. Carl Fürstenberg, whose voice would count when the supervisory board had to make up its mind, supported Deutsch's bid for leadership. As Walther was the obvious rival for the post Harden gradually took on the role of Deutsch's confidant, especially as Harden also backed Deutsch against Walther. BA Koblenz, Nachlass Harden 29, 2, Deutsch to Harden, 12 September 1912. The tensions between Harden and Rathenau—which had temporarily subsided after Lili Deutsch had passed Rathenau's letter on to Harden, earlier in 1912—erupted into hostility once Rathenau realized that Harden was not going to back him. Meanwhile Deutsch and Fürstenberg agreed that Deutsch should be Emil Rathenau's successor, and that if the latter would not resign a duumvirate might be feasible. Walther Rathenau opted for a delay and thus refused to discuss the situation with either Fürstenberg or Mamroth. BA Koblenz, Nachlass Harden 40, Fürstenberg to Harden, 21 September 1912.

10 October, Thursday. Evening, to Strasbourg.

12 October, Saturday. Early, Berlin. Confusion on account of the Balkan war.[118] Discussion with Deutsch, Fürstenberg.[119] Martin Beradt about *Zeit im Bild*.

15 October. Tuesday. At my advice Emil Rathenau sends Fürstenberg the letter about my joining the directorate of the AEG to replace him in his department.[120] Evening, discussion with Deutsch who is against it. Later, Fürstenberg at my house.

16 October, Wednesday. Morning, conferred with Fürstenberg about my taking over the chairmanship. 3.30 p.m., Fürstenberg, at Victoriastrasse. Agrees to 3 December (general meeting). 4.30 p.m., meeting of the supervisory board of the AEG.[121]

26 October, Saturday. Since then extremely strenuous work. Early, in the Grunewald, then *Mechanik des Geistes* for an hour, then work

[118] The BHG had taken part in several financial operations in the Balkans. Fürstenberg, *Carl Fürstenberg*, p. 535; Fürstenberg, 'Erinnerung', pp. 52 and 58.

[119] No result was reached at this talk. They were also probably preparing the meeting of the supervisory board's committee which took place on 14 October. This accepted an investment programme which was worth about 14.5 million marks, for which Walther had launched a new rights issue worth 25 million marks. AEG Archiv. Protokoll Buch I/62. Meeting of the supervisory board's committee, 14 October 1912.

[120] Rathenau told Deutsch about his father's letter to Fürstenberg. At their meeting Rathenau told Deutsch that his father had asked him to join the board of directors in order to gain some assistance. When Emil would finally withdraw from the AEG Walther would resign from the board, but only to become chairman of the supervisory board. Although Walther disliked the idea of joining the board again he was prepared to do so, but only if he became chairman of the supervisory board and board of directors as well. This would not mean that he would take over his father's position as Generaldirektor, but he would chair the meeting of the directors. This last condition was out of the question for Felix Deutsch, and he rejected two of Rathenau's further proposals. Firstly he could not accept that Emil Rathenau needed the assistance of his son on the board, as there were enough competent men already. Secondly he could not tolerate Walther being a member of the board of directors in his own right. Walther tried to change his mind but Felix Deutsch was adamant, and irritated Walther thoroughly when he mentioned that he had suffered enough by being passed over because Walther was Emil's son. In the last resort Walther referred to the possibility of his father resigning prematurely, but this did not impress Felix Deutsch. They had talked for an hour and a quarter. After that Walther saw Fürstenberg, and they together went to see Emil Rathenau on the next day. Walther's plan was buried, but it was agreed between the three of them that Walther would become chairman of the supervisory board at the annual general meeting on 3 December 1912. BA Koblenz, Nachlass Harden 29, 2, Deutsch to Harden, 16 October 1912. See also Hellige (ed.), Rathenau–Harden. Hellige has included Deutsch's letters in his edition.

[121] AEG Archiv, AR, 16 October 1912. Neither at the meeting of the committee nor at the plenary session of the supervisory board was the new arrangement officially discussed. But it is very likely that the members of the supervisory board were sounded out unofficially. The main business was Walther Rathenau's investment programme.

till 7 or 8 p.m. every day. In between at Landau's about Berliner Elektrizitätswerke, struggles with Deutsch about negotiations with Wermuth. His unfriendly answer yesterday at Bethmann's reception. This afternoon he came to complain about Emil Rathenau's letter to Wermuth, which was written by me. I proved to him that he was wrong. Spoke our minds generally. I complained forcibly that in the summer he suggested Fürstenberg for the chairmanship of the AEG although he had told me that only I was under consideration.[122] He admitted that no one else could lay claim to it. He also admitted having been 'vague' when he spoke to Fürstenberg. Finally he departed in a very subdued manner.

At the dentist each lunch-time. In between drawn by Max Liebermann for Hauptmann.[123] With Hauptmann to *Henry IV*, Part II (Deutsches Theater).[124]

Today, first visit from Dernburg since 1908, about oil monopoly.[125]

1813 appeared in the *Zukunft* the day before yesterday.[126]

4 November, Monday. At the club with Otto Kahn.

5 November, Tuesday. Emil Rathenau hands over to me a copy of his letter to Ballin with enclosure. Evening, Sternheim and Unruh.

6 November, Wednesday. Evening, Wassermann.

7 November, Thursday. Lunch at Bodenhausen's. Left for Milan.

8 November, Friday. Reached Milan at about 4 p.m.

[122] Deutsch may have mentioned to Fürstenberg in the summer that he would like him to become chairman of the supervisory board in order to check Walther's advance, but on 21 September Deutsch wrote to Harden that he was very much in favour of Walther getting the post. BA Koblenz, Nachlass Harden 29, 2.

[123] This drawing has recently been republished by Buddensieg and Rogge, *Industriekultur*, p. D 325.

[124] One of Max Reinhardt's specialities was directing Shakespeare's plays.

[125] The oil monopoly was to be set up in the same way as the planning for the electricity monopoly, i.e. under mixed ownership. The planned oil monopoly was directed against Standard Oil, the American combine which was predominant in Germany. It was, however, rejected by the Centre Party and the SPD on 30 January 1913, because they did not want to replace one monopoly by creating another which would benefit mainly the Deutsche Bank and its oil company the Deutsche Petroleum AG. See the chapter about the oil monopoly in Blaich, *Kartell und Monopolpolitik*, pp. 185–206.

[126] See fn. 106 above.

9 November, Saturday. Morning. At Compania Edison, Negri meeting.[127] Afternoon and evening at Joël's, Sviluppo.[128] In between, Brera.

10 November, Sunday. Early, to Bodio with Frey and Zander. Evening, Basle.

11 November, Monday. Laufenburg meeting until 4.30 p.m. 5.13 p.m. to Frankfurt.

12 November, Tuesday. Frankfurt. Morning, Lahmeyer; lunch at Salomon's, Dr von Trenkwaldt. Afternoon, Lechwerke. Evening, Konschewski. 10.36 p.m. to Berlin (general meeting and election at Berliner Elektrizitätswerke).[129]

13 November, Wednesday. Early, Berlin; evening, Jonas.

3 December, Tuesday. Presided over AEG general meeting. Then elected chairman.[130] Lunch at the club with Ballin.[131] Evening, at Mendelssohn's.

---

[127] With the aid of the Banca Commerciale Italiana the AEG tried to co-operate with the Società Generale Italiana di Elettricità Sistema Edison. Earlier projects were the construction of the tramway system for Milan and Rome. However, nothing came of it. Instead there was strong competition between the AEG and the Italian company which Rathenau tried to replace by a renewed attempt at co-operation.

[128] See diary entry for 1 March 1911 and fn. 19 above.

[129] Rathenau joined the supervisory board of the BEW.

[130] At the meeting of the supervisory board which had followed the general meeting Hollman resigned from his chairmanship. Then Ballin took over Fürstenberg's role as spokesman. The latter was not present, and Ballin proposed that Rathenau be elected chairman. Ballin told the meeting that Fürstenberg had declined because of his leading position in the AEG's banking consortium. Rathenau accepted and 'declared it to be his duty to be at his father's disposal at every point'. It was also agreed, due to Fürstenberg's earlier proposal, to increase the number of the representatives of the supervisory board by one committee member. This had become necessary to balance Walther's position since he regarded himself not only as the representative of the supervisory board but also as his father's agent on the supervisory board. AEG Archiv, AR, 3 December 1912.

[131] Four days later Ballin responded to a letter from Harden. Ballin had believed that the dispute at the top of the AEG had been sorted out, but he now heard from Harden that Deutsch still felt bitter about the arrangements. Ballin knew no more than that Deutsch wanted to give the briefing at the annual general meeting, but this was successfully resisted by Walther, who as chairman insisted on his right to undertake the briefing and answer the questions. Ballin sided with Walther over this incident, although he could understand Deutsch's desire, since by giving the briefing he could make public his keenness to take over Emil Rathenau's position. The fact that Emil Rathenau was accustomed to give the briefing was a personal privilege granted to him as the founder and moving spirit behind the AEG. BA Koblenz, Nachlass Harden 5, Ballin to Harden, 7 December 1912. The *Berliner Tageblatt*, while commenting on the change-over at the top of the AEG, stated that it was unusual for the son in family dynasties to take over the chairmanship of the supervisory

7 December, Saturday. Lunch with Hauptmanns and Hofmannsthal at the club.

With the Hauptmanns several times before then. One evening, with them and Heimann, after which mad excursion to the Admirals-garten-Bad [place of amusement] until 5 a.m.

Morning, in the Grunewald, then worked; in the Bank at about 11 a.m. Evenings, mostly at home.

10 December, Tuesday evening. Visit from Lili Deutsch. First lengthy encounter for a year. Try to clear things up. Calm atmosphere. She holds Harden responsible for everything. And it was Harden and Fürstenberg who prevailed on Felix Deutsch to lay sole claim to authorization and general management. Pointed explanation: I would not allow my rights to be infringed upon.[132] Harden has sent Ballin's letter about his discussion with me to Fürstenberg.[133]

13 December, Friday. Evening, Harden telephones, asks for a rendez-vous. I call on him. Discussion about various confidential matters, including AEG.

14 December, Saturday. Postscript. Consultation with Prof. Fränkel. He advises cutting smoking down to a minimum. Since then I have completely abstained. Nevertheless a test of will-power!

15 December, Sunday. Evening, Lili Deutsch telephones, furious. Harden had forced on her the contents of our conversation, ten-dentiously distorted. I have written to Harden with a categorical demand for an explanation.[134]

16 December, Monday. Harden replies at length, contradicting Lili Deutsch's story. I send her a copy. In the evening she sends the copy back, writes reproachfully, but uncertainly, wants to see me tomorrow. I decline and say I have had enough of these intrigues.

board, a post which was normally reserved for retiring founders and fathers. Hellige (ed.), Rathenau–Harden; *Berliner Tageblatt*, 3 December 1912.

[132] Those agreed upon by the annual general meeting and the meeting of the supervisory board on 3 December 1912.

[133] This is the letter mentioned in fn. 131 above.

[134] Rathenau's question to Harden ran: 'Dear Friend, Is it true that you have reported today, in detail over the telephone to the other party [Lili Deutsch], our confidential conversation of the day before yesterday? With best wishes, Yours W. R.' For Rathenau's letters to Harden, see Hellige (ed.), Rathenau–Harden. The resulting animosity between the former friends was partly based on Rathenau's new position in the AEG, but in particular arose out of intrigues based on what people were supposed to have said about the competition between Rathenau and Deutsch.

Unpleasant correspondence with Harden, which I finally brought to an end after a very vexing, unjust letter on 29 December. Conciliatory, calm but resolute.[135]

From *26 December*, Thursday, to *28 December*, Saturday, at Freienwalde.

27 December, Friday. Evening, with Bethmanns at Hohen-Finow. Occasion: I had replied to his warm letter saying thank you for the *1813* poems with a political discussion (England) and a reference to Erzberger's threat.[136]

No one there apart from the children. In his study talked about its redecoration (symptom of retirement ?!), then politics.

Admitted to conflict with Tirpitz in the spring.[137] More than a battleship involved. Haldane's proposals were unacceptable. Not prepared to move away from France or declare neutrality.[138] Germany would have to sacrifice the supplementary Navy Bill. England reserves rearmament to itself, only promised more concessions in Portuguese East Africa, which were, however, not to be realized for the time being.[139]

I replied: a definitive breach of the Triple *Entente* cannot be demanded; the conclusion of a 'reinsurance treaty *à la* 1889' would

[135] Rathenau did not leave things there, but asked Harden to authorize him to deny any allegation that firstly Harden had talked about Rathenau in a negative way only a fortnight before and that secondly he had mocked Rathenau about his relationship with the management of the AEG. (Rathenau to Harden, 16 December 1912.) Harden's letters have not survived, but he obviously did not satisfy Rathenau's requests. Furthermore, he must have written a fairly aggressive letter to which Rathenau replied after he had been in Essen. The latter tried to prevent a break-up of their friendship by asking Harden to have another talk to sort things out and forget them. (Rathenau to Harden, 20 and 21 December 1912.) Harden did not comply, and refused to dance to Rathenau's whistle. Rathenau repeated his request for a frank discussion on 26 December and asked Harden not to mention any more the letter he had written to Lili Deutsch in 1908. Harden did not feel in a conciliatory mood, and Rathenau wrote on 29 December: '. . . the wounding harshness of your words can mean nothing else but the desire to end our friendship. I submit with a heavy heart. We were united for eighteen years, and I think of that time gladly, with gratitude and affection. Farewell, Maxim.'

[136] Erzberger threatened to withdraw his party's support for government policy should the repeal of the Jesuit Law be refused. No trace has been found so far of Rathenau's letter to Bethmann.

[137] For the conflict see Tirpitz, *Politische Dokumente*, vol. i, pp. 314-38; Görlitz (ed.), *Der Kaiser*, pp. 112-19; Gutsche, *Aufstieg und Fall*, pp. 94-8; Berghahn, *Germany and the Approach of War*, pp. 117-124.

[138] The formula of neutrality proposed by the Chancellor was too comprehensive for the British Cabinet because it would have restricted England's ability to support France. *Grosse Politik*, vol. xxxi, pp. 95-229; *British Documents*, vol. vi, pp. 666-761; Cecil, *Ballin*, pp. 193-7.

[139] After the Second Morocco Crisis had faded away, negotiations for the renewal of the Anglo-German treaty of 1898 regarding the fate of the Portuguese colonies in Africa were resumed.

have to suffice.[140] I mentioned the folly of Austrian policy which had called in its debts too late. Had she made her claims at the beginning of the war she might have retained Salonika.[141] (On this question, where was there an advantage for us?)

Bethmann questions this. I remark that every audacious enterprise in the last 30 years has succeeded: Korea,[142] Morocco,[143] Tripoli,[144] the Balkans,[145] Cuba,[146] the Philippines,[147] etc. Every Balkan port was important for supplies in case of war.

Bethmann admits to being concerned about this question.

I say: the Franco-German rift, now Anglo-German, prevents both powers deriving advantage from any complications. England got Egypt and Cyprus out of the 1878 Balkan war,[148] now we are both of us going away empty-handed.

Bethmann emphasizes the current agreeable manner of negotiating with England and hopes this habit will be advantageous.[149]

Then, domestic affairs. He hoped to do away with the Jesuits Law by means of 'abolition'. Hertling had hampered this.[150] The Reichstag would vote for the repeal in January. He had to vote against it in the Bundesrat. Because of His Majesty, of course. Saxony would be against it too.

He knows of no compensation for the Centre [Party], but asks me to sound out Erzberger.

---

[140] The Reinsurance Treaty of 1887 assured Russia of German neutrality in a defensive war against Austria. The same applied in the event of a German defensive war against France.

[141] Austria had agreed to cede Salonika to Bulgaria if Bulgaria would comply with certain Romanian territorial claims.

[142] Korea had been a Japanese protectorate since 1905, but was annexed by Japan in 1910.

[143] The French march on Fez initiated the conquest of strategic points in Morocco, and led France to set up a protectorate over the whole of Morocco in 1912.

[144] The capture of Tripoli in the war between Italy and Turkey.

[145] The liquidation of Turkey's European possessions in the First Balkan War.

[146] The conquest of Cuba in the Spanish-American war. In 1898 the United States set up a protectorate over Cuba.

[147] In 1898 Dewey's squadron conquered the Philippines, which were awarded to the United States at the Peace of Paris.

[148] Britain gained Cyprus in the Anglo-Turkish Agreement of 4 June 1878, in exchange guaranteeing Asiatic Turkey against Russian attacks. Egypt was occupied by the British in 1882 when a nationalist movement threatened British interests in Egypt.

[149] The Chancellor was referring to Anglo-German co-operation, during the London Conference of Ambassadors, in settling the Balkan crisis, and also to the negotiations regarding the hypothetical partition of Portuguese and Belgian possessions in Africa.

[150] Hertling's Government in Bavaria had, after the fall of Podewils's Liberal Cabinet, taken over the Liberals' reinterpretation of the Jesuits Law (decree by Wehner, Minister for Education). Hertling sought to obtain the readmission of the Jesuit Order. The Chancellor had opposed the Bavarian interpretation (speech in the Reichstag of 4 December 1912). The Bundesrat had likewise voted against the Bavarian Government on 28 November. And so the Bavarian initiative fell through.

DIARY FOR 1913

6 January, Monday. Evening, Erzberger to dinner.

8 January, Wednesday. Evening, 6.15 p.m., at Bethmann's. 'I called Erzberger's attention to the fact that Delbrück had become a major.[1] He did not want him as Chancellor. I asked why he made things difficult for Bethmann. The Kaiser was against the Jesuit Law. Erzberger denies this. [In] 1902 the Kaiser offered to repeal the Jesuit Law [in exchange] for the Navy Bill, the Centre refused.[2] Erzberger considers acceptable the solution which Professor Delbrück recommended in the *Preussische Jahrbücher*, p. 167.'[3]

Bethmann knew the proposal; obviously pleased to hear that it was acceptable to the Centre. But he saw difficulties in proposing it to the Reichstag.

I advised against this. The Reichstag should vote the repeal and Bethmann should keep himself at a distance. Then, months later, the Bundesrat should vote for Delbrück's modification.

Bethmann agrees. Only the Centre should not hurry the matter too much.

I said I could not harangue Erzberger again without attracting attention; I do not recommend making it an official matter on that account. Bethmann agrees.

Talk about Jagow. Not a *Junker*. Kaiser not particularly enthusiastic. Handling of the Press.

Ended 6.45 p.m.

11 January, Saturday. Last attempt, by letter and telegraph, to reach an agreement with Harden. His last letter, at 11 o'clock in the evening, curt.[4]

[1] Clemens von Delbrück was mentioned with reference to his political position and his speech which appeased the Centre Party and was supposed to moderate the conflict between Bavaria and the Reich regarding interpretation of the Jesuits Law.

[2] In 1903 the Bundesrat prevented the repeal of the Jesuits Law. In 1904, as a compromise, Article 2 (deportation) was dropped.

[3] Hans Delbrück had suggested reformulating Article 1 of the Jesuits Law. Freedom of movement should now be granted to individual Jesuits, while establishments and educational institutions were to continue to be prohibited. *Preussische Jahrbücher*, vol. cliii (1913), pp. 164–7.

[4] After the New Year Rathenau received a letter from Harden which he answered on 3 January 1913, addressing his friend as 'Dear Mr Harden'. Harden must have accused Rathenau of dishonesty and of plotting with Lili Deutsch behind his back. Rathenau tried to put the record straight by telling Harden what he had discussed with her on 10 December 1912, the last time he had seen her. He also told Harden what she had related to him later

12 January, Sunday. Visit from M., briefed him as my second. If Harden should want a discussion, M. was to declare himself ready and suspend his mandate.

M. at Harden's at 3.00 p.m. Harden, at first very tense and polite, declares that he has to look into details. M.—contrary to the agreement—declines abruptly. Harden refuses, vehemently, to give an explanation; M. passes on the challenge to pistols, which Harden declines. Duration of the conversation—apparently about a minute.

Evening, to Deutsch's to let them know.

January, February, March, my father suffered another severe relapse. Recovered after weeks, but decidedly weaker.

Intensive work; at the same time *Mechanik der Seele* Book I finished, II almost.[5]

In his book *Zur Mechanik des Geistes oder Vom Reich der Seele* [*On the Mechanism of the Spirit: or concerning the Kingdom of the Soul*] Rathenau contrasts the 'intellect', which is more concerned with practical goals, with the 'soul' which serves no ulterior aim, but leads the way to a kind of contemplation on a higher level. This polarization is for Rathenau the essential division in human life. He fears that under the impact of modern technical

over the telephone about Harden's account to her of the meeting Rathenau and Harden had had on 13 December. Rathenau alleged that he broke off the telephone conversation with her after he had accused her of destroying his friendship with Harden. Again Harden's answer to this letter is not known, but in a letter to Harden on 7 January 1913 Rathenau drew up an account of their dispute. The balance was, as might be expected, in Rathenau's favour. In his letter of reply Harden stood by his accusations and taxed Rathenau with intriguing against him with Lili Deutsch. Yet, as his general tone was more conciliatory, Rathenau tried to put pressure on him by drafting a settlement proposal. Rathenau believed that if this were rejected he would have no alternative other than to settle the conflict by means of a duel. Thus the telegram of 11 January ran: 'See last chance of peaceful agreement if both sides simultaneously consider all accusations, reproaches, harshness, injuries, retracted, settled and forgiven, and if both parties pledge themselves unconditionally never to refer to this statement or to the events which lay behind it without mutual consent. We would try to unite ourselves as soon as possible in new, dignified, and understanding circumstances. Request telegraphic answer: agreed or declined.' In a letter of the same day Rathenau elaborated his terms and undertook to ask Felix Deutsch that nothing negative about Harden would emanate from his house. The telegram continued that if, however, Harden found Rathenau's proposals unacceptable then Rathenau would have to challenge him to a duel. He also announced the visit of his second. In the Diaries the second is called M. This could possibly have been Mutius or Mumm, both friends of Rathenau. There are apparently no more communications between the two until Rathenau sent Harden a telegram on 24 December 1913 with seasonal greetings. It is not clear what caused Rathenau to do this. BA Koblenz, Nachlass Harden. See now Hellige (ed.), Rathenau-Harden.

[5] For an interpretation of the book, see Kessler, *Rathenau*, pp. 81-98 and pp. 117-28; Joll. *Three Intellectuals in Politics*, p. 87; Schulin (ed.), *Walther Rathenau. Hauptwerke und Gespräche*, pp. 530-55. See the latter for the reviews the book received and Rathenau's remarks about his book.

life the realm of the soul will disappear. By materializing the spirit and by spiritualizing matter he tries to show a way out of this dreaded dilemma. The solution is the 'mechanization of the spirit'. Three basic spiritual experiences are part of this mechanization: 'the ability to divide, the ability to combine and the ability to reciprocate'. All three should contribute to the deepening effect the mechanization should have. If mechanization were achieved, then it might be possible for the soul to govern all branches of political and economic life. He ended his philosophical book with these words: 'Thus we stand at the gates of that kingdom which is not of this world but which yet has its beginning there, the kingdom which is known by its evangelists as the kingdom of heaven and the kingdom of God, and which in this poor worldly book hovers above us as the Kingdom of the Soul.'

The book was published, again by Samuel Fisher, in the autumn of 1913. It did not have the impact of the previous one, partly because it was more philosophical and partly because the outbreak of the First World War pushed it into the background. The first edition of 3,000 copies was not sold out until 1917. Although the theme of the book had kept him occupied, according to Kessler, since 1906, it took him only about twelve months to write it. He dedicated it pompously to the 'new generation', though it was clear that only a few would read it. The reviews were not very critical and revealed a mixture of surprise and respect. Only the *Berliner Zeitung am Mittag* mocked the new 'ethical pathos of a man representing the Berlin idealism'. The *Gegenwart* praised the book as a crucial event because an industrialist had written about idealistic philosophy. The critic Emil Ludwig found Rathenau's method noteworthy. He stated that, unusually, Rathenau had felt his way back from a general perception of society to the inner structure of an individual, rather than the other way round: by analysing the collective mentality he hoped to give an insight into the spirit of the individual. Robert Musil on the other hand criticized Rathenau for dividing spirit and reason. Musil thought that Rathenau's attempt to distil the spirit out of experience had been a worthy but not particularly useful effort. To him Rathenau's mysticism was still far too rational and not sufficiently penetrating. Rathenau himself was very hurt by Musil's criticism, especially as he regarded the book as his best, and emotionally had been very much involved in it. But it is true that it is vague, unsystematic, very subjective, and also very optimistic about the distant future. He may have been right in calling his book a reflection of his relationship with Lili Deutsch, but it appears to be more the dialectic sublimation of his previous political, industrial, and human frustrations.

[*12 January* continued] Easter article *Neue Freie Presse*: 'Eumenidenopfer'.[6]

In this article Rathenau complained of the audacity with which the Army Bill of 1913 and the levy to pay for it were linked to events in 1813. He saw the success of 1813 as resulting from the reform movement in Prussia of the years

---

[6] 'Das Eumenidenopfer', *Neue Freie Presse*, Vienna, 23 March 1913; Rathenau, *Gesammelte Schriften*, vol. i. On 3 April 1913 Bodenhausen told Hofmannsthal that the article was 'well worth reading'. Bodenhauser-Degener (ed.), *Briefe der Freundschaft*, p. 142. See also Kessler, *Rathenau*, pp. 169–72.

before. But the financial 'sacrifice' would still make sense if the Army Bill
were followed up with domestic political reforms. The aim of those reforms
should be the abolition of the 'most rampant injustice', namely elimination of
the dominating influence of the Prussian aristocracy and the principle of having
only a conservative government. Thus Rathenau wrote: 'Class rule manifest in
inadequate selection [of personnel] and weak politics, the conservatism of the
leaders, unequal burdens: that is the twofold injustice and twofold danger to our
country.' As steps on the road to basic reforms Rathenau demanded a change
in the distribution of constituencies and in the 'unjust electoral law in Prussia'.
Rathenau blamed these circumstances on an indolent middle class which tolerated
those injustices. He in no way justified the existing situation but rather emphasized
that 'a wrong tolerated does not make a right'. Finally he warned against the
idea that a serious political crisis or the effects of war could not be overcome
unless politics were conducted dynamically within a reformed constitution.

'But when the hour of destiny is nigh it will be understood that any undertaking
remains a straw in the wind unless it basically rests on a doubly reinforced
foundation: vigorous politics and a just constitution. The passion which is today
slave to the interests of material life will give way to concern for the welfare
of society and the State, and obsolete rights and privileges will perish together
with the rotten edifice of our industrial system. What seemed secure for aeons
to come will collapse in an hour; what seems today a presumptuous demand
will then seem an obvious assumption. At a time like that, of real sacrifice and
of true self-denial, the forces that are the nation, the Government, and the
Crown fuse together into a closer union and are rejuvenated, whether serving in
the defence forces, the assault troops, or in retaliation. But until then we must
celebrate 1813 and remember 1806.'

[*12 January* continued] Death's harvest: Hollmann, Mrs Magnus,
Delbrück, Fischel, Mrs Schwabach.

At the news of Mrs Schwabach's death I described why I was
amazed at lunch at Victoriastrasse. I had seen her the day before
in the Charlottenburger Chaussee, between Siegesallee and the
Brandenburger Tor, getting into her car with a lady, while I drove
past in my car, about a yard away. She looked at me, I greeted her
and went past. I was astonished at how well she looked.

That very afternoon I discovered that she had been in bed for
over a week before she died; she had not left her bed. I saw her at
1.00 p.m.; I have not learned at what time she died.

6 April, Sunday. Lunch in the Grunewald. Dernburg and wife for the
first time in four years, Secretary of State von Jagow, Police Commissioner von Jagow, Schroeders, Kardorffs, Hitz, Begas, Edith and
Fritz Andreae, Justi. After lunch, Robert von Mendelssohn.

9 April, Wednesday, to *12 April*, Saturday. Conferences daily with
Monnier and Count Pourtalès, later Joerger as well, about the future

organization of Delbrück Schickler & Co.[7] I first advised them to [try] Schuster; negotiated with him in vain. Then to von Gontard, who agreed enthusiastically with my suggestion; but he is only available in a year.

13 April, Sunday, to *20 April*, Sunday. Negotiations with Wermuth and city councillors about the Berliner Elektrizitätswerke.

Prince Henckel, who has been ill, asks me to visit him and wants me to join the Schlesische Zink-Gesellschaft [Silesian Zinc Company],[8] to represent his interests.

Visit and ecstatic letters from Christian Leyst, a clever but overexcited and apparently interested person.[9]

Influenza.

The trial run of the *Imperator* postponed.[10]

Bach, Beethoven, Brahms concerts.

23 April, Wednesday. Evening, lecture at Kraetke's. Conversation with Jagow. Advised him to broach the question of the Dardanelles, to contrast the Powers with Russia; furthermore to strive for a colonial conference with England.

Conversation with Conze about the Südwest-Afrikanisches Bodenkredit Institut [South West African Real Estate Bank].[11]

25 April, Friday. Lunch at von Siemens's. [To Lake] Wannsee with d'Albert.

From *24 May*, Saturday onwards at Freienwalde, with interruptions.

7 July, Monday. To Hamburg; evening, on board the *Imperator*.

8 July, Tuesday. Morning, Kaiser's arrival. Evening, 10.00 p.m., at his table in the smoking room with Fürstenberg, Ruperti, Rantzau, Professor Brauer. First, politics: satisfied with the Bulgarians' defeat.[12] Then stories told, mostly very *risqué* . . .

---

[7] See diary entry for 11 January 1911.

[8] Rathenau then joined the Schlesische AG für Bergbau und Zinkhüttenbetreib as a member of its supervisory board. The company was founded in 1853, and by 1913 had a joint-stock capital worth almost 30 million marks.

[9] See Rathenau, *Briefe*, vol. i, p. 119, Rathenau to Leyst, 3 May 1913.

[10] The *Imperator* was the first of HAPAG's three new fast steamers. The *Vaterland* and the *Bismarck* were to follow.

[11] Private capital refrained from granting credit on real estate. For this reason the Chancellor suggested to the Kaiser, in a report on 5 March 1913, the setting-up of a state-owned land bank. Its capital was to amount to 10 million marks and be defrayed by raising a loan on the colony. ZStA Merseburg, Rep. 89, VII *Schutzgebiete*, 4.

[12] The Second Balkan War began with a surprise attack by Bulgaria on Serbia and Greece

Kaiser tells jokes, *inter alia* Irish ones in dialect. *'At 4 o'clock "domen" was blown to Hell.'*[13]—Of a Swedish Countess who had twins several times: whether she had them every time? No, hundreds of times, she said, nay thousands of times nothing happens at all.— A woman asks: Impotency. Is that higher than Excellency?— A doctor says: Yes, I must operate on you straight away. But on your nose. Return journey 9 July.

15 July, Tuesday. Meeting of the AEG's supervisory board. Emil Rathenau attended for the first time.[14]

on 29 June 1913. Bulgaria had to sue for peace on 30 July after Romania and Turkey had joined the other two powers. At the beginning of July the German Government had rejected an Austrian invitation to support Bulgaria. *Grosse Politik*, vol. 35, pp. 122 ff., Zimmermann to Treutler, 4 July 1913; Hallgarten, *Imperialismus*, vol. ii, p. 410. Salonika was at this time occupied by the Greek army. The Serbian army had repulsed the Bulgarian attack and was advancing.

[13] The joke does not make sense in this form. The Kaiser was well known for telling *risqué* stories. Vierhaus (ed.), *Spitzemberg Tagebuch*, p. 564; Görlitz (ed.), *Der Kaiser*, p. 35.

[14] AEG Archiv, AR, 15 July 1913. At the meeting Rathenau welcomed his father and commented on the effects of the Balkan Wars. The AEG had to make several thousand workers redundant although sales were higher than in the previous year. However, the Wars had shaken the confidence in an undisturbed future, so investments in the car factory and for a new iron foundry had to be postponed.

DIARY FOR 1914

At the end of January or the beginning of February a memorable conversation with Bethmann in von Winterfeldt's presence. He asked (perhaps somewhat rhetorically) whether one should demonstrate consistency or opportunism in national affairs. I replied: these opposites are not the whole problem. What the country demands above all is clear direction. Also he might, in a speech, outline his programme for both foreign and domestic policies.

He thought this was possible for foreign policy, difficult but not impossible for domestic policy. He then turned to the Conservatives who want to eliminate him, above all Heydebrand,[1] whose intransigence caused a lively discussion which lasted until 11.30 p.m., while the guests in the room with the fireplace became embarrassed. The conversation took place in the entrance hall where the tapestries hang.

The wife of von Moltke, Chief of the General Staff, wanted to make my acquaintance in order to talk about [Rathenau's book] *Mechanik des Geistes*. We met at Baroness von Schröder's.

Mrs von Moltke invites me to hear Steiner's lecture, receives me at the architect's house as the protectress of her flock and introduces me to Steiner.

23 February, Monday. Count Rödern, Secretary for Alsace, at the club for lunch. Asked about Leoni. Means of winning-over Alsace culturally: academy, societies. I suggested Marx to him to succeed von Back.

Evening, von Jagow alone to dinner in the Grunewald. I advised him to take advantage of the complications in Mexico to invervene.[2]

---

[1] Bethmann's attitude in the Zabern Crisis had appeased the Conservative opposition. Even if they left him in no doubt of their antagonism, nevertheless it was Heydebrand, above all, who at this time wanted to prevent jabs at the Chancellor and who wanted to support him in the campaign against expanding the power of the Reichstag. ZStA Potsdam, Nachlass Westarp 1, Heydebrand-Westarp correspondence of December 1913; private information from Dr Fritz Klein; Zmarzlik, *Bethmann Hollweg*, p. 129; Pogge von Strandmann, *Die Erforderlichkeit des Unmöglichen*, pp. 28 ff.; Gutsche, *Aufstieg und Fall*, pp. 102–7.

[2] In the last few years before the war German economic interest in Mexico had increased considerably. At the turn of the year the Huerta Government, recognized and supported by Germany, met with increasing difficulties from revolutionaries. Germany's attempt, together with other European powers, to take action against the United States and the insurgents it supported, had just failed. Katz, *Deutschland, Diaz und die Mexikanische Revolution*, pp. 262–316.

Austria's mistakes in the Balkan War.[3] Trieste as a German naval base. The Kaiser's visit to the [German] Foreign Office. Crown Prince. Tirpitz.

24 February, Tuesday. 1 p.m., Solf and Erzberger to lunch in the Grunewald. It was agreed, at my suggestion, that Rechenberg should become director general of the Regie if the shareholders would accept him.[4] Furthermore, that the supervisory board should consist of 4 shareholders and 4 Government nominees, one of them a Commissioner with a veto. The position of the director general to be similar to that of the president of the Reichsbank.

Afternoon, agreement on the financing of the Neukölln–Gesundbrunnen overhead railway. Evening, at Kessler's, Hotel Adlon, with André and wife (American). Craziest American luxury. Then wintergardens. Finally *souper* at the Esplanade [Hotel] before which I took my leave.

12 March, Thursday. Lecture and lunch at Breitenbach's, the Kaiser present. After the meal he only spoke to Hoffmann, then to Breitenbach and myself until the end. First electricity, then Alsace.[5] 'Two Chancellors have lain at my feet to obtain the constitution.' 'Country vitiated to its very core.' 'A Chinese wall will have to be put up between us and France.' 'We can no longer count on a safe deployment [of troops].' 'A military directive has been in existence for 12 to 15 years that no one knew anything about: after sunset troops were only allowed to go out with their hands on their bayonets—, because the *Wackes* [disparaging word for Alsatians] were drawing

[3] The non-exploitation of the situation for its own advantage, i.e. the elimination of Serbian threats to Austrian aspirations in the Balkans.

[4] Monopolistic selling organization for the diamond industry, combining the interests of most of the diggers of South West Africa, which had been founded in 1909 by Fürstenberg at Dernburg's suggestion. Rathenau had a share in this plan (Rathenau, *Briefe*, vol. i, p. 72, Rathenau to Dr S., 26 January 1910). See diary entry for 25 July 1908.

In 1914 the South West African administration took over the Regie's shares for just over 2 million marks (nominal value). Consequently the colonial administration became the dominant influence. ZStA Merseburg, Rep. 89H, VII Schutzgebiete 4, Direct report to the Kaiser, 12 February 1914. A month later Solf reminded Erzberger of his undertaking to support Rechenberg. But because of his former policy in East Africa, opposition in the Reichstag proved to be too strong for Rechenberg to be appointed. BA Koblenz, Nachlass Solf 102, Solf to Erzberger, 25 March 1914.

[5] The Zabern Crisis had led to considerable tension between political and military circles. In 1914 the military way of thinking asserted itself when the country's political problems were being considered. When the Governor of Alsace-Lorraine, Count von Wedel, retired he was succeeded by von Dallwitz, the Prussian Minister of the Interior. The Secretary for Alsace-Lorraine, Zorn von Bulach, was replaced by Count Roedern. Zmarzlik, (*Bethmann Hollweg*), pp. 124–30; Wehler, 'Der Fall Zabern'; K. Stenkewitz, '*Immer feste druff!' Zabernaffäre 1913*.

the soldiers' weapons from behind to stab them in the back(!).'
I tried to object that only an upper-class group of 1,000 people in
Strasbourg and Mulhouse had disturbed the peace—, in vain. 'He
had hesitated for months about removing Zorn von Bulach who had
told him a hundred times that he would let himself "be chopped to
bits" for him.'

13 March, Friday. Privy Councillor Albert calls on me for a thorough
discussion of the Electricity Bill, which was drawn up according to
my suggestions.[6] New proposals *ad notam*. Talk regarding the 1921
Exhibition, about which he reported to Valentini favourably.

Rathenau had thrown light on German domestic and foreign policy in seven
longer articles, six of which appeared in the Viennese *Neue Freie Presse* before
the First World War.[7] The reason for publication in a Viennese newspaper was, as
he wrote to Ballin, 'that I am reluctant to provide Germany with inflammatory
material and am therefore seeking to restrict readership as far as possible to
those who are really interested, who for the most part have access to the *Neue
Freie Presse*.'[8] The questions which Rathenau repeatedly touched on in his
articles concerned the bureaucratization of politics, the lack of qualities of leadership in Germany, the unequal distribution of burdens in the State, the concentration of power in the hands of a small but powerful class, the political
indolence of the middle classes, the economic materialism, the impotence of the
Reichstag, Germany's loss of its position of hegemony in European politics,
and the lack of political goals. Alongside these repeated criticisms of the
political and social conditions in Wilhelmine Germany he developed ideas which
dealt *inter alia* with Anglo-German relations, with France's policy of alliances,
with the general usefulness of colonies, with a central European customs union,
and with the Monroe Doctrine. In a further article, which he published on
31 July 1914, Rathenau tried to clarify the situation, which bore in it the danger
of a 'world war'.[9] He did not see the altercation over the committee of investigation in Serbia as grounds for war, but held that war would be justified if Russia
claimed the right of arbitration over Austria's decisions.

August. Soon after the beginning of the war I took two steps:
    1. I offered the Chancellor my services[10] and worked out for him
a scheme for a customs union between Germany, Austria–Hungary,
Belgium and France.

---

[6] See diary entry for 4 January 1911 and fn. 19.
[7] 'Politik, Humor und Abrüstung' (12 April 1911), 'England und wir, eine Philippika'
(6 April 1912), 'Politische Selektion, die Auslese in der Diplomatie' (16 May 1912), 'Den
Finger auf die Wunde' (August 1912), 'Das Eumenidenopfer' (23 March 1913), 'Deutsche
Gefahren und neue Ziele' (25 December 1913), 'Parlamentarismus' (12 April 1914).
[8] Rathenau, *Briefe*, vol. i., p. 103 Rathenau to Ballin, 3 June 1912.
[9] 'Ein Wort zur Lage', *Berliner Tageblatt*, written on 29 July 1914. This and the articles
mentioned in fn. 7 above are reprinted in the *Gesammelte Schriften*, vol. i., and in the
Nachgelassene Schriften.
[10] On 4 August he wrote to Franz Blei that he 'had considered the idea but not yet come

Rathenau's ideas on *Mitteleuropa* were largely based on his pre-war concepts. In his article 'Deutsche Gefahren und Neue Ziele' [German Dangers and New Aims], published in December 1913, he emphasized the political necessity of a central European customs union which the Western European states would eventually have to join. While he regarded a union of this type as desirable from the industrial point of view, he also indicated that it would reduce 'the nationalistic hatred of the states'. According to Rathenau the reason for all the struggles, alliances, and different domestic developments was indirectly linked to questions of 'power, imperialism and expansion'. However, he believed that the structure of the economy lay at the root of these questions. 'If Europe's economy merges into a community—and that will happen earlier than we think— politics will merge too. That would not mean world peace, nor disarmament, nor slackening, but the moderation of conflicts, the saving of energy and a joint civilization.'

Shortly after the outbreak of the war, and presumably before Bethmann's departure to Koblenz on 16 August 1914, Rathenau may have had one or more talks with the Chancellor which included plans for a future *Mitteleuropa*. He evidently sent a memorandum to Bethmann about a customs union between Germany and Austria–Hungary, which the latter passed on to the Secretary of the Interior, Delbrück. This memorandum has not yet been found. All we have is Delbrück's detailed reply and comments which he passed on to the Chancellor on 3 September 1914.[11] Delbrück rejected Rathenau's plans because to him they did not take into account sufficiently the financial, legal, and domestic problems in Germany. Because of this disregard for domestic problems he did not agree with Rathenau's emphasis on the importance of industry. Although he denied any novelty in Rathenau's plans, which he had compared with similar projects already sixty years old, he admitted that the idea of forcing a customs union upon Austria during the war was new. However, Bethmann accepted Rathenau's basic ideas when he pointed out to Delbrück that *Mitteleuropa* as well as a customs union with Austria could only be realized by a *Friedensdiktat*, or through Germany's political superiority.[12] It is likely that Rathenau knew that Bethmann had passed on his memorandum to Delbrück, and the latter's reaction to it. Presumably in order to counter Delbrück's influence, and knowing that he had to compete with many other influences on Bethmann, he sent another letter to the Chancellor on 28 August, in which he mentioned the three issues that would arise from a peace settlement: *Mitteleuropa*, peace with France, and

to a decision whether it might not be more appropriate to join the army. At a time like this a business occupation fails to satisfy and even working in Staff or in [Government] offices means nothing.' Rathenau, *Briefe. Neue Folge*, pp. 206 f. The letter to the Chancellor referred to in the Diaries must have been written on or after 4 August; but whether it had actually been sent off is questionable. This was not the letter containing his ideas about a customs union with Austria to which he refers in his letter to Mutius. Rathenau, *Politische Briefe*, p. 8, Rathenau to Mutius 7 September 1914.

[11] ZStA Potsdam, RK 2476, Delbrück to Bethmann Hollweg, 3 September 1914; Fischer, *Griff nach der Weltmacht*, p. 108; Zechlin, 'Deutschland zwischen Kabinettskrieg und Wirtschaftskrieg', pp. 398, 401, and 423; Ritter, *Staatskunst und Kriegshandwerk*, vol. iii., p. 43 and 594.

[12] ZStA Potsdam, RK 403, Bethmann to Delbrück, 16 September 1914; Klein (ed.), *Deutschland im Ernsten Weltkrieg*, vol. i, pp. 369 f.

financial re-organization of the world trade and industry.[13] 'I do not consider it audacious,' he wrote,

'but rather timely, to think in terms of a future peace settlement with France, even if conquest only comes after a difficult time with England. I have laid before the Deputy Minister of War, under whose orders I am organizing the War Raw Materials Department, all the technical considerations regarding our relationship with England, which he found interesting. I dare to believe that ways exist to thwart England's far-reaching designs without endangering our fleet. I would ask your Excellency not to consider it presumptuous of me if I *again* refer to the fact that a central European customs union would be the greatest civilizing achievement that the war could bestow on our history.

'Financial reorganization of world trade and industry seems to me a further element in consolidation.

    1. France and Belgium should *ipso jure* open their markets, which have hitherto been closed to us, to all German loans, exempting [them] from taxes.

    2. New Russian stocks and shares should only be quoted in both countries after joint agreement between Germany and France.

    3. Until the end of the Japanese war no Power, which is allied to us or makes peace with us, is to accept Japanese stocks and shares. After peace with Japan, conditions similar to 2. shall come into effect.

Because America cannot play the international money-lender for a long period, and England must look to her own affairs, financial control over the armaments system would fall to us.

'These considerations and the technical transmission of war contributions—which, at forty thousand million francs, would not cover our indirect costs—demand a completely new kind of regulation of the international credit system. I am, together with one of our leading political economists, doing some research into this matter. I would like to ask for a later opportunity to submit the result to your Excellency.'

On 4 September the Chancellor asked Mutius to reply to the letter and to ask Rathenau to submit his new plans.[14] Rathenau replied to the Chancellor's letter on 7 September with a longer statement.[15] Rathenau wanted to win France over to a 'voluntary peace' because neither war contributions nor the transfer of colonies would be possible so long as the war with England continued. Occupation and the transfer of property in France would, in Rathenau's opinion, be more trouble than they were worth. After peace had been made with France, he believed, an economically united Europe could be created under German leadership, which would counterbalance England and America on the one side Russia on the other. 'The sacrifice which we would have to make, would mean renouncing territorial gains in France and reducing contributions.' Peace with France would deprive Russia of its financier and England of its excuse for

---

[13] ZStA Potsdam, RK 2476, Rathenau to Bethmann Hollweg, 28 August 1914; wrongly dated and misplaced in Rathenau, *Politsche Briefe*, pp. 18 f.

[14] Zechlin, 'Deutschland zwischen Kabinettskrieg und Wirtschaftskrieg', pp. 395 f.; ZStA Potsdam, RK 2476.

[15] Fischer, *Griff nach der Weltmacht*, pp. 108 f.; Zechlin, 'Deutschland zwischen Kabinettskrieg und Wirtschaftskrieg', pp. 426 ff; Rathenau, *Politische Briefe*, pp. 9–16, Rathenau to Bethmann, 7 September 1914. See also ZStA Potsdam, RK 2476.

entering the war. Rathenau believed that there were four necessary preconditions for dealing with England:

1. bombing the 'nerves' of British cities,
2. the use of French ports to destroy the Atlantic blockade,
3. threatening the British position in the Mediterranean, especially Egypt, Gibraltar, and Suez,
4. the economic unification and emancipation of *Mitteleuropa*.

The importance of a customs union would be greater than the partition of France, the liquidation of the British Empire, and the take-over of colonies. Germany's isolation as a central power would disappear if its neighbours could be integrated 'organically'. Rathenau had started from the assumption that Britain could not be completely defeated without a military conquest. Therefore he rejected the idea that the defeat of France would result in Britain suing for peace. He also did not share the common belief that England would suffer economically more than Germany. Although the British economy would suffer initially it would soon recover because it had the world market at its disposal. It would sell 'its goods and its normally unsaleable goods' at monopoly price level and survive, while Germany would run out of supplies. The German long-term economic vulnerability would even strengthen the British determination to continue the war. If all this were right then it would be very difficult to dictate a peace to France, especially as annexations and occupations were more burdensome than useful. Therefore a 'voluntary peace' like the one with Austria in 1866 would be more beneficial, because *Mitteleuropa* would have a real chance.

Bethmann did not in fact read this letter until 11 September, just two days after he had put his war-aims proposal before Delbrück, but it can be safely assumed that Rathenau's two earlier memoranda had been read by the Chancellor and that they had an important bearing on the drawing-up of his by now well-known war-aims programme.

In contrast to his pre-war ideas and the earlier two memoranda Rathenau mentioned in this one the integration of France, whereas in December 1913 he had argued that a central European customs union based on the central powers would lead, come what might, to an association with the Western states. In early September Rathenau may have believed that he would gain French co-operation for his plan, but Bethmann Hollweg knew that *Mitteleuropa* would only come about 'under the pressure of political superiority' after a military victory. This would equally apply to Austria–Hungary joining *Mitteleuropa*.[16]

[*August* continued]

2. I went to Colonel Scheüch in the Ministry of War and explained to him my ideas for the organization of raw materials.

---

[16] See diary entry for 25 July 1912 and Rathenau's article 'Deutsche Gefahren und neue Ziele', reprinted in *Gesammelte Schriften*, vol. i.; Delbrück, *Die wirtschaftliche Mobilmachung*, pp. 127 f.; Zechlin, 'Deutschland zwischen Kabinettskrieg und Wirtschaftskrieg', pp. 423–30; Fischer, 'Weltpolitik', pp. 322–9; Gutsche, 'Die Beziehungen zwischen der Regierung Bethmann Hollweg'; Klein (ed.), *Deutschland im Ersten Weltkrieg*, vol. i, p. 360; Fischer, *Krieg der Illusionen*, pp. 745 ff.; Erdmann (ed.), *Kurt Riezler*, pp. 198 f. and p. 208; Gutsche, *Aufstieg und Fall*, pp. 148 ff; Gutsche, 'Mitteleuropaplanungen'; Gutsche, 'Zur Mitteleuropapolitik der deutschen Reichsleitung'; Mader, 'Europapläne und Kriegsziele Walther Rathenaus'.

Recently found evidence suggests more clearly how the central organization which was to deal with Germany's raw materials during the war came into existence. Previously, nearly all accounts had been based on the report Rathenau gave to the Deutsche Gesellschaft on 20 December 1915, published a year later.[17] But once the Moellendorff Papers became available certain doubts were cast upon Rathenau's version.[18]

In 1920 the question of whose brainchild the War Raw Materials Department was led to a controversy between Rathenau and the former AEG employee and later Under-Secretary, Wichard von Moellendorff.[19] Both men claimed the honour of founding the Department and displayed a high degree of sensitivity over this issue. When the early correspondence between Rathenau and Moellendorff was published in the *Post* in January 1920 Rathenau was criticized for not fully recognizing Moellendorff's part in establishing the Department. In a letter to Moellendorff Rathenau tried to put the record straight, but recently Lothar Burchardt threw doubt on the accuracy of Rathenau's facts.[20] Since then enough evidence has come to light to support Rathenau's version. He had actually talked to a member of the Reichstag, one day after the British declaration of war and the beginning of the British blockade, about the effects on the supply of raw materials and foodstuff to Germany. This politician was Felix Schwabach, who advised him on 5 August to see Colonel Scheüch, the head of the War Department, who happened to be Schwabach's friend.[21] Rathenau then asked Scheüch to see him. His letter must have passed over Scheüch's desk on 7 August and a first meeting was arranged for the evening of the next day.[22] A few hours before their meeting Moellendorff's first letter arrived at Rathenau's office, in which he asked Rathenau to approach the War Ministry and suggest that a centre for the registration and distribution of scarce raw materials be organized.[23] He was very concerned about copper and lead, as the AEG used 14 per cent of Germany's annual consumption of these two metals. He also knew that his concern about the AEG would be shared by Rathenau. Rathenau replied to Moellendorff on the same day, before he went to see Scheüch.[24] He only mentioned the need to requisition copper, lead, and other raw materials in Belgium and Northern France. He thought that Moellendorff's proposal for a centralized distributive system would become effective too late as it would be superseded by events, presumably a German victory.

When Rathenau met Scheüch they apparently discussed three schemes,

---

[17] Rathenau, *Deutschlands Rohstoffversorgung*, Berlin 1916. Reprinted in *Gesammelte Schriften*, vol. v.

[18] Burchardt, 'Walther Rathenau und die Anfänge'.

[19] Ibid., pp. 190–4.

[20] BA Koblenz, Nachlass Moellendorff 52, Rathenau to Moellendorff, 29 January 1920. The letter is published in Burchardt, 'Walther Rathenau und die Anfänge', pp. 195 f.

[21] Schulin, *Walther Rathenau Repräsentant, Kritiker und Opfer seiner Zeit*, p. 64. See also Schulin (ed.), *Walther Rathenau. Hauptwerke und Gespräche*, pp. 706 f., Max Scheler and Hulten-Czapski.

[22] Burchardt, 'Walther Rathenau und die Anfänge', p. 178. Stamped on Rathenau's letter of 9 August 1914 is a reference to Scheüch's department and the file which must have been opened after Rathenau's letter had arrived at the Ministry of War. This date is given as 7 August.

[23] Ibid., p. 174.

[24] Ibid., p. 175. BA Koblenz, Nachlass Moellendorff 52, Rathenau to Moellendorf, 8 August 1914. See also Rathenau, *Politsche Briefe*, pp. 6 f., Rathenau to Moellendorff, 8 August 1914.

Rathenau's requisitioning, Moellendorff's central distributive system, and the purchase of raw materials abroad. Scheüch must have found their talk sufficiently important to ask the War Minister, Erich von Falkenhayn, to see Rathenau on 9 August. Rathenau then raised both proposals with him, and later that day wrote his memorandum, which until recently was regarded as lost. However, a copy has now been found.[25] In the memorandum Rathenau started from the assumption that the war would last several months; industry in general and the war industry in particular needed special raw materials. To replace imports would be one thing, but it would be even more important to use the existing stock efficiently. Therefore he recommended 'that the existing amount be registered, that its use be controlled and where necessary that there must be intervention on behalf of the State'. He wanted to apply the same method in the occupied areas. To achieve all this he proposed the establishment of a raw materials office within the War Ministry. This office should collect a list of those firms which wanted to use scarce raw materials, calculate the requirements, and decide on their use. If one firm were suddenly to need more, then the office would be empowered to transfer the necessary amount from one firm to the other. The office would extend its power to the occupied areas in the same way. It was considered that manpower for the running of the office would pose no problems. Finally Rathenau discussed whether the planned office should be attached to the Ministry of the Interior or the War Association of German Industry. He preferred that private industry should remain in an advisory capacity, since the Ministry of the Interior would be too inflexible to handle this. The War Ministry would be better suited, in his eyes, especially if the extension of the office's function in the occupied areas were taken into account. Finally he summed up the advantages of his proposals: 'A sudden lack of scarce raw materials for war production would not occur, an arbitrary use of these materials would be avoided, and the production of substitutes for raw materials as well as for war goods in general would be increased.' Obviously Rathenau had not yet been given the green light for the setting-up of such an office, but the first discussion with Falkenhayn had gone much further and into more detail than has hitherto been thought.

It is likely that Rathenau received Moellendorff's second letter before he saw Falkenhayn, but this would not have influenced Rathenau very much, as this second letter did not add anything new to the first one.[26] Rathenau's memorandum to Falkenhayn may be a mixture of his original proposal and Moellendorff's first letter, but it contained so many ideas which were not part of Moellendorff's plan that Rathenau has to be credited with a far greater contribution to the origins of the War Raw Materials Department than has recently been allowed. Nevertheless, it was probably Moellendorff who first mooted the idea of an organization which was to operate on a large scale. But there is nothing in

[25] BA–MA (Militärarchiv) Freiburg, R 48/v. 918, Rathenau to Falkenhayn, 9 August 1914. Burchardt published in 'Walther Rathenau und die Anfänge', p. 179, a copy purporting to be page 6 of Rathenau's memorandum. In fact this page is composed of a section of pages 3 and 4 as well as the final paragraph of page 6. I am grateful to Professor Michael Geyer for letting me see a transcript of Rathenau's memorandum.

[26] Moellendorff's letters are in BA Koblenz, Nachlass Rathenau 2, Moellendorff to Rathenau, 8 August 1914, and BA Koblenz, Nachlass Moellendorff 52, Moellendorff to Rathenau, 9 August 1914. Both letters have been published in Burchardt, 'Walther Rathenau und die Anfänge', pp. 194 f.

Moellendorff's letters which would justify the conclusion that his contribution to the founding of the later department was greater than Rathenau's. In any case, as Moellendorff was not present at the talks at the War Ministry and did not know the contents of Rathenau's memorandum, he was hardly in a position to claim sole fatherhood.

On 10 August Rathenau informed Moellendorff, in all fairness, that he had mentioned the latter's proposal and his own to the War Ministry, which still seemed to be reluctant to accept their suggestion.[27]

Rathenau also told Moellendorff that the proposal for an organization which would register and secure raw materials might be acceptable to the administration, but not the proposal to control the production costs. Despite the date on this letter, it looks as if Rathenau had written it before he drafted his memorandum on 9 August, since he does not mention his memorandum or his talk with Falkenhayn.

Rathenau went again to the War Ministry on 10 August to elaborate on his proposal. It was probably also on that day that Falkenhayn asked him whether he would be prepared to head the planned department. Since it was envisaged that the interview would last a mere fifteen minutes it is possible that Rathenau had agreed, even on the previous day, to organize such a department, and that the interview served merely as confirmation.[28] Three days later Falkenhayn set up the War Raw Materials Department and appointed Rathenau and Colonel Oehme as joint chiefs.[29] The purpose was to register raw materials necessary for military purposes, at home, in the occupied territories, and possibly in Austria. Military needs were to dictate their usage. The department was directly responsible to the War Minister and his representative.

A day later Rathenau wrote and told his friend Stehr about his aims in his new work.

'If I listen to my innermost being, I know that in so doing I am making myself into the tool of a process of development through which I am contributing to the overthrow of the gods to whom, before August 1914, the world prayed, a world to which I belong and through which I became what I am: an individualist. That is what, together with the difficulty of the task, weighs me down at this late hour, my friend. I come to you like a Saul who has indeed long been ready to recant and yet hesitates because he feels that, in seeking the salvation he is determined on, he is leaving behind a world that is more colourful, more varied, and, all in all, probably richer and happier than that which is now dawning. For paradise will not come in the world which is now being formed; on the contrary: we stand before an immeasurable period of intellectual and material reshuffling, a period, I hardly dare to express it, that will seem to many [to mark] the decline of Europe. Yet where the old crumbles, new can rise, and human, like national history, is never born of beginnings but only of violent commotion.'[30]

[*August* continued] Falkenhayn, the Minister of War, sent a telegram asking me to a further discussion on 10 August. The War Raw Materials

[27] Rathenau, *Politische Briefe*, pp. 7 f., Rathenau to Moellendorff, 10 August 1914.

[28] BA–MA Freiburg, R 48/v918, Wild von Hohenborn's note.

[29] BA Koblenz, Nachlass Rathenau 2, Falkenhayn to Rathenau, 13 August 1914.

[30] Meridies-Stehr (ed.), *Hermann Stehr–Walther Rathenau*, pp. 26 f., Rathenau to Stehr, 14 August 1914.

Department was founded on the 13th and its organization entrusted to me as chairman. Colonel Oehme became nominal head of the department. As colleagues I brought with me Prof. Klingenberg, von Moellendorff, Ehrenthal (from the Aero Club), Geitner, later Tröger (AEG), Nürnberg (Siemens & Halske), Schönbach from Leipzig. Soon the department had 40 officials; it founded the Kriegsmetall AG [War Metals Company], the Kriegschemikalien AG [War Chemicals Company, the Kriegswollbedarf AG, [War Wool Supply Company], the Kammzug AG [Worsted Yarn Company], the Juteabrechnungsstelle [Jute Clearing House], clearing houses for rubber, flax, tin-plate, leather.[31] An organization for Belgium came

[31] On 14 August the KRA began to work. As Moellendorff put it, 'speed was more important than absolute accuracy'. (Burchardt, 'Eine neue Quelle zu den Anfängen der Kriegswirtschaft'.) First the stocks of raw materials needed to be assessed, and a questionnaire was sent out to 900 firms. The next step consisted of setting up a system by which the use of raw materials could be controlled. Instead of letting the ministerial bureaucratic machine, as Rathenau called it, organize the distribution of raw materials, he followed up the suggestion made in his memorandum of 9 August and developed a plan of co-operating with industrial associations. Once the principle of 'mixed' organizations was adopted Rathenau used his experience with the Diamantenregie in South West Africa, the Strasbourg Electricity Works and the projected Imperial Electricity Monopoly to set up war corporations and clearing-houses for less important raw materials. The war corporations would have the character of mixed ownership companies, run as they would be by both State and private industry.

The war corporations had all the trimmings of a joint-stock company, but did not pay out dividends nor distribute profits. They had a board of directors and a supervisory board. In addition there was a committee of valuation and distribution which was to mediate in the case of conflicting interests. It consisted of Government officials and members chosen from the chambers of commerce. State officials who were members of boards and committees were equipped with the power of veto. The war corporations had the task of registering, buying, distributing, and selling raw materials.

By the beginning of October three war corporations had come into existence, and by early 1915 this number had doubled. Later that year about a hundred raw materials were being controlled. The regulation of prices and the development of ersatz materials were the most difficult problems. Although the KRA succeeded in promoting the production of saltpetre by the Haber-Bosch nitrogen fixation method, the general operation of the KRA and its relationship with the interests concerned were far from smooth. There was a constant barrage of complaints, mainly from Southern Germany and small companies. And there was clearly a well-founded reason for the general distrust of the KRA. For instance, the chairman of the supervisory board of the Metal Company which had been founded on 2 September 1914 was Heinrich Peierls, director of the AEG, the State Commissioner was Walther Rathenau himself, another member of the supervisory board was Carl von der Herberg, managing director of Felten & Guilleaume. The Frankfurt Metall-Gesellschaft was represented by one of its directors, Schwarz, and Max von der Porten, who was the second State Commissioner. Thus it appeared that the Metal Company was dominated by the AEG and the Metall-Gesellschaft.

A number of industrialists did not at all agree with the management of German raw materials. Bodenhausen complained about Rathenau: 'He is playing such a highly ambiguous, completely unclean role in this that I do not want to see him again at all.' Bodenhausen-Degener, *Briefe der Freundschaft*, p. 176, Bodenhausen to Hofmannsthal, 13 October 1914. The banker Max Steinthal defended Rathenau when he was criticized by Eich, who wanted

into existence; it was taken over by Colonel Oehme, who was replaced
by Colonel Dahlmann.

Meanwhile Wild von Hohenborn and von Wandel succeeded
Falkenhayn as Deputy [Ministers of War].[32]

Wahnschaffe is taking a lively interest in the customs union.[33]
There was a dinner at the Auto Club at which Lewald, Delbrück,
Drews, Johannes, Richter were present;[34] after initial opposition the
idea gained ground; von Rechenberg was drawn into working for us
at the Imperial Office of the Interior.[35] Delbrück travelled to Headquarters to discuss the matter with Bethmann. As the official advisers
were consulted opposition grew. Finally, on 30 October, there was
a meeting of the [Prussian] State Ministry; the customs union was
rejected.[36]

As a consequence of his correspondence with Bethmann Hollweg about the
'war aim' *Mitteleuropa*, the Secretary of the Interior, Clemens von Delbrück, was
given the task of sounding out in his department the possibilities for a *Mitteleuropa* with a customs union with Austria-Hungary at its centre.[37] At the
beginning of October, when Delbrück visited the Chancellor in Coblenz, he
pointed out to him the great difficulties involved in working out a plan for such
a customs union.[38] A few days later the departmental work was concluded, and
Delbrück summed up the results on 20 October 1914.[39] He was against a union
with Austria at this time because it would reduce the commercial flexibilities
of German traders, and boost cheap Austrian imports. In addition he objected
to being politically linked to a partner whose power was crumbling. Delbrück

him to support the Mannesmann group. Despite his diplomacy and his caution, Steinthal
thought that 'he was now the man who was most persecuted with enmity because naturally
he cannot please all the interests concerned'. Pogge von Strandmann, *Unternehmenspolitik
und Unternehmensführung*, p. 92. For the latest accounts on the organization of war raw
materials see Burchardt, 'Eine neue Quelle zu den Anfängen der Kriegswirtschaft'; Ott,
'Kriegswirtschaft und Wirtschaftskrieg 1914-1918'; Feldman, 'The Political and Social
Foundations of Germany's Economic Mobilization'; D. G. Williamson, 'Walther Rathenau
and the KRA'; Baudis, 'Die Herausbildung der staatsmonopolistischen Kriegswirtschaft',
in Baudis and Nussbaum, *Wirtschaft und Staat*.

[32] Falkenhayn was Minister of War until 21 January 1915. His representative Wild von
Hohenborn took over, and von Wandel became his representative.

[33] ZStA Potsdam, RK 403, Wahnschaffe to Rathenau, 14 September 1914.

[34] The same dinner is recorded by Riezler in his diary with a different emphasis. Neither
Rathenau nor Riezler mentions the other in their diaries. Erdmann (ed.), *Kurt Riezler*,
p. 225.

[35] Rechenberg was employed to work on the September Memorandum.

[36] The meeting of senior officials actually took place on 21 October 1914. Zechlin,
'Deutschland zwischen Kabinettskrieg und Wirtschaftskrieg', pp. 425 and 436.

[37] Ibid., pp. 419-27; Ritter, *Staatskunst und Kriegshandwerk*, vol. iii, pp. 43 and 594;
Erdmann (ed.), *Kurt Riezler*, p. 214.

[38] Erdmann (ed.), *Kurt Riezler*, p. 214. See also Delbrück, *Die wirtschaftliche Mobilmachung*, pp. 127 f.

[39] Zechlin, 'Deutschland zwischen Kabinettskrieg und Wirtschaftskrieg', pp. 434-9;
Erdmann (ed.), *Kurt Riezler*, p. 214.

then repeated the arguments of the other side which had been represented by Rechenberg and which were to some extent identical with those in Rathenau's letter to Bethmann Hollweg on 7 September.[40] Two days later Bethmann asked Delbrück to work out some guide-lines in case of a sudden peace settlement.[41] Bethmann wanted to avoid any surprises, and among other things pointed out that a close economic union with Austria was still at the centre of his plans. This time Delbruck proposed instead of a 'customs union' a 'customs alliance' of several states with common external tariffs and internal customs freedom.[42] Even this alliance could only be realized after a German victory. He feared that even the proposed alliance could be restricted to Austria and Belgium, although it would be essential to win the world markets for German exports. Therefore Delbrück recommended the continuation of the policy of trade treaties, which should not exclude the possibilities of tariff arrangements in certain fields.

After that Rathenau's project seems to have been put into cold storage, but a year later it was decided that the plan for a customs league with Austria should be revived.[43]

[*August* continued] Harden sounded me out through Fritz Andreae's mediation; relations were re-established after both sides had made a declaration: that it was a matter of honour never to treat private affairs in public.[44]

Up till now only Harden, Theodor Wolff and a few others stand

---

[40] Zechlin, 'Deutschland zwischen Kabinettskrieg und Wirtschaftskrieg', pp. 434 f.

[41] Gutsche, 'Zur Mitteleuropapolitik der deutschen Reichsleitung', pp. 98 f. See also Gutsche and Kaulisch (eds.), *Herrschaftsmethoden des deutschen Imperialismus*, pp. 206 f. Bethmann's letter is published here.

[42] Gutsche, 'Zur Mitteleuropapolitik der deutschen Reichsleitung', p. 99, Delbrück to Bethmann Hollweg, 30 October 1914.

[43] Ibid., p. 100, meeting about relations with Austria, 9 November 1915. See also Gottwald, 'Gemeinsamkeiten und Unterschiede in der Mitteleuropapolitik der herrschenden Klasse'.

[44] After the outbreak of the war, and presumably because of it, Harden tried to improve his relations with Rathenau through Rathenau's brother-in-law. The first letter Harden sent was on 29 September 1914. A year before that the relationhip had begun to deteriorate. Harden's relationship with Felix Deutsch was never repaired, whereas his relationship with Ballin improved after July 1913 once Harden had explained to Ballin about 'his divorce from Walther Rathenau'. Hellige (ed.), Rathenau–Harden. Lili Deutsch told her brother that she had experienced more with these men 'who are driven by ambition and the wish for power' than she could read in novels. In March 1913 she wrote to her brother: 'I am sorry I cannot tell you the details about the tragicomedy which took place between Harden, Walther and us. I don't believe that similar things happen very often; all good and bad demons were in motion. The result is now—Harden is separated from us and Walther; Walther has challenged Harden to a duel; and finally Walther is on loyal and dignified terms with Felix; Walther and I myself in a transitory stage. I like it best this way. It was no longer possible to keep Walther as well as Harden; Harden has behaved badly and Walther was a coward; I am most blameworthy, but also showed the greatest courage and the instinct to steer safely through all of it.' And a few months later in August she wrote: 'Between Walther and myself many things are destroyed; there was always something tragic in our relationship; perhaps old age will bring a beautiful clarity.' Schulin, *Walther Rathenau. Repräsentant*, pp. 59 f.

out against the prevailing optimism.[45] Even Hauptmann is caught up in it.

In the summer the idea of a free, international association grew among van Eeden's friends: Gutkind, Buber, Rang, Borel, Bjerre, Rolland, Tagore, and others were to belong to it and meet in the autumn at Forte di Marmi.

Some interesting war correspondences ensued, in which four or five members including myself participated.[46]

The outbreak of war interrupted my new work.[47] The war claims all our thoughts. Deeply oppressed by the arbitrariness of its causes, dampened hopes.

On *2 November*, Monday. At noon, lunch at Henckel von Donnersmark's. Also there: ladies, Count Monts, Count Moltke, Count Luxburg. Relatively lighthearted.

In the evening Mrs von Moltke sent for me. At 5.30 p.m. I entered the General Staff for the first time.

She alleged the reason for the visit was to warn me against Mrs von Schröder, who was not much better than a spy. Then she told me—almost abruptly—in the deepest distress, that she was travelling to Homburg that evening to look after her husband who was to convalesce at the castle as the Kaiser's guest.

Moltke has been shelved since the retreat (4 Sept.).[48] Lyncker conveyed the order to him to report sick. He went to the Kaiser, gave him an idea of the impression this would create abroad, received

---

[45] Rathenau expressed his worries about the future in his birthday telegram to Harden. Hellige (ed.), Rathenau–Harden, Rathenau to Harden, 20 October 1914. Theodor Wolff also noted the enthusiasm of Gerhart Hauptmann and Fritz von Unruh. Köhler, *Der Chefredakteur*, pp. 171 f.

[46] Van Eeden and Stefan Zweig had asked Rathenau to collaborate in Romain Rolland's Peace Movement. Rathenau had declined because of too much work. Rathenau, *Briefe*, vol. i, pp. 167 ff., Rathenau to van Eeden, and p. 170, Rathenau to Zweig, both letters 24 October 1914. See Loewenberg, *Walther Rathenau and German Society*, p. 117.

[47] In the summer of 1914 Rathenau wrote about one quarter of his third major book, which he published in 1917 under the title *Von kommenden Dingen* [Of Things to Come]. There are many references in the first pages to the pre-war world which could not have been written after the outbreak of the war, yet he did not change them during the next two years. Although he may have been unhappy about the interruption of his writing, he soon realized that his work in the KRA gave his ideas a much stronger push in the direction of his brand of 'socialism'. In order to underline the difference between the new world which would be brought about by the war and the old pre-war conditions he left his pre-war references unaltered. Schulin (ed.), *Walther Rathenau. Hauptwerke und Gespräche*, pp. 555–8.

[48] The order to von Kluck's army to retreat in the battle of the Marne was given by Lieutenant Colonel Hentsch, authorized by Moltke on 10 September 1914. On 14 September Lyncker transmitted the order to Moltke to retire and on 15 September Falkenhayn gave up the plan to circumvent the French left wing. At the same time Quartermaster-General von Stein was relieved of his post.

a vague answer. Stayed at headquarters. Falkenhayn took over his responsibilities, set aside Quartermaster-General von Stein. Moltke received no more reports. His aides-de-camp were transferred. He was only an onlooker at Falkenhayn's briefings (whom Mrs von Moltke calls Falkenstein). But he remained involved in the siege of Antwerp. 'For seven weeks', she said, 'the Kaiser did not know who was commanding the war.' After the fall of Antwerp Moltke was awarded the Iron Cross, First and Second Class; the Kaiser was very friendly.[49]

Finally the subject was broached. The Kaiser is supposed to have been under the impression that Falkenhayn was only 'deputizing' for Moltke.[50] But that day Moltke really did collapse owing to his liver complaint. The Kaiser visited him at his bedside, brought him flowers, sent him to Homburg. Evidently the mistake is Moltke's and his wife's. The Kaiser obviously wanted to drop him once and for all, but apparently could not find the words to express this clearly at the meeting.

Mrs von Moltke bitterly accuses Falkenhayn, Bethmann and Lyncker.

She tells how, at the beginning of the war, she had heard a frightful scene in her *salon* (the room with three windows to the right of the room where she received me) which adjoined her husband's study. Raised voices, 'I won't stand for it' and 'I forbid you', in the tone in which one shouts at a dog. Her husband came out pale; she then heard that it was Lyncker who was making the scene, apparently because of a direct report to the Kaiser, about which Lyncker had known nothing.

I calmed her and said that her husband should clear up this intolerable situation; it was more dignified to go down in the conflict than to remain in an impossible position.

At any rate, according to this, Moltke's position seems to have been finished long ago.

---

[49] Antwerp fell on 9 October 1914.
[50] Görlitz (ed.), *Regierte der Kaiser?*, pp. 57 f.; Janssen, *Der Kanzler und der General*, pp. 15–19. Moltke was officially Chief of the General Staff until 3 November 1914. See now Lange, *Marneschlacht und deutsche Öffentlichkeit*.

NOTES ON 1915

Journey to Kovno. Thursday evening, 18 November to Monday morning, 22 November 1915

Although Rathenau's far-reaching *Mitteleuropa* concept was not followed up he continued to believe in the necessity of an economically unified Europe.[1] However, the KRA kept him extremely busy until he resigned in March 1915. The reasons for his retirement have never been very clear. But already in September 1914 he had written to Mutius that he aimed at putting the KRA on its own feet and then withdrawing from his work.[2] By February 1915 he felt he had completed his task there. In a letter to Fanny Künstler he wrote: 'At last I see light in my work. Organization is as good as done; I can leave the management to others. By the middle of March, at the latest, I think I will have handed everything over to my colleagues and successors.'[3] Although the War Ministry asked Rathenau to stay he left his appointment on 31 March 1915. The Deputy Minister of War, Wandel, thanked him officially for what he had done.

'At your suggestion and with your co-operation the organization most vital to the national defence effort was brought into being and directed to its present state of perfection. I can now no longer oppose your wish to resign from the War Ministry now that the path has been smoothed out for the task of the War Raw Materials Department. I do not need to emphasize how difficult it is for me to accept your leaving us after almost eight months working here in the military administration. I am compelled, Dr Rathenau, to tell you that by the devotion and sacrifice you have shown in your work for the well-being and military preparedness of our army and our country you have won our sincerest thanks. I may yet hope that the severence of your formal ties with it has not broken your links with the War Ministry, but that you will be prepared to make your expert advice and rich experience available for furthering your work.'[4]

As well as Wandel and Wild von Hohenborn, friends had tried, in vain, to persuade Rathenau to stay in office.[5] Yet it was not just the fact that he had completed his task of organizing the department which prompted him to resign, but, according to Kessler, it was also the backbiting, intrigues, bureaucracy, excessive work-load, and opposition to him by a few circles in heavy industry which determined his move.[6] Kessler's point is strengthened by the fact that in the meetings of the budget committee of the Reichstag in the middle of March 1915 Rathenau was attacked for profiteering, as he had been in December 1914. Moreover, in a letter to Wild von Hohenborn he expressed a further motive when he wrote that a department 'which is greater in the number of its officials

---

[1] Interview with the *Neue Freie Presse*, 18 April 1915.

[2] Rathenau, *Politische Briefe*, pp. 8 f., Rathenau to Mutius, 7 September 1914.

[3] Rathenau, *Briefe*, vol. i, p. 178 f., Rathenau to Fanny Künstler, 21 February 1915.

[4] BA Koblenz, Nachlass Rathenau 2, Wandel to Rathenau, 31 March 1915; ibid., Wild von Hohenborn's letter of the same day.

[5] Hutten-Czapski, *Sechzig Jahre*, vol. ii, p. 152.

[6] Kessler, *Rathenau*, pp. 190 and 240; Gutsche (ed.), *Deutschland im Ersten Weltkrieg*, vol. ii, p. 115.

and in the amount of work it accomplishes than a normal ministry, cannot be continued on the free lines of an affiliation but must have close and strong administrative links with its central office'.[7]

This statement puts a rational gloss over the reasons for his resignation. Already in this letter he mentions that the 'necessary decision to sacrifice the person to the cause was made easier by the fact that the organizational work was completed'.[8] He implies that he may not have wanted to resign when he actually did. Although it is clear that he wanted to leave his job soon, it was political and industrial pressure which speeded up his decision. There was mounting criticism because he continued to hold his offices in industry and banking, and retained his special links with the AEG. Many people suspected him of favouring the AEG when it came to contracts and to the supply of raw materials. Even his father hoped he would work longer for the KRA so that the AEG would benefit from it.[9] It is very likely that the AEG empire gained from the involvement of several AEG people in the KRA, but they must have made every effort to conceal such advantages. But even if the AEG benefited only in the same way as everyone else it was an obvious charge to be made against Rathenau.

Initially Erzberger, who had himself suggested a plan of how to organize the continuous supply of raw materials, approved of Rathenau's appointment: 'Under the present circumstances I regard the existing organization as good and productive, especially as through Dr Rathenau, whom I have known personally for years, all guarantees are given that the Reich will not fare badly.'[10] A few weeks later the first attack came from several members of the Reichstag.[11] They doubted the usefulness of the organization and suggested that the existing departments in the War Ministry should have divided the tasks of supplying raw materials among themselves. Falkenhayn, inspired by Rathenau, defended the KRA by pointing out that the work was too new and too diversified for the existing departments to carry out.[12]

A fresh attack was launched by the Centre Party, which had been called upon to support the small and medium-sized firms against the large ones which appeared to be favoured by the KRA.[13] Erzberger changed his mind and called the KRA a 'failure'.[14] He was of the opinion that the system of registration and confiscation had been carried out inefficiently, and criticized the war corporations for helping the process of decentralization which pushed up prices. He was very scathing about Rathenau's arrangements of price ceilings and his continuous active involvement in industry. Erzberger asked Falkenhayn for an interview 'because he considered the solution of these problems as the most important task for domestic politics in the Reich'. This time it was Wild von Hohenborn who wrote the reply, again inspired by Rathenau.[15] He made it

[7] Rathenau, *Politische Briefe*, p. 37, Rathenau to Wild von Hohenborn, 1 April 1915.

[8] Ibid.

[9] See also Schulin (ed.), *Walther Rathenau. Hauptwerke und Gespräche*, pp. 558 f.

[10] BA–MA Freiburg, R 48/v. 918, Erzberger to Falkenhayn, 11 October 1914. I am greatly indebted to Professor Michael Geyer for letting me see his transcript of this letter, and several others concerning the criticism of the KRA.

[11] Ibid., memorandum to Falkenhayn about a meeting among members of the Reichstag, 28 November 1914.

[12] Ibid., copy of the reply, without a date.

[13] Ibid., copy of a letter sent to Erzberger on 5 December 1914.

[14] Ibid., Erzberger to Falkenhayn, 8 December 1914.

[15] Ibid., memorandum to Wild von Hohenborn, 1 January 1915.

clear that the KRA would be reformed in such a way that 'all persons who were working for the KRA on a voluntary basis', obviously including Rathenau, 'would gradually hand over their tasks to qualified officers'. Thus Erzberger was fended off, but four weeks later Schoeler, the Generalintendant on the Western Front, accused the KRA of using the raw materials from the occupied territories to serve the interests of the large firms only.[16] To meet this criticism it was recommended that all industrialists in decision-making posts be removed and retained in a consultative capacity only. Officers who were regarded as impartial were to take over all key posts in the KRA. This would also help the War Ministry when it had to account for all the goods under its own administration to the Reichstag after the war. Rathenau went along with this recommendation, but denied that any preferential treatment had taken place, adding that the existing State Commissioners would be able to prevent that.[17] He also reminded the Supreme Command of his intention to hand over his job to an officer the moment the organizational work was completed. Three weeks later he responded to the political and military pressures and resigned. But he did not sever all relations with the KRA. He continued to advise his successor, Major Koeth, whom he himself had proposed previously as official counselor, and he accepted Koeth's request that he should continue to work with the War Metals Company and Caoutchouk Clearing House.[18] Yet essentially his task as the 'economic general staff behind the front' had come to an end.[19]

The experience of his eight months in office left a deep impression upon Rathenau. It enabled him to develop his ideas for the post-war economy, and it also gained him considerable publicity when talking and writing about the work he had done.[20] He also left the KRA in good time to make a bid for a more powerful position within the AEG hierarchy when his father died on 20 June 1915.[21] This time the struggle was far less dramatic, but still irritated men like Ballin and Harden. Soon after his father's death the supervisory board was convened to discuss the new situation.[22] Rathenau then informed the meeting that in a preliminary discussion of the board's committee a letter of his father had been read out which by now was considered to be well known to the assembly. He then moved five points which were to be passed by the meeting:

1. His father's room would become his.
2. He would be entitled to visit the factories of the AEG.
3. He would be equally entitled to receive all statistical and other information. He would be able to convene the board of directors and take part in their meetings after having consulted the chairman of the board.
4. Deutsch was to take over the chairmanship of the board of directors.
5. Agreement was to be reached between the board of directors and Rathenau as to who would take over the jobs vacated by Emil Rathenau.

Rathenau emphasized that these five points would form the framework for co-operation between him and the board of directors for the time being. The supervisory board accepted this, but insisted that the rights and duties of the board

[16] Ibid., Schoeler to War Ministry, 19 February 1915.
[17] Ibid., Rathenau's memorandum, 19 March 1915.
[18] BA Koblenz, Nachlass Rathenau 2, Rathenau to Wandel, 3 May 1915.
[19] *Deutsche Export Revue*, 26 November 1915.
[20] Rathenau, 'Deutschlands Rohstoffversorgung', talk given to the Deutsche Gesellschaft, 20 December 1915. The talk was published as a booklet in 1916.
[21] Kessler, *Rathenau*, p. 249.
[22] AEG Archiv, AR-meeting, 8 July 1915.

of directors should not be curtailed. On the other hand the chairman of the supervisory board should be in close contact with the directors in order to help with the co-ordination of the technical and administrative management. In any case the supervisory board reserved its right to return to the subject and issue new instructions if this should prove necessary.

This arrangement largely depended on a good relationship between Rathenau and Deutsch. Both men had worked together well, and once the crisis of 1912/13 was over they continued to co-operate well. However, for Rathenau the new arrangement was not quite sufficient, and he wanted to give his new role a title. He wanted to be called 'president'. On 15 July Ballin informed Harden

'that it would be in Rathenau's interest to gain this title in agreement with the directors and not against their will.[23] Precisely because the supervisory board could pass on this title anyway, even without consulting the board of directors, and because it is an act of politeness, I think it necessary in the interest of the company not to undermine this politeness. [But] whatever the case for politeness may be Rathenau has decided this question in his favour already as he uses the title "Presidium" as his letter heading.'

Ballin and Harden were annoyed by Rathenau's vanity; Ballin had hoped that the tricks Rathenau used were a matter of the past.[24] However, their irritation was soon forgotten, especially since Deutsch did not object to this type of duumvirate, however much he may have felt irked by the title of president which was granted to Rathenau by the annual general meeting on 12 October. When, in 1921, Rathenau resigned from the AEG in order to become Minister for Reconstruction, Deutsch took over Emil Rathenau's old title 'General-director' and Fürstenberg chairman of the supervisory board, an arrangement Deutsch had advocated in the summer of 1912.

Rathenau was very pleased to become president. In a letter to Hutten-Czapski he wrote: 'I have found in my father's sphere of activity a substitute for my work at the ministry which I ended in the spring, after the material security for pursuing the war had been assured for years to come.'[25] Besides being president he became chairman of the supervisory boards of the BEW and the BHG. In this new position he was apart from Hugo Stinnes, the most powerful managerial entrepreneur in German industry.

In the field of politics he advocated the 'great breakthrough in the West', and for this purpose joined what had become something of a national pilgrimage to Kovno, the headquarters of Ludendorff. His visit to Ludendorff was decisive, since from that moment Rathenau belonged to 'the number of those who did all in their power to smooth his path to the Supreme Command'.[26] Yet his conversation with Falkenhayn shortly after his journey to Kovno seemed to serve the purpose of securing agreement between Falkenhayn and Ludendorff rather than of securing Ludendorff's supremacy.

[23] BA Koblenz, Nachlass Harden 6, Ballin to Harden, 15 July 1915.
[24] Ibid., Ballin to Harden, 18 July 1915. See also Hellige (ed.), Rathenau–Harden, Harden to Rathenau, 29 September 1915.
[25] Hutten-Czapski, Sechzig Jahre, vol. ii, p. 288, Rathenau to Hutten-Czapski, 21 August 1915.
[26] 'Schicksalsspiel', in Was wird werden?, collected in Harttung et al. (eds.), Walther Rathenau. Schriften, p. 290.

At Kovno station we were met (Councillor Deutsch and I) by
Captain Markau, who was at that time head of the telegraph department, and he accompanied us to the Hotel Levinsohn, which has
been requisitioned by the commandant. It is managed by a sergeant;
dirty and inadequate accommodation.

The next day's programme was arranged. Markau describes
personalities and relationships at Staff Headquarters, according to his
personal judgement.

20 November, Saturday. In the morning, inspected the Tillmann
factories.[27] Afterwards, long discussion in Markau's office about the
activities which were to be undertaken. Lengthy, fruitless telephon-
ing to get information about barbed wire manufacture in Libau.

Ludendorff let it be known that he would be available the whole
morning up to 1 p.m. Generally the degree of activity seems to be
relatively quiet at the moment.[28]

At 12 a.m. we called at Government House. After a few minutes
Ludendorff, who had just wound up a conference in the next room,
appeared. I explained to him what I had imagined would be his
wishes regarding production, and specified in a few minutes the procedure we had in mind. I proposed sending a letter to the Ministry
of War and a tender from Tillmann's, and concluded by referring
to the fact that it was therefore our business to prove to him that we
were determined to co-operate.

Ludendorff at once declared that he agreed with everything, and
the business conversation, in which Colonel von Eisenhardt-Rothe
had participated, came to an end; [the latter] I knew from the
Ministry of War.

We then moved on to a more general conversation. To begin with
Mr Deutsch spoke to Ludendorff about economic conditions in
Russia; Eisenhardt-Rothe spoke to me about the political situation
and prospects of peace, and told me that he wanted to continue this
conversation and would drive us out to the Kovno forts the next day.

[27] The practical purpose of Deutsch's and Rathenau's journey was the take-over of these
iron factories in Kovno and Libau. Tillmanns & Co. was a Rhenish screw-making factory near
Opladen. One branch of the family went to Kovno in 1868 and started a flourishing enterprise there. After the conquest of Kovno these factories were sequestered by the State of
Prussia and administered by the Supreme Command of the East. The result of the journey
was that the AEG and Felten & Guilleaume started the production of barbed wire at Libau.
Rathenau recommended the take-over of these factories by the AEG. This was accepted,
and Deutsch then asked Zapf to come to Berlin to finalize the arrangements. FG Archiv,
Deutsch to Zapf, 3 December 1915. The factory in Kovno was run by the German Tillmanns who received financial and managerial support from the AEG and Felten & Guilleaume.

[28] After the German-Austrian offensive in the summer the German Eastern Front did
not advance until June 1917.

We all then discussed the importance of Riga. I observed to Ludendorff that it would be hard for Russia to stand the shortening of its inadequate Baltic front. He agreed, but mentioned that he was not for the present thinking of capturing Riga.[29]

The gentlemen were summoned to table; we said goodbye after about an hour's conversation and after Ludendorff had invited us to dine at the Field Marshal's at 8 p.m.

In the afternoon we toured the town. I drafted the two letters that were to be sent off the next day.

At 8 p.m. we presented ourselves at the Villa Tillmanns. The villa is in the garden, a rather large brick building in the German executive style, over-furnished and with very little taste. The officers were together in the ante-room, first and foremost Ludendorff, Colonel Hoffmann, Prince Dohna, von Waldow, Kämmerer (aide-de-camp to the Field Marshal), and three artists who had come to paint and sculpt, namely Petersen, Lederer, and Metzner.

As soon as we had gone into the large drawing-room Hindenburg appeared. We were introduced and after a few minutes we went in to dinner. Hindenburg is big, and has rather run to fat, his hands are unusually plump and soft, the lower half of his head resembles the portraits, the upper half is completely different. His forehead is good, the setting of his nose and paticularly the nose itself very weak and undefined, his eyes swollen and dull—the last may be symptomatic of a temporary condition. His voice, soft, deep, elderly, his speech quiet and kindly.

Dohna sat on the Field Marshal's left, I on his right, then Ludendorff and Deutsch; opposite Hindenburg sat His Excellency Surgeon-General Kern.

Hindenburg drank to the guests. Conversation was conducted in a cordial and friendly way yet remained unproductive. His remarks had little colour, and towards the end when I told him about the great unanimity of popular feeling, such as had not been seen in Germany since the time of Luther, and of Blücher, he remarked, in his unpretentious and friendly way, that he did not deserve this enthusiasm, but probably ought to fear that it might arouse envy and ill will in the country.[30] I was rather astonished at this apprehension and tried to divert his attention; he came back to it again.

Conversation to the right was livelier. Ludendorff thanked me for

[29] Riga was not captured by the Germans until the battle of 1–3 September 1917. See also Janssen, *Der Kanzler und der General*, p. 136.

[30] Relations between Falkenhayn and Hindenburg had become exceptionally strained in the summer of 1915. Janssen, *Der Kanzler und der General*, pp. 154 f.; Hubatsch, *Hindenburg und der Staat*, p. 15.

the letter I had written to him.[31] We got on to talking about his answers and the general situation. I expressed the wish that the Supreme Command in the West could be taken over by Hindenburg and his staff; he explained that this was completely out of the question and hinted at the reasons.[32] He agreed with me regarding the political situation, the disinclination on the part of those concerned to conclude peace and the risks involved in any delay.

After dinner I next spoke to Hoffmann in an adjoining room. We renewed our acquaintance and our conversation immediately turned to Hindenburg. He asked for my impression, which I, to some extent, gave him while I expressed the idea that the great qualities of temperament of an elderly, quiet, right-thinking man promoted the consolidation of great forces; at which he immediately and with great enthusiasm referred to Ludendorff's qualities. He would not accept the example I had put forward—Bismarck's relationship with the old Kaiser—and suggested that the more passive qualities that I had mentioned presented a truer picture.

We then moved into the big room where we all sat in a circle round a table with cigars and beer. I was again placed next to Ludendorff and now he described in detail relations with the Austrians, who had let themselves be completely vanquished at Ivangorod and made the first encirclement of the Russians impossible;[33] then he turned to the second attempt at encirclement in July, which was

[31] The initiative for a correspondence with Ludendorff came from Rathenau, who had simultaneously forwarded to Ludendorff his memorandum to Bethmann Hollweg of 30 August 1915. ZStA Potsdam, RK 2444; Rathenau, *Politische Briefe*, pp. 45–9. The Chancellor had commented on it: 'Thanks. I cannot go into these completely vague concepts myself [text unclear]'. Zechlin, 'Deutschland zwischen Kabinettskrieg und Wirtschaftskrieg', p. 49. Ludendorff on the other hand responded to Rathenau's ideas on 6 September 1915. He considered making concessions to Russia to be a mistake. 'I do not know', he continued, 'what the Supreme Command is doing. I cannot, therefore, express my opinion frankly. At any rate I hope for an offensive in the West. I hope that something decisive will happen there now, since operations here have taken the known course.' BA Koblenz, Nachlass Rathenau 2. Some of the letters in the correspondence seem to have been lost. The next letter of Rathenau's that was sent (to Ludendorff) is dated 6 November 1915. Rathenau, *Politische Briefe*, pp. 50 f. In it Rathenau rejected concessions towards England and America. He did not believe in a separate peace with Russia and therefore pinned his hopes on a breakthrough in the West and peace with France. Hence he welcomed Ludendorff's repeatedly expressed idea of an attack in the West.

[32] The antagonism between Falkenhayn on the one hand and Hindenburg and Ludendorff on the other was probably decisive in this respect.

[33] In the battle of Ivangorod (22–6 October 1914) the Austrian First Army was routed and consequently the German Ninth Army had to fall back. Thus the first plan to encircle the Russian armies west of Warsaw had failed. Ludendorff believed that he could have annihilated the Russian army by means of a second large-scale encircling movement in the Kovno-Vilna direction in July 1915. Hoffmann, *Der Krieg der versäumten Gelegenheiten*, pp. 114 f.; Janssen, *Der Kanzler und der General*, pp. 134 f.; Ritter, *Staatskunst und Kriegshandwerk*, vol. iii, pp. 84–8.

thwarted by the removal of troops. He cannot see another opportunity to destroy the Russian army.

I told him about the Russians' military preparations, which he knew about and which he calmly awaited, particularly as he does not intend to advance any further.[34]

He then turned to his alleged loss of nerve, which he explained, and said (verbatim): 'I would not be able to fight the battle of Tannenberg over again today.'[35] Then he commented on this battle, which was not due to a fixed plan, but rather to decisions made instinctively at the time; only the first Masurian battle had been based on a more or less predetermined plan.[36] We reverted again to the general situation and the necessity of an offensive in the West.

At about 10.15 p.m. all the officers took their leave to go back to work at Government House. Hindenburg, Kämmerer, Dohna, and the civilians remained.

But beforehand it had been arranged that Hoffmann was to take over as guide instead of Eisenhart-Rothe who could not accompany us the next day.

Conversation slackened now. I stood to one side for a longish time with Lederer, who was just as disappointed as I was in the outward impression made by Hindenburg. Then we spoke about more general topics. I brought up the subject of Napoleon's campaign. Hindenburg expressed his opinion without being particularly critical, and only observed that Napoleon had stayed on in Moscow too long.[37]

The party broke up at 11.30 p.m.

We collected Hoffmann at 10 a.m. on Sunday. He took me in the first open car; the other followed with Mr Deutsch and Markau.

First we inspected the Russian trenches and obstacles, then Fort 2 with the scars of the 42 cm. shells; then Fort 1 which has a view across the Niemen to the town.[38] With the help of a map Hoffmann explained the details of the operations to us.

During the drive, which lasted more than two hours in cold weather, we talked uninterruptedly about political and personal relations. Hoffmann had already seen service under Prittwitz; when he proved a failure Ludendorff was appointed.[39] Hindenburg was put

[34] The Russian offensive, in the Vilna area, did not take place until the middle of May 1916.

[35] The battle at Tannenberg took place between 26 and 31 August 1914. A battle plan had certainly already been drawn up before Ludendorff arrived.

[36] The first battle at the Masurian Lakes lasted from 6 to 15 September 1914.

[37] Napoleon entered Moscow on 15 September 1812 and the retreat began on 19 October 1812.

[38] Kovno had been captured on 17–18 August 1915.

[39] Ludendorff had been appointed on 22 August 1914. Hindenburg had replaced Prittwitz as Commander-in-Chief.

at the head of the army because he was the oldest general. The battle at Tannenberg had been completely planned when they both arrived; it was won by Ludendorff's inspiration.[40] (Ludendorff had described to me the previous evening how, if the Russians had moved in from the North, which was hourly to be expected, the outcome would have been quite different.[41]) Falkenhayn's relations with Ludendorff were discussed in detail. There have already been bitter arguments here, though not with Hindenburg who, being extremely loyal, tends to acquiesce.[42] Falkenhayn's influence over the Kaiser is very great; at every review the Kaiser first asks if Falkenhayn has any other wishes. As seating was being decided in the Kaiser's railway carriage Ludendorff was placed at his side. This was not acceptable to the Kaiser because he was keeping the place for Falkenhayn who did not, however, come. Falkenhayn will oppose Ludendorff's transfer to the Western Front with all the means at his disposal.

Our opinions on the overall situation were very similar, the only difference being that at headquarters people are expecting peace with Italy.[43]

They are unanimous (even Ludendorff) in estimating that with regard to the Serbian campaign everything depends on whether the French and English can also be beaten in the same way.[44] Hoffmann, like the others, agreed with me that a peripheral victory would never end the war, and that everything depended on the central operations in the West, and also that this should not be delayed too long.

Hoffmann's view is that the army can be left at maximum strength for another seven months. The infantry in the east is beginning to weaken, particularly because of a shortage of officers. It is proposed to raise the quality of the troops in the winter by means of exercises. Everything is aimed at preparing strong winter positions.

Hoffmann asked me in great detail about the problem of Polish annexation. I replied that in my opinion our war aim consisted in

[40] Ludendorff, *Meine Kriegserinnerungen 1914–1918*, pp. 36 f. At this time Hoffmann worshipped Ludendorff and despised Hindenburg.

[41] Rennenkampf's army.

[42] This was certainly not the case, especially if one takes Hindenburg's demands for Falkenhayn's dismissal into account. Ritter, *Staatskunst und Kriegshandwerk*, vol. iii, pp. 67–72.

[43] Italy had entered the war on 23 May 1915 on the side of the Allies.

[44] The Serbian campaign began on 6 October 1915. On 14 October the Bulgars attacked the Serbs. By the beginning of December Serbia was virtually defeated. Harden and Rathenau shared the opinion that it would be preferable to make a concentrated attack in the West and to come to an agreement with Serbia. Hellige (ed.), Rathenau-Harden, Harden to Rathenau, 2 October 1915 and Rathenau to Harden 11 October 1915.

separating Russia from the Quadruple *Entente* and allying it to us, that everything else should be subordinated to this problem, even the annexation of Poland.[45] The latter was, nevertheless, still feasible, if it did not leave an irreparable breach with Russia, and did not make our work of colonization fail once again. The problems are infinitely more difficult than in Alsace; the Jewish problem, particularly, is almost insoluble.

Ludendorff intends, above all, to win land in order to increase the number of troops available in the future, yet he agreed with Hoffmann that first of all we must strive for [better] relations with Russia.[46] He would very much like to see Courland annexed.

Finally I mentioned that perhaps the most satisfactory political solution consisted in leaving the Tsar suzerainty over Poland on the understanding that it would receive an autonomous constitution, for then the insoluble problem and the precarious situation in the border country would revert to Russia.[47]

Hoffmann did not reject this idea out of hand, as the question of peace conditions was generally discussed in the whole circle without preconceptions.

What is admirable is the team-work in this circle, which obviously derives its great stability and its incomparable strength from the outstanding qualities of each individual and from Hindenburg's fatherly personality. Their collaboration is exemplary, so too is the mutual trust and high esteem, yet it seems to me beyond doubt that Ludendorff's is the spirit that dominates this circle and is openly acknowledged as such.

At 1.40 p.m. we left Kovno in an overloaded, unlighted military train, arrived at 5 p.m. at the equally dark station at Eydtkuhnen, and were back in Berlin at 6.20 a.m.

As we said goodbye Hoffmann promised me that if ever I thought of coming to Kovno again he would drive me to the front, even though it was a question of almost 24 hours' driving.

Berlin, 22.11.1915

[45] It is not clear whether Rathenau meant just the frontier strip or the whole of Poland. Rathenau considered Russia's disengagement from the *Entente* to be crucial.

[46] Ludendorff had been recommending the annexation of the frontier strip and the founding of a Polish state under German suzerainty since August 1915. Conze, *Polnische Nation*, p. 80; Geiss, *Der polnische Grenzstreifen*, p. 34 and p. 37; Fischer, *Griff nach der Weltmacht*, p. 251.

[47] For Russia's lack of interest in a separate peace see Scherer and Grunewald (eds.), *L'Allemagne et les problèmes de la paix*, p. 154, Ballin's note of a conversation with Andersen on 9 August 1915; Zechlin, 'Der Grossherzog von Hessen und die Bemühungen um den russischen Sonderfrieden', in *Krieg und Kriegsrisiko*, pp. 279-89.

Interview with General von Falkenhayn, Chief of the General Staff

28 November, Sunday. The conversation lasted from 10 till 11 o'clock. At that time Jagow was announced and came in while I was taking my leave.

Falkenhayn gave me a cordial welcome and asked me to express my observations and opinions to him quite freely. I began by trying to describe to him, on the basis of information I had gathered, the climate of opinion in England, France, and Russia. The culmination of this exposition was that it was becoming quite clear that they firmly intended to prolong the war so that Germany should gradually exhaust itself, so that its conduct of the war should be drawn further away from the centre, [and] its defence network became looser; but there should be no support for the hope that successes gained on the periphery would bring about any desire for peace on the part of the Allies, particularly England.

Falkenhayn mentioned that this opinion was not very different from his own, but since I had talked about waging war on the periphery he asked me whether I did not perhaps consider the Serbian campaign an urgent necessity. I replied that it seemed desirable to me on the understanding that we did not tie down greater numbers of troops on the Greek frontier than the French and English, and that I considered the alliance with Turkey valuable.

He replied very energetically that he saw it as a great chance to strengthen Turkey as a 'loyal' ally, particularly as hitherto the manufacture and supply of ammunition had been inadequate there.

I answered that Turkey could grasp the idea of loyalty only in the sense of interest, and mentioned interviews that had taken place with Enver and Talaat which clearly showed a lack of complete submissiveness on the part of the Turks.

Against this Falkenhayn recounted how two days previously, at Orsova, he had spoken to Enver who had offered him divisions for the West.[48] The Kaiser had been in favour of taking them, but Falkenhayn had declined because he could not envisage an outright loss in officers, guns, and munitions in equipping these 150,000 men. One might just as well have sent Russian prisoners to the Front, he maintained. Nevertheless, this incident showed Turkey's wish to reciprocate.

He then turned again to the contrast between peripheral and central operations, and I expressed, as cautiously as possible, my firm conviction that only a breakthrough in the West could alter the situation quickly and permanently to our advantage. I estimated the total

---

[48] The conversations at Orsova took place on 25 and 26 November 1915.

to be involved at 1 million men; the country's [production] of ammunition could be increased many times. A breakthrough would in any case be more difficult if it were attempted a year later because only a limited amount of manpower could be withdrawn from the present war economy. He seemed to share the last opinion, meanwhile he pointed out that the French, with a greater number of guns than we possessed altogether, had tried a breakthrough which had failed.[49] We could indeed provide munitions, meanwhile the capacity of the guns would be limited.

Talk now turned to Austria and to our continually deteriorating relations, which he knew about. But he could not, as he said, burden himself with diplomatic negotiations along with his main task.[50]

I pointed out that our relations with Austria were not so much a question of negotiation as a question of will, and that the negotiations about Serbia and Poland that were now under way would have to be decided by us in the end, because Austria could no longer today, as it had done at times, threaten a separate peace.

He agreed. He admitted that in some respects Austria had been treated too softly. This was due to the character of those people entrusted with the political tasks. Meanwhile he would point out that at present all political questions are decided by the military side, that is to say by him.[51] He is not prominent in this regard because, as a convinced monarchist, he stands for the idea of the Kaiser making the final decisions; the practice hitherto had allowed him a uniformity of action.

In conclusion he came back again to the question of a breakthrough, and doubted whether France, which had in this war retained a significant residue of noble qualities, could be influenced psychologically by a thrust on Paris. He agreed with me that at present everything was dependent on psychological appearances, but he could imagine that a decisive operation like that could equally well take place in the East.

I mentioned that in our experience of the French character there

[49] The French and British autumn offensive in Champagne and Artois that had begun on 22 August did not, however, lead to a breakthrough. Falkenhayn seemed at this time to have already abandoned the idea of a German breakthrough battle. Janssen, *Der Kanzler und der General*, pp. 181 ff.

[50] For the extremely strained relations between Conrad and Falkenhayn in the autumn of 1915 see ibid., pp. 142, 152 f., and 163 f.; see also the German negotiations for an alliance with Bulgaria, ibid., p. 153; for the political difficulties between Germany and Austria see Ritter, *Staatskunst und Kriegshandwerk*, vol. iii, pp. 134 f.

[51] Wild von Hohenborn, the Minister of War, had described Falkenhayn as a 'disciple of the political and military Generalissimo'. Janssen, *Der Kanzler und der General*, p. 165; see also Bethmann Hollweg's clash with Falkenhayn over the question of the claim to leadership. Ritter, *Staatskunst und Kriegshandwerk*, vol. iii, pp. 101 ff.

is a tendency to hysterical extremes which are unknown in England; they can certainly also be demonstrated in Russia by some people, though not by the country as a whole.

To that he replied that he, nevertheless, saw certain signs that war-weariness was growing in Russia, which made a swing in attitude seem possible. He did not expect the same of England.

I had explained that after a breakthrough in France a war to the end was likely with England, and would not threaten us economically.[52] He did not seem to dismiss this idea and finally expressed the conviction, which he had discussed with me, that even if the war was of long duration we would be able to sustain it at home and abroad without difficulty.

As we said goodbye he thanked me for my organization, which he appreciated highly, and declared that he was interested and satisfied by my information and opinions.[53]

Berlin, 28.11.1915

Conversation with Gerard, United States Ambassador

Today Gerard gave me the following documents to read: a letter of 7 September from Sir Edward Grey's secretary, Drummond, to a Mr Howard Taylor enclosing a note signed by Drummond, and also: a letter from Taylor to Gerard.

In Drummond's accompanying letter, which is written on Foreign Office paper, he says that he is transmitting the enclosed note to Taylor in order to establish his (Drummond's) participation in the conversation held previously; apart from that he refers cautiously to the *Entente*'s Agreement of 5 September 1914.[54]

The note mentions that a neutral person called on Grey, not at the order of the German Chancellor, but with his knowledge; the neutral person is not named.[55] He informed him that the following three points represented the Chancellor's opinion:

[52] In his memorandum of 7 September 1914 Rathenau still held the opposite view. He believed then that Germany would suffer from a blockade in the long run.

[53] On 8 January 1916 Rathenau informed Ludendorff of his conversation with Falkenhayn. In the published version of his letter Rathenau only mentions that he talked about the mood abroad. Rathenau, *Politische Briefe*, p. 54, Rathenau to Ludendorff, 8 January 1916.

[54] Martens, *Nouveau Receuil Général*, 3rd series, x, pp. 324 ff.; by the agreement none of the *entente* powers could conclude a separate peace.

[55] The reference is probably to the Danish Privy Councillor Andersen, who stayed in London from 9 to 17 June and from 24 to 31 August 1915. Andersen travelled to London a third time on 20 November 1915, and he found that the atmosphere had changed since the summer. 'Everywhere where the talk was of the war he had heard but one word, "endure".' Scherer and Grunewald (eds.), *L'Allemagne et les problèmes de la paix*, pp. 236 f.; Brockdorff-Rantzau to the Auswärtige Amt, 10 December 1915. For Bethmann's political ideas at this time see Fischer, *Griff nach der Weltmacht*, p. 240.

(a) Belgian independence,
(b) Compensation claims,
(c) Return of German colonies.

Grey had remarked on this, that the demand for compensation was *really an insult*, because a nation paying compensation has to work like a slave for the recipient of the compensation. He referred, moreover, to the Agreement of 5 September and indicated that the end of the war was not close enough for final negotiations to be begun.

Meanwhile he pointed out that the *restoration* of Belgian independence was an essential condition.

Then he talked about *reparation* for Belgium, and intended that it should go to a court of arbitration.[56]

He pointed out that both sides desired guarantees of future peace, and maintained that they were the subject of later negotiations, likewise a guarantee of Belgian independence.[57]

Allied agreement was made a prior condition to a meeting with the Chancellor in Holland, though it was evident from the formula that a refusal was not contemplated.[58]

Territorial and other questions should remain held over to a general congress.

The following seem to me worth noting:

1. A meeting and exchange of views is not refused.

2. War reparations will apparently only be bluntly dismissed in so far as England is concerned.

3. Belgian independence remains a condition, yet its integrity is not mentioned, thus the question of the Congo and possible frontier changes is still open.

4. The reference to territorial questions is ambiguous, because he does not specify to what extent the claims of the Allies will be taken into consideration.

5. It is characteristic that no mention of France or Russia was made at all.

In Taylor's handwritten covering letter there is another hint at apparent willingness for a conference in Holland.

Berlin, 4.12.1915

---

[56] Scherer and Grunewald (eds.), *L'Allemagne et les problèmes de la paix*, pp. 166 f., Bethmann's note after a conversation with Andersen on 2 September 1915.

[57] The demand for guarantees of peace, and guaranteed Belgian independence, implied England ending the war victoriously. Taylor, *English History*, pp. 50 f.

[58] The idea of an Anglo-German conference had come from House. Scherer and Grunewald, (eds.), *L'Allemagne et les problèmes de la paix*, pp. 127 f., Bernstorff to Bethmann Hollweg, 23 June 1915.

NOTES ON 1916

Talks with Colonel House, Ambassador Gerard, and Foreign Secretary Jagow

Rathenau and Colonel House met for the first time during House's visit to Berlin in March 1915. House recorded his impressions in a letter to President Wilson:

'I met last night an able and sane man by the name of Dr Rathenau. I am told that he has great power in commercial Germany. He has such a clear vision of the situation and such a prophetic forecast as to the future that I wonder how many there are in Germany that think like him. It saddened me to hear him say that, as far as he knew, he stood alone. He said he had begun to wonder whether all the rest were really mad, or whether the madness lay within himself . . . . It was almost pathetic to hear him urge us not to cease in our efforts to bring about peace.'[1]

Shortly after Rathenau had sent his open letter to Colonel House in December 1918 he mentioned in a letter that he had had 'several, detailed conversations' with House, 'in which I described to him the situation of the country and the war and we both came to the conclusion that Wilson must end the war in friendly co-operation with Germany.'[2] House had declared 'that he had not received such complete and credible information on the present situation from anyone but [Rathenau] . . .' and had asked him 'to write as soon as President Wilson should intervene; the beginning of the submarine war had prevented this.'

I

I had to decline an invitation to dinner, so Gerard left me the choice of two lunches—Friday and Saturday—to meet House.[3] I chose Saturday,[4] and found a small gathering.

After the meal House kept me back in the dining-room while the guests moved into the front room and the table was cleared. He had been in Paris for only one day, whereas he had spent several days in London, and so did not know much more about the atmosphere in France than that it had become rather more unfriendly, and began to talk about Grey and his aims. He fears Grey will have to go and that his successor will be less inclined to negotiate. He considers that Grey himself is ready to conclude a peace, and, what is more, under

[1] Seymour (ed.), *The Intimate Papers of Colonel House*, vol. i, p. 406, House to Wilson, 21 March 1915.

[2] Rathenau, *Briefe*, vol. ii, pp. 90 f., Rathenau to W. L., 17 December 1918.

[3] House's second trip to Germany lasted from 26 to 30 January 1916.

[4] 29 January 1916. Rathenau had to delay a meeting with Dehmel and his wife in order to go to Gerard's. Hamburgische Staats- und Universitätsbibliothek, Nachlass Dehmel 16.204, Rathenau to Dehmel, 28 January 1916.

the unchanged, original English conditions, namely: surrender of Belgium and northern France without compensation.

When I objected, he remarked that we would be left a free hand in Russia; in particular he considered an independent Kingdom of Poland to be desirable and achievable.[5] Further compensations would be found in Asia Minor. Our colonies would be restored, so far as England could arrange it; furthermore, there would be compensations to be gained (Belgian Congo, etc.). He can see no fear of France being disappointed,[6] but America would, above all, use all its power to guarantee the so-called freedom of the seas and to eliminate every future possibility of a blockade war.

I did not conceal what disappointment this opinion would be bound to arouse here, and recommended to him to come to Europe again in a year's time, in the belief that by then the situation might be somewhat clearer.[7]

The Ambassador came in and asked House to come to Zimmermann who was waiting for him in the front room; meanwhile the Ambassador stayed with me in the dining-room together with Grew, who had come in at the same time as he had. The Ambassador now spoke about the situation regarding the *Lusitania*, which had become critical.[8] He had received a report from Washington according to which Bernstorff and Lansing have agreed on a formula. He fears that, if this formula is not accepted, difficulties will ensue.[9] In order to show us the text he went down to his chancery, but it was still locked up. He tried again, in vain, a while later; then a secretary came and produced the document.

Gerard took us into a pantry, gave me the document, and I read it out. When I had got to the place where illegality is mentioned, I said to him that I felt that this sentence would, under any circumstances, have to be struck out, which annoyed him, particularly because Grew agreed with me. I now suggested to the Ambassador

[5] In his talk with Bethmann Hollweg, House had also apparently demanded the evacuation of Poland. Görlitz (ed.), *Regierte der Kaiser?*, p. 152; Fischer, *Griff nach der Weltmacht*, pp. 361 f. At any rate the remark that Germany would be left a free hand in Russia and the demand for the evacuation of Poland are contradictory.

[6] Although Rathenau apparently asked about French war aims House did not mention the return of Alsace-Lorraine, which was, however, the subject of the Grey-House memorandum of 22 February 1916. Seymour (ed.), *The Intimate Papers of Colonel House*, vol. ii, pp. 170 f.

[7] In this matter Rathenau found himself in agreement with Grey, who had described House's proposals as 'preposterously inadequate'. Northedge, *The Troubled Giant*, p. 17.

[8] The *Lusitania* was sunk on 7 May 1915.

[9] The exchange of Notes between Germany and America dealt on the one hand with the limitation of submarine warfare, and on the other with American compensation claims and also limitation of English blockade regulations regarding neutral shipping. Fischer, *Griff nach der Weltmacht*, p. 358; Link, *Wilson*, vol. iv, pp. 80–100.

that he should approve this one amendment and, should he have further difficulties, he should decide upon simultaneous publication of the German reply and the American Note to England, so that, on the supposition that the latter would be strongly worded, public opinion would, in this way, receive appropriate satisfaction. He heartily agreed with this idea.[10]

II

31 January, Monday. I had made an appointment with Jagow and visited him that evening from 5.30 to 6.30 p.m.

I told him the substance of my interview with House and concluded by saying that it was up to the [German] Foreign Office and Bethmann to decide whether the proposals might form the basis of a discussion.

To my astonishment Jagow took the latter as a matter of course, stressed that the case interested him in so far as no proposal of a positive nature had hitherto been received from England. There was however a serious consideration in evaluating the conversation with House, because, as he alleged, House had said to him that not only would Grey's time be up in a short while but that he was completely isolated, even in England.[11]

I had no reason to express my opinion on this because I had merely seen it as my duty to present my information about the situation, and therefore suggested to Jagow that he should discuss the facts of the case with Bethmann, which he intended to do that very evening.

I also reported to him the conversation concerning the *Lusitania*. He agreed with me regarding the unacceptable sentence and my suggestion of publishing the English Note [and German Note] at the same time.[12]

Berlin, 2.2.1916

[10] Gerard had not apparently altered the Note. For the modification proposed by Jagow, Link, *Wilson*, vol. i, p. 94.

[11] It is unlikely that House had not discussed the same questions with Jagow on 28 January 1916 as with Rathenau. Seymour, *The Intimate Papers of Colonel House*, vol. ii., pp. 142 f. Hence it seems as if Jagow wanted to avoid discussing the British proposals with Rathenau. For Bethmann's reaction to the talk with House, see Fischer, *Griff nach der Weltmacht*, pp. 361 f.

[12] Rathenau proposed that the German Note to America be published at the same time as the American one to England.

NOTES ON 1917

As well as being President of the AEG Rathenau had, since 1917, become increasingly prominent as a publicist. When his friends advised him to go into politics he replied that he 'stood further away from everyday politics than ever before' and did not want this to change.[1] It was enough for him 'to contribute towards planning for a distant future; he gladly left the present to those more competent.' Whilst he was really at least as able to deal with the present, he liked to think of his next book as being orientated towards the future, as its title suggests, and Utopian in character. He was unable to finish *Von kommenden Dingen* in 1915, and took another four months in the summer of 1916, to complete it. In his own estimation 'it will undermine the last bit of my bourgeois existence. So let it be.'[2] He realized that he would create a stir because of his authorship and because of the book's tendency. Although only a few German papers had briefly reported about his work for the KRA in 1914/15, public knowledge of him grew when the London *Times* quoted from an American journalist, Raymond G. Swing, who had reported in a very appreciative way about Rathenau from Berlin:

'It is an interesting story, this miracle of industry, this inventiveness, this genius of organization. It is a story which explains the fall of Warsaw and the great Eastern offensives and the impregnable Western line. And when the Falkenhayns, the Hindenburgs and the Mackensens, are thought of as great German soldiers, one person must be set beside them, the German business-man, Dr Walther Rathenau'.[3]

And *The Times* added its comments:

'One wonders what would have been the reception accorded to an English Rathenau (and we have such brains among us) were he today, after 14 months of comparative adversity, to offer his services to our Government . . . It is not too late to put at least the internal direction of the War Office into the hands of one of our English Rathenaus . . .'.

Both articles had some impact on the City, and *The Times* reported about that as well.

In Germany Swing's article was discussed in the two major liberal newspapers *Vossische Zeitung* and *Kölnische Zeitung*.[4] Partly influenced by the reception of Swing's article in the German newspapers and partly by Rathenau's own talk about the KRA, *Die Zukunft* published Emil Ludwig's praise of Rathenau's work in the KRA.[5] He received even further publicity when he was allowed to

---

[1] Rathenau, *Briefe*, vol. i, p. 261, Rathenau to Baroness von Schröder, 28 April 1917.
[2] Rathenau, *Politische Briefe*, p. 66, Rathenau to Steinbömer, 21 October 1916.
[3] *The Times*, 11 October 1915. See Gottlieb, *Walther-Rathenau-Bibliographie*, pp. 131 ff.
[4] 28 October 1915. See also D. G. Williamson, 'Pro and contra Rathenau', p. 35.
[5] *Die Zukunft*, 29 September 1916. Emil Ludwig had sent the MS to Rathenau in May and had asked him whether he could help with the publication. Rathenau thought (Rathenau, *Briefe*, vol. i, p. 212, Rathenau to Ludwig, 17 May 1916) that none of the papers he knew well would publish it. Nevertheless Ludwig sent it to Harden, who published it after insisting on a few alterations. On 30 September Rathenau, after he had received a copy, thanked

publish his talk in October 1916.[6] The small booklet acted as an ideal curtain-raiser to *Von kommenden Dingen*, which finally appeared in March 1917. Several months beforehand he had been depressed because he had not received the public acknowledgement he had expected for his work in the KRA. He complained to Gerhart Hauptmann 'that he was as good as expelled from bourgeois society [and] banned by the authorities'.[7] He was grateful for the letters of thanks for his services by Bethmann Hollweg, Falkenhayn, Wild von Hohenborn, and Wandel, but they did not quite make up for his impression that he was being ostracized as a non-bureaucrat and a non-military outsider who had successfully intervened in the organization of the German war machine. This began to change, however, after his talk about the KRA had been published, and even more so after his book had appeared. During the first three months 24,000 copies were sold, another 17,000 by the end of 1917, and 65,000 copies altogether by July 1918.[8] No longer was he merely well known: he was famous. In 1921 an English translation was published under the title *In Days to Come*, followed by a French one.[9]

In his book Rathenau dwelt on the subject of his two previous books, but concentrated more than before on the development of a system of economic equality and social liberty. The ultimate goal remained the moral regeneration of the social and economic orders, so as to counterbalance what Rathenau called increasing mechanization. He held the process of mechanization to be responsible for the dehumanization of life, and described the process 'in its excesses . . . as the cause of imperialism and nationalism and therefore of war'.[10]

As usual, Rathenau's ideas were very much part of a general discussion which was going on and which must have influenced the writing of his book. The economists Johann Plenge, Edgar Jaffé, and to some extent even Werner Sombart had written about the forthcoming end of the individualistic free-market economy, and Wichard von Moellendorff had published his book about *Deutsche Gemeinwirtschaft* (German Corporate Economy) in which he pointed out that the war corporations could become the first pattern of the job-orientated estates of the future.[11] In addition, several politicians, economists, and industrialists were occupied in outlining the future economic order in the transitory stage from war to peace.[12] There was also widespread public discussion about what Germany should look like after the victory which everybody was still expecting. In his book Rathenau did not want to take part in this discussion, which was being strongly coloured by the general debate about the war aims. He set goals for which everybody should strive: the abolition of poverty and the creation

Harden and said that his mother was very pleased with it. Hellige (ed.), Rathenau–Harden, Rathenau to Harden, 30 September 1916. Hellige also quotes Ludwig's memoirs, *Geschenke des Lebens*, p. 482.

[6] *Deutschlands Rohstoffversorgung*. In an appendix Rathenau published the letters of thanks by Wild von Hohenborn and Wandel (31 March 1915) and the comments of Wild von Hohenborn, Wandel and Bethmann Hollweg about his talk. (25 and 10 January, and 15 July 1916).

[7] Schulin (ed.), *Walther Rathenau. Hauptwerke und Gespräche*, p. 562, Rathenau to Hauptmann, 21 August 1916.

[8] Ibid., p. 563.

[9] Ibid., p. 585.

[10] Rathenau, *Briefe*, vol. i, p. 329, Rathenau to Georg Vogt, 29 October 1917.

[11] Schulin (ed.), *Walther Rathenau. Hauptwerke und Gespräche*, p. 561.

[12] Zunkel, *Industrie und Staatssozialismus*, pp. 53–68.

of human freedom.[13] If people could change their ethical attitudes according to his suggestions, then they might be able to achieve these goals. For Rathenau it was more important to change human nature than to reform the political and economic institutions. Nevertheless, he believed that certain economic and political conditions, once they had been reformed, could bring about a transformation of human ethics, and once ethics begin to change, a reform of the social and economic order would come about more easily. This dialectic process would, he considered, be speeded up by the effects of the war, which would not allow a simple return to the *status quo ante*. For him the 'spirit of the 1914' was the basis and the beginning of a new attitude towards the problems of the individual, society, and the State. The new spirit would lead to a real people's community which in turn would create a corporate economy. Together both would build up a people's state. While discussing this he also dealt with questions of social policy, analysed social reality as he saw it, and discussed the implications of socialism and capitalism.

The book was widely reviewed by all political parties and prominent individuals. Liberals criticized Rathenau for his abolition of the inheritance laws, for his wish to create a super-state which would leave all power in the hands of the bureaucrats, for his insistence on an equality of opportunities, and for his emphasis on education.[14] Others criticized him for wanting to control capitalism and monopolies and thus throttle economic life. The Social Democratic *Vorwärts* regarded Rathenau as old-fashioned, one whose criticism of capitalism sounded rather like curses from the Old Testament.[15] Obviously Rathenau's rejection of socialism was unacceptable; and it was pointed out that though he criticized similar institutions as the SPD he mixed his ideas with religious and ethical demands and certain Utopian concepts. The trade-union paper *Die Gewerkschaft* praised Rathenau for his criticism of inherited wealth, but pointed out that he 'does not attack the basis of the capitalist society, private ownership of the means of production and the capitalist economy'. As the paper noted, Rathenau criticized consumption, but not production.

Among Conservatives and industrialists his book met with strong criticism.[16] It was regarded as dangerous because it came close to advocating 'socialism'. It was considered that Rathenau's arguments against the inheritance laws, against saving, and against monopolies and speculation might destroy the existing culture. The anti-Semitic stance of certain conservative reviewers put Rathenau into the same category as Karl Marx. One of them hoped that 'the cosmopolitan bourgeois circles to which Rathenau belongs will have no more influence on our people after the war than before it'. Jewish circles reacted positively, and one reviewer in the *Neue Jüdische Monatshefte* thought that Rathenau embodied the

[13] For the latest discussion of this book see Berglar, *Walther Rathenau*, pp. 152–80; Schulin (ed.), *Walther Rathenau. Hauptwerke und Gespräche*, pp. 588–92; Joll, 'Walther Rathenau—Intellectual or Industrialist?', pp. 53–7.

[14] See the reviews by the Liberals, Ernst Troeltsch, Leopold von Wiese, Eugen Geiger, Robert Friedberg, Schulin (ed.), *Walther Rathenau. Hauptwerke und Gespräche*. pp. 588–92.

[15] Friedrich Stampfer in *Vorwärts* and *Die Gewerkschaft*, and Wally Zepler in the *Sozialistische Monatshefte*. Ibid.

[16] *Deutsche Arbeitgeber-Zeitung*, Ludwig Lorenz in *Bühne und Welt*, M. H. Boehm in *Die Grenzboten*. Ibid.

Jewish division between capitalism and socialism, although he held that Rathenau was not sufficiently critical of the capitalist society.[17]

In the judgement of some prominent contemporaries the book provoked a twofold reaction: it was attractive for its openness about certain problems which were widely felt, and repellent at a personal level. Thus Hoffmannsthal wrote to Bodenhausen that he had 'been put off by certain parts of Rathenau's book . . . Then I came upon it here but did not open it immediately. At the specific request of Nostiz who wanted to discuss it with me, I then read the last 120 pages of the book, and must at least withdraw my [previous] opinion of the ideas expressed there (called "Der Weg des Willens"), or completely withdraw my prejudice. These 120 pages are consistent, solid and seem to me remarkable. They give one something.'[18] In his letter in answer to this Bodenhausen described how he had read Rathenau's book with reluctance.[19] 'At times, after finishing ten pages,' he continued,

'I have had to keep on resisting the temptation to hurl the book into a corner and thus to give vent to my indignation with the arrogant author . . . . The pompous self-satisfaction, this unabashed arrogance are wholly distasteful to me. "I erect arcs of thought [Gedankenbögen] (sic), it is for you to extend them." No, I can't go along with that. There are so many good thoughts in it, most of them obviously quite self-evident, but good, they are there after all; why then all this odious rigmarole! I am convinced he believes in his decisive mission in world history; I am convinced he has no inkling of the contradictions between his teaching and his life; all the worse for him. But I may be unjust. . . .'

Just as during the war Rathenau made suggestions in his writings and developed concepts which allowed him to appear as a reformer and a prophet, so too in political life he made proposals regarding the political and economic conduct of the war which showed him to be an admonisher and a realist. One of Rathenau's aims was fulfilled when Hindenburg and Ludendorff took over the Supreme Command. He wrote to his friend Wilhelm Schwaner that he had uttered a sigh of relief when Hindenburg was appointed, 'and yet! . . . I feel . . . too late!'[20] His scepticism did not immediately interfere with his belief that dictatorship by Ludendorff could prevent catastrophe. Moreover, he hoped that Ludendorff would put through measures of domestic reform which he considered absolutely necessary. While Rathenau was still hoping that Ludendorff would provide resolute leadership, his criticism of the effectiveness of submarine warfare was taking up an increasingly large part of his thoughts. He took advantage of the 'Olympian's' presence in Berlin to submit his economic considerations and his doubts as to the success of submarine warfare to Ludendorff.

First Talk with General Ludendorff, 16 February 1917

I called on Excellency Ludendorff at 12.30 p.m. at the General Staff where Headquarters has been located for the past few

---

[17] Alfred Lemm in Neue Jüdische Monatshefte. Ibid. See also for the reviews D. G. Williamson, 'Pro and contra Rathenau'.

[18] Bodenhausen-Degener (ed.), Briefe der Freundschaft, p. 230, Hofmannsthal to Bodenhausen, 17 May 1917.

[19] Ibid., Bodenhausen to Hofmannsthal, 30 June 1917.

[20] BA Koblenz, Nachlass Rathenau 6, Rathenau to Schwaner, 2 September 1916; Gutsche (ed.), Deutschland im Ersten Weltkrieg, vol. ii, pp. 407 f., 462 f., 720.

days. Colonel von Bartenwerffer was present during the conversation.

After a very friendly reception I commented on the state of the war economy as it appears to me from numerous indications. I described the cause of the production crisis: the execution of the Hindenburg Programme[21] had not led to new basic attitudes and new principles. On the contrary it had been commenced before everything was fully thought through.[22] No one had borne in mind that a country which is absolutely occupied with making supplies for the war is not ready to be launched into a gigantic construction programme. Industrialists had been chivvied into building a great number of new factories whch are just begun or half-finished today. The fact that the raw materials absorbed by this building would also contribute to the volume of trade in commodities in circulation had not been taken into consideration. Transport conditions had been accepted as they were, with no thought for the increased quantity [of goods] in circulation and increased production. The Auxiliary Service Law [*Hilfsdienstgesetz*][23] had suffered similarly; it too had originated from a sound and feasible idea, but that had been transformed into a legislative monster, so that today 150,000 people would be needed to carry it out and so it has in practice become unworkable. One of the causes of disorganization lies in over-organization, in the way committees and advisory bodies are constantly expanding, in the way attention is continually paid to deputies, interested parties and parliaments, so that things have now reached the stage where directions and principles cannot be adhered to because of committee meetings, conferences, and the work of organization.

Ludendorff agreed with me on all these points,[24] and said that the problem had much embittered the days he had spent here, and he

---

[21] The Hindenburg Programme was set up by the third Supreme Command. The Programme was to help increase the manufacture of weapons and munitions. On the strength of this the War Office was founded, in October 1916, and Groener was appointed as head on 1 November. Among the departments subordinate to the War Office were the KRA and the Weapons and Munitions Procurement Office. Feldman, *Army, Industry and Labor*, pp. 149–96; Hiller von Gaertringen (ed.), *Wilhelm Groener*, pp. 328–73.

[22] The Hindenburg Programme foundered because the quotas of explosives to be produced for the spring of 1917 could not be met. This failure was due to the excessive demands of the Programme and lack of organization. Feldman, *Army, Industry and Labor*, pp. 266–73. See also Feldman, 'The Political and Social Foundations of Germany's Economic Mobilization', pp. 134–42. Baudis and Nussbaum, *Wirtschaft und Staat*, pp. 283 ff.

[23] The Auxiliary Service Law came into force on 5 December 1916. It did not fulfil the hopes expressed in the law, because the shortage of labour remained a problem. Feldman, *Army, Industry and Labor*, pp. 301–48; Armeson, *Total Warfare and Compulsory Labor*, chs. 4, 7, and 8; Baudis and Nussbaum, *Wirtschaft und Staat*, pp. 285–8.

[24] Ludendorff passed on some of Rathenau's complaints to Groener that very day. Hiller von Gaertringen, *Wilhelm Groener*, p. 358. In his letter Ludendorff did not refer to Rathenau but mentioned summarily 'several industrialists'.

did not contemplate the situation with the same confidence as he had had a few months previously.[25] I seized on this, saying that I had opposed the submarine war for the very reason that America could greatly increase its munitions production, and because I did not dare to hope that we could be at all successful in completely cutting off supplies of American munitions. The English would doubtless draw up a scale of risks, and put munitions and raw materials at the top of the list of defence necessities, so that these ships would make their way with the utmost care and at relatively little risk.[26]

Ludendorff now asked what measures I could recommend to him. I named three. First of all, a definite curtailment of building operations (this, he told me, was already being dealt with);[27] then the ruthless closure of all peacetime businesses; finally, and above all, a radical reform of the organizations,[28] in the sense of putting an end to the committees and advisory bodies so that the individual bodies would be in a position to work alongside each other unhindered, and so that a strong, uniform policy could manage business from one place.[29]

Ludendorff mentioned that he had already, months ago, brought the dangers which were threatening to the attention of the Minister of Railways, who had not taken his warnings seriously.[30] I replied to this that it was for that very reason that I had welcomed Groener's appointment, because it seemed to express the wish to have transport put, as it were, under the control of an important military specialist. It was, therefore, all the more astonishing that it was precisely in

[25] One of the reasons for Ludendorff's pessimism was the shortage of munitions; added to this the American declaration of war and the imminent withdrawal to the Siegfried Line; and on top of this the fact that the resumption of unlimited submarine warfare revealed the desperate situation of the army in the west.

[26] Ludendorff hoped that submarine warfare would provide relief for the Western Front. Feldmann, *Army, Industry and Labor*, pp. 270 f.; Kaulisch, 'Die Auseinandersetzungen über den uneingeschränkten U-Boot-Kriet', pp. 109 f.

[27] For Ludendorff's decree of 6 February 1917, see Feldman, *Army, Industry and Labor*, p. 269.

[28] Groener had been working on the 'concentration of resources' since December. Ibid., pp. 273–83.

[29] The measures recommended by Rathenau were not carried out. On 19 March 1917 he wrote to Ludendorff: '. . . even if the frost crisis is less severe, nevertheless, the conditions we discussed at our last meeting have not since changed. The economic situation in which we find ourselves, the personal relations we spoke about, make any further expansion of our armaments industry impossible. This will become quite apparent in the course of next winter. New principles will have to be enforced in all respects, if there is to be a further demand for increased productivity, which will probably occur, seriously, at the beginning of next year.' Rathenau, *Politische Briefe*, p. 106, Rathenau to Ludendorff, 19 March 1917.

[30] The Minister of Public Works, Paul von Breitenbach, was hardly involved in the working out of plans at all. The transport crisis had become increasingly serious since the summer of 1916. Ibid., pp. 253–7.

the field of transport that organization had so completely collapsed.[31]

Ludendorff replied that he had to work with the men he had been given and constantly had to endure serious clashes with the bureaucrats at various levels, Chancellor, and ministers. I pointed out to him that in fact he was unconsciously exercising a dictatorship, and that if he would rely on his actual power he would have the support not only of the parliaments but of the whole of public opinion against the authorities. I reminded him that whenever a bill is submitted to the Reichstag, the first question asked is whether or not the official moving the bill has the backing of the Supreme Command.

Ludendorff spoke again about the difficulties and dangers of the problem, which I corroborated by saying that, should no decisive remedy be forthcoming from this central position, we should have to fear a catastrophe. However, I hoped that remedial measures would be sufficient. It was not possible for me to go into further details since I had not had any detailed knowledge for some time now. Thus I was like a doctor who makes a diagnosis by recognizing the strong symptoms of an illness without having examined the patient with a stethoscope.

In conclusion I asked Ludendorff whether he wished me to carry on making occasional reports in the future. He replied that he had found my letters valuable and wished them to continue.[32] The conversation lasted until 1.15 a.m.

Berlin, 16.2.1917

Discussion with Bethmann Hollweg, Helfferich, and Wahnschaffe, 2 May 1917

Rathenau considered Helfferich to be an opponent of his, since he held him to be responsible for the optimistic attitude to the outcome of unrestricted submarine warfare, and it was clear to Rathenau that submarine warfare was not going to be as successful as expected. 'At the time (1916)', so he wrote to Ballin, 'when we were still working against the submarine war, the Navy was flatly told: you only have to name a number of tons, we will work out the consequences. Helfferich, then, is responsible for the consequences.'[33] In a letter to Steinbömer a few days later Rathenau criticized the belief in 'the forecasts by the Navy for 1 August. . . . What is most remarkable is that these forecasts were not issued by the Navy at all but by Helfferich.'[34] Helfferich

---

[31] Rathenau had obviously expected that Groener would use his experience as director of the Field Railways Section (General Staff) when he took over the War Office. Baudis and Nussbaum, *Wirtschaft und Staat*, pp. 289–95.

[32] Rathenau's letters to Ludendorff from August 1916 onwards are printed in Rathenau, *Politische Briefe*, and some of them are reprinted in Eynern, *Walther Rathenau.*

[33] Rathenau, *Politische Briefe*, p. 138, Rathenau to Ballin, 18 May 1917.

[34] Ibid., p. 143, Rathenau to Steinbömer, 26 May 1917.

had undertaken to translate tonnage sunk into a victory, so Rathenau wrote to Seeckt.[35] Rathenau first discovered in August from Count Zech that Helfferich was opposed to the submarine war and the hopes which were based on it. 'I just don't understand it!', he wrote to Steinbömer.[36] Helfferich had in fact prepared, for the conference between the Chancellor and the Supreme Command on 9 January 1917, a short memorandum which opposed the Navy's point of view.[37] Thus he seemed to have reversed his earlier opinion, put forward in a memorandum in September 1916.[38] By the end of January 1917, he had changed his attitude again, and revised 'his earlier statistical estimate of the English economic situation'.[39] Rathenau had not taken Helfferich's opposition to the submarine warfare at the beginning of January very seriously because he could not imagine that Helfferich could be sceptical about the forecasts by the Navy.

In a letter to Wandel in January 1918 Rathenau refers to the discussion he had with Bethmann, Helfferich, and Wahnschaffe about the organization of the peace economy.[40] He does not mention the discussion about submarine warfare, but reveals that it was Count Roedern who had suggested to Rathenau that he send a memorandum about the topic of the future economy to the Chancellor. Rathenau also mentions in his letter the presence of Roedern, whom he does not specifically mention in the note below. However, apart from a number of small points, letter and note are identical. Rathenau wrote the letter to prove his distrust of Helfferich by pointing out that he changed his mind yet again. During their discussion Helfferich had, to Rathenau's surprise, declared that he had already introduced measures which would herald the new organization of the post-war economy. Helfferich quoted the soap industry for which he had actually set up an obligatory syndicate.[41] After Bethmann's fall he declared, however, that he was strongly in favour of a return to 'a free and unrestricted economy' once peace had arrived. Rathenau believed that force of circumstance would prove Helfferich wrong.

1 May, Tuesday. In the evening, Under-Secretary of State Wahnschaffe telephoned; that the Chancellor had read my memorandum with particular interest and wanted to discuss it in an intimate circle.[42] He asked me to dine with him the following evening

---

[35] Ibid., p. 149, Rathenau to Seeckt, 26 June 1917.

[36] Rathenau, *Briefe*, vol. i, pp. 306 f., Rathenau to Steinbömer, 22 August 1917.

[37] Ritter, *Staatskunst und Kriegshandwerk*, vol. iii., p. 379; J. Williamson, *Karl Helfferich*, pp. 192 f.

[38] Ritter, *Staatskunst und Kriegshandwerk*, vol. iii, p. 328.

[39] Ibid., p. 404.

[40] Rathenau, *Briefe*, vol. i, pp. 355 ff., Rathenau to Wandel, 26 January 1918.

[41] See also, Zunkel, *Industrie und Staatssozialismus*, pp. 65 f.

[42] The reference is to the memorandum of 26 April 1917 which he had sent to Bethmann. Rathenau, *Politische Briefe*, pp. 111–19. In it Rathenau tried to outline the main features of an economic and social order for the time after the war. He shifted his emphasis from striving for *Mitteleuropa* and a customs union with Austria to the reform of German economic life. He thought it necessary to increase production, to raise wages and the standard of living, and to give the trade unions a 'productive sphere of action', This could only be achieved if the whole of the economy were thoroughly rationalized and based on the determined co-operation between 'national professional organizations' and the state bureaucracy. He rejected a socialist and planned economy and continued to express his

(Wednesday, 8 p.m.) and would also in that case invite Helfferich and Rödern.

To my question as to whether Wahnschaffe himself would be present, he answered that he had not so far received an invitation, nevertheless he would probably come after dinner.

On Wednesday morning the invitation was again confirmed by the Chancellor's private office.

Apart from the gentlemen mentioned, I also met Miss von Pfuel, Count and Countess Zech and Wahnschaffe, who had meanwhile received his invitation.

At dinner I sat between the Chancellor and Countess Zech and conversation, which Helfferich kept steering towards political and business matters, naturally turned to submarine warfare. I said jokingly to Helfferich, who was sitting diagonally opposite to me and who was bringing up the familiar arguments, that I believed his predictions would be completely borne out: by the New Year 120-150 per cent of the English merchant fleet would be sunk, nevertheless England would still be feeding herself and shooting. The Chancellor remained very reserved; Helfferich repeated his arguments and I asked him whether he was aware of England's daily subsistence level, expressed in tons. This was not the case, and those present seemed rather surprised when I gave the figure of 12,000 tons —that is to say, the contents of one big, two medium or three smaller ships.[43]

After dinner the Chancellor took me into a side room, and our conversation regarding the submarine question was continued confidentially; I will refrain from giving an account of it.

We then gathered, after the ladies had withdrawn, in the room with the fireplace, and the Chancellor opened the conversation on purely business lines by asking me to give a summary of the contents of my memorandum. I carried out this request by talking for about half an hour, and when I had finished everyone waited for

belief in the self-regulatory force of the economy. However, free competition and free demand should be replaced by a general assessment of the needs of the economy and society. He pointed out that England was moving in the direction of a thorough rationalization of the economy, but he criticized the developments there as being too rigid and compulsory: they put industry under state supervision and distribute production by decree.' At the same time the British Government was trying to win labour over to co-operate voluntarily. Rathenau thought this feasible, as the increase of efficiency was linked to rising incomes. He hoped to be able to prepare similar measures in Germany while the war was still in progress, because wartime regulations made structural reorganizations easier.

[43] In Britain it was, however, stated that the country needed to import an 'irreducible minimum of 1,900,000 tons' a month. Marder, *From the Dreadnought*, p. 185. See also fn. 65 below.

Helfferich's reply with close attention. To my astonishment he declared that he agreed with all that I had said, but that the Home Office had already taken steps along my lines, particularly to centralize industry, namely the soap, shoe and textile industries.[44]

I replied that this was necessitated by the shortage of raw materials, and these were on the whole wartime measures which did not signify a fundamental change in peacetime. As against these opportunist measures I demanded a wholesale transformation of our economic life, and saw this as the way, above all, to improve the living conditions of the lower classes and to create a large and productive sphere of activity for their political representatives.

Now the Chancellor, with a warmth that I had never seen in the course of ten years, took up the ideas, declaring that for the first time it was now possible to give the German people the great opening and base of activity they had been waiting for. This was the chance to compensate the nation for its war effort and to guarantee it an award in domestic politics in peace-time, and it was his opinion that the new economic structure would have to be introduced in the form of a great proclamation.[45]

Helfferich put up a most decided fight against this by putting forward his varying and conflicting arguments: for one thing, he said, things were better done quietly (which I had accepted for wartime, rejected for peacetime), for another he referred to mounting socialization in the Reich, which stood in contradiction to his general approval of the project. The dispute moved back and forth for quite a time, in the course of which I reminded him of his pledge to pay war compensations, which he had made months before in the Reichstag.[46] and finally came to the question of whether a similar socialization process would be necessary for agriculture.

Wahnschaffe asked whether it was then worth while giving workers

[44] See fnn. 40 and 41 above. There was a joke about Helfferich's about-turns based on the popularized version of Luther's words at Worms, 'Hier stehe ich, ich kann nicht anders' [Here I stand fast, I cannot do differently]. The joke ran: 'Hier statiske ich, ich kann auch anders. Gott Helf er sich! Amen!' [Here I quote statistics, I can do it quite differently]. J. Williamson, *Karl Hefferich*, pp. 198 f.

[45] The Chancellor had already cautiously referred in the Reichstag and the Prussian Chamber of Deputies on 27 February and 14 March 1917 to the necessity of a domestic reorganization. A day before his discussion with Rathenau the Chancellor declared in the Prussian Ministry of State that a parliamentary system was impracticable in Germany and Prussia, and that he would not appoint members of parliaments to ministerial posts. For this reason he seemed to endorse Rathenau's proposals for the economy, hoping this would divert attention from the wish to reform the government system. Rathenau, on the other hand, made it clear that the quality of the Reichstag would improve if it had to deal with more important tasks. Rathenau, *Politische Briefe*, p. 126, Rathenau to Wandel, 1 May 1917. See also Gutsche, *Aufstieg und Fall*, p. 211.

[46] Helfferich's speech in the Reichstag on 30 November 1916.

a share in the profits of estates, whereupon, again to my astonishment, the Chancellor said that he himself could see no drawback to this and would grant such a share to his workers without any further ado.

The conversation had lasted from 8.45 to 11.45 p.m. and was finally brought to a close by the Chancellor on a note of fundamental agreement.[47]

Berlin, 5.5.1917

Second Talk with General Ludendorff, 10 July 1917

Shortly before Rathenau went to Kreuznach he met Bülow. It is likely that he kept a record of their talk, but it has not survived. However, in a letter to Harden Rathenau refers to his talk with Bülow, who 'has only one wish—"to make peace"—and he expresses his wish by proving: neither Bethmann could do it, nor Zimmermann, nor x, nor y. To me it proves one thing: he believes peacemaking to be a comfortable and popular job; his opinion of the situation must be a similar one. I disturbed him when I explained how Talleyrand had made peace (by sacrificing the *usurpateur*); but he was in no way upset about this; instead he even seemed to experience undreamt-of pleasures.'[48] There is no obvious clue as to why Rathenau went to see these politicians. Perhaps he entertained the vague hope that he would be assigned an important task or qualify for a political job in the near future.

After their meeting in Kovno in the autumn of 1915 Rathenau and Ludendorff corresponded with each other. At the end of June 1917 Rathenau reminded Ludendorff that in spite of the Navy's calculations and expectations his forecast regarding submarine warfare had proved correct, and that contrary to the hopes of the Supreme Command 'submarines should not be relied on to end the war.'[49] Three days later Ludendorff answered: 'With regard to the submarine warfare our views are not in agreement. It is already working.'[50] Rathenau may have mentioned the subject to Ludendorff again, since on 8 July Ludendorff, apparently unsolicited, asked Rathenau to visit him in Kreuznach, at a time when the crisis round the Chancellor had reached its height.[51]

The conversation between Rathenau and Ludendorff tarnished their relationship. Rathenau's uncritical admiration for Ludendorff came to an end, and thereafter Rathenau probably only wrote two more letters. A few weeks

---

[47] A few days after the discussion Rathenau sent Bethmann another memorandum, the contents of which he had discussed with Adolf von Harnack beforehand to test his ideas. He recommended that Austria and Turkey should make peace with Russia, to release resources for the war against England and France. The transfer of Russian goods via Austria to Germany, and the resumption of the German industrial penetration of Russia, would be welcome in business circles. The separate peace with Russia would allow France to leave the war after it had successfully accused Russia of treason. All this would initiate the termination of the war. Rathenau, *Politische Briefe*, pp. 128–34, Rathenau to Bethmann, 8 May 1917.

[48] Hellige (ed.), Rathenau–Harden, Rathenau to Harden, 7 July 1917.

[49] Rathenau, *Politische Briefe*, p. 148, Rathenau to Ludendorff, 25 June 1917.

[50] BA Koblenz, Nachlass Rathenau 2, Ludendorff to Rathenau, 28 June 1917.

[51] Ibid., Ludendorff to Rathenau, 8 July 1917; Gutsche (ed.), *Deutschland im Ersten Weltkrieg*, vol. ii, pp. 747 f.

later he summed up his opinion of the new Chancellor, Michaelis, and the increased influence of the Supreme Command with the words: 'The new regime does not disappoint me; it is an adequate expression of the philistinism which rules the country and [it reminds me] of a (diluted) beery substitute for politics.'[52]

10 July, Tuesday.[53] I arrived at Kreuznach at 8.15 a.m. and was met at the station by Captain Blankenburg. We breakfasted at the Oranienhof, on the upper floors of which are the office rooms, and I was told that Excellency Ludendorff would await me at 9.30 a.m.

The conversation began with a very friendly welcome and a request to speak completely frankly and unreservedly as usual. In accordance with the wish I had expressed in my telegram no one else was present during the conversation.

I began by asking if I might be allowed, to begin with, to take issue with Ludendorff himself. I said to him that in this critical situation the Pan-Germans were using the Supreme Command as the focus not only of tendencies hostile to peace, but of reactionary tendencies as well; referred to the concept of the Hindenburg Peace, to the Hindenburg Telegrams answering various annexationist chambers of commerce, and to Hindenburg's and Ludendorff's journey to Berlin on 8 July which was interpreted as meaning that they had wanted to induce the Kaiser to reject reforms.[54]

Ludendorff interrupted me here while he said that the journey had been made in another connection, it had been requested by telegram by the Minister of War, von Stein, who had feared that the war credits would be rejected.[55] They had travelled to Berlin to give

---

[52] Rathenau, *Politische Briefe*, p. 158, Rathenau to Steinbömer, 9 August 1917.

[53] Paragraphs from these notes and two verbatim accounts which are not included here were published in 'Was wird werden?' and reprinted in Harttung *et al.* (eds.), *Walther Rathenau. Schriften*, pp. 290–5.

[54] On the issue of the necessary combination of the war aims question with domestic policy and administrative reorganization Ludendorff was on the side of the Pan-Germans, Conservatives, and the representatives of the Victory or Hindenburg Peace, who unequivocally rejected any parliamentarization or democratization of Germany's political structure. However, during their stay in Berlin the two military leaders made several members of the Reichstag believe they wished some of them to take part in the Government. As Bethmann had rejected this idea they tried to curry favour with the Reichstag. In any case Ludendorff was not strongly opposed to putting the Government on a broader base without introducing parliamentarism. Fischer, *Griff nach der Weltmacht*, pp. 149–40; Erdmann (ed.), *Kurt Riezler*, p. 439; Gutsche, *Aufstieg und Fall*, p. 213.

[55] For Ludendorff's and Hindenburg's journey to Berlin and their planned meeting with Erzberger and Stresemann see Fischer, *Griff nach der Weltmacht*, pp. 514 f.; Ritter, *Staatskunst und Kriegshandwerk*, vol. iiii, pp. 566 ff.; Görlitz (ed.), *Regierte der Kaiser?*, pp. 300 f. The journey was designed to oust Bethmann, who had fallen out with the Centre Party, the Progressives, and the SPD because he objected to their peace resolution and their parliamentary demands. He had met strong Conservative opposition when he succeeded in convincing the Kaiser that he (Bethmann) had issued an order for the Ministry of State to draft a bill for introducing an equal franchise in Prussia. With the support of the

information to the Reichstag, if it was desired, not, of course, 'in a forum', but in free discussion with visitors. This, however, had been prevented.[56] (And here surely, Ludendorff concealed an important detail from me. The Minister of War had certainly telegraphed in the alleged sense, yet had expressly added that the danger lay in the Erzberger Resolution and it was most earnestly to be desired that this should be averted.)[57]

I now went on to describe the general situation, and emphasized the principle that today it was not just a question of finding measures for the present but also of planning for the more distant future. If one fixed one's eye on this future, then the present appeared in a new light. To describe that future: after the war Germany will have liabilities totalling at least twelve thousand million marks a year, as long as no war indemnity is forthcoming. But receiving a war indemnity is harder than winning great stretches of territory (this was confirmed). The necessity of raising the income of the lower classes by least 50% must be added to the twelve thousand mark burden, for the cost of living has risen and will remain high, and the trenches cannot be paid for with a deterioration of the standard of living. Given this premise the economy will be burdened with at least another seven thousand five hundred million marks a year, so that as against a total production worth forty-five thousand million marks, Germany will be faced with burdens totalling twenty thousand million marks, not taking into account those expenses which might arise from the necessity of providing for an army of unemployed.

This situation demands immense economic changes. But such changes must correspond to the political ones. These political changes must take place now and quietly, so that they do not occur later on in a period of political upheaval.

Add to this that the question of the origins of the war will be broached. After the war the legend cannot be sustained that Germany was insidiously attacked by four powers. Every one will see that Austria's ultimatum to Serbia was in fact excessively harsh, that it was an unbelievable stroke of luck that 90% of this ultimatum was accepted, undeservedly so, and they will see through the even more

parties and the Conservatives Ludendorff tried to topple Bethmann for a second time a few days later.

[56] It is altogether possible that the invitation to Ludendorff and Hindenburg to dine with the Kaiser on 8 July was meant to prevent them both from meeting Ebert and Scheidemann. Ritter, *Staatskunst und Kriegshandwerk*, vol. iii, pp. 566 f.

[57] Rathenau was correctly informed. The contents of Stein's telegram related to Erzberger's speech in the Central Committee of the Reichstag on the proposal for a peace resolution.

incredible deception that this acceptance was followed by the Austrian declaration of war.[58]

Here Ludendorff interrupted me and asked whether I knew something about the connection between our policy and these events. He apparently knew nothing about it himself.

I now described to him the events in Potsdam on 4 July,[59] my conversation with Bethmann at Hohen-Finow during the week which followed,[60] Jagow's efforts to get the ultimatum before it was sent off, the arrival of the ultimatum in Berlin twelve hours before it was handed over in Belgrade, and then went over the subsequent events very summarily.[61] This information made an unmistakable impression on Ludendorff. I now continued by further justifying from this the necessity for political change.

Ludendorff now asked me whether more efficient political forces might then be expected from such a change, bearing in mind that the Reichstag was not at its height. I admitted this possibility, and also went on to discuss the likelihood that the new parliamentary ministers would begin by doing stupid things, and that this could lead to a

[58] Rathenau had already referred to the myth of being attacked, in a letter to Wandel. Rathenau, *Politische Briefe*, p. 127, Rathenau to Wandel, 1 May 1917. For the German policy during the July crisis of 1914 which pressed for an armed conflict on the continent and consciously drew on itself the risk of a world war, see Fischer, *Griff nach der Weltmacht*, ch. 2. For the text of the Austrian ultimatum and the Serbian reply, see Geiss (ed.), *Julikrise*, vol. i, p. 233 and pp. 400–3; Fischer, *Krieg der Illusionen*, pp. 663–738; Röhl (ed.), *1914: Delusion or Design?*, pp. 21–8; Gutsche, *Aufstieg und Fall*, pp. 113–37.

[59] Bethmann Hollweg, Zimmermann, and the Generals Plessen, Lyncker, and Falkenhayn, with several admirals from the Admiralty, met at the Neue Palais in Potsdam on 5 and 6 July 1914. On 6 July the Kaiser gave Austria a 'blank cheque' to attack Serbia. On 4 July Bethmann had gone to Hohenfinow only to leave it for Potsdam on the next day. See Fischer, *Griff nach der Weltmacht*, pp. 60 f.; Geiss, *Julikrise*, vol. i, pp. 58 f. and pp. 79–117; Erdmann, 'Zur Beurteilung Bethmann Hollwegs', p. 536; Stern, 'Bethmann Hollweg and the War: the Limits of Responsibility; Jarausch, 'The Illusion of Limited War'; Erdmann (ed.), *Kurt Riezler*, pp. 183–93.

[60] Rathenau may have seen Bethmann twice in July but he only talked in detail about his second visit, namely the one on 23 July 1914. He wrote to Steinbömer about this visit in September 1917 after he had again seen Bethmann: 'In the midst of it I could not restrain myself; calling to mind the Austrian conversation I asked bluntly: why did you not forbid the declaration of war after the undeserved triumph of this Habsburg ultimatum? I expected an answer along the lines that it was inadmissible to allow the brother-empire to weaken morally, and such like. I was mistaken. He looked straight ahead into the darkness and was silent, probably for more than a minute. Was it an apology? Was it an accusation? It was not ill-feeling; that was clear from the unchanged mood of our flagging conversation.' Rathenau, *Briefe*, vol. i, pp. 316 f., Rathenau to Steinbömer, 16 September 1917. Rathenau did not share the general fear that Austria would break away from the alliance with Germany. Perhaps he realized it was merely propaganda.

[61] The German Foreign Office had known the main features of Austria's ultimatum to Serbia since 12 July. The ultimatum was to be handed over either before or after Poincaré's visit to Russia. Geiss, *Julikrise*, vol. i, pp. 147 f. The text of the ultimatum was received in Berlin on 22 July, more than twenty-four hours before it was handed over. Ibid., p. 266 and pp. 273–6; Fischer, *Griff nach der Weltmacht*, p. 69.

complete reactionary relapse, but that an improvement in the quality of the Reichstag could be expected later on, and with it also of the leading personalities, taking the level of German intelligence into account. In any case the leadership could not remain the way it was, and in this Ludendorff agreed with me very emphatically, while particularly bringing the person of the Chancellor into discussion, and gave one to understand that Bülow, for instance, seemed much more suitable to him.[62]

From the present domestic situation I inferred that even if the population were to hold out for some time under greatly increased pressure—and a revolutionary movement or general strikes were hardly to be expected initially—the imminent concessions represented the minimum, and next summer or autumn, if the war, as I expected, were to continue, a further movement would probably arise, which might then bring about the ultimate result.[63] It seemed to me that the present political task was to keep all these things in hand.

I now turned to the situation abroad and explained the hitherto still unshaken bond of the *entente* which, with America's entry, had secured the strength of a common idea, namely that of a crusade against autocracy. I stressed the dangers of American entry which I saw, not in the sending of troops, but in economic aid, and contrasted it with the value of the submarine war, which I wanted to discuss further. The idea that any member of the *entente*—say England—would disengage itself for economic reasons, for example because of the danger of a future shortage of tonnage, should be dismissed because in this war all economic considerations have been allowed to give way in the face of the problem of survival.

These thoughts led on to the submarine war. I began by saying that Hindenburg's declaration in Vienna struck me as very regrettable, inasmuch as it abandoned a decisive land war and left everything

[62] The opposition to Bethmann favoured two candidates. The Supreme Command and some members of heavy industry supported Bülow whereas the Conservatives pressed for Tirpitz. Ludendorff would have accepted Tirpitz, but the Kaiser wanted to reassert his influence in the face of his diminishing power and prestige. As a compromise candidate Michaelis was put forward, and was acceptable to Ludendorff. Ritter, *Staatskunst und Kriegshandwerk*, vol. iii, pp. 570 f. and 578 f.; Gutsche (ed.) *Deutschland im Ersten Weltkrieg*, vol. ii, pp. 747 f.; Weber, *Ludendorff und die Monopole*, pp. 100–7.

[63] Like Bethmann Rathenau believed in political concessions to avert a revolution or at least a general strike. However, the more stable the military situation proved to be for the Central Powers in the winter of 1917/18, the more unyielding was the attitude of the Supreme Command to the question of reform. The series of strikes in Berlin and other German towns in January and February 1918 alarmed the military leadership, but it was confident that this movement would die down the moment the spring offensive began in the West. See also Feldman, *Army, Industry and Labor*, pp. 442-58.

to submarine warfare.[64] This was carrying everything to extremes again, and with regard to this optimistic attitude I referred to my statements in Berlin in February or March, when I first predicted to Ludendorff that I considered a conclusive result, such as had been prophesied for August, as out of the question.

I criticized isolated examples of the monthly figures of sinkings, while I put forward the opinion that the monthly figures could only be regarded as maximum figures because they were based on what are essentially estimates. Above all, I went into the principles underlying the whole calculation, by which it stands or falls: that of about twenty million tons [of shipping] England must, it is supposed, retain at least 60% as indispensable for so-called military purposes. These twelve million tons represent a reserve that can be called on, not only for transporting troops, horses or guns, but also largely for munitions and food; so if one thinks, not in terms of eight million, but rather of sixteen million tons of shipping as freely disposable, the calculation appears considerably different from the way Helfferich presented it. The Navy maintains that the millions [of tons] that it sinks every month include 500,000—600,000 tons of English freightage. If one reduces these 500,000-600,000 tons to about 400,000, which might be nearer the truth, that would represent five million [tons of shipping] a year.[65] So it would take one and a half

[64] The reference is probably to Ludendorff's and Hindenburg's telegrams of 22 and 23 December 1916. In them they stated quite clearly that without unrestricted submarine warfare defeat was inevitable. Submarine warfare was, they said, Germany's last card. Fischer, *Griff nach der Weltmacht*, pp. 407 ff.; Kaulisch, 'Die Auseinandersetzungen über den uneingeschränkten U-Boot-Krieg', pp. 110 ff.; Ritter, *Staatskunst und Kriegshandwerk*, vol. iii, pp. 368 ff. For Rathenau's conversation with Ludendorff on 16 February 1917, see pp. 215–18.

[65] The most successful months in the submarine warfare were the seven months from February until August 1917. The real figures contrast with the official ones: the official ones are those in brackets.

February	499,430 BRT	(781,000)
March	548,817 BRT	(885,000)
April	841,118 BRT	(1,091,000)
May	590,729 BRT	(869,000)
June	669,218 BRT	(1,016,000)
July	534,799 BRT	(811,000)
August	477,338 BRT	(808,000).

In 1917 5,938,023 BRT (gross tonnage) of allied and neutral merchant shipping was sunk. British losses represented about 60 per cent of the total losses. This figure contrasted with British shipbuilding at the rate of 1,163,000 tons a year. British, neutral, and allied losses for the whole war ran to 11,948,702 BRT (gross tonnage) while British losses amounted to 7,760,000 tons exclusive of warships. In the years 1915–18 shipbuilding produced 3,770,000 tons worth of freightage in Britain. The net loss was made up by the arrival of the American fleet and the high rate of shipbuilding in America. The number of ships which could carry freight was further reduced because of repair work. For the German figures see Herzog, *60 Jahre deutsche U-Boote 1906–1966*, pp. 110–13; Fayle, *The War and the Shipping Industry*; Ritter, *Staatskunst und Kriegshandwerk*, vol. iii,

years to reduce the sixteen million tons of available shipping by a half, and that presents a completely different picture. For submarine warfare would only be effective if it achieved its goal in a few months, as one had in fact assumed it would. But if it drags out over a long period of time when the enemy faces the difficult but certainly not insurmountable task of producing, with an annual turnover worth one thousand million marks, five million tons of new freightage a year. All these considerations seemed completely new to Ludendorff, at least he had never contemplated them from this point of view before.[66] I was therefore able to carry on with my conclusions. These concerned chances of peace.

If peace is not to be attained in a year then the question will arise as to whether it would prove more advantageous for us in 1921 rather than in 1920, in 1919 rather than in 1918.

Ludendorff did not deny this. So we could discuss under what circumstances a dictated peace would be at all possible. I took 1871 as an example. I noted the following points: the whole intelligentsia of a nation gathered together in the capital, the country overrun by victorious enemy armies, complete indifference on the part of other nations. The capital blockaded, cut off from food and enduring several months of famine. But these circumstances were not enough—the threat of the commune was still to come, and even then the peace was not a completely dictated one: the amount of the war indemnity was negotiated, although it was possible to lop off a large amount of territory.[67]

The occupation of Paris alone would probably not be enough to satisfy the desires of our annexationists; the occupation of London would probably have to be added as well. In these circumstances one would probably have to accept, come what may, the ideas of an agreed peace; but this would exclude any annexation whatsoever.

We then turned to the various territories. Ludendorff admitted that Poland was of no value to us. He protested against the fact that the Polish settlement was blamed on him when it had already been

---

pp. 372 f. See Taylor, *English History*, pp. 84 f. with reference to Lloyd George's share in introducing the convoy system. Marder, *From the Dreadnought*, vol. iv, pp. 102 f. and pp. 276 ff.

[66] Ludendorff was probably relying on the estimates of the so-called Kalkmann Memorandum of 22 December 1916, which called for unrestricted submarine warfare from 1 February 1917. Ritter, *Staatskunst und Kriegshandwerk*, vol. iii, p. 370; J. Williamson, *Karl Helfferich*, p. 190.

[67] At the Peace of Frankfurt between Germany and France on 10 May 1871 Germany annexed Alsace-Lorraine and received five thousand million francs as a war 'indemnity'.

arranged between Bethmann and Burian before he came to office (before 12 August 1916, if I understood correctly).[68]

He sees the possession of Courland as strategically more worth while, to ward off future invasions of East Prussia. But above all he stressed frontier adjustments in the West, so that, as he said, in the next war the French would not destroy our industry at Aachen straight away. In reply I repeated my conviction that any annexation was impossible, but also remarked that if the war went on for another two years we need not worry about our industry at Aachen because we would have no idea whether there would still be any industry there.[69] I then mentioned the arguments which were used to acquire Metz (a saving of 300,000 men) by which I inferred that military arguments can be overtaken by the way affairs develop generally.[70]

Ludendorff now explained that he was not at all opposed to a negotiated peace, and never had been; that he merely considered the mood in the country as important and that one had only to bring the negotiator to him.[71] He had been asking Bethmann to do this for a year, but he had not been able to bring anyone. I answered that I did not consider mood as an applicable measurement. I held the view that the English way was better, that of constantly pointing out to the nation the seriousness of the situation. We had emasculated opinion by three years of deception, at least thirty illusions had come into being during that time and were completely believed.[72] This was one of the reasons why there were repercussions now. It

[68] The Vienna Agreement of 11-12 August 1916 between Burian and Bethmann Hollweg led to the proclamation of the Kingdom of Poland on 5 November 1916. Ludendorff had, in the hope of obtaining Polish soldiers, advocated the setting-up of a miniature Poland under German supervision. After the attempt to establish Polish units had proved a failure Ludendorff withdrew from the plan for an independent Poland. Conze, *Polnische Nation*, pp. 194-226 and p. 259; Geiss, *Der Polnische Grenztreifen*, pp. 107-15; Ritter, *Staatskunst und Kriegshandwerk*, vol. iii, p. 283 f.

[69] On the question of war aims the opinion given by the Supreme Command on 23 December 1916 laid the foundation for the Kreuznach Conference of 23 April 1917. This war aims programme went further than that advocated by Bethmann, but he signed it and believed that it could be realized if Germany won outright. Fischer, *Griff nach der Weltmacht*, pp. 444-60; Ritter, *Staatskunst und Kriegshandwerk*, vol. iii, pp. 503-27; Gutsche, *Aufstieg und Fall*, p. 208.

[70] At the Peace of Frankfurt France had had to hand over the fortress of Metz to Germany. Apparently Bismarck yielded less to military and more to nationalist pressure. Lipgens, 'Bismarck, die öffentliche Meinung und die Annexion von Elsass und Lothringen 1870'. For contrary views see Gall, 'Die Annexionspolitik von 1870/71'; Becker, 'Baden, Bismarck und die Annexion von Elsass und Lothringen'.

[71] Ludendorff's assertion does not ring true in this form because he had just (on 7 July) rejected a British offer of a negotiated peace. Fischer, *Griff nach der Weltmacht*, pp. 506-10.

[72] Erzberger concluded his conversation with Bauer on 10 June, regarding the critical military situation and the failure of the submarine war, by saying that it was essential to set up a central propaganda institute, 'a sort of spiritual War Food Office'. Ibid., p. 507.

was a pity that the nation did not know how to distinguish between
a military and a political victory, and that it could not for once
understand that when one had been winning all along one could not
now finally dictate a peace.

Ludendorff did not contradict a single point and repeatedly
asserted that he himself neither maintained the annexationists'
point of view, nor did he intend to interfere in political developments, and with that our conversation, which had meanwhile gone
on for an hour and a half—briefly interrupted twice, by a telephone
call from the Crown Prince who announced his departure to Berlin,[73]
and by a call from Groener—moved into its last phase. I said to
Ludendorff that whatever the future Government looked like, close
co-operation between it and the Supreme Command, that is himself,
was absolutely indispensable for the good of the country.[74] He
underestimated his power, as I had already told him months before;
he possessed an authority close on dictatorship and with it responsibility as well, and the historiography would hold him to it.

He replied that I still overestimated his power, that he could
not approach the Kaiser and that he was hemmed in on all sides.

I answered by emphasizing the incredibly confused leadership
in our power structure: the Under-Secretaries of State are power-
less because the Chancellor is above them. The Chancellor cannot
do anything if he does not have the sanction of Headquarters. At
Headquarters Ludendorff is hampered by Hindenburg, who switches
over to the Kaiser whenever he taps him on the shoulder. The Kaiser
himself thinks that he is obeying the constitution and thus the circle
is complete. However, here it is a question not of 'uniform hierarchy' but rather of world history. Gradually, and we had contributed to this, alongside the Hindenburg legend the reality of
Ludendorff's achievements and of his effectiveness had penetrated
[the consciousness], not it is true of the nation, but of the great
mass of the educated classes. Even he could now stand on his own
and did not require protection from above, and this ensured his
independence of responsibility.[75] At this Ludendorff raised a small
objection which did not however concern the ideas expressed, but

[73] For the Crown Prince's journey to Berlin, see Ritter, *Staatskunst und Kriegshandwerk*, vol. iii, pp. 577 f. On behalf of the Supreme Command the Crown Prince worked for
the dismissal of Bethmann. He saw Count Westarp, Stresemann, Erzberger, and David who
were all in favour of Bethmann's dismissal.

[74] Erzberger had already referred, at the Inter-Party Committee of 6 July, to close
co-operation between the Supreme Command and the 'future' government. Epstein, *Erzberger*, pp. 185-193; Morsey, *Die Deutsche Zentrumspartei*, pp. 54-67; Matthias and
Morsey (eds.), *Der Interfraktionelle Ausschuss*, vol. i, pp. 7 and 25.

[75] Despite the fact that Rathenau began to be aware of Ludendorff's machinations
he still believed in him as an organizational saviour.

was always to the effect that I overestimated his influence. Otherwise he was disposed to collaborate with any future Government excepting one which vacillated like the present one. Obviously it would be asking the superhuman to demand that along with running the war he should also take on responsibility for the political situation. But he did not exclude the thought that unity was essential.

His goodbye was in the same vein as his welcome.

After lunch I had received the following dispatch from Berlin, which a friendly source, the only one who knew I was at Kreuznach, had sent me, signed as we had agreed:

'Developments upset by National Liberal refusal to give an explanation before parliamentarization.[76] They want it done the other way round but are prepared, on the basis of the explanation, to join the Government and support it. Negotiations continue. Central Committee adjourned without debate after a statement from the Chancellor that he was still unable to give any particulars of the changes.[77] Pressure from that end for speedy conclusion might be advisable.[78] Schmidt.'

I had myself announced to Ludendorff again. He received me immediately, after two gentlemen had left him, at about 5.30 p.m. He thanked me for transmitting the dispatch, which I gave him for his information together with the naïve postcript, and he reverted again to the morning's conversation, saying that he could not altogether go along with my exposition on one point and that was the question of submarine warfare. I asked him what made him say that, and he replied that he could not give me reasons. It was an inner feeling, the same feeling that had decided him in his strategic measures. I replied that I would not venture to speak of strategic matters in his presence, but that these questions seemed to me matters of calculation and economics, in which for my part I saw a part of my life's purpose, and which I therefore also for my part believed I grasped with an intuitive feeling. So everything will probably now have to remain deferred until the final decision.

In concluding, the conversation ran once again, though more

[76] At the Inter-Party Committee meeting of 6-10 July the National Liberals had refused to support the Peace Resolution and had instead pressed for the immediate introduction of parliamentarization. On 9 July their party's central committee decided not to support the Peace Resolution, a decision which was repeated on the next day, yet then the party seemed ready to collaborate 'within the framework of the Resolution', if parliamentarization were introduced. As Bethmann was unwilling to do so the National Liberals intended to force his resignation this way. Mathias and Morsey (eds.), *Der Interfraktionelle Ausschuss*, vol. i, pp. 11-32; Deist (ed.), *Militär und Innenpolitik*, pp. 779 ff. See also J. Williamson, *Karl Helfferich*, pp. 218-38.

[77] The possible appointment of a few parliamentarians to governmental posts.

[78] This seems to be a reference to Ludendorff's threat to resign, made on 12 July. The Chancellor saw no chance of successfully resisting the Supreme Command and the Reichstag and resigned on 13 July.

briefly, on the same lines as the final thoughts of the morning's conversation.

I took my leave at about 6 p.m.

Berlin, 12.7.1917

A year and a half later Rathenau referred to the talk he had had with Ludendorff in two letters. In the first one he wrote: 'In July I visited Ludendorff in Kreuznach in order to make clear to him the hopelessness of the submarine warfare, during a talk lasting three hours in the morning and the afternoon, to change his mind over his conditions for peace and to make him accept a peace of understanding.'[79] In his second letter Rathenau said:

'I have a high opinion of Ludendorff's strategic greatness and his will to power and believe that if he had followed my advice in July 1917 when I explained to him the political situation and the problems of the submarine warfare everything could have been saved. It is bad that he was wrongly advised and that he was not able to avoid this advice by knowing his counsellors better.'[80]

Rathenau disapproved of Ludendorff's Pan-German environment and wanted his 'hero' to be more independent. But Rathenau's picture of Ludendorff remained on the whole positive. He appreciated the latter's willingness to correspond with him despite his anti-Semitic stance, his understanding of organizational questions, and his courage when making decisions. His last two known letters to Ludendorff reflect what he wanted to see in the General. In July 1918 he appealed to him for help.[81] Aircraft production was hampered by a bottleneck affecting the output of engines. The AEG did not have enough skilled labour to meet the new production targets. It is not known what Ludendorff did, but it is likely that he met Rathenau's wishes for the release from the front of a number of skilled labourers. The second letter did not deal with practical matters. When Ludendorff interfered in public with the negotiations with President Wilson he asked the army not to capitulate without being consulted by Prince Max von Baden. On hearing this the Chancellor threatened to resign. This step led to Ludendorff's enforced resignation on 26 October 1918. Probably on the same day Rathenau wrote his last letter to the General which he delivered himself. Only the general contents are known.[82] It must have been a very emotional and enthusiastic letter and must also have expressed in a tactful way that Rathenau's illusions were destroyed after the General's collapse on 29 September 1918. Rathenau's belief in Ludendorff's genius was damaged; he was no longer the courageous 'hero' whom Rathenau had to some extent typified in his writings before he had even met him.

[79] Rathenau, *Briefe*, vol. ii, p. 91, Rathenau to W. L., 17 December 1918.

[80] Ibid., p. 111, Rathenau to Breucker, 15 January 1919.

[81] Rathenau, *Politische Briefe*, pp. 182 ff., Rathenau to Ludendorff, 4 July 1918.

[82] Hillard (Steinbömer), *Herren und Narren der Welt*, pp. 232–5. For Breucker's reference, see Schulin (ed.), *Walther Rathenau. Hauptwerke und Gespräche*, p. 782.

NOTES ON 1918

Germany's imminent defeat on the Western Front after 8 August 1918, the collapse of the front of the Central Powers in Macedonia, and finally Bulgaria's decision to surrender on 26 September caused Hindenburg and Ludendorff on 28 September 1918 to ask the political leaders in Berlin to seek an end to the war. During the previous days in September the idea of bringing about peace through the mediation of President Wilson had gained ground. Now, because of Bulgaria's action, the policy makers in Berlin speeded up the replacement of Count Hertling by Prince Max von Baden as Chancellor, and approached Wilson on 3 October with the request for an armistice and a subsequent peace. This was based on Wilson's Fourteen Points which he had declared as a possible peace formula on 8 January 1918. A day before Wilson's reply to the German message became known, Rathenau opposed the German initiative in his article 'Ein dunkler Tag' in the *Vossische Zeitung* of 7 October 1918.[1] He was against taking premature steps regarding peace, and expected that in his Note Wilson would make far-reaching demands, which, as he saw it, would have to be rejected by an appeal to the last reserves of strength of the whole nation. He therefore suggested 'a national defence, the rising up of the nation'. He closed the article with the words: 'It is peace we want, not war. But not a peace of surrender.'

Just a day before the article appeared, Rathenau's plan for a *defense nationale* was the theme of a war cabinet meeting.[2] A day later his suggestion was also debated in the joint cabinet.[3] As a result Scheüch was delegated to discuss these plans with Rathenau on 8 October.[4] On that occasion he told Scheüch that he reckoned with the mobilization of between one and one and a half million additional soldiers for the last stand he thought the country should make. He also recommended revising the peace of Brest-Litovsk and of putting an end to the submarine warfare. Furthermore he thought that parliamentarization of the War Office was necessary, i.e., its transformation into a 'ministry

[1] The article has been reprinted in *Walther Rathenau. Schriften*, pp. 296 f. An English translation has been published in the *Memoirs of Prince Max of Baden*, vol. ii, pp. 55 ff. Rathenau's article did not come out of the blue. In two earlier articles on 30 September and 4 October 1918 he pursued a similar line. In the first one he argued against defeatism and moral collapse. He encouraged the Germans to hold out until the Allies realized that they could not destroy Germany. In the second one he pleaded for the mobilization of all resources to fight for a 'dignified peace'. Rathenau, *Nachgelassene Schriften*, vol. i, pp. 63–9. The titles of the articles are 'Festigkeit' and 'Die Stunde drängt'. See also Petzold (ed.), *Deutschland im Ersten Weltkrieg*, vol. iii, p. 465; Ritter, *Staatskunst und Kriegshandwerk*, vol. iv, pp. 417 and 428; Schwabe, *Deutsche Revolution und Wilsonfrieden*, pp. 88–144. See also Hellige (ed.), Rathenau–Harden, Rathenau to Harden, 9 October 1918. Harden took a different line from Rathenau and suggested an early peace to avoid the revolution which he saw coming. In fact Harden polemicized openly against Rathenau in two speeches he gave on 11 and 19 October 1918. He also submitted a lengthy memorandum to Prince Max on 14 October with the motto: 'The Empire of [18]70 is dead. The new one will be more healthy and more beautiful. Upward!' But unlike Rathenau's views Harden's only had a weak echo.

[2] Matthias and Morsey (eds.), *Die Regierung des Prinzen Max von Baden*, p. 92. Meeting on 6 October 1918.

[3] Ibid., p. 103. Meeting on 7 October 1918.

[4] Rathenau, *Politische Briefe*, pp. 188–91, Rathenau to Scheüch, 9 October 1918.

of defence made up of citizens and soldiers'. In the subsequent conference at the Chancellor's, Rathenau's plan for a *levée en masse* was discussed. Ludendorff and Scheüch rejected his idea of a great voluntary army.[5] Yet at the meeting of the War Cabinet on 10 October it was suspected that General Hoffmann and the High Command were in fact still supporting Rathenau's ideas.[6]

Without giving up the point of view he had expressed in the *Vossische Zeitung*, Rathenau was also planning demobilization, the main aim of which was to avoid disturbances and to secure the position of German industry.[7]

Meanwhile, the German Government prepared its answer to Wilson's Note which had become known on 12 October. Two days later Wilson's second Note was sent to Germany, and this was interpreted in Berlin as being much tougher than the first one. The German Government had to decide whether it wanted to continue on the road of a Wilson-inspired peace or risk the failure of the peace initiative. Following the first option meant acceptance of Wilson's military and political demands, which also implied admitting military defeat openly. While the politicians favoured the first step the military changed their mind and showed themselves willing to continue with the war. However, in the German reply of 20 October the politicians prevailed.

Four days earlier, when pessimism in Berlin ran strong, the Foreign Secretary, Wilhelm Solf, tried various means to impress the American Government with the German disappointment about Wilson's second Note.[8] After a conversation with Solf on 16 October Rathenau drafted the letter to President Wilson which appears below and which was to deal 'not with diplomatic negotiations any more, but with the emotional upsurge of popular opinion'.[9] Yet he admitted that he did not expect the letter to have any great effect. He also made it clear that he did not believe in the appeal to Wilson, and 'thought that every day was lost which we did not use for reconstructing our war organization'.[10] To Rathenau the drafted letter and his own concern were not mutually exclusive.

Solf answered Rathenau on 23 October, a few hours before Wilson's third Note was published in Washington.[11] Solf was at this moment still full of hope that he would be able to moderate the Wilsonian conditions for armistice and peace by diplomatic negotiations. So he wrote:

'I understand your train of thoughts very well. It contained much that was tempting for me too . . . But I do not think that now is the right time for an appeal given the way you have drafted it and the way it affects me strongly as a human being. We have sinned too much in the opposite directions for the world to believe us! The English will say *the devil is sick, the devil monk will be* and Wilson, who has difficulties in upholding his thoughts about peace against the victorious army leaders, will be obliged to reject the answer from man to

[5] Matthias and Morsey (eds.), *Die Regierung des Prinzen Max von Baden*, pp. 118 and 122 f. Conference of 9 October 1918.

[6] Ibid., pp. 126 f.

[7] Rathenau, *Politische Briefe*, pp. 195–200, Rathenau to Scheüch, 15 October 1918. Rathenau had discussed demobilization with the War Minister on that day.

[8] Schwabe, *Deutsche Revolution und Wilsonfrieden*, p. 135.

[9] BA Koblenz, Nachlass Solf 124, Rathenau to Solf, 17 October 1918. An abbreviated letter was published in Rathenau, *Briefe*, vol. ii, pp. 68 ff. See also Petzold (ed.), *Deutschland im Ersten Weltkrieg*, vol. iii, p. 471.

[10] This passage was omitted from the published version.

[11] BA Koblenz, Nachlass Solf 124, Solf to Rathenau, 23 October 1918; Vietsch, *Wilhelm Solf*, p. 202.

man and from nation to nation and to demand instead realistic replies to his Notes.'

Rathenau remained convinced that more advantageous terms for the armistice would have been possible if the political and military leaders had not panicked. As late as January 1919 he was still objecting to the signing of the armistice on 11 November 1918.[12] A very similar situation occurred with the terms of the Versailles Peace Treaty. He rejected them and tried to persuade the Government not to sign the treaty, but as before his arguments were not followed.[13] It appears that he was more motivated by patriotism than by realism.

Walther Rathenau's Letter Drafted for Prince Max von Baden to send to President Wilson (not dispatched)

Dear Mr President,

The form of your last Note does not make it easy for me to give you an answer.[14] As I trust your and the American nation's feeling for humanity, justice and non-partisanship, as you express it in your messages and speeches, I have decided to abandon the form of diplomatic negotiation and speak to you and the American nation as man to man and as people to people without reservation as my responsibility to God and to the people whom I serve demands.

I have decided to give you an answer which goes beyond the text of your question and to tell you all that you, the Americans and all the other nations ought to know. The German people are willing to undergo basic reforms and have taken this process in hand. This reform is a social, political and moral one. I speak on behalf of the people and their legitimate representative body.

Our constitution has been altered.[15] The people have taken their fate into their own hands and we govern ourselves on a democratic basis. Today there is no single power which can make its own decisions and which in turn will decide matters for the people; and there will never be such power again. I have always objected to the unrestricted submarine warfare which has separated us from the American people.[16] The unrestricted submarine warfare has ceased, the necessary orders have been given to the commanders.[17]

[12] Rathenau, *Nachgelassene Schriften*, vol. i, p. 96, Rathenau to *Frankfurter Zeitung*, 30 January 1919.

[13] Hellige (ed.), Rathenau–Harden, Rathenau to Harden, 20 May 1919. See especially the editor's comments; Rathenau, *Nachgelassene Schriften*, vol. i, pp. 102-5, Rathenau's article 'Das Ende' in *Die Zukunft*, 31 May 1919.

[14] Wilson's Note of 14 October 1918.

[15] In fact the constitutional reforms were to become law on 28 October 1918.

[16] Max von Baden, *Erinnerungen*, pp. 52-65.

[17] In the German memorandum of 20 October Wilson was informed that German submarines would no longer attack passenger ships.

I disapproved of the peace treaty of Brest-Litovsk because it did not do sufficient justice to the principle of national self-determination.[18] It has been declared void except for the first article which stipulates that Germany and Russia want to live in peace.[19] The High Command has resolved and taken all measures to save all those parts of France and Belgium which have been affected by war. We have accepted the fourteen points of your message of 8 January and are resolved to make peace on that basis.

Our offer of an armistice was not made with the aim of gaining time or altering the existing balance of forces or preparing in any way for an extension of the war. We are prepared to offer guarantees for that, but they must not violate the honour of the army and the people. I am expecting just proposals about this.

If you and the American people thought it more useful to negotiate about peace without armistice I would deeply regret it for humanitarian reasons and would greatly deplore any human sacrifice which would result from the continuation of hostilities; however we would be prepared to choose this path if need be.

I think I can testify to God and humanity that the German people have expressed through this letter their unreserved willingness to accept all your peace terms. Nobody can or may demand that our people accept conditions which are beyond the limits of justice and violate its honour. We do not assume that such conditions would be imposed by you, Mr President and the American nation. If any side expects us to accept them, then we shall fight and die for the honour of our people if God inflicts us with this fate. I myself should then leave this office which has been entrusted to me by the German people, with the one wish, to join the lines of my brethren and save the country or die.

17.10.1918

[18] The Peace Treaty of Brest-Litovsk had been signed on 3 March 1918. For Prince Max's attitude see his *Erinnerungen*, pp. 186–210.

[19] A revision had not taken place because diplomatic relations were broken off on 5 November 1918. Rosenfeld, *Sowjetrussland und Deutschland*, pp. 130 f.

NOTES ON 1920

During the revolutionary days in Berlin in November 1918 Rathenau had the feeling that he was missing out on what could have become a radical transformation of German society. Somehow he expected to be more in the centre of events; but he was not being passed over, as he sometimes thought. Outside Berlin he was quoted, by several people involved in the revolution, as their hero. He may not have been aware of this fact, but he knew perfectly well that he was a public figure. He had even become the object of political jokes. Thus Winterfeldt wrote to Seeckt during the war that 'above the war when it was won there would gleam a symbol—a huge W.R.—which some would take to mean Wilhelm Rex, and others Walther Rathenau . . .'[1]

Rathenau was clearly well known, but he was also one of the most controversial personalities in German public life. His role during the war as head of the KRA, his admiration for Ludendorff, his position in industry, and his newspaper article of 7 October 1918 were all obstacles to his being asked to join politics at a very high level. To some he was the capitalist who had prolonged and profited from the war, and advocated useless resistance, to others he was a 'socialist' or a dangerous economic reformer. His efforts to enter politics suffered from these contradictions. They were the reason why his candidature for the National Assembly in early 1919 fell through, why he was not a member of the First, but only of the Second Socialization Commission from April 1920, and why when his name was proposed to the National Assembly as a possible presidential candidate it was met with laughter.

However, he was not excluded from the political scene, nor did he withdraw into self-imposed political exile. His position as one of Germany's most important industrialists would have made any such considerations impossible. He belonged to the very small group of leading industrialists who concluded the Stinnes–Legien Agreement on 15 November 1918 which formed the basis for the Zentralarbeitsgemeinschaft (ZAG—Central Working Community) and which institutionalized collaboration between employers and trade unions in social and economic matters.[2] It was mainly due to Rathenau, for instance, that after great difficulties the eight-hour working day was accepted. To him the Agreement was a step in the right direction because it was to demonstrate that the only viable power left in Germany was that of the 'united employers and workers'. This power was to organize demobilization in conjunction with the State. It all seemed to be heading towards his New Economy, provided ethical attitudes would undergo fundamental changes. This latter point was so crucial to him that when the Minister of Economics, Rudolf Wissell, presented a socialization bill to the Reichstag and accused Rathenau of wanting to change the German economy into a large AEG, he reacted furiously to this misrepresentation of his ideas.[3] When Wissell and his Under-Secretary Moellendorff pointed

[1] Rabenau (ed.), *Seeckt*, vol. i, p. 325.

[2] Feldman, 'The Origins of the Stinnes–Legien Agreement', and 'German Business beween War and Revolution'; Zunkel, *Industrie und Staatssozialismus*, pp. 188–200; Feldman, *Iron and Steel in the German Inflation*, pp. 82 ff.; Baudis and Nussbaum, *Wirtschaft und Staat*, vol. i, pp. 332–8.

[3] Feldman, *Iron and Steel in the German Inflation*, pp. 100–6; Baudis and Nussbaum, *Wirtschaft und Staat*, vol. i, p. 362. See also Kessler, *Rathenau*, pp. 274 f.

out that they, in contrast to Rathenau, were most concerned with the welfare of human beings it was all too easy for Rathenau to put them right.

However, the demands of November 1918 and the plans Wissell and Moellendorff put forward allowed Rathenau to rescue his ideas in the face of a political challenge by putting them aside for the future when ethical attitudes would have changed. By not translating and adapting his ideas to the revolutionary situation he missed the chance of finding a direct entry into politics through his activities as a publicist. Certainly he was able to increase his reputation as an important author on social, economic, and political matters, but the way into practical politics came primarily through his importance as an industrialist.

In March 1919 he was called upon to lend his advice as an expert in electrotechnology to the German peace delegation bound for Versailles. This was the first public task given to him after his attempts to set up the Demokratischer Volksbund (Democratic People's League) and enter the National Assembly had ended in failure. During the remaining months of 1919 he was occupied with preparing the AEG for the post-war inflationary world, and preserving it against the onslaught of the steel industry in general and Hugo Stinnes in particular.

Besides his industrial and political activities he continued to write books and articles. His plan to give the Allies complete responsibility for governing Germany, unless the Peace Treaty were altered, met with little attention. Late in 1919 Ludendorff misrepresented to the Reichstag committee enquiring into the reasons for Germany's defeat a remark Rathenau had made in his pamphlet *Der Kaiser*, published earlier that year, in such a way as to make him appear a saboteur of the moral war effort. The same circumstances which made him well known were used by his enemies to denigrate him. He published so much in 1918 and 1919 that it was relatively easy to select remarks to use in the political struggle or to criticize him. Within two years of the first edition of the *Gesammelte Schriften* (September 1918), he wrote *An Deutschlands Jugend* (1918) and an essay *Der Kaiser* (March 1919), and published his plans for *Der Neue Staat* (May 1919) and *Die Neue Gesellschaft* (September 1919). The *Kritik der dreifachen Revolution* (1919) and *Was wird werden?* were to follow.[4]

The reviews and reaction which Rathenau's *Neue Wirtschaft* received during 1918 caused him to link his concepts to the *Neue Staat* and *Neue Gesellschaft*. The liberal economist Wiese criticized Rathenau's system:

'There are many strange contradictions in this system. From the political point of view it is partly cosmopolitan, partly very nationalistic; economically speaking it is partly a product of the spirit of the market economy, partly— particularly in its practical demands—directed towards a 'communal economy'; [his system] is in social-political terms a genuine product of capitalism, while at the same time the author has moved towards state socialism of the purest kind.[5]

In his booklet *Der Neue Staat*, Rathenau recommended a socialized *Volksstaat*. He rejected party democracy, but believed that the entire State had to be penetrated by 'organic democracy and socialism'. Professional parliaments and professional associations would have to exist side by side with the political parliament. This implied that both the State and the economy would have to be reorganized at one and the same time. Finally he confessed that he was fascinated

[4] Kessler, *Rathenau*, pp. 241–89; Berglar, *Walther Rathenau*, pp. 244–51.
[5] Berglar, *Walther Rathenau*, p. 178; (Wiese, Freie Wirtschaft).

by early communist Russia. Although he wanted to co-operate with all nations. 'our leaning will be towards Russia'; he did not want to imitate Bolshevism, but did hope that Germany together with Russia would be the protagonists of the spirit of a new era.

The last work of this tryptich dealt with *Die Neue Gesellschaft*. The new economy and the new State would form the new society which would be held together by solidarity instead of 'proportionate figures of the interests concerned'. The new society would live in a harmonious *Volksstaat*, in which its citizens would be educated to live for the common good (*Gemeinsinn*). One of the main aims of the new society would be to break the vicious circle of inherited poverty and deprivation. He also aimed for 'equalization of labour' by which manual workers and white-collar workers would exchange their work-places for a short while. He also advocated the introduction of a one-year labour service for young men and women. As long as socialism believed in a division of labour it would not be able to cope with the problem of poverty. Through his 'equalization of labour' and the labour service he hoped to help the change in the ethical attitudes which would be the precondition for his ultimate goal, the spiritualization of human beings.

Even his last Utopian booklet *Die Neue Gesellschaft* sold well, but it is difficult to decide how popular Rathenau was. He himself felt isolated, mainly because he had hoped to become more popular through his writings and had not in fact achieved this. He may have again played with the idea of retirement, but he could not contemplate it. His industrial activities kept him busy, and through them he kept in touch with politics and remained a man of mark to politicians.

The Kapp Putsch

During the Kapp Putsch Rathenau seems to have tried to mediate between the legal Government which, except for Eugen Schiffer, had fled to Stuttgart, and the putschists who were led by the commander of a Reichswehr district, General von Lüttwitz, and the former Prussian civil servant, Wolfgang Kapp. The putsch was the first attempt to overthrow the Republic. It had been caused by the democratic development, by the demand of the Versailles Treaty for a heavy reduction of Germany's armed forces, and the Government's attempt to disband two naval brigades near Berlin. When the two brigades had marched on Berlin, the Government departed to Stuttgart and thus left the capital to the putschists. However, they encountered a general strike called for by the trade unions, and an unhelpful attitude by the civil service and the army. When it became obvious that the power basis was too narrow for the putschists and that Kapp and Lüttwitz did not wield any authority they left Berlin and fled the country. The putsch had collapsed.

The Ministry of the Interior telephoned at lunch-time, 1 p.m.:[6] at Minister von Jagow's behest Colonel Bauer requested an interview

---

[6] The phone call and the subsequent conversation took place on Tuesday, 16 March 1920. Rathenau had been slow to hear the news: on the 13th Rathenau was still apparently

at 6 p.m. that evening at the State Chancellery. In answer to an enquiry it was said that other gentlemen from the tram and overhead railway [companies] had been summoned as well. It was also established, by other means, that von Borsig and von Gontard were also invited. Von Borsig had asked if he might bring Mr Pfeil and Dr Levy with him.

The gentlemen arrived at 6 p.m. that evening. Confusion in the entrance hall like in November 1918. No one knows what is going on. We are asked to announce our presence in writing. Word is sent round: Colonel Bauer cannot be found.

While we waited in the ante-room I talked to the gentlemen and was able to establish that Mr Pfeil maintained, to a certain extent, the same position as the new Government. When I remarked that if the two Governments did not arrive at an agreement immediately, then an uprising would come by the end of the week, he excitedly declared that in that case each and every man would just have to shoulder his gun and set off together with the army against the 'common enemy'.[7]

Finally we are led into a small sitting-room in the right wing and are told that Kapp will receive us. A few minutes later he enters, introduces himself to each of the gentlemen, declares he knows nothing about the invitation but that he wants to give us some interesting information. The news has just come in that there will be a joint attack by the Independents and the Communists during the night;[8] he considers it his manifest duty to defend the country against the 'common enemy'; every precaution has been taken. Then, since he asked the gentlemen to express their opinion, I said that the danger existed that it was not just the 'common enemy' that would be fought but that a great part of the working class, indeed of the middle classes themselves, would join the revolutionary elements. It would be necessary to establish the extent of forces available. This would show that part of the flat country (East Prussia, Pomerania, Silesia) was on the side of the military, west of the Elbe and in the south the situation was different.[9] I do not believe that they have a true picture of the balance of forces.

uninformed as to what had happened in the centre of Berlin. Schulin (ed.), *Walther Rathenau. Hauptwerke und Gespräche*, p. 809.

[7] Rathenau shared the apprehension that a radicalization of the general strike, called out on 13 March, could bring about an uprising of the Left. Under the increasing pressure of this threat efforts were made in Berlin to reach an agreement with the putschists.

[8] Lüttwitz and Kapp tried to impress those present with the ultimatum issued by the Left, in the hope of being able to use the anticipated wave of anti-communism for their own purposes. This threat was, however, not taken very seriously by the Ministry of Defence. Erger, *Der Kapp–Lüttwitz-Putsch*, pp. 255 ff.

[9] Even Schiffer still believed at this moment that Kapp had the East securely in his

Mr Pfeil replied that he was of the same opinion as the 'Imperial Chancellor', that one must set off against the 'common enemy'.[10]

Kapp answered that he believed the situation was rather different from the way I had presented it, but that to discuss it would be going too far. He thanked me and said goodbye to me particularly courteously, and said that he had long awaited the opportunity to make my acquaintance.

We now had ourselves announced to Bauer again; firstly because we had been asked to and secondly because Mr von Borsig wanted to show him the list of Independent ministers (from Däumig to Cohn).[11]

Bauer received us in the Chancellor's big ante-room. He cleared coffee cups from the table and placed us in Bülow's faded damask armchairs. In the middle of the room, his back turned to us, sat a gentleman who looked very like Kapp and was apparently taking notes.

Bauer has aged a lot, stoops, and seems tired out. We immediately turned the conversation to the settlement with Stuttgart.[12] I asked what was preventing it; he answered: stubbornness. I asked: doesn't it finally come down to questions of prestige? He denied this.

I seized this opportunity and said: if it were absolutely certain that questions of prestige did not come into consideration, then it would have to be possible to arrive at an understanding, so long as none of the gentlemen were by any chance making personal demands. This was also denied.

'What then do you want?' I asked.

'The troops, obviously, must know that they have not been abused. No one must be brought to account.'

'In other words: amnesty?' I asked.

'The word amnesty only applies to crime', he replied.

'Let's drop the word. It is a question then of impunity, or to put it even more impartially: no one is to be called to account for the actions of the last six days?'[13]

hands. Ibid., pp.. 249 and 252 ff. Already General Maercker had told Kapp between 14 and 15 March that 'Germany is at the moment divided into two parts. One is the whole of Western and Southern Germany and the other Northern and Eastern Germany. If this situation is not brought to an end quickly then there will be a fight between Reichswehr and Reichswehr and this must be avoided at all costs.' Carsten, *Reichswehr und Politik*, p. 97.

[10] Rathenau did not call Kapp 'Chancellor', although Harden maintained this later, but he called Jagow 'Minister'. Harden, 'In der Mördergrube', *Die Zukunft*, 1 July 1922.

[11] With the news of the ultimatum came the announcement that the workers had already formed a new government with Däumig and Cohn. Erger, *Der Kapp–Lüttwitz-Putsch*, p. 255.

[12] After a settlement had been rejected by the Government in Stuttgart the right-wing parties and the Reichswehr in Berlin worked together for a settlement.

[13] Six days previously, on 10 March, Lüttwitz had presented his demands to President Ebert as an ultimatum. On 11 March, after his demands had been rejected, he ordered Ehrhardt's Brigade to occupy Berlin. Erger, *Der Kapp–Lüttwitz-Putsch*, pp. 121 and 125.

'Yes, that's it', he said.

'Have you said this to Schiffer?' I asked.[14]

'No,' he answered. 'Why, Schiffer doesn't come over here.'

'So it is a question of prestige,' I said. 'Why don't you go over to Schiffer?'

'I cannot leave my military post,' he replied.

'Are you prepared to reach an agreement with Schiffer on the telephone?'

'Certainly.'

'Shall we tell him that?'

'Yes, please do.'

So, I summed up:

'Would you be satisifed if the purely technical demands (new general election, presidential elections, specialist ministers, etc.)[15] were voluntarily carried out by the old Government? You are making no personal claims, nor are you taking matters of prestige into consideration? You are merely demanding impunity for the parties concerned?'

'Yes, indeed.'

'Shall we pass this on?'

'Certainly.'

We now went over to Schiffer at Voss Strasse, although most of the gentlemen had little inclination to do so and would much rather have let me go alone. But I wanted to have witnesses.

We found Schiffer in his study with his Under-Secretary, also Albert and Oeser. I reported on the course of events and asked Schiffer if he was prepared to come to an agreement by telephone. He agreed to do so. At this moment Südekum came and was of the opinion that this was redundant because an agreement had already been reached.[16] He reported, furthermore, on the Independents' mad behaviour. A few minutes later several gentlemen arrived and were shown into the next room. I think it was Schlicke. In any case Göhre was there and came into the study later on. Südekum was summoned away to a State Ministry meeting.

Meanwhile I had taken Oeser and Schiffer aside separately and told them that Bauer gave one the impression of a broken man who was

[14] On the same day Stresemann had also tried to arrange a conversation between Bauer and Schiffer. The time-sequence of Rathenau's and Stresemann's attempts to mediate is not clear. Ibid., p. 255.

[15] In their effort to mediate, the right-wing parties hoped to be able to move the Government in Stuttgart to accept these basic demands as well as an amnesty for all political activities since 9 November 1918.

[16] Südekum had mistakenly taken the news that Kapp and Lüttwitz were ready to resign as meaning that the resignation had already taken place. Erger, Der Kapp–Lüttwitz-Putsch, p. 257.

ready to capitulate. He should not be driven to desperation by formalities; it should be settled immediately.

Schiffer went to the gentlemen in the next room and asked me to telephone Bauer meanwhile. But the connection could not be made.

Meanwhile a Conservative minister came in—at first I thought it was Heinze, because he knew me, but I could not remember him, so it must have been someone else.

The rest of the industrial gentlemen had left.

Suddenly Schiffer came back and said: there has been a great misunderstanding here; it turns out that Heinze and Düring were on the stairs bringing a message from Kapp; Südekum said to them, 'Why, that has been superseded because we have positive news at the Reichstag that Kapp has just resigned.'[17] At this the gentlemen immediately turned round. Meanwhile the news of Kapp's resignation was spread about, but this news was false.

Another attempt was made to telephone Bauer;[18] but at that moment Major Pabst was announced, coming at Bauer's orders.[19] As he came in I took my leave, for my task had been accomplished. But from the self-conscious way in which this young major made his appearance I had to conclude that the whole affair was still not going quite smoothly.

The two defects in the affair were:
1. Südekum's misunderstanding,[20]
2. The breakdown in the telephone connection.

Berlin, 16.3.1920

The Spa Conference

After the Kapp Putsch the Government was reshuffled. In the new Cabinet Josef Wirth became Finance Minister. So far it is not quite clear how Wirth and Rathenau came to know each other, but it is generally assumed that it was Wirth who enabled Rathenau to join the Second Socialization Committee, the Economic Council, and, as a technical adviser, the delegation for the Spa Conference.[21] The conference had been arranged to reach agreement between the Allied and German delegations about German disarmament and coal deliveries in execution of the reparations clauses of the Treaty of Versailles. It was the first time that Germany was admitted to negotiations about Versailles. The

[17] Ibid.

[18] Bauer was finally able to reach Schiffer at about midnight. Schiffer still insisted on Lüttwitz's resignation. Ibid., p. 260.

[19] Major Pabst arrived at the Ministry of Justice at 8 p.m. with orders from Kapp and Lüttwitz to negotiate, but not to tender their resignations. Ibid., pp. 259 ff.

[20] Despite Südekum's misunderstanding Kapp resigned on the morning of 17 March and Lüttwitz later that afternoon. Ibid., pp. 263–78.

[21] Kessler, *Rathenau*, pp. 291 f.

clash during the conference between Stinnes and Rathenau over the amount of coal Germany should deliver to France emphasized the difference between a policy which aimed at preventing an occupation of the Ruhr (Rathenau) and one which was prepared to risk an occupation (Stinnes). Eventually the financial advisers Bonn, Melchior, and Rathenau made the German Government accept the Allied demand for a delivery of two million tons of coal per month, in order to avoid the Allies marching into the Ruhr. Wirth later claimed that the 'policy of fulfilment' was born at Spa.[22]

The remark may indicate how strongly he agreed with Rathenau, but the notion of fulfilment had existed since 1919 and had also been proposed by Maximilian Harden. If there was agreement between Wirth and Rathenau, it was on the tactics of how to treat the Allies. Thus whenever there was a danger of more serious measures being taken against Germany, as, for example, with the occupation of the Ruhr, the idea of fulfilment was put forward more firmly, and whenever the German position appeared to be stronger, the case for the preservation of German sovereignty or honour was made, so that the policy of fulfilment could be reduced in its scope. In line with this general approach, the Fehrenbach Government did not come forward with any detailed schemes or proposals. It tried to exploit the threat of Soviet Russia appearing on Germany's eastern borders after initially defeating Poland during the Russo-Polish war. But the Allies were not to be blackmailed over the issue of reparation. When it became known that plans for an actual occupation of the Ruhr were prepared and that the Allies were willing to carry them out, the German delegation agreed to deliver coal to France on a regular monthly basis in return for food shipments to German miners.

The outcome of the conference confirmed the view among French politicians that 'the literal execution of the Treaty [of Versailles] is a chimera', and that it would be more sensible to come to an arrangement with German industry on how best to co-operate economically.

When we arrived at Spa on Friday, 9 July at 4 p.m. (Dernburg, Stauss, Stinnes, Wiedfeldt, von Flotow),[23] we discovered at the station that the military agreement had been concluded.[24] Gessler was about to depart. At the Hotel Annette et Lubin we found out that the coal and reparations negotiations were to begin.

Early on Saturday I visited Malcolm—up to then there had been no unofficial contact with the English at all—and asked him:

[22] Ibid., pp. 297 f. G. Soutou, 'Die deutschen Reparationen und das Seydoux-Projekt'; Trachtenberg, *Reparation in World Politics*, p. 159 and the subsequent section on the Seydoux Plan; Wulf, *Hugo Stinnes*, pp. 210 ff.

[23] The Spa Conference lasted from 5 to 16 July 1920. The agenda included four points: 1. execution of the military clauses of the peace treaty, 2. the reparations question, 3. the coal question, 4. the war-crimes proceedings. For the latest account of the Spa Conference in English, see Trachtenberg, *Reparation in World Politics*, pp. 144-54, and Wulf, *Hugo Stinnes*, pp. 196-221.

[24] Germany's demand for an army of 200,000 men had at this time been rejected by the Allied Supreme Council. Under threat of further occupation of German territory Germany was given until 1 January 1921 to reduce its army to 100,000 men. The German delegation finally accepted the Allied demand on 9 July 1920. Gründer, *Walter Simons*, pp. 109-14.

1. Why was only the question of disarmament to be dealt with and not that of joint consultation on public safety and the policing of the country (gendarmerie or constabulary)? He answered that topics of this kind had not been proposed.[25]

2. I asked why the brusque form of an ultimatum had been chosen, and what reasons lay behind its being so particularly ill-humoured. At this he showed me in his printed records a letter dated 5 March from General Nollet who asked for the abolition of compulsory military service. I replied that our constitution did not include military service; furthermore the Treaty of Versailles formed part of State legislation.[26] But he replied by saying that the *Entente* had for particular reasons set store by the proclamation of a special law regarding abolition. The letter of 5 March had only been answered on 8 May. Reference had been made to the fact that a Reichswehr law was under discussion in the Reichsrat,[27] that it included abolition, but the State law had now been passed and so nothing further had been heard of the matter. This had contributed especially to the ill-humour.

When I asked Colonel Michelis the next day, he confirmed this connection and emphasized that the military authorities had reminded the Treasury of its urgency; but there the matter had been dealt with as a formality. I informed the [German] Foreign Office of all this, but only found out later in Berlin that the Foreign Office had been dealing with it for some time and in particular that General Malcolm had been to Mr von Haniel to remind him.

The next few days were devoted primarily to the Coal Committee which was deliberating with an Allied Coal Commission,[28] but could not come to any agreement. The German side offered 1.1 million tons a month. There is no doubt that the misunderstanding lay in the fact that our Government identified itself completely with the Coal Committee.[29] This misunderstanding was worsened by the fact that

[25] The German Government tried to avoid this topic because the police were organized on military lines. Then the Prussian Minister of the Interior, Severing, was called to Spa. He appeared relaxed about the whole question and argued that the disarmament of the people could be carried out within six months. Moreover Simons had pointed out that if public order were in danger Germany would not be bound by its contractual obligations, because the peace treaty was based on the assumption of a domestic peace. Ibid., pp. 113 f.; Salewski, *Entwaffnung und Militärkontrolle*, pp. 126-37.

[26] See *Reichsgesetzblatt*, 1919, p. 687.

[27] A defence law came into effect on 23 March 1921. It included, *inter alia*, the provisions of the Versailles Peace Treaty.

[28] On 10 July the French President, Millerand, had proposed that agreement should be reached with Germany by means of conferences of experts. The experts on each side were to form a commission. Thus there was a German Coal Committee and an Allied Coal Commission.

[29] The reference is to the German Coal Committee.

a formal Cabinet resolution regarding its attitude to the German coal offer was never even extracted: on the contrary, reference was repeatedly made to the votes of the experts. Thus the opinion arose on the other side, not altogether unjustly, that the Government had put all its power in the hands of the coal lobby. This impression was considerably heightened by Stinnes's speech,[30] which was seen as the military–industrial spirit flaring up again. This explains why the Allies' proposals took on the form almost of an ultimatum.

After the Allied proposal had been handed over, negotiations on Wednesday, if I am not mistaken, came more or less to a complete standstill.[31] So I went to Malcolm off my own bat and arranged with him that a meeting would take place between Simons and Lloyd George or Millerand. It seems that a similar suggestion had been put forward by the Dutch journalist Blankenstein.[32] The result was that the well-known meeting between Simons and Lloyd George took place that afternoon.[33]

Counter-proposals were worked out again on Thursday that went a long way towards meeting the Allied point of view.[34] They were transmitted on Friday morning. During Wednesday night, between 11 p.m. and 2 a.m., two Englishmen and an Italian (Wise and Giannini) came to see me. We discussed the question of Upper-Silesian compensation in great detail and above all the permissible limits or margin of error which could be regarded as unobjectionable. Unfortunately the results of this [discussion] could not be put to use on account of the speeding-up of the negotiations.

On Friday, both in the morning and in the afternoon, I had an hour and a half's interview with Lord d'Abernon at the

---

[30] Stinnes made his speech on 10 July. It caused anger and concern among the Allies because of its hostile tone, and feelings of pride among right-wing Germans. Simons explained Stinnes's behaviour by pointing out that he was in the habit of addressing board meetings in a similar way. D'Abernon, *An Ambassador of Peace*, vol. i, p. 64; Gründer, *Walter Simons*, p. 113; Wulf, *Hugo Stinnes*, pp. 206 f.

[31] Negotiations had run into difficulties already on Tuesday (13 July) because the German side initially rejected the Allied demand for 2 million tons of coal. Thereupon the occupation of the Ruhr district was threatened.

[32] See Blankenstein's article about Rathenau, 'Rathenau van nabij'. *Nieuwe Rotterdam Courant*, 27 June 1920; Schulin (ed.), *Walther Rathenau. Hauptwerke und Gespräche*, p. 818.

[33] The talk between Lloyd George and Simons took place on 14 July. See now Gründer, *Walter Simons*, pp. 118 f. Lloyd George told Simons that the Allies were going to insist on a delivery of 2 million tons of coal per month. If this were not forthcoming, the Ruhr district would be occupied. To give this threat more substance Marshal Foch and Field Marshal Wilson were called to Spa. Marc Trachtenberg has called this meeting a secret one but does not supply any evidence as to why this should have been so. Trachtenberg, *Reparation in World Politics*, pp. 150 f.

[34] At the same time Bonn had also attempted to bring about an Anglo-German accommodation. Trachtenberg, *Reparation in World Politics*, pp. 120 ff.; Bonn, *So macht man Geschichte*, pp. 244–53.

Hotel Britannic during which he occasionally left the room for twenty minutes to harmonize the discussions with Lloyd George's intentions.[35] The results are contained in the appendix. It was a question, once more, of the wording for Upper Silesia, and also of Paragraph VII of the French proposals (occupation), and finally, of revising the question of German security. At lunch-time I conveyed the results to the Cabinet in whose discussion I took part.[36] The formula agreed to on Upper Silesia[37] was undoubtedly more strongly worded than the one which Lloyd George, in the heat of the final negotiations, made verbally and which we accepted.

At my suggestion Lloyd George sent his card to [Foreign] Minister Simons, which he had hitherto neglected to do, and at the same time to the Chancellor.

The German delegation's decisive meeting took place on Friday afternoon at 5.30 p.m. at the Hotel Annette et Lubin, where the Cabinet was joined by all the experts (coal and finance) for a consultation. In his opening speech Simons laid particular stress on the necessity of not giving in and was most forcibly backed by Stinnes. To begin with it seemed as though all the experts were of the same opinion. The Cabinet had obviously expected this too. The picture changed when three of the financial experts took the floor (Dernburg, Bonn, and I). I directed a precise question to Stinnes, whether in the event of French occupation the French had less chance of receiving the 2 million tons a month than if the agreement were signed. Stinnes candidly admitted that the French would easily be able to procure this amount themselves.[38] Thus a new situation arose, for it now appeared conclusive that, should the proposal be rejected, we would gain nothing materially. However, there was a much greater chance that the French would not just take the 2 million tons but as much again over and above that, as originally guaranteed them by the Treaty of Versailles, that is, 3.2 million tons a month.[39] To the objection that it would be impossible to transport this quantity, came the necessary reply that they would probably be in a position to appropriate this or an even greater amount and sell it to Germany at the world market price. This would solve the problem of war reparations in a purely administrative way, quite

[35] The conversation with D'Abernon occurred at the time when Bonn was trying to let Lloyd George have the German Note of reply. Bonn, *So macht man Geschichte*, pp. 249 f.

[36] P. Wulf has been unable to trace any reference to this and the next meeting in the official records. Wulf (ed.), *Das Kabinett Fehrenbach*, pp. 66 f.

[37] The question was to what extent could Germany draw on Upper Silesian coal for reparations deliveries.

[38] Presumably the argument with Stinnes, reported by Bonn as having taken place that evening. Wulf (ed.), *Das Kabinett Fehrenbach*, p. 247.

[39] Eventually Germany accepted the Allied demand of a monthly delivery of 2 million tons of coal beginning on 1 August and continuing, initially, for the next six months.

apart from the fact that France would find herself in possession of all of the central European coal deposits and would thus exercise an economic dictatorship alongside her military and political one.

The Cabinet was visibly staggered; Fehrenbach observed in alarm that there were differences of opinion among the experts, which he had obviously not expected. The Cabinet continued its deliberations at the Villa Sorbière. In the evening the results of the negotiations became known. Stinnes's indignation and threats exceeded all bounds; he openly declared that northern Germany would have to be prepared to accept moderate deliveries and threatened to stir up serious political, and social, particularly anti-Semitic conflicts.[40]

During all this time the financial discussions had made very little progress. Contrary to the vote of a section of the experts an offer was transmitted without the figures having been filled in. The result was that a mixed Commission was nominated, which only met once in fact, yet which had the very painful task of supplying the figures of the German offer.[41] So we were in the position, as it were, of having to finish off an unsatisfactory task under the eyes of our opponents. Therefore, in my conversations with Lord d'Abernon I put it to him that these negotiations in Spa should on no account be continued. And there was little inclination to do so since France had accomplished her programme both in the matter of disarmament and of coal.[42] What was remarkable was the effective support which was accorded us, not out of friendship but out of self-interest, by the English, who notably intervened so that the occupation should not take place;[43] they were of course deeply committed to the French.

Berlin, 23.7.1920

[40] For Stinnes's polemics against the Spa Agreement as well as against Rathenau and Bonn, see Wulf (ed.), *Das Kabinett Fehrenbach*, p. 250. Kessler, *Rathenau*, p. 298. See there also Stinnes's remark about Rathenau's 'soul of an alien race'. See now Wulf, *Hugo Stinnes*, pp. 215 f. Rathenau had described Stinnes after the incident with the words: 'When he says Germany he means coal. Agreement with Russia means to him petrol, mangan, and pit-wood. When he recommends submarine warfare with a patriot's glowing eyes, he is reflecting on how soon after the sinking of so many ships his own tonnage will increase in value ... He is a man of purpose, and beyond God and godliness, but would, if he had swallowed up the whole of the German economy into his stomach and bowels, still have himself celebrated as the saviour of the Fatherland.' Harden, *Köpfe*, reprinted by H. J. Fröhlich, p. 152; de Mendelssohn, *Zeitungsstadt Berlin*, p. 230. On the avoidance of naming any figures, see Bergmann, *Der Weg der Reparation*, pp. 60 f. and 64 f.

[41] This commission met on 11 July.

[42] At Lloyd George's suggestion it was decided to postpone the discussion of the reparations issue to an international conference which was to take place in Geneva. Bergmann, *Der Weg der Reparation*, p. 65.

[43] See Bergmann's similar judgement, ibid., p. 58. See also Northedge, *The Troubled Giant*, pp. 168–71, with reference to the published documents. The conference has been interpreted as a modest success for Simons because he was able to avoid the occupation of the Ruhr and gain considerable prestige in Germany. He was also able to reduce the coal deliveries from 2.4 to 2 million tons per month. Gründer, *Walter Simons*, pp. 123 ff.

A Visit to the Italian Ambassador

At 6 p.m. on the afternoon of 26 July I visited the Italian Ambassador[44] to tell him the following:

My visit is a purely personal one. I do not know what our Government thinks of the matter I propose to put before you.

Discussions at Spa have confirmed my impression that France does not intend to take her reconstruction in hand on quite the scale or as systematically as we had originally believed. It seems much more as though France wants to compensate her industrialists, leave the rebuilding of their factories to them on a privately financed basis, and perhaps at the same time erect a few sample works in towns and in the countryside to satisfy public opinion.

I take it that Italy intends to plan her reconstruction more thoroughly, more efficiently, and more systematically. Collaboration beween German and Italian entrepreneurial forces would therefore be desirable. Requirements in both the countries concerned should be met as far as possible. This would result in close co-operation between German and Italian industry, but also, at the same time, a certain independence for Italy from foreign supplies and financing. Hence it seems to me desirable that German and Italian work parties should make contact with one another. This would best take place through the agency of the Italian Government, so that those groups will be involved which the Government deems desirable.

One could envisage the inclusion of a French group in this co-operative undertaking, and thus there would be a reciprocity for Italy, in so far as there would in this case be a reason for Italian co-operation in French reconstruction.

The Ambassador was exceptionally enthusiastic in agreeing with my ideas. As he expressed it, 'votre idée me sourit [plaît] beaucoup', and said he intended, in representing it to his Government, to be quite committed to the idea. He added that co-operative societies had been set up in Italy to study reconstruction in Russia; there had also been discussions in this respect with the Diskontogesellschaft. Perhaps these co-operative societies could be used in the sphere of joint Italo-German action.[45]

He promised news in a few days which, should I by then have gone to Freienwalde, he intended to bring out there.

Berlin, 27.7.1920

---

[44] De Martino.

[45] Rathenau's repeatedly-expressed proposals for the joint reconstruction of Europe through collaboration by business enterprises were part of his later plan to pay reparations by delivery in kind. Rathenau also included Russia in his reconstruction plans. He hoped to secure the Russian and Italian markets for German industry in general and for the AEG in particular.

NOTES ON 1921

Gradually Rathenau became more and more involved in politics. On 24 July 1920 he had made his first appearance in the Provisional Reich Economic Council. In December he delivered a speech at the Democratic Party Conference in Nürnberg. He also continued to be adviser to the Government on reparation questions after the Spa Conference, but did not attend any other international conferences. He worked out an index-scheme for the expected conference in Geneva which he defended at several preparatory meetings. However, the conference was cancelled; instead the Allies convened a conference in Brussels. Rathenau had agreed to go, but in the end his presence was not required. In addition, Stinnes intervened at a Reichstag meeting to prevent Rathenau from going. Nevertheless, the Government again asked Rathenau to act as a member of a working party to prepare the crucial London Conference at which the reparation settlement was going to be fixed for Germany.[1] The opinions of the working party were very much divided. Rathenau advocated an international reconstruction loan of 8,000 million marks which was to be raised in Germany. Moreover, Germany should take over up to 43,000 million marks of the Allied debts to the United States. All in all Rathenau proposed an effective annual payment of about 1,950 million marks for forty-one years. This plan, the so-called 'Rathenau Proposal', was rejected by the other German experts and the German Foreign Office, but was eventually accepted by the Cabinet and the party leaders just before the breakdown of the London Conference (1–7 March 1921). His plan arrived in London too late to prevent the breakdown of the negotiations, and certainly could not prevent the occupation of the towns of Duisburg, Düsseldorf, and Ruhrort, which took place on 8 March.[2] The German Foreign Minister, Simons, did not consider that there was a chance that Rathenau's Proposal would be accepted or that there would be an adjournment of the conference. So on 7 March Simons rejected what he regarded as excessive demands. He was praised for his stand in Germany, but it provided the French Government with the pretext to execute the plan Marshal Foch had put to Briand on 19 January 1921 of occupying three German towns on the right side of the Rhine. Foch wanted to demonstrate to the Germans that the terms of the Peace Treaty had to be followed. The occupation of the three German towns was part of his plan, developed in 1919, to separate the Rhineland from Prussia and possibly even from Germany.[3] Once the London Conference was over Foch tried to push the French Government into stepping up their plans for the occupation of the Ruhr, but it was another two years before they were finally carried out.

During the following weeks the German Government tried to enlist American

---

[1] Schröder, *Otto Wiedfeldt*, p. 122. D. G. Williamson, 'Walther Rathenau: A Study' pp. 332–8. The preparatory meetings took place on 9 and 21 February 1921.

[2] Laubach, *Die Politik der Kabinette Wirth*, pp. 35 f.; Gründer, *Walter Simons*, pp. 185 ff.; *Documents on British Foreign Policy*, 1st Ser. xv.; Middlemas (ed.), *Whitehall Diary*, vol. i, pp. 130 f.. See also Rathenau, *Briefe*, vol. ii, pp. 306 ff., Rathenau to Braun, 2 and 21 May 1921; Felix, *Walther Rathenau*, pp. 16 f.

[3] For the French side see now Bariety, *Les Relations Franco-Allemandes*, pp. 68–73. See also Trachtenberg, *Reparation in World Politics*, pp. 202–11.

mediation through the Vatican, but the Americans did not want to intervene at this stage. Undeterred by this first reaction Simons then asked the President on 20 April to mediate directly between the Allies and Germany. But the Americans turned down Simons' request, although they might have been willing to consider such a direct appeal if it had come secretly through diplomatic channels like the Vatican. Nevertheless, they indicated that they were willing to join the negotiations with the Allies if Germany made 'clear, definitive and adequate proposals'.[4] On 24 April Simons offered the Allies through America a payment of 50,000 million marks or annuities totalling 200,000 million marks. The Allies rejected the offer on 3 May and the Fehrenbach Government resigned a day later. Meanwhile, by the end of April final conditions for German payments had been thrashed out in London and were presented to Germany in the form of the well-known Ultimatum of 5 May 1921 which pegged the reparation debt at a level of 132,000 million marks. This was less than the demand of 226,000 million marks which had been made at the Paris Conference earlier in 1921 and which Simons had firmly rejected.

The undated 'draft' below appears to be notes or guidelines for a discussion of the 'Rathenau Proposal' with political leaders just before, or more likely during the early stages of, the London Conference in March.[5]

Commentary on a Proposal regarding Allied Reparations Demands

1. Reparations must be regarded not simply as a material, but also as a moral duty in that they bring about the reconciliation of nations.

2. Given the Allies' excessive demands one can hardly expect any positive results in London. Germany will, nevertheless, have to exert itself to the utmost limits of its capacity to maintain its position even after negotiations have broken down.

3. The task of reparations cannot be discharged without American co-operation.

4. One means of discharging this debt lies in taking over a substantial part of the Allied debts to America.

In this way

    i. floating a new loan will be avoided,

    ii. the payment of a modest rate of interest as demanded by the Americans will bear fruit.

5. The offer to take over the American debt must come from us. It is a mistake to wait for Allied initiatives, since in that case the chief benefit —low interest rate and modest repayments—would be lost to us.

---

[4] For a new appraisal of the German approach to the United States, of its failure, and of its effects on German-American relations, see Link, *Die amerikanische Stabilisierungspolitik*, pp. 44–52. See also Laubach, *Die Politik der Kabinette Wirth*, pp. 9–19. For a link between Simons's American initiative and the German domestic scene, see Gründer, *Walter Simons*, pp. 193–209.

[5] Gründer, *Walter Simons*, pp. 170 ff.; Felix, *Walther Rathenau*, pp. 20 ff.

[6] Zsigmond, *Zur deutschen Frage*, pp. 72–90; Link, *Die amerikanische Stabilisierungspolitik*, pp. 33–86.

6. Offering a maximum of one thousand million [marks] a year undervalues Germany's capacity.[7] After our economic apparatus has been reconstructed, which is certain, I think, in the course of the year, our surplus production will be even greater. I do not share the assumption that it is easier for us to pay two thousand million marks for the first two years; on the contrary, it would be desirable if our burden could be lightened for the first years.

7. World trade arrangements must be initiated so that, by eliminating any appearance of *dumping*, the German surpluses over and above those required for reparations payments can be guaranteed on the world market.[8]

8. Should the Allied demands remain unacceptable, then the Government will remain firm, and the German nation will have to accept the consequences.[9] They will be borne if it can be proved that our offer represents the absolute limit of what is feasible.

The Negotiations with Loucheur at Wiesbaden

On 2 May the American Secretary of State, Hughes, had informed the German Government: 'This government finds itself unable to reach the conclusion that the proposals afford a basis for discussion acceptable to the Allied government.'[10] The message sealed the Government's fate and Fehrenbach resigned, not in protest against the Allies' rejection but because the right-wing People's Party withdrew its support from the Government.[11] By 10 May a new Coalition Government (Social Democrats, Democrats, and Centre Party) under the chancellorship of the former Minister of Finance, Joseph Wirth (Centre), was formed, and it accepted the London Ultimatum.[12] It was hoped that a new Cabinet might have a better chance of retaining Upper Silesia, whose fate was going to be decided later that year. The post of the Minister for Reconstruction had not been filled by the time Wirth announced his Cabinet of the eleventh hour to the Reichstag. Apparently Wirth offered the post to Rathenau a day later, but Rathenau refused.[13] So Wirth had to shop around for a bit longer, offered

[7] While the Allies demanded three thousand million marks a year, the German Government was willing to offer 1.4 thousand million marks on 6 March. See *Documents on British Foreign Policy*, 1st ser., xv, and Gründer, *Walter Simons*, pp. 183–6.

[8] See for the position of the trade, Bergmann, *Der Weg der Reparation*, pp. 83 f.

[9] Rathenau held a similar attitude when the London Ultimatum was issued on 5 May 1921. See his article, 'Ja oder Nein', of 10 May 1921, *Nachgelassene Schriften*, vol. i, p. 244.

[10] Felix, *Walther Rathenau*, p. 20; Gründer, *Walter Simons*, pp. 206 f.

[11] Trachtenberg, *Reparation in World Politics*, p. 213.

[12] Morsey, *Die Deutsche Zentrumspartei*, pp. 382–5; Laubach, *Die Politik der Kabinette Wirth*, pp. 23 ff.

[13] Laubach, *Die Politik der Kabinette Wirth*, pp. 29–37; Felix, *Walther Rathenau*, pp. 64 ff. Apart from any other reason it is possible that Rathenau wanted to win time after his two pronouncements as to why Germany should not accept the Ultimatum. On 7 May he declared in public that 'we would be dishonest if we sign' and on 10 May he published the above-mentioned article (see fn. 9). Rathenau, *Gesammelte Reden*, p. 222.

the Krupp-director Widfeldt a ministerial post, but had no success there either.[14] Another industrialist was asked in vain, but after the Foreign Ministry had been accepted by Rosen, Wirth renewed his efforts for Rathenau. The pressure increased and Rathenau came round eventually to accepting the Ministry for Reconstruction, late on either 27 or 28 May, under the condition that he might build up close co-operation with the Finance and Foreign Ministries.

Rathenau was also in favour of winning the support of the People's Party; but he proved to be unsuccessful in this because the Party firmly rejected Wirth. On 29 May Wirth announced that Rathenau had passed his acceptance to the Reichstag. By this time Rathenau had abandoned his earlier opposition to the London Ultimatum.[15] In his first speech in the Reichstag Rathenau launched the 'policy of fulfilment' by which he wanted to demonstrate Germany's willingness to comply with the demands for reparation payments as well as its incapacity to pay. He also wanted to free Germany from its isolated position and make it a fully recognized partner in international affairs. He emphasized the need for 'coming together with other nations' and for helping to 'reconstruct France'. By that time Rathenau must have received hints that the French were willing to discuss practical reconstruction measures.[16]

The reconstruction of destroyed northern France had already been mentioned in the discussions at the London Conference when Lloyd George had suggested to an acquiescing Briand that 'France might accept a large proportion of payment in the form of labour and material'.[17] On 23 April 1921 the German Chancellor Fehrenbach had sent a Note to the Reparations Commission in which he stressed the German preparedness for helping in the reconstruction of northern France with materials and workers.[18] The Note made a good impression in France, and Loucheur, the Minister of the Liberated Regions, followed up the idea, and accepted in principle the offer of erecting 25,000 wooden houses in 1921.[19] The *rapprochement* made progress when a member of the German War Damages Committee, Wolf, suggested to Rathenau a meeting with Loucheur. On 3 June Loucheur expressed his interest in Rathenau's views; on the same day Briand told Loucheur how an American general had told him of Rathenau's desire to meet Loucheur, while the French Ambassador in Berlin, Laurent, suggested the same.[20]

A day later Wolf expressed to Loucheur his personal wish that both ministers should meet. Loucheur replied that the initiative must come from Rathenau.[21] Since Rathenau had demanded the same of Loucheur, at least officially, intervention by Wolf and Laurent assumed an increased importance. Thus Laurent reported to Paris on his conversation with Rathenau that 'he [Rathenau] had distinctly asked to see him [Loucheur]'. It seems that both Rathenau and Loucheur were prepared for a meeting, yet felt that Wolf and Laurent had to

---

[14] Schröder, *Otto Wiedfeldt*, p. 124.

[15] See Rathenau's speech on 22 May 1921. Rathenau, *Gesammelte Reden*, p. 194; Laubach, *Die Politik der Kabinette Wirth*, p. 37.

[16] Felix, *Walther Rathenau*, p. 74. On 19 March Rathenau still held the view that the French were unwilling to go ahead with a reconstruction programme. See also Bariety, *Les Relations Franco-Allemandes*, p. 76.

[17] *Documents on British Foreign Policy*, 1st ser., xv, p. 288, 4 March 1921.

[18] Laubach, *Die Politik der Kabinette Wirth*, p. 42.

[19] Ibid.; Felix, *Walther Rathenau*, pp. 74 f.

[20] Felix, *Walther Rathenau*, p. 75; De Launay (ed.), *Loucheur. Carnets Secrets*, p. 84.

[21] De Launay (ed.), *Loucheur. Carnets Secrets*, p. 84.

take the steps to initiate it. When finally both men met secretly in Wiesbaden on 12 June 1921, they started the first direct talks between a French and a German minister after the war.

The day after my Reichstag speech[22] Laurent came to see me and told me that a completely new situation had now been created and he considered it imperative that I should see Loucheur.[23]

I replied that my predecessor[24] had received a refusal from Loucheur; that could not happen again, so the initiative must come from Loucheur himself. Neither Paris nor Berlin could be considered, the choice was between Cologne and Wiesbaden. Two days would be needed for the talks.

Laurent wrote to Paris along these lines and was back again to see me on Wednesday 8th, and informed me that Loucheur was coming, as arranged, under the pretext of a French art exhibition at Wiesbaden, and could make two days available.[25] It was agreed that Loucheur would send his card to me at a hotel yet to be designated; I would send him a card immediately on arrival.[26]

Since I knew in advance that I would not find Loucheur's card at the hotel I was prepared to send a card, without turning down the corner, to him at his hotel, asking at what time the rendezvous we had agreed to was to take place. And that was how it turned out. The answer came in a letter written by his secretary,[27] which, in the politest way, contained the phrase 'votre visite comme vous le lui avez demandé', but also at the same time, to make up for such tactlessness, Loucheur's visiting card with the corner turned down.

I referred to these formalities later as little as I did to the interviews which he gave to the French press and which were aimed at representing the visit along the lines of *Maria Stuart*, Act III.[28] I limited myself to the occasional remark that I had taken note of the comments in the Paris newspapers and had for my part forgone joining in the debate but had only given a single interview to *le*

[22] Rathenau's speech of 2 June 1921, in which the policy of fulfilment was officially inaugurated. Rathenau, *Gesammelte Reden*, pp. 199-204; *Reichstag Berichte*, vol. 349, p. 3743.

[23] See p. 253.

[24] Otto Gessler had been Minister of Reconstruction from 1919 to 1920. The office had remained vacant until Rathenau took it over.

[25] On 8 June Loucheur explained to Wolf that only technical questions could be discussed at a meeting with Rathenau. The French Cabinet also agreed to this stipulation two days later. De Launay (ed.), *Loucheur. Carnets Secrets*, p. 86.

[26] Loucheur had awaited Rathenau's card 'as agreed' in order to send his own to Rathenau immediately on receiving it. Ibid., p. 86.

[27] Maurice Petsche.

[28] Schiller's drama with the famous encounter of the rival queens Mary Stuart and Elizabeth I.

Matin, and read the rough draft to him which was signed by the editor.

The talks took place on Sunday morning from 11 a.m. to 1 p.m. and in the afternoon from 3.30 p.m. to 7 p.m., and the next day from 11.30 a.m. to 1 p.m. and from 3 to 3.30 p.m. They were carried on exclusively between Loucheur and myself; Bergmann and Guggenheimer were present only at the concluding talk, to make the final agreements for the working programme. It was originally envisaged that the second day would be spent on special questions. By mutual agreement this was abandoned because, compared with the general discussions, these questions hourly lost in importance.

The conversations proceeded on a more than courteous, one might say cordial note; there was never a moment of tension.

Sunday morning [12 June 1921]. Loucheur greeted me by talking about my industrial and literary activities of which he professed to have detailed knowledge, and proved himself to be an adherent of advanced economic systems. He spoke warmly of the Chancellor's policy and of international, particularly French, impressions of my Reichstag statements.

I replied with similar courtesies and went on to describe the international economic situation: the disappearance of large numbers of consumers, the reshifting of the programme of world requirements because of changes in social stratification, mistaken policy regarding raw materials on the part of the World Powers, with all of which he heartily agreed.

Then the theoretical side: relations between [our] two countries, one of which is constantly working and paying, the other receiving. This situation is untenable and destructive for both countries. The danger presented by Europe's far too small export markets; the danger presented by a surging American economy and particularly by the dollar. Criticism of dollar payments, at which he interjected that he could not understand the measures taken by the Reparations Commission, namely the conversion of payments into dollars.

The need for mutual help in restoring the economies of both these extensively damaged countries to working order, the need to convert German payments as comprehensively as possible into deliveries in kind, and the need to study the requirements of an inter-European economic life.

Loucheur: he proposed to concentrate France's efforts essentially on its agricultural products, to introduce a stringent protective tariff system, only to maintain such industry as was absolutely necessary for exploiting agricultural products and for keeping the population prosperous. He wanted to suppress the *rentier* concept which I had referred to as dangerous for France.

My answer: by concentrating on agriculture in France the country will lose its technical *standing*; the Boer Republics were an extreme example [of this]. America is the only country that can work on new inventions spending ten to twenty years on a project costing dozens of millions.

Intermezzo: Loucheur recalls our industrial past. It was precisely this consideration that led him to conclude the agreement with General Electric, to channel American technology to Europe. He knew that I had negotiated the same agreement for Germany a few months before.[29]

He completely agreed that countries linked, as it were, by communicating pipes could not live by mutual exploitation; pumping the one dry would lead to the other being pumped dry; only the third complex, possibly America (perhaps even England) would profit by it.

I now moved on to the Cabinet's situation: a small majority, every intention of energetically fulfilling [their obligations], yet this could only be done in agreement with the Allies as to what form reparations would take. If the Cabinet's foreign policy remained without result from Germany would be obliged to follow another policy for a long time. The 26% Index[30] completely ruinous; it devalues German bonds in French possession, devalues German credit, imposes a penalty on exports, and must therefore result in the attitudes of successive governments changing as they argue now for, now against an export policy. All this to the detriment of her neighbours.

Loucheur: he had in fact devised the Index, yet had regarded it as far from perfect. Deeply regretted Simons's policy. He had expected a broad programme of payments in kind, but he had not been offered one. A programme of payments in kind would have enabled him to negotiate with the Allies a revision of the 52% share in indemnities which did not favour Franco–German relations,[31] but it had not come to that. The 52% share only gave France a relatively small claim to yearly payments and therefore made German deliveries

---

[29] The pre-war arrangement between the AEG and GE about technical co-operation and a partitioning of overseas markets was renewed in 1920 and signed on 2 January 1922. Link, *Die amerikanische Stabilisierungspolitik*, p. 70; Brinkmeyer, *Die Rathenaus*, pp. 55 f.

[30] According to the London Payments Plan Germany was to pay two thousand millions marks to redeem the bonds handed over to the Reparations Commission. To this was added 26 per cent of the value of German exports on the basis of an index yet to be agreed.

[31] France had never fully accepted the 52 per cent share in reparations payments coming from Germany. The French share had been stipulated at the Spa Conference in accordance with the so-called 'Spa Key'. Simon, *Reparation und Wiederaufbau*, pp. 102 f.

on a larger scale difficult unless special methods of payment could be found.

Loucheur went into his political situation: great difficulty in convincing the Chamber [of Deputies] of the necessity of payments in kind. Popular notion of a stream of gold which one had but to take delivery of. Similar notion in the press and among the public. Policy is, however, only made in the lobbies [of the Chamber]. There he had managed to convince a number of deputies.

Brief conversation about his speech at Valenciennes in which he had cleverly said to French industrialists: keep your sights rather on the world market than on the reparations contest with the Germans, otherwise you will lose your international position.[32]

He describes the work of reconstruction. In the *département* of the Somme 1.75 million *quintaux* [175,000 tonnes] of corn ostensibly already being harvested as against 2 million in peacetime. 90% of the fields have been restored to use. (This statement is undoubtedly an exaggeration.)

He estimates the total amount of payments in kind still outstanding at twenty-five to thirty thousand million francs. He believes that he can assume ten thousand million gold marks as the upper limit of total German payment, which seems to me considerably too high.

The likelihood of a labour supply is considerably less. Loucheur had originally reckoned on 100,000 workers;[33] he believes he can think in terms of a maximum of 25,000 for four or five months a year, partly because of the rapid rate at which work on the land has progressed and partly because there can be no thought of systematic rebuilding of the cities. French law prescribes, and French character wants it that way, that every house must be rebuilt on its old foundations and as nearly like the original as possible. This necessitates complicated work on the site and in the midst of a city population which is partly housed in cellars and provisional dwellings.

Hence two main technical problems will arise:

1. ensuring that French orders in Germany can be dealt with on a large scale so that the questions of financing and price can be taken into account;

2. the labour force on the spot which will be complicated by social and wage relationships.

[32] Loucheur had made a similar speech before the Senate on 31 May. *Schulthess*, 1921, p. 95.
[33] On 30 March 1921 Loucheur had complained about Germany's lack of will to rebuild, but had opposed the use of German labour on a large scale. Ibid., p. 80. For a reconstruction project in northern France (eleven villages) which was to be carried out in co-operation by German and French trade unions, see Potthoff, *Gewerkschaften und Politik*, pp. 239–44.

Another area that was touched on was the question as to when reparations work should end; and, also in the future, of converting gold payments into payments in kind and, in fact, with the idea

(*a*) of continuing coal deliveries for several years possibly through an agreement regarding ore deliveries,[34]

(*b*) of making France into a market for German nitrogen and excluding nitrogen produced overseas,

(*c*) of reaching an agreement on potash.

I pointed out that all these problems were primarily the concern of the Ministry of Economics, and that free initiative on the part of industry must not be forestalled, but, above all, that the danger threatening in Upper Silesia could result in us not being at all in a position to continue producing even the quantities of coal we need. If we must, on the whole, come to terms with the danger that a part of the Silesian coalfield might fall into Polish hands, I pointed out that the foundation on which our industry is based would in the long or the short run be destroyed.

Loucheur did not refuse to talk about this topic (as one reads in the Paris newspapers), but said: Whatever the decision was regarding Upper Silesia, over which he had no influence, there would be concern that precise dispositions were made in order to retain industry and to make materials available to German economic life. I rejected this eventuality as impossible and stuck to my view that only a German Upper Silesia is of any value to Germany and Europe.[35]

Finally we discussed the possibility of so financing German payments in kind that, in the case of large orders whose value far exceeds that of the annual instalments, they could be carried over to future annual instalments. Here I indicated that I could see that it was possible to make joint financial arrangements like this which simultaneously encompassed this kind of financing and the problem of the 26% Index.

In the course of this conversation Loucheur emphasized that the aviation question was among those points which caused alarm in France. People had the impression that military aviation was being strengthened under the cloak of civil aviation. I did not go into this issue but only remarked that it would be best for civil aviation, inasmuch as it was not a question of manufacture but of its running, if it could be made into international air transport companies.[36]

---

[34] On the question of German coal–French iron-ore, see Zsigmond, *Zur deutschen Frage*, pp. 123–49; Bariety, *Les Relations Franco-Allemandes*, pp. 150–63.

[35] According to notes in Loucheur's diary the Upper Silesian question was discussed on Sunday afternoon. De Launay (ed.), *Loucheur. Carnets Secrets*, p. 89.

[36] Rathenau had that morning also emphasized the need to increase German exports

Sunday afternoon (3.30 to 7p.m.). Loucheur opens the afternoon session with the following statement: there is on the French side not just 'bonne volonté' but 'la volonté, la volonté ferme' to achieve a strong, peaceful, and profitable co-operation. He wants true peace; he knows that France is capable 'de nous embêter, même de nous embêter journelement'; he does not want that under any circumstances; he wants to make the deliveries easier for us in every respect.

France's relationship with England is a very close and friendly one, he would not jeopardize it. (The fact that he particularly stressed this allows one to draw conclusions.) Then he began to boast rather— the only time throughout the conversations—and said: before the change occurred in German policy he had really believed that war would come again. Today he felt his mind was at rest and began to emphasize his confidence in Wirth's government again. Dr Rosen's appointment had certainly revived some memories of earlier days.

I used this opportunity to explain fully how, not just in the Cabinet, but throughout the country, the appointment of Dr Rosen, who had during the war made such an exceptionally great contribution towards overcoming international dangers, was regarded as a guarantee of a friendly and conciliatory policy, and that the Chancellor, who had had a completely free hand in choosing the Foreign Minister, had called on the very man who in his opinion offered the strongest guarantee for the execution of his policy as a whole.

Loucheur, it seemed to me, was pleased to learn this.

Loucheur then moved on to problems relating to the *main d'œuvre* [labour force], and was of the opinion that only 5,000 workers would have to be brought in to begin with, and those in two places: 2,000–3,000 at the one and 1,000 at the other. For the present he was reckoning on eight million man-hours.

Now came the difficulties. Agreements had been reached at Geneva regarding working conditions; the French Government could accept two of these: (1) parity of wages with the French rate, (2) German workers to be members of German trade unions.[37]

On the other hand the entry of German workers into French unions must be prohibited at all costs. The situation was particularly difficult because French law guarantees membership and cannot be changed.

and reduce imports. Apart from that he had stressed Wirth's struggle with the right-wing radicals, who complicated the policy of fulfilment. In conclusion he had also mentioned the international reconstruction association, which probably went back to the suggestion in the summer of 1920 for the setting-up of an international syndicate. Loucheur noted in his diary that he had let Rathenau talk for two hours without interruption. Ibid., pp. 87 f.

[37] See Loucheur's speech in *Schulthess*, 1921, p. 80.

I replied that this difficulty might be overcome if the French Government exerted moderate pressure on its trade unions that they should not insist upon entry; for I think that our trade unions would have no particular cause for joy if our workers were drawn into the very radical French organizations.

We touched on further difficulties regarding the right to strike— the problem here was to make appropriate provision for courts of arbitration—, then regarding lodging, since it did not seem desirable to him to have German workers travelling freely around the country.

Against this I stressed that it would not be expedient to lock up German workers in concentration camps or similarly confined conditions; a suitable compromise would have to be sought; likewise suitable accommodation would have to be provided by building simple estates.

The question of pay was brought up. If wages had to be paid in francs on a level with the French rate there would be no saving. It would be difficult, on the French side, to explain the reasons for employing Germans at a time when there was a work shortage.

We considered examining to what extent rations could be deducted in kind from the franc wages, supplies which could perhaps be partly provided from Germany so that the balance owing to the workers could be credited to them in marks.

Now the conversation turned to the question: prices for payments in kind. Under no circumstances may prices higher than those current in France be approved. But difficulties already began to arise here, for the wooden houses being offered were up to 20% more expensive than the French ones tendered. Here Loucheur laid his table of submissions before me, which appeared to prove this fact on paper with regard both to area and volume.[38]

Against this I asserted that one should never expect objective tenders from a side which is not on the look-out for orders and which wants very much to prevent foreign deliveries. Loucheur had himself admitted to me, that morning, that when the French steelworks seem to be making a tender at 500 francs, they in fact add on 150 francs. The house tenders were obviously a case of the same thing. But I was prepared to have these tenders verified, so long as not merely the tables, but also the specifications and designs were sent to me; he promised to do this.

We touched on similar difficulties regarding wood deliveries.

Now we examined a positive way of determining objective prices in the future, and the method was in fact this: one would attempt

[38] De Launay (ed.), *Loucheur. Carnets Secrets*, p. 90.

to start from the established gold prices of 1914 and multiply them by the Index numbers which were valid at the moment of delivery.[39] We discussed the possibility of setting up an international scientific and objective Index Bureau.

In [their] debate about possible payments in kind the following categories were discussed:

Bricks: they discussed whether coal should be delivered to French brickworks and wages be paid for the production of these bricks or whether [German] brickworks should be set up.

Furthermore,

Lime and Cement.

Loucheur also seems to estimate the possible demand for these materials rather too highly at 300 million gold marks.

Regarding the delivery of catalogue items like windows, doors, metal fittings, plumbing materials, we aimed at setting up local organizations so that the *sinistré* [victim of war damage] would apply to a French office and, on the basis of his claim, have a *bon* [voucher] drawn up for specific deliveries. He would then take himself to the adjacent German office to put in his order for the items noted. As soon as the German delivery has been made the French department will stamp the voucher with a notice of receipt which immediately makes it equivalent to a payment into the French Government's settlement account.

We then discussed whether as well as these vouchers, which we called *bons forcés, bons libres* should be issued, with which the *sinistré* could buy in Germany whatever he pleased. This only seemed practicable in certain exceptional cases where it was a question of special orders rather than routine materials.

Using this opportunity I asked Loucheur for an authoritative statement regarding the present system of compensation in France, which he described as follows:[40]

There are 2.8 million *sinistrés*; about 800,000 of them have been dealt with provisionally by means of *sentences rendues*. In the last analysis the *commissions cantonales* have jurisdiction over these *sentences rendues*.

When Loucheur came to office five months previously, 40,000 judgements were conferred monthly; he had seen to it that this figure had now risen to 100,000. Thus the preliminary decisions will all have been made in twenty months.

Two *titres* are handed over to the *sinistré*. One represents the '*valeur 1914*', and the other the '*majorisation*', that is to say the established increase in value. Twenty-five per cent of the first bond

[39] Ibid.   [40] Ibid., p. 89.

is paid out immediately, the *sinistré* can withdraw the remainder
(75% of the *valeur 1914* plus *majorisation*) in monthly instalments
to be formally declared to him beforehand in proportion to the
rate at which the rebuilding is progressing.

But the investigation takes up a great deal of time and therefore
provision has been made so that in isolated cases advances of 60%
of this amount can be paid out without further investigation. The
remainder can only be refunded after a final verification.

This explains the pressure on the capital of a number of construction companies, to which I had alluded, because I knew that
companies like these were seeking capital in neutral countries abroad
as well as in Germany itself. The construction companies have
advanced an estimated one thousand five hundred million francs
and do not know how they can obtain this capital and the further
amounts that are required.

This fact presented an opportunity to bring up the question
whether it would not be advisable to bring a large-scale Franco-
German construction company into being. Loucheur had no fundamental objections to this possibility provided that such a company
had the right to place about 10% of its commissions in France.
He mentioned that German firms of building contractors had written
him a letter proposing a company like this and had furnished the
signatures of three of the big banks (the Dresden Bank among them
apparently) as a guarantee. These banks had it in mind to be paid in
German *bonds*.

Because I had doubts about this step I asked Loucheur to give
me a copy of the letter, which he consented to do. (The redemption
of German *bonds* without cogent reason must, in my opinion, be
prevented because otherwise the remaining eighty-two thousand
million bonds will only be directed at the underwriter.)

Loucheur put the State's monthly expenditure on *sinistrés*
at 600 million francs, which contrasts with the 700 million francs
spent monthly by the contractors, so that the capital strain on
the entrepreneurial companies increases by 100 million francs
a month.

A transitional phrase, which I can no longer recall, led me to speak
of the gap in the west and to describe the dangers of 1919/20 which
were repeating themselves today.[41] Loucheur assumed the position
that the dossiers regarding customs and imports, to which access
had been won, had made it clear that there had hitherto been a

---

[41] Ibid., p. 88. The gap in the west refers to the deficiencies of the customs frontier in
the Rhineland between France and Germany. Laubach, *Die Politik der Kabinette Wirth*,
p. 48.

discrimination in handling, to France's disadvantage. I contested the likelihood of this by referring to the fact that, unfortunately, France produced those very goods which Germany was determined, in her present situation, to forgo. Example: claret and champagne. Pressure is brought to bear on us to import these products and then there are complaints afterwards that we consume them. Loucheur admitted this but thought that a way must be found to regulate French imports by means of quotas, but not to exclude them altogether. He believed that Seydoux was ready, at any time, to study regulations of this kind which were, as I remarked, the affair of the Ministry of Economics. There was then renewed discussion about further coal deliveries to be made when the task of reparation works was ended. Loucheur puts France's constant coal deficit at fifteen to twenty million tons a year and does not see any reason why this product should henceforward be imported from England so long as Germany was ready and able to supply it.

Monday morning (11.30 a.m.) [13 June 1921]. The original programme for this talk was: individual problems in consultation with the experts. But because it seemed important to continue discussing the whole range of general problems and since neither side intended to upset the course of the general negotiations by any disagreement on details, the individual deliberations were waived and the main programme put together again as follows:

Negotiations were to be conducted in Berlin by Prangey and Léfebvre. But because it was not to become known that the gentlemen were spending weeks, so we presumed, in Berlin for this purpose, the official address for the negotiations was to be at Mr Bergmann's in Paris. Loucheur envisages three weeks for the negoatiations themselves. I considered this limit to be far too short. We were unanimous in our intention to speed things up.

I. Conditions financières.[42]

A solution must be found for financing those payments which exceed a minimal annual amount to be delivered, which had in earlier conversations been set tentatively at one thousand million gold marks a year. The French intention is to anticipate later annuities; perhaps there is an idea slumbering in the background, though it is not explicitly indicated, of settling the account by means of *bonds*, which we would reject.

[42] The following five items are only briefly mentioned. See also de Launay (ed.), *Loucueur. Carnets Secrets*, p. 92. Loucheur had drawn up yet a sixth point: proposal for future methods of payment (coal, nitrogen or potash etc. . . . .).

II. Fourniture par l'Allemagne des matières nécessaires pour la réconstruction des régions devastées (payments in kind).

Here it is a question of determining the formalities, either as from town to town, according to the negotiations on Sunday, or by having the orders collected and transmitted to Germany through an international company.

III. Règles à trouver pour la fixation des prix.

The first question to be studied here is that of the Index and the Bureau des Etalons.[43]

IV. Études de l'emploi de la main d'œuvre allemand (deployment of labour).

This includes problems of social classification, wages, lodging and— the possibility of an international company was considered.

V. Récupérations et restitutions forfaits affaires.

The well-known pending problems of restitution and substitution. It has been explicitly agreed that these go alongside and should not influence the course of the main negotiations.

Questions to be worked on which are principally of interest to other central authorities:
1. The gap in the west.
Loucheur suggests negotiations with Seydoux which could be conducted by Bergmann and a delegate from the Ministry of Economics.
2. The problem of bringing the coal and ore industries nearer together, which is going to be promoted chiefly by Loucheur's influence on French industrialists and which will, it is hoped, draw French and German industrialists together (Economic Ministry's concern).
3. Nitrogen, potash.
The same.

In conclusion the question of joint handling of Russian interests was also discussed, where the possibility of international consortia like the Chartered Companies was borne in mind.

But these questions were considered less urgent at the moment.

Loucheur intends, as soon as studies in Berlin and Paris have reached a certain degree of settlement, to suggest a further meeting at Wiesbaden in the middle of July, so long as neither the Chamber [of Deputies] nor public opinion presents him with any trouble.

Monday afternoon. The dates of the meeting and the way the negotiators will be organized was discussed again in consultation

---

[43] International Bureau of Weights and Measures.

with Messrs Bergmann and Guggenheimer. The problem of supplying bricks and glass for windows was also touched upon again.[44]

Berlin, 14.6.1921

Rathenau must have been satisfied with his success. A dialogue had been established with the French Government and some progress had been made towards undermining the London payments plan, whilst creating an improved atmosphere. Rathenau had also been able to stress the need for the retention of Upper Silesia in order to carry out the coal deliveries agreed upon at Spa. Whatever he may have known about the different currents in French politics he was probably aware of the fact that the occupation of the Ruhr had been averted by the negotiations preceding the Wiesbaden Agreement. Thus he could pride himself on having contributed to the preservation of the unity and sovereignty of Germany.[45] Moreover, he and Loucheur had set the pattern for bilateral agreements which could well lead to the formation of a Franco-German *détente* against Britain. Only when the League of Nations decided in favour of a partition of Upper Silesia on 20 October 1921, when Germany asked for a moratorium for paying reparations in the autumn of that year, and when the international situation changed, did Rathenau turn more towards Britain. When this change of direction did not yield all the expected results, he shifted the emphasis of his foreign policy to Soviet Russia to counterbalance dependence on the West. The result of this policy was the Agreement of Rapallo during the international Genoa Conference in April 1922.

On his return from Wiesbaden, Rathenau began to exploit his success with Loucheur in order to gain support for his fulfilment policy before arranging an agreement. First he won the support of the Cabinet, then he gave three well-received talks to the Reparation Committee of the National Economic Council on 16 June, 27 July, and 9 November 1921. He also spoke successfully to the Industrial Association in Munich on 28 September.

After four months of negotiations, during which Rathenau and Loucheur met for a second time on 25 and 26 August, the Wiesbaden Agreement was finally signed on 6 and 7 October 1921. The aim was to replace the export tax by a delivery in kind to France worth seven thousand million gold marks over a period of four and a half years. The Agreement had a mixed reception in Germany and in other countries in political as well as in industrial circles,

---

[44] De Launay (ed.), *Loucheur. Carnets Secrets*. Ibid., p. 91. Deliveries of potash were to be added. Furthermore it was agreed that Bergmann was to be in Paris on 24 June. Bergmann took the opportunity to ask if he might inspect the damaged areas. Loucheur advised against it; he also thought that it would not be a good idea if Rathenau went to Paris. Summing up Loucheur sketched his impressions of the Wiesbaden meeting: 'One showed goodwill and even made an effort to achieve concrete results. Rathenau had lots of contradictory ideas. He said nothing which seemed to me definitely likely to succeed, but one may hope. Only at the end of June will we know whether this hope is justified.' Ibid., p. 92.

Rathenau summed up the results of the talks at Wiesbaden in a letter to Oscar von Miller. He thought the outcome should not be overestimated. 'Our task was to establish a work programme; nothing more than this was achieved, but contact was indeed established, which will probably be useful for making progress . . .'. Rathenau, *Briefe*, vol. ii, p. 322, Rathenau to Miller, 18 June 1921. Rathenau's report to the Cabinet is to be found in Schulze-Bidlingmaier (ed.), *Die Kabinette Wirth I und II*, pp. 64 ff.

[45] For a discussion of French politics, the Wiesbaden Agreement, and the eventual fall of Briand in January 1922, see Bariety, *Les Relations Franco-Allemandes*, pp. 82-101.

and only by the end of March 1922 did it find the approval of the Allies. However, only a relatively small amount of products was ever handed over to France.
Recently it has been suggested that Rathenau's 'willingness to sign texts was not
entirely serious' because the 'budgetary problems were already unusually
critical'.[46] This assertion has been made with reference to Wiesbaden without,
however, making it clear that the export tax was to be replaced by delivery in
kind. Consequently the Agreement would not have affected the budget on the
scale suggested. The reason why the signing of the Agreement was delayed on
the German side was heavy-industrial—and especially Stinnes's—opposition
to it.

Plan for a Visit to Paris

During the negotiations preceding the Wiesbaden Agreement it became obvious
that the Reparation Commission and other countries showed a growing interest
in the bilateral Franco-German dealings. This was presumably the reason why
the plan for Rathenau to visit Paris came up, although it was not, in fact, realized this time.

Yesterday evening at Councillor Wilson's in Wannsee I met the members of the Reparations Commission with the exception of the
Italian.[47]

The Reparation Commission's desire to see me in Paris was repeated
and we talked

(*a*) about a pretext

(*b*) about a formula.

With reference to this I explained to the gentlemen, in response to
their question about the 26% Index, the possibility of making the
Index 'uninteresting', and in connection with this, the possibility
of not—as they suggested—making the German bonds *marchand-
able*, but rather of finding a substitute for the lack of market possibilities.[48] They seemed to find this very interesting.

Bemelmans visited me at lunch-time today after having made an
appointment beforehand, to inform me of a letter from Delacroix
to Theunis which he had with him, and we agreed on the following
points regarding my possible trip to Paris:

1. The price question provides the pretext. Price discussions with
   Loucheur only relate to deliveries to France; it will be easy to dis-
   cuss price questions regarding other countries as well with the
   Reparations Commission.

---

[46] Trachtenberg, *Reparation in World Politics*, p. 218. For Stinnes's opposition, see
Wulf, *Hugo Stinnes*, pp. 317-24; Laubach, *Die Politik der Kabinette Wirth*, pp. 42 ff.,
48 f., 73-9; Felix, *Walther Rathenau*, pp. 74 ff., 84 ff.

[47] Alberto Pirelli. See also Laubach, *Die Politik der Kabinette Wirth*, pp. 44 ff.

[48] The interest on the bonds was at 5 per cent.

Yet these questions would only be touched on in the first session, and then a press release would be agreed on, stating that the talks had proceeded amicably and would be continued through deputies.

2. It will be so arranged that the Reparations Commission inform me that they would like to meet me in Wiesbaden. To this I would reply that, to save five gentlemen a journey, I would be prepared to come to Paris.

3. The real subjects of the conference would be the questions of the Index and advance payment of interest on the bonds.

Yet these questions would not be discussed at the official session, but rather unofficially and confidentially between the six [of us].

4. As a precondition I indicated Loucheur's agreement. Dubois, the chairman, will sound him out.

Berlin, 25.6.1921

Conflict over Troop Transports to Upper Silesia

After the result of the plebiscite held in Upper Silesia on 20 March 1921, and after the suppression of the third Polish uprising in June 1921, German–Polish relations continued to remain strained. In view of the increasing unrest among the German population and the imminent decision by the League of Nations about the partition of Upper Silesia, the French Government proposed sending troop reinforcements there. On 16 July Laurent, the French Ambassador, handed Rosen, the German Foreign Minister, a Note in which the disarmament of the German Self-Defence Units and the Free Corps Units in Upper Silesia, as well as arrangements for the speedy transport of French troops, were demanded.[49] In Germany it had still been hoped that a partition could be avoided altogether. Thus the French request was a reminder that France was going to insist on a partition, a blow for Wirth and Rathenau who had hoped otherwise. The contents of the French Note were discussed at the meeting of the Cabinet that same day.[50]

The German answer to the French Note was transmitted on Friday or Saturday.[51]

23 July, Saturday. At lunch-time Laurent made a vehement scene to Rosen and demanded an immediate statement as to whether

[49] *Schulthess*, 1921, vol. ii, pp. 290 f. See also the chapter on Upper Silesia in *Laubach, Die Politik der Kabinette Wirth.*
[50] BA Koblenz, R43I/1369, Cabinet Minutes, 16 July 1921; Laubach, *Die Politik der Kabinette Wirth*, p. 59.
[51] 23 July 1921.

Germany would consent to the transporting of troops to Silesia or not.[52]

The Cabinet met in the afternoon and discussed the letter which Rosen was to write to Laurent.[53]

Differences of opinion: the Chancellor and I advocate moderate interpretation, the President, Bauer, Rosen, Giesberts argue for a harsher version, which was adopted. Against this it was pointed out that there was some doubt about its ironic undertone and about damage to French prestige. It was decided, in my absence, to make the letter to Laurent public.

25 July, Monday.[54] Laurent appeared at the Chancellor's and at Rosen's and made an even bigger scene, which Rosen described graphically, and demanded *oui ou non, immédiatement* and *incessament*.[55] Apparently this made a very strong impression. In this connection the Chancellor, Rosen and I discussed whether one ought, on the strength of this, to give in. I proposed asking London and Rome first how the Governments there regarded the legal question. This proposal was accepted.

26 July, Tuesday.[56] The answers had arrived from Rome and London. The first read completely colourlessly. The English answer recommended us not to adhere to the legal point of view and made quite clear no conflict of opinion was to arise within the *Entente* on account of the impending problem.

We now had to consider a draft from the [German] Foreign Office of a new letter to Laurent. This draft struck the Cabinet, quite rightly, as illogical, because it declared it did not want to stick to the legal point of view but would submit to the decision of the Supreme Council (which was no concession, since there existed an obligation to do this).[57]

[52] Laurent informed Rosen as late as 23 July that France intended to send a division to Upper Silesia. Rosen, *Aus einem diplomatischen Wanderleben*, vol. iv, p. 327.

[53] There is no record in the minutes of the Cabinet meeting on 23 July of a discussion of this letter. However, it seems that Rathenau had not remembered the dates of the events of the next few days correctly, since the Cabinet minutes of 25 July touch on the question that Rathenau had entered under 23 July. Cabinet Minutes of 25 July 1921. See also Laubach, *Die Politik der Kabinette Wirth*, p. 59. According to Rosen's memoirs he had in fact promised a letter to Laurent. Rosen, *Aus einem diplomatischen Wanderleben*, vol. iv, p. 327.

[54] In the private print Rathenau mistakenly dated the following entry 24 July.

[55] Rosen, *Aus einem diplomatischen Wanderleben*, vol. iv, pp. 328 ff.

[56] Rathenau mistakenly dated the following entry 25 July.

[57] The Cabinet resolved to abide by the legal interpretation it had communicated earlier —according to which France could not by itself send troops to Upper Silesia without the

The Cabinet then agreed to a very brief draft which I have written down here and which only contained the following ideas:

A new situation has arisen due to the imminent assembly of the Supreme Council[58] and due to the fact that the problem will be laid before it. We, therefore, expect the question to be postponed until then.

27 July, Wednesday.[59] The [German] Foreign Office submitted the draft of the letter for further discussion. It was maintained that my draft was too harsh. One criticized the expression of our expectations as being already too hard for French prestige. After a long debate we agreed on a combination of the two drafts.

Meanwhile, news arrived that Laurent had made an appointment to see the Chancellor in the afternoon. This evoked a certain amount of excitement in Rosen who now declared that the situation was so critical that it made no difference which of the drafts was chosen.[60]

That evening, after Laurent had put forward the same point of view to the Chancellor as the day before and had requested a definite reply by 12 noon the next day, a new draft was submitted by the [German] Foreign Office. It concerned three instructions which were to go to Rome, London and Paris.[61]

Our representatives in London and Rome were commissioned to protest against 'breaking the law' and 'oppression'; the Embassy in Paris was to ask categorically whether the ultimatum would be kept to. (This after a request for postponement had, that morning, been considered 'too harsh'.)[62]

I was with the Chancellor when this draft was submitted by Assessor Meyer. Chancellor and President refused to send the letter, which was called an Ems Telegram.[63]

agreement of the Supreme Council—yet without wanting to make the legal standpoint seem too harsh. Rosen claims that it was he who informed the British side and asked for its help. Curzon's reply 'not to press unduly the legal point of view', which is quoted by Rosen, is identical to Rathenau's above-mentioned remark.

[58] The Allied Supreme Coucil was to have met on 4 August. In fact it met on 8 August. I. Schulze-Bidlingmaier, who has been unable to find Rathenau's draft in the Cabinet Papers, has overlooked the passage here which indicates the gist of Rathenau's ideas. Schulze-Bidlingmaier (ed.), *Die Kabinette Wirth I and II*, p. 153.

[59] In the private print Rathenau mistakenly dated the following entry 26 July.

[60] An English Note was transmitted to Briand that day in which the sending of French troops was to be postponed until the Supreme Council met. *Schulthess*, 1921, vol. ii, p. 291. Rosen does not mention this escalation at all.

[61] Rosen's reference to the instructions to the embassies can be found in Rosen, *Aus einem diplomatischen Wanderleben*, vol. iv, p. 329.

[62] Schulze-Bidlingmaier (ed.), *Die Kabinette Wirth I and II*, p. 154.

[63] The telegram of 13 July 1870 led to the outbreak of war between France and Germany.

28 July, Thursday. 8 o'clock in the morning, conference between Ebert and Wirth. A new draft was submitted. Laurent was urgently requested not to carry out his threats and first to allow the preceding letter to be sent to Paris.[64] (This after the Ems Telegram of the evening before.)

The Chancellor also refused to have this letter sent off.

My arguments went as follows: Laurent's move was a *bluff*, since (i) no ambassador would, at a time like this, arbitrarily keep back a document like that overnight, (ii) it is not in his power 'to propose measures' in a question which is more Anglo-French than Franco-German and which Briand was empowered to settle.

These two arguments revealed the weakness of the French Government which had commissioned Laurent, obviously because other means were lacking, to act rigorously.

In order to be quite sure I sought the Chancellor's agreement to my arranging an informal talk with Laurent.

I commissioned Haniel to say to him that I had not yet had any definite news of Tannery's arrival.

That evening, at 7 p.m., Laurent came to me. An hour-long, very friendly conversation, from which the following emerged:

(1) Paris is in a great predicament.

(2) Laurent's moves were unofficial.

(3) A solution is being sought.

Thus confirmation of the hypothesis. In answer to his question, I spoke personally and under the proviso that:

(1) The question must be raised above considerations of prestige.

(2) It must, together with the crucial question about Upper Silesia, be solved through direct talks with France. At 8 p.m. I reported to the Chancellor.

29 July, Friday. 9.30 a.m., visit Laurent. 'In *re* Tannery.' I said: *réflexion faite* I stick to my point of view. Industrial questions could even be discussed. I had seen the Chancellor but not asked him.

Laurent declared he would go to Paris.

10 a.m., at the Chancellor's who asked me to report also to the President. 12 a.m., with the President.[65]

---

[64] The reference is to a combination of both the drafts of 27 July 1921 which Laurent had not immediately sent on. See also Rosen, *Aus einem diplomatischen Wanderleben*, vol. iv, p. 331. Generally the British intervention on behalf of Germany against the French was considered to be a success. See also Rathenau, *Politische Briefe*, pp. 302 f., Rathenau to Müller, 18 August 1921. Rosen's interpretation in his memoirs, and his claim to be the instigator of this diplomatic success, seem to be neither correct nor justified in view of Rathenau's description.

[65] The Cabinet resolved, on 1 August, to publish the Joint Note from the Ambassadors

The Supreme Council of the Allies had turned the problem of solving the Upper Silesian question over to the Council of the League of Nations on 12 August 1921; the Council, after it referred the problem to a subcommittee, accepted the recommendation submitted two months later by the Committee of Four that Upper Silesia be partitioned. On 20 October, the German Ambassador in Paris was informed of the decision of the Allied Conference of Ambassadors which followed the recommendation of the Council of the League of Nations.[66] Rathenau had advocated the idea of resignation since 10 October when the plan to partition became known. Two days later he had told the cabinet:

'that he agreed with Minister Rosen's reasons for resigning, which were based on foreign policy. To these should be added serious domestic reasons. No one would understand if the Cabinet stayed together after territory had been taken from us. There was a point at which logic ceased to operate and emotion took over. The Cabinet would no longer enjoy the respect of the nation. This was a question of character. Logic would have to give way to character. Determination and emotion were decisive at a moment like this. He also believed that there was still a 25% chance that resignation would influence London. The position of the present Reich Cabinet was different from that of the earlier ones. It was the first to earn for itself a position of international confidence. Its resignation would, however, have a different effect from the resignation of earlier Cabinets. Foreigners were indifferent to these earlier Cabinets. He recommended resigning today, while their hands were still free. If they did not they would eventually be forced to resign. One thing should be quite clear to them: Upper Silesia had become a national palladium.'[67]

To his regret, despite his warning, the Cabinet only resigned on 22 October as a sign of protest. But the decision was by no means unanimous. Neither the Social Democrats nor several other members agreed with this step. When Wirth accepted the task on 25 October of forming this second Cabinet he was unable to offer a post to Rathenau as the Democratic Party had not joined the coalition. Rathenau agreed with the position of the Democrats, since their decision, which depended on that of the People's Party, was not to take part in a Government which had accepted the *entente*'s partition of Upper Silesia.[68]

Although Rathenau had been left free to decide whether or not to join the Cabinet, because he was not a member of the parliamentary faction of the Democratic Party, he submitted 'willingly to party discipline'.[69] 'My resignation was due to the necessity of holding on to Gessler and, through him, the

---

in which Germany was requested to facilitate troop transports to Upper Silesia should the case arise. BA Koblenz, R43I/1370, Cabinet Minutes of 1 August 1921.

[66] *Schulthess*, 1921, vol. i, p. 291, and vol. ii, pp. 292 f; Morsey, *Die Deutsche Zentrumspartei*, pp. 414–17; Laubach, *Die Politik der Kabinette Wirth*, pp. 93–7. See also now Campbell, 'The Struggle for Upper Silesia'; Rosen, *Aus einem diplomatischen Wanderleben*, vol. iv, pp. 400 ff.; D'Abernon, *An Ambassador of Peace*, vol. i, pp. 216–22.

[67] BA Koblenz, R43I/1371, Cabinet Minutes, 10 and 12 October 1921; Laubach, *Die Politik der Kabinette Wirth*, pp. 95 ff.; Felix, *Walther Rathenau*, pp. 103 f.

[68] Rathenau, *Politische Briefe*, p. 315. Rathenau to Koch, 31 October 1921; Morsey, *Die Deutsche Zentrumspartie*, p. 219; Laubach, *Die Politik der Kabinette Wirth*, pp. 102 f.

[69] Rathenau, *Politische Briefe*, p. 316. Rathenau to Koch, 31 October 1921; Laubach, *Die Politik der Kabinette Wirth*, p. 105.

generals of the little army,' he wrote at the beginning of November.[70] Although Rathenau did not approve of the party's decision his resignation from the Cabinet was not altogether unwelcome to him. On the domestic scene it was important that he no longer had to identify himself with acceptance of the Upper Silesian 'Diktat'. Yet the international situation made fulfilment and reparation policy the only viable possibilities with regard to the West. And it was in France that Rathenau's resignation had an effect. So Briand told the Senate on 27 October: 'I see with disquiet that Rathenau has not been brought in.'[71]

Apart from party discipline there may have been other reasons for not 'bringing in' Rathenau. The tasks which the German Government faced made it perhaps necessary to have someone of Rathenau's international reputation as an unofficial envoy. He could help Wirth and his policies by dealing directly with other Governments about the next reparation issues.

[70] Rathenau, *Politische Briefe*, p. 318. Rathenau to Batocki, 3 November 1921.
[71] Felix, *Walther Rathenau*, p. 104.

RATHENAU'S TALKS IN LONDON
AND PARIS, 1921–1922

Rathenau's First Journey to London

A few weeks after the Government crisis in October 1921, Rathenau, in his new role as unofficial envoy for the German Government, was to be responsible for negotiations with the Allies for the deferment of the reparations payments which were due, and he was to establish contact with the English and the French Governments. It was already clear to the German Government, soon after the first thousand million had been paid, that they would meet with difficulties in paying the next instalment. In the tug of war with the Reparations Commission over payment of the next instalment Wirth had informed the Commission that Germany would apply for credit abroad so as to be able to fulfil its obligations.[1] But that was not the only reason why Rathenau went to England at the end of November; there was also the matter of sounding out the possibility of a moratorium as well as discussing economic policy in general. On the English side the position had changed during the summer of 1921. More and more members of the British Government became convinced that Germany needed some sort of relief and that an international conference might be convened to solve or ease the situation of international debts. On 28 November Rathenau arrived in London, invited by the British Government supposedly to negotiate for a loan but really for a moratorium or what the British preferred to call a temporary reduction.[2] Moreover, it was hoped that the Germans would agree to the stabilization of the mark which was to be achieved by a balanced budget and a full deflationary programme. Although it was realized that most German industrialists regarded inflation as a weapon against the Treaty of Versailles, Rathenau was seen as a more flexible representative of this group who had demonstrated his willingness to solve the reparations problem by international co-operation. He was the best German the British could use to counterbalance the French demands for a strict control over Germany's economic affairs.

29 November, Tuesday. Treasury 4 p.m.: Sir Robert Horne, Sir Basil Blackett, Sir Robert Kindersley, Stanley Baldwin.
Questions: German situation.—English difficulties—Loucheur—
What proposals for reparations.
Answer: I. Condition of Germany.
II. Reparations.

---

[1] *Schulthess*, 1921, vol. i., p. 337; Laubach, *Die Politik der Kabinette Wirth*, pp. 122–6. This search for money had become even more necessary after German industry had virtually turned down the demand by Wirth for a credit. Ibid., pp. 118–22; Schröder, *Otto Wiedfeldt*, pp. 125–30.

[2] For Rathenau's visit to London, see Laubach, *Die Politik der Kabinette Wirth*, pp. 131–4 and Felix, *Walther Rathenau*, pp. 112 ff.; Trachtenberg, *Reparation in World Politics*, pp. 226–32; Wulf, *Hugo Stinnes*, pp. 290–3, 300 ff., 324.

With regard to I. Unfavourable balance of payments.

(*a*) comment on imports.

(*b*) comment on exports.

Deficit.

Inflation and consumer resistance. Consequences.

Interjection: German employment.[3]

Answer: Explanation. Flight from the mark. Examples. Why exports had not risen. Prohibition.[4]

Objection: Large exports to England. *Toys.*[5]

Answer: Other industries inadequate.

Objection: 'French would say': Government is preventing exports (foreign trade departments). To hoard up riches. Sham bankruptcy.

Answer: Interested in exports. Task of the foreign trade departments.

Objection: Artificial purchasing power and increased consumption. *Subsidiary policy* (price reductions).

Answer: Primarily: not inflation, but rather a balance of payments deficit.

Protection for the small pensioners' incomes.

Prospect of balancing budget endangered by sale of marks.

Controversy: Inflation or balance of payments deficit.

With regard to II. Theory to pay reparations in kind. Scope and conditions. Wiesbaden. Hypothesis and likelihood of the analogy. Russia.

III. Political situation. Danger of the Ruhr-loans.[6]

Objection: Uncertainty. Universal controls. Which products? Sugar? Potash?

Answer: Only those which do not prevent regular exports. Additional exports.

Adjourned until Thursday at 10 a.m.

Before that talked to Blackett.

Stinnes's railway plans.[7] Future. Blackett: '*I simply listened.*'

[3] In contrast to Britain, where there were about one million unemployed, the number who drew unemployment benefits in Germany had dropped to 150,000 by the end of 1921. This figure dropped further to 12,000 in 1922.

[4] This is a reference to the prohibitive effect on exports caused by the Allied tax of 26 per cent.   [5] Germany exported more machines to Britain (in value) than toys.

[6] Plan for a loan which would use part of the German industrial capital as security. For the so-called Hachenburg Plan, see Laubach, *Die Politik der Kabinette Wirth*, pp. 120 f. Rathenau feared industry would suffer when it wanted to buy foreign raw materials.

[7] Stinnes had it in mind to turn all the railways of Central Europe over to private enterprise. He countered the governmental demand for a loan from industry with a demand to go private. Stinnes had been in London from 19 to 23 November 1921. See Raphael, *Hugo*

1 December, Thursday. 10 a.m., Treasury. Horne, Blackett, Baldwin at the beginning.

Various questions: Who are the consumers of German industrial products? German taxes too low? Subsidies? Exports?

Reparations. Blackett gave an account of Stinnes's plans. Not at the moment. Proposals? Sugar? Potash?

Detailed answers: records promised.[8]

General topics: 15 January. City refuses.[9] Everything else depends on it.

Loucheur Agreement: credits to be revised.

Second *delivery in kind* Agreement can only be made in connection with reparations problems as a whole, because public opinion and the conscientiousness of the debtor demand it.

Answer: Approval for the French Agreement,[10] which England *encouraged*. However, the date for revision premature. Counter-proposal: *Suppose that you ask for [a] moratorium and we agree under conditions* (delivery in kind.)

My answer: We could discuss making a *preliminary agreement* which took the question of our productive power into consideration and was linked to the possibility of a moratorium. We must in any case avoid overburdening ourselves or agreeing to overburden ourselves.

Question: What commodities can we supply? Sugar? Potash?

Answer: One can only give a *negative description*.

And that is: (i) Not those goods that are indispensable.

            (ii) Not those that will compete with us on the world market.

          (iii) Not such as we are at the moment exporting for payment and whose proceeds we need. Consequently: additional commodities and additional exports.

Objection: But those are precisely the commodities which England manufactures; objections from industrialists.

Answer: That is right. There will just have to be frank discussions

---

Stinnes, pp. 165–71. See now Wulf, *Hugo Stinnes*, p. 290, with reports about Stinnes's visit published in German newspapers.

[8] The reference is to the German trade records which Rathenau was wanting from the Cabinet. In the City the argument was gaining ground that German reparations ought to be restricted to timber, potash, sugar, and coal. *The Times* reported McKenna's speech, 16 June 1921. Felix, *Walther Rathenau*, p. 106.

[9] Germany requested a loan of 550 million gold marks to pay off the next instalment by 15 January 1922. A rejection was expected and was then to be used as an argument for a moratorium. Laubach, *Die Politik der Kabinette Wirth*, pp. 128 f.; Felix, *Walther Rathenau*, pp. 112 f.

[10] Wiesbaden Agreement of 6 and 7 October 1921.

with industry: do you want such and such work to be carried out which we can only do with German help; in that case you will also receive orders, otherwise it will not be forthcoming. Horne gets up and stands by the fireplace, the talk continues as a *friendly conversation* and in strict confidence.

Question: Whether I will rejoin the Government.

Answer: Silesian experience. England and ourselves both deceived in the same way. (Horne agrees.) Threat of danger in the Ruhr. Detailed explanation. Defence? Credit? What means?

Horne hopes I can take office again. I doubt whether England is interested in a democratic regime. It is confirmed that she is.

Continuation of conversation planned. Prime Minister.[11]

1.30 p.m., Embassy, with Schwabach; give an account of the discussions so far. Chancellor's telegram and answer: summary: Ruhr question.[12]

4 p.m., collected by General Allen and taken to American Ambassador Harvey.

Results from Washington.[13]

  1. Disarmament at sea.
  2. China in the hands of Balfour and Hughes.
  3. Evidence that America and England can enforce everything.
  4. Attempt at disarmament on land: France's isolation.

How can the Ruhr expedition be prevented? Actual and legal situation ascertained.

2 December, Friday. 8.15 p.m., dined at Sir Philip Sassoon's—he was not present—with Lloyd George and Sir Robert Horne.

Explained the situation.

Question: Why, given its low exports, did Germany have no unemployed, but was instead fully employed?

Answer: Flight from the mark, temporary.

[11] On the same day Horne reported to the Finance Committee of the Cabinet. He 'had had several interviews with Herr Rathenau and had been very favourably impressed with his strength of character [and] ability . . . Herr Rathenau would only be prepared to resume office in the German Government if he could see some sign of hope.' Apparently this was a further argument to ease the pressure upon the Germans. See also Felix, *Walther Rathenau*, p. 113. PRO Cab 27/71.

[12] Rathenau received an invitation to dine with the Prime Minister and replied at 7.15 that evening: '*I thank you for your kind letter. As Mr. Simon telephoned an hour ago, I shall be highly pleased and honoured to meet the Prime Minister at Sir Philip Sassoon's house at dinner, tomorrow, Friday night at 8.15.*' House of Lords Records, F/53/3/12.

[13] The Washington Disarmament Conference lasted from 21 November 1921 to 6 February 1922. At the same time as a general limitation on naval armament, the United States and England agreed to parity in battleships. The aim of both powers was to maintain China's independence and integrity. Japan, therefore, had to negotiate directly with China over Shantung and Kiaochow. France's attitude was a contributory factor to the failure to reach an agreement to limit military armaments.

'What is the value of money in Germany?' Balancing the budget in Germany. He had seen Stinnes at a private house; the latter had told him that Germany has a million too many employed in national enterprises including the railways. They had to be dismissed. The following year England was going to dismiss some 100,000 state employees. England had raised freight rates up to net costs. Stinnes's railway project would take a long time. The East European project was still hanging fire. Perhaps one would get the Austrian railways but the Czech, Yugoslav, Polish, etc., would be hard. How did Germany expect to make out in the next two years? Germany faced greater danger than at any time since 1807.

Answer: That depends, to a great extent, on England's attitude.

Lloyd George: England wanted a strong, healthy, blooming Germany. It would be a disaster for Europe if Germany were to be *broken up*. He would exert all his power to bring about Germany's recovery.

Answer: One should never forget that Germany had saved the West from Bolshevism.

Lloyd George: Agreed completely. The earlier efficient, reliable Germany had risen up again, but there was great danger.

Answer: The Powers have done little to help Germany. Burdens, disappointments, daily pin-pricks, right up to the present day, e.g., police, above all Silesia.

Lloyd George: Stirred up by the Geneva decision.[14] This would finish the League of Nations. He was *deeply ashamed* by the outcome. He had done what he could.

Answer: I had been pessimistic since the day of the Paris decision.[15] Criticized the proceedings in Geneva. Three Envoys who were accredited in Paris, Example 'Guatemala'. No parties admitted. No investigation.[16] Asian and South American.

Lloyd George: confirmed this.

Answer: I was astonished by Balfour.[17]

Lloyd George: Balfour had been trusting. He did not want to intervene. France had intervened. Whether we had filed a petition to be allowed to plead our case at Geneva?

Answer: I thought so. I thought I remembered that it had been

[14] Decision of 12 October 1921.

[15] The Upper Silesia problem was handed over by the Supreme Council to the League of Nations on 12 August 1921.

[16] Polish and German experts were heard by a committee of experts of the Committee of Four. The Committee was composed of envoys from Belgium, Brazil, China, and Spain.

[17] D'Abernon, *An Ambassador of Peace*, vol. i, pp. 216 and 221.

quite explicitly rejected, while it was pointed out that Poland could not plead its case either.[18]

Lloyd George: He was sure we had not submitted an application.

Answer: I will find out about it.

Upper Silesia had (i) taken our international credit away,[19]

                 (ii) bewildered our people about the Government. Radical right and left.

People reproach us for having a weak Government and repudiate it daily. A Ludendorff Government could not have had worse treatment.

Lloyd George: wants the Government and all the parties which have democratic and parliamentary principles strengthened.

Answer: The opposite has happened. Lack of success all along the line, cold praise now and then, which does more harm than good.

Lloyd George: It was extremely difficult. Foch had Briand in his hand, he wanted the Rhine, Confederation of the Rhine, secession of Bavaria, which could not be won back for generations, religious segregation. Example—Ireland. Foch had hoped for a rejection of the Ultimatum.[20] Briand had mobilized. England had preserved the Ruhr up to now. Whether [she could] this time as well was questionable. Whether I saw a way of satisfying France?

Answer: No. There are only two ways: loan or moratorium. 1. Has been rejected by Norman today, with an open explanation. The only remaining possibility is, 2. In order to carry that out, a concession would have to be made to France.

Lloyd George: Which?

Answer: France is disappointed by the rejection of the Guarantee Pact[21] and because they have been denied a share of the thousand million marks.[22] France will have to be given a priority. Belgian priority goes too far.[23]

[18] Neither country pleaded before either the Council of the League of Nations or the Committee of Four.

[19] Rathenau had hoped that this region would add to Germany's position as international debtor.

[20] London Ultimatum of 5 May 1921. See now Bariety, *Les Relations Franco-Allemande*, pp. 68–90. Apparently Bradbury and Horne believed that France wanted to march into the Ruhr even in December if Germany voluntarily defaulted. However, the French Government did not seriously plan to occupy the Ruhr at this moment. Like the British the French were much more interested in Germany improving her financial position so that she could pay reparations. Trachtenberg, *Reparation in World Politics*, pp. 227 ff.

[21] The Inter-Allied Financial Agreement of 13 August 1921 was not ratified by France.

[22] France received nothing of the first payment of 1,000 million marks on 31 August 1921, because half of it went to England for unpaid occupation expenses, the other half went to Belgium on account of the Belgian priority agreed to at Spa. Bergmann, *Der Weg der Reparation*, pp. 65 and 142.

[23] Belgian priority amounted to 2,000 million marks.

Lloyd George: it is a stupidity. Wilson is taken with the idea. He is not averse to giving France priority. Would one year be enough?

Answer: That would not help at all. Belgium still has 1,250 million to receive. We need a moratorium at the same time.

Lloyd George: He could imagine a priority lasting two years, so that England would receive absolutely nothing for two years. Perhaps a two-year moratorium for us. Horne was to consider this. How much could we pay if need be?

Answer: The Reparations Commission receives about eighty million a month from us so far as I remember. Also some payments in kind. A definitive settlement would only be possible with help from America.

Lloyd George: He would have liked to go to America. But hesitated because it would look as though he wanted England's debt to be remitted. England was owed more by her Allies than she owed to America. He would like all the debts in the world to be renounced. Only he thought it just that the devastated areas should be rebuilt by Germany.

Answer: That is why I made the Wiesbaden settlement.

Lloyd George: That was right.

Answer: Now I am attacked because I have annoyed England.

Lloyd George: That is utter nonsense.

Answer: I wished Lloyd George were going to America. I do not share his hesitation. A very influential American personality whom I could not name had told me the following: (Harvey's four points).

Lloyd George: He wished very much that he could talk things over with Hughes. He was the most important American statesman. Harding was *narrow*, but very well-intentioned, respectable and clever.

Answer: It must be made clear to America that it can only be cured by sacrifice. Symbol: Rheingold, Fafner, Mime.[24]

Lloyd George: Agreed. To Horne: Whether Briand was back yet?— Yes.[25]

Briand was France's foremost politician. Clemenceau was stronger. But no one handled Parliament better than Briand. Long digression on France.

France was not a democracy. It was Paris and a bureaucracy. The provinces were pacifist, but they did not exist. France had never altered itself.

[24] A reference to the first part (*Das Rheingold*) of Wagner's opera *Der Ring des Nibelungen.*

[25] On 2 December Briand returned from his visit to America which began on 29 October.

France (Briand) was disappointed in America. Briand had not been *'in the picture'* (remarkable translation, hitherto unknown to me, of 'im Bilde sein'). France was now rather annoyed with England. But now comes a rather strange statement (which perhaps masks a certain apprehension)—France knew that England could at any moment deliver the full armour of Power against France, even if she did not have a standing army; above all, she would never pick a quarrel simultaneously with both England and America.

(All this very much in contradiction to the alleged concern over the Ruhr, the latter seems to be the truer factor.)

He wanted to suggest to Briand that they could meet. Possibly at Sassoon's house by the sea. He should bring Loucheur. What was my impression of Loucheur.

Answer: Brief character sketch.

Lloyd George: *You may put him and Stinnes in one box.*

Answer: *Do you mean, and close it?*

Lloyd George: *Certainly. Who, do you think, would kill the other?*

He had talked to Stinnes about Russia. Russia must be made accessible immediately. He would talk to Krassin. Krassin was not a Bolshevist.

Answer: Krassin was absolutely the right person for negotiations. I have also always advocated the opening-up of Russia.

Lloyd George: Germany had lost more from the collapse of the east than England, which had its export outlets in the colonies and in the west, but opening up [eastern Europe] was necessary for the world.

Long discussion about Russia. I talked about club-rule (Tartars, Varangians, Lenin), transformation of Bolshevism, new bourgeoisie, Cheka, need for international chartered companies, Loucheur's interest, risk, etc.

Horne wants to bring an English group together.

Chance of linking up with *reparations in kind.*

World situation as a whole. My statements about double collapse: international division of labour and the world manufacturing programme.

With it the continuation of the war. Unemployed soldiers. Prohibitive tariffs. Example of the electric light bulb.[26]

Why no joint projects? Mistakes continued.

Lloyd George: We have drawn together. Spa was a beginning. To be sure, Stinnes's behaviour was *truculent.* (Horne: Millerand turned

[26] A reference to the AEG's and Siemens's joint effort to compete with Phillip's expansion in Europe.

his back on him.) Simons had come to grief in London. One would have to talk in the smallest of circles. Possibly with Briand next. He wanted to take only Horne with him. Perhaps I could come along too. (??) Main thing was to get through the next two years.

Horne was to talk it over further with me and report to him. How long was I staying? Perhaps he would see me again. He had had an urgent desire to talk to me, etc. (All in all: much that was very valuable, but put across with Lloyd George's famous powers of fascination, which make too many concessions to the desire for an easily flowing conversation.)

Farewell at 11 p.m.

Addendum: Talk about monarchy, with anecdotes of the English radical gathering. Socialists as a national party.

3 December, Saturday. 1.30 p.m. At Churchill's.

Present: Churchill, brother and Mr Montagu. Russia—He was a *reactionary*. Nevertheless we agreed. France. *No desertion.*[27] General feeling in the country. Opposite to 1815. (Secret Anglo-French Treaty.)[28] Whether I would go back *into office*? Churchill proposed a three-cornered meeting with Loucheur—America becoming *balance of power*. After the two guests had taken their leave I put forward my proposals.

1. '*No*' to be said to France more often.

2. Against hypocrisy and collective guilt.

He quoted Burke: *You cannot frame a . . . against a nation*, (debt or blame?) sounded like *dike*.[29]

Finally he showed me his pictures in the studio.

6 p.m., Rechnitzer, introduced by Andreae at Sir Basil Zaharoff's behest.

French proposition rejected. 1.5 commission![30]

5 December, Monday. 1.30 p.m. With Lord Chancellor, Viscount Birkenhead and Sir Charles Dunn. Equivocal atmosphere and discussion. Copy of Havenstein's[31] had been sent from Stinnes by special envoy (Freytag) to Dunn, and from him to Birkenhead.

Finally Dunn, who drove me to the hotel, suggested that

---

[27] See Churchill's speech of 29 November 1921. *Schulthess*, 1921, vol. ii, pp. 51 f.

[28] Anglo-French Guarantee Pact, January 1921.

[29] 'I do not know the method of drawing up an indictment against a whole people.' About the same time Churchill used the phrase which characterized his attitude towards Germany: 'kill the Bolshie and kiss the Hun.'

[30] It is not clear which transaction is being referred to.

[31] Havenstein's request for a loan of 550 million gold marks.

Stinnes and I should come to England together in the future. I did not oppose this.

Meanwhile Wirth and Rathenau decided by telegram what measures the German Government would be prepared to agree to in return for the Allies' meeting them half-way, namely 'cessation of subsidies, balancing the budget, closing down of printing presses'.[32] Everything else depended, according to Rathenau, 'on talks between the Allies'. With this plan the British demands were to be met. Apart from that Wirth agreed to draw up a budget for the term of respite. In conclusion Wirth commented on Rathenau's reduced offer of money: 'Your summing-up regarding the possibility of payment seems too optimistic to me.' Wirth warned Rathenau not to offer too much and advised him to wait for English counter-proposals.

9 December, Friday. 10 a.m., message from Petsche that Loucheur is setting off at 2 p.m., cannot talk with me at 6 p.m.

10.30 a.m. Second discussion with Petsche about journalists. He mentions deliveries of railway carriages and possibility of discussion with Loucheur.

11 a.m., with Loucheur. A notice that is to appear in the press has been agreed upon at Chequers.[33]

1. Wiesbaden talks,

2. Introducing reparations,

3. Briand's invitation.—Discussed meeting in Paris. 12 a.m. At Sir Basil Blackett's. Montagu appeared after a few minutes and remained. Message from Horne.

1. Confirmed Loucheur's message.

2. Briand-Lloyd George meeting is to take place on 17th or 18th either at Chequers or at Lympne. I was to be in London on 17th in order, possibly, to take part.

3. English agenda. All international debts and reparations are to be cancelled. France is to retain reparations for reconstruction. England is to receive certain sums for *actual damages*. Small nations to be compensated.—Occupation expenses to be limited, occupation to be reduced.—Trade agreements between England, France, America, Germany.—America is to convoke an Economic Congress.—Norman calls this 'America and England summoning their debtors'.—Loucheur has admitted that present German contribution are impossible.

[32] Laubach, *Die Politik der Kabinette Wirth*, p. 133; Rathenau's telegram to Wirth, 6 December 1921, PA Bonn, Friedensvertrag Allg. 7, iv, Wirth to Rathenau, 8 December 1921.

[33] Loucheur had a conversation with Lloyd George and Sir Robert Horne at Chequers on 8 December. See Loucheur's report in de Launay, *Loucheur. Carnets Secrets*, pp. 185-8. See also *The Times*, 10 December 1921; Felix, *Walther Rathenau*, p. 115.

1 p.m., Embassy, report to Sthamer and Dufour.
7 p.m., Anthony Rothschild at the hotel. Blackett telephones:
petition for respite to be lodged by Friday.[34]

Rathenau left London for Berlin on 10 December. Shortly after his arrival
he interpreted his visit as a success at a meeting at Cabinet level.[35] The fact that
Briand had accepted Lloyd George's invitation for talks on reparations in
London seemed to him like the beginning of a 'revision of Versailles'. Consequently the German application for a moratorium was dispatched with some
optimism on 14 December to the Reparations Commission. According to this
request Germany offered far lower sums (150 to 200 million marks) for the next
payment instalments, due in January and February. The Commission replied
quickly, but only to point out that no time limit was mentioned for the
moratorium and Germany had given no indication as to how much she held
in foreign currency. The German side was slow in answering these queries
because Berlin first wanted to know the outcome of the Briand–Lloyd George
talks in London.

Meanwhile the Cabinet in London planned its meeting with Briand. It was
agreed there that Germany should not pay more 'than she can afford'.[36] Horne
believed that 'undoubtedly her inability to pay was due to a very large extent
to her own action'. For him it was a fact 'that the German Government was
a very weak government, in fear of Bolshevism on the one hand, and a revival
of Prussianism on the other'. A moratorium had to be granted, but only on
certain conditions which had been discussed with Rathenau. With regard to the
economic reconstruction of Eastern Europe, 'it was clear that the rehabilitation
of Russia could only be properly effected by Germany'. The result of the
meeting was that pressure was to be put on France to grant the moratorium.

Rathenau's Second Journey to London

18 December, Sunday. Arrived four hours late, 11.30.

19 December, Monday. 11 a.m., Treasury: Blackett. Sketched plan:
Sixty-five thousand million marks of German debts divided among
all the Allied debtors. England and France are remitting their share
of about twenty-five thousand million.—My objection: No cash
for France. Suggestion: Liquidate part of the twelve thousand million worth of A-Bonds.

Reparations Commission Note. Complained about reckless tone.[37]

[34] The request for a moratorium had been handed over on Wednesday, 14 December
1921. *Schulthess 1921*, vol. ii, p. 332.
[35] Schulze-Bidlingmaier (ed.), *Die Kabinette Wirth I und II*, pp. 463 ff. (12 and
13 December). This was followed by a Cabinet meeting on the next day, ibid. pp. 468 ff.
[36] PRO, (ab. 23/27), 16 December 1921.
[37] The Reparations Commission answered the German Note of 14 December on
16 December. *Schulthess*, 1921, vol. ii, pp. 272 f. Meanwhile Wirth informed a meeting at
Cabinet level that Rathenau intended to use his second journey to change the character

Delai de grâce. He: 'to win time'. My message about France's apparent intention not to give back Upper Silesia. Ended at 12 a.m.

Embassy. Report. Fischer from Paris. Lunch at Embassy. 4 p.m., Treasury. Horne and Blackett. Why only 200 million offered?[38] Difficulty regarding rest of plan: America. European conference perhaps. Germany's inclusion recommended. Plan sketched out: A-Bonds for loans. B-Bonds as cheque for goods.

What could we supply as 'delivery in kind'? Little. Need to boost English industry. French objections: large assets. Where from? Not from exports, since 40% are handed over and 60% needed for raw materials. From foreign purchases of shares? No, they are equivalent to the restocking of our portfolios.——Whether to meet Briand? Lloyd George requested my presence.

6 p.m. Ate with Fischer at the hotel. Discussed the figures.

20 December, Tuesday. 4.30 p.m. After a secret invitation (Grigg), 25 Park Lane (Sassoon). Present: Horne, Blackett, Sir Laming Worthington-Evans, Loucheur, Avenol.

Horne: at Lloyd George's request a discussion on Russian action. England, France, Germany. The 'Dioscuri' should be questioned.[39]

Loucheur: the syndicate should be expanded for the whole world. Individual companies to be established for special purposes. Well-known political anxieties about Russia (acknowledgement of debts, etc.).

I agree with Loucheur about expansion. Proceed immediately with regard to Russia. Principles:

    I. Transport the most important.

    II. Transport to be linked to investment because of self-payment of freight charges.

    III. No new concessions to be developed, but rather the existing ones to be re-established.

    IV. Consequently agreement with previous owners.

    V. Hence a new political aspect: reintroduction of private rights by action, consequently acceptable to France. General agreement. Details.

Private Control. Controversial issue on account of German

of the talks in London. He wanted them to become more official and he also hoped to negotiate with France. Schulze-Bidlingmaier (ed.), *Die Kabinette Wirth I und II*, p. 475.

[38] When requesting a moratorium on 14 December Germany offered to pay 150–200 million marks.

[39] For this complex question see the chapter 'Die Erfüllungspolitik und die "russische Frage" ' in Zsigmond, *Zur deutschen Frage*, pp. 179–205. For Horne's report, see *Documents on British Foreign Policy*, 1st Ser., xv, pp. 776 ff.

participation. It was demanded that Germany should make available half of the proceeds of its share for paying reparations. I declined: incompatible with *Private Control*, insignificant dividends.

Worthington-Evans suggests: All three should give half of their profits.

Loucheur declined: The others could not pay for Germany.

I [said it was] acceptable, with modifications. Each Government will receive on paper, for securing the *Charter*, one half of 5 per cent. Possibly Germany could renounce part of this bonus. The question remains open.

7.30 p.m. Blackett's visit to the hotel. He recounts how the French had that morning proposed: fifty-three thousand million A-Bonds for themselves, eighty-thousand million B-Bonds for the others.

Rejected by Lloyd George.—He hands over the *draft* of the conditions. Against this we are supposed to get through 1922 with payments of 500 million marks, Wiesbaden and the *Recovery Act*.[40]

10 p.m.- 2 a.m. Worked out, with Fischer and Simon, the points of the *draft* which will be handed over to Blackett at 9.30 a.m. on the morning of the 21st.

21 December, Wednesday. 9.30 a.m. Montagu Norman. He should intervene with Horne over the conditions of the Reichsbank.

22 December, Thursday. 10 a.m. at Blackett's, 32 Tite Street, with Norman.

Document of the Anglo-French agreement. Invitation to Paris.

23 December, Friday. 1.50 p.m. left from Victoria Station.[41]

Rathenau returned to Berlin and on 26 December reported to the Cabinet about the Lloyd George–Briand agreement. He thought that it would be implemented at the meeting of the Supreme Council in Cannes which had been arranged by the two Prime Ministers.

[40] This sum was to be paid in four instalments by 15 April; this issue figured importantly at the Cannes Conference. Bergmann, *Der Weg der Reparation*, pp. 146 f. In the report on the meeting the French proposal and Lloyd George's rejection are not mentioned. Moreover, in addition to the reparation instalments, 220 million marks had to be paid for the occupation army. *Documents on British Foreign Policy*, 1st Ser., xv, pp. 800 f. The reparation sum was increased from the German offer of 200 million to 500 million marks. The extra 300 million marks were to come from the gold the Reichsbank held. See also Middlemas (ed.), *Whitehall Diary*, vol. i, pp. 186 f.

[41] For Rathenau's second journey to England, see also Laubach, *Die Politik der Kabinette Wirth*, pp. 138 ff. Rathenau reported about the results on 26 and 27 December. Schulze-Bidlingmaier (ed.), *Die Kabinette Wirth I und II*, pp. 481–9.

In London Rathenau had been invited to Paris to discuss more detailed plans for a syndicate which was to aid Russia in its reconstruction.[42] The invitation had come from the British side because Loucheur still felt unable to invite him himself. Neither in London nor in Paris did Briand dare to see Rathenau, although they had met in 1910 over the Mannesmann affair.

In order not to fall out with the Reparations Commission, for its queries had not been answered yet, the Commission was asked to discuss them with Rathenau in Paris. This was accepted.

Rathenau's Visit to Paris

29 December, Thursday.
    Arrived 11.30 a.m., Hotel Crillon.
      1.30 p.m., Embassy. Dubois letter.
      5.30 p.m., Fischer.
      6.30 p.m., Sir Robert Kindersley.
      10.30–12 p.m., Sir Basil Blackett.[43]

30 December, Friday.
    10 a.m., Fischer.
    11 a.m., at Dr Mayer's.
    4 p.m., with Sir Worthington-Evans, plan not to reply to the Note.[44]
    5 p.m., with Sir John Bradbury and Kemball, Astoria.
    7.30–8.45 p.m., with Bemelmans and Delacroix, Astoria.

31 December, Saturday.
    10 a.m., Fischer, Trendelenburg.
    11 a.m., Secretary Raggi.
    1.15 p.m., Hotel Ritz with Beaverbrook, Bonar Law.
    3 p.m., with Worthington-Evans. Kindersley, Blackett, Sir Alan Smith. Problem of rates of exchange in the syndicate.[45]

[42] For the Anglo-French negotiation on the syndicate for reconstructing Russia see *Documents on British Foreign Policy*, 1st Ser. xv, pp. 806–35; Zsigmond, *Zur deutschen Frage*, p. 211.
[43] Two conversations had taken place between Rathenau and Blackett on that day. BA Koblenz, Kleine Erwerbungen 442, Rathenau to Mayer, 30 December 1922. The British delegation stayed at the Hotel Crillon.
[44] The German Government did not intend to answer the three questions of the Reparations Commission in its Note of 16 December 1921. Zsigmond, *Zur deutschen Frage*, p. 199. Lord D'Abernon noted in his diary: 'I hear from Paris that Rathenau was left entirely alone by the French for the first four days after his arrival. They did not even return his cards. Briand was furious about his being in Paris, said it was an English trick— an endeavour to force his hand.' D'Abernon, *An Ambassador of Peace*, vol. i, p. 243. It was true that Rathenau met Loucheur four days after his arrival.
[45] The reference is to the European syndicate for economic reconstruction in eastern Europe.

4 p.m., with Bemelmans, Gut (Theunis's secretary), two industrialists.

5 p.m., with Salvago Raggi, who had been at the hotel at 3.30 p.m. Misunderstanding by the German chargé d'affaires in Rome.[46]

7 p.m., Stahl (*Frankfurter Zeitung*).

7.30 p.m., with Kindersley.

8 p.m., with Boyden (Majestic). Whitehouse. Evening, drafted dispatch.

1 January [1922], Sunday.
  11.00 a.m., Embassy, telegram about Raggi.
  8.00 p.m., At Mayer's. Hösch.

2 January, Monday.
  10.30 a.m., André Gide.[47]
  11.00 a.m., Haguenin.
  12.00 a.m., Goll.
  4.00 p.m., Raphael.
  5.45 p.m., Loucheur.

3 January, Tuesday.
  11.00 a.m., Countess Castellane.
  12.15 a.m., Embassy.
  3.15 p.m., Herbette.
  4.30 p.m., Salvago Raggi.
  6.15 p.m., Prangey.
  8.00 p.m., Aubrun.

4 January, Wednesday.
  Telegram Haniel (Belgian Mark Agreement).[48]

[46] Konstantin von Neurath. Rathenau also negotiated with the Italian side in order to delay an Italian demand for a 'Wiesbaden Agreement' (delivery in kind). Laubach, *Die Politik der Kabinette Wirth*, p. 141.

[47] Felix, *Walther Rathenau*, p. 118. Gide put the meeting a day later (3 January). They talked for an hour at the Hotel Crillon. Gide, who had met Rathenau before, complained that Rathenau left his hand on his arm for nearly the whole time, and noted 'manières trop cordiales'. Rathenau's refrain was: 'All Europe is plunging into the abyss.' Schulin (ed.), *Walther Rathenau. Hauptwerke und Gespräche*, p. 847. On 4 January the Cabinet in Berlin accepted the draft agreement about the liquidation of former German property in Belgium. Schulze-Bidlingmaier (ed.), *Die Kabinette Wirth I und II*, pp. 498 ff.

[48] The Belgians were supposed to be the main obstacle to an agreement in Cannes because they felt their priority with regard to the reparation payments to be endangered. In order to mollify Belgian resistance, the Germans offered to negotiate an agreement (delivery in kind) with them. In Cannes the Belgians nevertheless pushed up the sum from 500 million to 720 million marks in order to increase the pressure on Germany. Laubach, *Die Politik der Kabinette Wirth*, pp. 141, 159 f.

11.00 a.m., Raggi, till 1.15 p.m.
1.30 p.m., Embassy.
5.30 p.m., Raggi.
7.00 p.m., Zöpfl.

5 January, Thursday.
10.00 a.m., Trendelenburg.
10.30 a.m., Wertheimer, Stock Lossa, Louvre.
3.30 p.m., Fischer.
4.00 p.m., Herbette.

6 January, Friday.
10.00 a.m., Carolan.
11.00 a.m., Tschenkeli (Georgia).
12.00 a.m., Embassy.
7.20 p.m., Departure.[49]

Negotiations with the Reparations Commission in Paris[50]

1. Mayer's letter to Dubois.[51] Without mentioning it, Fischer wrote an accompanying letter suggesting that I visit, which was withdrawn too late.

2. Reparations Commission arranged a session on 29.12.21. at 4 p.m.—because there was a chance of 'information'.

3. It received none, instead a question: Answer or not.

4. It was asked to express itself officially and gave an enigmatic answer. This was misunderstood and repeated.

5. Our reply is promised at least by 'the day after tomorrow' (Saturday 31 December).

6. Fischer makes an enquiry to Berlin.

7. Fischer hands a letter over on Saturday; Reparations Commission dilemma whether or not to publish it.

8. Bradbury says on Friday evening, Boyden on Saturday evening, that no answer will be requested.

[49] Rathenau informed the Cabinet about his stay in Paris on 8 January 1922. Schulze-Bidlingmaier (ed.), *Die Kabinette Wirth I und II*, p. 506.

[50] The ten points are concerned with whether and how the German Government should reply to the three questions of the Reparations Commission Note of 16 December 1921. See fnn. 35 and 42 above. On the German side there was a considerable amount of anxiety as to what would happen if the forthcoming Cannes Conference produced no results and Germany had not paid anything by 15 January. It was feared that the Reparations Commission might invoke penal clauses. Laubach, *Die Politik der Kabinette Wirth*, pp. 139 f.

[51] As a result of Rathenau's discussions with the Commission it became clear that the Commission could not reply to the German request until it received a reply to its Note of 16 December. It looks as if the Germans had replied, but the Commission could not agree on a joint decision until 13 January 1922 in Cannes. Ibid., p. 136 and fn. 32.

9. Fischer reports to Berlin on Saturday 31st, to get authorization for an answer 'first week in January'.[52]

10. Monday, Haguenin reports discord.[53]

[52] This is presumably Fischer's report, in which he points to the 'feared mechanism of the penal clauses' if Germany did not pay. Laubach, *Die Politik der Kabinette Wirth*, p. 139.

[53] It was obvious that the French would see through the German delaying tactics.

NOTES ON 1922

Back from his talks in Paris Rathenau informed the Cabinet in Berlin on 8 January 1922 about their outcome.[1] On the same day the Supreme Council in Cannes asked the German Government to send a delegation to the conference to discuss the reparation problem. Rathenau naturally headed the German delegation, which arrived in Cannes on 11 January. Lloyd George had been there since 26 December and Briand joined him on 4 January. When the French President, Millerand, and other members of the French Cabinet in Paris objected to the planned moratorium Briand returned to Paris, on the same day as Rathenau arrived. In the face of mounting opposition in Cabinet and Parliament to his policies Briand resigned, on 12 January, because the opposition insisted on more guarantees that Germany would resume payments once the financial crisis was resolved. The news of Briand's dramatic move came through while Rathenau was telling the Allies in a long speech full of economic statistics that Germany was unable to pay, and that even the realization of the London agreement between Lloyd George and Briand of December 1921 would mean a doubling or trebling of taxation. This would ruin the German economy completely.

At Cannes Rathenau also tried to convince the Reparations Commission of Germany's financial difficulties. He apparently argued very persuasively and left a good impression with the members of the Commission. Nothing definite, however, could be decided once Briand had resigned.[2] As a short-term measure the Commission decided on 13 January that Germany should pay 31 million gold marks every ten days starting on 18 January. There was no longer any insistence that the instalments of 500 million marks which Germany should have paid on 15 January, of 260 million due on 15 February, and the next 500 million fixed for 15 April should be paid at all.

The Commission's arrangement expired on 21 March when it was superseded by the granting of a provisional moratorium which was to last until 31 May. Attached to this scheme of payments was a package of financial and economic reforms, the success of which was to form the basis for a settlement valid for the time after 31 May.

Thus the Cannes Conference did not bring about a solution of the reparation problem, but the rigidity of the London payment plan of May 1921 gave way to a more flexible approach. Rathenau had successfully demonstrated that his policy of fulfilment could lead to a revision of the reparations payments and ultimately to a revision of the Versailles Peace Treaty. Although the two goals could not be realized in the immediate future, the first steps had been taken. However, even for Rathenau the path to revisionism proved to be very testing for his patience. Bearing in mind the growing nationalism and anti-Semitism at home it was an arduous task to sell the policy of 'small steps'. Rathenau's policies became even more difficult for the German public to understand when it became clear that fulfilment and revisionism were intertwined with the utilization of Germany's special relationship with Soviet Russia. It was not

---

[1] Laubach, *Die Politik der Kabinette Wirth*, pp. 139 f.
[2] Ibid., pp. 141 ff.; Felix, *Walther Rathenau*, pp. 122 f.

easy for them to realize that Rathenau was using the project of a Recon-struction Consortium as a vehicle to organize co-operation with the Allies. From the co-operation a different climate was to follow in which it would be easier to arrange a gradual reduction of the burden of reparation pay-ments. During the following weeks after the Cannes Conference it became increasingly clear that this plan was in danger because of Poincaré's lack of interest in the Consortium, although he initially pursued the same reparation policy as Briand.[3]

Back in Berlin, after the Cannes Conference, Rathenau was praised for his efforts and his success and was even presented with Meissen porcelain by Presi-dent Ebert.[4]

After the Cannes Conference it was obvious that Rathenau would lead the German delegation at the forthcoming international economic conference at Genoa. At the end of January rumours ran strong that the vacant post of Foreign Minister would be filled by him, especially as it was hoped that he might help to solve the pressing problem of reparations. Meanwhile, the German Government had to draft its deflationary programme, which was sent to the Reparations Commission on 28 January. When Rathenau was appointed Foreign Minister on 31 January 1922—a post which he accepted only after some hesitation and with certain doubts about what he might be able to achieve— reparations policy remained his foremost task.[5] In addition he approved of the German-Russian *rapprochement* which took shape during December and January and which he had supported for the last three years.

The problems Rathenau faced were rather difficult to solve. The relative weakness of the German economy virtually excluded an American loan; and a reduction of the reparations was blocked by Poincaré. Thus the repara-tion issue in general and the Franco-German relations in particular dominated and poisoned the international scene. By mid-March Franco-German tensions had grown considerably. Yet Poincaré intended to make the existing schemes of payments in kind work, although they were apparently opposed by the British representative on the Reparations Commission; the French Govern-ment was even in favour of an international reparations loan. But the work of the Committee of Experts which had been convened for 24 May, was marred by the Franco-British polarization. Unlike Lloyd George, Poincaré was not prepared to envisage a revision of Versailles and the London pay-ments plan of May 1921, despite his willingness to help Germany econom-ically.[6] To Rathenau's disappointment he did not want to realize that a strict adherence to the London payments plan ruled out an international loan and thus an economic recovery if a deflationary policy was to be avoided. Disagreement over aims and solutions led to a deterioration in the Franco-German relations which had improved so dramatically after Rathenau had joined the Cabinet under the banner of 'fulfilment' at the end of May 1921.

[3] Bariety, *Les Relations Franco-Allemandes*, pp. 91-101; Trachtenberg, *Reparation in World Politics*, pp. 237 ff.
[4] BA Koblenz, Nachlass Rathenau 2, Ebert to Rathenau, 16 January 1922.
[5] Kessler, *Rathenau*, pp. 322 f. Rathenau, *Politische Briefe*, p. 326, Rathenau to Mayer, 1 February 1922; Morsey, *Die Deutsche Zentrumspartei*, pp. 445 f.
[6] Bariety, *Les Relations Franco-Allemandes*, pp. 92 f.; Trachtenberg, *Reparation in World Politics*, pp. 247 f.

Conversation with the French Ambassador Laurent, 15 March 1922

Laurent visited me today at 12.30 p.m. and said he wanted to have three conversations with me one after the other: one on behalf of his colleagues, one as Ambassador and one as Charles Laurent.

On behalf of his colleagues he wanted to give me the accompanying Note, which I read over and to which I replied that I would give him my answer in the third conversation.

As for 2, he handed over the accompanying French Note[7] to which he got the same answer.

As for 3, I did not even let him say a word, but instead spoke to him as follows:

The depreciation of the mark represents our most severe anxiety at the moment. He will have been convinced that wages and salaries had still not adjusted to the new rate of exchange. It will, furthermore, have become quite clear to him what the threateningly dangerous rise in commodity and food prices means. I used Sunday's meeting in the Lustgarten as an example. Very serious times were ahead. There could be all kinds of surprises and disturbances. Above all I felt very pessimistic about the popular mood. Uncertainty meant that no general opinion had as yet been formed regarding the Reparations Commission and Genoa, but there was a danger that a deep and generally felt bitterness would bring up the question of which foreign power was now to blame. England would not incur blame because England had proposed Genoa and defended it and behaved with great restraint. The United States had assumed an exceptional position towards the whole of Europe and not an unfriendly one towards ourselves. The remaining states conducted themselves quietly. France was different. Along with the well-known charges which can be laid to France's account, a system of Notes has now been launched which, if the public ever got to know about it, would arouse feelings of great bitterness. I hold back these Notes, as far as I am able, to prevent too great a feeling of bitterness arising. But I cannot prevent a more peremptory attitude towards France being demanded from the Government. If this debate were accompanied by an outburst of general despair it would lead to consequences which would be disadvantageous to both countries. But it is now no longer possible, even physically, to sustain the wave of Notes. I am having statistics drawn up of how many serious Notes have recently arrived. He would be astonished at the number.[8]

---

[7] French Note of 15 March 1922; Zsigmond, *Zur deutschen Frage*, p. 213.

[8] In his Reichstag speech on 29 March 1922 Rathenau mentioned a hundred Notes. Rathenau, *Cannes und Genua.* See also Laubach, *Die Politik der Kabinette Wirth*, p. 169.

I could add that the whole office is kept busy day and night answering this hailstorm of Notes. I myself had the greatest difficulty during the past few days in reaching agreement with the Länder on an acceptable answer to the Nollet Note.[9] This task cost me days of work and now I am being flooded out with new papers. His Government should realize that the game they are playing is more than dangerous, and if it is continued then neither I nor my successor will be in a position to maintain that calm which has hitherto been preserved with effort. Even in the last few days I had considerably promoted the negotiations with Mr Gillet.[10] In so doing I had once more exposed myself to serious political dangers which consist in the fact that since it has finally been acknowledged that the Wiesbaden Agreement is of no use whatsoever to France, I will be blamed for having made it acceptable [to France]. I shall not be able to continue this work if there is no clear sign of a decrease in tension between France and Germany. That is why I am not inclined to follow up Poincaré's request to go to Paris. Obviously Poincaré does not see the conditions in Germany from the right angle. Perhaps he believes that he is doing me a favour if he invites me to Paris. Quite the contrary in fact. I should be exposing our policy to serious risks if I once more emphasized my conciliatory attitude to France so clearly,[11] and the result would be that Mr Poincaré would think he had done me a favour if he vouchsafed me twenty-five minutes conversation. Perhaps at Genoa, or after Genoa, I would have an opportunity to see him more informally. Given the existing state of tension which constitutes an absolute threat of danger, and which is characterized by the hailstorm of Notes, I would not go to Paris.

Laurent, who had become very thoughtful, found no arguments with which to invalidate my statements. He only said that the French Government had most urgently requested the Reparations Commission to reach a decision as soon as possible so that the potentially dangerous exchange rate of the mark would at least be slowed down. He was most insistent that I should, nevertheless, go to Paris. Talking to him would certainly be useful, but all the world problems could only be settled if a *détente* were to develop between France and us, and that could only be brought about by personal contact.

I answered by asking him first of all to transmit the whole content of our conversation to Poincaré, adding his own judgement of our

[9] Nollet's Note of 22 February 1922 concerning the military organization of the Schutzpolizei [ordinary police], which was answered on 15 March.

[10] The Gillet-Ruppel Agreement of 15 March 1922 regarding German payments-in-kind to France.

[11] For criticism of the Cabinet's francophile tendency, see Morsey, *Die Deutsch Zentrumspartei*, p. 446.

circumstances, every aspect of which he was indeed in a position to form an opinion upon, to tell him why I hesitated to go to Paris now, and to ask him whether he would really expect that any visible decrease in tension would result from a conversation between us. Meanwhile, I urgently asked him to see to it that the system of Notes should cease as soon as possible, since if developments should take a crooked turn, they could no longer be held back.[12]

He said goodbye in a very friendly way, declaring again: what does a conference like Genoa mean? The European situation depends only on the relationship between Germany and France, and if this can be improved we shall advance further than by any other means.

At a Cabinet meeting on 24 March Rathenau reviewed the basic arguments on fulfilment policy.[13] He was more open about the underlying tactical considerations than he had been ten months earlier. He insisted that the policy was 'no end in itself' but a ploy to win the co-operation of at least one ally for the path towards revision. There had been one alternative after the London Ultimatum, either to fulfil or to strengthen the front against Germany.

To his mind a similar situation existed after Stinnes's speech at the Spa Conference in 1920. The fulfilment policy so far carried out had had some success, but a firmer policy was now needed to counter the intransigence of the Allied Reparations Commission, provided it did not provoke the Allies. Moreover, the Anglo-French rift would make it worthwhile to try and see 'how far the ice is capable of bearing the load'. A pure policy of fulfilment would not lead to the desired results, as the right-wing parties correctly pointed out. 'Fulfilment' meant a flexible policy without the endorsement of 'a continuous absolute Yes'. He had always expected that the policy's limitations would become obvious and he was thus now prepared to take risks. However, he expected certain positive results from a change in tactics. Rathenau's change of emphasis in his tactics vis-à-vis the Allies is all the more interesting as it foreshadows the German expectations of the Genoa Conference, the Rapallo Agreement, and finally even on personal lines, a rapprochement between Rathenau and Stinnes on the eve of the former's assassination.

Rathenau considered that one of his main tasks was to obtain a substantial reparations relief at the Genoa Conference. Over the previous weeks he became more and more concerned that the question of reparations was not to be discussed. He is supposed to have warned the French politician Thomas: 'When that decision is taken from the Chair at Genoa I shall pick up my papers, walk out and return home.'[14] But his fears were not justified because the Reparations Commission were expected to make demands which would be likely to keep the issue alive, although officially reparations were not to be discussed. In its answer of 21 March to the German Note of 28 January, the Commission provisionally accepted the London agreement, but declared that the planning for

---

[12] For Rathenau's pessimistic frame of mind, see Kessler, *Tagebücher*, pp. 276 f.
[13] Schulz-Bidlingmaier, (ed.) *Die Kabinette Wirth I und II*, p. 636, 24th March 1922.
[14] Middlemas (ed.), *Whitehall Diary*, vol. i, p. 195.

the budget was unsatisfactory, and demanded an increase in taxation of sixty thousand million (paper) marks.[15]

After lengthy discussion in the Cabinet the German Government rejected the tax demands and the bid for financial control. This was in a Note on 7 April, and was only handed over on the opening day of the Genoa Conference. The Note has been aptly called 'the first grand attack by the Wirth–Rathenau Government on the London Payments Plan of 1921'.[16] Despite Germany's strong words and despite its improved standing at the Conference, an arrangement with the Reparations Commission had to be reached by the end of May. Otherwise the penal clauses would have come into effect, and this could have led to the feared occupation of the Ruhr. Eventually the Government had to accept most of the demands though some concessions were granted to the Germans. Without any prospect of financial help the tactics seemed, during the last weeks of Rathenau's life, to have been to delay German financial, fiscal, and economic bankruptcy by adhering to 'fulfilment'; this really aimed at delaying all payments. The German request for a moratorium had made it clear that fulfilment really implied an unwillingness to pay more. Rathenau's last notes before his assassination revealed a similar conclusion.[17] After Rathenau's death the Wirth Government continued to negotiate for further reductions and another moratorium. Reparations and fulfilment policy, relief, and finally abolition continued to dominate the politics of the Weimar Republic.

[15] Laubach, *Die Politik der Kabinette Wirth*, pp. 148 ff. and 163 ff.
[16] Ibid., p. 171; Bergmann, *Der Weg der Reparation*, pp. 153 ff.
[17] Rathenau, *Politische Briefe*, p. 343.

RATHENAU'S MEMBERSHIP OF SUPERVISORY BOARDS OF JOINT-STOCK COMPANIES 1907–1922

The corporate basis of Rathenau's influence is indicated in parentheses and italic following the name of the company. Either the translation of the name or the company's main line of business is provided where it seems to be useful.

Allgemeine Elektrizitätsgesellschaft Berlin, (AEG), [General Electric Company]

AEG-Lahmeyer Werke AG, Frankfurt (*AEG*); dynamos

AEG-Schnellbahn AG, Berlin (*AEG*); underground trains

Allgemeine Lokal- und Strassenbahn-Gesellschaft, Berlin (*AEG*); financial holding company for tramway constructions

Bank für Elektrische Unternehmungen (Elektrobank), Zürich (*AEG*)

Baumwollspinnereien, Erlangen (*BHG*); cotton mill

Baumwollspinnereien, Unterhausen (*BHG*); cotton mill

Bayerische Elektrizitäts Lieferungs-Gesellschaft, Bayreuth (*ELG*); [Bavarian Electrical Supply Company]

Berliner Elektrizitätswerke (BEW), Berlin (*AEG*)

Berliner Handelsgesellschaft, Berlin (*BHG*); bank

Berg- und Metallbank AG, Frankfurt (*BHG*); bank

Blechwalzwerk Schulz-Knaudt, Essen (*BHG*); sheet metal rolling mill

Braunkohlen- und Brikett-Industrie, Berlin (*BHG*); lignite coal for power-stations

Brown, Boveri & Cie (BBC), Mannheim (*AEG*); turbine construction

Capito & Klein AG, Düsseldorf (*AEG*); sheet metal rolling mill

Compania Barcelonesa de Electricidad, Barcelona (*Elektrobank*)

Compania Sevillana de Electricidad, Sevilla (*Elektrobank*)

Deutsche Niles Werkzeugmaschinenfabrik, Berlin (*AEG*); tool-making

Deutsch-Überseeische Elektrizitäts-Gesellschaft, Berlin (*AEG*); holding company for constructing and running power installations, mainly in South America

Deutsche Werft AG, Hamburg (*AEG*); shipyard

Deutsch-Niederländische Telegraphengesellschaft, Berlin (*Felten & Guilleaume*); undersea cables

Deutsch-Südamerikanische Telegraphengesellschaft AG, Berlin (*Felten & Guilleaume*); undersea cables

Elektrowerke AG, Berlin (*AEG*); generating and supplying electricity in central Germany

Elektrizitäts Lieferungs-Gesellschaft (ELG), Berlin (*AEG*); financial holding company with managerial tasks

Elektrizitätswerke und Strassenbahn Abo, Berlin (*ELG*); electrical supply and tramway company

Elektrizitätswerke und Strassenbahn Königsberg, Königsberg (*ELG*); electrical supply and tramway company

Elektrochemische Werke AG, Berlin and Bitterfeld (*AEG*)

Elektro-Nitrum-AG Rhina, Baden (*AEG*); saltpetre production

Elektro-Salpeter-Werke AG, Zschornewitz (*AEG*); saltpetre production

Elektrotreuhand AG, Hamburg (*AEG*); a type of mortgage bank

Felten & Guilleaume Carlswerk AG, Köln (*AEG*); wires and cables

Gebrüder Körting AG in Körtingdorf, Hanover (*AEG*); gas engines

Gesellschaft für Elektrische Unternehmungen, Berlin (*AEG*); holding company

Glashütten AG, Weisswasser (*AEG*); electric bulbs

Glockenstahlwerke AG, Remscheid (*AEG*); electric steel processing

Th. Goldschmidt AG, Essen; chemical plant

Hamburger Hochbahn AG, Hamburg (*AEG*). fast electric urban trains

Hohenlohewerke AG, Berlin (*BHG*); coal and zinc mines

Internationale Kohlebergwerke AG, St. Avold; coal mining

Land- und Seekabelwerke AG, Köln (*Felten & Guilleaume*); land and sea cables

Lech Elektrizitätswerke, Augsburg (*Elektrobank*)

Leipziger Elektrische Strassenbahn AG, Leipzig (*ELG*)

Linke-Hofmann-Werke für Waggonbau, Berlin (*AEG*); engines, carriages, machines

Ludwig Löwe & Co. AG, Berlin (*BHG*); ammunition and armaments

Märkisches Elektrizitätswerk AG, Berlin (*AEG*); electrical supply

Mannesmannröhren-Werke AG, Düsseldorf (*BHG*); steel tubes

Neue Oberlausitzer Glashüttenwerke Schweig & Co. AG, Weisswasser (*AEG*); electric bulbs

Norddeutsche Seekabelwerke AG, Nordenham (*Felten & Guilleaume*); cables

Oberrheinische Kraftwerke AG,Mühlhausen (*Elektrobank*)

Oberschlesische Elektrizitätswerke AG, Kattowitz (*Gesellschaft für Elektrische Unternehmungen*);electrical supply Oberschlesische Kleinbahn AG (AEG); tramways

Permutit AG, Berlin (*AEG*); water filtration

Planiawerke AG für Kohlefabrikation, Plania/Ratibor (*AEG*); carbon brushes

Rheingau-Elektrizitätswerke AG, Eltville (*Elektrobank*); electrical supply

Rütgerswerke AG, Berlin (*AEG*)

Russiche Eisen-Industrie AG, Gleiwitz (*BHG*); iron industry

Rybniker Steinkohlen-Gewerkschaft, Berlin (*BHG*); mining

Schlesische AG für Bergbau und Zinkhüttenbetrieb (*BHG*); mining

Schlesische Elektrizitäts- und Gas AG, Breslau (*Gesellschaft für elektrische Unternehmungen*); electrical and gas supply

Schlesische Kleinbahn AG, Kattowitz (*AEG*); tramways

Schweigsche Glas- und Porzellanwerke, Weisswasser (*AEG*); insulators

Solinger Kleinbahn AG, Solingen (*AEG*); tramways

Spinnerei und Buntweberei Pfersee, Augsburg; cotton mill (*BHG*)

Stahlwerke Richard Lindenberg AG, Remscheid (*AEG*); electro-steel processing

Stein- und Ton-Industriegesellschaft 'Brohltahl', Köln (*Felten & Guilleaume*)

Strassburger Elektrizitätswerk AG, Strassburg (*Elektrobank*); electrical supply

Thiederhall AG Thiele, Braunschweig; potash

Treuhandbank für die elektrische Industrie AG, Berlin (*Felten & Guilleaume*). mortgage bank

Tschöpelner Werke AG, Muskau (*BEW*); lignite coal

Vereinigte Lausitzer Glaswerke, Weisswasser (*AEG*); electric bulbs

(In addition Rathenau was a member of the boards of a number of limited companies.)

BIBLIOGRAPHY

Archival Sources

State Archives

Bundesarchiv Koblenz
Bundesarchiv-Militärarchiv Freiburg
House of Lords Record Office, London
Ministère des Affaires Étrangères, Paris
Politisches Archiv des Auswärtigen Amtes, Bonn
Public Record Office, London
Staats- und Universitätsbibliothek, Hamburg
Zentrales Staatsarchiv, Potsdam
Zentrales Staatsarchiv, Merseburg

Private Archives

AEG-Archiv, Braunschweig and Frankfurt
Felten & Guilleaume Carlswerk AG Archiv, Köln–Mülheim
Historiches Archiv der Gutehoffnungshütte, Oberhausen
Friedrich Krupp GmbH Archiv, Essen
Mannesmann Archiv, Düsseldorf
Werner von Siemens Institut für die Geschichte des Hauses
Siemens, München

Achterberg, E., *Berliner Hochfinanz. Kaiser, Fürsten, Millionäre um 1900*, Frankfurt 1965.
Armeson, R., *Total Warfare and Compulsory Labor: A Study of the Military-Industrial Complex in Germany during World War I*, The Hague 1964.
Austen, R., *Northwest Tanzania under German and British Rule. Colonial Policy and Tribal Politics 1889–1939*, New Haven 1968.
Baden, Prinz Max von, *Erinnerungen und Dokumente*, Berlin 1927. (English translation, 2 vols., New York 1928.)
Bald, D., *Deutsch–Ostafrika 1900–1914. Eine Studie über Verwaltung. Interessengruppen und wirtschaftliche Erschliessung*, München 1970.
Bariety, J., *Les Relations Franco-Allemandes après la Première Guerre Mondiale*, Paris 1977.
Barkin, K. D., *The Controversy over German Industrialization 1890–1902*, Chicago 1970.
Baudis, D., and Nussbaum, H., *Wirtschaft und Staat in Deutschland vom Ende des 19. Jahrhunderts bis 1918/19*, Berlin 1978.
Becker, J., 'Baden, Bismarck und die Annexion von Elsass und Lothringen', *Zeitschrift für die Geschichte des Oberrhein*, 115, 1967.
Berghahn, V., *Germany and the Approach of War in 1914*, London 1973.
Berglar, P., 'Harden und Rathenau. Zur Problematik ihrer Freundschaft', *Historische Zeitschrift*, 209, 1969.
—, *Walther Rathenau. Seine Zeit. Sein Werk. Seine Persönlichkeit*, Bremen 1970.

Bergmann, C., *Der Weg der Reparation. Von Versailles über den Dawesplan zum Ziel*, Frankfurt 1926.

Bernhard, H. (ed), *Gustav Stresemann. Vermächtnis*, vol. ii, Berlin 1932.

Bertram, J., *Die Wahlen zum Deutschen Reichstag vom Jahre 1912. Parteien und Verbände in der Innenpolitik des Wilhelminischen Reichs*, Düsseldorf 1965.

Bismarck, O. von, *Die Gesammelten Werke*. xv, *Gedanken und Erinnerung*, Berlin 1932.

Blaich, F., *Kartell- und Monopolpolitik im Kaiserlichen Deutschland. Das Problem der Marktmacht im deutschen Reichstag zwischen 1879-1914*, Düsseldorf 1973.

—, *Der Trustkampf (1901-1915). Ein Beitrag zum Verhalten der Ministerial-bürokratie gegenüber Verbandsinteressen im Wilhelminischen Deutschland*, Berlin 1975.

Bodenhausen-Degener, D. Freifrau von (ed.), *Hugo von Hofmannsthal, Eberhard von Bodenhausen. Briefe der Freundschaft*, Berlin 1953.

— (ed.), *Eberhard von Bodenhausen. Ein Leben für Kunst und Wirtschaft*, Düsseldorf/Köln 1955.

Böhme, H., *Deutschlands Weg zur Grossmacht. Studien zum Verhältnis von Wirtschaft und Staat während der Reichsgründungszeit 1848-1881*, Köln/Berlin 1966.

Bongard, O., *Staatssekretär Dernburg in Britisch- und Deutsch-Südwestafrika*, Berlin 1908.

—, *Die Studienreise des Staatssekretärs Dernburg nach Deutsch-Ostafrika*, Berlin 1908.

Bonn, M. J., *So macht man Geschichte. Bilanz eines Lebens*, München 1953.

Böttcher, H. M., *Walther Rathenau. Persönlichkeit und Werk*, Bonn 1958.

Bourdon, G., *L'Énigme allemande. Un enquête chez les Allemands, ce qu'ils pensent—ce qu'ils veulent—ce qu'ils peuvent*, Paris 1913.

Boveri, W., *Ansprachen und Betrachtungen*, Zürich 1954.

Brinckmeyer, H., *Die Rathenaus*, München 1922.

British Documents on the Origins of the War, see Gooch and Temperley below.

Buddensieg, T. and Rogge, H., *Industriekultur. Peter Behrens und die AEG. 1907-1914*, Berlin 1979.

Bülow, Bernhard Fürst von, *Denkwürdigkeiten*, 4 vols., Berlin 1931.

Burchardt, L., *Friedenswirtschaft und Kriegsvorsorge. Deutschlands wirtschaftliche Rüstungsbestrebungen vor 1914*, Boppard 1968.

—, 'Walther Rathenau und die Anfänge der deutschen Rohstoffbewirtschaftung im Ersten Weltkrieg', *Tradition*, 15, 1970.

—, 'Eine neue Quelle zu den Anfängen der Kriegswirtschaft in Deutschland 1914. Das Tagebuch Wichard v. Moellendorff vom 13 August bis zum 14 October 1914', *Tradition*, 2, 1971.

Burger, H. (ed.), *Hugo von Hofmannsthal—Harry Graf Kessler Briefwechsel 1898-1929*, Frankfurt 1968.

Burte, H., *Mit Rathenau am Oberrhein*, Heidelberg 1948.

Campbell, F. G., 'The Struggle for Upper Silesia 1919-22', *Journal of Modern History*, 42, 1970.

Carsten, F. L., *Reichswehr und Politik. 1918-1933*, Köln 1964.

Cecil, L., *Albert Ballin. Business and Politics in Imperial Germany. 1888-1918*, Princeton, 1967.

Christie, R., 'The Electrification of South Africa', unpublished thesis, Oxford 1979.

Collier, P., *Germany and the Germans from an American Point of View*, London 1913.

Conze, W., *Polnische Nation und deutsche Politik im Ersten Weltkrieg*, Köln 1958.

Crothers, G. D., *The German Elections of 1907*, New York 1941.

D'Abernon, Edgar V., Viscount, *An Ambassador of Peace: Pages from the Diary of Viscount D'Abernon Berlin 1920-1926*, 3 vols., London 1929/30.

Deist, W. (ed.), *Militär und Innenpolitik im Weltkrieg 1914-1918*, 2 vols., Düsseldorf 1970.

Delbrück, C. von., *Die Wirtschaftliche Mobilmachung in Deutschland*, Berlin 1924.

Denkmalsausschuss (ed.), *Entwürfe zum Bismarck-Nationaldenkmal auf der Elisenhöhe bei Bingerbrück*, Düsseldorf 1911.

Dernburg, B., *Kapital und Staatsaufsicht. Eine finanz-politische Studie*, Berlin 1911.

—, 'Östliche Wirtschaftsfragen', *Koloniale Rundschau*, 4, 1912.

Dessoir, M. and Muthesius, H., *Das Bismarck-Denkmal*, Jena 1912.

Documents on British Foreign Policy, see E. L. Woodward and R. Butler below.

Doss, K., *Das deutsche Auswärtige Amt in Übergang vom Kaiserreich zur Weimarer Republik. Die Schülersche Reform*, Düsseldorf 1977.

Drechsler, H., 'Jacob Morenga: A New Kind of South-West African Leader', *African Studies*, Leipzig 1967.

Dresdner, A., *Industrielle. Vertreter der Industrie und des Handels in Wort und Bild*, Berlin, n.d.

Durieux, T., *Eine Tür steht offen. Erinnerungen*, Berlin 1954.

Eley, G., *Reshaping the German Right. Radical Nationalism and Political Change after Bismarck*, London/New Haven 1980.

Ensor, Sir Robert, *England 1870-1914*, repr., Oxford 1966.

Epstein, K., *Matthias Erzberger and the Dilemma of German Democracy*, Princeton 1959.

Erdmann, K. D., 'Zur Beurteilung Bethmann Hollwegs', *Geschichte in Wissenschaft und Unterricht*, 15, 1964.

— (ed.), *Kurt Riezler. Tagebücher, Aufsätze, Dokumente*, Göttingen 1972.

Erger, J., *Der Kapp-Lüttwitz-Putsch. Ein Beitrag zur deutschen Innenpolitik 1919/20*, Düsseldorf 1967.

Eynern, M. von (ed.), *Walther Rathenau. Ein Preussischer Europäer. Briefe*, Berlin 1955.

Fayle, E., *The War and the Shipping Industry*, London 1927.

Federn-Kohlhaas, E., *Walther Rathenau. Sein Leben und Wirken*, Dresden 1928.

Feis, H., *Europe, the World's Banker, 1870-1914*, New Haven 1930.

Feldman, G., *Army, Industry and Labor in Germany 1914-1918*, Princeton 1966.

—, 'German Business between War and Revolution: The Origins of the Stinnes-Legien Agreement', G. A. Ritter (ed.), *Entstehung und Wandel der modernen Gesellschaft*, Festschrift für Hans Rosenberg, Berlin 1970.

—, 'Big Business and Kapp Putsch', *Central European History*, 4, 1971.

—, (assisted by I. Steinisch), 'The Origins of the Stinnes-Legien Agreement: A Documentation', *Internationale Wissenschaftliche Korrespondenz zur Geschichte der deutschen Arbeiterbewegung*, 19/20, 1973.

—, 'The Political and Social Foundations of Germany's Economic Mobilization 1914-1916', *Armed Forces and Society*, iii, 1976.

Feldman, G., *Iron and Steel in the German Inflation 1916-1923*, Princeton 1977.

— and Homburg, H., *Industrie und Inflation. Studien und Dokumente zur Politik der deutschen Unternehmer 1916-1923*, Hamburg 1977.

— and Nocken, U., 'Trade Associations and Economic Power: Interest Group Development in the German Iron and Steel and Machine Building Industries 1900-1933', *Business History Review*, 49, 1975.

Felix, D., *Walther Rathenau and the Weimar Republic. The Politics of Reparation*, Baltimore 1971.

Fischer, F., 'Weltpolitik, Weltmachtstreben und deutsche Kriegsziele', *Historische Zeitschrift*, 199, 1964.

—, *Griff nach der Weltmacht. Die Kriegszielpolitik des kaiserlichen Deutschland 1914-1918*, 4th. edn., Düsseldorf 1969.

—, *Krieg der Illusionen*, Düsseldorf 1969.

Frauendienst, W. (ed.), *Bismarck. Die Gesammelten Werke*, vol. vi c, Berlin 1935.

50 Jahre AEG, Berlin 1956.

Fürstenberg, H., *Carl Fürstenberg. Die Lebensgeschichte eines deutschen Bankiers*, 2nd edn., Wiesbaden 1961;

—, *Erinnerungen. Mein Weg als Bankier und Carl Fürstenbergs Altersjahre*, Wiesbaden 1965.

Gall, L., 'Die Annexionspolitik von 1870/71', *Historische Zeitschrift*, 206, 1968.

Gann, L. and Duignan, P., *The Rulers of German Africa 1884-1914*, Stanford 1977.

Geiss, I., *Der polnische Grenzstreifen 1914-1918. Ein Beitrag zur deutschen Kriegszielpolitik im Ersten Weltkrieg*, Lübeck/Hamburg 1960.

— (ed.), *Julikrise und Kriegsausbruch 1914. Eine Dokumentensammlung*, 2 vols., Hanover 1963/4.

Görlitz, W. (ed.), *Regierte der Kaiser? Kriegstagebücher des Admirals von Müller*, Göttingen 1959.

— (ed.), *Der Kaiser. Aufzeichnungen des Chefs des Marinekabinetts Admiral Georg Alexander von Müller 1914-1918*, Göttingen 1965.

Gooch, G. P. and Temperley, H. (eds.), *British Documents on the Origins of the War 1898-1914*, 11 vols., London 1926-38.

Gottgetreu, E., *Maximilan Harden. Ways and Errors of a Publicist*, London 1962.

Gottlieb, E., *Walther-Rathenau-Bibliographie*, Berlin 1929.

Gottwald, H., 'Gemeinsamkeiten und Unterschiede in der Mitteleuropapolitik. Ein Betrag zur Stellung der verschiedenen Strömungen der deutschen Sozialdemokratie zur imperialistischen Aussenpolitik', W. Gutsche (ed.), *Studien zur Geschichte des deutschen Imperialismus. Jahrbuch für Geschichte 15*.

Grosse Politik der Europäischen Kabinette, see J. Lepsius *et al.* below.

Gründer, H., *Walter Simons als Staatsmann, Jurist und Kirchenpolitiker*, Neustadt 1975.

Gutsche, W., 'Die Beziehungen zwischen der Regierung Bethmann Hollweg und dem Monopolkapital in den ersten Monaten des ersten Weltkrieges', Habilitationsschrift, Berlin 1967.

— (ed.), *Deutschland im Ersten Weltkrieg*, ii, Berlin 1968. See for the other two volumes F. Klein and J. Petzold.

—, 'Mitteleuropaplanungen in der Aussenpolitik des deutschen Imperialismus vor 1918', *Zeitschrift für Geschichtswissenschaft*, 20, 1972.

Gutsche, W., *Aufstieg und Fall eines Kaiserlichen Reichskanzlers: T. von Beth-mann Hollweg 1856-1921*, Berlin 1973.

—, 'Zur Mitteleuropapolitik der deutschen Reichsleitung', W. Gutsche (ed.), *Studien zur Geschichte des deutschen Imperialismus. Jahrbuch für Geschichte*, 15, 1977.

—, (ed.), *Studien zur Geschichte des deutschen Imperialismus von der Jahr-hundertwende bis 1917. Jahrbuch für Geschichte 15*, Berlin 1977.

—, 'Einige Bemerkungen zur wirtschaftliche Vorbereitung des deutschen Imperialismus auf den ersten Weltkrieg', *Zeitschrift für Geschichtswissen-schaft*, 25, 1977.

— and Kaulisch, B. (eds.), *Herrschaftsmethoden des deutschen Imperialismus 1897/98 bis 1917*, Berlin 1977.

Hallgarten, G F., *Imperialismus vor 1914*, 2 vols., 2nd edn., München 1963.

Harden, M., *Köpfe*, 4 vols., Berlin 1910-24, repr. by H. J. Frölich, Hamburg 1963.

Harttung, A., Jenne, G., Ruland, M., and Schmieder, E. (eds.), *Walther Rathenau. Schriften*, Berlin 1965.

Hauser, O., *Deutschland und der english-russische Gegensatz 1900-1914*, Göttingen 1958.

Heckart, B., *From Bassermann to Bebel*, New Haven 1974.

Hellige, H. D., 'Wilhelm II und Walther Rathenau', *Geschichte in Wissenschaft und Unterricht*, 196, 1968.

— (ed.), 'Rathenaus Briefwechsel mit Maximilian Harden', forthcoming.

Hentschel, V., *Wirtschaft und Wirtschaftspolitik im Wilhelminischen Deutsch-land. Organisierter Kapitalismus und Interventionsstaat?*, Stuttgart 1978.

Herzog, B., *60 Jahre deutsche U-Boote 1906-1966*, München 1968.

Hillard (Steinbömer), G., *Herren und Narren der Welt*, München 1955.

Hiller von Gaertringen, F., *Fürst Bülows Denkwürdigkeiten*, Tübingen 1956.

— (ed.), *Wilhelm Groener. Lebenserinnerungen. Jugend. Generalstab. Weltkrieg*, Göttingen 1957.

Hoffmann, M., *Der Krieg der versäumten Gelegenheiten*, München 1924.

Hubatsch, W., *Hindenburg und der Staat*, Göttingen 1966.

Hutten-Czapski, Bogdan Graf von, *Sechzig Jahre Politik und Gesellschaft*, 2 vols., Berlin 1936.

Iliffe, J., 'The Organization of the Maji Maji Rebellion', *Journal of African History*, 8, 1967.

—, *Tanganyika under German Rule. 1905-1912*, Cambridge 1969.

Jäckh, E. (ed.), *Kiderlen-Waechter, der Staatsmann und Mensch. Briefwechsel und Nachlass*, 2 vols., Stuttgart/Berlin 1924.

Janssen, K.-H., *Der Kanzler und der General. Die Führungskrise um Bethmann Hollweg und Falkenhayn (1914-1916)*, Göttingen 1967.

Jarausch, K. H., 'The Illusion of Limited War: Chancellor Bethmann Hollweg's Calculated Risk, July 1914', *Central European History*, 2, 1969.

Joll, J., *Three Intellectuals in Politics*, London 1960.

—, 'Rathenau and Harden: A Footnote to the History of Wilhelmine Germany', M. Gilbert (ed.), *A Century of Conflict 1850-1950, Essays for A. J. P. Taylor*, London 1966.

—, 'Walther Rathenau—Intellectual or Industrialist?', V. R. Berghahn and M. Kitchen (eds.), *Germany in the Age of Total War*, Festschrift for Francis Carsten, London 1981.

Kaelble, H., *Industrielle Interessenpolitik in der Wilhelminischen Gesellschaft. Zentralverband Deutscher Industrieller 1895-1914*, Berlin 1967.

Kallner, R., *Herzl und Rathenau. Wege jüdischer Existenz an der Wende des zwanzigsten Jahrhunderts*, Stuttgart 1976.

Katz, F., *Deutschland, Diaz und die mexikanische Revolution. Die deutsche Politik in Mexiko 1820-1920*, Berlin 1965.

Kaulisch, G., 'Die Auseinandersetzungen über den uneingeschränkten U-Boot-Krieg innerhalb der herrschenden Klasse im zweiten Halbjahr 1916 und seine Eröffnung im Februar 1917', F. Klein (ed.), *Politik im Krieg 1914-1918. Studien zur Politik der deutschen herrschenden Klassen im ersten Weltkrieg*, Berlin 1964.

Kayser, A., *Reise nach Ostafrika*, Berlin 1892.

Kennedy, P., *The Rise of Anglo-German Antagonism 1860-1914*, London 1980.

Kern, B., *Weltanschauungen und Welterkenntnis*, Berlin 1911.

Kessler, Harry Graf, *Walther Rathenau. Sein Leben und sein Werk*, Berlin 1928 (English translation 1929), repr. with a commentary by Hans Fürstenberg, Wiesbaden 1962.

Klein, F. (ed.), *Politik im Krieg 1914-1918. Studien zur Politik der deutschen herrschenden Klasse im ersten Weltkrieg*, Berlin 1964.

— (ed.), *Deutschland im Ersten Weltkrieg*, Berlin 1970. See for the other two volumes W. Gutsche and J. Petzold.

Kocka, J., 'Siemens und der aufhaltsame Aufstieg der AEG', *Tradition*, 3/4, 1972.

— and Siegrist, H., 'Die hundert grössten deutschen Industrieunternehmen im späten 19. und frühen 20. Jahrhundert. Expansion, Diversifikation und Integration im internationalen Vergleich', N. Horn and J. Kocka (eds.), *Recht und Entwicklung der Grossunternehmen im 19. und frühen 20. Jahrhundert. Wirtschafts-, sozial- und rechtshistorische Untersuchungen zur Industrialisierung in Deutschland, Frankreich, England und den USA*, Göttingen 1979.

Köhler, W., *Der Chefredakteur. Theodor Wolff. Ein Leben in Europa 1868-1943*, Düsseldorf 1978.

Lange, K., *Marneschlacht und deutsche Öffentlichkeit 1914-1939*, Düsseldorf 1974.

Laubach, E., *Die Politik der Kabinette Wirth 1921/22*, Lübeck/Hamburg 1968.

Launay, J. de (ed.), *Louis Loucheur. Carnets Secrets 1908-1932*, Brussels/Paris 1962.

Lepsius, J., Mendelssohn-Bartholdy, A., and Thimme, F. (eds.), *Die Grosse Politik der Europäischen Kabinette 1871-1914*, 39 vols., Berlin 1922-7.

Lichtwark, A. and Rathenau, W., *Der rheinische Bismarck*, Berlin 1912.

Link, A. W., *Wilson. Campaigns for Progressivism and Peace 1916-1917*, Princeton 1965.

Link, W., *Die amerikanische Stabilisierungspolitik in Deutschland 1921-1932*, Düsseldorf 1970.

Lipgens, W., 'Bismarck, die öffentliche Meinung und die Annexion von Elsass und Lothringen 1870', *Historische Zeitschrift*, 197, 1964.

Loewenberg, P., 'Walther Rathenau and German Society', unpubl. thesis, Berkeley 1966.

— 'Walther Rathenau and Henry Kissinger: The Jew as a Modern Statesman in Two Political Cultures', *Leo Baeck Memorial Lecture*, 24, 1980.

Louis, W. R., *Ruanda-Urundi 1884-1919*, Oxford 1963.

Ludendorff, E. (ed.), *Urkunden der Obersten Heeresleitung über ihre Tätigkeit 1916-18*, 3rd edn., Berlin 1922.

—, *Meine Kriegserinnerungen 1914-1918*, Berlin 1941.

Mader, U., 'Europapläne und Kriegsziele Walther Rathenaus', W. Gutsche (ed.), *Studien zur Geschichte des Deutschen Imperialismus. Jahrbuch für Geschichte*, 15, 1976.

Mann, G., 'Am Hofe Walther Rathenaus', *Die Zeit*, 23 February 1968.

Marder, A., *From the Dreadnought to Scapa Flow. The Royal Navy in the Fisher era, 1904-1919*, 5 vols., London 1961-70.

Maschke, E., *Grundzüge der deutschen Kartellgeschichte bis 1914*, Dortmund 1964.

Matthias, E. and Morsey, R. (eds.), *Der Interfraktionelle Ausschuss 1917/18*, 2 vols., Düsseldorf 1959.

— and — (eds.), *Die Regierung des Prinzen Max von Baden*, Düsseldorf 1962.

Medalen, C., 'Capitalism and Colonialism. The Career of Bernhard Dernburg', unpublished thesis, Harvard 1973.

Mendelssohn, P. de, *Zeitungsstadt Berlin. Menschen und Mächte in der Geschichte der deutschen Presse*, Berlin 1959.

Mendelssohn-Bartholdy, A., *The War and German Society. The Testament of a Liberal*, New Haven 1937.

Meridies-Stehr, U. (ed.), *Hermann Stehr-Walther Rathenau: Zwiesprache über den Zeiten. Geschichte einer Freundschaft in Briefen und Dokumenten*, München 1946.

Meyer, H. C., *Mitteleuropa in German Thought and Action 1815-1945*, The Hague 1955.

Michels, R., *First Lectures in Political Sociology*, Minneapolis 1949.

Middlemas, K. (ed.), *Thomas Jones. Whitehall Diary*, 2 vols., London 1969.

Mielke, S., *Der Hansa-Bund für Gewerbe, Handel und Industrie 1909-1914*, Göttingen 1976.

Morselli, G., *Contro-passato prossimo*, Milan 1975.

Morsey, R., *Die deutsche Zentrumspartei 1917-1923*, Düsseldorf 1966.

Mortimer, J. S., 'Commercial Interest and German Diplomacy in the Agadir Crisis', *Historical Journal*, 10, 1967.

Müller, A., *Die Kriegsrohstoffbewirtschaffung 1914-1918 im Dienste des deutschen Monopolkapitals*, Berlin 1955.

Namier, Sir Lewis, *Vanished Supremacies. Essays on European History 1812-1918*, London 1958.

Newbury, C., 'Partition, Development, Trusteeship: Colonial Secretary Wilhelm Solf's West African Journey, 1913', R. Louis and P. Gifford (eds.), *Britain and Germany in Africa. Imperial Rivalry and Colonial Rule*, New Haven and London 1967.

Nocken, U., 'Corporatism and Pluralism in Modern German History', D. Stegmann, B. J. Wendt, P. C. Witt (eds.), *Industrielle Gesellschaft und Politisches System. Beiträge zur politischen Sozialgeschichte*. Festschrift für Fritz Fischer, Bonn 1978.

Northedge, F., *The Troubled Giant. Britain among the Great Powers 1916-1939*, London 1966.

Nussbaum, H., *Unternehmer gegen Monopole. Über Struktur und Aktionen antimonopolischer bürgerlicher Gruppen zum Beginn des 20. Jahrhunderts*, Berlin 1966.

Nussbaum, H., 'Versuche zur reichsgesetzlichen Regelung der deutschen Elektrizitätswirtschaft und zu ihrer Überführung in Reichseigentum 1909 bis 1914',
Jahrbuch für Wirtschaftsgeschichte, 2, 1968.

Oncken, E., *Panthersprung nach Agadir. Die deutsche Politik während der Zweiten
Marokkokrise 1911*, Düsseldorf 1981.

Ott, H., 'Kriegswirtschaft und Wirtschaftskrieg 1914-1918. Verdeutlicht an
Beispielen aus dem badisch-elsässischen Raum', E. Hassinger, J. H. Müller,
and H. Ott (eds.), *Geschichte—Wirtschaft—Gesellschaft*, Festschrift für
Clemens Bauer zum 75. Geburtstag, Berlin 1974.

—, Privatwirtschaftliche und Kommunal- (Staats)-Wirtschaftliche Aspekte beim
Aufbau der Elektrizitätswirtschaft. Dargestellt am Beispiel des Strassburger
Elektrizitätswerkes', *Aus Stadt- und Wirtschaftsgeschichte Südwestdeutsch-
lands*, Festschrift für Erich Maschke zum 75. Geburtstag, Stuttgart 1975.

Paret, P., *The Berlin Secession. Modernism and Its Enemies in Imperial Germany*,
Cambridge (Mass.), 1980.

Petzold, J. (ed.), Deutschland in Ersten Weltkrieg, iii, 2nd edn., Berlin 1970.
See for the other two volumes F. Klein and W. Gutsche.

Pinner, F., *Emil Rathenau und das elektrische Zeitalter*, Leipzig 1918.

Pfeiffer-Belli, W. (ed.), *Harry Graf Kessler. Tagebücher 1918-1937*, Frankfurt
1961.

Pogge von Strandmann, H., 'Rathenau, die Gebrüder Mannesmann und die
Vorgeschichte der Zweiten Marokkokrise', I. Geiss and B. J. Wendt (eds.),
Deutschland in der Weltpolitik der 19. und 20. Jahrhunderts, Festschrift
für Fritz Fischer zum 65. Geburtstag, Düsseldorf 1973.

—, 'Grossindustrie und Rapallopolitik. Deutsch-sowjetische Handelsbezie-
hungen in der Weimarer Republik', *Historische Zeitschrift*, 222, 1976.

—, 'Widersprüche im Modernisierungsprozess Deutschlands. Der Kampf der
verarbeitenden Industrie gegen die Schwerindustrie', D. Stegmann, B. J.
Wendt, P. C. Witt (eds.), *Industrielle Gesellschaft und Politisches System.
Beiträge zur politischen Sozialgeschichte*, Festschrift für Fritz Fischer zum
75. Geburtstag, Bonn 1978.

—, *Unternehmenspolitik und Unternehmensführung. Der Dialog zwischen
Aufsichtsrat und Vorstand bei Mannesmann 1900-1919*, Düsseldorf
1978.

—, 'Rapallo—Strategy in Preventive Diplomacy', V. R. Berghahn and M. Kitchen
(eds.), *Germany in the Age of Total War*, London 1981.

—, 'Rathenau zwischen Wirtschaft und Politik', O. Franz (ed.), *Am Wende-
punkt der europäischen Geschichte*, Göttingen 1981.

—, *Imperialismus an grünen Tisch. Der Kolonialrat in der deutschen Politik
1890-1914*, forthcoming.

—, *Grandmaster of Capitalism. Walther Rathenau, a Wilhelmine Industrialist*,
forthcoming.

— and Geiss, I., *Die Erforderlichkeit des Unmöglichen. Deutschland am Vorabend des Ersten Weltkrieges*, Frankfurt 1965.

Potthoff, H. *Gewerkschaften und Politik zwischen Revolution und Inflation*,
Düsseldorf 1979.

Rabenau, F. von (ed.), *Seeckt. Aus meinem Leben 1918-1936*, Leipzig 1940.

Raphael, G., *Hugo Stinnes. Der Mensch. Sein Werk. Sein Wirken*, Berlin 1925.

Rathenau, W., *Die Absorption des Lichts in Metallen*, Berlin 1889.

—, *Impressionen*, Leipzig 1902.

—, *Reflexionen*, Leipzig 1908.

Rathenau, W., *Zur Kritik der Zeit*, Berlin 1912. Reprinted in E. Schulin (ed.), *Walther Rathenau. Hauptwerke und Gespräche*.

—, *Zur Mechanik des Geistes oder Vom Reich der Seele*, Berlin 1913. Reprinted in E. Schulin (ed.), *Walther Rathenau. Hauptwerke und Gespräche*.

—, *Deutschlands Rohstoffversorgung*, Berlin 1916.

—, *Von Kommenden Dingen*, Berlin 1917. Reprinted in E. Schulin (ed.), *Walther Rathenau. Hauptwerke und Gespräche*.

—, *Die Neue Wirtschaft*, Berlin 1919.

—, *Am Deutschlands Jugend*, Berlin 1918.

—, *Der Kaiser. Eine Betrachtung*, Berlin 1919.

—, *Der Neue Staat*, Berlin 1919.

—, *Kritik der dreifachen Revolution. Apologie*, Berlin 1919.

—, *Die Neue Gesellschaft*, Berlin 1919.

—, *Was wird werden?*, Berlin 1920.

—, *Cannes und Genua. Vier Reden zum Reparationsproblem*. Berlin 1922. Reprinted in W. Rathenau, *Gesammelte Reden*, Berlin 1924.

—, *Gesammelte Reden*, Berlin 1924.

—, *Briefe*, 2 vols., Dresden 1926.

—, *Neue Briefe*, Dresden 1927.

—, *Briefe. Neue Folge*, Dresden 1928.

—, *Gesammelte Schriften*, 5 vols., Berlin 1918 and 1925.

—, *Nachgelassene Schriften*, 2 vols., Berlin 1928.

—, *Politische Briefe*, Dresden 1929.

—, *Gesammelte Schriften*, 6 vols., Berlin 1929.

Redslob, E. (ed.), *Walther Rathenau. Blanche Trocard*, Berlin 1947.

Reiss, K. P. (ed.), *Von Bannermann zu Stresemann. Die Sitzungen des national-liberalen Zentralvorstandes 1912-1917*, Düsseldorf 1967.

Rich, N., *Friedrich von Holstein. Politics and Diplomacy in the Era of Bismarck and Wilhlem II*, 2 vols. Cambridge 1965.

Rich, N. and Fisher, M. (eds.), *The Holstein Papers*, 4 vols., Cambridge 1955-64.

Riedler, A., *Emil Rathenau und das Werden der Grosswirtschaft*, Berlin 1916.

Ritter, G., *Staatskunst und Kriegshandwerk. Das Problem des Militarismus in Deutschland*, 4 vols., München 1954-68.

Röhl, J., 'Staatsstreichplan oder Staatsstreichbereitschaft? Bismarcks Politik in der Entlassungskrise', *Historische Zeitschrift*, 203, 1966.

—, *Germany without Bismarck. The Crisis of Government in the Second Reich 1890-1900*, London 1967.

—, (ed.), *1914: Delusion or Design? The Testimony of two German Diplomats*, London 1973.

Rogge, H., *Holstein und Harden. Politisch-publizistisches Zusammenspiel zweier Aussenseiter des Wilhelminischen Reichs*, München 1959.

Rosen, I., *Aus einem diplomatischen Wanderleben*, vols. iii and iv, Wiesbaden 1959.

Rosenfeld, G., *Sowjetrussland und Deutschland 1917-1922*, Berlin1960.

Salewski, M., *Entwaffnung und Militärkontrolle in Deutschland 1919-1927*, München 1966.

Scherer, A. and Grunewald, J. (eds.), *L'Allemagne et les problèmes de la paix pendant la Première Guerre Mondiale*, Paris 1962.

Schiefel, U., *Bernhard Dernburg 1865-1937. Kolonialpolitiker und Bankier im Wilhelminischen Deutschland*, Zürich, 1975.

Schmitz, H., *Schloss Freienwalde*, Berlin 1928.

Schnee, H., *Als letzter Gouverneur in Deutsch-Ostafrika. Erinnerungen*, Heidelberg 1964.

Schröder, E., *Otto Wiedfeldt. Eine Biographie*, Essen 1964.

Schulin, E., 'Die Rathenaus—Zwei Generationen jüdischen Anteils an der industriellen Entwicklung Deutschlands', W. E. Mosse and A. Paucker (eds.), *Juden im Wilhelminischen Deutschland 1890-1914*, Tübingen 1976.

— (ed.), *Walther Rathenau. Hauptwerke und Gespräche*, München and Heidelberg 1977.

—, *Walther Rathenau. Repräsentant. Kritiker und Opfer seiner Zeit*. Göttingen 1979.

Schulthess, Europäischer Geschichtskalender, München 1918 ff.

Schulze-Bidlingmaier, I. (ed.), *Die Kabinette Wirth I und II*, 2 vols., Boppard 1973.

Schwabach, P. von, *Aus meinem Akten*, Berlin 1927.

Schwabe, K., *Deutsche Revolution und Wilsonfrieden. Die amerikanische und deutsche Friedensstrategie zwischen Ideologie und Machtpolitik 1918-1919*, Düsseldorf 1971.

Seidenzahl, F., *Hundert Jahre Deutsche Bank 1870-1970*, Frankfurt 1970.

Seymour, C. (ed.), *The Intimate Papers of Colonel House*, 2 vols., London 1926.

Sheehan, J., *German Liberalism in the Nineteenth Century*, Chicago 1978.

Simon, H. F., *Reparation und Wiederaufbau*, Berlin 1925.

—, *Aus Walther Rathenaus Leben*, Dresden 1927.

Smith, W., *The German Colonial Empire*, North Carolina 1978.

Sombart, W., *Die Juden und das Wirtschaftsleben*, 2nd edn., München/Leipzig 1918.

Soutou, G., 'Die deutschen Reparationen und das Seydoux-Projekt', *Vierteljahrshefte für Zeitgeschichte*, 23, 1975.

Stegmann, D., *Die Erben Bismarcks. Parteien und Verbände in der Spätphase des wilhelminischen Deutschlands*, Köln/Berlin 1970.

Steinberg, J., 'Diplomatie als Wille und Vorstellung: Die Berliner Mission Lord Haldanes im Februar 1912', H. Schottelius and W. Deist (eds.), *Marine und Marinepolitik im Kaiserlichen Deutschland 1871-1914*, 2nd edn., Düsseldorf 1981.

Stenkewitz, K., '*Immer feste drufff!' Zabernaffäre 1913*, Berlin 1962.

Stern, F., 'Bethmann Hollweg and the War: The Limits of Responsibility'.

Stoecker, W. (ed.), *Drang nach Afrika*, Berlin 1977.

Strobel, A., 'Die Gründung des Züricher Elektrotrusts. Ein Beitrag zum Unternehmergeschäft der deutschen Elektroindustrie 1895-1900', E. Hassinger, J. H. Müller, and H. Ott (eds.), *Geschichte—Wirtschaft—Gesellschaft*, Festschrift für Clemens Bauer zum 75. Geburstag, Berlin 1974.

—, 'Zur Einführung der Dampfturbine auf dem deutschen Markt 1900 bis 1914 unter besonderer Berücksichtigung der Brown, Boveri & Cie AG Baden (Schweiz) und Mannheim', *Landesgeschichte und Geistesgeschichte*, Festschrift für Otto Herding zum 65. Geburstag, Stuttgart 1977.

Tardieu, A., *Le Mystère d'Agadir*, Paris 1912.

Taylor, A. J. P., *The Struggle for Mastery in Europe 1848-1918*, repr. Oxford 1957.

—, *English History 1914-1945*, London 1965.

Tetzlaff, R., *Koloniale Entwicklung und Ausbeutung. Wirtschafts- und Sozialgeschichte Deutschostafrikas 1885-1914*, Berlin 1970.

Thompson, L. M., *The Unification of South Africa 1902-1910*, London 1960.

Tirpitz, A. von, *Politische Dokumente*, i, *Der Aufbau der deutschen Weltmacht*, Berlin 1924.

Trachtenberg, M., *Reparation in World Politics. France and European Economic Diplomacy, 1916–1923*, New York 1980.

Trebitsch-Lincoln, J. T., *Der grösste Abenteurer des 20. Jahrhunderts! Die Wahrheit über mein Leben*, Wien 1931.

Uhsadel, W. (ed.), *Friedrich Naumann. Werke*, 6 vols., Köln 1964–9.

Ullmann, H. P., *Der Bund der Industriellen*, Göttingen 1976.

Vierhaus, R. (ed.), *Das Tagebuch der Baronin Spitzemberg*, Göttingen 1960.

Vietsch, E. von, *Wilhelm Solf. Botschafter zwischen den Zeiten*, Tübingen 1961.

Walker, M., *Germany and the Emigration 1816–1885*, Harvard 1964.

Weber, H., *Ludendorff und die Monopole. Deutsche Kriegspolitik 1916–1918*, Berlin 1966.

Weber, M., 'Der Nationalstaat und die Volkswirtschaftspolitik', in *Gesammelte politische Schriften*, 2nd edn., Tübingen 1958.

Wehler, H. U., 'Der Fall Zabern', *Die Welt als Geschichte*, 23, 1963.

Weinberger, G., *An den Quellen der Apartheid. Studien über koloniale Ausbeutung und Herrschaftsmethoden in Südafrika und die Zusammenarbeit des deutschen Imperialismus mit dem englischen Imperialismus und den burischen Nationalisten (1902–1914)*, Berlin 1975.

Wermuth, A., *Ein Beamtenleben*, Berlin 1922.

Wernecke, K., *Der Wille zur Weltgeltung. Aussenpolitik und Öffentlichkeit im Kaiserreich am Vorabend des Ersten Weltkrieges*, Düsseldorf 1969.

White, D., *The Splintered Party. National Liberalism in Hessen and the Reich, 1867–1918*, Cambridge, Mass. 1976.

Willequet, J., *Le Congo Belge et la Weltpolitik (1894–1914)*, Brussels 1962.

Williamson, D. G., 'Walther Rathenau: A Study of his political, industrial and cultural activities and of his reputation in contemporary Germany 1893–June 1921', unpublished Ph.D. thesis, London 1972.

—, 'Pro and Contra Rathenau: The Controversy in the German Press 1914–1918', *Wiener Library Bulletin*, 28, 1975.

—, 'Walther Rathenau: Patron Saint of the German Liberal Establishment (1922–1972)', *Leo Baeck Yearbook*, 20, 1975.

—, 'Walther Rathenau: Realist, Pedagogue and Prophet, November 1918–May 1921', *European Studies Review*, 6, 1976.

—, 'Walther Rathenau and the KRA August 1914–March 1915', *Zeitschrift für Unternehemensgeschichte*, 23, 1978.

Williamson, J., *Karl Helfferich 1872–1924. Economist, Financier, Politician*, Princeton 1971.

Wilson, K., 'The Agadir Crisis; the Mansion House Speech and the Double-Edgedness of Agreements', *Historical Journal*, 15, 1972.

Witt, P. C., *Die Finanzpolitik des Deutschen Reiches 1903–1913*, Lübeck 1970.

Woodward, E. L. and Butler, R. (eds.), *Documents on British Foreign Policy 1919–1939*, London 1946 ff.

Wulf, P. (ed.), *Das Kabinett Fehrenbach*, Boppard 1972.

—, *Hugo Stinnes. Wirtschaft und Politik 1918–1924*, Stuttgart 1979.

Young, H. F., *Maximilian Harden. Censor Germaniae. The Critic in Opposition from Bismarck to the Rise of Nazism*, The Hague 1959.

Zechlin, E., 'Deutschland zwischen Kabinettskrieg und Wirtschaftskrieg. Politik und Kriegsführung in den ersten Monaten des Weltkrieges 1914', *Historische Zeitschrift*, 199, 1964.

Zechlin, E., *Krieg und Kriegsrisiko. Zur deutschen Politik im Ersten Weltkrieg. Aufsätze*, Düsseldorf 1979.

Zimmermann, A., *Mit Dernburg nach Ostafrika*, Berlin 1908.

Zmarzlik, H. G., *Bethmann Hollweg als Reichskanzler 1909-1914. Studien zur Möglichkeiten und Grenzen seiner innenpolitischen Machtstellung*, Düsseldorf 1957.

Zsigmond, L., *Zur deutschen Frage 1918-1923*, Budapest 1964.

Zunkel, F., *Industrie und Staatssozialismus. Der Kampf um die Wirtschafts-ordnung in Deutschland 1914-1918*, Düsseldorf 1974.

BIOGRAPHICAL INDEX

Page references are to the introduction, the text, and the notes.

Abercorn, Duke of (1838-1913), President of the British South Africa Company, 63

Aehrenthal, Alois Count von (1854-1912), Austro-Hungarian Foreign Minister (1906-11), 168

Ahrens, Gustav (1860-1914), banker (BHG), 96, 108, 109, 117

Albert, Eugen d' (1864-1932), pianist and composer, 110, 179

Albert, Heinrich (1874-1938), assistant to the German Commissioner for the World Fair at St. Louis (1904); head of the Reich Chancellery (1919-21); Treasury (1922-3); Ministry of Reconstruction (1923), 149, 183, 242

Albert, King of Saxony (1828-1902), reigned from 1873, 125

Alberti-Sittenfeld, journalist with the *Berliner Morgenpost*, 30

Alberts, 101

Ali Seid (*1885), Sultan of Zanzibar (1902-11), 37

Allen, Henry T. (1859-1930), American General at Koblenz (1919-23), 276

Alma-Tadema, Sir Lawrence (1836-1912), painter, 64

Andersen, Danish Privy Councillor, 204, 207

Anderson, Roy Dunlop (*1878), District Commissioner, 33

André, Arnold, tobacco industrialist, 182

Andrea del Castagno (1423-57), painter, 129

Andreae, Fritz (1873-1950), banker; married Edith Rathenau (1883-1952), 5, 99, 102, 103, 107, 116, 122, 149, 165, 178, 192, 281

Angelico, Fra (1387/8-1455), painter, 129

Annunzio, Gabriele d' (1863-1938), poet, 113

Arnhold, Eduard (1849-1926), coal magnate, 162

Arnim, Bettina von (1785-1859), Goethe's ward, 140, 141

Arnswaldt, Bertha von (1850-1919), 102, 151

Asch, Robert (1859-1929), doctor, 159

Aselmeier, Consul, 30

Asquith, H. H. (1852-1928), Prime Minister (1908-16), 133, 147

Aubrun, French civil servant, 287

Augusta, Queen of Prussia and German Empress (1811-90), reigned 1861-88, 166

Avenol, Joseph L. (1870-1952), French financial delegate in London (1916-23); reparation expert; Deputy Secretary-General of the League of Nations (1933-1940), 284

Bach, Johann Sebastian (1685-1750), composer, 179

Back, Karl A. (1834-1917), Mayor of Strasbourg, President of the Upper Chamber of the Landtag of Alsace-Lorraine (1911), 181

Baden, Prince Max von (1867-1929), Imperial Chancellor (1918), 232, 233, 234, 235, 236

Baden-Powell, Robert Stephenson (1851-1941), General, 69

Bagot, Walter L. (*1864), General Manager of the Victoria Falls and Transvaal Power Company, 67

Bahr, Hermann (1863-1934), author, 144

Baker, Guy S. (*1882), forest officer, Colonial Office, 33

Baker, Sir Herbert, architect, 65

Baldwin, Stanley (1867-1947), President of the Board of Trade (1921-2), 273, 275

Balfour, Arthur J. (1848-1930), Prime Minister (1902-5); Foreign Secretary (1916-19); Lord President of the Council (1919-29), 276, 277

Ballin, Albert (1857-1918), Managing Director of HAPAG, 29, 60, 106, 130, 135, 144, 146, 148, 151, 152, 168, 170, 171, 172, 183, 197, 198, 204, 218

Baltzer, Franz (*1857), railway expert, 30, 116

Barrère, Camille (1851-1940), French Ambassador in Rome (1898-1924), 127

Bartenwerffer, Major-General Paul G. von (1867-1928), Director of the Political Department of the General Staff, 216

Basch, Emanuel (*1868), Mayor of Bulawayo and Justice of the Peace, 70

Bassermann, Ernst (1854–1917), National Liberal politician, 96, 105, 132

Bauer, Gustav A. (1870–1944), Social Democrat; Reich Chancellor (1919–20); Minister of Transport (1921); thereafter Vice-Chancellor and Minister of the Treasury, 268

Bauer, Max (1867–1929), artillery officer, adviser to Ludendorff, 229, 239, 240, 241, 242, 243

Baur, 109

Beak, George B. (1872–1934), Vice-Consul in Katanga (1908–11); later Consul-General in the United States, 64

Beaverbrook, Lord (1879–1965), British newspaper publisher; Minister of Information (1918), 286

Bebel, August (1840–1913), Chairman of the SPD (1815–1913), 96

Beck, photographer, 30

Beethoven, Ludwig van (1770–1827), composer, 122, 179

Begas, Carl (1845–1916), sculptor, 149, 156, 178

Behmer, Marcus (1879–1958), drawer and etcher, 146

Behn, Fritz (*1878), sculptor, 140, 152

Behrens, Peter (1869–1940), painter and architect, 116, 123, 145

Bell, Charles (*1853), Civil Commissioner and Resident Magristrate, 66

Bell, Henry Fitzgerald (1880–1910), colonial civil servant, 33

Bellini, Giovanni (1430–1516), painter, 111

Below-Rutzau, Gustav von (1855–1940), Prussian Envoy to Stuttgart (1907–15), 160

Bemelmans, Belgian representative on the Reparation Commission, 266, 286, 287

Bénac, André-Jean (1858–1937), President of the Paris Electricity Company; President of the Paris–Lyon Railway, 162

Beradt, Martin (*1881), lawyer, 98, 169

Bergman, B. A., Deputy Mayor of Upington, 71

Bergmann, Karl (1874–1934), banker (Orient Bank) (1911); representative on the Reparation Commission; Under-Secretary in the Treasury, 255, 263, 265

Berliner, Alfred, Managing Director of Siemens-Schuckert (1903–12), 152

Bernhard, Georg (1875–1944), social thinker and publicist; editor-in-chief of the Vossische Zeitung (1913–30); member of the Reichstag (1928–30), 165

Bernheimer, 140

Bernstorff, Johann Count von (1862–1939), Ambassador in Washington (1908–17); Ambassador in Constantinople (1917–18), 210

Bestelmeyer, German (1874–1942), architect, 102, 107

Bethmann, Renate von, née Countess Harrach (*1882), 151

Bethmann Hollweg, Theobald von (1856–1921), Prussian Minister of the Interior (1905); Secretary of the Interior (1907–9); Imperial Chancellor (1909–17); married Martha van Pfuel (1856–1914), 93, 94, 96, 102, 104, 105, 114, 125, 126, 132, 133, 134, 135, 136, 144, 146, 148, 149, 151, 152, 158, 163, 164, 167, 170, 173, 174, 175, 181, 183, 184, 185, 186, 191, 192, 194, 206, 207, 208, 210, 211, 213, 219, 220, 221, 222, 223, 224, 225, 226, 229, 230, 231

Bethusy-Huc, Valeska Countess von (1849–1926), authoress, 151

Birkenhead, Lord (1872–1830), Lord Chancellor (1918–22), 281

Bismarck, Otto Prince von (1815–98), Imperial Chancellor (1870–90), 102, 124, 127, 166, 167, 201, 229

Bismarck, von, a member of the Bismarck family, 156

Bjerre, Paul (*1876), Swedish doctor, philosopher, 193

Blackett, Sir Basil (1882–1935), financial expert; Treasury representative in Washington (1917–19); adviser to the Viceroy of India (1922); Director of the Bank of England (1929–31), 273, 274, 275, 282, 283, 284, 285, 286

Blanche, Jacques Emile (1861–1942), painter, 99

Blankenburg, Captain, 223

Blankenstein (1880–1964), Dutch journalist, correspondent of the Nieuwe Rotterdamsche Courant, 246

Blaserna, Pietro (1836–1918), physicist, 127

Blei, Franz (1871–1942), author, 144, 152

Bleloch, William E. (1863–1946), geologist, 71

Blücher, Prince Gebhard von (1742–1819), General and Field Marshal in the wars against Napoleon, 200

Blüthgen, Clara (1856–1934), authoress, 96

Bockys, farmer, 71

Boddien, Franziska von, née Schröder (1872–1944), 124, 146

Bode, Arnold W. von (1845–1929), art historian, Director-General of the Berlin museums (1906–20), 160

Bodenhausen, Eberhard Freiherr von (1868–1918), member of the board of directors of Krupp (1906–16); married Dorothea Countess von Degenfeld-Schonburg (*1877), 99, 103, 104, 108, 109, 111, 114, 115, 117, 123, 131, 132, 137, 138, 139, 140, 146, 170, 177, 190, 215

Böder, Gustav (1860–1910), colonial civil servant, 36

Böhm, farmer, 41

Bötticher, Karl H. von (1833–1907), Secretary of the Interior (1880); Lord Lieutenant of Saxony (1897–1906), 125

Bohlen-Halbach, Gustav Krupp von (1870–1950), 12, 109

Bollert, National Liberal Reichstaf deputy, 106

Bonar Law, Andrew (1858–1923), leader of the Conservative-Unionist Party (1911–21); Prime Minister (1922–3), 286

Bongard, O., journalist, 30, 41, 61, 71

Bonn, Moritz J. (1873–1966), political economist, publicist, and politician, 244, 246, 247

Borchardt, Rudolf (1877–1945), scholar and poet, 128

Borel, Henri (1869–1933), Dutch author, 193

Borsig, Ernst von (1869–1933), industrialist, 240, 241

Bosch, Jonkheer Willem van den (1848–1914), Dutch Royal Chamberlain, 118

Botha, Louis (1862–1919), Commander-in-Chief in the Boer War after 1900; Prime Minister of the Transvaal (1907); Prime Minister of South Africa (1910–19), 68, 69

Bourdon, Georges (1868–1938), journalist, 162

Boveri, Walter (1865–1924), industrialist, 113

Boyden, Ronald W. (1863–1931), unofficial observer for the United States Government at the Reparation Commission (1920–3), 287, 288

Bradbury, Sir John (1872–1950), economic expert, financial adviser to the British Government (1914–1918), delegate to the Reparation Commission (1919), Chairman of the Food Council, 278, 286, 288

Brahm, Otto (1856–1912), theatre director, founder of the Freie Bühne association, 117, 118, 145, 146

Brahms, Johannes (1833–1897), composer, 179

Brauer, Ludolph (1865–1951), surgeon, 179

Breitenbach, Paul von (1850–1930), Minister of Public Works (1906–18), 182, 217

Breithaupt, Ernst (*1861), National Liberal politician; publisher, 129, 130

Briand, Aristide (1862–1932), French statesman, 125, 253, 265, 269, 272, 278, 279, 280, 281, 282, 283, 284, 285, 286, 290, 291

Brill, Heinrich A. (*1876), District Officer (1908–11); department head in the Ministry of Reconstruction (1920), 73

Brion, antiquary, 112

Bronn, H., Consul, 31

Bronsart von Schellendorff, Bernhard (1866–1952), Major, 143

Bronsart von Schellendorff, Günther (1868–1947), General, 143

Brüning, Gustav von (1864–1913), chemicals manufacturer (Höchst), 114, 117, 120

Bruhn, Bruno (1872–1925), member of the board of directors of Krupp, 114, 138

Bruhns, Leopold P. (*1884), art historian, 108

Buber, Martin (1878–1965), philosopher, 193

Bülow, Bernhard Prince von (1849–1929), Imperial Chancellor (1900–9); married Maria Princess di Camporeale (1848–1929), 27, 28, 29, 41, 44, 47, 48, 72, 75, 76, 77, 93, 94, 96, 105, 124, 125, 126, 127, 128, 132, 133, 135, 141, 145, 163, 166, 168, 222, 226, 241

Bülow, Carl von (1846–1921), Prussian General, 114, 118, 140

Burchardt, Georg, author, 144, 151

Burian von Rajecz, Stefan Count (1851–1922), Austro-Hungarian Foreign Minister (1915–16 and 1918), 229

Burke, Edmund (1721–97), statesman and political writer, 281

Caillaux, Joseph (1863–1944), Radical Socialist, Finance Minister, several times between 1909 and 1914. Prime Minister (1911–12), 120

Cambon, Jules-Martin (1845–1935), French Ambassador in Berlin (1907–14); Chairman of the Conference of Ambassadors (1919–31), 120, 140, 147, 157, 158, 160

Cambon, Paul (1843–1924), French Ambassador in London (1898–1914), 147

Caprivi, Leo Count von (1831–99), Imperial Chancellor (1890–4), 163

Carolan, 288

Cartwright, Sir Fairfax (1857-1928), British Ambassador in Vienna (1908-13), 133, 134

Cassel, Sir Ernest J. (1852-1921), banker, 62, 64

Cassirer, Lotte, née Jacobi (*1881), married Hugo Cassirer, 118

Cassirer, Paul (1871-1926), art publisher, married Tilla Durieux, 108, 156

Castellane, Countess, 287

Cauer, Wilhelm (*1858), engineer, railway expert, 106

Cave, Sir Basil (1865-1931), Consul-General, 37

Centurione, 109, 126, 128

Chamberlain, Houston Stuart (1855-1927), anti-semitic author, 142, 143

Chamberlain, Joseph (1836-1914), British Colonial Secretary (1895-1903), 62

Chelius, Oskar von (1859-1923), composer, 104, 105

Chopin, Frederic (1810-1849), composer, 110

Christian, Johannes, Chief of the Bondelzwarts, 72

Christophe, 144

Churchill, John (1880-1947), Winston Churchill's brother, 281

Churchill, Winston (1874-1965), President of the Board of Trade (1908-10); Home Secretary (1910-11); First Lord of the Admiralty (1911-15); Minister of Munitions (1917-18); Secretary for War and for Air (1918-21); Colonial Secretary (1921-2), 62, 147, 152, 281

Clemen, Oskar (1866-1947), art historian; married Elisabeth von Wätjen, 102, 103

Clemenceau, Georges (1841-1929), French Premier (1906-9, and 1917-20), 279

Codrington, Robert (1869-1908), civil servant, 70

Cohn, Oskar (1869-1935), Reichstag deputy (1912-18); USPD member of the Reichstag and member of the Prussian Chamber of Deputies (1921-4), 241

Coleman, John W. (*1860), postmaster, 66

Collier, Price (1860-1913), journalist; married Katharine Dalano, 137, 138, 139, 140, 142, 143, 145, 146

Colombo, Giuseppe (1836-1921), engineer and chemist, 129

Conrad von Hötzendorf, Count Franz (1852-1925), Colonel-General, Chief of the Austro-Hungarian General Staff (1906-17), 206

Conti, Ettore (*1871), engineer and industrialist, 129

Conze, Peter (*1860), Director in the Colonial Office (1907); Under-Secretary in the Colonial Office (1911-15); Commissioner for Damages Abroad (1920), 179

Coquelin, Jean (1865-1944), actor, 127

Cova, 111, 150

Crewe, Lord (*1858-1945), Irish Viceroy (1892-5); Colonial Secretary (1908-10); Secretary for India (1910-15); Ambassador in Paris (1922-8), 62

Currie, Henry A. F. (1866-1912), General Manager of the Uganda Railway, 38

Curzon, George Nathaniel Lord (1859-1925), Foreign Secretary 1919-24, 269

D'Abernon, Lord (1857-1941), British Ambassador in Berlin (1920-6), 246, 247, 248, 286

Däumig, Ernst (1866-1922), USPD and Communist member of the Reichstag (1920-2), 241

Dahlmann, Colonel, 191

Dallwitz, Johann von (1855-1919), Prussian Minister of the Interior (1910-14); Governor of Alsace-Lorraine (1914), 182

Darcy, Henry (1840-1926), French industrialist, 95

Dartnell, Sir John G. (1838-1913), General, 64

Daumier, Honoré (1808-79), French painter and lithographer, 122

David, Edward (1863-1930), Social Democrat, 230

Degenfeld-Schonburg, Ottonie Countess von, née Schwartz (*1882), daughter of Margarethe, née Schröder, 138, 140

Dehmel, Richard (1863-1920), poet, 99, 143, 144, 153, 168

Delacroix, Léon (1865-1929), Belgian politician, Minister of Finance, and Premier (1918-20), 266, 286

Delarey, Jacobus H. (1848-1914), General in the Boer War; politician (Het Volk), 68

Delbrück, Clemens von (1856-1921), Secretary of the Interior (1909-16); Chief of the Civil Cabinet (1918), 149, 175, 184, 185, 191

Delbrück, Hans (1848-1929), historian and political publicist, 175

Delbrück, Ludwig (1860-1913), banker, Keeper of the Privy Purse to Wilhelm II, 99, 117, 178

Delcassé, Theophile (1852-1923), French Foreign Minister (1898-1905); Minister of the Navy (1911-12); Ambassador in St. Petersburg (1913); Foreign Minister (1914-15), 120, 127, 167

Dernburg, Bernhard (1865-1937), Director of the Bank für Handel und Industrie (1901-6); Deputy Director of the Colonial Department (September 1906); Colonial Secretary (May 1907-10); member of the Prussian Upper House (1913); Minister of Finance (1919); Reichstag deputy, 27, 28, 29, 30, 41, 44, 47, 48, 60, 61, 65, 70, 71, 73, 75, 76, 77, 93, 103, 114, 115, 151, 155, 160, 165, 170, 178, 182, 244

Dernburg, Hermann (*1868), architect, 114, 118

Dessoir, Max (1867-1947), psychologist and art expert, 102

Deutsch, Felix (1858-1928), member of the board of the AEG; Chairman (1915-22); Managing Director (1922-8); married Lili Kahn (1869-1940), 22, 24, 77, 97, 98, 99, 104, 108, 110, 111, 113, 122, 123, 130, 131, 132, 139, 141, 143, 155, 156, 157, 158, 160, 165, 168, 169, 170, 171, 172, 173, 176, 177, 192, 197, 198, 199, 200, 202, 247

Dewey, George (1837-1917), American Admiral, 174

Dewitz, von, farmer, 74

Diezelsky, Georg von, landowner, 101, 102, 103, 104, 155

Dill, Ludwig (*1848), painter, 102

Dinglinger, Captain, 115

Dohme, Frau, married Richard Dohme, art historian (1845-93), 105, 139

Dohna-Schlobitten, Prince Richard von (1843-1916), 200, 202

Donatello, Donato di Niccolo (1386-1466), sculptor, 45

Donnay, Charles M. (1859-1945), French dramatist, 129

Drewes, Hans (*1880), engineer; Director of the Allgemeine Deutsche Kleinbahn AG, 108

Drews, Wilhelm (1870-1938), Under-Secretary; then Prussian Minister of the Interior (1917-18); President of the Prussian Supreme Court for Administrative Law (1921-37), 191

Drummond-Ramsay, Sir Arthur (1876-1935), British politician; Under-Secretary in the Foreign Office (1919-21), 207

Dubois, Louis (*1859), French deputy since 1910; Postmaster-General and Minister of Commerce (1919-20); Delegate to and Chairman of the Reparation Commission (1922-8), 267, 286, 288

Düring (*1885), Prussian Minister of Food and Agriculture (1920), 243

Dufour, Albert Freiherr von (1868-1945), Councillor at the German Embassy in London (1920), 283

Dunn, Sir Charles, 281

Dunning, Officer, 64

Durieux, Tilla (1880-1971), actress, 108, 118

Ebert, Friedrich (1821-1925), German President (1919-25), 224, 241, 268, 269, 270, 291

Edison, Thomas A. (1847-1931), engineer, 4

Edward VII, King of Great Britain and Ireland (1841-1910), reigned from 1901, 94, 114

Eeden, Frederick Willem van (1860-1932), Dutch poet and author, 157, 193

Ehrenthal, Bruno P. von (1879-1942), engineer, 190

Ehrhardt, Hermann, Captain, 241

Eich, Nicolaus (1866-1919), Managing Director of Mannesmann-Röhrenwerke (1900-19), member of the executive board of the Hansabund, 131, 190

Eilender, Walter, industrialist (Richard Lindenberg AG), 111, 123

Eisenhart-Rothe, Ernst von (*1862), General, 199, 202

Eitel, Albert (*1866), architect, 130

Ekkehard, (c.1260-1327), German mystic, 123

Eloesser, Arthur (1870-1938), theatre critic of the Vossische Zeitung, 118

Endell, Ernst M. (1871-1925), architect and designer (art nouveau), 103, 121, 139, 146

Endt, Hermann vom, architect, 103

Engeland, military staff doctor, 41

Engelhardt, Victor (1866-1944), industrialist, 103, 146

Enver, Pasha (1881-1922), Turkish Minister of War (1908-18), 205

Erzberger, Matthias (1875-1921), Reichstag deputy (Centre Party), Minister of Finance (1919-20); murdered, 99, 106, 109, 138, 173, 174, 175, 182, 196, 197, 223, 224, 229, 230

Escher, Nanny von, 137

Estdorff, Ludwig von (1859-1943), General, 72

Eulenberg, Herbert (1876-1949), author, 103, 121

Eulenburg, August, Count zu (1838-1921), Lord Chamberlain and Minister of the Royal Household, 101, 102, 111, 112

Eulenburg, Prince Philipp zu (1847-1921), Ambassador in Vienna (1894-1902); friend of Wilhelm II, 135

Ewers, Hans H. (1871-1943), poet, 99, 104, 121, 122, 137, 145

Ewest, 125

Eysler, Edmund (1874-1949), composer of operettas, 146

Fänder, A. AEG engineer, 102, 130

Falkenhayn, Erich von (1861-1922), Prussian Minister of War (1913-15); Chief of the General Staff (1914-16), 22, 188, 189, 191, 193, 194, 196, 198, 200, 201, 203, 205, 206, 207, 213, 225

Farrar, Sir George (1859-1915), mining magnate and politician, 68

Farrar, John P. (1857-1929), politician, 64, 69

Favreau, 132

Fehrenbach, Konstantin (1852-1926), Reichstag deputy (Centre Party), Reich Chancellor (1920-1), 244, 248, 251, 252, 253

Fink, Daniel, Rabbi, 115

Firle, Walter (1859-1929), painter, 114, 123, 124, 130, 132, 142, 149

Fischel, Arthur (†1913), bank director (Mendelssohn & Co.), 178

Fischer, Hermann (1897-1922), one of Rathenau's assassins, 11

Fischer, Johann D. (*1873), Under-Secretary in the Ministry of Finance (1921); represented the German Government at the Reparation Commission in Paris (1921-4), 284, 285, 286, 288, 289

Fischer, Samuel (1859-1934), publisher, 22, 135, 136, 144, 146, 149, 177

Fischer, Theodor (1862-1938), architect, 102

Fitzgerald, Sir Maurice (1844-1927), banker, 62

Fitzpatrick, Sir James, politician, 69

Flake, Otto (1880-1963), author, 144

Fletcher, Patrick (1867-1948), railway designer, 71

Flossmann, Josef (1862-1914), sculptor, 102

Flotow, Friedrich von (1812-83), composer, 103, 152

Flotow, Hans von (*1862), diplomat and banker, envoy in Brussels (1913-14), owner of Hardy & Co. bank, 244

Foch, Ferdinand (1851-1929), Marshal of France, 246, 250, 278

Fränkel, Professor (Medicine), 172

France, Anatole (1844-1924), poet, 113

Francke, Max (*1867), Director of the Goerz Mining Group, 67

Frank, Wolfgang (*1871), Consul, 67

Frankenberg und Proschnitz, Victor von (*1873), District Officer, 74

Frantzen, Jakob (*1865), paper manufacturer, 106

Frantzius, von, retired Director in the German Foreign Office, 128

Freitag, Pastor, 133

Frey, Emil, President of the Schweizer Kreditanstalt, 110

Frey, Julius, industrialist, 146, 150, 154, 171

Frey, Karl (1857-1917), art historian, 111

Freytag, 281

Fricke, Wilhelm (*1865), AEG engineer, 106, 113, 116, 137, 142, 145

Friedberg, Robert (1851-1920), National Liberal politician and economist, 214

Friedländer-Fuld, Friedrich von (1858-1917), coal magnate; married Milly Fuld, 104, 107, 115, 116, 117, 118, 121, 131, 145, 153

Friedmann, 123

Friedrich Wilhelm II, King of Prussia (1744-97), reigned 1786-9, 101

Friedrich Wilhelm IV, King of Prussia (1795-1861), reigned 1840-61, 141

Fürstenberg, Carl (1850-1938), banker in the BHG, 68, 96, 101, 104, 108, 111, 113, 118, 123, 145, 153, 155, 162, 168, 169, 170, 171, 172, 179, 182, 198

Fürstenberg, Prince Max Egon von (1863-1941), 104

Fuhrmann, Paul (*1872), Reichstag deputy (National Liberal Party) (1907-12); member of the Prussian Chamber of Deputies (1913-18), 122, 123, 129

Gabler, Ernst (*1872), painter, 106

Garré, Carl (1857-1928), surgeon, 165

Gaul, Georg A. (1869-1921), sculptor, 102, 114, 132, 144, 145, 150

Geiger, Eugen (1865-1944), 214

Geitner, Hugo (1879-1942), Rathenau's secretary, 121, 129, 144, 145, 165, 190

George I, King of the Hellenes (1845-1913), reigned from 1863, 168

George V, King of Great Britain and Ireland/Northern Ireland (1865-1936), reigned from 1910, 147

George, Prince of Greece (*1869), 168

Gerard, James W. (1867-1951), American Ambassador in Berlin (1913-17), 207, 208, 209, 210, 211

Gessler, Otto (1875-1955), Democratic politician; Lord Mayor of Nürnberg (1914-19); Minister of Defence (1920-8), 244, 254

Gevers, Willem Baron von (1856-1927), Dutch Envoy in Berlin (1906-22), 101, 102, 107, 114, 115, 118

Ghislandi, Fra Vittore (1655-1743), painter, 129

Giannini, Amedeo, 246

Gide, André (1869-1951), poet, 113, 287

Giesbert, Johann (1865-1938), Centre Party politician, Postmaster-General (1919-22), 268

Gillet, 293

Gilly, Freidrich (1772-1800), architect, 98

Glatzel, Walther, industrialist, 98, 104, 107, 155

Glynn, Major, 131

Gnauth, Feodor (1854-1916), Managing Director of Felten & Guilleaume (1910-16), 120, 123, 139, 143

Gobineau, Joseph A. Comte de (1816-1882), racialist author, diplomat, 16, 142

Göhre, Paul (1864-1928), Social Democrat; Under-Secretary in the Prussian Ministry of State (1919-23), 242

Göppert, Heinrich (*1867), State Commissioner of the Berlin Stock Exchange (1909-14); Under-Secretary in the Prussian Ministry of Commerce (1917); later Professor of Law, 114

Göring, electrical engineer (AEG), 102

Goethe, Johann W. von (1749-1832), 141

Götzen, Adolf Count von (1866-1910), Governor of German East Africa (1901-6), 44

Goldberger, Ludwig M. (1848-1913), co-founder of the Dresdner Bank; adviser to Caprivi; President of the Association of Berlin Businessmen and Industrialists, 98

Goldmann, 60

Goldschmid, Alfons, journalist, 165

Goldschmidt, Adolph (1864-1944), art historian, 142

Goldschmidt, Karl (1857-1926), industrialist, 130

Goldschmidt-Rothschild senior, Max von (*1843), banker, 115

Goll, Johannes, banker, 287

Gontart, Paul von (*1868), Managing Director of the Deutsche Waffen und Munitionsfabriken, 179, 240

Gottschalk, Fritz (1853-1913), economist, 117

Graaff, Sir David P. de Villiers (1859-1931), South African Minister-without-Pottfolio in Merriman's Cabinet; later several times Minister of Public Works, 64, 65

Grässel, Hans (1860-1939), architect, 137

Grew, Joseph C. (*1880), American diplomat in Berlin (1912-17); Under-Secretary in the State Department (1944), 210

Grey, Edward (1862-1933), British Foreign Secretary (1905-16); created Viscount (1916), 125, 147, 160, 207, 208, 209, 210, 211

Grigg, Sir Edward (1879-1955), Private Secretary to Lloyd George (1921-2), 284

Groeben, Theodor von der (1868-1952), District Officer, 73

Groener, Wilhelm (1867-1939), General, Head of the War Office (1916), 216, 217, 230

Grönvold, Bernt (*1859), Norwegian painter; married to Minka, 124, 143, 145

Grossberg, industrialist, 122

Grünfeld, Alfred (1852-1924), pianist, 104

Grunelius, Marie von, née Tachard (*1861), 123

Grunwald, 151

Günther, Hans von (1864-1934), Under-Secretary in the Ministry of State (1907); Lord Lieutenant of Silesia (1910), 105, 165

Guggenheimer, Emil, member of the board of directors of the MAN, 255, 265

Guilbeaux, Henri (1884-1938), French socialist, 107

Guilleaume, Émil (1846-1913), industrialist (Felten & Guilleaume), 108

Guilleaume, Max von (1866-1932), industrialist (Felten & Guilleaume), 100, 108, 111

Guilleaume, Theodor von (1887-1933), industrialist (Felten & Guilleaume), 100, 107, 111

Gut, Belgian official, 287

Guthmann, oculist, 130

Gutkind, 157, 193

Gutmann, Eugen (1840-1925), banker (Dresdner Bank), 29, 132

Gwinner, Arthur von (1856-1925), banker (Deutsche Bank), 29, 150, 152

Haas, Robert (†1938), engineer, 122, 123

Haber, Fritz (1868-1934), chemical industrialist, 117

Hagen, Louis (1855-1932), banker and 'industrial matchmaker', 100, 102, 107, 130

Haguenin, Émile, French unofficial Envoy in Berlin; representative of the Allied Committee of Guarantees in Berlin, 287, 289

Hahn, Hermann (1868-1945), sculptor, 102, 103, 107, 115, 124, 137, 140

Halberstadt, farmer, 75

Haldane, Richard (1856-1928), British Secretary for War (1905-12); created Viscount (1916); Lord Chancellor (1912-15), 62, 146, 147, 148, 151, 173

Haller, Gerda, née von Wätjen (1886-1965), wife of the sculptor Hermann Haller (1880-1950), 108, 113, 114, 116

Hamsphon, Johann (1840-1926), member of the board of directors and later of the supervisory board of the AEG, 109, 132

Hanenfeldt, Paul von (*1877), officer, 71

Hang, Alfred, Consul in Zanzibar, 37

Haniel von Haimhausen, Edgar (1870-1935), diplomat; Under-Secretary in the Auswärtige Amt (1920); Reich representative in Munich (1923-30), 245, 270, 287

Harden, Maximilian (1861-1927), editor of Die Zukunft, 15, 28, 29, 60, 65, 76, 77, 94, 95, 96, 97, 99, 100, 105, 107, 113, 114, 133, 135, 139, 140, 143, 144, 155, 156, 157, 158, 160, 165, 166, 167, 168, 169, 170, 171, 172, 173, 175, 176, 192, 197, 198, 212, 213, 222, 233, 241, 244

Hardenberg, Karl A., Prince (1750-1822), Chancellor (1810-22), 164

Harding, Warren G. (1865-1923), Republican President of the United States (1921-3), 279

Hardt, Ernst (1876-1947), poet, 111, 115, 136

Harnack, Adolf von (1851-1930), Protestant theologian, 222

Harrach, Ferdinand Count (1832-1915), historical painter; married Countess Pourtalès, 129

Harrach, Hans A., Count (*1873); married Helene, Countess von Arco-Zinneberg (*1877), 111, 112, 129, 145, 146, 148, 151

Harris, farmer, 71, 74

Hartmann, Alma von (1854-1931), wife of Eduard von Hartmann, 101

Hartmann, Gustav von (1856-1943), Consul General, later Councillor, 30

Harvey, George (1864-1928), American Ambassador in London (1921-4), 276, 279

Hassinger, Director of the Otavi Gesellschaft, 74

Hauptmann, Benvenuto (*1900), Gerhart Hauptmann's youngest son, 136

Hauptmann, Carl (1858-1921), author, brother of Gerhart, 117

Hauptmann, Gerhart (1862-1946), author, married Margarethe Marschalk (1875-1957), 97, 100, 104, 106, 109, 110, 113, 123, 135, 136, 150, 160, 161, 170, 172, 193, 213

Hauptmann, Ivo (*1886), painter, 136

Havenstein, Rudolf (1857-1923), President of the Seehandelsbank, later the Reichsbank (1908-22), 118, 281

Heeringen, Josias von (1850-1926), Minister of War (1909-13), 153

Hegel, low-ranking civil servant, 166

Heilbut, Emil (1861-1921), art-critic, 117

Heimann, farmer, 71

Heimann, Moritz (1868-1925), author and editor for Fischer-Verlag, the publishing house; G. Hauptmann's brother-in-law, 132, 136, 145, 172

Heinemann, Elkan, banker and industrialist, 97, 132

Heinitz, von, farmer, 73

Heinlein, 142

Heinze, Rudolf (1865-1928), Under-Secretary in the Turkish Ministry of State (1916); Minister of Justice in Saxony (1918); Reich Minister of Justice (1922-3); member of the Reichstag (1907-23), 243

Helfferich, Karl (1872-1924), colonial civil servant (1901); Director of the Deutsche Bank (1906); Secretary of the Treasury (1915); Secretary of the Interior (1916); member of the Reichstag (1920-4), 218, 219, 220, 221

Hely-Hutchinson, Sir Walter (1849-1913), Governor of Cape Colony (1901-10); married May Justice, 64, 65

Henckel von Donnersmarck, Guido Prince (1830-1916), Silesian industrialist; married Katharina von Slepzow, 98, 104, 113, 144, 154, 156, 179, 193

Henckel von Donnersmarck, Valentin Count (1869-1940), Lord Chamberlain, 30, 41, 61, 74, 74, 75

Hennig, Alfred, Director of the Planiawerke, 109, 111, 131, 132

Hentsch, Lieutenant-Colonel, 193

Henwood, Charlie (*1857), Mayor of Durban, 66

Herberg, Carl von der (1862–1926), Director of Felten & Guilleaume, Managing Director (1921–6), 120, 190

Herbette, French Ambassador in Brussels (1922), 287, 288

Hermann, farmer, 73

Hertling, Georg Count von (1843–1919), Centre Party politician; Minister President of Bavaria (1912); Imperial Chancellor (1917–18), 174, 233

Herz, Paul, businessman, 144

Herzfeld, Marie, 139

Heydebrand und der Lasa, Ernst von (1851–1924), politician; leader of the Conservative Party, 125, 181

Heydebreck, Joachim von (1861–1914), officer, 74

Heye, Hermann (1865–1941), Managing Director of the Gerresheimer Glasshütte, 162

Heyking, Edmund Baron von (1850–1915), diplomat; married Countess Flemming, 113, 116, 151

Heymel, Alfred W. von (1878–1914), author, 138, 140, 143, 146, 152

Hildebrandt, District Officer, 75

Hill, Sir Clement (1845–1913), First Superintendent of African Protectorates in the British Foreign Office (1400–5), 39

Hille, low-ranking civil servant, 30

Hindenburg, Sophie von, née Countess zu Münster (1871–1933), married Konrad von Hindenburg (1839–1913), 108, 117, 121, 124, 140, 143, 149

Hindenburg und von Beneckendorff, Paul von (1847–1934), General, Chief of the General Staff (1916–18); German President (1925–34), 200, 201, 202, 203, 204, 215, 223, 224, 226, 230, 233

Hirschhorn, Friedrich (1862–1947), Director of the De Beers Company, 69, 71

Hirst, Francis W. (1873–1953), editor of The Economist, 152

His, Wilhelm (*1863), doctor, 160, 165

Hitchins, Charles (*1846), Minister of Public Works in Natal, 66

Hitz, Dora (*1856), painter, 117, 121, 122, 139, 178

Hoensbroech, Paulus Count von (1887–1931), farmer, 74

Hösch, Leopold von (1881–1936), diplomat, Councillor at the German Embassy in Paris (1921–3); Chargé d'Affaires in Paris (1923–4); Ambassador in Paris (1924–32); Ambassador in London (1932–6), 287

Hoffmann, Ludwig (1852–1932), architect and town-planner, 102, 182

Hoffmann, Maximilian (1869–1927), General, 200, 201, 202, 203, 204, 234

Hofmann, Julius (1859–1916), editor of the Münchener Allgemeine Zeitung, 105, 145

Hofmann, Ludwig von (1861–1945), painter, 160

Hofmannsthal, Hugo von (1874–1929), poet, 104, 106, 109, 138, 140, 143, 172, 177, 215

Holländer, Felix (1867–1931), drama producer and journalist, 98, 136, 151

Hollmann, Fritz von (1842–1913), Admiral, Secretary of the Navy (1890–7), 106, 114, 117, 144, 146, 171, 178

Holstein, Friedrich von (1837–1909), Councillor in the Auswärtige Amt (1876–1906), 127, 128, 135

Holzmann, Wilhelm (†1913), industrialist, 144, 146

Horne, Sir Robert (1871–1940), Minister of Labour (1919–20); President of the Board of Trade (1920–1); Chancellor of the Exchequer (1921–2), 273, 275, 276, 278, 279, 280, 281, 282, 283, 284, 285

Hornung, journalist, 30, 41

House, Edward M. (1867–1931), Colonel, President Wilson's personal representative, 209, 210, 211

Huck, newspaper editor, 103

Hülsen-Haeseler, Dietrich Count von (1852–1908), General; Chief of the Military Cabinet (1901–8), 126

Hültscher, District Officer, 74

Huerta, Victoriano (1854–1916), President of Mexico, 181

Hugenberg, Alfred (1865–1951), member of the board of directors of Krupp (1909–18); leader of the German Nationalist Party, 100, 101

Hughes, Charles E. (1862–1948), American Secretary of State (1921–5), 252, 276, 279

Huhn, Arthur E. von (1851–1934), editor of the Kölnische Zeitung, 132, 150, 160

Hull, Henry C. (1860–1932), Chancellor of the Exchequer in Both's cabinet; Minister of Finance from 1910, 68, 69

Hulse, 130

Humboldt, Hans P. Freiherr von (1857–1940), Consul General in Cape Town; later German Envoy in Lima, 65

Hutten-Czapski, Bogdan Count von (1850–1937), Marshall of Posen Castle and member of the Colonial Council, 118, 144, 160, 198

Illich, Domäneupächter (domain tenant), member of the Colonial Council, 47

Ilse, Lieutenant Colonel, 116, 144

Israel, James (1848–1925), surgeon, 159, 160, 165

Jänecke, Max (1869–1912), newspaper publisher and National Liberal politician, 100

Jaffé, Edgar (1866–1921), economist, 213

Jagow, Gottlieb von (1863–1935), Ambassador in Rome (1909); Foreign Secretary (1913–16), 107, 126, 127, 175, 178, 179, 181, 205, 209, 211, 225

Jagow, Traugott von (1865–1941), Police Commissioner of Berlin (1909); leading civil servant of Breslau district (1916–19); accomplice in the Kapp Putsch (1920), 108, 109, 133, 178, 239, 241

Jahn, L., 98

Jameson, Sir Leander S. (1853–1917), Prime Minister of Cape Colony (1904–1908), 60

Jeidels, Otto, AEG director, 143

Joel, Karl (1864–1934), philosopher, 123, 155, 168

Joel, Otto, director of the Banca Commerciale in Milan, 111, 150, 160, 171

Joerger, Carl, banker, 99, 178

Johannes, Hermann, head of the Commercial Department in the Auswärtige Amt, 191

Johnston, Reginald E. (1847–1922), banker, 62

Jolles, Oskar (1859–1929), industrialist, 107

Jones, co-founder of the Freie Bühne, 171

Jonina, Baroness de, 140

Jordan, Paul (1854–1937), member of the board of directors of the AEG (1883–1920), 111, 116, 130

Jung, Gustav, industrialist, 103

Jungheinrich, 66

Justi, Ludwig (1876–1957), Director of the Berlin National Gallery, 139, 142, 143, 144, 146, 178

Kämmerer, 200, 202

Kahigi (†1916), Sultan of Bukoba, Paramount Chief of the Haya, 40

Kahn, Otto, American banker, Lili Deutsch's brother, 170, 192

Kalkreuth, Leopold Count von (1855–1928), painter, 102, 106, 107, 129, 137, 152, 168

Kampf, Arthur (1864–1950), painter, 107

Kandt, Moritz (1865–1917), lawyer, 149

Kapp, Wolfgang (1858–1922), leading civil servant in East Prussia, leader of the Kapp Putsch, 239, 240, 241, 242, 243

Kardorff, Konrad von (1877–1945), painter, 106, 107, 108, 145, 156, 178

Karsavina, Russian ballerina, 146

Kaulitz-Niedeck, Rosa (*1881), authoress, 118

Kayser, Paul (1845–98), Head of the Colonial Department (1890–6), 27

Kehr, Paul F. (1960–1944), archivist and historian, 128

Kemball Cook, Sir Basil (1876–1949), Delegate to the Reparation Commission (1921–6); captain of industry, 286

Kemman, Gustav (*1858), engineer, expert on electric railways, 106

Kern, Surgeon-General, 200

Kern, Berthold von (1848–1915), philosopher and doctor, 106

Kern, Erwin (1898–1922), naval officer, one of Rathenau's assassins, 11

Kessler, Harry Count von (1868–1937), author, diplomat, Rathenau's biographer, 10, 105, 109, 111, 113, 115, 116, 117, 118, 120, 138, 141, 177, 182, 195

Keyserling, Eduard Count von (1855–1918), author, 104, 148

Khevenhüller, Count, 101

Kiderlen-Wächter, Alfred von (1852–1912), Envoy in Bucharest (1895); Foreign Secretary (1910–12), 115, 134, 135, 137, 140, 147, 148, 152, 157, 158

Kindersley, Sir Robert (1871–1954), Director of the Bank of England (1914–46); member of the Bankers' Committee for German Finances, 273, 286, 287

Kirdorf, Emil (1847–1938), industrialist (Gelsenkirchner Bergwerks AG), 29, 102, 107, 134, 137

Kleefeld, Kurt von (1881–1934), Director of the Hansabund, 107, 114, 115, 117, 123, 124, 131, 136, 140

Kleist, Ewald von (1868–1938), member of the supervisory board of Felten & Guilleaume, 100

Kleist, Heinrich von (1777–1811), poet, 136

Kleist, Rudolf von (1875–1945), officer, 73

Kliemke, Director of the Deutsche Bank, 30

Klingenberg, Georg (1890-1925), member of the board of directors of the AEG, 109, 112, 117, 190

Klinger, Max (1857-1920), painter and sculptor, 102, 137

Klingler, Karl (*1879), violinist, 122

Klöckner, Peter (1863-1940), industrialist, 97, 99, 104, 119, 122

Kluck, Alexander von (1846-1934), Field Marshal, 193

Königsheim, Ludwig, 110, 129

Körber, Ernest von (1850-1919), Austro-Hungarian Minister of Commerce (1897); Chief of the Joint Ministry of Finance (1905); Austrian Prime Minister (1916), 166

Körting, Berthold (1839-1919), industrialist, 99, 100, 139, 165

Körting, Ernst Sr. (1842-1921), industrialist, 10

Körting, Ernst Jr., industrialist, 97

Koeth, Joseph (1870-1936), succeeded Rathenau in the KRA; Head of De-mobilization Office; Minister for Economic Affairs (1923), 197

Kohler, Joseph (1849-1919), philosopher, poet, and journalist, 97, 99, 113

Kovovtsov, Count V. N. (1853-1943), Russian Premier (1911-14), 163

Kolb, Annette (1875-1967), authoress, 144

Kolbe, Frau (1881-1927), singer, married to the sculptor George Kolbe (1877-1947), 115, 116

Konschewski, M., Director of the Stein und Ton Industrie Gesellschaft, Brohltal, 115, 120, 123, 143, 165, 171

Kopp, Georg von (1837-1914), Cardinal and Prince-Bishop of Breslau, 118

Korn, Friedrich Alfred Krupp's private secretary, 144

Kraaz, Johannes, architect, 98

Krätke, Reinhold (1845-1934), Postmaster-General (1901-17); member of the Colonial Council (1891-1908), 104, 179

Kranold, Viktor von (1838-1923), Railway Director and member of the supervisory board of the Dresdner Bank, 162

Krassin, Leonid B. (1870-1926), Chairman of the Soviet Supreme Economic Council (1917); People's Commissar for Foreign Trade (1920); Ambassador in Paris (1924), and in London (1925), 280

Krebs, 144

Kreis, Wilhelm (1873-1955), architect, 102, 138

Kretschmar, Herman (1848-1924), musicologist, 124

Kries, businessman, 73

Kröpelin, Herman, 149

Krüger, Moses, farmer, 71

Krüger, Paulus (1825-1904), President of the Transvaal (1883-1902), 68, 167

Krüger, senior, 71

Krüger, low-ranking civil servant, 30, 41, 62

Krupp, Friedrich Alfred (1854-1902), industrialist, 144

Kühn, Hermann (1851-1937), Under-Secretary in the Treasury (1910); Secretary of the Treasury (1912-15), 105

Külz, Wilhelm (1875-1948), local politician, administrative expert in South West Africa (1907-8); member of the Reichstag (1920-33); Reich Minister, 74

Künstler, Fanny (1867-1923), authoress, 195

Kuntze, Friedrich (*1881), Professor of Philosophy, 123

Kunze, Bruno (1854-1935), engineer, 145

Kyser, Hans (1882-1940), author, 100, 103, 105, 113, 116, 117, 121, 122, 145

Labò, 110

Lambert, 145

Lamont, William J. (1870-1918), Adviser to the Liberian Government on customs problems from 1906, 64

Lancken-Wakenitz, Oskar von der (1867-1939), Councillor at the German Embassy in Paris (1908-13), 109, 120

Landau, Hugo (†1921), industrialist and banker; co-founder of the AEG and BEW, 115, 170

Landauer, Edgar (*1888), businessman; attached to the Treasury during the First World War, 122

Langwerth von Simmern, Ernst Freiherr (1865-1942), Councillor in the Auswärtige Amt (1910); Head of the Political Department (1916); Under-Secretary (1919); Ambassador in Madrid (1920); Commissioner for Occupied Territories at Koblenz and Wiesbaden (1925-30), 109, 111

Lansing, Robert (1864-1928), American Secretary of State (1915-21), 210

Larsen, Karl H. (1860-1931), Danish author, 122

Latouche, Gaston (1854-1913), painter, 99

Laurent, Charles, French Ambassador in Berlin (1919-22), 253, 254, 267, 268, 269, 270, 292, 293, 294

Lavigerie, Charles (1825-92), founder of a religious order; Cardinal (1882), 40

Lécomte, Raymond (1857-1921), French diplomat, 135

Lederer, Hugo (1871-1940), painter and sculptor, 200, 202

Léfebvre du Prey, Edmond (*1866), French Minister of Agriculture (1921-2), 263

Legien, Karl (1861-1920), Reichtag deputy (SPD), trade union leader, 237

Lehmann, Else (1866-1940), actress, 100, 146

Lehndorff, Heinrich Count von (1829-1905), General and Adjustant-General to Wilhelm I, 166

Lehndorff, Margarethe Countess von (1858-1928), Lady-in-Waiting to the Empress Auguste Viktoria, 101

Lehndorff, Paula Countess von (*1889), 101

Leidig, Eugen (*1861), industrialist, 129

Leishman, John (1857-1924), American Ambassador in Berlin (1911-13), 139

Lenin, (Ulyanov) Vladimir Ilyich (1870-1924), Chairman of the Council of People's Commissars; founder of the Soviet Republics, 280

Leoni, Walter (†1914), local politician, 96, 105, 106, 108, 121, 131, 150, 181

Lepsius, Reinhold (1857-1922), portrait painter, 116, 142

Lesczynski, Paul von (1830-1918), General, 135

Lessing, Ernst (*1870), architect, 117

Levy, Max (*1869), industrialist, 240

Lewald, Theodor (1860-1947), German Commissioner for the World Fair in St. Louis (1904); Director of the Interior (1910); Secretary of the Interior (1920); Plenipotentiary in the negotiations with Poland regarding Upper Silesia (1921); member of the board of the BHG, 144, 149, 191

Leyst, Christian, poet, 179

Lichnowsky, Prince Karl von (1860-1928), Ambassador in London (1912-14); married Mechthild Countess von Arco-Zinneberg (*1879), 104, 112

Lichtenberger, Henri (1864-1941), Professor of German Literature, 113

Lichtwark, Alfred (1852-1914), art historian, 102, 103, 129, 145, 149, 168

Liebermann, businessman, 66

Liebermann, Max (1847-1935), painter, 5, 99, 105, 106, 113, 130, 143, 170

Lindenberg, Richard (1869-1925), industrialist, 95, 123, 130, 137

Lindequist, Friedrich von (1862-1945), Governor of German South West Africa (1905); Under-Secretary in the Colonial Office (1907); Colonial Secretary (1910-11), 70, 137

Lindner, Heinrich (†1917), Managing Director of the Bergwerksgesellschaft Hibernia, 108

Lindsay, politician, 69

Lingner, K. A. (1861-1916), industrialist, 118

Linsing, Lieutenant, 73

Lipper, Father, priest, 72

Lloyd George, David (1863-1945), President of the Board of Trade (1905-8); Chancellor of the Exchequer (1908-15); Minister of Munitions (1915-16); Secretary for War (1916); Prime Minister (1916-22), 133, 147, 246, 247, 248, 253, 276, 277, 278, 279, 280, 281, 282, 283, 284, 285, 290, 291

Lobengula, 70

Loebell, Friedrich W. von (1855-1931), Head of the Chancellor's Office (1904); Lord Lieutenant of Brandenburg (1909); Prussian Minister of the Interior (1914-17), 76, 93, 125

Loën, Leopold Freiherr von (1817-95), General, 167

Loerke, Oskar (1884-1941), author, 144, 145

Loewe, Alfred, Director of the Strassburger Elektrizitätswerke [Strasbourg electricity works], 112

Loewe, Isidor (1848-1910), industrialist, 115

Loucheur, Louis (1872-1931), French, Minister in various cabinets (1918-30), 253, 254, 255, 256, 257, 258, 259, 260, 261, 262, 263, 264, 265, 267, 273, 275, 280, 281, 282, 284, 285, 286, 287

Ludendorff, Erich (1865-1937), Quartermaster-General (1916-18), member of the Reichstag (1924-8), 198, 199, 200, 201, 202, 203, 204, 207, 215, 216, 217, 218, 222, 223, 224, 225, 226, 227, 228, 229, 230, 231, 232, 233, 234, 237, 238, 278

Ludwig, Emil (1881-1948), author and publicist, 144, 150, 177, 212

Lueg, Heinrich (1840-1917), industrialist, 111

Lüttwitz, Walther Freiherr von (1859-1942), General, 239, 240, 241, 242, 243

Luini, Bernadino (c.1480-1532), painter, 111

Luther, Martin (1483-1546), founder of Protestantism, 200, 221

Luxburg, Karl Ludwig Count von (1872–1956), diplomat, 193

Lyncker, Moritz Freiherr von (1853–1932), General; Chief of the Military Cabinet (1908–18), 193, 194, 225

Macaulay, Thomas Babington, Baron (1800–59), English historian and politician, 93

Mackay, Charles (†1933), Mayor of Port Elizabeth (1908–9), 66

Mackensen, August von (1849–1945), Field Marshal, 148

Maercker, Georg, Ludwig (1865–1924), General, 241

Magnus, Nina (†1913), actress, married to the banker Georg Magnus (†1924), 178

Maillol, Aristide (1861–1944), sculptor, 113

Malcolm, Sir Neill (*1869), British General, head of the Military Mission in Berlin, 244, 245, 246

Malcolme, Sir Dougal (1877–1955), politician, Director of the British South Africa Company (1913), 63

Malcolmess, Hermann (1848–1921), wool merchant, 66

Mamroth, Paul (1859–1938), member of the board of directors and later of the supervisory board of the AEG, 99, 105, 148

Mangili, 129

Mann, Heinrich (1871–1950), author, 99

Mannesmann, Max (1857–1915), inventor of seamless steel tubing, 9, 94, 95, 101, 134

Mannesmann, Reinhard (1856–1922), industrialist, 9, 94, 95, 101, 134

Marignolle, Curzio (1546–1606), author, 129

Markau, Captain, 199, 202

Marschalk, Max (1863–1940), music critic, 132

Marschall von Bieberstein, Adolf Freiherr (1842–1912), Baden Envoy to Berlin (1883); Foreign Secretary (1890); Ambassador in Constantinople (1897); Ambassador in London (1912), 148, 160, 167

Martino, de, Italian Ambassador in Berlin (1920), 249

Marx, Karl (1818–1883), philosopher, 142, 214

Marx, Paul (1861–1911), editor-in-chief of the Tag, 104

Marx, Salomon (*1866), banker and journalist, 100, 116

Marx, Wilhelm (1851–1924), Lord Mayor of Düsseldorf, 116, 130, 181

Mascagni, Pietro (1863–1945), composer, 150

Matarée, Friedrich W. (*1845), wool merchant, 65

Mathis, Karl W. (1845–1917), District Court President, 129

Matuschka, Franz Count von (1859–1943); married Alice Schalscha von Ehrenfeld (*1869), 114, 115

Mau, Friedrich, servant, 30, 62

May, Daniel, Magistrate in Upington, 71

Mayer, Wilhelm (1874–1923), Centre Party politician; Secretary of the Treasury (1919–20); Ambassador in Paris (1920–3), 271, 286, 287, 288

Mayrisch, Emile (1862–1928), Luxemburgian industrialist, 137

Meinecke, Friedrich (1862–1854), historian, 166

Melchior, Carl (1871–1933), banker, partner in Warburg & Co.; expert at the Reparation Conferences at Brussels, Spa and Genoa, 244

Mendelssohn, Franz von (1865–1935), Vice-President of the Berlin Chamber of Commerce, 122

Mendelssohn, Paul von (*1875), banker, 113, 151

Mendelssohn, Robert von (1858–1917), banker; married Guiletta Gorgiani, (*1871), 121, 122, 123, 155, 171, 178

Mendelssohn-Bartholdy, Albrecht (1874–1936), historian, international lawyer, 25

Merkel, Hermann (*1871), Rathenau's servant, 62

Merker, Moritz von (1867–1908), Captain, 44

Merriman, John X. (1841–1926), Prime Minister of Cape Colony (1908–10), 64, 65

Merton, Walter (†1937), banker with the BHG (1911–13), industrialist, 94, 118, 123

Methuen, Lord (1854–1932), General in the Boer War, captured in 1902, 68, 69

Metternich, Paul Count von Wolff, German Ambassador in London (1900–12), 148, 151

Metzner, Franz (1870–1919), sculptor, 200

Meyer, low-ranking civil servant, 269

Michaelis, Georg (1857–1936), Permanent Undersecretary and later Imperial Chancellor, 223, 226

Michaelis, Karl T. (1852–1914), pedagogue and philosopher, 109, 142

Michaelis, Sophus (1865–1932), Danish poet, 139

Michelis, Lieutenant-Colonel, Chief of the Army Peace Committee, 245

Michels, Robert (1876–1936), sociologist, 25

Mietzl, Austrian Military Attaché, 128

Miller, Oskar von (1855–1934), engineer, founder of the Deutsches Museum, 149, 265

Millerand, Alexandre (1859–1943), first French Socialist Minister (1899–1904); Minister in various cabinets (1909–19); President of the Republic (1920–4), 245, 246, 280, 290

Minghetti, Donna Laura, née Acton (†1915), Prince Bülow's mother-in-law, 127

Miquel, von, Landrat, 44

Miquel, Johannes von (1828–1901), Prussian Minister of Finance, 125, 126

Moellendorf, Wichard von (1881–1937), AEG engineer; Under-Secretary in the Ministry for Economic Affairs (1919); author, 99, 187, 188, 189, 190, 213, 237, 238

Moltke, Friedrich von (1852–1927), Prussian Minister of the Interior (1907–10); Lord-Lieutenant of Schleswig-Holstein (1914–19), 104

Moltke, Hellmuth von (1848–1916), Chief of the General Staff (1906–14), 181, 193, 194

Moltke, Kuno Graf (1847–1923), General, 193

Monet, Claude (1840–1926), impressionist painter, 99

Monnier, 152, 162, 178

Montagu, Edwin S. (1879–1924), Under-Secretary in the India Office (1910–14); Secretary of State in India (1917–22), 281, 282

Monts, Anton Count von (1852–1930), Envoy in Munich (1895–1902); Ambassador in Rome (1902–9), 126, 127, 193

Moor, Sir Frederick R. (1853–1927), Prime Minister of Natal (1906–10), 66

Morenga, Jacob, Chieftain of the Namara in South West Africa, 41

Morowitz, 64

Morselli, Guido (1912–73), Italian author, 25

Rosenthal, businessman, 66

Mosler, Eduard (1873–1939), banker (BHG, Deutsche Bank and Diskontogesellschaft), 96, 117, 121, 130, 132, 138, 139, 153, 156

Mühlberg, Otto von (1843–1934), Under-Secretary in the Auswärtige Amt (1900–7; Prussian Envoy to the Vatican (1908–18), 124, 128

Müller, Felix von (1857–1918), Envoy in Stockholm (1905–7), Envoy in The Hague (1908–15), 141

Müller, Karl (1852–1940), church historian, 152

Müller, Otto (*1870), Director of the BHG (1904–22), 143

Mullins, Alfred (1846–1910), General Manager of the Africa Bank, 64

Mumm von Schwarzenstein, Alfons Freiherr (1859–1924), Ambassador in Tokyo (1906–11); Ambassador in Kiev (1918), 145, 150

Muro, Bernado de (1881–1955), singer, 150

Murray, Gilbert (1866–1957), British classical scholar, 113

Musil, Robert (1880–1941), author, 177

Mutahngarwa of Kiziba, Sultan of Bukoba, 40

Muthesius, Hermann (1861–1927), architect, 102

Mutius, Gerhard von (1872–1934), diplomat; Chancellor's representative at Headquarters (1914); Envoy to Oslo (1918); Chairman of the German Peace Delegation (1920), 105, 184, 185, 195

Mutzenbecher, Kurt von (1866–1938), Manager of the Wiesbaden theatre, 146

Mutzenbecher, junior, 111

Nachmann, Isaak (1816–1870), banker, 5, 120

Nansen, Peter (1861–1918), Danish author, 144

Napoleon I (1769–1821), French Emperor, reigned 1804–14, 68, 202

Nast, 128

Nathan, Sir Matthew (1862–1939), Governor of the Gold Coast (1900); Governor of Hong Kong (1903); Governor of Natal (1907–9); Governor of Queensland (1920–5), 66

Naumann, Friedrich (1860–1919), politician and publicist, Reichstag deputy 1907–19, 17, 99, 100

Neame, Laurence E. (1875–1964), journalist, 64

Negri, Francesco (1841–1924), inventor, 128, 129, 171

Nernst, Walther (1864–1941), physicist, 103

Neurath, Konstantin Freiherr von (1873–1856), German Chargé d'Affaires in Rome (1921–30), 287

Nicholas II, Tsar of Russia (1868–1918), reigned 1894–1917, 163

Nieske, 142

Nietzsche, Friedrich (1844-1900), philosopher, 16, 113

Nijinski, Vaslav, Russian ballet dancer, 113, 146

Nischwitz, Hugo (*1875), Managing Director of the Vereinigte Lausitzer Glaswerke AG, 118, 144, 148, 155

Nötzel, Max (*1876), colonial civil servant, 34

Nollet, Charles M. (1865-1941), French General; Chief of the Allied Control Commission from 1919; Minister of War (1924-34), 245, 293

Norman, Montagu (1871-1950), Governor of the Bank of England (1920-44), 278, 285

Nostiz-Wallwitz, Alfred von (1870-1953), administrative official in Saxony; Envoy to Vienna (1916); married Helene von Hindenburg (1878-1944), 109, 124, 215

Nürnberg, Heinrich, banker and engineer, 190

Nyarabambave of Ihangiro (1875-1911), Sultan in the Bukoba District, 40

Oats, Francis (1848-1918), Managing Director of the De Beers Company, 69, 71

Oehme, Walter, Colonel, 189, 190, 191

Oeser, Rudolf (1858-1926), Prussian Minister of Public Works (1919-20); Reich Minister of the Interior (1922-3); Reich Minister of Transport (1923-4), 242

Olfers, Marie von (1826-1924), authoress, 140, 141

Olivier, son of General Jan H. Olivier, 65

Oppenheim, Simon Freiherr von (1864-1932), banker and member of the Colonial Council, 145

Oppenheimer, Franz (1865-1943), economist and sociologist, 141, 144, 145, 157

Orange-Nassau, Princess Pauline of (1800-6), 101, 107, 111, 112, 114, 118

Oriolla, 141

Orlik, Emil (1870-1932), painter, 105

Oswald, Wilhelm von (1853-1936), industrialist, banker, 109, 137

Pabst, Waldemar (1881-1972), Major, 243

Pacelli, Eugenio, Monsignor (1876-1958), Papal Nuncio in Germany (1918-30); later Pope Pius XII, 125

Palestrina, Giovanni Pierluigi da (1526-1594), Italian composer, 128

Panzera, Francis W. (1851-1917), Native Commissioner, 69

Pariser, doctor, 162, 164

Pauli, Gustav (1866-1938), art historian, 145, 162

Peierls, Heinrich (*1867), director of the AEG, 190

Perponcher-Sedlnitzki, Wanda Countess von (1840-1911), Head Lady-in-Waiting to the Empress Augusta, 116

Peters, Carl (1856-1918), colonial politician, 46

Petersen, Walter (*1862), painter, 200

Petsche, Maurice (1895-1951), Secretary to Loucheur, 254, 282

Pfeil, Robert, Director of Siemens & Halske AG, 240, 241

Pforr, Philipp (1865-1949), Director of the AEG, 111

Pfuel, Clara von (*1863), sister-in-law to Bethmann Hollweg, 104, 220

Phillips, Sir Lionel (1855-1936), mining magnate; took part in the Jameson Raid, 67

Pichon, Stéphan (1857-1933), French Minister for Foreign Affairs (1906-11), 94, 109

Pirelli, Alberto, 266

Pissaro, Camile (1830-1903), painter, 99

Platen, Count, 141

Plenge, Johann (1874-1963), economist, 213

Plessen, Hans von (1841-1929), Colonel-General; Adjutant-General to Kaiser Wilhelm II, 225

Plieniger, Theodor, Managing Director of the Chemische Fabrik Griesheim-Elektron, 111

Plieninger, Director of the Diskontogesellschaft, 154

Ploetz, Karl (1819-1881), author of school books, publisher, 98

Podewils, Klemens Count (1850-1922), Bavarian Prime Minister, 174

Poincaré, Raymond (1860-1934), French statesman; Premier and Minister for Foreign Affairs (1912); President of the Republic (1913-20); Premier (1922-4 and 1926-9), 225, 291, 292

Pollak, Anton (*1865), invented phototelegraphy, 111

Ponsonby, Ashley, Secretary to the Governor, 66

Porten, Max von der, industrialist, 190

Posadowsky-Wehner, Arthur Count von (1845-1932), politician, 126, 149

Pourtalès, Hubertus Count von (1863-1949); married Margarete Freiin von Schickler, 99, 152, 178

Prächtel, 118

Prangey, 263, 287

Preussen, Prince Heinrich von (1862-1929), brother of Kaiser Wilhelm II, 104

Preussen, Princess Wilhelmine von (1774-1837), wife of the Dutch King Wilhelm I, 101

Prittwitz und Gaffron, Max von (1848-1917), Colonel-General, Commander-in-chief of the 8th Army in East Prussia in 1914, 202

Quade, Lieutenant-Colonel of the Colonial Troops, 30, 41

Quast, Wilhelm A. von (1849-1919), member of the Prussian Chamber of Deputies, 146

Quilitz, Hans, industrialist, 123

Radowitz, Josef M. von (1839-1912), Ambassador in Constantinople (1882); Ambassador in Madrid (1892-1908), 101

Raggi, Salvago, Italian Delegate of the Reparation Commission, 286, 287, 288

Raikes, A. E. (*1867), Brigadier, 37

Rang, pacifist, 193

Rantzau, Kuno Count zu (1843-1917), diplomat, 105, 151, 179

Raphael, Gaston, politician and journalist, 287

Rath, Walther vom (1857-1940), industrialist and banker; married Maximiliane Meister, 102, 107, 109, 114, 143

Rathenau, Emil (1838-1915), industrialist; founder of the AEG, Walther Rathenau's father, 4, 5, 6, 7, 8, 9, 18, 64, 67, 100, 106, 111, 113, 121, 130, 138, 141, 150, 159, 160, 163, 165, 168, 169, 170, 171, 176, 180, 197, 198, 213

Rathenau, Erich (1872-1903), engineer, Walther Rathenau's brother, 5, 102, 144

Rathenau, Fritz (1875-1949), Councillor in the Prussian Ministry of the Interior, 98

Rathenau, Mathilde (1845-1926), Walther Rathenau's mother, 5, 10, 39, 64, 65, 100, 113, 130, 159, 164

Ratibor and Prince of Corvey, Viktor A. Duke of (1847-1923), industrialist, 156

Rechenberg, Albrecht Freiherr von (1861-1935), Consul-General in Warsaw (1900); Governor of German East Africa (1906); Centre Party member of the

Reichstag (1913-18); Envoy to Warsaw (1922), 27, 34, 35, 41, 44, 70, 137, 138, 139, 151, 156, 182, 191, 192

Rechnitzer, Leopold, banker, 281

Redlich, Karl (1860-1918), engineer, 111, 131

Reibnitz, Johannes von (1882-1939), officer; farmer; leader of the Silesian Farmers' League, 75

Reicke, Georg (1863-1923), Deputy Mayor of Berlin 1903-20, poet, 109, 145

Reimer, Erich, Consul in Pretoria, 68

Reinhardt, Max (1873-1943), Director of the Deutsche Theater in Berlin, 99, 136, 151, 170

Reinhardt, junior, 107

Reinsch, Paul (*1869), American Professor, later American Envoy in China, 139, 152

Rennenkampf von, Russian General, 203

Reuter, Gabriele (1859-1941), author, 144

Reyersbach, Louis J. (1869-1927), mining magnate; President of the Chamber of Mines 1907-27, 67

Rheinbaben, Georg Freiherr von (1855-1921), Prussian Minister of Finance (1901-1910), Lord Lieutenant of the Rhine Province, 107

Rhodes, Cecil (1853-1902), Prime Minister of Cape Colony (1890-6); founder of Rhodesia, 62, 65, 70

Richter, Cornelia (1842-1922), married to Gustav Richter senior; kept a salon in Berlin, 115

Richter, Ernst (1862-1935), Under-Secretary in the Ministry of the Interior; Reich Minister of Finance (1921-5), 191

Richter, Eugen (1838-1906), left-wing liberal politician, member of the Reichstag 1867-1906, 47

Richter, Gustav (*1867), sculptor, son of the well-known portrait painter Gustav Richter (1823-1884) and Cornelia Meyerbeer (1842-1922), 108, 111, 115, 120

Richter, Raoul (1871-1913), Professor of Philosophy, also son of Gustav and Cornelia Richter. Raoul R. was married to Lina Oppenheim, 108, 111, 113

Richter, Theodor, factory owner, 123

Riedler, Alois (1850-1936), machine-building expert, engineer, Professor, 109

Riesser, Jacob (1853-1932), banker (Darmstädter Bank), and founder of the Hansabund, 131, 132

Riezler, Kurt (1882-1955), diplomat, 114

Rissik, Johann F. (1857-1925), Minister for Land and Native Questions (1907); First Civil Servant of the Transvaal (1910-17), 68

Robinson, Charles P. (*1866), politician, 66

Rodin, Auguste (1840-1917), sculptor, 99

Rödern, Siegfried Count von (1870-1953), Secretary of Alsace-Lorraine; later Secretary of the Treasury, 181, 182, 219, 220

Rödiger, Paul (*1859), Chairman of Brown, Boveri & Co., 132

Rössler, Carl (1864-1948), author, 142

Roetger, Max (1860-1923), Chairman of the Central Association of German Industrialists, President of the Hansabund (1909-11), 131

Roetger, Landrat in Teltow, 117

Roland-Lücke, Ludwig (1853-1917), National Liberal politician, banker, 130

Rolfes, Werner, Consul, 66

Rolland, Romain (1866-1945), author, 193

Rosen, Friedrich (1856-1935), diplomat, Envoy to Tangier and Lisbon; Minister for Foreign Affairs (1921), 160, 253, 259, 267, 268, 269, 271

Rosenberg, Hermann (†1918), banker (BHG), industrialist, 113

Rossi, Luigi (*1867), lawyer and politician, 129

Rothe, Karl (*1865), member of the board of directors of the Leipziger Hypotheckenbank, 130, 136, 145, 157

Rothschild, Alfred von (1842-1918), banker, 147

Rothschild, Lionel Walter von (1868-1937), banker, 283

Ruperti, Oskar, senior, merchant (saltpetre), 179

Ruprecht, Toni, actress, 117

Russel, Sir Alexander F. (1876-1952), judge, 65

Saenger, Samuel (1864-1944), author, Envoy in Prague (1919-21); joint-editor of the Neue Rundschau, 100, 101

Saldern, Sieghard von (1881-1963), officer, 75

Salomon, Bernhard, industrialist, Managing Director of the Lahmeyer Werke, 112, 115, 122, 124, 129, 146, 158, 171

Salomonsohn, Arthur (1859-1930), banker (Diskontogesellschaft), 115

Sarasin, Paul (1856-1929), author, 113

Sarre, Friedrich (1865-1945), art historian, 114, 160

Sassoon, Sir Philip (1888-1939), Member of Parliament (1912-39), 276, 284

Sattier, Joseph (1867-1931), painter, 112

Sauer, Johannes W. (1850-1913), Minister of Agriculture in the Merriman Cabinet (Cape Colony) (1908-10), 64, 65

Savage, Samuel R. (1859-1920), Mayor of Pretoria (1907-8), 68

Sazonov, Sergei D. (1860-1927), Russian Minister for Foreign Affairs (1910-16), 163

Schadow, Johann G. (1764-1850), sculptor, 107

Schad-Rossa, Paul (*1862), painter, 115

Schäfer, Wilhelm (1868-1952), poet, 121, 152

Scheffler, Karl (1869-1957), author and artist, 107

Schneidemann, Philipp (1865-1939), Reichstag deputy (SPD), member of the Provisional Government (1918-19), Reich Minister President (1919), 224

Scherl, August (1849-1921), newspaper publisher, 105, 106

Scheüch, Heinrich (1864-1946), General and Prussian Minister of War (1918-19); Chief of Staff at the War Office (1914), 186, 187, 188, 233, 234

Schickler, Ferdinand Freiherr von (1835-1909), banker and historian. His daughter Marguerite Freiin von Schickler (1870-1956) married Count Hubertus von Pourtalès, 99

Schiffer, Eugen (1860-1954), German Minister of Justice (1919-21), 239, 242, 243

Schinkel, Karl F. (1781-1841), architect and painter, 98, 114

Schlenther, Paul (1854-1916), author, 146

Schlippenbach, Marianne Countess von (*1852), 149, 151

Schlüpmann, Hermann (1873-1944), railway expert, 61, 71, 117, 135

Schmidt, Albert (1841-1913), architect and painter, 102

Schmidt, Paul (*1872), District Officer, 72

Schmitz, Bruno (1858-1916), architect, 149

Schoder, industrialist, 124

Schoen, Wilhelm Freiherr von (1851-1933), Foreign Secretary (1907); Ambassador in Paris (1910-14), 126, 151

Schön, Lieutenant, 41

Schönaïch-Carolath, Heinrich Prince zu (1852-1920), National Liberal politician, 101, 156

Schönbach, Georg (*1870), Chairman of the United Wool Traders (1900-27); Head of the wool section of the War Office, 190

Schorlemer-Lieser, Clemens Freiherr von (1856-1922), Prussian Minister of Agriculture (1910-17); Lord Lieutenant of the Rhein Province, 144

Schott, Walter (*1861), sculptor, 151

Schröder, Mary Freifrau von, née Donahue (1856-1925), married Heinrich Freiherr von Schröder, 142, 143, 148, 156, 181, 193

Schröder, Rudolf A. (1878-1962), poet, 117, 138, 178

Schröder, Dr, 164

Schubert, manufacturer, 30

Schuckmann, Bruno von (1857-1919), Governor of German South West Africa (1907-10), 68, 72, 73, 74

Schumacher, Fritz (1869-1947), architect and town planner, 102

Schumann, Robert (1810-1856), composer, 122

Schuster, Sir Felix (1854-1936), banker, 62

Schuster, 112, 158, 179

Schwabach, Leonie (†1913), 101, 145, 178

Schwabach, Paul von (1867-1938), banker (banking firm S. Bleichröder); married Eleonore Schröder (1869-1942), 29, 62, 98, 118, 124, 145, 158, 276

Schwaner, Wilhelm (1863-1944), Völkisch author, 215

Schwarz, industrialist, 190

Schwerin, Count, 99

Severing, Carl (1875-1952), Social Democrat, 245

Scotti, 129

Seekt, Hans von (1866-1936), Chief of the General Staff (1919); Head of the Reichswehr (1920-6), 219, 237

Seid, Chalid (1874-1927), eldest son of Sultan Seid Bargash of Zanzibar; made two unsuccessful attempts (1893, 1896) to gain the throne of Zanzibar, 35

Seidl, Gabriel von (1848-1913), architect, 106, 137, 139

Seiring, lawyer, 118

Selbourne, Lord (1859-1942), Under-Secretary in the Colonial Office (1895); First Lord of the Admiralty (1900); High Commissioner (1905-10), 65, 67

Selchow, Hedwig von (1851-1934), 168

Semon, 64

Senden, Karl O. Freiherr von (1863-1942), officer, 101

Sering, Max (1857-1939), economist, 142

Severing, Carl (1875-1952), Social Democrat, Prussian Minister of the Interior, 245

Seydoux, Jaques, French politician, Under-Secretary in the Ministry for Foreign Affairs, 264

Shaw, George Bernard (1856-1950), author, 144

Siemens, Carl Friedrich von (1872-1941), industrialist, 179

Siemens, Georg von (1839-1901), banker, 135

Siemens, Werner von (1816-92), scientist, engineer, and entrepreneur, 4

Sierstorpff, Adalbert Count von (*1856), Vice-President of the Royal Automobile Club, 146

Simon, Hugo Ferdinand (*1877), diplomat, 112, 276, 285

Simon, James (1880-1941), musician and philanthropist, 199, 146

Simonius, Alfons, President of the Schweizer Bankverein, 113, 162

Simons, Walter (1861-1937), Minister for Foreign Affairs (1920-1); President of the Supreme Court of Justice (1922-9), 245, 246, 247, 250, 251, 281

Simson, August von (1837-1927), industrialist, 157

Sinclair, Upton (1878-1968), author, 157

Slevogt, Max (1868-1932), painter, 122

Smith, Sir Allan (†1941), representative of the Employers Organization, Member of Parliament (1919-23), 286

Smuts, Jan C. (1870-1950), Boer officer; South African Minister of Defence (1910); Prime Minister of South Africa (1919-24 and 1939-48); Commander-in-Chief in East Africa (1916-18), 68, 69

Solf, Wilhelm (1863-1936), Governor of Samoa (1900); Colonial Secretary (1911); Foreign Secretary (1918); Chargé d'Affaires and Ambassador in Tokyo (1920-8), 27, 107, 118, 139, 159, 182, 234

Soliman bin Nasr el Lemke, Wali of Dar es Salaam; former Arab governor, 35

Solomon, Sir Richard (1850-1913), Minister in the Botha Cabinet; High Commissioner in London for the Union of South Africa (1910-13), 68

Sombart, Werner (1863-1941), political economist and sociologist, 99, 111, 123, 142, 213

Speck von Sternburg, Hermann Freiherr (1853-1908), Ambassador in Washington (1903-8); married Lilian Langham (*1879), 151

Spengel, Herman G. (*1865), engineer of the Victoria Falls and Transvaal Power Company, 67

Spengler, Oswald (1880-1936), philosopher, 142

Spieker, Friedrich A. (*1854), President of the Zentralverband für Innere Mission, Director of Siemens & Halske AG., 104

Spitzemberg, Hildegard von (1843-1914), widow of the Würtemberg Envoy in Berlin, 114

Stadthagen, Arthur (1857-1917), Social Democrat, member of the Reichstag 1890-1917, editor of the *Vorwärts*, 125

Stahl, Fritz (*1864), journalist, 287

Stampfer, Friedrich (1874-1957), Social Democrat, journalist, 214

Staudt, Richard (†1955), textile industrialist, 116

Stauffer-Bern, Karl (1857-1891), painter, 137

Stauss, Emil G. von (1877-1942), Managing Director of the Deutsche Bank, 244

Stead, William T. (1849-1912), journalist, 62

Stehr, Hermann (1864-1940), author, 149, 189

Stein, Carl (1857-1921), engineer; Director of the Gasmotorenfabrik Deutz, 142

Stein, Hermann von (1854-1927), Quartermaster-General; Prussian Minister of War (1916-18), 193, 194, 223, 224

Stein, Ludwig (1859-1930), sociologist and politician; editor of the monthly magazine *Nord und Süd* (1911); managed the Mittwochgesellschaft which he had founded with Stresemann and Rathenau, 98, 141, 159

Steinbömer, Gustav (1881-1972), pen-name Hillard, author, 218, 219, 225

Steiner, Rudolf (1861-1925), founder of Anthroposophy, 181

Steinert A. (1864-1913), theatre director, 117

Steinthal, Max (1850-1940), banker, 191

Stern, Julius (†1914), banker and industrialist, 101, 117, 143

Sternheim, Carl (1878-1942), author and playwright, 106, 107, 136, 140, 142, 146, 161, 162, 164, 170

Sthamer, Friedrich (1856-1931), Mayor of Hamburg (1920); Ambassador in London (1920-5), 283

Stieglich, administrative official in Saxony, 41

Stinnes, Hugo (1870-1924), mining magnate, industrialist, 8, 9, 12, 21, 24, 198, 237, 244, 246, 247, 248, 250, 266, 274, 275, 280, 281, 282, 294

Stock-Lossa, correspondent of the Wolff-Telegraph-Bureau, 288

Stolberg-Wernigerode, Prince Wilhelm zu (1870-1931), Second Secretary at the German Embassy in London, 62

Storz, V., journalist, 30, 41, 115

Strauss, Emil (*1866), author, 132

Strauss, Richard (1864-1949), composer, 111

Stresemann, Gustav (1878-1929), National Liberal Reichstag deputy; leader of the Deutsche Volkspartei; Reich Chancellor (1923); Foreign Minister (1923-9), 12, 223, 230, 242

Strübe, Hermann (1879-1960), poet and painter, 153, 158, 162

Stuck, Franz von (1863-1928), painter, 102, 137

Stucken, Eduard (1865-1936), author, 132, 151

Stümer, Willibald von (1870-1945), colonial civil servant, 40

Stumm, Wilhelm von (1869-1935), Councillor; Director in the Auswärtige Amt; later Envoy, 62, 151, 152

Stumpf, Johannes (*1862), electrical engineer, 109

Sudermann, Hermann (1857-1928), author, 151

Südekum, Albert (1871-1943), journalist and politician; Prussian Minister of Finance (1918-20), member of the PSD, 242, 243

Suse, Dr, 140

Swing, Raymond G., journalist, 212

Sydow, Reinhold von (1851-1943), Prussian Minister of Commerce (1909-18), 114, 160

Szögney-Marich, Ladislaus Count von (1841-1916), Austro-Hungarian Ambassador in Berlin (1892-1914), 101

Tagore, Sir Rabindranath (1861-1941), Indian poet, 193

Talaat Pasha, Mehmed, Turkish Minister of the Interior (1914-17); then Grand Vizier, 205

Talleyrand-Périgord, Duc de Sagan, Louis de (1811-98), 147, 222

Tannery, Jean, member of the French Ministry of Finance, 270

Tatishchev, Ilya, Russian military representative in Berlin, 104

Tattenbach, Count Christian von (1846-1910), diplomat, Envoy in Lisbon, Ambassador in Madrid, 128

Taylor, Alfred J. (1862-1941), Native Commissioner, 70

Taylor, Howard (1865-1920), lawyer and politician, 207, 208

Techow, Ernst W. (*1901), one of Rathenau's assassins, 11

Theiler, Sir Arnold (1867-1936), biologist, 68

Theunis, Georges (1873-1944), Belgian Premier (1921-4 and 1934-5), 266, 287

Thomas, Albert (1878-1932), French Socialist, 294

Thüngen, Nadine Freifrau von, née Radowitz (1871-1935), 111

Thurn und Taxis, Albert Prince von (1867-1952), 101

Thyssen, August (1842-1926), industrialist, 12, 134

Tieck, Ludwig (1773-1853), poet, 140

Tillmann, industrialist, 199

Tirpitz, Alfred von (1849-1930), Secretary of the Navy (1897-1916), 173, 182, 226

Tittoni, Tommaso (1849-1931), Italian Minister for Foreign Affairs (1903-5, 1906-9), 167

Tönnesen, Director of the South West Africa Company, 75

Toeppen, journalist, 30, 41

Trebitsch, Siegfried (1869-1956), Austrian author, 116

Trendelenburg, Ernst (*1882), Under-Secretary in the Ministry of Economics, 286, 288

Trenkwald, Hermann von (*1866), museum director in Vienna, 177

Trippensee, Albert, Director of the Stein und Ton Industrie Gesellschaft, Brohltal, 114, 123

Tröger, Richard, Professor, 190

Troeltsch, Ernst (1865-1923), philosopher, 214

Trollope, Anthony (1815-82), author, 69

Trowitzsch, National Liberal politician, 130

Tshchenkeli, Akaki (1876-1959), President of the Transcaucasian Republic (1918), 288

Tschirschky und Bögendorff, Heinrich von (1858-1916), Foreign Secretary (1907); Ambassador in Vienna (1908-16), 126

Tuaillon, Louis (1862-1919), sculptor, 102, 107, 129

Türken, 160

Twombley, painter, 150

Unruh, Fritz von (1885-1970), poet, 140, 152, 156, 157, 158, 159, 160, 161, 162, 170

Unsworth, Isaac (1860-1931), Colonel in the Salvation Army, 64

Valentin, Julius, co-founder of the AEG, 112

Valentini, Rudolf von (1855-1925), Chief of the Civil cabinet (1908-18), 93, 183

Varnbüler von und zu Hemmingen, Axel Freiherr von, Württemberg Envoy in Berlin (1894-1918); married Natasha Gavrilink, 104, 105, 114, 115, 124, 135, 146, 152, 157

Varnhagen von Ense, Karl A. (1785-1858), diplomat and author; married Rahel Levin (1771-1833), 141

Veltheim, Karl von (1858-1943), officer and Chamberlain at the court of Brunswick, 75

Velde, Henry van de (1863-1957), architect and designer, 113

Verhaeren, Émile (1855-1916), Belgian poet, 151

Victor Emanuel II, King of Italy (1820-78), reigned from 1861, 126

Victor Emanuel III, King of Italy (1869-1947), reigned 1900-46, 128

Victoria, Queen of Great Britain and Northern Ireland (1819-1901), reigned from 1837, 167

Vietsch, Wilhelm von (1877-1925), 74, 108

Villiers, Lord Henry de (1842-1914), judge, President of the Constituent Assembly in South Africa (1909), 68

Voigts, farmer, 73

Vollmöller, Hans, 106

Vollmöller, Karl (1878-1948), author, 99, 100, 104, 105, 106

Vuillard, Edouard (1868-1940), painter, 99

Waechter, Sir Max (1837-1924), author, 147

Wätjen, Hermann von (1851-1911), engineer and town councillor; married Clara Vautier (*1862), 103, 108

Wahnschaffe, Arnold (1865-1946), Under-Secretary in the Chancellor's Office (1909-17), 48, 105, 160, 164, 191, 218, 219, 220, 221

Waldow, von, 200

Waller, Herman (1873-1922), banker (Diskontogesellschaft), 115, 116, 117

Wallot, Paul (1841–1912), architect, 102

Walser, Karl (1877–1943), painter, 98, 102, 113, 145

Wandel, Franz G. von (1858–1921), General and Deputy Minister of War (1914–16), 185, 191, 195, 213, 219, 225

Wassermann, August von (1866–1925), doctor; married Dora Bauer, 109, 128, 136

Wassermann, Jakob (1873–1934), author, 136, 144, 170

Waterbury, 162

Weber, Max (1864–1920), economist and sociologist, 142

Wedekind, Frank (1864–1918), playwright, 99

Wedel, Prince Karl (1842–1919), Governor of Alsace-Lorraine (1907–14), 182

Wehner, Anton Ritter von (1850–1915), Bavarian Minister of Education (1903–12), 174

Weinberg, 115

Weiner, M., Viennese author, 98

Weiss, Emil (1875–1942), painter, 109, 116

Weissbach, wife of Franz W. (1865–1944), orientalist, 142

Wells, Herbert George (1866–1946), author, 113

Wendelstadt, Julie Freifrau von (1871–1942), 138

Wermuth, Adolf (1855–1927), Under-Secretary of the Interior (1904); Secretary of the Treasury (1909); Lord Mayor of Berlin (1912–20), 96, 97, 105, 108, 149, 170, 179

Wernher, Sir Julius C. (1850–1912), diamond magnate and financier, 64

Werthauer, Paul (*1858), lawyer in Berlin (industry and banks), 117

Wertheimer, Fritz (*1884), journalist, 288

Westarp, Kuno Count von (1864–1945), Conservative politician, 230

Whitehouse, J. Howard, American diplomat, 287

Wied, Prince zu (*1872), 126

Wied, Prince Wilhelm (1877–1946), Prince of Albania (1914), 107

Wiedfeldt, Otto (1871–1926), member of the board of directors of Krupps; railway expert; Ambassador in Washington (1922–6), 244, 253

Wiens, Arnold, industrialist, Chairman of the Bitterfeld Industrialists, 106, 111, 124, 136, 142, 143, 145

Wiese, Leopold von (1876–1970), sociologist, 214

Wild von Hohenborn, Adolf (1860–1925), Director of the General War Department in the Prussian War Ministry; Prussian Minister of War (1915–16), 191, 195, 196, 206, 213

Wildhagen, landscape painter, 30, 41

Wilhelm, I, King of the Netherlands (1772–1844), reigned 1814–40, 101

Wilhelm I, King of Prussia and German Emperor (1979–1888), reigned 1861–88, 141, 166, 201

Wilhelm II, King of Prussia and German Emperor (1859–1941), reigned 1888–1918, 10, 41, 48, 60, 75, 76, 94, 107, 111, 114, 126, 127, 128, 130, 133, 135, 144, 146, 147, 148, 151, 152, 160, 161, 163, 167, 174, 175, 179, 180, 182, 193, 194, 203, 205, 206, 223, 224, 225, 226, 230

Wilhelm, Crown Prince of Prussia (1882–1951), 182, 230

Wilhelmina, Queen of the Netherlands (1880–1962), reigned 1890–1948, 101, 115

Wilkins, Erwin (*1868), member of the Colonial Council, 30

Wille, Bruno (1860–1928), author, 143, 144

Wilson, Sir Henry (1864–1922), Field Marshal, 246

Wilson, Hugh R. (1885–1946), American diplomat, 266, 279

Wilson, Thomas Woodrow (1856–1924), President of the United States (1913–21), 209, 232, 233, 234, 235, 236

Winchester, Marquess of (1862–1962), 62, 67

Winterfeld, Karl Detlef von (1868–1945), colonial civil servant, 34

Winterfeldt, Hans Karl Djtlof von (1862–1937), General, 237

Winterfeldt, Joachim von (1865–1945), Lord Lieutenant of the Province of Brandenburg; Conservative member of the Reichstag (1908–18), 181

Wintzer, Wilhelm (*1867), journalist, 129

Wirth, Joseph (1879–1956), Centre Party politician; Reich Chancellor (1921–2), 2, 24, 243, 244, 252, 253, 259, 267, 268, 269, 270, 271, 272, 273, 276, 282, 295

Wise, Edward F. (1885–1933), economic adviser to the British Government, 246

Wissell, Rudolf (1869–1962), trade unionist, Minister of Economics (1919), Minister of Labour (1928–30), 237, 238

Witting, Richard (1856–1923), industrialist, brother of Maximilien Harden, 117

Wölfflin, Heinrich (1864–1945), art historian, 142, 145

Wolf, Julius (1862-1937), economist, founder of the Central European Economic Union, 153

Wolf, 253, 254

Wolff, Theodor (1868-1943), editor-in-chief of the *Berliner Tageblatt*, 106, 118, 120, 146, 192

Wolff-Zitelmann, Hans, industrialist in Upper Silesia, 115

Wolkenstein, Maria Countess von (1842-1922), 151

Worthington-Evans, Sir Laming (1868-1931), British Secretary for War (1921-2 and 1924-9), Postmaster-General (1923), 284, 285, 286

Zaharoff, Sir Basil (1850-1936), banker, 281

Zander, Carl (1867-1920), industrialist, AEG, 102, 103, 107, 111, 114, 116, 121, 122, 124, 129, 130, 136, 138, 139, 143, 144, 146, 148, 150, 155, 158, 160, 161, 171

Zapf, Georg (1867-1943), Managing Director of Felten & Guilleaume, 102, 122, 137, 138, 145, 151, 161, 199

Zech, Julius Count von (1885-1945), diplomat; married Ilsa von Bethmann Hollweg, 219, 220

Zelter, great-grandson of Goethe's friend; married to a friend from Rathenau's youth, 105

Zepler, Wally (*1865), socialist authoress, 214

Zimmermann, Adolf, journalist, 30, 41, 47, 106

Zimmermann, Arthur (1864-1940), diplomat, Director of the Political Department of the Auswärtige Amt (1910); Under-Secretary of the Auswärtige Amt (1911); Foreign Secretary (1916-17), 210, 222, 225

Zimmermann, Eugen, journalist, 30, 132

Zoelly, Swiss engineer, 139

Zoepfl, Gottfried H. L. (*1867), economist; member of the Economic Department of the German Embassy in Paris (1920-2); later Professor of Economics, 288

Zorn von Bulach, Hugo Freiherr (1851-1921), Under-Secretary of Alsace-Lorraine (1895-1909); Secretary of Alsace-Lorraine (1909-14), 182, 183

Zweig, Stefan (1881-1942), author, 106, 107, 110, 151, 193

GENERAL INDEX

Bold type indicates footnotes where fuller information on a particular subject is given. An asterisk preceding an entry indicates that Rathenau was a member of its supervisory board. *See* pp. 296-8 for a list of joint-stock companies on whose boards Rathenau served between 1907 and 1922.

*Abo, Finland, electrical power station at 112, 152
Aciéries Réunies de Burhach-Eich-Dudelange (ARBED) 137 n. 223
Africa:
 German colonial policy in 27, 28, 47, 60-2, 76, 135 n. 212, 155 n. 64, 163-4, 208, 210
 R's comments on 47, 49-59, 76, 77, 78-92, 153
 R's visits, *see* East Africa, Rhodesia, South Africa, South West Africa
Africa Bank 64
African Concessions Syndicate 63 n. 16
Agadir crisis 133 n. 205, 134, 167
Agrarian League 96 n. 17
Aircraft industry 115 n. 122, 144, 153 **n. 58,** 232, 258
*Aktien-Hütte, see Vereinigte Lausitzer Glaswerke
*Allgemeine Elektrizitätsgesellschaft (AEG) 2, 4, 7-8, 24, 77, 95, 99, 102 n. 49, 104 n. 62, 105 n. 65, 106, 110 n. 89, 113 nn. 105 and 106, 115 nn. 117 and 118, 122, 116, 117, 118, 121 n. 151, 122, 130, 131 n. 199, 137 n. 223, 138 nn. 226 and 227, 142, 144, 169, 170, 171, 180, 187, 190 n. 31, 196, 238, 280 n. 26
 Emil Rathenau's position 4, 7, 168-70, 171 nn. 130 and 131
 R's position and policies 2, 7, 8, 9, 18-19, 24, 93, 114 n. 114, 165 n. 103, 168-71, 172, 173 n. 135, 196, 197-8, 238
 expansion 7, 8, 64 n. 17, 93, 136, 138 n. 227, 169 n. 119, *and see following five sub-entries*
 subsidiaries: Aluminium Industrie 7; Elektrochemische Werke 7, 106 n. 70; Elektrizitäts Lieferungs-Gesellschaft 117 n. 130, 152 n. 48; Deutsch Überseeische Elektrizitätsgesellschaft 97 n. 24
 mergers: Brown, Boveri & Cie 8, 113 n. 105; Union Elektrizitäts-Gesellschaft 8, 64 n. 17, 112 n. 102, 115

n. 117, 117 n. 135; Felten & Guilleaume 8, 93, 97 n. 22, 100 n. 42, 107, 112 n. 104, 114 n. 114, 120 n. 148, 123, 137 n. 223, 138 n. 227, 149 n. 37
 part controlling interest in: Elektro-Stahl Gesellschaft 95, 109 n. 83; Elektro-treuhand AG 149 n. 36; Ozon Gesellschaft 132 n. 203; Treuhandbank für die elektrische Industrie 149 n. 37; Gasmotoren Körting (electrotechnical branch) 97 n. 25; Vereinigte Lausitzer Glaswerke 100 n. 40, 106 n. 68, 151 n. 43; Schlesische Kleinbahnen 108 n. 79; Schweigsche Glas- und Porzellanwerke 151 n. 43; company for constructing underground railways (AGE-Schnellbahn AG) 157 n. 72; Tillmann factories 199 n. 27
 links and other relations with power station companies: Abo (Finland) 152 n. 48; Berliner Elektrizitätswerke (BEW) 161 n. 88; Elektrische Kraftwerke Baku 122 n. 160; Laufenburg (Switzerland) 112 n. 102, 120 n. 146; Märkisches Elektrizitätswerk (MEW) 115 n. 121, 136; Eheingau Elektrizitätswerke 117 n. 130; Saar-Elektrizitäts-Gesellschaft 112 n. 103, 116 n. 128; Schlesische Elektrizitäts- und Gas AG 114 n. 112; Strasbourg Power Station Company 22, 96 n. 19, 112 n. 103; Victoria Falls Power Company (Rhodesia) 62, 67 n. 27; electrification in Italy 110-11 nn. 92 and 93, 171 n. 127; electrification in Spain 116 n. 124
Allied Coal Commission 245
Allied Conference of Ambassadors, and Upper Silesian question 271
Allied Supreme Council:
 policies on reparation and Upper Silesia 268, 269, 271, 277 n. 15, 285, 290
 on German disarmament 244 n. 24
Alsace-Lorraine, relations with Germany 127, 132, 133, 181, 182-3, 204, 210 n. 6, 228 n. 67

Aluminium Industrie 7, 109 n. 83
Ampère Gesellschaft (Ampère Co.) 122
Anglo-French Guarantee Pact (Jan. 1921) 281 n. 28
Anti-Semitism, as motive for assassination of R 11
Antweiler clay works 151
Armistice terms, R opposed to 235, 236
Arnimscher Opalglaswerke (Arnim Opal Glassworks) 123
Association of German Jews, see Verband Deutscher Juden
Aumetz-Friede 97, 99
Austria-Hungary 126 n. 176, 168, 174, 179-80 n. 12, 182, 183, 184, 186, 189, 191-2, 201, 206, 222 n. 47, 224, 225 and nn. 58-61
Auxiliary Service Law, see Hilfsdienstgesetz

Baden power station 112 n. 103
Baku Electrical Power Station, see Elektrische Kraftwerke Baku
Balkan Wars:
    1878 Balkan War 174
    First Balkan War 1912, 168 and n. 116, 169, 174
    Second Balkan War 1913, 179-80 n. 12, 182
    effects on AEG 180 n. 14
Baltischport, meeting of Tsar and Kaiser (4-6 July 1912) 163 n. 95
Banca Commerciale Italiana 171 n. 127
Banca di Roma 148
*Bank für Elektrische Unternehmungen, Zurich, see Elektrobank
Banque de l'Union Parisienne 162 and n. 90
Barcelona, see Compañia Barcelonesa de Electricidad
Bavaria 278
    conflict with Reich over Jesuits Law 174 n. 150, 175 n. 1
Belgian Congo 135, 208, 210
Belgian Mark Agreement 287
Belgium 183, 185, 187, 190-1, 192, 208, 210, 236, 277 n. 16, 278, 279, 287 n. 48
    African possessions 135, 174 n. 149, 208, 210
*Berg- und Metallbank AG, Frankfurt, see Metall-Gesellschaft
Bergmann Elektrizitäts Unternehmungen (Bergmann Electrical Enterprises) 138 n. 227, 150, 152
Berlin opera house, plans 160 and n. 84
Berlin Sezession (artists' association) 9, 99 and n. 34, 122
*Berliner Elektrizitätswerke (BEW) (Berlin

Electricity Works) 9, 161, 170, 171, 179, 198
*Berliner Handelsgesellschaft (BHG) 8, 9, 28, 29 n. 6, 48, 96, 104 n. 60, 109, 114 n. 115, 117, 118 n. 137, 123, 143 n. 6, 145, 155, 169 n. 118, 172, 198
    commercial and banking interests 73 n. 47, 77, 97 n. 25, 115 n. 123, 143 n. 5, 149
Berliner Tageblatt, comments on AEG changes (1912) 171 n. 131
    publishes 'Ein Wort zur Lage' (1914) 183 n. 9
Berliner Zeitung am Mittag, reviews Mechanik der Seele 177
Bismarck Memorial competition, see National Bismarck Memorial competition
Bitterfeld, see Elektrochemische Werke, Bitterfeld and Rheinfelden
Bitterfeld-Dessau overhead electric railway 118
*Blechwalzwerk Schulz-Knaudt, see Schulz-Knaudt
Bosnia, annexation by Austria 125, 126 n. 176, 128 n. 188, 167
Brazil 277 n. 16
Brest Litovsk, Peace of, R favours revision 233, 236
British South Africa Company 62 n. 8, 63, 64, 70 n. 42
*Brohltal Stein- und Ton-Industriegesellschaft (Brohltal Stone and Clay Industrial Company) 120 n. 150, 123, 162
*Brown, Boveri & Cie (BBC) 8, 110 n. 89, 113 nn. 105 and 106, 131-2, 162
Bulgaria 168 n. 116, 174 n. 141, 179-80 n. 12, 203 n. 44, 206 n. 50, 233
Bund der Industriellen, Der (League of Industrialists) 130 n. 194

Cameroons 134, 135 n. 212
    see also New Cameroons
Cannes Conference on reparations Jan. 1922, R attends 2, 287 n. 48, 288 n. 50, 290-1
Caoutchouk Clearing House (set up by KRA) 190, 197
*Capito & Klein AG 105, 131
Carl Spaeter, iron and steel traders, Koblenz 109 n. 88
Central power station, Genoa, see Sampierdarena Centrale, Genoa
Central Railway (German), Dar es Salaam to Lake Tanganyika 27, 36 n. 23, 47

Central Working Community of the German Commercial and Industrial Employers and Employees, *see* Zentralarbeitsgemeinschaft

Centralverband deutscher Industrieller (Central Association of German Industrialists):
backs R as possible candidate for Reichstag elections 129
breach with Hansabund 131 n. 197
sends commission to South West Africa 60 n. 1

Centre Party 125, 137 n. 221, 145 n. 14, 146, 170 n. 125, 174, 175, 196, 223 n. 55, 252

Chartered Company, *see* British South Africa Company

Chemische Fabrik Griesheim Elektron (Griesheim Elektron Chemical Works) 7

Chilean Electrical Tramway and Light Company 130 n. 195

China 138 n. 224, 276, and n. 13, 277 n. 16

Clearing houses set up by KRA:
flax 190
jute 190
leather 190
rubber (Caoutchouk Clearing House) 190, 197
tin plate 190

Coal Committee (German) 245

Coal deliveries as reparations 243–4, 245–8, 258

Collart, *see* Jules Collart steel plant, Steinfort (Luxemburg)

*Compañia Barcelonesa de Electricidad (Barcelona Electrical Company) 116

Compania Edison, *see* Società Generale Italiana di Elettricità Sistema Edison

*Compañia Sevillana de Electricidad (Seville Electrical Company) 116

Congo:
Belgian 135, 208, 210
French 135 n. 212, 158

Conservative Party 137 n. 221, 145 n. 14, 146 n. 20, 181, 214

Courland, Ludendorff favours annexation of 204, 229

Crete 168 and n. 115

Cuba 174 and n. 146

Cyprus 174 and n. 148

Daily Telegraph affair 77
Dardanelles 179
Darmstädter Bank 103
De Beers Mining Company 68 n. 29, 69, 73 n. 47

Delbrück bank, R's part in merger with Schickler bank 9, 93, 99, 160

Delbrück Schickler & Co. 179

Democratic Party, R a member after the war 9, 250, 252, 271

Demokratischer Volksbund (Democratic People's League), R's failure to establish 238

Deutsch-Atlantische Telegraphengesellschaft (German Atlantic Telegraph Company) 151 n. 42

Deutsch-Ostasiatische Bank (German Far Eastern Asiatic Bank) 103 n. 57

*Deutsch-Überseeische Elektrizitäts-Gesellschaft (DUEG) (German Overseas Electricity Company) 97, 104, 130, 150

Deutsche Bank 30, 97 n. 24, 104 n. 60, 170 n. 125

Deutsche Edison-Gesellschaft (German Edison Company, founded by Emil Rathenau and Siemens) 4

Deutsche Gesellschaft:
R a member of 10
R's report on KRA, published 1916 as *Deutschlands Rohstoffversorgung* 187, 197 n. 20, 212–13

Deutsche Kolonial-Eisenbahnbau- und Betriebsgesellschaft (German Colonial Railway) 73 n. 47

*Deutsche-Niles-Werkzeugmaschinenfabrik (German Niles machine tool factory) 122, 136, 156

Deutsche Petroleum AG 170 n. 125

Deutsches Theater 107 n. 74, 114, 140

Diamantenregie 73 n. 47, 182, 190 n. 31

Disarmament, R's views 119–20, 152, 154, 161, 163

Disarmament, of Germany by Versailles Treaty 244 n. 24, 245, 248, 267

Disarmament Conference, Washington (21 Nov. 1921–6 Feb. 1922) 276 n. 13

Diskontogesellschaft (Diskonto Bank) 75 n. 49, 96 n. 20, 98 n. 31, 130, 154, 249

Dresdner Bank, 98 n. 31, 262

Düsseldorf occupied by French (8 Mar. 1921) 250

Duisburg occupied by French (8 Mar. 1921) 250

East Africa:
German policy in 27–8, 47, 61, 118
railway construction in 27, 37 n. 31, 49, 56, 60
R and Dernburg's tour (1907) 9, 27–59

East Africa (cont.):
    R's Notebook 33–47
    R's Report 34 n. 17, 48–59
East African Railway Company 30
Eastern Asia, report by Dernburg on journey
    to China and Japan 103 and n. 57
Economic Council, see Provisional Reich
    Economic Council
Egypt 30–1, 133 n. 205, 174, 186
Electricity Bill (1914) 183
    see also State monopoly in electrical
    supply industry
Elektrische Kraftwerke Baku (Baku Elec-
    trical Power Station) 122
Elektrische Werke Bitterfeld (Bitterfeld Elec-
    tricity Works), see Elektrochemische
    Werke
*Elektrizitäts Lieferungs-Gesellschaft (ELG)
    (Electricity Supply Company) 116–
    17 and n. 130, 123, 124, 152 nn. 48
    and 49
*Elecktrobank, Zurich (Bank für Elektrische
    Unternehmungen) 9, 110 n. 92, 112
    n. 103, 113 n. 105, 115 n. 117, 116
    n. 124, 120 n. 148, 146, 149 n. 37,
    164
*Elektrochemische Werke, Bitterfeld and
    Rheinfelden 7, 106, 109, 138, 152
*Elektro-Nitrum AG Rhina 120 n. 146
*Elektro-Stahl Gesellschaft (Electro-Steel
    Company) 95, 109 and n. 83, 148
*Elektrotreuhand AG (Electrical Mortgage
    Bank) 149
Emil-Rathenau-Foundation, founded by R
    after his father's death 9
Erlangen, lock-out of textile workers by
    Weber & Ott (1911) 122
Escher-Wyss factory, Zurich, 100 n. 42,
    110, 112 n. 104, 139 n. 233, 143 n. 4
Eulenburg affair 76, 135

Felten & Guilleaume Carlswerk AG (before
    1905):
    origins of firm 108 n. 78
    founds Deutsch-Atlantische Telegraphen-
    gesellschaft (1899) 151 n. 42
    founds Norddeutsche Seekabelwerke
    (1899) 151 esp. n. 42
    gains control of Land- und Seekabel
    Werke (1905) 152 n. 50
    acquires manufacturing side of W. Lah-
    meyer & Co (1905) 112 n. 104,
    120 n. 148
*Felten & Guilleaume Carlswerk AG (after
    1910) 9, 93, 97, 100, 104 n. 62,
    112 n. 102, 124, 130, 132 n. 203,
    136 n. 220, 137, 149, 156, 199 n. 27

    need for steel supply 97 n. 22, 104 n. 62,
    109, 120 n. 149, 137 n. 223
    negotiations for Collart steel plant 137,
    138, 139, 143 n. 4, 145 nn. 16, 17,
    156 n. 66
    and Escher-Wyss 100 n. 42, 110 n. 89,
    112 n. 104, 139 n. 233, 143 n. 4
    and Main Kraftwerke 114 n. 114
    possible merger with Krupp 100–1 esp.
    n. 44, 137 n. 223
    and Tronto power station 100, 107, 108
    n. 77, 112 n. 104
Felten & Guilleaume-Lahmeyerwerke AG
    (1905–10):
    founds Treuhandbank für die Elektrische
    Industrie (1909) 149 n. 37, 156 n. 66
    majority shareholding acquired by AEG
    (1910) 8, 93, 97 n. 22, 138 n. 227,
    149 n. 37
    sells Lahmeyer dynamo factory to AEG
    (1910) 93 n. 1, 120 n. 148, 123 n. 164
Finland, electrical power station at Abo
    112, 152
France:
    Moroccan policy 94–5, 120 n. 145, 127,
    132, 133 n. 205, 134, 136 n. 219,
    137 n. 221, 167, 174 n. 143
    relations with Germany: pre-war 128,
    135 n. 217, 154, 163, 167–8, 174,
    182, 228 n. 67, 229 n. 70; during
    war 184–6, 187, 201 n. 31, 203, 205,
    206, 207, 208, 209, 210, 222 n. 47,
    228, 236; post-war 244, 247–8, 249,
    253–66, 267–70, 272–83, 283–5,
    286, 289 n. 53, 291, 292–4
    relations with Great Britain 134, 147,
    149, 152, 160, 173, 183, 248, 259,
    291, 294
    reparations: coal deliveries 244–8, 265;
    joint reconstruction 249, 253–66,
    275, 279, 282; moratorium on pay-
    ments 265, 273, 275, 278–9, 283–5,
    290–1, 295
    threatened occupation of the Ruhr 244,
    246 nn. 31 and 33, 247, 250, 265
    and Upper Silesia 265, 267–72, 277, 284
Franz Mine 115, 117
Freie Volksbühne, see Volksbühne
Friedmann-Quilitz's commission case (1911)
    123
Fürstenkonzern, see Hohenlohe group

*Gasmotorenfabrik Körting (Körting Gas-
    Engine Works) 97 n. 25, 100 n. 43,
    116, 118, 139, 156, 165
Gebrüder Körting AG, see Gasmotorenfabrik
    Körting

Gegenwart, reviews *Mechanik der Seele* 177

General Electric Company (USA) 256 and n. 29

General Electric Power Company 63 n. 16

General strike, during Kapp Putsch 239, 240 n. 7

Genoa, Italy, electrical undertakings backed by AEG 110-11, 150

Genoa Conference (1922) 265, 291, 292, 293, 294, 295

George Allen & Unwin, publishes English translation of *Von Kommenden Dingen* (1921) 9

German East Africa, *see* East Africa

German East African Company 57

*Gesellschaft für Elektrische Unternehmungen (GESFÜREL) 112 n. 102, 115 and n. 117, 117 n. 135

Gibraltar 186

Gillet-Ruppel Agreement about German payments in kind to France (15 Mar. 1922) 293 n. 10

*Goldschmidt, Theodor, *see* Theodor Goldschmidt AG, Essen

Great Britain:
as colonial power 50, 52, 55, 59, 60-1, 62, 63, 81, 84, 87, 88, 89, 154, 174, 179
economic problems of analysed by R 15, 61
relations with France 134, 147, 149, 152, 160, 173, 248, 259, 291, 294
relations with Germany: pre-war 61, 62, 65 n. 20, 105 n. 63, 133-4, 146 n. 23, 147, 148, 151, 152 n. 53, 153-4, 163, 167, 168, 173, 174, 179; during war 185-6, 187, 201 n. 31, 203, 205, 207, 208, 209-10, 211, 217, 219, 220, 222 n. 47, 226, 227, 229 n. 71; post-war 244, 246-7, 248, 265, 268, 269, 273-83, 283-5, 286, 292

Greece 168 nn. 115, 116, 179 n. 12, 205

Griesheim Elektron Chemical Works, *see* Chemische Fabrik Griesheim Elektron

Gross-Schönebeck railway 157

Guarantee Pact, *see* Inter-Allied Financial Agreement

Gutehoffnungshütte (steel-making and manufacturing group), attempted merger 8, 24

Hachenburg Plan 274 n. 6

Halle, electrical power station in 103

Hamburg–Amerika–Packetfahrt–Aktiengesellschaft (HAPAG), trial run of steamer *Imperator* 179

Hansabund 96 and n. 17, 103, 114, 115, 118, 130 n. 194, 131, 132 and n. 202

R suggests political aims for 131

Hansing (firm trading in East Africa) 37

Hermann Eckstein & Company, Transvaal mining group 67 n. 27

Héroult system of steelmaking 95, 109 n. 83

Hilfsdienstgesetz (Auxiliary Service Law of 5 December 1916) 216 and n. 23

Hindenburg Peace 223

Hindenburg Programme 216 and nn. 21 and 22

Hindenburg Telegrams (22, 23 Dec. 1916) 223, 227 n. 64

Höchst laboratory for nitrogen fixation 120

*Hohenlohe group (Hohenlohewerke AG/ Fürstenkonzern) 104 n. 60

Holland, *see* Netherlands

Imperator, HAPAG steamer 179

Imperial Electricity Monopoly proposed 190 n. 31
see also State monopoly in electrical supply industry

Industrial Association, R's speech to (1921) 265

Inter-Allied Financial Agreement (13 Aug. 1921) 278 n. 21

*Internationale Bergwerksgesellschaft (International Mining Company) 162

Italy:
war with Turkey over Tripoli 148 and n. 32
during 1914–18 war 203
post-war 287 n. 46
industrial co-operation with proposed by R (1920) 249
visits to by R 30, 109, 110-11, 124-9, 150, 170-1

Ivangorod, battle of (Oct. 1914) 201

Japan 174 n. 142, 185, 276 n. 13

Jesuits Law, abolition of 173 n. 136, 174 and n. 150, 175

Jewish campaign 109, 112

Jewish problem in Poland 204

Jewry, Society for the Preservation of Traditional 115

Jews, Association of German 119
see also Rathenau, Walther, *under* attitude to Judaism, publications

Jules Collart steel plant, Steinfort (Luxemburg) 137 **n. 223**, 138, 139, 143 n. 4, 145 nn. 16 and 17, 151, 156 n. 66, 162 n. 89

Juteabrechnungsstelle (Jute Clearing House), set up by KRA 190

Kammerspiele (Theatre Workshop) of Deutsches Theater 107

Kammzug AG (Worsted Yarn Company), set up by KRA 190

Kapp Putsch, R's attempt to mediate 9, 239-43

Klöckner, possible steel suppliers 97 n. 22, 99, 104 n. 62

Kölnische Zeitung, comments on 1915 *Times, The*, article on R 212

*Königsberg electricity company (Elektrizitätswerke und Strassenbahn, Königsberg) 152

*Körting, see Gasmotorenfabrik Körting

Köslin paper factory 143 n. 5

Korea 174

Kovno, R's visit (1915) 198-204

Kreditanstalt (Credit Institution), Zurich 110

Kriegschemikalien AG (War Chemicals Company), set up by KRA 190

Kriegsmetall AG (War Metals Company), set up by KRA 190, 197

Kriegsrohstoffabteilung (KRA) (War Raw Materials Department) 2, 9, 22, 185, 186-91, 195-7, 216 n. 21
  controversy over origin 187-9
  R's resignation as head of KRA, 195-7
  subsidiaries and clearing houses 190
  criticism of 190 n. 31, 195-7

Kriegswollbedarf AG (War Wool Supply Company), set up by KRA 190

Krüger telegram 167

Krupp 8, 24, 100-1, 105 n. 65, 114 n. 115, 137 n. 223, 138 n. 226, 139 n. 229
  possible mergers 8, 24, 100-1, 137 n. 223, 139 n. 229

*Lahmeyer Werke AG:
  W. Lahmeyer & Co. 120 n. 148
  founds Lech Elektrizitätswerke, Augsburg (1903) 136 n. 220
  manufacturing side merged with Felten & Guilleaume (1905) 112 n. 104, 120 n. 148
  AEG acquires Lahmeyer dynamo factory, Frankfurt (1910) 93 n. 1, 112 n. 104, 120 n. 148, 123 n. 164
  R on board of AEG-Lahmeyer Werke AG 171

*Land- und Seekabelwerke AG (Land and Sea Cable Works) 152

Laufenburg, Switzerland, power station at 112 n. 102, 120 n. 146, 139, 150, 158, 171

Lausanne, Peace of (Oct. 1912) 148 n. 32

Lausitz electricity company 152

*Lausitz Glass Works, see Vereinigte Lausitzer Glaswerke

League of Nations Council:
  and Upper Silesian question 265, 267, 271, 277, 278 n. 18
  Committee of Four 271, 277, 278 n. 18

*Lech Elektrizitätswerke (Lech Electrical Works), Augsburg 136 n. 220, 171

Lenz & Company, interest in S W African diamond fields 73 n. 47

Lessingtheater-Ensemble 150, 151

Libya 148 n. 32

*Lindenberg, Richard, see Stahlwerke Richard Lindenberg AG

Lingner Werke (manufacturers of Odol mouthwash) 118

*Loewe Group, see Ludwig Löwe & Co. AG

London:
  visit to by R and Dernburg (1908) 60, 61-4
  visits to by R (29 Nov.-10 Dec. 1921) 273-83; (18-23 Dec. 1921) 283-6

London Agreement between Lloyd George and Briand on reparations (16 Dec. 1921) 283, 285, 290, 294

London Reparations Conference (Mar. 1921) 2, 250-1

London Ultimatum on reparations (5 May 1921) 251, 252, 253, 265, 278, 290, 291, 294

Lothringischer Hüttenverein (Lorraine Steel Mill) 104

Louis Peter AG, Frankfurt (rubber goods factory) AEG negotiations with 115, 116, 117, 118

*Ludwig Löwe & Co. AG 117, 130, 155

Lusitania:
  sinking of, 210 and nn. 8 and 9, 211
  subsequent American and German Notes on 210-11

*Märkisches Elektrizitätswerk AG (MEW) 115 n. 121, 117, 136, 155

Main-Kraftwerke (Main Power Station) 114 n. 114, 117 n. 130

Maji-Maji rising 27, 35 n. 19, 44 n. 48

Malkasten (Düsseldorf artists' association) 103

Mannesmann brothers, R's negotiations about mining concessions in Morocco on their behalf (1910) 9, 94-5, 101 n. 47, 114, 134, 286

*Mannesmann Group (Mannesmannröhren-Werke AG) 8, 101 n. 47, 113 n. 109, 118, 190-1 n. 31

Mansion House Speech 133 nn. 205 and 208, 147 n. 25

Maschinenfabrik Augsburg–Nürnberg (MAN), attempted merger 8, 24
Masurian Lakes, 1st Battle (Sept. 1914) 202
*Metall-Gesellschaft (Berg- und Metallbank AG, Mining and Metal Bank) 73 n. 47, 77, 94, 190 n. 31
Mexico, R recommends German intervention (1914) 181
Milan, Italy:
    electrical undertakings in 111, 150, 171
    visits to by R 111, 129, 150, 170-1
Mining concessions, Morocco, R's negotiations (1910) 9, 94-5
'Mitteleuropa' concept, R advocates 153 n. 55, 163 n. 97, 184-6, 191-2, 195, 219 n. 42
Mitteleuropäischer Wirtschaftsverein (Central European Economic Association) 153 n. 55
Moltke–Harden trials 76, 143 n. 4
Moltke Memorial 160
Monopolies, see State monopoly in electrical supply industry and oil, State monopolies
Montags-Zeitung, publishes R's article 'Judentaufen' (1911) 98
Montenegro 168 n. 116
Morocco:
    1905 crisis 28, 127-8, 135 n. 217, 167 n. 113
    1911 crisis 120 n. 145, 126 n. 179, 132-3, 134, 136, 147 nn. 26 and 29, 167, 173 n. 139, 174
    R's negotiations about mining concessions 9, 94-5

N process (?nitrogen fixation process) 117
National Bismarck Memorial competition (R on committee) 102-3, 107, 115, 129, 136-7, 138
    R and Lichtwark publish Der rheinische Bismarck (Feb. 1912) 102 n. 52, 138 n. 228, 145, 148, 149, 151, 160
National Economic Council, Reparations Committee, R's 1921 talks to 265
National Liberal Party 9, 95, 96 n. 18, 102, 105-6, 122, 123, 125, 129, 130 n. 194, 132 n. 202, 137 n. 221, 138 n. 225, 145 n. 14, 146, 214, 231
    R a possible candidate for in 1912 Reichstag elections 9, 95, 105-6, 122, 123, 129, 130 n. 194
Netherlands 208
    return of remains of Princess Pauline of Orange-Nassau to Delft by R 101, 107, 111, 112, 114, 115, 118
'Neue Ära, Die' (R's 'manifesto', pub. in the

Hannoverscher Courier, 1907) 28-9, 106
Neue Freie Presse (Viennese newspaper), publishes R's articles 119, 153, 155, 160, 177, 183
Neukölln-Gesundbrunnen overhead railway, financing of 182
New Cameroons 135 n. 212, 158 n. 76
Niederdeutsche Bank, Dortmund (Lower German Bank), collapse of 104 n. 60
Nietzsche Memorial Committee (R a member) 113 and n. 107, 118
*Niles, see Deutsche–Niles-Werkzeugmaschinenfabrik
Nitrogen-fixation process 120 n. 146
    see also N process
Nollet Note on military organization of Schutzpolizei (22 Feb. 1922) 293
Nord und Süd 141, 161
    publishes R's article 'Den Finger auf die Wunde' 161
*Norddeutsche Seekabel Werke AG (North German Sea Cable Works), Nordenham 151

*Oberschlesische Elektrizitätswerke (Upper Silesian Electricity Works) 156
*Oberschlesische Kleinbahn AG (Upper Silesian Light Railways) 153
    see also Upper Silesia
Oder Zeitung, opposes R as National Liberal candidate (1911) 129
Officine Elettriche Genovesi (Genoa Electrical Works) 110, 111, 150
Ostbank für Handel und Gewerbe (Eastern Bank for Trade and Commerce) 115 n. 123
Otavi-Minen- und Eisenbahngesellschaft (Otavi Mining and Railway Company) 75 n. 49, 77, 79
Otavi Railway 74 and n. 48, 75 n. 49
Ozon Gesellschaft (company to purify drinking water in Paris and St Petersburg) 132

Paris, visits by R:
    (1910) 9, 94-5
    (1912) 161-2
    (29 Dec. 1921-6 Jan. 1922) 286-9
Paris Conference on reparations (1921) 251
Peace Movement (Romain Rolland) 193 n. 46
Peace moves 192, 207-8, 209-11, 228, 229 n. 71, 232, 233, 234-6
Peace resolution in Reichstag (July 1917) 224 n. 57, 231 n. 76
People's Party 252, 253, 271

*Permutit AG 153, 157
Persia, Russian policy in 105 n. 63
Peter, *see* Louis Peter AG, Frankfurt
Philippines, 174 **n. 147**
Phillips, expansion in Europe 280 n. 26
*Planiawerke AG für Kohlefabrikation
    (Plania Works) 109 and n. 87, 111
    n. 99, 113, 120
Poland 167, 203-4, 206, 210, 228-9, 244,
    258, 267, 277 n. 16, 278, *see also*
    Upper Silesia, proposed partition
Polish Central Co-operative Bank 48
Portuguese East Africa 173
Portuguese possessions in Africa 173 n. 139,
    174 n. 149
Potsdam, meeting (5-6 July 1914) 225 and
    n. 59
Premier Company (Transvaal diamond
    mining company) 68 n. 29
Preussische Jahrbücher, suggestions about
    Jesuits Law 175
Princess Pauline of Orange-Nassau's grave,
    Schloss Freienwalde 101, 107, 111,
    112
    return of remains to Delft 101, 107,
    111, 112, 114, 115, 118
Privatization of railways of Central Europe
    proposed by Stinnes (1921) 274, 277
Progressive Party 96 n. 18, 105, 145 n. 14,
    223 n. 55
Provisional Reich Economic Council, R
    a member 243, 250

Quadruple *Entente*, 204, 207, 226
    Agreement of (5 Sept. 1914) 207, 208
    see also France, Great Britain, Italy,
    Russia

Rand Central Electric Works 63-4 n. 16
Rand Mines Ltd. 64 n. 17, 67 n. 27
Rand Mines Power Supply Company 67
    n. 27
Rapallo Agreement, signed by R (16 Apr.
    1922) 22, 265, 294
Rathenau, Walther:
    background and education 4-6
    career: joins Aluminium Industrie 7;
        managing director Elektrochemische
        Werke (1893) 3, 7; joins AEG board
        of directors (1899) 7; resigns (1902)
        7; on board BHG 8; joins BBC 8;
        vice-chairman AEG supervisory board
        (1910) 8; chairman AEG supervisory
        board (1912) 8, 171; for pre-war
        career in industry *see also* under
        separate companies, listed 296-8;
        talks with Bülow (1911) 124-7,
    (1912) 166-8; talks with Bethmann-
    Hollweg (1911) 132-5, (1912) 151,
    163-4, 173-4, (1913) 175, (1914)
    181; talks with Jagow (1913) 179,
    (1914) 181-2, (1916) 211; talks with
    the Kaiser (1912) 146-8, (1913)
    179-80, (1914) 182-3; proposes
    customs union, 183-6; proposes war-
    time control of raw materials for
    industry 22, 186-9; head of KRA
    (Aug. 1914-Mar. 1915) 2, 9, 22, 185,
    189-90, 195-7, 212-13, 237; presi-
    dent of AEG (Oct. 1915) 2, 8, 197-
    8; talks with and support for Luden-
    dorff (Nov. 1915) 198, 199-200,
    201-2, 204, (Feb. 1917) 215-18,
    (July 1917) 222-32; interview with
    Falkenhayn (Nov. 1915) 205-7; talks
    with US Ambassador (Dec. 1915)
    207-8, (Jan. 1916) 210-11; talks
    with Col. House (Jan. 1916) 209-
    10, 211; *Times, The*, article on R
    (Oct. 1915) 212; talk with Bethmann
    Hollweg, Helfferich, Wahnschaffe
    (May 1917) 218-22; draft letter to
    President Wilson (Oct. 1918) 234-6;
    member of 2nd Socialization Com-
    mission (Apr. 1920) 2, 9, 237, 243;
    adviser to Versailles peace delegation
    (Mar. 1919) 238; attempts to mediate
    during Kapp Putsch (Mar. 1920)
    9, 239-43; delegate to Spa Confer-
    ence (July 1920) 2, 243-9; talk with
    Italian Ambassador (July 1920) 249;
    member of Provisional Reich Eco-
    nomic Council (July 1920) 2, 243,
    250; adviser on reparations 2, 250;
    draft proposal on reparations (1921)
    251-2; talks with Lloyd George and
    others, London and Paris (1921-2)
    273-89; Minister for Reconstruction
    (May-Oct. 1921) 2, 9, 24, 198, 252-
    71; negotiations with French Minister
    of Liberated Regions (June 1921)
    254-65; signs Wiesbaden Agreement
    (6-7 Oct. 1921) 2, 265-6; plans visit
    to Paris about reparations (June 1921)
    266-7; problem of Upper Silesia
    267-71, 276; resignation 271-2;
    negotiations in London on reparations
    and economic problems (Nov.-Dec.
    1921) 2, 273-83, 283-6; negotiations
    in Paris with Reparations Commission
    (Dec. 1921-Jan. 1922) 2, 9, 286-9;
    heads German delegation to Cannes
    Conference (Jan. 1922) 290-1;
    Foreign Minister (31 Jan.-24 June

1922) 2, 9, 25, 291-5; talk with French Ambassador (Mar. 1922) 292-4; signs Rapallo Agreement with Russia (April 1922) 22, 265, 294; assassination 10-11

honours and rewards: Order of the Crown, Second Class (1907-8) 48, 94; Order of the Red Eagle, Second Class (1910) 77, 94; Star to the Order of the House of Orange (1910) 94, 101, 118; War Merit Medal (1910) 94; Iron Cross, Second Class (1910) 94; French clock 99; Meissen porcelain 291

journey to German and British East Africa (1907) 9, 27-47; Notebook 30-47; 'Report on the Development of the German East African Colony' 34 n. 17, 48-59; places mentioned or visited: Amani Regional Institute 45, 46, 56, Bomole, Mt. 46, Bukoba 39, 40, Central African Rift Valley 38, Dar es Salaam 34-6, 37, 47, Entebbe 39, Gilgil 38, Kahigi 40, Kihuui 45, Kilimanjaro, Mt. 36 n. 23, 38, Kilindini 33, Kisumu see Port Florence, Kwai 47, Lushoto see Wilhelmsthal, Missungi 44, Mombasa 33, 36 n. 23, 37, 41, 45, Mombo 46, 47, Morogoro 47, 56, Msimbazi see Simbasi, Muheza 45, Mwanza, 40, 41, 43, 44, Nairobi 38, Nakuru 38, Niussi 46, Port Florence (Kisumu) 39, 45, Sadani 47, Shirati 45, Simbasi/Sibasi (now Msimbazi, Dar es Salaam) 36 n. 22, Tabora 36 n. 23, 41, 42-3, 56, Tanga 34, 36 n. 23, 45, 47, Usambara Mts. 45 n. 52, 46 n. 57, Usambara plantation district 36 n. 23, 49, 56, Usambara, West 46, Victoria Nyanza, Lake 36 n. 23, 39, 45, Voi 38, Wilhelmsthal (now Lushoto) 46, 47, Zanzibar 33, 34, 36-7

journey to London (1908) 60-4; 'Remarks about England's Present Situation' 60-1

journey to South Africa (1908) 9, 60, 64-9, 70-1; Rhodesia 70; German South West Africa 71-5; Memorandum on South West Africa 75-92; places mentioned or visited: Berseba 73, Bethanie 72, Bloemfontein 69, Brakpan, power station at 67 n. 28, Brakwasser 72, Britstown 70, Buchholzbrunn 72, Bulawayo 70, Cape Point 65, Cape Town 63, 64, 65 n. 20, 68 n. 34, 71, Chaimaites 72,

Draghoender 71, Drijhoek, Bondel reserve 72, Durban 63, 66, 67 n. 25, East London 66, Gabis 72, George 65, Germiston 67, Gibeon 73, Gröndorn 73, Grootfontein 75, Houwater 70, Johannesburg 67, Kanus 72, Karibib 74, 75, Karibib marble quarries 79, Keetmanshoop 72, 73, Khan area copper fields 79, Kimberley 69, 70, Kubub (?Küibis) 72 n. 46, Livingstone 70, Lüderitz Bay 68 n. 34, 72-3, 79, Mafeking 69, Majuba Hill 67, Maltahöhe 73, Matopo Hills (Rhodes's grave) 70, Mossel Bay 65, Naawte, Great and Little 72, Nachab 71, 72, Okahandja 74, Okanjande 75, Okasise 74, Omaruru 74, Osoana (?Osona) 74, Otavi 74, 75, Otjikokoseo 75, Otjiwarongo 74, 75, Oudtshoorn ostrich farms 65, Pietermaritzburg 66, Port Elizabeth 66, Pretoria 68, Prieska 71, Rehoboth 74, Seeheim 72, Shark (Haifisch) Island deportation and concentration camp 82, Simmerpan, power station under construction 67 n. 28, Somerset West, dynamite factory 65, Swakopmund 74 n. 48, 75, Tses 73, Tsumeb 74, Tsumis 73, Ukamas 71, Upington 68 n. 34, 71, Victoria Falls 70, Walfis Bay 64, 65, 75, Warmbad 72, Waterberg 75, Windhoek 74

journey to Paris on behalf of Mannesmann brothers (1910) 9, 94-5, 114

journey to Switzerland (1911) 109-10

journey to Italy (Feb. 1911) 110-11; (May-June 1911) 124-9; conversation with Bülow 124-7

journey to Italy (Feb. 1912) 150; (Nov. 1912) 170-1

journey to Paris (1912) 161-2

journey to Kovno (1915) 198-204; talks with Ludendorff 199-200, 201-2, and Hoffmann 201, 202-4

journey to Kreuznach (1917) 222-32; talks with Ludendorff 223-31, 231-2

journey to Spa (1920) 2, 243-9

journey to Wiesbaden (1921) 254-66; talks with Loucheur 255-65

journey to London (29 Nov.-10 Dec. 1921) 273-83; (18-23 Dec. 1921) 283-6

journey to Paris (29 Dec. 1921-6 Jan. 1922) 286-9

journey to Cannes (1922) 290-1

personality and private life: attitude to Judaism 6, 97 n. 28, 98, 99, 105,

Rathenau, Walther (*cont.*):
109, 112, 115, 116, 119, 128; *cultural and intellectual interests*: artistic and architectural 10, 98 n. 32, 108, 111, 112, 118, 124-7, 129, 156, 160, literary 106, 107, 110, 117, 121-2, 135, 137, 139, musical 10, 104, 108, 110, 111, 122, 150, 151, 152, 160, 179, theatrical 99, 100, 103, 104, 105, 107, 111, 113, 114, 136, 140, 142, 146, 150, 151, 170; supports Berlin Sezession 9, 99, 122; supports Schiller Foundation 9, 152; establishes Emil-Rathenau-Foundation 9; on committee of Bismarck National Memorial 102-3, 107, 115, 129, 136-7, 138; dreams and psychic experiences 111, 120-1, 157, 178; *relations with*: father 4-5, father during latter's illness 159-60, 164-5, 168 n. 117, 169, 170, 171 nn. 130 and 131, 176, mother 4-5, Bernhard Dernburg 27, 28, 29, 47-8, 60-2, 73 n. 47, 76-7, 93, 151, 155, 170, 178, Felix Deutsch 165 n. 103, 168 n. 117, 169 n. 120, 170, 171 n. 131, 172, 176, 198, Lili Deutsch 97 n. 27, 108 n. 81, 155-6, 157, 158, 172, 175 n. 4, 176, 177, 192 n. 44, Maximilian Harden 29 n. 8, 60 n. 2, 76, 94, 97, 132 n. 202, 133 n. 205, 139-40, 143 n. 4, 144 n. 10, 155-6, 165 nn. 103 and 105, 166 n. 106, 168 n. 117, 172-3, 175-6, 192, 197, 198, 212 n. 5, 233 n. 1; *see also* entries in Biographical Index
    political ambitions 9, 13, 15, 18-21, 24-6, 95, 105, 141, 212; political manifesto 'Die Neue Ära' (1907) 28-9, 106; possible National Liberal candidate for 1912 Reichstag elections 9, 95, 105-6, 122, 123, 129, 130 n. 194; fails to enter National Assembly (1919) 237, 238; rejected as presidential candidate for National Assembly 237; fails to establish Demokratischer Volksbund 238
    policies: *colonial*: 27, 47, 48, 49-59 (report on German East Africa), 60, 76, 77, 78-92 (report on South West Africa), 159 n. 80, 183, memorandum on England's economic and colonial problems 60-1; *domestic*: pre-war parliamentary, franchise and constituency reforms 17, 146, 164, 178, wartime control of raw materials for industry 186-91, 212-13, post-war economy 17, 197, 213, 214, 219-22, 224, 237, 238-9, 255, 273-8, 280, 290, 291, 292, 295, post-war parliamentarization and democratization of Germany 221 n. 45, 223 nn. 54 and 55, 231, 233, 235, 238, Jesuits Law 173 n. 136, 174 **n. 150**, 175; *foreign*: arms limitation and disarmament 119-20, 161, 163, 185, war strategy 198-204, 205-7, 215-31, 233, 234-6, 'Mitteleuropa' and Central European customs union 163, 183, 184-6, 191-2, 195, 219, post-war international economic and political reorganization 185, 249, 255-6, attitude to peace negotiations 233-6, reparations policy 2, 9, 243-8, 249 n. 45, 250, 251-2, 253-65, 266-7, 273-83, 283-5, 286-9, 290-1, 292-4, 294-5, 'fulfilment' policy 244, 253, 272, 290, 291, 294-5, policy towards Austria-Hungary 183, 184, 206, policy towards France 163, 183, 184, 185-6, 201 n. 31, 203, 205, policy towards Great Britain 153-4, 161, 163, 183, 185-6, 201 n. 31, 203, 205, 207, policy towards Russia 22, 204, 222 n. 47, 233, 236, 239, 265, 280, 283, 290, 291, 294; *industrial*: integration in electrical and electro-technical industry 8, 22, 114 n. 114, mergers (*see also under individual companies*) 7, 8, 9, 24, 93, 100, favours state monopoly of electrical supply industry 13, 22, 96 n. 19, 97, 105, 108, 121, 131, 182, 183, 190 n. 31, as employer 18-19, 237, party to Stinnes–Legien Agreement 9, 21, 237, attempts to limit power of steel industrialists 24, 238; opposition from other industrialists 13, 20, 21, 22, 23; *see also* Rathenau, Walther, social and political philosophy
    publications: *Impressionen* (1902) 3 n. 2, 9; *Reflexionen* (1908) 3 n. 2, 9, 158 n. 78; *Zur Kritik der Zeit* (Criticism of the Age) (1912) 9, 109 n. 85, 119 n. 144, 123 n. 167, 135, 136, 139 n. 230, 142-3, 144, 149, 158 n. 78, 165-6 n. 105; *Der rheinische Bismarck* (with Lichtwark, 1912) 102 n. 52, 138 n. 228, 145, 148, 149, 151, 160; *Zur Mechanik des Geistes oder Vom Reich der Seele* (The Mechanism of the Mind) (1913)

9, 116, 169, 176-7, 181; *Deutsch-lands Rohstoffversorgung* (1916) 187, 197 n. 20, 213; *Von Kommenden Dingen* (*In Days to Come*) (1917, English translation 1921) 9, 17 n. 25, 20 n. 30, 193 n. 47, 212, 213-15; *Die Neue Wirtschaft* (The New Economy) (1918), 9-10, 21 n. 31, 238; *Der Neue Staat* (The New State) (1919) 10, 238; *Die Neue Gesellschaft* (The New Society) (1919) 10, 238, 239; *An Deutsch-lands Jugend* (1918) 6 n. 7, 238; *Der Kaiser* (1919) 238; *Kritik der dreifachen Revolution* (1919) 238; *Was wird werden?* (1920) 238; *Gesammelte Schriften* (5 vols., 1918) 238; play, *Blanche Trocard* (privately printed 1887) 158 n. 74; poems, *1813* (1912) 165, 166 n. 106, 170, 173; *articles*: 'Die Neue Ära' (*Han-noverscher Courier*, 1907) 28-9, 106, 'Englands Industrie' (1906) 15, 'Judentaufen' (*Montags-Zeitung*, 9 Jan. 1911) 98, 'Staat und Judentum' (3 articles, *Der Tag*, 2, 4, 16 Feb. 1911) 97 n. 26, 98-9, 102, 104, 105, 107, 108, 123 n. 167, 'Politik, Humor und Abrüstung' (*Neue Freie Presse*, 12 Apr. 1911) 119-20, 163 n. 98, 183 n. 7; 'England und wir, eine Philippika' (*Neue Freie Presse*, 6 Apr. 1912) 153-4, 155, 160, 183 n. 7, 'Politische Selektion, die Auslese in der Diplo-matie' (*Neue Freie Presse*, 16 May 1912) 183 n. 7, 'Den Finger auf die Wunde' (*Nord und Süd*, Aug. 1912) 161, 183 n. 7, 'Das Eumenidenopfer' (*Neue Freie Presse*, 23 Mar. 1913) 177, 183 n. 7, 'Deutsche Gefahren und neue Ziele' (*Neue Freie Presse*, 25 Dec. 1913) 147 n. 30, 183 n. 7, 184, 186 n. 16, 'Parlamentarismus' (*Neue Freie Presse*, 12 Apr. 1914) 183 n. 7, 'Ein Wort zur Lage' (*Ber-liner Tageblatt*, 29 July 1914) 183 n. 9, 'Ein dunkler Tag' (*Vossische Zeitung*, 7 Oct. 1918) 233, 237, 'Festigkeit' and 'Die Stunde drängt' (30 Sept. and 4 Oct. 1918) 233 n. 1, 'Das Ende' (*Die Zukunft*, 31 May 1919) 235 n. 13, 'Ja oder Nein' (10 May 1921) 252 n. 9
residences: Bitterfeld flat 10; Victoria-strasse, Berlin flat 10, 106, 157, 159; Schloss Freienwalde 10, 93, 94, 101,

114, 156, 157, 159; build house in Berlin-Grunewald 10, 93, 98 n. 32, 101, 102, 111
social and political philosophy: 'mechan-ization' and the quality of life 142-3, 176-7, 189, 213; moral re-generation to counter mechanization 17-18, 176-7, 213-14, 237; war an inevitable stage in national develop-ment 153-4; arms control to limit sovereignty of state and tendency to war 119-20, 152, 153-4, 161, 163; Utopian post-war social political and economic system 184, 185, 195, 213, 214, 221-2, 224, 237, 238, 239, 249, 252, 255; industry and the state 13, 14-16, 17-18, 20-1, 22, 23, 25-6; 'Physiologisches Theorem / Symbion-tentheorem' (physiological/symbiotic theory) 109, 121
Reconstruction Consortium/Syndicate for Russia 284-5, 286, 291
Regie, *see* Diamantenregie
Reichstag elections (1912) 95, 96, 143, 143-4 nn. 6, 7, and 11, 145
Reinsurance Treaty with Russia (1887) 167, 173, 174 n. 140
Reparations:
Spa Conference (1920) 2, 243-8, 250
Paris Conference (1921) 251
London Conference (1921) 2, 250-1, 253
London Ultimatum (5 May 1921) 251, 252, 253, 265, 278, 290, 291, 294
Wiesbaden Agreement (1921) 265-6
Cannes Conference (1922) 290-1
Genoa Conference (1922) 291, 292, 293, 294, 295
R as negotiator: at Spa 2, 243-8, 250; 'Rathenau Proposal' 250-2; recon-struction of Europe (reparations in kind) 249, 253-66; negotiations with Loucheur (June 1921) 253-65; plans to see Reparation Commission in Paris 266-7; talks in London about deferment of payments 273-83, 283-6; talks with Reparation Commission in Paris (1921-2) 286-9; as Foreign Minister 291-5
*Rheingau-Elektrizitätswerke (Rheingau Electricity Works) 117 and n. 130, 152
Rheinhausen steel plant (Krupp), possible merger 101
Rhodes Group 75 n. 49
Rhodesia, visit by R and Dernburg (1908) 70

*Richard Lindenberg, see Stahlwerke Richard Lindenberg AG
Riga, strategic importance discussed by R and Ludendorff 200
Ringen clay pit 151
Rixdorf–Gesundbrunnen underground railway 157
  see also Neukölln–Gesundbrunnen overhead railway
Romania 174 n. 141, 180 n. 12
Rombacher Hütte, Lorraine (blast furnace plant) 109 n. 88, 137 n. 223
Rote Tag, Der 104 n. 61
  see also Der Tag
Ruanda, closed to Europeans 56
Ruhr, possible Allied occupation 244, 246 nn. 31 and 33, 248 n. 43, 250, 265, 276, 278, 280, 295
Ruhr loans 274
Ruhrort occupied by French (8 Mar. 1921) 250
Russia 10, 167 and n. 114, 168, 179, 183, 185, 281
  relations with Germany pre-war 105, 163, 174 n. 140
  relations with Germany during war 199, 201 nn. 31 and 33, 202, 203, 204, 205, 207, 208, 210, 222 n. 47; Treaty of Brest–Litovsk, R favours revision 233, 236
  post-war reconstruction 249, 264, 274, 283, 284, 286, 291
  Russo–Polish war 244
  R in favour of normalization of relations with Soviet Russia 22, 239, 265, 280, 290, 291
  R signs Rapallo Agreement (16 Apr. 1922) 22, 265, 294
Russian ballet, R's reactions to 146
*Russische-Eisen-Industrie AG 154
*Rybniker Steinkohlenwerke (Rybnik Colliery) 115 n. 123, 130, 154

Saar-Elektrizitäts-Gesellschaft (Saar Electricity Company) 112 n. 103, 116 n. 128, 117
Salonika 174, 179–80 n. 12
Sampierdarena Centrale, Genoa, AEG provides electricity supply 111, 150
Schaaffhausener Bankverein (Schaaffhausen Bank) 98, 108
Schickler bank, R's part in merger with Delbrück bank 9, 93, 99, 160
  see also Delbrück Schickler & Co.
Schiller Foundation 9, 152
*Schlesische AG für Bergbau und Zinkhüttenbetrieb 179

*Schlesische Elektrizitäts- und Gas AG (Silesian Electricity and Gas Company) 114 n. 112, 156
*Schlesische Kleinbahn AG (Silesian Light Railways) 108, 117, 122, 142, 153, 165
*Schlesische Zink-Gesellschaft (Silesian Zinc Company), see Schlesische AG für Bergbau und Zinkhüttenbetrieb
Schneider–Creusot 94, 95, 162 n. 90
Schöneweide, AEG's cable and wire factory at 102, 165
Schuckert, AEG rejects R's proposed take-over of 7
*Schulz–Knaudt, steel rolling mill taken over by Mannesmann (1914) 113, 153
*Schweig-Unternehmungen (Schweig Enterprises) 137
*Schweigsche Glas- und Porzellanwerke (Schweig Glass and Porcelain Works) 116, 151
  see also Schweig-Unternehmungen
Schweiz negotiations 149
Schweizer Kreditanstalt 112 n. 102
Schweizerische Bankverein (Swiss Banking Association) 112 n. 102
Serbia, and Balkan Wars 168 n. 116, 179–80 n. 12, 182 n. 3, 183
  Austrian ultimatum to 224, 225 nn. 58, 59 and 61
  during war 203 and n. 44, 205, 206
Seville, see Compañia Sevillana de Electricidad
Sezession, see Berlin Sezession
Sidara agricultural institute, Natal, R's visit 66
Siemens 4, 7, 110 n. 89, 115 n. 121, 132 n. 203, 138 n. 227, 149 n. 36, 280 n. 26
Silesia, see Oberschlesische, Schlesische, Upper Silesia
Social Democratic Party (SPD) 16, 19, 96, 106, 125, 141, 144 n. 7, 145 n. 14, 170 n. 125, 214, 223 n. 55, 252, 271
Socialization Commissions 237
  R on Second Socialization Commission 2, 9, 237, 243
Società Generale Italiana di Elettricità Sistema Edison 171 n. 127
Società per lo Sviluppo delle Imprese Elettriche in Italia (Development Company for Electrical Printing Machines in Italy), Milan 111, 150, 171
*Solinger Kleinbahn AG (Solingen Light Railway) 116, 122, 155

South Africa:
  visit by R and Dernburg (1908) 9, 60, 64-9, 70-1
  constitutional problems (conversation in London with Dr Jameson) 62-3
  electricity supply industry in 67 nn. 27, 28
  mining: gold 62, 67, 68 n. 34, diamonds 62, 68, 69, asbestos 71, copper 71
  visits to native reserves 66, 69
South West Africa, visit by R and Dernburg (1908) 63, 65 n. 20, 68 n. 30, 71-5
  R's report on 75-92, 159 **n. 80**
  war in (1904-7), 27, 41 n. 41, 76, 80-2, 90
  native peoples of 79-80, 81-2, 83, 85-6, 90
  white settlers in 88
  mining: diamond fields (Lüderitz Bay) 73, 77, 79, (Diamantenregie) 73 n. 47, 182; copper (Otavi and Khan area) 77, 79
  marble quarries (Karibib) 79
  visit by Commission for Central Association of German Industrialists, 60 n. 1
  visit by Wilhelm Solf, Colonial Secretary, 27 n. 3
South West Africa Company 74 n. 48, 75 n. 49, 90
  see also Südwest-Afrikanisches Bodenkredit Institut
Spa Conference on reparations (July 1920), R technical adviser to delegation 2, 243-8, 250, 278 n. 22, 280, 294
Spaeter, see Carl Spaeter
Spain 277 n. 16
  see also Compañia Barcelonesa de Electricidad and Compañia Sevillana de Electricidad
Speyer-Ellissen Bank 103 n. 56
*Spinning mills 107, 137, 146
*Stahlwerke Richard Lindenberg AG 95, 109 n. 83
Standard Oil 170 n. 125
State monopoly in electrical supply industry, supported by R 13, 22, 96 n. 19, 97, 105, 108, 121, 131, 182, 183, 190 n. 31
State monopoly in oil 170 **n. 125**
State monopolies 96
*Stein- und Ton, see Brohltal Stein- und Ton-Industriegesellschaft
Stinnes-Legien Agreement, supported by R 9, 21, 237
*Strassburger Elektrizitätswerk AG (Strasbourg Electricity Works) 22, 96 n. 19, 112 n. 103, 190 n. 31

Submarine warfare 209, 210 n. 9, 217 nn. 25 and 26, 218-20, 222, 226-8, 229 n. 72, 235
  R opposed to, 215, 217, 218-19, 220, 222, 227-8, 231, 232, 233, 235
Südwest-Afrikanisches Bodenkredit Institut (South West African Real Estate Bank) 179
Suez 31, 186
Sulzer, Swiss machine building company 113 and n. 106
Supreme Council, see Allied Supreme Council
Sviluppo, see Società per lo Sviluppo delle Imprese Elettriche in Italia
Switzerland, visits by R 109-10, 112, 158, 164, 171
  see also Laufenburg, Switzerland, power station at

Tag, Der, publishes article by R 104, 105, 108, 115
Tannenberg, Battle of (Aug. 1914) 202, 203
Tate Gallery, London, visit by R 63
Telegraph companies 152
*Theodor Goldschmidt AG, Essen 130, 131 **n. 199**, 139, 156
*Thiederhall AG, Thiele 121, 148
Tillmanns & Co., factories at Kovno and Libau, R recommends take-over by AEG 199 **n. 27**
Times, The, article on R (Oct. 1915) 212
Titanic, wreck of 162
*Treuhandbank für die elektrische Industrie (Mortgate Bank for the Electrical Industry) 149, 156 n. 66
Trieste, as German naval base 182
Tripoli, war between Italy and Turkey over (1911-12) 148 n. 32, 174
Tronto power station, North Italy 100 n. 42, 107, 108 n. 77, 112 n. 104
*Tschöpelner-Braunkohlenwerke (Tschöpeln Lignite Works) 100, 121, 143
Turkey:
  Agreement with Great Britain (1878) 174 n. 148
  war with Italy over Tripoli (1911-12) 148 n. 32, 174 n. 144
  Balkan Wars (1912, 1913) 168 n. 116, 174 n. 145, 179-80 n. 12
  ally of Germany in 1914-18 war 205, 222 n. 47

Uganda Railway (British) 36 n. 23, 37, 38 n. 33, 39 n. 38, 45, 49, 52
Ullstein Publishers 103 n. 56
Union des Mines Marocaines 94-5

Union Elektrizitäts-Gesellschaft (UEG), taken over by AEG (1904) 8, 64 n. 17, 112 n. 102, 115 n. 117, 117 n. 135

Unione Italiana Tramways Elettrici, 110 n. 92, 111, 139, 150

United States of America 10, 15, 154, 170 n. 125, 174 nn. 146 and 147, 181 n. 2, 185, 201 n. 31, 255, 256, 281

peace initiatives 209-11 (Col. House's talks with R, Jan. 1916), 233-5 (possible mediation of President Wilson, Oct. 1918), 234-6 (R's draft reply to Wilson's Note, Oct. 1918) enters war 217, 226, 227 n. 65

peace settlement, disarmament, and reparations 250-2, 276 n. 13, 279-80, 282, 284, 292

Upper Silesia:

and coal reparations 247 n. 37, 258, 265

proposed partition 246, 247, 252, 258, 265, 267-72, 277, 278, 284

Urundi, closed to Europeans 56

Vatican 251

Verband Deutscher Juden (Association of German Jews) 119

Verein zur Erhaltung des überlieferten Judentums (Society for the Preservation of Traditional Jewry) 115

*Vereinigte Lausitzer Glaswerke (United Lausitz Glass Works) 100 n. 40, 106, 123 n. 169, 151

Vereinigung Rheinischer Elektrizitätswerke (Union of Rhenish Electricity Works) 96

Versailles, Peace Conference and Treaty 235, 239, 245, 273

R a member of advisory committee to German delegation (1919) 238

reparations clauses, 243-4, 247, 290

revision of treaty sought by R 290, 291

Victor Emmanuel II, R attends dedication of memorial (1911) 128

Victoria Falls Power Company 62, 63-4 n. 16, 64 n. 17, 67 nn. 27 and 28, 77, 96 n. 19

becomes Victoria Falls and Transvaal Power Company (1909) 67 n. 28

Volksbühne (People's Theatre) 99

Volksstaat, ideal propounded in R's later books 238-9

Vossische Zeitung:

negotiations for its sale 103 n. 56

comments on 1915 Times article on R 212

publishes articles by R 233, 234

Wallace Collection, London, visit by R 63

War Association of German Industry 188

War Ministry, R's relations with 185-9, 195-7, 199

War Office (Kriegsamt) (established Oct. 1916) 216 n. 21, 233

War Raw Materials Department, see Kriegsrohstoffabteilung

Washington Disarmament Conference (Nov. 1921-Feb. 1922) 276 n. 13

Weapons and Munitions Procurement Office 216 n. 21

Weber & Ott, textile firm, Erlangen, 1911 strike and lock-out 122 n. 163

Welt am Montag, Die, see Montags-Zeitung

Wernher, Beit & Company, London banking house 64 n. 17, 67 n. 27, 69, 97 n. 24

Westfälische Drahtindustrie (Westphalian Wire Industry), taken over by Krupp (1911) 101 n. 44

Westphalian Coal Syndicate 161 n. 88

Wiesbaden Agreement, signed by R 2, 265-6, 279, 293

Zabern Crisis (1913) 133 n. 206, 181 n. 1, 182 n. 5

Zeit im Bild, controversy over Zur Kritik der Zeit (1912) 165-6 n. 105, 169

Zentralarbeitsgemeinschaft (ZAG) (Central Working Community of the German Commercial and Industrial Employers and Employees) 21, 237

Zentralverband deutscher Industrieller (Central Association of German Industrialists), see Centralverband deutscher Industrieller

Zukunft, Die (ed. Harden) 76, 98 n. 28, 155 n. 64

publishes articles by R 3, 9

publishes extracts from R's report on German East Africa 49 n. 68

publishes R's poems 1813 166 n. 106, 170

publishes Emil Ludwig on R's work for KRA 212

see also Biographical Index under Harden

Zurich, visits by R 109-10, 164

Zurich Elektrobank, see Elektrobank